Paths in the Rainforests

Paths in the Rainforests

Toward a History of Political
Tradition in Equatorial Africa

Jan Vansina

The University of Wisconsin Press

The University of Wisconsin Press
114 North Murray Street
Madison, Wisconsin 53715

Maps by Claudine Vansina

Library of Congress Cataloging-in-Publication Data
Vansina, Jan.
Paths in the rainforests: toward a history of political
tradition in equatorial Africa / Jan Vansina.
428 pp.   cm.
Includes bibliographical references.
1. Africa, Sub-Saharan—Politics and government. 2. Africa,
Central—Politics and government. 3. Bantu-speaking peoples—
Politics and government. 4. Bantu languages—History. I. Title.
DT352.65.V36   1990
967—dc20   90-50100
ISBN 0-299-12570-X
ISBN 0-299-12574-2 (pbk.)   CIP

Contents

Maps and Figures

Maps

Figures

Preface

Imagine that Caesar arrived in Gaul and landed in Britain in 1880, a mere century ago, and that your known history began then. You were not Roman, your language was not Latin, and most of your cherished customs had no historical justification. Your cultural identity was amputated from its past. Would you not feel somewhat incomplete, somewhat mutilated? Would you not wonder what your cultural heritage was before Caesar? Unimaginable? Yet that is the situation of the So in Zaire, whose record seems to begin only with Stanley in 1877; of the Tio in Congo, who trace their past back only to the arrival of de Brazza in 1880; and indeed of most of the peoples living in the vast stretches of equatorial Africa. It hurts to be told by foreign scholars that, in earlier days, the ingenuity of your forebears was so constrained by "cultural tradition" that people were condemned to repeat themselves endlessly, to be stuck in the same rut for time immemorial. This simply flows from rank incomprehension. It is no consolation to be told by others that, because there are no written sources, no past can be recovered, as if living traces of that past were not part and parcel of daily life.

Such a situation poses a challenge. Any attempt to meet it will be most significant to the peoples in equatorial Africa themselves, and especially to their intellectuals. Beyond this consideration, the existence of such a gap in everyone's knowledge about our common past should be in itself of interest to historians everywhere, for the past of equatorial Africa is as relevant to the human experience as any other. Moreover this situation is not unique to equatorial Africa. It exists in many other parts of the world where the usual sources used by historians are lacking. Part of the challenge is to find a methodology that will make better use of other traces of the past than written documents or oral traditions. If that methodology is fruitful and valid in equatorial Africa, it can be equally fruitful and valid in similar situations elsewhere in the world. These considerations are powerful voices calling for research to recover the past of equatorial Africa.

This book grew out of such research. It consists of an introduction to the relevant questions, and an exposition of the data known today. Ideally this work should be published in French, the working language common to almost every country in the area, and the exposition should be much longer. I wanted to do this but practical realities intervened. It seemed unwise to write a three-volume introduction in French and then rely on the hazards of the publishing market to find an outlet for it. On second thought it was perhaps better to write a condensed account, highlighting the essentials, one that would stand a reasonable chance of being published in the near future. After all, the results are also of interest to those scholars who face similar questions elsewhere in the world.

While the book was taking shape, I became more and more impressed by the fact that the past of equatorial Africa exemplified the workings of a powerful endogenous process, a cultural tradition that had its roots some 4,000–5,000 years ago, and that had maintained itself by perennial rejuvenation, until it withered as a result of the colonial conquest. Cultural tradition is a process that is often invoked, but little understood. Historians and anthropologists have, on the whole, shunned the study of such phenomena that stretch over thousands of years and span vast regions. Unwittingly, this research drew me into a study of this topic. The main outline of the past in equatorial Africa is a story about tradition. Hence I had stumbled on yet another *ex post facto* reason for writing this account and directing it to an audience of professional anthropologists and historians.

Later, as the manuscript progressed, it became clear that one could present an essential outline of its results in a much shorter compass than had been planned. Yet there are drawbacks. The exposition is condensed, hence harder to follow, and only a fifth of the bibliography extant could be cited, making this book less of a guide to the whole existing literature than I had wished. But the advantages outweigh the drawbacks. The major segments of the overall argument stand out more clearly, and the book is much better centered on the history of the overall tradition. And, admittedly, the length of this work is more amenable to publishers than a longer study would be. I hope that it can be published in a French version as well, to serve the audience most concerned with the substance of its contents.

This book became an *introduction,* not just because it is more condensed than the work originally planned, but in more fundamental ways as well. It focuses on institutional history, on the past of societies. Historians always have to make such heartrending choices. The past is too complex to be rendered in all its richness, with all its interconnections, in a single book. Moreover, to refuse a clear choice means that the fabric will remain on the loom forever. One can always spend another decade teasing out further evidence, especially if one uses linguistic methods. But to do this hinders the progress of scholarship by delaying the communication of the result of ongoing research.

The choice I made can easily be defended. First, the greatest contribution of this tradition to the general experience of humanity may well lie in the sociopolitical realm. Second, the reconstruction of a sociopolitical history, at least in broad outlines, is an urgent and essential task, when one first broaches a hitherto unknown area. Third, as previous authors specifically doubted that there had ever been any sociopolitical change here since Neolithic times, there is an appealing irony in focusing first on this facet of the past.

This choice does not mean, or even imply, that other aspects of the past are less important. For instance, from time to time I underline the role played by economic factors such as production and trade. Other similar topics are then not entirely neglected, but a great deal more can be achieved than has been presented in this work. Hence I ask the reader to remember that, as far as substance goes, this book is merely an introduction, a first glimpse into a lost world.

But the book does not just recount an institutional history. It is also concerned with methodology and with some issues that relate to the philosophy of history. Hence, as an anonymous reviewer of the manuscript put it, three strands are intertwined here: a tale, a study in methodology, and reflections about history and tradition. The book begins by introducing its methodology. Then, from chapters 2 through 8, it tells a story of the institutional past. The third strand opens with a discussion about reality at the outset of chapter 3, continues at the end of each section with reflections about the tale as it unfolds, and culminates in the last chapter.

Madison, September 1989   Jan Vansina

Acknowledgments

There is no better chrestomathy of clichés than in the acknowledgments pages. Yet such acknowledgments are no less sincere for being banal. The *topoi* merely reflect the common condition of the writer. We are all dependent on institutions to provide us with the means to do research and with access to the information required. We are all but a thread in a collective fabric of people from technical helpers such as typists to assistants, colleagues, hosts in a foreign culture, friends, family, and our predecessors. However trite, to recognize those who helped along the way is only proper and a source of grateful satisfaction.

For over a decade, the unwavering commitment of the Graduate School of the University of Wisconsin–Madison and the William F. Vilas Trust for the University of Wisconsin have literally made it possible for me even to think that a long-range project such as this could be pursued. A Guggenheim award, an A. Von Humboldt Prize, and later a J. D. Mac Arthur Professorship further facilitated and accelerated the pace of the research. Together these institutions provided both the free time and the means needed for this project.

Although this study benefited from past fieldwork experience, it has been specifically based on library resources and archives. Among these, perhaps the greatest contribution came from the Memorial Library of the University of Wisconsin, and especially from its interlibrary loan service. Year after year it continued to deliver obscure but important references. An equally important input was provided by the Royal Museum of Central Africa in Tervuren (Belgium), where I have been able to work off and on for close to forty years now. Further assistance in Belgium came from the Library of the Foreign Ministry in Brussels and from the De Cleene papers, deposited at the library of the Catholic University at Leuven. In France the collections of the Centre de recherches africaines at the University of Paris 1 were quite useful. I am especially grateful to the Office de la Recherche Scientifique et Technique d'Outre-mer (ORSTOM) for providing practical help and access to relevant information in Paris, Brazzaville, and Libreville. I also recall with gratitude a stay at the Frobenius Institut in Frankfurt, which allowed me to see the notes of Leo Frobenius. In Gabon, the National

Library, the University Omar Bongo, and the Centre de Saint Exupéry all gave access to relevant holdings.

And now to people. First let me mention Ms. Laurie Heiser, who typed most of the text, no mean feat given the hazards she faced as she met a welter of typos, erratic commas, and illegible handwriting.

A decade-long procession of research project assistants, almost all doctors now, has worked on this project. Their input varied with their personalities and talents. The most valuable contributions came from the work of Agayo Bakonzi, Elizabeth Eldredge, Jan Ewald, James Giblin, Susan Grabler, Sebagenzi wa Lulenga, Martial Treslin, Peter Vansina, and Michèle Wagner.

A number of central and equatorial African students in Paris have shared their research experience with me, and in some cases checked some of my more general propositions in light of their own research. I am indebted to all of them, and rather than mention only some names I wish to assure them that I equally remember everyone's interest and kindness to me.

Although this was the kind of study which often sounded esoteric to them, nevertheless a host of colleagues has encouraged me and offered valuable clues. Again the list is too long to mention all of them. But I cannot omit to thank particularly Professors and Doctors Yvonne Bastin, Bernard Clist, André Coupez, Pierre de Maret, Jean Devisse, Claire Grégoire, Beatrix Heintze, David Henige, Bogumił Jewsiewicki, Albert Maesen, Claire Nasse, Emiko Ohnuki-Tierney, Claude-Hélène Perrot, Michael Schatzberg, Huguette Van Geluwe, Pierre Van Leynseele, and Jean-Luc Vellut. I also remember what I owe to the multitude of those forebears who studied this area before me. The bulk of that debt is shown in the references, even though I had to limit their number.

This book owes much to three revered mentors, now deceased. Daryll Forde taught me the full scope of anthropology. Malcolm Guthrie put comparative Bantu on a footing which made its findings accessible to historical research for all of us, and I am fortunate that he initiated me to comparative Bantu. Yet I owe much more to Emiel Meeussen. Meeussen was a genius in linguistics generally, and in Bantu studies in particular. He allied cold rigorous logic and a no-nonsense honesty in evaluating research to a warm disposition and an astonishing breadth of scholarly interests. He was the sort of person that becomes a role model. Luckily he was also blessed with endless patience, and he needed it as he tutored this wayward amateur in the study of comparative linguistics and of Bantu languages.

My good friends Professors Robert Harms and Joseph Miller graciously read the first very rough draft of this study, commented ruthlessly, and thereby helped me immeasurably. As the saying goes, they are not to blame for any shortcomings in this book, but they deserve praise for whatever readability it has!

A work of this nature must rely on many maps to get its message across and the mapmaker is a partner in its creation. The maps render what they should accomplish better than I had imagined possible before-hand. That achievement I owe to my alter ego, Claudine.

Note on Spelling

African items are written according to the following conventions:

Place names have been spelled according to the national conventions involved. Thus *u* in Zaire is *ou* in Congo. The rivers bordering Zaire and Congo or the Central African Republic have been spelled Zaire, Malebo Pool, Ubangi, and Bomu.

Personal names and ethnic names have been rendered by the conventions of the Africa alphabet of the International African Institute but without indication of tone. Hence: *Douala* for the city and *Duala* for the people. Nouns in Bantu languages begin with a class prefix. The prefixes for populations are usually *mu-* (singular) and *ba-* (plural). According to a convention observed in most writing about Bantu speakers, these prefixes are omitted in ethnic names. Hence Kongo stands for *mukongo* or *bakongo*. This convention has been followed here only insofar as the prefixes involved are *mu-* and *ba-*. All other Bantu prefixes are incorporated into the ethnic name. Hence *Mituku, Bolia*, and *Mabodo* although *mi-*, *bo-*, and *ma-* are prefixes. Prefixes have been preserved in all non-Bantu ethnic names. Hence, for instance, *Mangbetu* and *Azande*, not *Ngbetu* or *Zande*.

Other words in African languages are transcribed in the Africa alphabet, with the following restrictions. Semantic high tone in Bantu languages, *where it is known,* is marked with an acute accent. No tones are marked in the other African languages cited, although these are also tonal. Distinctions between implosive and explosive consonants have been ignored, although they occur in a few languages. Distinctions between vowels of the second and third degree in Bantu languages are correctly rendered only in the Appendix. Elsewhere the distinction between ε as in "pet" and *e* as in "eight" or ɔ as in "cross" and *o* as in "rose" are ignored. Distinctions between degrees as well as tension of vowels in other African languages are not rendered. This is particularly relevant with regard to words in the southern central Sudanese languages. It has recently been discovered that their vowel systems are quite complex and involve several uncommon features that are still being studied by specialists.

Reconstructed linguistic forms are rendered in the Africa alphabet and starred: e.g., **-ntu* ("entity"). Although they do affect meaning, the relevant class indications are omitted except in the Appendix. For the example above, class ½ specifies the meaning of *-ntu* as "person," class ⅞ gives it the meaning "thing," and class 14 either "personhood" or "the notion of entity." Readers using M. Guthrie, *Comparative Bantu,* or E. Meeussen, *Bantu Lexical Reconstructions,* should be aware that the vowels of the second and the third degrees are transcribed there according to a convention different from that of the Africa alphabet and hence here. Where a common nonreconstructed form is given, no asterisk precedes the form given. Thus *-bugo* ("plantain"). This form is not a reconstruction, but rather a root found in a particular language or in a set of particular languages.

The conventions adopted involve a number of compromises dictated by practical considerations ranging from cost to the state of the raw data used. Most readers will not require the precision which can be achieved by a full transcription, and at each point the arguments used have been checked against the fullest transcriptions available.

Paths in the Rainforests

One

Voids and Blinders, Words and Things

Ainsi nous est apparue une première province que nous appelons *Afrique centre-équatoriale* et qui pourrait être appelée la région *anhistorique* de l'Afrique Noire car aucun état important ne s'y est développé.[1]

PREAMBLE

There exists in Africa a huge area—as large as the arable part of West Africa to the west of the lower Niger, as large as the United States east of the Mississippi, almost as large as western Europe—which remains *terra incognita* for the historian (map 1.1). Maps of Africa generally depict this as a green mass, since the area is mostly covered with the rainforests of equatorial Africa. Such forests and their approaches cover all of southern Cameroon, Gabon, Equatorial Guinea, and Congo, half of Zaire, and spill over into the Central African Republic and Cabinda in Angola (map 1.2). Today some 12 million people live there and ethnologists count up to 450 ethnic groups there.[2]

Why has this part of the world remained without a historiography? Some blame only the lack of historical sources. Others held and still hold that the peoples living there "were too busy surviving in such a hostile environment" to change. Peoples there supposedly still live today as they have done for centuries or millennia. They have supposedly "preserved prehistoric civilizations until our own day."[3] That cliché is particularly cherished by writers about pygmies, but it is also applied to farmers in the area.[4] In other words, environment determines history and the unlucky peoples here have no history because they have never changed.

To Europeans the African communities seemed minuscule in size and so unstructured as to deserve the epithet of "anarchies"[5] or the more euphemistic "segmentary societies." Both foreign observers and the in-

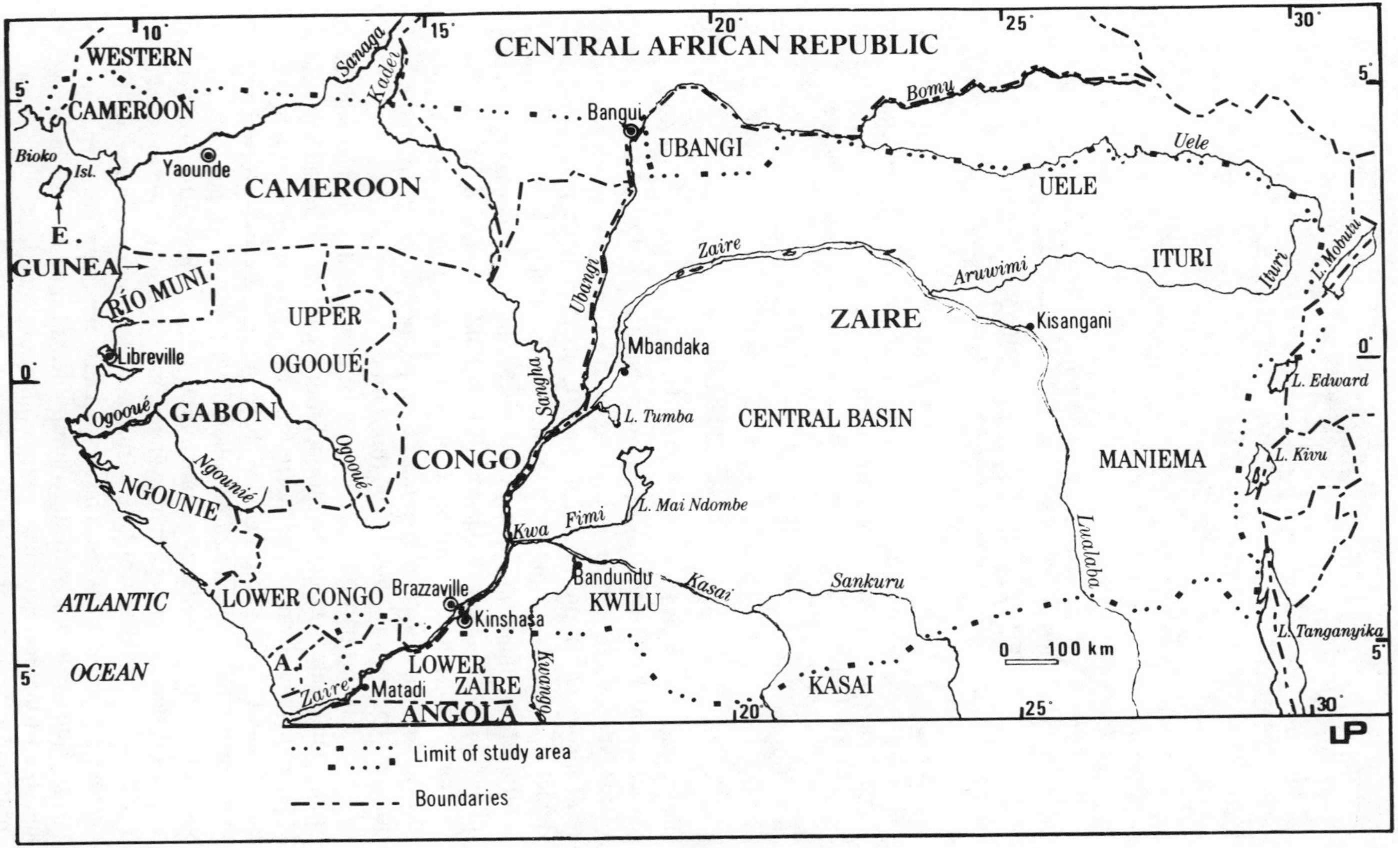

Map 1.1. Equatorial Africa

habitants thought that society here was congruent with kinship, not with kingship, in sharp contrast to the adjoining regions of the great lakes or the savanna to the south. The history of these peoples was that of the demographic growth of kinship groups. When a lineage became too big it split "just as an amoeba does" into two or more smaller lineages, a never-ending process of quasi-biological growth.[6] There was therefore no history except for the gyrations and migrations of "clans" or "tribes," which were the perennial units of society.[7] Moreover the peoples of this huge area seemed as similar to each other as the trees in their forests. Many ethnographers lumped all of them together in a single cultural whole.[8] They matched a never-changing, monotonous, dark, debilitating juggernaut of a rainforest. No wonder that ways of life were unrefined in such a "terrifying" or "brutalizing" environment, which smothered any puny attempt at change.[9] Were these people in the forest huddled like penguins on their ice floes, perfectly adapted to their surroundings but incapable of leaving the ice floe?

Such a dismal dismissal is mistaken. But it does explain why such a large portion of Africa has been neglected for so long. Perhaps the major deleterious influence of the rainforests has been to deter scholars.[10] In fact, the rainforest habitats differed from place to place, and the societies differed more among themselves and were far more complex than has been realized. Indeed the differences between ways and styles of life here are both the proof and the product of ceaseless change over millennia. There is no doubt then that there is more to the past of the rainforests than gyrations and migrations. There is a political, social, and economic history to be recovered here, along with a history of ideas, values, and ideology.

But is this past common to all or to most of the peoples in the area? Are we not falling into a determinist trap by delimiting an area and then looking at it as a single unit of study because it happens to be covered with rainforests, whatever its myriad habitats and the diversity among its inhabitants? Are we not creating a false unity? I do not think so. Despite all the internal differences, the cultures and societies of the area constitute a unit when compared with the outside. The area contrasts with all the surrounding ones by its system of food production. Its decentralized, yet large-scale, social and political institutions strongly contrast to those of the great lakes to its east and the savanna to its south. Its overall pattern of settlement in villages rather than in dispersed settlements contrasts with the savanna to its north and the great lakes to the east. Moreover almost all the people of the rainforests speak related languages of a group called western Bantu. Their northern and eastern neighbors do not. Their southern neighbors do, but those languages show a strong influence of eastern Bantu languages.[11] Such contrasts, however, are merely the symptoms of a common cause. These cultures and societies are the heirs of a single ancestral society and culture whose carriers expanded into the area four to five millennia ago. The forest people share a common tradition. That, more than their habitats, explains their basic unity. Thus tradition, more than environment, will be the focus of this book. People, not trees, will be its heroes. ·

This study, then, tells the story of the equatorial African tradition, and it would be helpful to understand the characteristics of the phenomenon called "tradition" in general, a phenomenon that has gone almost unnoticed in anthropology since the days of A. Kroeber. Only a few

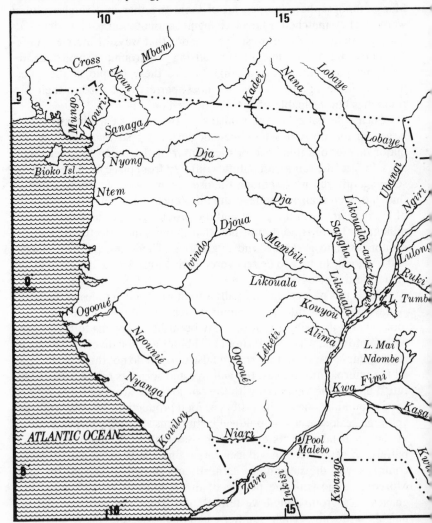

Map 1.2.   General orientation

archaeologists have even used the term.[12] And yet it underlies so much anthropological reasoning that the concept should be examined over and over again. "Tradition" is not just "continuity" and certainly not "unchanging," although that idea is so ingrained that most writers use the adjective "traditional" as a synonym for "unchanging." How and in what sense can tradition be both "continuity" and yet "change"? The answers will gradually appear as the cultural history of the area unfolds. The issue of tradition can then be addressed in the last chapter.

There is, then, a past to be found in the rainforests of equatorial

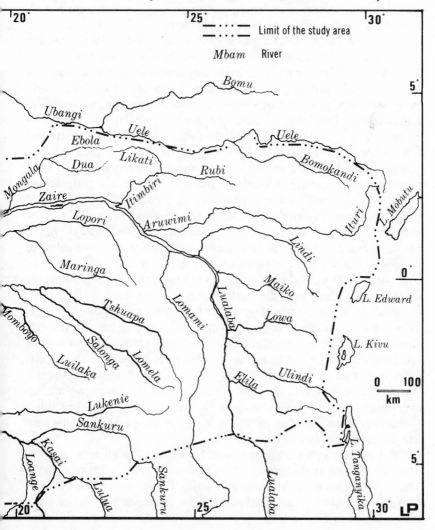

Africa. But can it be found? Where are the records that document it? A sheaf of writings that deal with portions of the coast before 1880, a large collection of oral traditions limited to at best the last two centuries before the colonial conquest, a meager scattering of excavated archaeological sites.[13] How can these document a past so deep over so large an area? Would it not be wiser to abandon this project, to wait a generation for archaeological data to accumulate? I do not think so. There can be no archaeology without interpretation, and interpretation escapes ethnocentrism only by relying on other information relevant to the past. Hence the blossoming of such activities as ethnoarchaeology, which studies the here and now to interpret the long ago.

Written records, archaeological objects, and oral memories are the direct and indirect traces of the past which historians are wont to use. They do not suffice for this endeavor. One must look for other traces of the past. And there is a world of them. Every object we use, nearly everything we say, everything we do, and almost everything we think and feel carries the imprint of the past. Imagine how rich scholars would be if every little thing had a tag on it with the date and place of its appearance. What a wonderful surrealistic world it would be where the ancient Egyptian practice of shaving jostles with the medieval properties of lanolin purified in the twentieth century, and the mirror would talk of the invention of polished metal, silvering processes, and industrial rationalization! But the world is not like that. There are no tags with dates and places for inventions. Only written records tell us that the colors worn by the fan of one soccer team are those of seventeenth-century Spain and the colors of its opponent those of Carolingian Lotharingia; only archaeology tells the Chinese that chopsticks were used in Han times; only oral tradition tells the Arnhemlander where the world began.

And yet, there are tags. Some have become famous. Genes are tags. They tell us what the biological history has been of every plant, every animal, and every person. But famous as they are, they are not universal; they can document only certain biological processes. One needs other tags, tags that exist for everything, tags that duplicate the world. But do they exist? Yes, they do. These tags are the words we use for everything, be it object, activity, thought, or feeling. So when other sources are wanting, why not try to tease out the past from language, why not turn to words as history?

But ethnographic, linguistic, and biological data all seem flawed. They are of twentieth-century or, at best, nineteenth-century vintage. They are anachronistic and every historian knows that anachronism is Clio's deadly sin.[14] Can anachronisms be overcome? Genetics have shown how they can be for biological materials. A living cell testifies to its ancestors of long ago. And so, too, language and specifically words carry an imprint from the past in the present, an imprint that can be put in its proper time perspective.

To achieve that goal much of the recovery of the past in equatorial Africa must be based on the evidence of language and especially words. The way to go about it seems simple enough. If one wants to study an object, one gathers the whole vocabulary that relates to the materials it is made of, the processes used in its manufacture, the vocabulary used to describe its shape, its use, and its collective social significance, if it has any. If one wants to study institutions, one gathers the vocabulary that relates to the institution under investigation. And then one studies the history of each word. The sum of the results should tell a great deal about the history of the object or the institution.

The techniques involved in such a study are not novel. Linguists have used them to reconstruct the history of languages themselves. But the methodology is new in the sense that the conclusions drawn from the technical analysis are different. The goal for which the techniques are to be used is different. Here one wants to reconstruct the past of a society and culture, not language itself. The methodological approach, then, is new. If the methodology is valid, all will be fine. The story to be told in later chapters will be credible "fact." But if the methodology is wrong, the tale is fiction and heavy-fisted fiction at that. The credibility of this book is of general interest to any anthropologist or historian who can use its methodology to solve problems elsewhere.

Now the reader sees the need for a discussion of techniques and methodology before anything else is said, and how unwise it would be in the end to skip this chapter. And even after this has been done, one still cannot jump right into the tale. Almost all the information used in this book came to me through the writings of others, rather than from direct observation, and it is important to explain how the reliability of those sources of information can be assessed.

WORDS AS HISTORY

The social and cultural differences among related peoples are a product of their past history. It would therefore seem proper first to document such differences precisely at a given moment of time and later to explain the differences as divergence from the original situation to the situations today. In practice one can take a single topic, say a set of comparable institutions, beliefs, or practices, examine it in all the related societies, and then align all the variants found. The variants would then be seen as a set of transformations from the single ancestral situation to the multiple contemporary ones. Each variant would be a step in a *logical* pathway of development, usually going from less complex to more complex. The pathway accounts for all the recorded differences in the set with the smallest possible number of transformations. Yet such an exercise is not a *historical* reconstruction. Historical and logical developments need not be identical. For example, it could easily be argued that marriage with bridewealth is a logical transformation of the practice of exchanging one woman for another. But it cannot be demonstrated by this deduction alone that the latter practice is in fact anywhere older than the former. A full list of all the forms of marriage which occur in the area and beyond merely establishes the parameters involved in the history of marriage forms within the region. Parameters are useful because they establish the boundaries of the general field in which the dynamics of change have been at work. But they cannot establish any historical sequence. This and other approaches based on spatial distributions of similar features have been attempted by historical anthropologists, but these approaches have remained unconvincing. There does not seem to be a way to avoid anachronism if one relies only on a comparison of contemporary cultural or social features.[15] Straightforward comparative ethnography cannot be used as a source of history.

Historical Linguistics

Comparative linguistics, in contrast, is a flourishing historical enterprise.[16] This flows from the fact that, unlike ethnographic data, which are the very fabric of collective life itself, language is an arbitrary, symbolic, and largely unconscious holistic system of communication with a high degree of internal inertia. Because of these properties it is impossible at any given moment to take a portion of even two languages and fuse them into a new one. Hence each language has one and only one ancestor. Related languages descend from a common ancestral language, the dialects of which have diverged beyond the pale of intercomprehension. Linguists establish a genetic relationship between languages by showing *systematic* phonological, morphological, and syntactic correspondences which cannot result from chance occurrence. They *prove* relationships by showing how a whole subsystem (usually the sound system) has changed in one language or language group as compared with another one by the operation of a sequence of single systemic changes, reflected in many features. Using such techniques they establish genetic family trees such as the Indo-European one, and they reconstruct features of the ancestral language, the so-called starred forms indicated by an asterisk before the reconstructed form. Even though linguists disagree as to how close such starred forms come to the once-spoken reality, experience has vindicated language reconstruction where ancient texts exist, and are still occasionally discovered, as happens in Indo-European and in the Semitic languages. This approach, called the tree model, privileges one facet of reality. Another one, the wave model, privileges another. It shows how change ripples through the languages of an area, affecting first one item, then a few which at first appear as "exceptions" to the overall norm but in the end lead to a replacement of the norm and trigger the single systemic change. Both models work together.

The Bantu family of languages was recognized as a language family over a century ago, and the common Bantu sound system, as well as large portions of its morphology, has been reconstructed.[17] But its internal family tree has been difficult to trace because frequent later borrowing among the related languages, a phenomenon called convergence, has obscured the lines of descent. Such a tree has finally been established in its overall outline by the use of lexicostatistics,[18] the first of a series of techniques involving vocabulary studies that will be discussed here. Lexicostatistics consists in the comparison of 100 (or 200) items of basic or culturally neutral vocabulary among related languages. Such items are supposedly resistant to replacement by new words. The rate of their replacement is low and constant over time. The percentage of similar items between two languages is therefore an index of their genetic closeness. The basic list of these words was elaborated from language families for which fairly deep historical records were available. Only if the form of an item in both languages compared is similar *and* the meaning identical does it score as a positive.[19] Some of the principles on which the technique is based are not valid. Change in basic vocabulary is not necessarily constant and the selected items are not always and everywhere culturally neutral.[20] Thus "moon" is a basic term in most languages, but in northeastern Zaire a cult linked to the new moon makes the term culturally loaded. Despite these flaws the technique does yield an approximate index of relationship. Its results must be followed up by more definite proof, usually by showing regular sound shifts.

Words and Things

Words are the tags attached to things. Among the various endeavors of historical linguistics, vocabulary studies (semantics) are the most rewarding to historians because of the special property of words as joiners of *form* and *meaning*. The form is an arbitrary linguistic feature, but the meaning refers to culture or society. Because the form is a linguistic feature, its historical study is as valid as any other linguistic inquiry and for the same reasons. But it follows from its link to a field of meaning or semantic field that the history of the *form* tells us something valid about the history of *meaning:* the institution, belief, value, or object to which the form pertains. The combination of linguistic and ethnographic data, called the study of "words and things," is fully validated by this property of the word.[21] One can therefore make use of ethnographic data for historical purposes after all. Indeed in the study of semantics one must do so.

Words have one of three origins: they are inherited from an ancestral language, they are the product of internal innovation, or they are loanwords, the product of external innovation. Thus in English "we" is inherited, "to interface" is an internal innovation, and "mutton" is a loan from French. Each of these possible origins yields historical data and each is discussed in turn. Inherited words are used to reconstruct the vocabulary of the ancestral language, the proto-vocabulary, as a lexicon of starred forms. The meanings attached to these forms testify to the way of life of the people who spoke that language. In Bantu studies M. Guthrie has published a dictionary of starred forms for "Common Bantu."[22] The meaning of each reconstructed form is established by a comparison of the meanings of its reflexes, that is, the forms found in modern languages. In cases where the meanings of the reflexes are identical, the meaning of the ancestral form is evident. For example, CS 174[23] *búa* means "dog" wherever it occurs in Bantu languages. But often the meanings of the reflexes are merely related. Thus CS 472–73 and 475 *-dáka* means "tongue" here, "throat" there, "voice" elsewhere, and "word" or "business" still elsewhere. Semantic shifts over time have widened the field of the original meaning of this term. To establish what that was, the possible histories of semantic shift have to be examined along with the spread of each variant. In the example, "throat" or "voice" was the primary meaning. Moreover, one must take related ancestral forms into account and treat the whole package together. For example, CS 208 *-bot-* meaning "to bear a child," "to bear fruit," must be considered along with CS 210.5 *-boto,* "relative," CS 211 *-bóto,* "seed," and ps 50 (p. 67) *-bóta,* "tribe" (sic). This collection of forms is, moreover, remotely related to CS 210 *-bótam,* "to crouch," since women gave birth in a squatting position, and in turn to CS 209 *-bót,* "to lie down," which seems to be derived from the first set. The original, central meaning of the first item, CS 208, becomes much clearer by charting the whole semantic field involved in its derived forms as well.

The proof that a reconstructed form really belongs to the ancestral languages flows from the distribution of its reflexes over the branches of the genetic tree. Thus CS 174 *búa* ("dog") is found in eastern Bantu languages as well as in western Bantu languages and therefore must stem from common Bantu. It often happens that a form is found only in western Bantu languages. Its ancestor must then have been an innovation from the time between the period of the ancestral language common to all Bantu languages and the ancestor common to western Bantu languages only. The reader will find many examples of this in the Appendix. But the evidence can be blurred. It is not uncommon for a proto–western Bantu form to be later borrowed by eastern Bantu languages bordering on western Bantu languages and vice versa. The reflexes on the genetic tree then give a false impression and lead the analyst to attribute the ancestral form mistakenly to proto-Bantu.

To guard against such errors it is necessary to take the geographically continuous or discontinuous nature of the spread into account. When the reflexes of a given form occur in a single solid distribution without any gaps one should suspect borrowing from a cradle somewhere in the area. Item 127 of the Appendix is a case in point. If one merely charted the presence of *-*gámbí* ("oracle") in both western Bantu languages and related non-Bantu languages, one would attribute a hoary antiquity to it. But the continuous distribution, coupled with the absence of the form in most branches of both western and eastern Bantu, leads to the conclusion that the form is a relatively recent innovation. Conversely, the discontinuous character of the spread of the reflexes greatly strengthens the conclusion that the item is ancestral. A rather spotty distribution of reflexes far apart in space and occurring in widely different branches is a very strong indication of the ancestral character of the underlying form.

These indications show that proto-vocabulary reconstructions are not always self-evident. It is not enough to turn to Guthrie's compendium and just follow his conclusions. A careful examination of the form (the "shape"), the meaning, and the distribution of the reflexes over space and in relation to the branches of the Bantu genetic tree is called for. But given such care, starred vocabulary items constitute very strong evidence.[24]

The reader will note that to reconstruct an image of proto-society and proto-culture, which is then contrasted with societies and cultures of recent times, involves circular reasoning, because the meaning of a "proto" item is set by a comparison of all its contemporary reflexes. But the circularity of the argument is often more apparent than real, if only because in one-on-one contrasts between an ancestral society and a single recent daughter society only a tiny amount of the data from the daughter society conditions the reconstruction of the ancestral society.

The second possible origin of words is internal innovation. In the narrow sense, an internal innovation is a new word created in a given language, practically always by derivation from an older form, either to replace an existing word or to name something new. In either case this tells something substantive about change in culture and society. Because the innovation is a derivation it also gives an insight into a pattern of thought. In Bushong *mwaamsh,* "wife," is an innovation. It is a noun in the class of persons derived from the causative of a verb *-am,* "to give," which preexisted. Hence: "the person that is the cause for giving," which refers to bridewealth. The Bushong were unique in the area with respect to monogamy. Still, even they had pawn women, *ngady,* a well-known term in western Bantu, which was their original designation for "wife."[25] At one time, therefore, a major change in their marriage practices took place. The new term occurs only in Bushong and is an innovation there. Thus, it was created after the separation of Bushong from even the closest related languages. Other data allow us to be more precise and date the change to the seventeenth century. The relative period of an innovation is obtained by showing at what point it occurs on the genetic tree, just as if it were an ancestral word. After all, even ancestral words were once innovations. If members of a subgroup of related languages have the term in common but other subgroups do not, the innovation occurred after the appearance of that subgroup.

The origin of a word as a loanword can be established in two main ways: by the spatially continuous distribution of the form over several languages, related or not, and by the presence of skewing, that is, anomalies with regard to sound or morphology for that language. Thus a district was called *kesé: ke* + root *-sé* in Buma, a regular reflex of CS 331 **-cé.* Boma has *nkesé,* "political domain": *n* + root *-kesé,* which is irregular. The item was borrowed, prefix and all, from Buma and given a new prefix. The situation lends credence to oral traditions which have Buma overlords conquering Boma lands.[26] Distribution maps make it fairly easy to establish the reality of loanwords, but give no clue as to their antiquity or the direction of their spread. One attempts to find the language of origin in which it was an innovation. Proof comes when one finds a cognate from which the form studied derives in only one language. That must be the language of origin. But this is not always possible. Often, especially for older loans, several languages qualify,[27] so that it is possible to give only a general idea of the area of origin. Sometimes cognates cannot be found, be it for lack of data or because the source of the item in the language of invention has died out. Other means are sometimes helpful. Thus Bushong *iloon,* "sword," is borrowed from Luba *cilonda,* "iron weapon." None of the languages which are closely related to Bushong has the term, but several of the Luba languages as far away as Shaba do. It is new in Bushong, ancient in Luba. Again, *itók,* "mat of type X" in Bushong, is a loanword from Luba *dítoko,* "mat of type X." One suspects this because there is a homonym *itók,* "antelope sp.," in Bushong and not in Luba. Many cases of homonymy are due to the borrowing of one of the pair of words. It helps, of course, that in this case the Bushong specify that this is a Luba-type mat! In the case of an origin in non-Bantu languages, it is often possible to spot borrowings because they carry morphemes (grammatical features) that are common there but not in Bantu and the reverse.

That is the case, for instance, with the *ne-* prefix of the Mangbetu group of languages and for Bantu prefixes in other languages.[28]

Loans can also be detected from the substance itself already borrowed. This occurs when an arbitrary system that cannot be duplicated by chance is involved, as in the case of language itself. Style and complex technology are often useful in this way. Thus objects with similar complex arbitrary shapes, such as throwing knives, are a case in point.[29] In the case of organisms, biological proof can be established if the biological origin of the organism is known, as is the case for most domestic plants. In such a situation the item named rather than the form establishes the origin and the direction of spread.[30]

Borrowing has always been going on. There are therefore loans of all ages, from very early items such as the banana to the modern *bulanketi* (blanket) or even *kokakola*. Many of the older ones have adapted to the norms of the language and are more difficult to discern in the absence of skewing,[31] but they leave continuous distributions across different branches of the genetic tree of western Bantu, a telltale sign. It is not easy to date borrowing. The total size of the distribution spread is a poor guide for this, as very recent items such as blankets can have spread over huge distances. Moreover, dating is complicated by several factors. A diffusion can start, stop, then start again perhaps centuries later. For the last few centuries oral traditions can offer some help with dating; known and dated spatial patterns (such as the routes of the slave trade) can be compared with the distribution of loanwords. Item 125 is an example of a word that partly spread with the slave trade. For earlier periods the date of the first innovation can be established by the presence or absence of the item over several languages of one branch or over several branches of the genetic tree, especially if the distribution is already discontinuous. The following example shows an often encountered situation. We have seen that in Bushong *mwaamsh*, "wife," is recent because it is found only in that language. But *ikul*, "ceremonial knife," is older. It occurs in most languages of the Mongo branch to which Bushong belongs and was an innovation at the level of that group from a verb whose reflex in modern Mongo is *kula*, "to hit." But in most Mongo languages, it now has the meaning "iron arrowhead." Was the meaning "knife" a Bushong innovation derived from that other meaning? It was not, because one of its closest genetic northern neighbors, Nkucu, has reflexes with the meaning "arrow" as well as "ceremonial knife." Was Nkucu then the place where the innovation occurred before Bushong split off? It was not. Far away, in Mongo itself, the meaning "knife" is preserved as an archaic form. In sum the word was coined in proto-Mongo times with the meaning "ceremonial knife." Later a new meaning, "arrowhead," was innovated in one of the Mongo languages in connection with a bridewealth practice and spread with the proliferation of that practice far and wide, reaching the Nkucu but not the Bushong. As the example shows, innovation in meaning can occur independently of formal changes.

Glottochronology

Dating linguistic change is crucial for the use of such data by the historian. As has already been shown, relative dating is tied in to the genetic tree of western Bantu languages, so that innovations and loans come before or after splits between language groups or languages. Glottochronology provides a formula for turning these relative successions into absolute dates. It claims that the basic vocabulary used in lexicostatistics changes at a constant rate of replacement. This rate was calculated from known language splits in branches of Indo-European and some other language families for which deep time-depths are available. The formula[32] allows one to convert any lexicostatistical percentage into years. Unfortunately, the dates arrived at are about a century or so too early, since they refer to differences that become established only *after* a split in related languages. Glottochronology has been rejected by most linguists because the rate of change is not constant.[33] Finally, languages do not split at a given date: they diverge over a period of time. Hence no calendar date will ever be correct, except as an indicator of a timespan. Over a very long run linguists acquire a sense of how much divergence could have occurred within a language family. Hence even those who denounce glottochronology still object to some new dating of proto-Indo-European as too late: "the differences between the subgroups are not as big as they could be expected to be," etc. They also forget that glottochronology works for the cases from which the formula is derived, even though it systematically underestimates the timespans involved. The whole debate suggests that glottochronology can be quite useful in cases where all other indications of absolute time-depth are lacking, even though it gives only "ball park" figures. If some of the time-depths for a given case that can be checked are reasonably close to the chronology derived from archaeological or other data, then the technique provides a roughly calibrated scale for those points where other chronological inputs are lacking. The situation is not all that different from that of the genetic time clocks used in cladistics.

For western Bantu one should use these dates as first approximations. Early archaeological evidence tallies with the scale based on the retention constant of 85.4 words per millennium within a century or two at the distant end and fewer at the near end. All the dates seem to be too late. Glottochronology is useful *for the time being,* because it yields an estimate of genuine time-depth. No one would have proposed a thirteenth-century A.D. immigration by Bantu speakers into Gabon had the glottochronological date of 1860 B.C. (30 percent) been known.

INFORMATION AND EVIDENCE

The strategy by which it is possible to reconstruct the past in equatorial Africa dictates what sources will be used. In a strict sense such sources must be written, oral, or objects. In practice almost all the ethnographic, linguistic, or biological evidence used in this study stems from written documents. Direct fieldwork experience and information straight from oral traditions form only a minute fraction of the documentation used here. Given the pivotal role written documents play in this research, their reliability merits some discussion, for no written record can ever be taken for granted, whatever the content and whoever the author. In past practice this has often been neglected.[34] This can be disastrous, as the following shows. It is a time-honored custom in administrations to plagiarize earlier reports. Thus the case of an administrator publishing a study in which he incorporated crucial data and interpretations culled from an earlier manuscript written by a colleague is not uncommon. Forgery is rarer but has occurred, at least forgery in the sense that the author falsely claimed that his information came from personal observation and direct oral inquiry. One of the works of H. Trilles, an otherwise reliable author, is a case in point. His ethnographic description of pygmies is in part a forgery. Its contents derive partly from his imagination, partly from observations made by his colleagues, and only for a tiny part from observed facts. This work enjoyed great authority and influenced a generation of theories in the history of religion before his deception was discovered.[35] A routine application of the rules of evidence would have uncovered the situation, but he was writing ethnography, and in practice ethnographic, anthropological, and linguistic studies were exempted from critical examination. Given such disturbing cases, it is certainly useful to discuss critically the major characteristics of the written documents which underlie this study.

The Pivotal Role of Writing

We owe the earliest written documents about the coast of equatorial Africa to Portuguese writers of the beginning of the sixteenth century. However, only a handful of sketchy observations are available for that century. After 1600 and the arrival of others on the coast, more documents become available but, with the exception of some relating to the kingdom of Loango, these are also only brief notes. In the eighteenth century the trickle of information about the peoples living on the coast actually becomes even thinner, to recover gradually after 1800; but even so, one must wait until the 1840s before a continuous series of writings becomes available for coastal Cameroon and the Gabon estuary. Sketchy information about the interior begins to be available from hearsay shortly after 1800, but reports of the first foreign travelers in the interior date only from the late 1850s (Gabon). This period ends in the 1880s. From then on, a continuous flood of written information becomes available.

The early sources were mostly written by outsiders such as seafarers, traders, and missionaries, and second-hand by at least one geographer. As writing was unknown in equatorial Africa, there are practically no insiders' reports.[36] Most of the documents are letters, travelogues, and manuals for trade. There are also a very few geographic descriptions, which were to develop in a full-fledged ethnographic genre after the 1840s.[37] After 1880 most documents flowed from the pens of administrators and missionaries, with notable contributions from the military, traders, travelers, physicians, and some scholars: geographers, anthropologists, and, later still, historians. Travel reports and ethnographic writing continued, but, in volume at least, administrative reports of all stripes soon outweighed all other data.

Before 1880 writings were modestly supplemented by rare objects for curiosity cabinets and even rarer reliable iconographic documents.[38] After the 1850s ethnographic collections were made and photography supplemented drawings.[39] The first archaeological objects were gathered in the 1880s and the first archaeological site was dug up in 1925.[40] The earliest known sound recordings date from 1910.[41]

With regard to their accessability, after 1880 it is useful to distinguish between published and archival records. In this regard three groups stand out. First, there is the mass of administrative records. Many, perhaps most, are not easily accessible. Second, there are linguistic, geographic, or ethnographic descriptions. Most of these have been published, although many a study by an administrator or missionary is still accessible only in manuscript. Third, there are learned monographs which use other primary or even secondary sources to arrive at scientific conclusions, as well as travelogues aiming at entertaining or impressing readers in Europe or America. Almost all of these are published and are the most accessible. Because of this and because they carry the greatest prestige, they have influenced later authors the most. Published linguistic and ethnographic monographs have exercised a similar influence, especially when written by academics. Administrative reports have been the least influential, except on colleagues in their own milieu. Unfortunately many theses produced during the 1970s and 1980s in the various institutions of higher learning in the area are not accessible.

Further relevant distinctions differentiate between sources which record events or a course of proposed action, sources which record existing situations, and sources which aim at "scientific" general conclusions. Then one must distinguish between primary sources which rely on observation and oral information and secondary sources which derive their information from other writings. These distinctions largely overlap with the three groups we have set up. Administrative reports are primary sources dealing with events and action. So are travelogues. Ethnographic, linguistic, and geographic descriptions are usually primary sources depicting situations. Academic studies are usually secondary sources which aim neither to tell of events nor to describe situations but to discuss their significance within some general theoretical framework. Paradoxically, then, from this point of view the most accessible writings are often the least valuable.

For this study I have used all the extant published materials for the area I could find, complemented by archival holdings, especially in regions for which the published record was sparse, and by accessible university theses from central Africa. Records of travel and ethnographies by nonspecialists are the most abundant of the printed sources. A small number consist of grammars or lexical material often from the pens of self-taught linguists. Historical monographs are rare. Given the approach outlined above, the reader would expect me to have privileged ethnographic descriptions. Yet, wherever possible, I have cross-checked these and the geographic descriptions with administrative records of actual events and travelogues, because these descriptions generalize and extrapolate from impressions, whether those of the author or the normative expectations of his informants. Still, ethnographies are crucial, especially for a study of "words and things." Yet it soon becomes evident that they raise major problems dealing with space, time, and authorship. I address these three points in the order cited to conclude with an assessment of the quality of the bodies of data available.

Tribes and Space

A convention of the ethnographic genre was that peoples constituted territorial groups called "tribes," which were the given units of observation. Tribes were of almost indeterminate age. Within a tribe everyone held the same beliefs and practices, and observations made in any part of the tribal territory were valid for any other part. Moreover, by definition, every tribe differed from its neighbors. Such notions, no doubt derived from European ideas of nationhood, were mistaken.

Actually, ethnic identities change over time. They are not givens and they do not necessarily correspond to homogeneous units of social institutions or culture. The study of ethnic identity over time belongs to the history of ideas. In practice many modern ethnonyms were of colonial vintage. The Bondjo ethnic group on the shores of the Ubangi River seems to have existed only in the minds of French administrators.[42] In the 1920s Belgian administrators argued for years about the status of "the Ngando": Should they be included in the Mongo ethnic group or kept separate? They concluded that Ngando were Mongo.[43] As a result, by the 1950s the Ngando of Equateur province felt themselves to be Mongo. They had adapted their vision of ethnic identity to colonial reality. In some groups no sense of ethnic identity existed beyond the village. Among the "waterpeople of the Ngiri" (an administrative label), precolonial ethnic identity was village identity. Thus the ethnic identity of the inhabitants of the village or town of Libinza was limited to their settlement.[44] Still, in the same general area, R. Harms has shown how the ethnic identities called "Bobangi" and "Irebu" have taken root and evolved over time since c. 1750.[45]

On the other hand, not all ethnic references are of colonial vintage, although older labels then began to include more or fewer groups than before. Thus many names of the peoples of southern Gabon are attested from the early nineteenth century onward and the cluster of ethnicities mentioned has remained stable since then.[46] Indeed some of those names go back to the seventeenth century, and one name is already mentioned c. 1500 in the first written report about the area. In sum it is not possible to make generalizations about ethnic consciousness, because every case is the product of its own history. Therefore ethnic units must be abandoned as unanalyzed units for study.

Moreover it is not true to say that the spatial distribution of social or cultural features is congruent with "tribes." Thus, "the Lele of Kasai are polyandric" misleads.[47] In reality a portion of the Ding, their western neighbors, and of the Kuba, their eastern neighbors, as well as a few villages of their southern Pende neighbors and perhaps one or two Ooli villages to their north, also practice polyandry. In contradistinction, a portion of the Njembe, who are considered Lele by some authors but not by others, did not practice polyandry.[48] Such examples vividly illustrate the danger of using ethnic groups as units of observation.

The ethnic unit cannot be used as a valid unit of observation, even though it has served as such in all the ethnographies. It is necessary to pinpoint the actual places where the observations have been made. The authors rarely give this information, so it has to be derived from other sources such as the preface to a monograph. By using the itineraries of travelers and the maps of government, mission, and commercial posts, and by localizing the place names cited in such sources, I have been able to fix the points of observation for almost all the data used in this study.

Given the requirements of spatial coverage needed for an approach using "words and things," it became essential to make certain that the whole territory was adequately covered. Reports about the mobility of concrete villages are very useful here. Such data suggest that, on the whole, one can extrapolate from a point of observation for an area with a radius of approximately 50 km around that spot, without missing major cultural and social variants.[49] Given the intensity of European administration and missionary activity, there are no "unknown peoples," no totally unknown major social or cultural variants. As early as 1908 in Uele, for instance, ethnographic studies were being made "chiefdom" by "chiefdom," sometimes village by village.[50] But not all this information is published, and not all written data were available to me. In this study the sampling procedure described was used to make certain that the area was covered adequately. Where the published record left gaps, archival materials were used to complement the basic grid. Despite this, four gaps bigger than a circle with a 50 km radius still remain, only one of which, in eastern Cameroon and northern Gabon, is sizable. All the gaps are in areas with fewer than one person per km², or in "dead zones," totally uninhabited areas.[51] Even so, reports by travelers through these areas were available, as are reports, however sketchy, for almost all ethnic groups reported to be living there.[52]

A determined attempt has been made to abandon ethnic nomenclature in this book whenever a phenomenon of ethnicity is not discussed or where the term is anachronistic. But this was not always possible. In the end I have had to compromise and use ethnonyms, albeit sparingly.

Time

Linguistic and ethnographic reports used the present tense, thus referring to the time when the text was written. But this present was held to be valid for "traditional times." By implication "traditional" refers to an epoch without change, covering precolonial times far into dim antiquity. Observers often left out of their accounts anything that referred to an obvious colonial practice. This applied even to photographs: no bicycles, no kerosene lamps, no office buildings, no policemen, etc. And, naturally, "traditional" clothing and housing was a must.[53] The authors seem to have believed that they had thus expunged any influence of the colonial conquest. They did not realize that the foundations of every local community had been drastically altered by the colonial conquest or that substantive culture was no longer a "pristine" precolonial culture.

Obviously one cannot accept such claims. The dates of observation and of writing must be taken into account. The abundant observations of Pechuel Loesche in Cabinda date from the 1870s. His ethnography may date from 1907, but his data are precolonial. In contrast, the excellent studies of W. De Mahieu in northern Maniema cannot be considered a direct report of precolonial usage or thought, because they are based on observations of the 1970s.[54] To evaluate the position of the data, as precolonial or colonial, one needs to know the local date of colonial conquest and the time elapsed since then. The date of the colonial conquest is the date when administrative control began to be exercised by tax collection, by the nomination of local authorities, and often by the conducting of a census. In most cases the colonial period started with a genuine conquest followed by military occupation. Military histories are invaluable for establishing such dates.[55] Any observation made before such a period is precolonial, including reports by the military engaged in the conquest. Thus the 1892 report by W. H. Sheppard of his trip into the Kuba kingdom of Kasai is precolonial, because the first conquest here started in 1899–1900. The 1885 date for the foundation of the Independent Congo State is irrelevant. E. Torday's observations of 1907–1908 among the Kuba fall in colonial times, but his report on the Lele (1907) is precolonial, because their country had not yet been occupied. By the same principle, reports from the 1860s for the Libreville area are already colonial.[56]

This date being established, one can then estimate whether the information of a given later author was obtained from people who were old enough at the moment of conquest to have known precolonial conditions. "Old enough" varies with the topic reported. Domestic conditions in the household are well understood even by young children, but some public developments can be grasped only by people in their twenties or even thirties. At best 50 years could pass before everyone alive at the time of conquest has passed away. For the Kuba this would be 1950. It is true that in 1953 I still found a few eyewitnesses of the battles of 1900, but only a single direct witness to a functioning precolonial society. Among the Tio north of Brazzaville this date should fall in 1942. In 1963 there were still two quasi-centenarians, however, who could tell me about some aspects of precolonial life. But what most people told then was already oral tradition: what they had heard from their parents and others of that generation. Such a generation lasts approximately 30 years. After 1970 one no longer expected to find Tio whose parents had experienced the precolonial period, except for a few very old persons. Most people now were grandchildren of the precolonials. Their information can be expected to be much less abundant or knowledgeable and much more stereotyped. As a result of all this, one can assess any text as falling into one of four groups: precolonial, based on the remembrances of precolonial witnesses, based on first-generation oral tradition, or based on second-generation oral tradition.

Another aspect of this question concerns the duration of the observations reported. In extreme cases the situations reported have changed while they were being observed. For instance, G. Hulstaert began to live in Mongo country in 1925 and was still living there in 1988! But in most cases the record is supplied by a traveler who stayed a few days or weeks, or by a resident who stayed a year or more but typically less than five. The less time spent observing, the less believable the author's generalizations will be, unless he or she records the opinion of an informant. A longer stay does not automatically mean that the report is more trustworthy. One of the factors involved is the amount of time available for observation the author-resident actually had. In practice one can distinguish between short visits (a month or less), year-long stays, and residence for more than a year. Because of the round of the seasons, the year is an important measure.

As for information about space, the data necessary to estimate time factors such as length of stay, date of conquest, and age of informants are not always clear from the document studied. All but the last point can often be elucidated, usually from the profession of the author. As to the age of the informants, one must assume them to be men in early middle age unless otherwise indicated.

The Question of Authorship

When one asks oneself who the author of a given text is, the answer can be much more complex than expected, for two major issues are involved: one is the status of the writer, the other the specific authorship of the information reported. Given the fact that most writings in the corpus deal with people writing about other cultures, a complex situation of authorship is the usual case.

The first question to ask here is what the writer/author reports for himself or herself and what is in fact information provided by an informant. The following example shows the complexity of a real case. Le Testu was an administrator in Gabon as well as an amateur botanist and, on occasion, a military man. He observed the plants in the kitchen gardens himself, but when, in his official capacity, he asked about questions of inheritance, he had to rely on informants. When he wrote about the Wanji rebellion his information came partly from archives, partly from witnesses, but one part is an account of his own military actions—a fact that he does not advertise.[57]

Most writers in the assembled corpus rely on nameless hidden informants. Only small bits of the data reported derive from direct observation. Most come from hearsay, from one or more informants often understood through an interpreter. One must therefore assess the role of interpreters and informants who were trying to explain phenomena familiar to them to exotic foreigners. They had their own interests, their own perceptions of situations and of norms, their own interpretations of events, and their own biases, all reflected in their testimony. Writers usually do not talk about these issues directly. Sometimes writers give the impression that they carefully checked the statement of one person against that of others. But our impression is that quite often they did not. They relied on friends or major informants, often on employees. Frequently it is not possible to know all this without visiting the place of observation itself, and even then it cannot always be known.[58] Usually one can be aware only that these documents, although written by foreigners, often carry more than just a flavor of insiders' views and interests. They can be quite partisan, and as a result quite misleading. This often becomes clear when independent texts are confronted with each other, and it is one of the reasons why it is imperative to compare all the available data about each place.

Beyond the question of who was responsible for the information comes the examination of the writer, the author who composed the text. It is easy to establish whether the writer is an African and an African of the region with which the report deals. The distinction of insider or outsider is a crucial one. Insiders do not misunderstand and are not often misinformed, but they often do not report on situations that are as self-evident to them as they are puzzling to outsiders. Their hidden agendas will be different from those of outsiders and may range from a general wish for recognition of the qualities of their people to quite partisan reporting, for instance, about political succession. Outsiders had to rely on inside informants, often on only a single major informant who remains unnamed, and they were likely to misinterpret what they saw and to misunderstand what they were told for lack of knowledge of the local language.

Language competence is also fundamental. How well did the outsider really know the local vernacular or the *lingua franca* that was being used? Did he or she in fact use the vernacular, a *lingua franca,* a European language, or did he or she employ an interpreter? Many writers do not tell you. The prefatory statements of those who do are often empty boasts or leave unclear what level of competence they had achieved. Most residents had only a rudimentary knowledge of African languages, except for missionaries who had to preach in the vernacular. And even they were not always fluent. Transients were not very proficient. They used interpreters, as did most anthropologists, at least for the first year or so of their stay. Often the text of the report reveals more about language competence than any statement does. The transcriptions of items, even proper names in the local or regional language, are often dead giveaways. The writer reveals even more when indulging in etymological reasoning or in general statements about the language. In such ways one can often infer some information in this matter. But once again, questions of language competence may come to the fore only during a confrontation of texts, especially when comparing reports of local insiders with those of outsiders.

The profession of the author is important. It gives a feeling for the circumstances under which the research was conducted and it discloses areas of expertise. Administrators tended to use their personnel as informants and to write about social institutions or law. Missionaries often used elders or converts as informants, and tended to focus on religion, the life-cycle, morality, and marriage. A physician is a good reporter about childbirth practices, a missionary usually is not. Common professions for the authors in our sources fall into the following groups: a set of administrators, agricultural and medical personnel, magistrates, and even some engineers, accountants, and postal officers; a set of missionaries of various denominations, congregations, and statuses; a set of traders; a set of professional scholars in academic positions. Then there are the sets of travelers, journalists, cineasts, sportsmen, sailors, adventure seekers, and a few European servants or untrained laborers.

One usually thinks that the academic specialist, especially the anthropologist, is infinitely better qualified and hence more reliable than others. An article about the X by an anthropologist must rank higher than even a short book about the X by the local missionary or administrator. The academic is trained for the task and held to be much less biased than the missionary or the administrator. Such reasoning fails to take into consideration that academics too have their biases and fads, their preferred topics, and their taboos. One scholar may be a devotee of kinship systems and will see ambiance only in local music or dance, another is enthralled by cosmologies and does not care for kinship terminology. Anthropologists, moreover, are not the only trained observers. It is easy to forget that others, such as physicians or students of law, or indeed Pecile, the farmer servant of P. de Brazza,[59] were also trained to observe, albeit to observe different things. As a result the rarity of writings by professional anthropologists is not nearly as great a handicap as one would think. Just like any other text their reports must be confronted whenever possible with the whole available record, whether emanating from specialists or not.

Last but not least, gender is given for every named writer. There are very few female authors and hence the corpus shows an obvious lack of data about women, their lives, and their points of view. Not a single text about women's associations in Cameroon, Gabon, or Congo comes from a woman, and, in consequence, very little is known about them, since men were prevented by their gender from learning about them. On the whole, gender did not handicap foreign women as much as foreign men because they were often treated as "honorary men,"[60] except when inquiries dealt with closed men's associations. Gender thus has affected the record more by leaving obvious gaps than otherwise. The issue has been less of a problem than professional or insider status and language proficiency when evaluating the value of the records.

The effect of nationality and creed has been small. Writers of many nationalities indeed reported on equatorial Africa, especially in the Independent Congo State. National bias is visible from time to time in the mutual recriminations and stereotypes of rival European nationals. But jointly held stereotypes about Africans overrode most national differences, with the notable exception of the account of Tippo Tib, a Zanzibari. A similar observation holds for creed. Catholics, Protestants, anti-clerical liberals, Marxists, and others quarreled among themselves, but once again shared stereotypes used to describe Africans overrode their differences.

Special Contents

From the point of view of contents, the student of precolonial history will have to pay special attention to ethnography, linguistic data, and reports about oral tradition, in addition to documents from precolonial times and archaeological reports. Given the scant number of documents dating from the sixteenth century through the 1850s and the fledgling state of archaeology, most of the relevant documents consist of linguistic data, reports on tradition, and ethnographic materials. Linguistic data form the smallest group among these. Most of those materials were composed by missionaries who needed them for their work.[61] Collections of oral traditions, including oral literature such as tales, proverbs, and poems, are even rarer.[62] They were not considered by most to be of practical interest to any colonial. The bulk of the data consists of ethnographic information and content summaries of oral traditions. They abounded especially in the Belgian Congo, because such data were required for the preliminary inquiries to establish any local administrative unit.[63] Moreover, ethnography appealed to the exotic tastes of readers in Europe, at the same time justifying a "civilizing mission."

The linguistic documents are the most specialized. They consist of rare grammars and dictionaries and more abundant vocabularies, as well as texts with translation. The difficulties of interpretation usually involve the erroneous transposition of European grammatical models to African languages, deficient transcriptions, and approximate glosses. For only a few languages do we have full-sized dictionaries and grammars, resulting from many years of study, usually by several persons. Typically, only one person recorded the language and produced a rudimentary grammar and a vocabulary, so that no direct assessment of the quality of the work is possible. Luckily, however, professional linguists have made at least brief notes for a majority of languages,[64] which can be used to assess the quality of other materials. Even though the quality of older materials is usually more deficient than that of more recent data, an early date of notation is still valuable, especially for vocabularies, since they carry so much ethnographic information.

The "words and things" approach ideally requires adequate lexical information for all the languages of the area. Some data for practically all the languages of the area can be found in comparative compilations such as Sir H. J. Johnston's.[65] But fuller and adequate ready-made vocabularies exist for only a fourth or so of the languages spoken in the area. It has therefore been necessary to construct relevant vocabularies by gleaning items cited elsewhere, usually in ethnographies or transcribed texts.[66]

Content summaries of oral traditions are often quite condensed, and they were collected as interviews in administrative settings, where the expected practical consequences influenced the outcome. For such reasons the two syntheses, based as they are on such administrative data and made by senior colonial officials for the people of the rainforests in Zaire, are highly unreliable.[67] Moreover such traditions were often recorded only in a lapidary form such as "According to tradition . . . ," followed by the conclusions of the writer. That simply does not give any scope to evaluate critically the content of the tradition. A full, taped record of tradition as presented in a normal performing context still remains the exception.[68]

The homogeneity of content of the vast mass of ethnographic reports, published or not, is astounding. Given the near infinity of possible observations that can be made about a culture or a society, it is totally unexpected. But there it is: not only do most texts follow the same order of presentation (environment, economy, society, politics, religion, arts) but also, within these rubrics, the same topics are highlighted. The situation is a happy one, for it ensures the comparability of information across space, which is essential to the approach advocated here. It is also fortunate that the attention is centered on the major sociopolitical institutions and the principles of substantive culture and ideology, which are to be stressed in this study. But why such a harmony? One understands that the administrative records—intent on showing that such-and-such a district forms an administrative unit, headed by so-and-so, a legitimate chief, and heir to previous chiefs, with such-and-such rights, privileges, and obligations—delved into political institutions and ideologies, but the phenomenon is much broader than this type of specialized document. Almost all the authors use the same mental schemes, the same models. The models are ethnographic questionnaires which flourished even before the onset of the colonial period[69] and form a single interdependent body of writing, elaborated by jurists (Germany), administrators (France, Belgium), sociologists, and ethnographers (Great Britain, Germany, Belgium). The most influential questionnaire may well have been the successive editions of *Notes and Queries in Anthropology*. It certainly is a representative example. Such questionnaires directly inspired only a fraction of the documents. Other authors copied the plan and contents of existing monographs. This homogeneity of interests and exposition also holds for professional anthropologists. The particular model is usually easy to spot. Only after independence did breaches appear in this type of reporting. The new administrations do not care for ethnography; national authors feel less constrained by the established practices and theoretical developments in anthropology; history and folklore begin to focus on new questions which require the gathering of other data.

Even though one rejoices about the comparability of the data, one should not ignore the drawbacks of such a situation. Any selection, any codification, orders data in advance, assigns relative importance, and incorporates prejudices. Although crude colonial prejudice in general is easily spotted nowadays, more subtle biases are not. Thus the assumptions that numerically small societies are simple, that there are tribes, that kinship operating through "lineages" (a "unilineal descent group") is their only cement, that only one form of legitimate marriage could exist (determined by European law), that agriculture was the only form of food production system, that religion formed a separate system grounded in dogma as it is in Europe, and so on, are all false. Such a-priorisms have continually falsified the realities of the past, as will become evident all along in this book.

Then there are the systematic omissions. It is, for instance, difficult to know the exact composition of households or villages. Exact data on social inequality, a description of the small gardens near the kitchen (also known as dawn gardens), a description of the bonds of friendship, the point of view and many details in the life of women, the variety of views people held about their own rituals, current aesthetic notions— these are some examples of other obvious lacunae. Although one can evaluate and use the data provided, the selectivity of these observers creates restrictions. Not only does one not know what they did not report, but also constant vigilance is required to keep one's epistemology from sinking into the familiar ruts of past inquiry. Hence the need to spot chance remarks and fleeting notes, which often will assume greater importance than long disquisitions on stereotyped themes.

Reliability of Bodies of Evidence

So far the issues addressed affect the credibility of individual documents. Beyond this, however, one must also assess the reliability of whole bodies of data. The strongest evidence of reliability is independent confirmation by other documents, just as the quickest way to spot problems of reliability is to spot discrepancies between documents. The notion of independence is a relative one. For instance, two writers may be different, never have known each other, and yet not be independent because their work belongs to the same genre or the authors belong to the same calling. To establish even a rough index of reliability, it is therefore necessary to take into account not just the quantity of documents available for cross-checking or the number of authors, but also their status and the type of document. In practice I have considered the following criteria for each observation spot in the whole area studied: quantity of materials, number of authors, their eventual relationships (e.g., as master and disciple, superior and inferior, as colleagues), the diversity of their backgrounds, their professional competence, their gender, their linguistic competence, their insider or outsider status, the length of their stay, the variety of genres, and the dates of observation. The result of the analysis appears on map 1.3, which gives the reader an indication of the quality of statements made about various portions of the whole area.

The map shows that four portions of the area are so well served in quantity, diversity, and quality, and have generated such a large and diverse bibliography that the study of the peoples involved has become highly specialized. One finds here every type of author, every genre of writing, information for every generation since c. 1885, every sort of competence. The fuller state of knowledge about the peoples there has often led to unwarranted generalizations applied to large, lesser-known portions of equatorial Africa, or even to the whole area.

Beyond this, there are 19 areas for which documents exist from the outset of the colonial period or before, documents by insiders and outsiders, professionals and nonprofessionals, where linguistic materials are adequate and data occur in the main genres. Only the lesser quantity of information distinguishes them from the first group. Two-thirds of them are located not far from the epicenters of the first group.

Informed readers would expect at this point at least to see a mention of pygmy studies, especially for those living in Ituri, in northern Congo, and eastern Cameroon. There exists an enormous literature indeed about pygmies, and the field certainly forms a subspecialty of its own in anthropology. But this corpus suffers from a fatal flaw: it studies only part societies. It studies the hunter gatherers, but not the farming people with whom they are linked. The overwhelming majority of writings are anthropological reports, and the bulk of the writers are anthropologists. There are no pygmy authors and no authors who come from the villages with which the hunter gatherers are linked. The main reason that pygmies have attracted such attention has been, first, their "exotic" appeal, and second, the assumption that somehow they represent the roots of humanity.[70] They are studied for their presumed potential to elucidate life at the dawn of humanity, not for their own sake. So, yes, there exists a vast amount of valid information, but it is always incomplete—the farmers are missing—and it is often flawed by strong preconceptions.[71]

Returning to a general assessment one then comes to a third set of areas for which most of the criteria mentioned are met, barring but one. Frequently there are no insider authors, or sufficient linguistic material is lacking. Normally this is associated with a substantial drop in the quantity of writings available as well. The data for the next class of areas become downright scanty. Often one deals with only one main author and with but an article or two. There is just enough to know the main

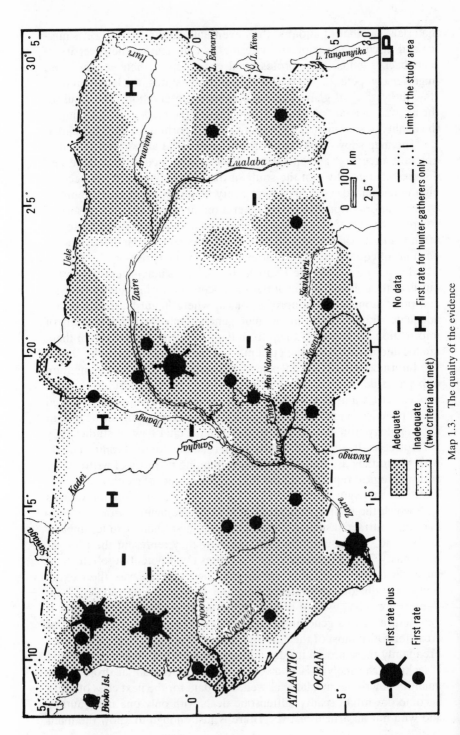

Map 1.3. The quality of the evidence

outlines of late precolonial societies and cultures, but not more. And then there are the four gaps, which have been mentioned before. As can be seen from the map, however, all in all the data are good enough over almost the whole area to provide a reliable base for this study.

RESEARCH DESIGN

Given the aims and approach set forth, one must now consider the research design used. The scholar working with "words and things" is like a mosaicist or a pointillist painter. He or she makes an image of the past by painstakingly fitting together small slivers of evidence exactly as tesserae finally yield a mosaic and dots of paint a picture. It is slow and tedious work, but the approach is incredibly fruitful and flexible. One can reconstruct the past in absolutely every detail that has been retained in the languages. Yet each detail involves one in a large mass of comparative research, because each distribution must be followed spatially as far as it goes. In short, the approach soon forces a researcher to limit his or her field. One cannot restrict the subject to too small an area, for the area must be sufficiently large to show the emergence of general trends and one must have full comparability for every word one uses. So one must also delimit the specific subject of research. Not every reconstruction is equally important. Some cultural and social features affect the whole profile of a way of living, others do not. Thus midwifery or football are interesting topics to pursue, but, at this point, and given the general goals of this study, political roles are more "significant."

In this study I have chosen to concentrate on the major lineaments of the original tradition: the economic, social, and political institutions, which shaped societies as a whole, and the key elements of worldviews and ideologies underlying cultural visions. All the ethnographic, semantic, and relevant linguistic materials for this huge area had to be assembled, first to establish what the key social and cultural institutions actually were, and then to strive for that completeness of documentation required by the "words and things" approach.

At that point a choice had to be made among various ways to reconstruct the past. I chose the following path: first to document the major social and cultural features of the peoples in the forests, just before the colonial conquest, and thus establish a baseline. Once in place this served as a jumping off point for "upstreaming," that is, for going backward in time,[72] using the information at hand from all kinds of sources. The key ingredient in this approach was the set of vocabularies, which yielded evidence of ancestral forms, borrowing, or innovations on a rough, relative time-scale. For a century and a half before the baseline, oral traditions were given due cognizance. Rare though the written

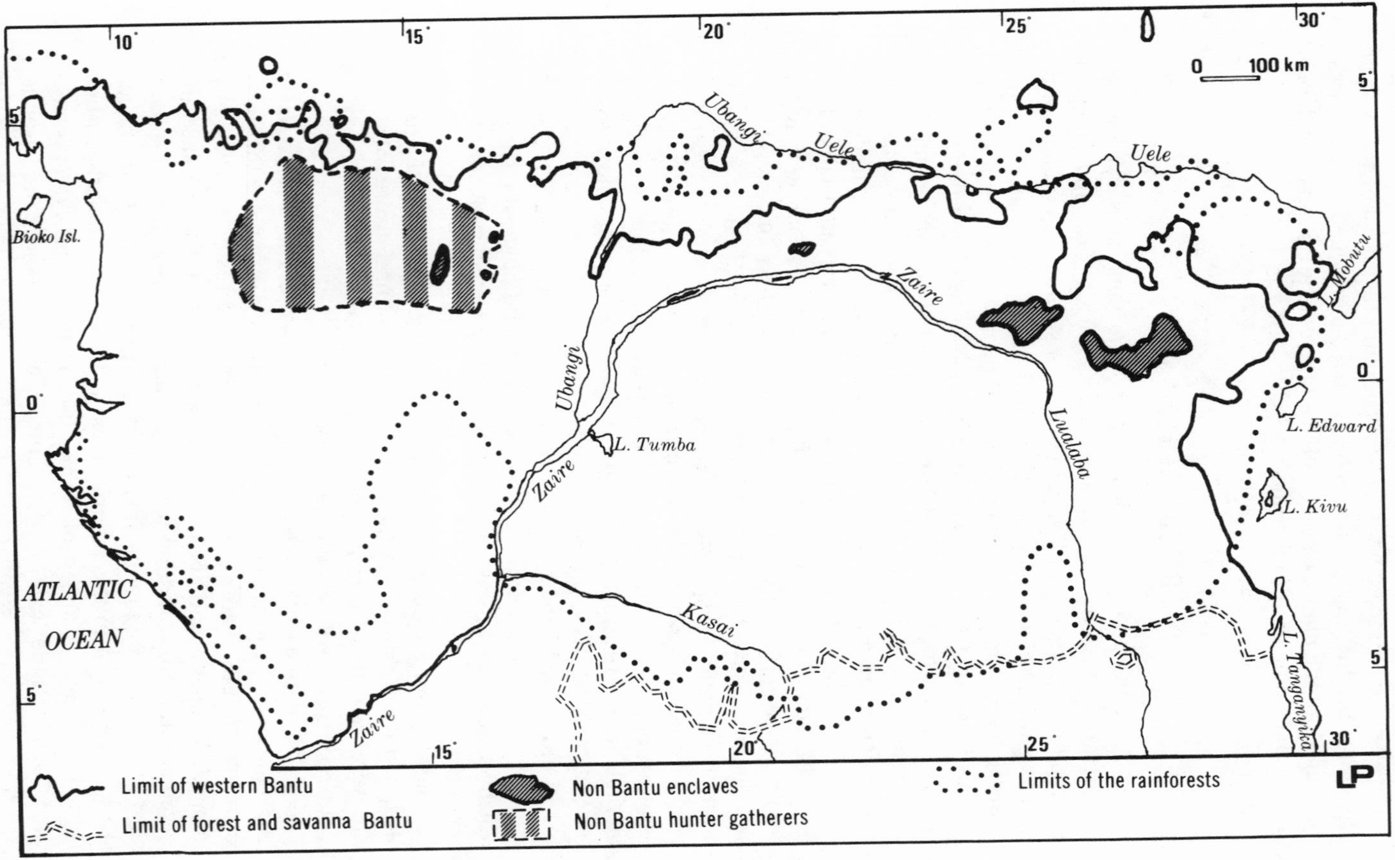

Map 1.4. Western Bantu languages of the rainforests

sources are, especially before 1850, they still tell us much about the intensity, the routes, and the impact of the slave trade, which affected much of the region after 1660. Biological data about plants and animals available were taken into account as well.

Upstreaming in this fashion, I have now reached backward to the first centuries after A.D. 1000. The "words and things" technique can be carried further back in time than this. In theory one could reach all the way to the first settlements of Bantu speakers. But as one moves further into the past, the amounts of data to be examined are more massive, and because the traces become fainter and fainter, the quality of the evidence must be better and better. Given the specific goals sought and the time available, the research was confined to only major features of culture and society, especially to institutions, and the upstreaming was halted at this point. More detailed semantic and sometimes ethnographic data will have to be available before one can safely resume further upstreaming.

Data at the other end of the spectrum of time involved complemented this approach (map 1.4). The process of settlement by Bantu-speaking farmers in the area was reconstructed from the genealogical model for western Bantu languages as known today; a study of their proto-vocabulary allowed the sketching of a profile of the society and culture of the ancestral community at the outset of its expansion. Taking into account the later immigration of eastern Bantu speakers south of the forest, as well as major early borrowings in food production and in metallurgy, the ancestral profile then allowed for the presentation of an inventory of the main features common to the societies and cultures of the area in the last centuries before A.D. 1000, with some indication as to their antiquity before that time. The reader is given a description of the starting era of the tradition, but should remain aware that this sketch does not constitute a baseline. For it does not describe a situation limited in time to a given generation, as the late precolonial baseline does. By its nature the proto-vocabulary represents a whole period rather than a point in time.

The results are presented in this book in the conventional order: from a beginning to an end, rather than against the current of time, and for good reason. The arrow of time is the historian's lodestar, because what comes later cannot affect what comes earlier. Still tradition, like Janus, has two faces, and the book shows them in succession: first the petrified face of continuity, then the mobile face of change. The technique of historical reconstruction involved differs for each face: the first is built up on semantic inheritance, the second on semantic innovation.

Two

The Land and Its Settlement

Nearly 5,000 years ago hunters and gatherers in the forests then covering part of what are now the Cameroonian grasslands began an experiment which went on for almost a millennium: They became more sedentary, acquired ceramics, and began to supplement their hunting and gathering practices with new ventures in agriculture and trapping. Slowly a new way of life took shape here. Once perfected, it allowed them to spread far and wide as colonists in search of a mythical land of plenty, following rivers and elephant trails through forests which were inhabited only by small numbers of scattered groups of hunters and gatherers and by fishermen. It was a slow "happening," but in the end they settled the whole of equatorial and central Africa. This chapter tells the story of this expansion. But first one must sketch the stage on which these actors were about to appear.

THE LANDSCAPES

The coordinates for this study are the area between longitudes 9° and 29° east, and latitudes 4° north, in places 5° north, and 4° south, but dipping sometimes as far as 6° south. This is the home of the largest block of rainforests in the world but one. In each spot of this large area, relief, soils, and climate largely produce a specific landscape. It was a landscape slowly changing not only as a result of the fluctuations of the climate, but also in response to the specific effect of flora and fauna striving toward optimal ecological conditions. The culling of selected plant and animal species by hunters and gatherers did not seriously disrupt the balance of nature, but when farming colonists arrived, they began to cut swaths into the forests. Their impact grew with their experi-

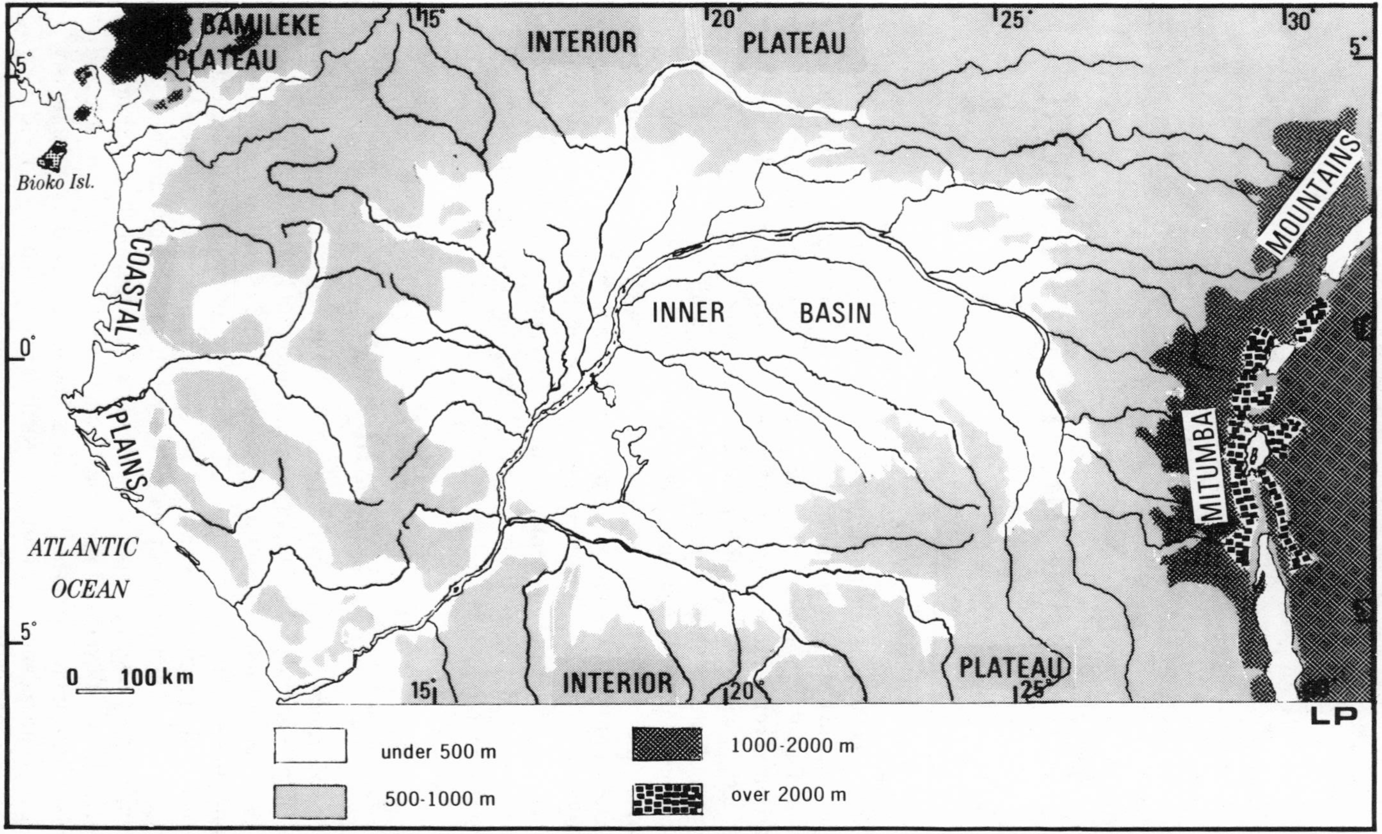
BAMILEKE PLATEAU
INTERIOR PLATEAU
15°
20°
25°
30°
5°
0°
5°
Bioko Isl.
COASTAL PLAINS
INNER BASIN
MOUNTAINS
MITUMBA
ATLANTIC OCEAN
0 100 km
INTERIOR PLATEAU
15°
20°
25°
LP
under 500 m
500-1000 m
1000-2000 m
over 2000 m

Map 2.1. Orography

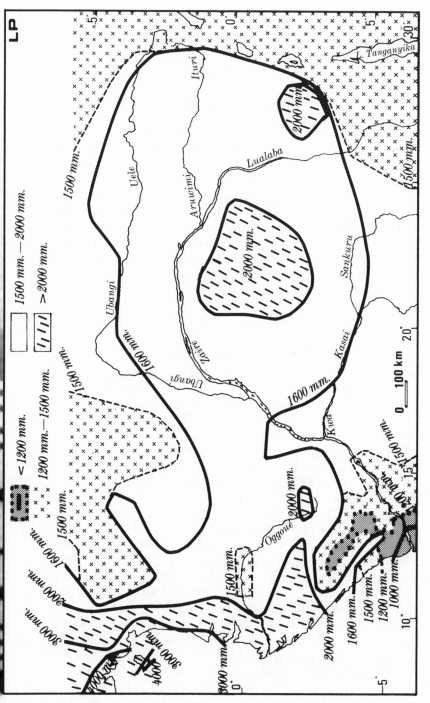

LP

< 1200 mm.

1200 mm.—1500 mm.

1500 mm.—2000 mm.

>2000 mm.

L. Tanganyika

Ituri

Uele

Aruwimi

Lualaba

Ubangi

Zaire

Sankuru

Kasai

Kwa

Oggoué

1500 mm.

1600 mm.

2000 mm.

3000 mm.

Map 2.2.   Rainfall

0   100 km

37

ence and confidence. The history of the landscapes is interdependent
with theirs, especially in the rainforests, perhaps the most complex set of
habitats in the world, and therefore among the least stable and most
vulnerable.[1]

Physical Geography

As map 2.1 indicates, the core of the area is constituted by the depression
of the central Zaire or Congo River basin, which is separated from the
Atlantic coast by a low mountain range not exceeding 1,000 m, and from
East Africa by the formidable mountain barrier which borders the Western Rift Valley. Toward West Africa the area is geologically bounded by a
line of high volcanoes which starts as the islands of Saõ Tomé, Principe,
and Bioko in the ocean, peaks in Mt. Fako (Mt. Cameroon) to run northwest toward the high Cameroon grasslands. The dominant soils are rich in
iron (ferralitic) and infertile. They are cut by swaths of waterlogged
(hydromorph) soils which are somewhat more fertile. Rich soils, whether
volcanic or not, are rare.[2]

The exuberant vegetation can survive on such soils only by constantly recycling organic materials before they are leached away by the
abundant rains. Although ferralitic soils are common, higher quality
veins of iron ore are not evenly distributed. Mineral salts are rare. They
are found in hydromorph soils, especially in marshes or, here and there,
as saline springs on the slopes of the eastern mountain range.

This geographic relief conditions the network of rivers. All the major rivers are barred by falls before reaching the ocean. The Zaire River,
the second largest river in the world by flow, and its navigable tributaries
drain the central depression. In the west the Mungo, Wouri, Sanaga,
Nyong, Ogooué, and Kouilou-Niari rivers are smaller than the main
tributaries of the Zaire. They are navigable only in stretches between
cataracts.

Given the location of the area astride the equator, it always lies
between extreme intertropical weather fronts. Most of the rains come
from the Atlantic during the summer in the northern hemisphere and
from the Indian Ocean during the summer in the southern hemisphere,
although even then the coastal regions still derive their rains from the
Atlantic.[3] Most of the area receives between 1,600 and 2,000 mm of rain
a year, a necessary condition for the sound development of rainforests
(see map 2.2). In the west, in the middle of the central depression, and in
the southeast, quantities over 2,000 mm are usual. Only lower Zaire and
the valley of the Kouilou-Niari receive much less: 1,200 mm and even
1,000 mm in places. Temperatures are also favorable for the development of rainforests, as they oscillate between 23°C and 27°C, the amplitude of daily oscillations being often superior to annual amplitudes.[4]

The single most crucial climatic variable for farmers is the annual round of seasons (map 2.3). There are two, a wet and a dry season. For the core of the area the dry season lasts two months or less, and even then approximately 50 mm of rain fall per month near the equator.[5] Thus "dry" is relative, but the seasonal phenomenon is real. The plants adapt their biological cycles to it. Map 2.3 indicates the length of the dry season in months. Farmers dread the absence or short duration of the dry season, wherever it is less than three months. In lower Zaire and lower Congo, with long dry seasons, prolonged drought can be a problem. Rain magic is meant to stop rain, but here rain magic is aimed at bringing rain. Everywhere the date for the onset of the main rainy season, the sheet anchor for the farming cycle, is anxiously awaited.[6]

Mythical Jungles and True Rainforests

Jungle is as much a myth as Tarzan is. The myth paints the rainforests as a single monotonous primeval environment, enormous in size, a "green hell," where wretched "Man" unceasingly wrestles to keep the ever-encroaching foliage at bay. This glaucous universe is impenetrable, and within minutes of entering this uncharted sea of green, one is lost. Buzzing with insects, exhaling weird miasmas, the rainforest stupefies, cripples, and kills. Only pygmies ever adapted to it and their adaptation stultified them. They became living fossils: human insects caught in the amber of the green sea.[7] The other forest dwellers are the dross of humanity dumped out of the way there by the better endowed.[8] This image merely expresses the European or North American hostility toward milieux that were utterly foreign to them. Stanley contributed much to its creation, especially by his description of the hardships he suffered when crossing the Aruwimi forests during his search for Emin Pasha.[9] Everything in this perception is wrong, except for the size of the rainforests. They do indeed cover some 15 million ha and stretch over a length of 3,400 km.

"Rainforest" is a general term to designate low altitude forests exposed to high rainfall, with stable temperatures in the 25°–27°C range, characterized by closed canopies, often disposed on several levels, and by evergreen or semideciduous trees. The expression "rainforest" encompasses a wide range of the most complex habitats in the world. For the botanist there is no monotony, but rather endless variation under these canopies. Most of these forests consist of such a diversity of flora that one is hard put to find a few trees of the same species per acre. Hundreds of species are associated in each local habitat, and the total number of species known for the whole area runs well over 10,000. Every local habitat is influenced by temperature, humidity, pluviosity, wind, exposure to the sun, and type and declivity of soil. No two locales

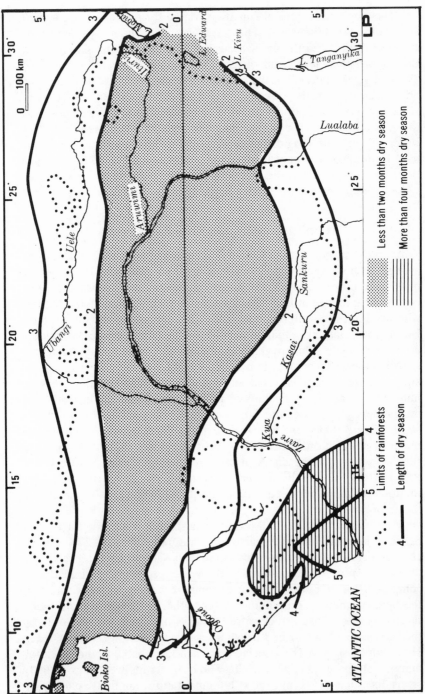

Map 2.3.   Seasons

Limits of rainforests
Length of dry season

Less than two months dry season
More than four months dry season

40

are identical. Hence a crowd of microbiotopes exist, all striving toward different biological climaxes. A single wood varies even from the crest of a hill to its foot. It differs on the ridge, it differs on the slope, and it differs near the brook at the base. It forms a *catena*, a chain of transitions between its aspects on the ridge and those near the water. The distribution of the fauna itself depends on such biotopes. To mention but a commonplace occurrence: on a single catena one finds wild pigs (*Phacochaerus*) and water chevrotain antelopes at the bottom, small duikers (Cephalophinae) on the slopes, and larger antelopes such as the bongo (*Boocercus eurycerus*) near the crests. Monkeys distribute themselves by height of canopy and by the frequency of the species of trees whose fruit they eat, hence also along the catena. And so it goes for every species, from the lordly elephant to the tiny shrew and the specialized microant. Forest people are well aware of this host of habitats varying by soil, place on a catena, and striving toward different biological climaxes.[10]

Some of the major contrasting types of habitats are coastal mangroves, sweet water marshes with raffia thickets, other marshes, floating meadows, permanently and temporarily inundated forests, forests on dry soils (evergreen or semideciduous, with or without stands of dominant species among which *Gilbertiodendron dewevrei* is most common), forests on rocky soils, forests covering a tortuous relief, and mountain forests culminating in the bamboo forests at an altitude of over 1,500 m, a paradise for gorillas. One must also mention the most notable ecotones or associations of diverse biotopes: the savanna/forest mosaics on the edges of the area; intercalary savannas scattered like ponds or lakes within the forest cover and often located on poor soils which cover a few acres or hundreds of square miles; denuded rocks and mesas; and the landscapes created by the mighty rivers, such as the Zaire at Lisala with its 40-km-wide expanse, its islands, its natural dikes, and its associated marshes beyond. One should not forget secondary forests, often typified at an early stage of regeneration by the fast-growing "umbrella tree" (*Musanga smithii*) or *Terminalia* spp.

An underestimation of this diversity leads to a flawed understanding of the interaction between people and their habitats. For example, C. Turnbull thought that all Mbuti of Ituri lived in a single biotope, and hence that the habitat played no role in the existence of two social types of Mbuti communities: net hunters and archers. But Mbuti live in three different biotopes and the choice of net hunting is closely related to one of them.[11] The historian in particular should furthermore be aware that some biotopes testify to former population densities through the relative impact of recent or ancient human farming activity.[12]

A reliable map of this host of habitats becomes quite cluttered, as a segment of a map by Letouzey shows (map 2.4b).[13] General maps for

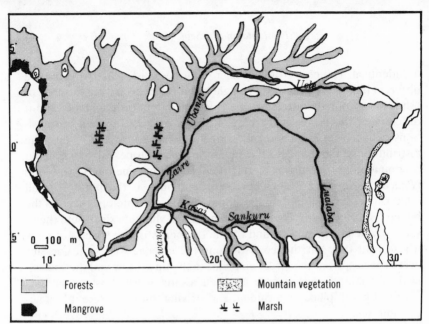

Map 2.4a. The rainforests: a simple view

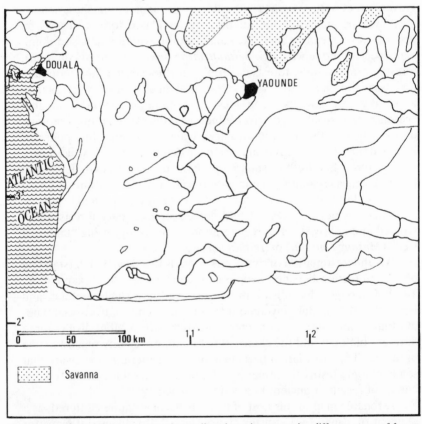

Map 2.4b. The rainforests: a complex reality—botanists recognize different types of forest vegetation in the outlined areas

the whole area of rainforests cannot render all this detail (map 2.4a). They are simplified and hence insufficient for any local study. But an indication of even the main natural conditions in the area as on map 2.5 stands in striking contrast to the uniform green of most atlases. It serves as a broad orientation, and as a reminder of the diversity of interaction between the habitats and the peoples who occupy them.

Are rainforests impenetrable? This varies from one biotope to another. The stereotype of description and photograph, the green wall on the edge of any clearing, such as for a road, relates to one small biotope only, just a few meters deep, where a riot of groundcover exists because it has access to sunlight. Behind this screen one meets sparse groundcover and people circulate easily. In general, relief can be more of a barrier to communication than vegetation. Rainforests are so named because they receive abundant precipitation. This precipitation, in turn, creates mighty rivers which can be used as highways, at least on sedimentary reliefs. Thus the Zaire River is navigable for 1,734 km from the Malebo Pool to Kisangani, the Kasai for almost 1,000 km, and the Sangha for 780 km. The Zaire River system formed one transportation network. Another one was constituted by the shorewaters of the Atlantic and the lower courses of the rivers that flowed into the ocean. As shown by the record of diffusion and population movements, the mountain wall on the eastern border of the area acted as a major barrier to travel. To a lesser extent, this also holds true for portions of the lower western mountain chain. Contrary to myth, then, no population in the area was ever isolated, "lost in the woods." In fact, ease of communication, especially within the Zaire basin, is a major geographic characteristic of the area.

Are forests healthy for people? Informed opinion is divided on this question.[14] The morbidity and mortality in the majority of rainforest environments is not significantly higher than elsewhere, although the agents of ill health are different. On the whole the comparison seems to favor primary rainforests on dry soil over savanna. But one must take other biotopes into account. Thus *Anopheles* mosquitoes do not thrive under closed canopies and hence there is no malaria, but open marshes are a haven for them. River banks and open fields, with crops whose leaves retain pockets of water, are good habitats for *Anopheles* and breeding grounds for malaria. The *Glossina* flies, carriers of sleeping sickness, require precise conditions of sunlight and humidity. Unfortunately most river banks in forested areas meet them.[15] Any general statement about the debilitating effects of forest or savanna expresses but prejudice. Only a study of the pathological agents in each precise biotope can answer such questions of health.

As to "menacing," the myth has it the wrong way around. "People kill the forest"[16] rather than the reverse. These rainforest habitats are

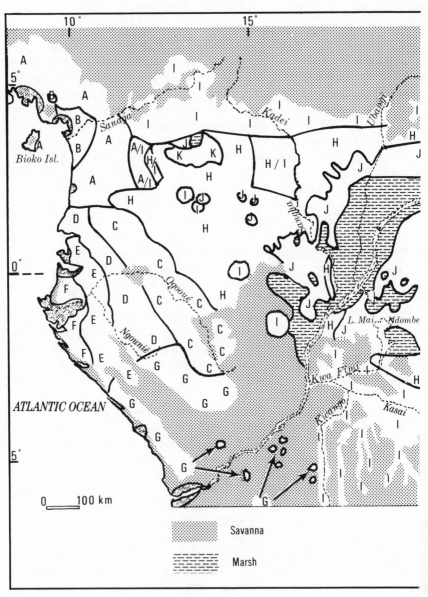

Map 2.5.   Vegetation

A.   Atlantic evergreen forest with *Caesalpiniaceae* in Cameroon

B.   Coastal forest of Cameroon

C.   Gabonese forest of the northeastern plateau

D.   Gabonese mountain forest with *Aukoumea kleinia*

E.   Gabonese lowland forest with *Aukoumea kleinia*

F.   Gabonese coastal forest with *Aukoumea kleinia*

G.   Rainforests of Mayombe

44

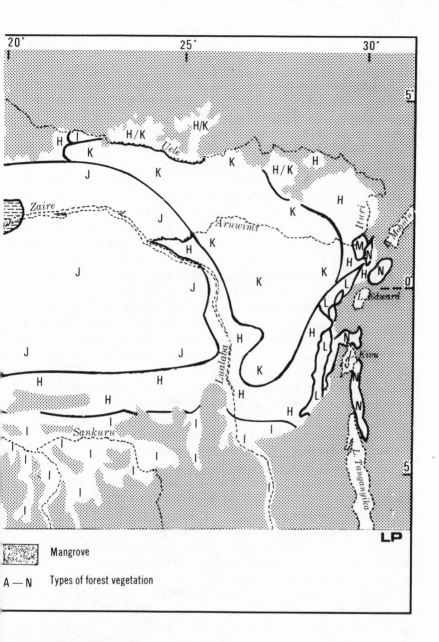

H. Guineo-Congolian rainforest: drier types

I. Dense wet subequatorial forest

J. Easily flooded rainforest in mosaic with K

K. Guineo-Congolian rainforest: wetter types with stands of *Gilbertiodendron dewevrei*

L. Dense dry mountain forest

M. Forest with *Cynometra alexandri*

N. Dense wet mountain forest

fragile and easily disturbed, precisely because of their complexity. Living in them requires no particular struggle but, rather, good care not to damage such habitats beyond repair. Population densities in the rainforests are usually quite low, not because these habitats are so difficult to live in, but because very few people can exploit them without forever altering them. That is, larger populations cut so many trees that the forests do not recover and the habitat is destroyed.

To insist on the "primeval" character of "virgin" rainforests is equally wrong. The rainforests have their history, even though that history is not yet well-known for lack of sufficient palynological data. Around 16,000 B.C. the climate here was at its most arid. Evergreen rainforests survived only in refuges surrounded by semideciduous habitats. By 10,000 B.C. the climate became wetter and the forests expanded until 3000 B.C., a millennium before the western Bantu expansion began.[17] Since then the expanse of rainforests has shrunk as the climate became drier and humans began to leave their mark. After the onset of our era, the amplitude of climatic oscillations subsided and the borders of the rainforests should have stabilized. But increased human intervention led to further irregular shrinking, especially along the northern and southern edges. These general indications are not valid everywhere; locally contrary movements have been recorded. Thus, on their eastern edge, forests were conquering savanna at Matupi after 1000 B.C.[18]

The other portions of the common stereotype do not merit further extended discussion. Because of their local diversity, forests do not disorient forest dwellers, especially the villagers who intimately know the domain of their settlement. Nomadic hunter gatherers find their way over long distances by reference to a gridwork of streams crossed and elephant trails.[19] Contrary to the stereotype, then, rainforest habitats are desirable environments, and the ancestors of the western Bantu speakers, seeking an easy living, thought so. In the end the whole ludicrous nightmare of rainforests as a dump for the rejects of humanity is shown up for what it is: environmental racist determinism.

On occasion, the area studied does spill over, beyond the boundaries of the habitats discussed, into savanna countries, especially in the southwest. Even though "savanna" is less misleading than "forest" as a general description, still the fauna and flora of various savannas and parklands vary according to altitude, rainfall, and soils. Different but similar habitats result, such as the coastal savannas or the savannas of the Niari Valley. Among these only the savannas of the five Bateke plateaus stand out, because of their lack of rivers. People there have been forced to develop innovative techniques to store and utilize rainwater.[20]

WESTERN BANTU EXPANSION

Early Inhabitants

Because the region adjoins East Africa, the birthplace of humanity, equatorial Africa has been inhabited since very early times, especially during periods when most of the area was covered by savannas. But traces of the most ancient Stone Age hunters and gatherers are rare (map 2.6). A few Oldowan pebble tools have been found at the Malebo Pool. At present Middle Stone Age and Late Stone Age sites are known from savannas all around the area. Tshitolian, a Late Stone Age industry that involved the production of microliths mainly for hafting and began c. 10,000 b.c., when more humid conditions returned to the region, abounded in the southern savanna areas, where it lasted until the arrival of the Bantu speakers.[21]

But there is no firm evidence so far for human settlement in rainforest environments. Sites now deep in the present forest may have been occupied when such places lay in savanna. The Middle Stone Age site on the road from Ouesso/Liouesso (north Congo) dates from a very arid period. The sites of Equateur, dated to later than c. 23,000 b.c. relate to a savanna environment. One suspects similar conditions for the surface finds at the confluence of the Lomami and the Zaire, near the Ituri, and at Angumu in northern Maniema. Late coastal sites near Libreville and Lope were also located in savannas.[22]

Still, the presence of human occupation over such a large portion of the area, before the forest expanded again after 10,000 b.c., leads to the suspicion that not all the inhabitants of the area retreated in the face of the encroaching forests, especially not in certain places, such as the habitats of the Zaire River bend or on the shores of the equatorial lakes. Therefore the first farmers may possibly have found fishermen as well as hunter gatherers in the area. Such people would not have looked like pygmies, because these habitats did not exert any pressure by natural selection toward such a physique. By the same token it is virtually certain that hunter gatherers of pygmy physique roamed the densely canopied forests, because as scholarly consensus has it, their physique results from an adaptation to such forests.[23]

The archaeological finds should not delude us about population density. Such densities were extremely low, probably better measured as persons per 10 or per 100 square kilometers than per 1 square kilometer. It is clear that pygmy populations were isolated, because the biological differences between surviving groups are so marked.[24] They therefore probably spoke languages that were quite different from each other, so that the search for "the pygmy language" will remain fruitless.[25] But one cannot be quite so certain about the isolation of people living near

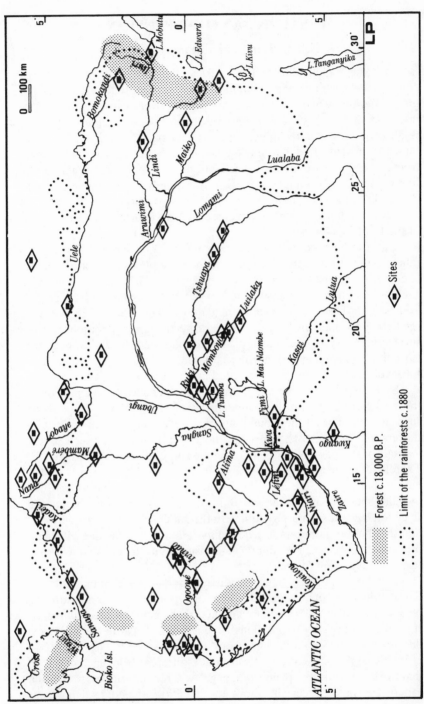

Map 2.6. Older Stone Age sites

Sites ◈

▦ Forest c.18,000 B.P.

⋯ Limit of the rainforests c.1880

watercourses. The inhabitants around Lake Tumba and the Ruki River imported their stone from 200–250 km away and those around the lower Gabon estuary imported stone from over 300 km away.[26]

However shadowy these populations may be in the extant record, and however tiny their numbers, they were the autochthons found by the main actors of this book, Bantu-speaking farmers and trappers, when they settled in the area. Traditions remember the aborigines as the teachers and guides, or in the lapidary words of one African author: "the pygmy acting as compass."[27]

Western Bantu Expansion

As has been known for over a century, almost all the peoples of the subcontinent south of a line from the lower Cross River to southern Somalia speak patently related languages. These have been labeled *bantu* ("people"), a term whose reflexes recur almost everywhere. The cradle of the Bantu languages must have been in Nigeria, in the Benue Valley, because the languages closest to Bantu are still spoken in that area. In that general area as well, the Bantu family split into two branches: eastern and western Bantu, a split dated by glottochronology to c. 3000 B.C. Western Bantu evolved east of the Cross River in western Cameroon, both on the then-forested Bamileke Plateau and on the lowlands near the ocean.[28]

The proto-vocabulary indicates that Bantu speakers made pottery and had begun to farm by this time. Indeed, it is striking that terms connected to the cultivation of cereal crops occur only in eastern Bantu, and terms dealing with the cultivation of the oil palm and yams occur in both branches, but most terms for root crop and tree cultivation are western Bantu. Given the natural habitat of these crops, early Bantu speakers must have been living near the margins of rainforests. The eastern Bantu later went on to live in savanna environments.[29] Proto-Bantu speakers farmed but they neither smelted nor used metals. All plausible items relating to metallurgy derive from activities such as "hammering," which may have belonged to the technology of stone knapping, or are later loanwords.[30] In other words, early Bantu speakers were "Neolithic." Sites relating to them would contain ceramics and stone tools, probably polished, as well as evidence for oil palm cultivation (yams do not leave traces for the archaeologist to find).

Western Bantu languages gradually occupied all of central Africa. This is best explained by assuming that their speakers spread farming into the whole area as they expanded. It follows that the major splits in western Bantu indicate the temporal and spatial succession of this expansion. The main outlines of the genealogical tree are now known (figure 2.1), and its spatial implications are set out on map 2.7 with the relevant dates.

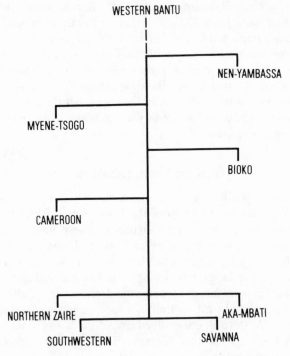

Figure 2.1. The western Bantu family of languages

Western Bantu did not split into branches of equal complexity. Rather, a succesion of splinter groups seems to have broken away from a main body. Among the early splits, some were caused by the isolation of small groups moving out of reach. That seems to be the case for the Bioko and the Myene-Tsogo group, who moved by sea. Later on, the Sekyani may well have seceded from the Cameroon languages by sea as well. But the impression of splinter groups moving out is usually spurious, created by the major thrust of the expansion itself. When splits occurred, most splits broke the so-called main body into nearly equal parts, one of which *later* expanded much more than the other.[31] At the time of the split itself, "the main body" is an anachronism.

The linguistic genealogy easily allows one to follow the main push of the expansion. Starting north of the lower Sanaga the main movement was southward to the lower Zaire. Once in the savanna areas to the south of the river, western Bantu speakers expanded to the southeast as far as the present Zambian-Malawian border area, the middle Zambezi, and the southern Kunene. Within equatorial Africa proper, the area west of the Sangha-Zaire was settled first. A major thrust eastward

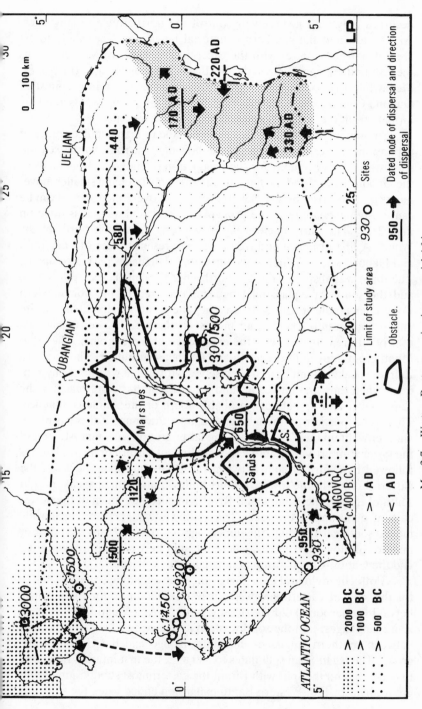

Map 2.7. Western Bantu expansion in equatorial Africa

51

occurred only with a three-way split of the northern Zaire languages, Aka-Mbati, and the southern equatorial languages. The whole forest area of northern Zaire, with the exception of southern Maniema, was then settled by speakers of the northern Zaire languages (map 2.8). Meanwhile the southwestern group of languages spread over most of Gabon, Congo, and lower Zaire. Southern Maniema was settled by farmers from the southern savanna at a much later date.

Not enough is yet known for us to be able to map detailed routes of expansion. One can only suggest the following: One route was by sea and southward. This accounts for the occupation of Bioko and the lands of the Gabon Estuary and the Ogooué Delta. Some later and smaller movements also occurred by sea. Several centers of overland dispersal can be cautiously postulated, by the principle of least removes, as is done on map 2.7.[32] The early nucleus lay in western Cameroon north of the Wouri. A first dispersal occurred near the present border of Cameroon and Gabon, where Cameroonian and other languages parted company. The three-way dispersion of the northern Zaire languages, Aka-Mbati, and the southern equatorial languages occurred in the northwestern Congo panhandle. East of this area lies the great Sangha-Ubangi-Zaire marsh and swamp, the second biggest in the world, a set of habitats utterly different from any in the experience of the migrants. The Aka-Mbati group moved to the north and northeast around it. The northern Zairian speakers familiarized themselves with this new aquatic environment when they first moved around it to the south, before reaching the Zaire River and its habitats, probably south of the Alima confluence. Then, one portion of them migrated into the inner Zaire basin and another went up the Zaire River. The latter group broke up first, west of the lower Itimbiri Valley, into a western and an eastern branch. That was followed by a further split between the Buan and Soan blocks of the eastern branch in the lower Itimbiri Valley. Later, Buan speakers split south of the middle Bomokandi River and occupied much of the northeastern quadrant of the area. The southwestern speakers meanwhile moved southward through the upper Ogooué Basin toward the lower or middle Kouilou-Niari Valley, where the split between the Kongo group and the Gabon-Congo group of languages took place.[33]

Glottochronological data give us the following time scales: 3000 B.C. for the split of eastern and western Bantu; 1560 B.C. for the advance beyond Cameroon; 1120 B.C. for the split of Aka-Mbati, the northern Zaire languages, and the southwestern languages; 950 B.C. for the split between southern languages, including Kongo and the Gabon-Congo group. The Buan-Soan split dates to 580 B.C., the first internal Buan one to 440 B.C., and the split with Biran, the easternmost subdivision of that group, by A.D. 170. Western Bantu expansion ended when the southern

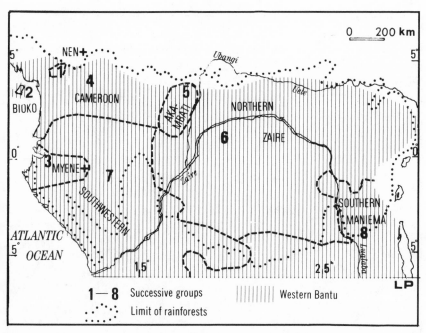

Map 2.8.   The major Bantu language groups in equatorial Africa

Maniema group differentiated from its nearest savanna neighbor as late as A.D. 330.

The dates available from Neolithic sites in equatorial Africa agree, on the whole, rather well with the glottochronological estimates (map 2.9). The earliest one is Shum Laka, where a date of 3000 B.C. corresponds to the passage of the people there to farming. Later the Obobogo cluster, south of Yaounde, is dated from c. 1500 B.C. onward, in line with the occupation of Cameroon. Tchissanga, a site north of Loango, where a language of the Kongo group is spoken now, dates to c. 600 B.C., which is later than the 900 B.C. date expected. A good fit is the date of c. 500 B.C. at Imbonga on the Momboyo River, where people speak a language belonging to the inner Zaire basin block, which broke away from the northern Zaire group c. 650 B.C. Several dates of around 400 B.C. for the Ngovo industry in the lower Zaire cataract area are not surprising.[34] The 1450 B.C. (+/− 70) date for a site on the Gabon fits with the glottochronological estimate of 1860 B.C. for the split of the Myene-Tsogo languages.[35]

Encouraged by the overall good, if loose, fit between carbon dates and glottochronological estimates, one is emboldened to use such estimates, pending further archaeological evidence. The estimates predict

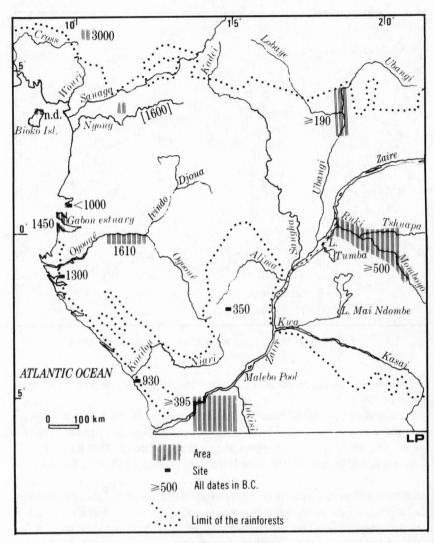

Map 2.9.   Neolithic sites

dates earlier than c. 1000 B.C. for colonization by farmers of the westernmost part of equatorial Africa, and earlier than c. 500 B.C., for their
settlement in the Itimbiri-Bomokandi area, in portions of the inner
Zaire basin, and in the lands north of the lower Zaire.[36] By A.D. 1
western Bantu speakers occupied the whole area except southern
Maniema.

Dynamics of the Expansion

Why and how did this expansion take place? We can at present only guess at the reasons why. Theories of overpopulation lack any support. It is likely that the expansion actually got underway by accident. With the existing system of food production, villages moved to fresh sites once or twice a decade. Good sites were at local environmental borders (eco- tones), near natural clearings, often provided with rivers, and suitable for the main crops. It is not too much to assume that people preferred sites away from sectors where the best spots were already occupied by other farmer trappers. To the contemporaries this migration was just natural drift. The calculated speed of the expansion between Sanaga and the coast of Congo, no more than some 22 km per 10 years, is quite consistent with this view.

But motives and means of the expansion did not remain unchanged over two millennia of expansion! Given what is known about the ances- tral social tradition and its emphasis on leadership by achievement, one expects some young and ambitious men to have struck out in search of a land of plenty, sometimes going much farther than usual. Some oceanic travel did take place, and in the Zaire bend and along its affluents most movement took place by water and was much faster than overland travel. The great variety of natural habitats deeply influenced the motiva- tions, and the manner and timing of further expansion. Some areas, such as the great swamp or the sandy and waterless Bateke plateaus, were at first avoided, while others, such as the forest-savanna margins in eastern Gabon-Congo south of the equator, were probably preferred.

Because of the duration of the expansion and the variety of habitats involved, it is unwise to rely on a single model of expansion. As a rough illustration, here are calculations of speeds of dispersal in three cases. The overall movement from the Sanaga River to the Congo coast took 600 years for 1,000 km as the crow flies, twice as far, let us say, on the ground, or approximately 33 km/decade, a speed consistent with the usual drifting. But along the stretch between the Congo panhandle and the confluence of the Alima with the Zaire, the northern Zaire language speakers ambled over 400 km (double to 800) in 470 years at the rate of only 17 km/decade. Yet later one of their fractions raced 900 km on the river in a mere 70 years from the confluence of the Alima and the confluence of the Itimbiri for an astonishing 128 km/decade. That light- ning migration followed the Zaire River upstream on a stretch where good dwelling sites on mounds or high banks were rare. The situation suggests first a very slow rate of movement as people were learning about the new aquatic habitats followed by a dash once they had achieved mastery over these environments.[37]

Whatever the real value of the numbers cited, migration rates definitely fluctuated widely and several sorts of expansion were at work
here. It is clear that the factors affecting migration rates included specifics on the practices of food production, nutritional and disease environments, demographic patterns, barriers between major types of natural
habitats where expansion was not possible for a while, and, last but not
least, the density of autochthonous populations, their relations with the
immigrants, and the probability of socio-dynamic change induced by
such contacts among the latter.

Farmers and Autochthons

Memories about expansions and migrations in the historical consciousness of the farmer trappers in equatorial Africa usually refer to more
recent times. Yet some dim remembrance of these remote ages may
have survived in a number of clichés about the habitats they encountered. These revolve around the autochthons, whom they met everywhere, although in small numbers. A common term, CS 1804–5 *-tuá,
for "bushpeople" (hunters and gatherers) survives. It now also often
designates "pygmy." The two meanings have fused in the many places
where later hunters and gatherers were pygmy.[38] In stories about settlement, pygmies are the guides who taught the immigrants how to cope
with various habitats within the rainforests, even in the great marsh. The
stories are all the more remarkable because, by the nineteenth century,
all surviving bands of pygmy hunters and gatherers were serfs for the
villagers, who held profoundly ambivalent views about them. They were
a despised, uncivilized, subhuman race, unfit for sexual congress with
any farming woman. Yet they were the fountain of civilization: the first
in the land; the inventors of fire; the teachers about habitats; the wise
healers with medicinal plants; sometimes even the first metallurgists;
and, on occasion, the first farmers. The inhabitants of the Kuba kingdom, for instance, so intertwined the very notion of untutored nature,
its bounty and its dangers, with the notion of pygmy hunter and gatherer
that the image of the powerful nature spirits was modeled after the ideal
pygmy, that the prohibition of incest was said to have been taught by
pygmies, and that any claim to mastery of the land had to involve the
legitimizing presence of a quintessential autochthon, a pygmy.[39]

Do these paradoxes not contain a dim remembrance of the crucial
role of autochthons during the expansion, when they tutored the newcomers in the ways of the various new habitats they encountered? If so,
how crucial their role must have been to have survived for millennia in
the collective memory, despite their despised place in the social order!
How crucial also then was the process of mastering each of the myriad
habitats encountered! Yet if the influence of these autochthons was so

momentous, why did their languages vanish, and why were most of them absorbed into the western Bantu way of life, without finally influencing it all that much? The nomadic hunter gatherers lived in relatively small bands at such low densities that distance made for regional isolation. When the farmers settled in compact semipermanent villages, these became the cultural focus for all the bands within reach. Their language may well have become the common language, used not only between villagers and hunter gatherers, but also among hunter gatherers speaking different languages. Yet during this whole period the number of immigrant settlements was puny relative to the huge areas over which they expanded, their prestige was counterbalanced by that of the knowledge autochthons had about the world around them, and the villages were held in check by the limited sets of habitats most suitable for their agriculture. All this only marginally affected the way of life of the autochthons, and one must conclude that their languages and cultures were hardly affected by the newcomers, until the immigrants had achieved a greater mastery of their habitats and grown substantially in numbers. Hence archaeologists continued to find Late Stone Age sites overlapping with Neolithic sites for many centuries.

Meanwhile the compelling western Bantu stereotype imagery about the earlier inhabitants has led scholars astray by picturing all autochthons as "pygmies." Whatever the reasons that collective memory held this image,[40] there probably were other aborigines, especially fisherfolk. The Bantu newcomers, already familiar with fishing and therefore competing for the ecological niches exploited by fishermen, must have clashed more with them.[41] In the end their ceramics, which provided for cooked food and hence better nutrition, more than their agricultural technology itself, may have given the Bantu speakers a demographic edge. They certainly did absorb the first fishermen. It is also just possible that the increased incidence of malaria caused by the cultivation of yams may have decimated the early fishermen, because yam fields create excellent conditions for *Anopheles* mosquitoes. But probably both groups lived side by side for centuries before this happened. Archaeologists may well uncover evidence for a transitional period and find traces of specific fishing technologies taken over from the early inhabitants by the later Bantu speakers.

FROM ANCESTRAL TO FOREST TRADITION

The western Bantu farmers brought with them a common ancestral tradition of culture and society, which they shared with their kinfolk in the southern savannas. But this tradition evolved. It assimilated various technological innovations and was affected by some features originating in groups with different ancestral traditions. As a result there emerged a single, special, and stable variant of the original heritage in the lands of the rainforests, which has been baptized as the equatorial tradition. This section successively sketches the impact of the new technologies and the interaction with other peoples before A.D. 1000.

The Adoption of Metals

The original expansion of western Bantu speakers in and around the rainforests resulted in the occupation of only those small portions of the area that held the best potential for yam and palm growing and for fishing. The total population must have grown only gradually and erratically. Not enough is known about concrete conditions to propose a demographic model. Even so one would expect a very irregular growth curve. Possibly demographic disasters occurred because the newcomers faced new disease environments. The autochthons may have been decimated by novel diseases carried by the colonists. All these are possible scenarios, but as long as the specific disease factors have not been identified, such assumptions cannot be made.[42]

Western Bantu expansion had not yet run its course when major technological breakthroughs began to alter the situation. The first one was the adoption of metallurgy (map 2.10). Iron smelting is attested in the great lakes area and in southern Nigeria at Taruga by the seventh or sixth centuries B.C, possibly as early as the ninth century in both cases.[43] The first smelting sites in northern Gabon may be earlier than the fifth century, when sites are well attested in Haut Ogooué. The earliest iron smelters lived on the inland plateau side of the Crystal and Du Chaillu mountains, and the technology spread unevenly from there.[44] By the onset of our era iron smelting was common west of the Sangha-Zaire. Farther east, the Batalimo (Maluba) complex (second century B.C. to fourth century A.D.) in the Ubangi Valley, however, still remained Neolithic in the fourth century A.D., and so far Eggert has found no traces of iron in Equateur before the thirteenth century A.D.[45] In the far east one early Iron Age Urewe site, estimated to be from the second or third century A.D., lies on the edge of the forest.[46] No conclusions can be drawn yet from these data. Much more excavation will be required before the picture will become clear. Linguistic data from the Buan group in Uele show the complexity of the chronology that can be expected. According to them iron began to be smelted and worked c. 400 B.C.[47] A study of Buan vocabulary shows that the first diffusion came from the east, but was soon followed by another diffusion from the west.

Despite the fact that iron smelting does not go back to ancestral Bantu times, a number of common terms such as "ore," "iron," "anvil," "hammer," "forging," "smith," "forge," and "charcoal" are widely

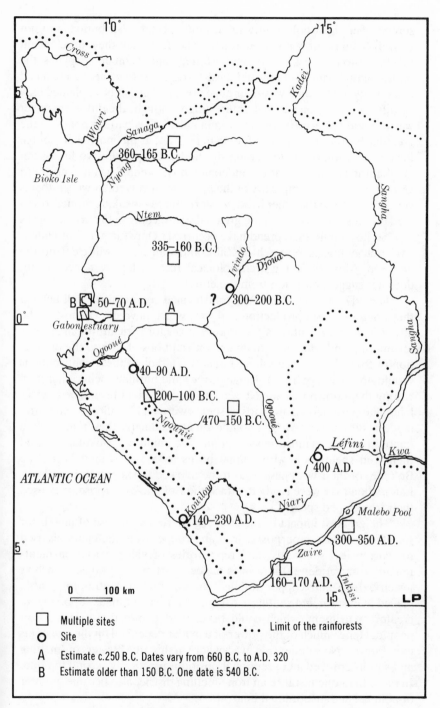

Map 2.10. The early Iron Age

59

spread over the whole Bantu area, although the distributions are not
entirely congruent with each other. The fact that they once meant
"rock," "stone block," "to work stone," and "ember" explains the
proto-Bantu forms. But how did these terms come to be applied to metal
technology in the same way over huge areas? That can be explained only
by diffusion from one center. Interestingly enough, the diffusions cover
western and eastern Bantu indiscriminately.[48] This pattern points to the
great lakes area, rather than Taruga in Nigeria, as the most likely source
for the diffusion of the technology in the Bantu-speaking world, assuming that the technique was not independently invented again in northern
Gabon. Given the complexity of the processes involved, however, that is
very unlikely. On the other hand, western Bantu–speaking farmers occupied the western borders of the great lakes area only in the first centuries
A.D. So how could this spread have occurred? Only further, more intensive archaeological research in Zaire and Cameroon will clear up the
question. Meanwhile the archaeological record, however incomplete,
does not suggest diffusion from the east.

The advent of the Iron Age transformed communities well beyond
the spheres of food production and war, which have drawn most of the
attention of commentators.[49] Cutlasses, axes for agriculture, and spears
for hunting and war were the main contributions of iron to the production of food and the provision of defense, although these contributions
should not be exaggerated. Ringing trees and burning them rather than
cutting them down with an axe was the most efficient technique to clear
land, and poisoned arrowheads or spears were highly efficient. Still, iron
made a difference. At Mondombe on the Tshuapa they remember a
famous ruse which illustrates the point. The immigrant Bokoka replaced
their iron spearheads with animal horns to convince their hosts, the
Bokone, of their weakness so as to be allowed to stay on Bokone land.
Later when they were ready to attack the Bokone by surprise, they used
their iron-tipped spears.[50]

The greatest impact of the Iron Age here was the use of metals for
social and exchange purposes. Iron and copper were the materials used
for currencies, standards, and repositories of value, social payments
ranging from bridewealth to fines or fees, and prestige objects, such as
jewelry. Iron and copper fulfilled the celebrated central role cattle
played in eastern and southern Africa. Their advent made it possible to
create a patrimony which could be converted into the acquisition of
people. Hence much of the power of a leader depended on the size of his
metal stores. No wonder that everywhere in this area masters of smelting
and smiths enjoyed an exceptional position, practically second to none.
In more than one instance an iron-smelting district also became a center
of political and institutional innovation.

Iron soon became indispensable and spawned a new organization of space. For although low-grade ores can be found almost anywhere, good ores are unevenly distributed. Where they occurred, smelting centers often appeared. The one near Lebombi in Haut Ogooué for instance, lasted for about 500 years in the first millennium A.D.[51] Hence iron and ironwares became the object of trade. Once iron was available, the resulting trade was all the more significant, because iron objects were both necessary for production and a commodity of prestige and hence power. Earlier the only trade in basic commodities had been the salt trade and a trade in stones or stone tools in places where the raw material was lacking. The rarity of copper ores made copper all the more valuable. It was the prestige good par excellence and was probably traded early on over great distances. Thus the Iron Age led to more intensive communication over longer distances and so to still more exchanges of both goods and ideas.

The Coming of the Banana

Yet the impact of metallurgy was on the whole perhaps smaller than that of the humble banana. The yield of bananas exceeds that of yams by a factor of ten, and is equalled only by the yield of manioc. Unlike yams or oil palms, bananas are ideally adapted to evergreen rainforests. Unlike yams, the absence of a dry season does not hurt them. One needs to clear only about two-thirds of the trees on the field, rather than clear it completely as is necessary for yams. That produces a microenvironment freer of *Anopheles* and hence of malaria, helps the forest to regenerate faster on the fallow field, and saves labor. Compared with yams, the crop requires less care after planting and its preparation for food saves much time. It was the ideal staple crop for agriculture in the rainforests, and it allowed farmers to colonize all of its habitats everywhere.[52]

Domesticated bananas originated in Southeast Asia or perhaps India. People brought them to Africa, but when and how is still a bone of contention. Genetically bananas belong to three families of which the ones labeled AAA and AAB are found in Africa. Each of the families contains many varieties (cultivars). AAB contains mostly plantains to be baked or made into flour and AAA mostly sweet bananas to be eaten by hand. AAB is the dominant banana in central and West Africa. AAA is dominant in East Africa. AAB is subdivided into three subfamilies: Horn, French, and Polynesian, the first two of which exist only in Africa; the third is not found there. Given the very great number of cultivars of AAA, AAB Horn, and AAB French found in Africa, bananas must have been introduced into Africa in remote times, but botanists cannot give precise estimates. Because Horn is a degeneration of French, but lives side by side with it in the Zaire basin, De Langhe suggests that (1) the cultivation of AAB plantains in central Africa is very old; (2) AAB was introduced twice consecutively, once for French and once for Horn; and (3) this occurred long before the arrival of AAA, which dominates in East Africa, despite the large number of cultivars of AAA bananas in Uganda and near Mount Kilimanjaro.[53]

Whereas it is not known how or when bananas reached Africa, the upper Nile Valley was an important center for their diffusion. Here AAB and AAA cultivars are both grown as staples. But the AAB spread into the rainforest area, and later to West Africa, while the AAA varieties spread into East Africa. Within central Africa the greatest variety of cultivated and feral variants in the AAB variety occurs in the northeast, where, for example, some 58 cultivars were actually cultivated near the Aruwimi-Zaire confluence (Olombo) and still others grew wild. The farther west one goes the fewer the number of cultivars. Near the Gabon estuary about 30 cultivars were known, including varieties introduced by Europeans, and in West Africa a mere handful are found. Conversely the greatest number of variants of the AAA family occurred in Uganda. That whole pattern is consonant with a proximate center of diffusion on the upper Nile and makes an introduction from northeastern Africa or from the East African coast probable.[54]

The linguistic evidence is by no means complete. The distribution of terms for the generic meaning "banana" refers to AAA east of the western rift and to AAB west of the rift. But even the terms for French, Horn, and AAA are not known for all the languages in the area. Terms for banana tree, where they differ from the term "banana," for banana groves, and for parts of the banana tree, have not been gathered everywhere. Guthrie noted that many Bantu languages have CS 1090, 1144, 1146, and 1146a *-ko, -kondo, -konde* ("banana," "plaintain,") and proposed a proto-Bantu origin for the term (map 2.11). However, this is not likely. With the generic meaning, the distribution of these terms covers a solid single area in western Bantu, whereas the reflexes in Uganda specifically refer to AAB only, not the staple AAA, and most of the reflexes in northern Swahili refer apparently to a single variety, although on the lower Tana *ningko* is the generic term. The term is not proto-western Bantu nor is its distribution consonant with proto-Bantu.

In the northeastern part of equatorial Africa and among most different language families near the upper Nile, the generic term is *-bugu* and related forms. This distribution results from active borrowing among diverse language groups including western Bantu languages. So far its language of origin remains unknown. The term also recurs as *i-buga* among the Saa between Kasai and Mfimi as a synonym for *inko,* and probably as *bugugu,* the name for a cultivar in Tsogho (Gabon).[55] This means that at one time *-bugu* was widespread in equatorial Africa and was later ousted by the *-kondo* group of terms, at least for the generic meaning "banana in general." The solid distribution of those forms in

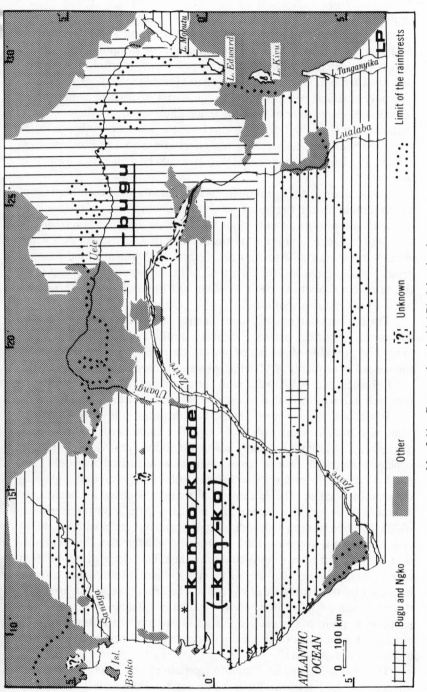

Map 2.11. Banana plantain (AAB): *-kondo, -bugu

equatorial Africa lends credence to that view. Yet the *-konde* forms occur in the northern great lakes area right to the upper Nile and in northern Swahili, which also is an indication of antiquity! One cannot escape the conclusion that both groups of terms referred to AAB and that both are old. One group referred to Horn and the other to French. The only satisfactory explanation in equatorial Africa is to assume first a diffusion of *-bugu* over at least the inner Zaire basin and the northeast, then its ousting by the *-kondo* forms from the south or southeast, forms which, in the final analysis may tentatively be traced to northern East Africa. The isolated *kondro* in Malagasy would be a loan from Swahili as well.

Furthermore, other generic terms in Maniema and in southern Cameroon remind us that the history of this terminology has been more than a simple tale of diffusion of *-bugu* and *-kondo* and their interrelationship. For instance, a group of terms of the form *-toto* for AAA is widespread in equatorial Africa, from Gabon to Maniema, and another group, *-poku/-bogo* for "banana tree," "banana grove," is found from the northern Gabonese coast to Kivu and the Uele area. These also attest to ancient distributions.[56]

The introduction of the banana in equatorial Africa clearly has been a complex historical process, involving multiple diffusions over wide areas and probably over long periods of time. The first crucial step was the spread of probably AAB-Horn as a staple crop from the upper Nile. AAB-French and AAA were later introductions. If this is correct, future research will show that *-bugu* refers specifically to AAB-Horn.

When and from where did the first diffusion into Africa occur?[57] The question is fraught with problems. The lands north and east from the upper Nile are not naturally hospitable to bananas. One is forced to conclude that, whatever the route, bananas were carried by people from patch to patch, from favorable habitat to favorable habitat, bypassing unfavorable locales. The earliest bit of written evidence for bananas in Africa is its reported presence in A.D. 525 at Adulis on the Red Sea, which was then trading with India, Ceylon, and indirectly with Southeast Asia. The text is accompanied by a drawing which makes the identification certain, if the drawing is contemporary. This sliver of information merely confirms the antiquity of banana cultivation in Africa, already indicated by the profusion of cultivars. The exact date of the arrival of the banana in Africa or in equatorial Africa is still unknown. The straws in the wind point to the early centuries of our era. If so, its diffusion in equatorial Africa could have been completed by the middle of the first millennium of our era.[58]

The dynamics of the first introduction of the AAB banana, reinforced by the later introductions, wrought major changes. Gradually yams were ousted as the staple over most of the area. Farmers could now settle everywhere and populations increased faster, to the growing inconvenience of the hunter gatherers. Clashes between them and the farmers therefore increased over time. The farmers now easily produced food surpluses for exchange with hunter gatherers and fisherfolk in return for their products. The specialization of food production, so striking in this area, intensified. The growing advantage of the farmers over the hunter gatherers gradually became such that autochthons were left with few choices. They could turn to agriculture and adopt the way of life of the farmers; they could stand their ground and fight for a time only, then flee to deeper forests until the farmers caught up with them again; or they could intensify their relations with the villages, accepting their bananas and their iron tools for the chase in return for meat. Whatever choice the hunter gatherers made, they were gradually but inexorably drawn into a dependent relationship. They lost their languages so thoroughly that only faint traces, if any, of their former speech remain. Today all "pygmy" languages are those of farmers and, well before 1900, hunting and gathering pygmy bands had disappeared over large portions of the area.[59]

New Neighbors

Western Bantu speakers were the first farmers to colonize the forests, but they did not remain in splendid isolation. Other farmers also immigrated near and, later, into the area. Their interaction with the first colonists must now be sketched. The earliest other farmers who had been expanding to the north of the western Bantu spoke languages of a family called eastern Adamawa, or Ubangian, which stands in a remote relationship to Bantu languages. This family comprises two main blocks: the Gbaya block now found north of the rainforests, from central Cameroon to within the Ubangi bend, and an eastern block, which first met western Bantu speakers on the forest fringes north of the Uele. These people were not well equipped for life in the forest although they also relied on yams as a staple. Later, perhaps in the last centuries B.C., a subfamily of the eastern block, the Ngbaka Mabo–Gbanziri group, settled in the area south of the bend of the lower Ubangi Valley and came into permanent contact with western Bantu speakers there.[60] Meanwhile in the northeast, the incoming Bantu farmers met speakers of several groups belonging to a totally foreign language family: southern central Sudanic. They were herders and growers of cereals, a way of life incompatible with life in the forest.[61] Later, when western Bantu speakers came up against the high mountains to the east around A.D. 1, they found eastern Bantu speakers, who had long been established there, and who were already using metals when the forest farmers arrived. But once again the eastern Bantu way of life based on cereals and cattle was totally unfit for life in the rainforests.[62]

After the turn of the era a number of significant changes took place. From A.D. 100 onward East African cereal growers moved into portions of Zambia and Shaba (southeastern Zaire) and then farther west toward the Atlantic Ocean, over the full extent of the savannas south of the rainforests. They mixed there with the older western Bantu speakers, whose yam and oil palm farming was ill adapted to the savanna habitats they found, so that they were restricted to gallery forests in the river valleys, whereas the cereal farmers could use the open savannas. By my guess the movement had run its course by A.D. 500, but only actual finds of cereals near the Atlantic will settle the question. These people spoke eastern Bantu languages and they left a strong eastern Bantu imprint on the western Bantu languages of all the savanna dwellers. They also introduced a new system of food production, based on cereals and hunting, which led to significant sociocultural innovations, so that before the end of the first millennium the peoples in the southern savanna had developed their own variant of the ancestral western Bantu tradition. This eastern Bantu expansion overlapped with the end of the western Bantu expansion west of Lake Tanganyika, so that the first farmers immigrating into the rainforests of southern Maniema were already a mixed population.[63]

Later, further major population movements occurred on the northern boundary of the forests (map. 2.12). Various peoples migrated from the savannas into the forests. Two blocks of Ubangian-speaking peoples were involved: the Mba-Mondunga subgroup and the Ngbandi subgroup. Speakers of the first group expanded to the southwest from the lower Bomokandi-Uele area, the Mba to settle north of Kisangani; the Mondunga first followed the Uele downstream then traveled from the lower Uele into the forests north of Lisala. In their movement westward along the Uele, they were followed by the Ngbandi group, who moved from the upper Uele to settle in the forests south of the upper Ubangi (see map 2.12).[64] The Ubangians moderately influenced the languages of the adjacent Bantu speakers all over northern Zaire, and were in turn influenced by them. Culturally, however, the western Bantu assimilated them to a large extent. Bantu speakers also assimilated most Mondunga and probably many Mba settlers, so that only two remnants of these language groups subsist today.[65]

Much more dramatic in the long run was the entry on the scene of a southern central Sudanic group whose language was related to the Mamvu-Balese subgroup. Such a language profoundly influenced those of all the western Bantu speakers of the northeast (especially Bali, Bira, and Komo), all the way to 1° south and as far west as the Lualaba River.

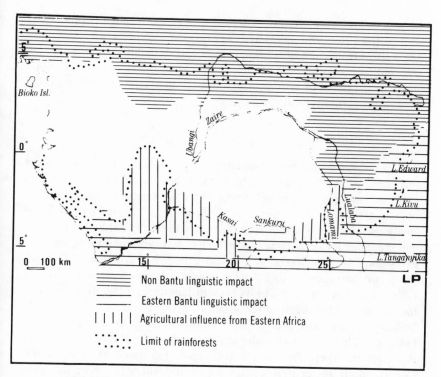

Map 2.12.   Major outside influences on the equatorial African tradition

These people imposed their basic social organization on the area, which as a result lost much of its ancestral western Bantu heritage. Still, in the end, the Sudanic newcomers fused with the original farmers. These Sudanic language speakers are not to be confused with the Balese, who entered the forests of Ituri only in the last few centuries.[66]

Unfortunately these population movements on the northern edge of the rainforests remain undated so far.[67] Clearly they were made possible by the adaptation of Ubangian and south-central Sudanese speakers to a forest economy, and the introduction of the banana may well have played a crucial role in these developments. The cradle for these movements lay in the northeastern corner of the area, the region where AAB bananas are called -*bugu*. Still, none of the Ubangian populations mentioned here use the term, although all the southern central Sudanese do.[68] The ease with which south-central Sudanese, Mba, and Mondunga speakers settled in the forests, despite the presence of western Bantu speakers, would still be best explained if they had acquired bananas before the Bantu farmers did, so that they were free to settle anywhere among the few niches occupied by Bantu farmers, who acquired the crop only at a later date. Again, the ancestors of the Nyanga people—who moved from the great lakes area to cross the mountain wall that separated them from the forests, where they had settled in a still-empty area by a glottochronological date of A.D. 200—may also have planted bananas. The ancestors of Tembo, who followed them later in the first millennium A.D., certainly cultivated them.

Equatorial Africa by A.D. 1000

The era of great expansions ended when the last flurry of colonization provoked by the adoption of the banana died out. As the evidence of glottochronological estimates shows, the area was fully settled perhaps by A.D. 500, certainly before A.D. 1000. By A.D. 500 well over half the smaller subgroups had begun to differentiate into individual languages, and the language centers were scattered all over the rainforests with few exceptions. By A.D. 1000 only a few subgroups had not as yet differentiated, and only one sizable area in southern Cameroon and northern Gabon had not yet acquired its present language distribution. By now the process of language differentiation involved only small districts.[69] Stability rather than expansion is therefore clear from the linguistic evidence. The scant archaeological data available do not conflict with this view, but there are still too few digs to say more, even in Gabon, Congo, and in the central Zairian depression where the more intensive surveys have been carried out.[70]

The end of the large-scale migrations opened up a new era in the history of these peoples. They had by now developed a detailed mastery of each of their habitats, and had forged the fundamental trading and other social links to other communities with different habitats, to acquire a wide resource base. Settlement was still sparse. Denser populations may have begun to build up in favorite locales, along the margins of the rainforests or within the Zaire bend, but it is unwise to extrapolate so far back, even from present vegetation patterns and certainly not from a map of differential densities c. 1900.[71] The population was no doubt still concentrated in clusters, even though these had multiplied. Indeed settlement in clusters was, in most regions, still the rule by the advent of the colonial conquest. By A.D. 1000 farmers had explored all the available land and tended to drift cyclically within a territory rather than search for unknown fertile and empty lands. What empty land remained was not as fertile as the settled districts were. Meanwhile, however, individual mobility remained high, for men as well as for women, and tended to even out differentials in population density within and between neighboring clusters of population.

Later population movements occurred on a small scale, involving relatively few people, usually from a single cluster, traveling over short distances, usually by intentional drift. Such population movements differed from the earlier dynamics in fundamental ways, not merely by their small scale and lesser frequency. They were triggered in most cases by relative overpopulation, and no longer by a search for an empty Eden. Even though local leaders did control the natural increase of population, still the population built up in the most favored habitats in answer to the competition that characterized the communities. The requirements for labor and for defense put a premium on numbers. Hence every leader wanted to increase the population he controlled. Eventually competition for resources among villages, and for authority within smaller groups, triggered the emigration of groups who wanted to lead a less-troubled life, or whose leaders wanted to play a more prominent role than they could hope to achieve in their communities of origin. Other population movements were induced by the desire to occupy key locations for trade or for the control of prized resources such as salt, metals, or oil palm trees.

Farmers took some 2,000 years to settle the rainforests of equatorial Africa, and then about another half millennium to absorb new technologies and to become finely attuned to all the potential of their habitats. They had come with a single ancestral tradition, the way of life and thought of their ancestors. The new habitats, the autochthons, the non-Bantu, the eastern Bantu farmers with their different legacies—each influenced the development of this ancestral tradition differently from place to place. But the growth of links by trade and by marriage exercised a counteracting converging effect. Local clustering of the population resulted in the appearance of differences in their way of life, and regional contacts tended to unify them again. On the whole, convergence was the stronger dynamic, as the far-flung geographical distributions of objects, practices, institutions, beliefs, and values show. The common ancestral tradition survived, was enriched, and was transformed. In A.D. 1000 the peoples of the rainforests still shared a common tradition that was largely ancestral, but their tradition had diverged from that of their kinfolk in the savannas to the south as a result of the very different natural surroundings, the economic adaptations made by the original farming colonists, and the influence of eastern Bantu speakers on the peoples of the savanna. Yet both the savanna and the forest traditions remained variants of the older ancestral heritage and, to a surprising degree, continued to cherish and hold in common the essential features of their ancestral culture.[72]

Three

Tradition: Ancient and Common

The life of the peoples in rainforests has been shaped by the continuity of their common tradition over four millennia, a continuity which resulted from the adoption of fundamental choices that were never questioned again, only elaborated over time as new situations seemed to warrant. This chapter focuses on that continuity. It therefore adopts a very long time perspective and concentrates on the structuring principles of society and culture. Although this perspective may seem contrived and too abstract to some, the data validate such an approach, because they reveal a substantial concrete content to the ancient and then common tradition. Such a continuity is no less a part of the historian's domain than is the study of shorter conjunctures, trends, or events.

Two sets of data attest to this tradition and its substance: the proto-vocabulary for the ancestral tradition and ancient loanwords on the one hand, and the features still shared by the nineteenth-century peoples in equatorial Africa on the other. The links that persist between such features and the early vocabulary establish the continuity. But before one gives an outline of the common tradition one must first address a crucial feature of the data.

REALITY AND REALITY

Not all data share the same status with regard to reality. They do not all refer to the same reality, and to neglect this feature is a recipe for certain error. Reality is multiple. Reality independent of any observer we can never know. Reality observed is always processed by the mind. Objects, situations, or actions are not just mentally recorded as items; they are recognized and catalogued with the help of information already in the mind, and significance is attached to them. They are, therefore, interpreted from the moment of perception onward. Now some interpretations are independent of culture, but most are not. Often it is impossible to distinguish between the record of action, situation, or object, and the cultural interpretation given to the observation, but sometimes one can. In such cases, I will use the expression "physical reality," in the sense that all observers, whatever their cultural background, agree on the action, situation, or object, not that it "really" exists in an absolute philosophical sense. Most records, however, are cultural interpretations, shared by the members of a community. They are "collective representations" and refer to a different reality. I will use "cognitive reality" to designate it. Physical and cognitive realities can diverge widely, and normally the latter take precedence over the former. But a tension exists between these two realities, for they are never totally congruent. A systematic divergence between the two realities could become conscious. In such cases cognitive reality is usually brought more in line with physical reality. Both physical and cognitive reality are equally valid at the ontological level. They are also equal realities for the historian because, although all motivation for action in the past derived from cognitive reality, action was taken in physical reality.

Beyond these two versions of reality lie the interpretations made by outside observers who are not actors in a given setting. They too are a reality. But their views are not a historical reality as long as they were not actors themselves in the time and situation studied. This also holds true for a set of generalizations called "theory," a body of collective representations held by the academic community.

The confusion between physical and cognitive reality has led to grievous error in the past. Another common source of error has been the assessment of outside reports. Early scholars often held such reports to render physical reality, which they do not, whereas recently scholars have assumed that they are only interpretations by outsiders, which is equally wrong. Although portions of these reports are indubitably interpretations by outsiders, large parts are in fact records by actors and render their cognitive reality. Such confusions seriously affected the validity of anthropological theory as it developed over time. In turn the theory of their own times shaped not just the interpretations that outsiders made but also the very substance of what they chose to observe.

The theme of this chapter, the continuity of tradition, is primarily a phenomenon of cognitive reality, but its sources include both cognitive and physical records. Among the sources, vocabulary testifies to cognitive and physical reality separately. An item meaning "sun" deals with physical reality, an item meaning "family" with cognitive reality. Similarly, ethnographic data relate to a mix of cognitive and physical realities, plus interpretations by outsiders, including the effect of theory on them.

COMMUNITIES AND BIG MEN

Three interlocking social groups formed the framework of the ancestral society: the district (A9),[1] the village (A3), and a large household establishment often called "the house" or the "hearth," which will be referred to as the House (A2). Their interrelations were quite flexible so that the system remained extremely decentralized. Each House freely chose which village its members wanted to belong to, and each village freely chose other villages as allies to make up a district. Over time the relative importance of the groups often shifted as one or another basic group gained in prominence at the expense of the others. At the extreme one group could be absorbed by another, as when a single House occupied an entire village or even a whole district. In a few cases the village or the district could even vanish.[2] The history of political organizations in the area shows the dynamic possibilities of this situation. Transformations of the ancestral pattern occurred as new patterns of interlocking ties between the basic groups developed. Thus despite the political differences between societies in the area, by the nineteenth century the basic groups were still present.

The loose nature of the system was enhanced by the fact that the House and the village were led by recognized leaders (A11) who achieved rather than inherited their status, but the district did not have a distinct leader (CS 1263–65). Leadership itself was a necessary institution, but who was to be leader was probably not institutionalized in the ancestral society. Men competed for leadership within each unit, and leaders of different units competed with each other, so as to increase their following at the expense of others. Competition was the counterpart of autonomy.

In some languages leaders are referred to as "great men," which recalls "big men," the technical term in anthropology for such leaders.[3] What it meant to be such a "big man" is well expressed in the invocations during a ceremony performed at puberty among the Djue of Cameroon when the grandparents gave charms to their grandson for a successful life.

The grandfather gave an ivory bracelet and said:
"This elephant which I put on your arm, become a man of crowds,
a hero in war, a man with women
rich in children, and in many objects of wealth
prosper within the family, and be famous throughout the villages."[4]

The grandmother gave a charm of success as a belt and said:
"Father, you who are becoming a man
Let toughness and fame be with you as this sap of the
Baillonella toxisperma tree is glued to this thread.
Become dominant, *a great man*,
a hero in war, who surpasses strangers and visitors;
prosper, Have us named!"[5]

The term for such a leader shares an etymology with terms meaning "fame," "honor," and also "to become rich," as in the grandfather's invocation.[6] In the languages of south-central Cameroon, a form of the word which intensifies its meaning still means "a rich man." Competition involved wealth with which to attract followers. This ancient link between leadership and the exchange of goods is evident from the term for "gift" (A105), which is derived from "to give away" and "to divide." These forms occur again and again in the political terminology of all Bantu-speaking lands. Similarly fame, "to be talked about," attracted followers, and to have many wives also built up a following. Finally the leader had to be a warrior, not to conquer, but to defend his achievements: "to surpass strangers and visitors."

Leadership status was accompanied by a set of symbols and basic values. The quintessence of leadership was the leopard (A16). To a lesser degree the fish eagle and the python (CS 159) were also the animal symbols of big men.[7] They were all carnivores, supreme in their respective realms, solitary predators and therefore potential competitors. The notion of a special variety of witch substance (A125), thought of as a special organ in the body of a leader, explains the exceptional success of big men. The practice of giving the pangolin (A17) to the big man, and the ritual surrounding it, probably reflects supernatural powers (pangolins were thought to be anomalous animals endowed with mysterious properties).[8] In the common tradition the ideology and ritual for leadership recalls the complex of belief, ritual, symbol, and etiquette that used to be labeled "divine kingship" but should more properly be called "sacred kingship."[9] Although in some cases such features may well be late borrowings from one or another kingdom, in general the royal ideologies seem to have developed out of less elaborate variants linked to local leaders. One should therefore interpret such typical cases of "sacred kingship" that occur, among others, in the Kuba kingdom, on Bioko, and in Loango, as enriched variants of what originally was an ideological complex justifying and legitimizing the authority of "big men."

The House

The basic level of social organization was that of the House, the establishment of a big man. Often it lasted beyond its founder's death and was taken over by another big man among its members. The House was always competing for membership with other establishments. In the common tradition the House was the unit of food production and usually comprised from 10 to 40 people, that is, a labor force close to the optimum for the collective labor requirements in agriculture (clearing brush), trapping, and hunting. Even in ancestral times its size must have been extremely variable, as it was in the nineteenth century. Most new Houses, then as later, probably began with a small membership, often at the limits of the possible; membership in old, established Houses may have run into the hundreds. Actual sizes for such remote times will eventually be known from the size of their settlements.[10] The big man was the magnet and the manager of the establishment. His House was a spatial unit within a village, demarcated in various ways.[11] Although part of a village, his House could always abandon one village to join another one. This often occurred when, as regularly happened, the village moved from one site to another.

Membership included kinfolk of the big man, but also friends, clients, and various dependents as well. Big men were usually polygamous and gave some of their wives as consorts to young clients in order to attract men to the House. The ideology of the House was based on the fiction that it was a family, that is, a bilateral group in anthropological parlance, or better yet, an "undifferentiated" group.[12] The "big man" was the father of all the others and hence the term for "his father" (CS 303, 2027, ps 76 [3:87]) probably was a term of address for the leader. The strongest evidence for undifferentiated descent are terms derived from the verb "to give birth to" (CS 208) and other derivations such as "relative" (CS 210.5) and "seed" (CS 211). These include "House" (ps 50 [3:67]) and many more reflexes not noted by Guthrie, which prove that this derived term is proto–western Bantu.[13] People did not think or act in terms of unilineal descent. The large number of nineteenth-century cases of kindreds rather than unilineal descent groups is an indication of this. Hence there were no lineages, because the definition of lineage requires that the group's descent be "unilineal," that is, counted through one gender only.[14] Consequently free men had a wide choice as to the establishment they cared to join. They could stay with their parents, move to their mother's brother's House, or to the Houses of any of their grandparents, to mention only the most usual possibilities. Hence CS 447,[15] meaning "home village," was a term separate from the general designation for "village." This flexibility, as well as the flux of the number of Houses within each village, made it easier to obtain a good fit between the requirements of labor for production and optimal returns per capita for work invested.

In contrast to this ideology of belonging, however, comparative ethnography discloses the existence of half a dozen or so unequal, exclusive social statuses, such as slave, client, protected/adopted person or group, serf (hunter and gatherer group), friend, and cadet in the sense of junior member. How elaborate such unequal statuses were in the ancestral tradition is hard to say. There are terms for dependent (A21), which implies out-of-group status, friend (A18), captive (A23), and serf (A22); in addition the concept of relative age (A20) was a discriminant in kinship terminology and also discloses inequality.

The terminology of kinship indicated a set of roles within the House because each kinship term implies expected behavior. The forms for adjacent generations—father, mother, and child—are well known.[16] The original forms for mother's brother and father's sister seem to have been male mother and female father, in which the gender terms also are proto–western Bantu. As in English, sister's son was designated by a compound form. In contrast with this set of terms, the set designating members of the generation of the individual speaking cannot as yet be reconstructed, although it is clear that relative seniority and polar terminology (special terms for members of the opposite sex to the speaker) were taken into account. A great deal of innovation affected these terms in later times, no doubt as the internal structure of Houses changed. Innovation is also striking in the designation of grandparent and grandchild.[17]

The system of classification underlying the terminologies is tentatively held to have been "bifurcating Hawaiian," despite the widespread presence in the region of "Omaha" and "Crow" systems. In the Hawaiian system a given term can designate only persons of the same generation. All persons of the same gender within the generation of the speaker share the same terms. Cousins are handled as if they were siblings. Bifurcation (differentiation) between father's and mother's sides of the family is indicated by the special terms for mother's brother and father's sister. In the Omaha and Crow systems, however, a given term can designate persons of different generations.

Kinship terminology systems are often thought to reflect the basic principles of the structure of descent groups.[18] The evidence from equatorial Africa does not support that position. True, a Hawaiian terminology fits well with an undifferentiated kinship system, except for the bifurcation. But the widespread presence of Crow and Omaha terminologies, or part Crow and Omaha terminologies, by the nineteenth century does not fit well. A Crow terminology should correspond to a matrilineal system and an Omaha terminology to a patrilineal system. Many of them do not. Wherever insiders have explained their reasons for the usage of Crow or Omaha systems here, they have stressed matrimonial exchange. And this, of course, also explains the bifurcation in the Hawaiian system. It all underscores the fact that the House was a unit for matrimonial exchange.

Western Bantu has two terms for marriage (A33–34): "to marry" and its derivation CS 17 "marriage," as well as CS 1175 "to marry." The terms for spouses CS 697 (A38) and CS 986 merely mean "male" and "female." One of two western Bantu designations for "in-law" (A37) derives from a verb CS 822 "to avoid," "to be forbidden." This refers to the correct behavior between in-laws of different gender in adjacent generations or of different seniority in the same generation. The other, CS 1092 "in-law," is derived from CS 1175.

The ethnographic record for the nineteenth century shows a whole range of types of marriages: sister exchange, delayed exchange (preferential marriages: various possibilities), marriage by capture, marriage by payment of compensation (bridewealth), marriage by gift to conclude peace, and cicisbeism (the gift of a wife by a man who had married her before). Several types of marriage existed in the same societies, and a few societies may have practiced all of them simultaneously. Anthropological theory has seriously underestimated the play of power and inequality with regard to marriage.[19] Marriages were the key to the reproduction of the House, and women were crucial to production as well. The very existence of a House depended on them, and no leader could remain indifferent to marriage and still be a leader. He handled the matrimonial transactions of his House and did so not only to increase the number of resident women, but also to attract the largest number of young men.

Hence multiple forms of "marriage" are to be expected. But specific forms of marriage cannot be linked to one or the other proto-term, even though some reflexes of CS 1175 mean "to give bridewealth" (A35). This has led some authors[20] to assert that CS 1175 originally referred to marriage by bridewealth. But its origin is CS 1092 "in-law," from which stems CS 1174 with the same meaning. The meaning "to give bridewealth" of some reflexes may just as well derive from "to marry." The whole set could derive, in fact, from CS 1091–92, 1173–74: "you," "he," in which the in-laws were the "you" or "he." CS 1092 "in-law" would derive from this, and the verb "to marry" and the noun "marriage" would be further derivations. Although these terms cannot be used to claim that the payment of marriage compensation belongs to the ancestral tradition, still the evidence shows that the practice of giving bridewealth is not limited to recent times.

The Village

The village was the unit of settlement in the ancestral tradition and remained so almost everywhere, in contrast with the adjacent areas in the north and east. In the nineteenth century the village was of variable size, with a median of just over 100 inhabitants, to judge by the few early available figures.[21] The earliest known village sites date back to neolithic times.[22] Their layout, as suggested both by comparative ethnography and the proto-terminology, is as follows.[23] Private rectangular dwellings lay along the sides of a street or plaza, the shape being indicated by CS 1790 and the saddle roof structure by ps 49 (3:66). Each quarter inhabited by a separate House was clearly indicated. Public buildings or sheds could be found on the plaza. Although no single term designates a men's clubhouse, there was probably one per village or one per House. Some sheds were used for industrial work, such as weaving or, later, smithing. The plaza, or a portion of it, was a place of authority (A5), probably where court cases were heard and major collective decisions taken. A second term (*-cenge* [A6]), refers to the plaza itself. Later some peoples used it to designate "dominant villages" or "capitals." The terminology for village (A3–4) contains several proto-terms. The oldest are CS 447/ps 482, ps 483 (3:142), "home, our village," and CS 818 and 936 "village." CS 192 may first have meant "path, road" and then "village," referring perhaps to the village "street."[24] CS 780 "village" derives from a primary meaning "settlement of a House (quarter)"; other derivations of the same yield "camp," "house," and much later "matriclan."

The village was an aggregate of Houses. It was rare in the nineteenth century to find a House so successful that it occupied a whole village, and it must have been even rarer in ancestral times.[25] The village was led by the big man who founded it, assisted by the big men of the other Houses who made up its council. Terms such as "palaver" (A24) and "to pay a fine" (A25) belong here. The headman of the village was due respect. In the common tradition the spoils of the emblematic animals, such as the leopard, went to him via the big man of the House, as long as a House stayed in the village. The village head also received a portion of the hunt in recognition of his status as master of the village domain. For the village, as the territorial unit, owned a domain and defended it against outsiders. Its raison d'être was common defense. The search for security led Houses to join in a village and every House needed a village to feel secure. The village was therefore the very foundation of society.

Yet a move destroyed the village at least once every decade. Its constituent Houses then left to join another settlement, and a new village was born out of a new aggregate of Houses. Thus this "very foundation of society" seems ephemeral. But just when one has been convinced of its fragility and wants to dismiss it as an ancillary institution to the House, one rediscovers that living in villages was essential.[26] Equatorial Africans were obviously well aware of the impermanence of villages, but their ideology stoutly denied this. It focused on the founding House in a village. Wherever that House settled after a breakup, there was the continuation of the former village and its territorial rights. In cognitive terms the village was as perennial as the House. Hence the sense of permanence, predictability, and security, false in physical reality, but essential for social life.

Although there is no direct proof that the image sketched in these paragraphs holds for the ancestral tradition, villages existed and often must have moved if only to assure a continued food supply. The use of one of the terms for "village" (CS 780 and many more reflexes) as a term for "camp" points to this. Again there is no direct evidence that villages were the territorial units responsible for common defense. Yet, this was universal in the nineteenth century and it could hardly have been otherwise in ancestral times. How could there be even a minimal spirit of cooperation in a village if people did not assist each other in defense? The perception of permanence is also universal in the nineteenth century. Even in early times people must have thought of villages as moving rather than dying.

Given these characteristics of the village, collective institutions, activities, and ideas which created an esprit de corps were important. Among these, circumcision may have played a major role. This was the chief rite of passage for boys and their formal induction into adult life. Initiation schools included instruction about the main principles underlying social life. Western Bantu did circumcise their children, as A26 shows. Other terms, probably derived from CS 1709 and 1711 "to cut," are found over the whole area. They designate either the circumcision proper, the accompanying initiation, or the boys to be circumcised.[27] In the nineteenth century, circumcision was often the centerpiece of a lengthy collective village initiation which was held every few years. But circumcision was not then practiced everywhere, and there were cases where initiations did not include circumcision. Most circumcision and initiation rituals were collective, but in a few cases, they were held for individuals or pairs of individuals only. The peoples of the middle Bomokandi circumcised and initiated all boys individually, while in northeastern Gabon the ritual was performed only for the sons of high-status parents. On the whole, however, the extant data suggest that collective circumcision with initiation rites for boys was ancestral.[28]

Collective initiation engendered comradeship and could lead to the creation of formal age grades across Houses. There is a term designating "age group" (A20), which derives from CS 1190 "to grow." In the nineteenth century the terminology to designate different ages took account of gender and varied somewhat in precision from group to group. Age grades for men then were far from universal. Where they were found, as in western Cameroon, or in northern and central Zaire, they played only a minor part in society, although the young men's age grade tended to be more important than is usually believed, for instance, among the people of the Ngiri River area. Among a very few people, age grades played a crucial role. This is so for the Lele of Kasai, where age grades more than

Houses determined the actual structure of the village, and assured its supremacy over both House and district. On the whole the presence of ritually privileged age categories such as "begetters" (fathers) and "begetters of children of different sex" in societies as far apart as the Lele and the Komo of northern Maniema suggests that in the late nineteenth century the role of age classes may well have been more important than ethnographers have reported.[29]

By the nineteenth century various other types of village associations were prominent in Cameroon and Gabon, western Congo and lower Zaire to the west, as well as in the whole of Maniema to the east, but not elsewhere. Many of the terms used for such associations are derivations of perfectly ordinary items for "group, assembly," and there may not have been a special designation for them in the ancestral language. It therefore remains unknown whether they existed in ancestral times. This is certainly unfortunate, because prominent associations provided the strongest institutional support for a common esprit de corps in the village later on.[30]

War has often occurred between villages in recent centuries. There were two sorts of war: "restricted war" (A27) and "destructive war" (A28). The first term is derived from a verb meaning "to throw" (CS 1633–64) from which CS 1631 "bow" (A31) also derives. In this sort of war, fighting was hedged by a stringent set of rules that served to limit the damage and the duration of each encounter. A formal declaration of war was followed by an agreement to meet on a given day near the borders of the domains involved. The elders of either group stopped the fighting, usually after one or two serious casualties had occurred. Peace negotiations and the settlement of the conflict that had provoked the fighting followed.[31] The term for a destructive war is derived from the verb "to burn" (CS 1870–71)[32] because the winner burned the village or villages of the loser. There were no limiting rules in such wars, even though data from the period of the European conquest show significant differences in strategy and tactics. Such wars were intended to destroy or to chase away the enemy, to take his lands, to plunder his wealth, often to take captives, and sometimes to subject opponent groups to dependent status. Destructive wars often involved sets of villages, and even sets of districts. In recent centuries they were infrequent,[33] and in early times they may have been even rarer, because competition for resources was less marked. This explains why no fortifications earlier than the last few centuries have yet been found, and why no ancestral terminology refers to them. Still, communal village charms for the defense and well-being of the village, implanted when the settlement was founded, were quite common, especially in the western half of the area, where the widespread ancient common term for "village charm" (A7; *-kínda) refers to them.[34]

Although the esprit de corps in a village flowed from common residence and common experience, ideology also contributed to it. Village communities were thought of as a single family whose father was the village headman, and the big men of each House were his brothers. The village was thus perceived as a House on a higher level. Although direct evidence in the ancestral vocabulary for this is lacking, shifts in the meanings of terms designating "house," "village," and "kin group" indicate as much. A single term can shift from one of these meanings to the others. Moreover, several terms are derived from meanings such as "hearth."[35]

The District

"The following day our march was through a similar series of villages, twelve in number, with a common well-trodden track running from one to another. In this distance sections of the primeval forest separated each village. . . ."

This quote is typical for observations made repeatedly by the earliest European travelers, who called such sections districts, regions, or lands. They often emphasized that settlements appeared in clusters with "desert" or "dead" areas in between.[36] Districts, however, have not been stressed by later writers. They were the first victims of the colonial order. When anthropologists or others later refer to them, they often talk of "maximal lineages," "subtribes," and the like. These are cognitive expressions of outsiders. They do not relate to the physical reality described by the first travelers. The district, unlike the House or the village, is known by a single ancestral term (A9); the expressions meaning "inhabitant of, member of group X" (A10) refer to the common sense of ethnicity among the inhabitants of a district. CS 343 was probably the original form. Some ethnographic data report that in the nineteenth century the inhabitants of some districts shared a tattoo so as to be immediately identifiable.[37] The district was the largest institutional organization of space known. A district came into existence when a group of neighboring villages began to rely more on each other for common defense, for trade, and for intermarriage than on other villages. Gradually they thus constituted an informal cluster and developed a sense of ethnicity, of "us" versus "them."

The district had no chief and need not have a principal village, although no doubt village size within a district varied considerably, even in ancestral times, and bigger villages carried more weight than smaller ones.[38] Nor were common meetings of the village headmen or the leaders of the Houses in the district necessary. Cross-cutting bilateral alliances sufficed. Although in theory some villages could belong to two or

more districts, in practice the uneven clustering of settlements over the
land prevented this, by separating clearly visible and named territorial
wholes. Only where population densities overall became high enough
were the boundaries blurred. The clustering of settlements also explains
why districts could be long lasting, even though villages were ephemeral.
Houses, it may be recalled, often abandoned one village for another or
attempted to attract Houses around them to found their own village.
Even so, usually more Houses apparently chose to stay within the lands
of a district than to leave the region altogether, and thus developed the
bonds of coresidence needed for the awareness of district identity.

It is therefore legitimate to describe the district as an alliance of
Houses, especially founding Houses, rather than of villages. The permanence of the district reflected a dynamic equilibrium: more of its original
Houses, especially the founding Houses, stayed within the district than
moved out of it. This alliance of Houses was formalized, even in ancestral times, by the institution which ethnographers usually refer to as
"clan." The proto-term for "clan" (A1) is CS 714, from which CS 665
with the same meaning is derived. CS 714 itself may be a distant derivation of CS 709 "to join by tying." Its meaning is also often rendered by
"tribe," thus directly referring to the people in a district.[39] In the nineteenth century clan members shared a name and story of origin; they
often had a common food taboo, less often a common tattoo. Clan
brothers were welcome in the Houses of the same clan in other villages,
but in most cases clanship was limited to this general sense of hospitality
and alliance only. Clans were seen as unalterable and permanent, given
by nature, because all of a clan's members were thought to be the
progeny of a single person. All the founding ancestors, one for each
affiliated House, were held to be equal siblings issued from a common
parent. Often the common story of origin related this claim. Clan affiliation actually changed over time, but the ideology was and still is so
strong that this continues to be denied by most people, whatever evidence may be adduced to the contrary.[40] Both the cognitive reality of
permanence and the physical reality of strong but changing alliances
between Houses existed in the ancestral tradition. Clan alliance provided an underlying flexible frame for solidarity within a district, and the
stress on the equality of all the Houses within a clan reflected the fact
that all the villages in a district were supposedly equal partners.

Like the village, the district was an organization for defense and
common security. Its solidarity was expressed in matters of war, especially destructive war. Villages within a single district fought only restricted wars. When a village in the cluster was attacked by outsiders it
called its allied villages to the rescue. This must have been the genesis of
many a destructive war. In addition the district was probably also crucial
as the arena for matrimonial alliances, not only because most spouses

came from within the district, but also because the frequency of such alliances then gave rise to a body of common customs in such matters. The unit was therefore essential for the reproduction of its constituent Houses. And lastly the district probably has always been important as a favorable framework for the mutual exchange of goods or raw materials from irregularly distributed resources, and thus played a major role in economic life.

This last comment may well remind the reader that a sketch of the fundamental social institutions in isolation is highly artificial. Society cannot be neatly cut away from its economics or for that matter from its worldview. So it is time to broach these subjects.

MAKING A LIVING

The Bantu-speaking colonists arrived south of the Sanaga with a single system of food production and acquisition that included farming as one element only, albeit a central element. After all, it is this element that distinguished them from the autochthons. They had already developed this system in the rainforests north of the Sanaga. With the help of the autochthons, they perfected it during their expansion to adjust for differences in rainfall and seasons, new flora and fauna. Activities to procure food formed an integrated system because the available time and labor for each component of the system was limited. These factors had to be carefully allotted according to season, according to technological and production levels, and according to the division of labor. Thus farming aimed at producing only some 40 percent of the food supply. Because certain crops attracted particular species of game, specialized traps were set up around the fields to protect them and to provide a steady supply of meat. During the one- or two-month-long fruiting season, gathering provided most of the vegetable food. The proper short seasons for the harvesting of caterpillars, honey, mushrooms, and termites were taken into account. In the dry season, villagers went to live for a month or so in outlying camps for collective fishing, hunting, and more gathering. Only the raising of goats, the lone domestic animal apart from the hunting dog, was not well integrated into the system. Major advantages of this food procurement system were the availability of food all year round, the quality of its nutritional balance, and the flexibility of the system, so that risks of food shortages were minimal compared with an almost exclusive reliance on farming. Finally this single system of food production was, at least in the nineteenth century, the same for all habitats with rainforest cover on dry soil. It belonged to their common tradition and, although its technology and some of its products were no longer those of ancestral times, in all essentials it still remained the ancestral system.

Farming

Farming was the centerpiece of the system.[41] Its staples were the oil palm (A61) and a yam: *Dioscorea cayenensis* Lam. (A66). Nuts of the oil palm have been found on many of the early sites.[42] But one should not leave it at that. Many more plants were involved. Among them the terms for beans (A67), calabash (A68–69), *Voandzeia* or a closely related groundnut (A71), and pepper (A74) are attested. The names of many others have not often been recorded or were lumped together under headings such as "greens" or "spinach," and so proto-terms for them remain unknown. Perhaps 10 more species of yams were cultivated at one time. They are now wild and some may always have been wild; others became feral, having "escaped" from the fields. Most were abandoned because of their low yields, and many of these are now gathered only during food shortages. People grew several more species of leguminous plants, as well as several species of gourds, among which *Cucumerops edulis* Cogn. may have been the most important, because of its fat content. Several species of *Hibiscus* and at least five species of *Amaranthus* seem to have been grown. "Spinach" is an English omnibus word that covers more than 10 other greens which grow on abandoned fields and are used for food. In earlier times some of these may have been formally cultivated.[43] Besides the oil palm, useful trees were grown, although not in orchards. Among these the "African plum" (*Pachylobus edulis,* or "safu," A49), *Canarium schweinfurthii,* three different species of kola, the raffia palm (A65), and various species of fig tree (usually *Ficus thonningii* Blume [A93] or *Ficus erystogmata*) were the most common. So far, however, only the fruits of *Canarium* have been found in early sites.[44] Contrary then to the impression that is sometimes given of people subsisting on boiled yam with palm oil sauce, the reality was utterly different even if one considers only the range of cultivated crops.

Some farming activities are present in the proto-vocabulary. They are "field in the forest" (A39), "to work on the field" (A40), its derivation ps 60 "field," and, in some languages, a machete for work in the field and two terms for "to plant" (A41–42), of which the second one seems specifically to refer to the burying of a cutting. Specific terms for farming tools have been identified as follows: A44, which now means "hoe" in many languages, originally meant "axe," as it is derived from CS 1703 "to cut." CS 372, now "axe," derived from CS 371 "to poke and ram in" (as one does with cuttings), probably referred to the digging stick (A45). CS 1640 refers to a raised platform (A47) on which to put root crops or carrying baskets. In the rainforest system the original basic tools seem to have been a digging stick and a hafted stone cutting "axe." The latter was replaced by the axe after metal tools became available, and the bushknife was then added to the set. Hoes were not used in forest farming, and terms to designate them now are derived from "axe." It is also striking that the whole early terminology associated with cereals, from sowing to weeding to winnowing to granary, is eastern Bantu. The mass of data allows one to conclude from negative evidence in this case: western Bantu originally did not grow cereals.

Every year a single, new, principal field was cut out of the forest. First the undergrowth was cleared, probably by both sexes, and then the men cut the large trees. This was done early enough in the main dry season to allow the debris to dry out. Then the men built a strong fence around the field, which was provided with traps to keep wild game out, whereupon both men and women planted the main yam crop as well as other smaller plants that matured faster, such as beans or gourds. The association of several plants on one plot is a major feature of forest agriculture. The crops were chosen so that they complemented each other either with regard to nutrition or often for shade. They supported each other's growth. Women followed up the planting phase by several weedings and by the harvesting of the associated crops, and the men planted the stakes to support the yam vines. Ten months after planting, the yams were harvested by both sexes and stacked. Then most of the field was left fallow, so that semi-spontaneous greens could develop there. But a small portion of the field was retained for another year and turned into a raised bed in which women planted a number of greens, gourds, and subsidiary crops. Then that too returned to a fallow state. Apart from crops in the kitchen gardens, rotation was not practiced. This stands in sharp contrast to agriculture in the savannas, where crop association was not much developed, but crop rotations were crucial. Gradually, secondary forest cover began to reclaim the fallow land, a process that might have taken up to 10 years.

Hence the House, which was the unit that managed plantations, needed about 10 times the amount of land annually under cultivation. With the passing of the years the distance between settlement and main field grew, until so much time was spent daily going to and returning from the main field that it became advantageous for a whole village to abandon the site and start anew elsewhere. Thus seminomadic settlement was built into this system of agriculture. And so it was too with regard to trapping and hunting, because, after only a few years, the game learned to avoid the vicinity of villages.[45]

Besides the main field every woman also had a kitchen garden, the *falga,* next to her house. This was fertilized with detritus of all kinds, and crop rotation was practiced here. One or a few specimens of useful plants such as peppers, greens, and medicinal plants were grown there. Historically these kitchen gardens are quite important because they served as experimental stations to test new plants. Here new crops and new varieties of old crops were tested for natural and labor-related requirements as well as for yields. But unfortunately very few of them have ever been reported.[46]

Finally, here and there, where marine salt was not available and other methods for extracting salt were not used, grasses or reeds with a high saline content were planted on plots in marshes or rivers, their natural habitats. These were harvested in the dry season, burned, and their ashes leached, to obtain the desired potassium salts.[47]

The main drawback to the field system was a labor bottleneck. The field had to be cleared during the dry season, in good time for the vegetation to dry thoroughly before the onset of the rains. The shorter the dry season, the more variable from year to year this crucial dry period was, and the shorter the dry season, the more it rained even during that time. So time was of the essence: the shorter the time available, the faster the land had to be cleared and the more collective labor that required. Moreover the duration of the dry season was also crucial for hunting and fishing. To maximize output there, collective labor was also needed. The main variables for the performance of the whole system, and especially for its farming component, were then the length of the dry season and the size of the labor force available for that time. The shorter the dry season, the larger the male work group for clearing the fields needed to be. Since the only fully reliable male group available for collective labor was the group of men belonging to the same House, the length of the dry season imposed a minimum size on this unit. The shorter the season, the larger the House had to be.[48]

The above description differs from most nineteenth-century practice in one major respect. The usual practice then was to burn the dried-out vegetal matter after a field had been cleared. This provided fertilizing ash. On the other hand, it also promoted the growth of weeds and increased women's work. Burning was not universal. Yam and banana fields do not really require it. And burning requires that the work be started a few days earlier to let the vegetation dry out so that it will burn well. When a season was not dry enough or long enough to allow burning—either of which was frequently the case, especially where the season is less than two months long—crops would fail. The extra time needed for drying meant a further increase in the size of the collective male labor force and in the minimum size of the House. Given such conditions it is surprising that so many burned their fields, not that some did not. The higher yields obtained with burning must have warranted running the risk incurred by the vagaries of the dry season. That is not evident in the case of bananas or yams. Hence the practice is best explained by the later adoption of new crops, such as maize, manioc, and American beans, which seem to have required burning. Therefore burning was probably not practiced in ancestral times.[49]

After the expansion of the first farmers into the rainforests, their agriculture evolved continually, albeit always within the parameters of the single-field system. We have seen that the first adoption of the banana was a major change. With yields 10 times those of any yam, less need for labor (clearing and weeding, as well as food preparation), a longer harvesting season, a secondary crop after the first harvest, and a faster regeneration of fallow land, during which time the field was ideal for trapping, the banana crop's effects were revolutionary, especially because it freed time for other economic pursuits and yielded surpluses for exchange with nonfarmers. And yet the banana did not become the only major staple everywhere. In the west and in some other regions, yams retained their place or retained at least the status of staple.

The first diffusion of the AAB banana was followed by at least one, and probably two others, one AAB set and one AAA.[50] By then, the invasion of other new Asiatic plants was probably underway as well. They came from India, carried by Muslims, or directly by boat from Southeast Asia.[51] From Asia came taro (*Colocasia esculenta*) and the water yam (*Dioscorea alata*), both useful crops in wet and very wet surroundings, respectively; the eggplant (*Solanum melongena* L.) of Indian origin, which was to establish itself everywhere as a major vegetable; and the sugar cane (A73; *Saccharum officinarum*), no more than a snack in most places, but a major crop in some areas, for example, on Bioko. And then there were lemons and oranges. All these plants are reported by early Muslim authors and a few were in the Middle East before then. They did not spread into central Africa all at once, nor did a single crop spread everywhere during a single diffusion. Thus in the western Zaire basin taro is a European import; in Cameroon it was older and probably of North African origin because its name *nkasi* is derived from the Arabic *Qulqash;* in Rwanda (*iteke*) it was a major and ancient crop.[52] Detailed studies for each of these plants still remain to be undertaken. They all fitted in with the preexisting system, in which most of them competed with older plants: taro with yams, for instance, and eggplant with gourds. They were all present in portions of the area probably as early as A.D. 1000 and certainly well before 1500. Even with the rudimentary knowledge we have about their spread, it is clear that the advent of these plants of minor importance indicates that agriculture remained dynamic. Perhaps every generation saw new plants being tried out. Yet at the same time the farming subsystem remained stable. These innovations provoked no agricultural revolution, as the banana had done, and as a number of American crops would do after 1600.

The eventual appearance here and there of other field systems deserves particular attention. More intensive farming was found by 1900 in several regions within the area. It was achieved by preparing the ground more thoroughly by mounding and ridging, by applying various forms of green fertilizer, and in places by adding new silt as soil. In most cases such developments occurred in the last few centuries. Most of these techniques seem to have developed for the growing of particular new plants, just as was surmised for the practice of burning. Thus cassava is often cited in connection with mounding or ridging. But in a number of cases intensive agriculture was a response to market conditions that appeared in the last two or perhaps three centuries.[53]

The single-field system was dominant in the rainforests, but it was not the only one in central Africa. Two others developed from or alongside it. To the south of the rainforests there was a field system based on the use of two fields annually, one in the forest (often gallery forests) and one in the savanna. The second one, completely managed by women, was used in the beginning for *Voandzeia* groundnuts and related crops. It corresponds perhaps to the second-year crop in the rainforests. The other field was cleared annually by men and planted with cereal crops. Bananas remained a secondary crop in stands near the villages. In this two-field system the association of minor crops with the major staples was, at least by 1900, much less developed than in the single-field system. Crop rotation was universal, and fields remained in use for two or more years as new crops took the place of the older ones. Still another system, called Sudanese agriculture by agronomists, developed on the northern fringes of the rainforests in the Ubangi and Uele lands. This was based on the exploitation of a field—if possible one cleared from forested land—until after several years the soil was truly exhausted and the forest vegetation could no longer reclaim it. The crop rotation of the two-field system to the south also occasionally caused such extreme soil depletion. But there it was not a systematically pursued effect as it was in the north. As a result of the two-field system and especially of Sudanese agriculture, wide swaths of rainforest were turned into savanna over time. No wonder that the vegetation maps for central Kasai, portions of Kwilu, the lands north of the middle Sanaga and Ubangi, and north of the lower and middle Uele River show evidence for a steady recession of the rainforests. As expected, this recession was more radical in the north than in Kasai or in Kwilu, where interdigitated gallery forests, and sometimes hilltop woods, survived to provide the forest component of the two-field system.[54]

Finding Food

The other major components of the early western Bantu system—gathering, trapping, hunting, and fishing—were practiced by the autochthons long before the arrival of farmers. Almost certainly the newcomers borrowed from the autochthons on all these counts, although solid evidence for this is still not available. Probably the Bantu speakers also introduced some new techniques, however, and they perfected the way in which these activities were linked to farming to form a new system. The closest links were forged between farming, gathering, and trapping. Hunting and fishing were only indirectly involved. As to husbandry, it was an innovation in the area, but it was also an activity that atrophied when sheep and cattle, unsuited to most habitats here, were left behind.

Such was the role of gathering in the equatorial tradition that even after 1900 the economy of some groups "reminds one strongly of a gathering economy."[55] Gathering for food was a highly complex endeavor, presupposing a great deal of knowledge and a clear strategy of use. The complexity appears from the amazing range of products gathered. They included: leaves to be used as greens, providing minerals, vitamins, and sometimes vegetal protein; fruits with their lipids and vitamins; roots with their carbohydrates; ants, larvae, caterpillars, termites, snails, crabs, mollusks, and fish, all sources of concentrated animal protein; mushrooms, with their mineral salts and vitamins; honey (A79) with its sugars; and drugs such as kola and the hallucinogen *iboga,* famous in Gabon. As late as the nineteenth century, gathered products remained essential to providing a balanced daily ration in protein, lipids, vitamins, and minerals. One people in Ubangi, for instance, routinely gathered 9 types of fruit, 8 types of snails, 13 of termites, 22 of caterpillars, 2 types of honey, and 32 of mushrooms. These people were not exceptional. Indeed the observer did not mention leaves or roots, and the number of fruits is much smaller than elsewhere.[56] Such an account still leaves out the myriad products used as raw materials for material culture and as medicine. The botanist Chevalier mentioned two of the more exotic ones, a fern used in the construction of traps and a mushroom used to make ceremonial belts, as illustrations of the encyclopedic knowledge about the natural environment held by equatorial Africans.[57]

Hundreds of plants and dozens of animals were used, and hundreds more had been observed and labeled. The depth and systematic nature of this knowledge was and still is vastly underrated by ethnographers.[58] Such scientific knowledge for knowledge's sake is an essential ingredient in understanding the relation of these peoples with their habitats. It provided them with a wide range of choices according to social or cultural goals.

The strategy of use consisted in supplementing agriculture on the one hand and in drastically cutting the risks involved in farming on the other. A seasonal calendar for gathering was set up so that, at each moment, gathered food complemented grown produce, and together they provided the requirements for a balanced diet. Series of wild products with the same nutritive input but available at different times were set up as substitutes. In various regions people left the village to camp in the forests at the height of the fruiting season and then again in the dry season, the latter being the best time for large-scale hunts and fishing in brooks and ponds. This not only diminished a heavy reliance on farm produce and the climatic risks involved, but it also freed up more time for gathering than more intensive agriculture would have left available.[59]

The specifics of the gathering activities differed from place to place because the habitats differed, although mainstays such as kola, safu (A49), palm wine, *Canarium* fruits, and the fruits of *Irvingia gabonensis* were used over large areas. Apart from *Canarium,* there is no direct evidence for their use in early times. How much knowledge and how many of these practices were derived from the earlier hunter gatherers and how many were added later? Eventually detailed collection of field data and biological vocabularies may well lead to the discovery of a long list of common wild foodstuffs and techniques for gathering them. This sort of data will then provide some answers to questions such as the above, or perhaps invalidate the usual assumption that, as farming improved, gathering declined.

Certain crops attracted certain animals: thus bushpigs love root crops and antelopes vegetable leaves. Such observations were used to tie trapping directly to farming. The fields were protected by traps especially designed for the major predators expected, as all traps (A48) were adapted to the game one wanted to catch. The Djue of the upper Dja River used 11 main types of traps, and similar or even higher numbers are found elsewhere. Thus a yam field also produced bushpigs and beans produced antelopes. Elaborate trapping systems were also set up elsewhere and could control whole landscapes, at the price of a big labor investment by men. The principles and perhaps the major types of traps certainly go back to the ancestral tradition, as is shown by the proto-vocabulary CS 1661 "trap," and CS 1698 "to set a trap," both derived from CS 1657 "to walk." However, subsequent innovation and diffusion, rather than ancestral legacy, certainly explains the widespread similarities of game traps or fish traps.[60]

The Bantu speakers brought some of their hunting techniques to their new homelands and borrowed others from the hunter gatherers who lived there before them. Given the size of the labor unit required, such loans are more likely to have involved individual hunting, or hunting in small groups, rather than large-scale collective hunting. Its techniques were either imported or invented *in situ.*[61] Collective hunting (A50) with nets (A51) was a dry season activity, usually carried out in the weeks before the farming cycle began, but not otherwise linked to it. In the nineteenth century hunting with nets was widespread in the dry season. It was a cooperative and exciting endeavor, usually involving all the men of the village. One-day net hunts were organized from the village, usually on special occasions such as an initiation, a funeral, a marriage. Longer, more intensive expeditions occurred when the villagers left for hunting and gathering camps. Like restricted war such hunts were a major occasion for manifesting the esprit de corps of a village; great feats of hunting were remembered for a long time, and hunts, like wars, were hedged about by ritual. Despite their prestige, however, the returns per participant of such hunts were often lower than those from trapping, and always less predictable. The fun and the spectacle may explain why the practice was so cherished. The element of chance in turn makes clear why some peoples used a net hunt as a divination device, a barometer of their relations with supernatural beings.[62] The equivalent of the excitement of net hunting in the open savannas north and south of the forests was the dry season fire drive. The grass was set on fire and everyone in a village lined up opposite the advancing line of fire to catch and kill the fleeing game.[63]

In most forest societies individual hunting, and hunting in small groups without nets, occurred occasionally all year around. This was usually an occupation for youths and semi-specialized experts. In the nineteenth century not all societies were equally involved in hunting. Some, such as the peoples of northern Gabon and the Boyela of the upper Lomela and northern Maniema, hunted much more than others. Without exception, such people lived in areas of very low population density, and practiced a very undemanding agriculture based on banana fields. Full-time groups of nomadic hunters, who did not farm at all, were found by 1900 in many parts of the area. They were all linked to specific farming villages, and the farmers considered them to be serfs. Most, but probably not all of these groups, were physically pygmy. Although many groups may well have been the descendants of autochthonous hunting groups, some probably were descendants of farmers, devoted to hunting, who, under exceptionally favorable conditions, abandoned agriculture altogether.[64]

Two very different kinds of fishing were probably practiced from the beginning. One was just a specialized form of trapping, a collective activity for women and children often practiced during the dry season. The techniques included damming, traps, the use of scoops, and the use of stunning drugs such as those derived from *Tephrosia vogelii* Hook. f. They were similar from one end of the area to the other. The other approach presupposed a sizable amount of equipment and consisted of systematic fishing on the navigable rivers. The proto-vocabulary (A54–60) testifies to riverine fishing by line from a dugout, but not to fishing with nets, although nets were probably used. Indeed, even before the expansion, specialized fishermen may have plied the ocean shores or the Mungo, Wouri, and Sanaga rivers.[65] Soon after their expansion some of the colonists became specialized fishermen, in particular along the Zaire River and its major tributaries. Linguistic groups there split into languages of fishermen and languages of landlubbers, as long ago as the beginning of our era.[66] Fishing technologies for use on major rivers were complex, capital intensive, rapidly changing, and widespread.[67]

The immigrant farmers crossed the Sanaga with only the dog (A75, 52) and the goat (A76). Their forefathers had some cattle and perhaps sheep, but there was no place for them in the forest. Goats eat shrubs and leaves, but cattle and sheep eat grass, and in most of the rainforest areas grass was rare. The next domestic animal to appear was the fowl (A77). Its bones have been found on sites dating from around A.D. 1000 in Rwanda and in southern Zaire.[68] By the nineteenth century goats and fowl were the main domestic animals. Unlike the dog, these animals were not integrated into the overall food procurement system, even though either could be important as festive and sacrificial meat and, in places, goats were a store of wealth. Sheep in small numbers are then reported, here and there, especially on the margins of the rainforests or in savannas; pigs (A78) were also raised in portions of the southern and western savannas. These are late introductions unintegrated into production, and often a flock of sheep or herd of pigs remained merely an expensive substitute for wild pigs and antelopes.[69]

Industries

The incoming Bantu speakers introduced not just farming into this area but also at least one new craft: ceramics. Both vocabulary and direct archaeological finds attest to this. They may have introduced raffia weaving (A89–92) and the extraction of salt (A80) as well. Their technology of basketry plaiting (A87) may have been more advanced than was known hitherto in the area, and they certainly built more solid houses. It is not evident, however, that leatherworking, woodworking, the making of bark cloth (A94), and sewing (A88) were more advanced than the technology in use before their arrival.[70] The technology of iron smelting (A97–103) was acquired from the last centuries B.C. onward. These industries and associated technologies did not remain static for thousands of years, as can be deduced from the distributions for objects of material culture and their associated terminologies. But despite its obvious importance this history still remains unknown and unstudied.[71]

A distribution study of objects leaves the impression that the peoples of the forests were highly interested in technology. They especially loved gadgets for fishing, hunting, and gathering, and they seem to have frequently invented more efficient tools. The drive to improve was rooted in a desire to achieve higher returns, but not at any cost. The available evidence shows what almost amounts to an obsession to achieve optimal, not maximal, returns. As it happens, the technology of traps provides us with a particularly telling example of this principle of optimal returns. H. Koch showed that the Djue of southeastern Cameroon had the choice between building highly effective trapping systems with palisades crossing whole valleys from ridge to ridge or forgoing the barricades and placing only flimsy traps instead. The former solution yielded more meat but took more time and collective labor to set up than the alternative. A single expert could do that in a day or two. Most Djue used the first technique, yet the virtuoso trappers used the second. The loners obtained a higher return of meat per person working than their fellows, and they spent less time on the project. The expert solution was the optimal one. In terms of returns, the flimsy work made more sense than the fine trap and the sturdy palisade.[72]

The search for optimal returns for labor, rather than technical perfection, acted as a powerful incentive for innovation, and was the strongest engine of diffusion in all technological fields. It explains, for instance, why around 1900 the Djue borrowed a crude, large, meshed hunting net from their neighbors, the Bulu, although they had other types of net as well. This one was more efficient for catching bushpigs at lower labor costs. Similar considerations explain why standardized small, flimsy, and foldable fishtraps were much more common on the Zaire River than giant weirs and fixed traps. Closely intertwined with the system of production, with the endeavor to create substitutes for scarce resources, and with the drive to invent labor-saving devices, industrial technology was part of the wider system and remained within the overall choice of a mode of living made by the ancestral founders of this tradition.

Exchange and Trade

Exchange occurred within communities as gift (A104), with a connotation of "occasional gift," and as a related activity: "to borrow," "to lend" (CS 376). A second term for "to give" and "gift" (A105) has a connotation of "division of spoils" and a political connotation linked to big men. Such terms differ from an equally ancient term (A106) related to gift exchange between communities, involving trade or not. According to Guthrie, CS 490 "to buy" arose in western Bantu and is older than CS 414 "to buy." CS 490 might well be common Bantu given the presumably related CS 494 "poor person," CS 495 "affair," CS 496 "fault," CS 497 "debt," and CS 498 "penalty,"—all in eastern Bantu—even though CS 876 "buy" or "sell" is the oldest common Bantu form. The very succession of three early forms for "trading" points to its dynamic character, changing with the times.[73]

Trade of some sort existed in the area well before the Bantu speakers arrived and has done so ever since. The irregular distribution of necessary resources has always been an incentive to trade, as is shown by the export of stone from Mayombe to the Loango coast, from the middle Ogooué to the coast of Gabon c. 350–300 b.c., and from the area around the mouth of the Kasai River to Lake Tumba well before then.[74] The need for finery is shown by a find such as the mother-of-pearl fragment left in the cave of Ntadi Ntadi (c. 390–15 b.c.), far from the sea in lower Zaire.[75] Socially such exotic luxuries were often quite significant as visible signs of the wealth and power of the big men who owned them, enhancing their prestige and their authority. And then there were the necessities, such as good salt (A80) for food and redwood powder (A83) for skin care.

The semantic evidence for successive changes in the vocabulary associated with trade testifies to continuing endeavors to overcome the limitations of the habitats within the reach of each participating group. But surely the evidence must also be linked to the ongoing competition among big men who "divided" and "gave away" goods since early times, and built up hoards of treasure as a war chest in their endless struggles. A major use of such treasures, from an early date on, may have been to fund matrimonial compensation as well. Last but not least, trade has been a major avenue for stimulating innovation and diffusion, because ideas always accompany trade.

From later practice one may surmise that the commodities traded included such necessities as farm produce, metals, metal objects, salt, fish and seafood, raffia cloth, pottery, canoes, camwood powder, palm oil, perhaps mats and baskets, and a few rare luxury items such as conus shells and rare furs.[76] As to an early slave trade, there is clear linguistic evidence only for pawning in early times, but not for a trade in people as commodities.

Similarly there is no early linguistic evidence for most specialized commercial institutions, such as caravans, markets, potlatch, currencies, and the names of market weekdays. One regional term for market is derived from the common meaning "beach" (CS 205), recalling the exchange of fish for vegetal food between fishermen and landlubbers on beaches. Then there is a term for "friend" (A18), which in recent times was used between big men who were business associates or between host and trader. The institution paralleled clanship by creating links between two Houses, but differed from clanship in limiting such a link to their leaders. Bloodbrotherhood may be a later development of it.[77]

Unlike basic production patterns, most trading patterns tend to change rapidly over time. They are a major dynamic for change. Their relevance in a study about tradition is how they alter it, rather than how they perpetuate it. Time and time again, trade was a major engine of sociopolitical innovation through its links with leadership. Hence the recovery of its past, especially through archaeology, is exceptionally important.[78]

THE MEANING OF THE WORLD

Worldviews are essential to the creation and maintenance of tradition. They are the cognitive substance that gives meaning and aims to life. To claim a common cultural tradition for the peoples of the rainforests, one must demonstrate that the fundamental axioms of the worldviews of different western Bantu–speaking peoples are the same and to what degree they are the same. To assume this merely on the basis of a common linguistic ancestry is not sufficient grounds for claiming a whole common cultural heritage. Instead one must prove by the use of reconstructed vocabulary that this common tradition truly is a heritage of the group that spoke the ancestral language. A particular difficulty in this case stems from the fact that the worldview was never systematized as dogma. To participate in common ritual mattered more in a community than any divergence of belief about this ritual. Nevertheless basic concepts were shared and formed a coherent if open-ended whole, so that a consistent account of them can be given.[79]

The early western Bantu speakers believed that the "real" world went beyond the apparent world. In this "real" world the spirits of heroes (A113, 115), sentient beings with anthropomorphic attributes, were powerful.[80] Although some reflexes of the proto-term now refer to nature spirits, the original concept referred to heroes. A nice insight into ancestral thought stems from the realization that CS 619 "hero" derives from CS 617–18 "to extinguish," "to get lost," "to become extinguished."[81] The notion was first linked to the spirit of a long-deceased leader, whose personality and perhaps even whose name had been forgotten and then rediscovered when he wrought wonders. That is the first meaning of the Greek word for hero. The spirit offered protection in return for worship. His cult, manifested at a shrine through prayer, libation, or sacrifice, by or on behalf of the leader of the House or village, undoubtedly bolstered the legitimacy and the authority of the big man in charge, whether the spirits were held to be heroes worshiped by their very successor in office or nature spirits.

The ancestral tradition also knew another type of spirit (A114), which in contrast to A113 was a nature spirit. Such a spirit was linked to a village domain or to the lands of a district. In the nineteenth century one even finds a hierarchy of such spirits in part of the area. Compared with the peoples of the southern savanna, in equatorial Africa nature spirits were prominent.[82] The term may also have referred to a portable shrine or charm for such a spirit. By the seventeenth century it was used in lower Zaire and lower Congo for both the charm and the supernatural force believed to reside in it.

One of Guthrie's proto-terms glossed "God" (A116),[83] and was probably not western Bantu. Recent missionary activity has affected both its meaning and expanded its geographic distribution so much that special caution is indicated. Still, even before the arrival of missionaries, the term was widespread in the westernmost part of the area, and it must be of considerable antiquity. It referred to a particularly powerful or "supreme" spirit, perhaps the first of all ancestors,[84] perhaps a first Creator spirit, perhaps a prime cause. Most of the other terms translated as "God" refer to first spirits thought to have created all others. In some cases a connection with the sun is indicated.[85] This notion of "fountain and origin" differs from the general concepts of spirits. It sounds like the logical conclusion of speculation about the worldview, an impression reinforced by the perfunctory character or even the total absence of a cult for the Creator.

In the ancestral tradition people also believed in charms (A117). One set of terms (CS 787) has the same root as CS 786, meaning "ritual expert," "medicine man." Another set (CS 1730) derives from CS 1729 "tree" and refers to vegetal matter, which still constitutes the bulk of the pharmacopoeia. Charms were always perceived as tools. No one worried excessively about the precise nature of their wonderful power. Whether it was *sui generis*, derived from heroes, the recent dead, or nature spirits, or had some other origin was of interest only to ritual practitioners with a speculative bent. Charms worked when the correct ingredients were correctly gathered, the correct words spoken, and above all when the medicine man and the customer or owner observed the correct ritual taboos (A121–22). There are no proto-vocabulary items referring to the creation and transfer of such charms. Charms were very versatile tools, used as an adjunct to the most varied practical activities. They could be collective or individual, and could exert momentary or durable effects according to goal. Not surprisingly the crucial collective charms were those that coped with crucial problems: control of the rains, defense of the village (A7), help in war and hunting, and, not least, detection and eradication of witchcraft, a central part of the collective representations everywhere.

Words for bewitching (A123), witchcraft (A124), and witches are all built on the same semantic root. Witches were those people, women or men, who had the ability to kill others out of envy by wishing them evil, consciously or unconsciously. Such killings were thought to occur frequently, and witchcraft was suspected on the occasion of every death. Witchcraft incorporated the notion of absolute, malicious evil, and held that pure evil always was the work of humans, and only of humans. A corollary of this belief was that one should never give cause for envy. One should never stand out, one should always share. In sum witchcraft was an ideology of equality and cooperation. Quite paradoxical for societies built on competition between big men and on inequality of status! Yet the ideology was in tune with the stress on equality between social units and on the need to pretend at least superficially (as in the use of kinship terminology) that social inferiors were equals. Nevertheless, in recent times, most accused witches were social inferiors, such as women, slaves, or clients. They were suspected most precisely because they had no other reliable means of redress for injustices committed against them. This reasoning effectively exposed the pretense of equality. It is not surprising then that a wave of witchcraft accusations often resulted from high social tensions and caused further tension at the same time.

Witchcraft occurred because some people had a bewitching substance (A125) inside their bodies. Among those thought to be witches were big men. In a celebrated article McGaffey has shown that beliefs about leadership in the whole area assumed that big men were successful because they had extraordinary supernatural powers, identical with and often superior to those of witches.[86] A leader was always a focus of envy. A battery of charms helped him to repel the attacks of witches, and his own witchcraft killed competitors or subjects. His success was attributed to the favor of supernatural agencies, a favor won by furtive human sacrifices through witchcraft "at night." Such beliefs explain why competing leaders often used accusations of witchcraft against each other. In practice, then, accusations of witchcraft included both ends of the social scale: the hapless and the successful.

Beyond these basic notions each society in recent centuries held further rich beliefs and rituals about witchcraft and witches. In the western half of the area it was then thought that the power of witchcraft was caused by either a special organ or a little animal in one's belly. Autopsies were practiced to determine if someone had been a witch while alive or had died bewitched. Everywhere a luxuriant folklore told of witches' Sabbaths, their astral bodies, their appearance at night, and their familiars such as the owl—a folklore that was usually richer than any other concerning supernatural beings.

Diviners were crucial for the detection of witches. The term for them (ps 47 [3:64]) was a derivation of A129 "to cure," "to divine." The term includes both divination and healing, because diagnosis of the supernatural causes of an illness was the first step toward recovery. Using dreams (CS 672–74), charms, oracles (A127–28), or sometimes a trance, the diviner could "see" what was happening in the supernatural and determine the cause of illness: for example, a broken taboo and the displeasure of a nature spirit or a hero, a charm, or a witch. When witchcraft was involved, a formal accusation was lodged by the relatives of the patient or the deceased person. The suspected witch then had to demonstrate his or her innocence. This was done by the poison ordeal. The accused drank the poison. If innocent, he vomited the poison; if guilty, he could not and showed signs of poisoning, whereupon the bystanders lynched him and the body was burned in order to annihilate its ancestral spirit. There are three interlocked proto–western Bantu terms for "poison oracle" (A128), designating two plants used in the process and the oracle itself. This situation suggests an ancestral origin for the poison ordeal.[87]

These principles of the ancestral worldview lay at the very core of cognitive reality in general, and hence of the motivation for action. The mix of well-informed pragmatic action, the application of charms, and the appeal to spirits, in any technological field, including medicine, never ceases to fascinate the outsider. Medicine is perhaps the most obvious field for appeals to the supernatural. This was so not only because to conserve people's lives was a primary goal in these societies but also because illness was the quintessential manifestation of abnormality,[88] and abnormality always resulted from the neglect of spirits or attacks by witches. In the nineteenth century, curing was a process of restoration pursued by the patient, the specialist, and the support group within the House of the patient. Most curing interventions were public performances, often to the sound of music, and some were spectacular. Medicines (A118), administered in various ways and an essential part of most interventions, were always charms as well. They were accompanied by taboos (A122) for the patient, often by taboos for the healer, and sometimes by taboos for the support group.[89]

Charms (A117) were the most versatile instruments to address abnormality, and the more important the collective issue, the more important the collective charm. Charms for rain, charms to defend the village, charms for war, and charms to expel witches were universal in the nineteenth century. The dynamics of religious thought and practice to cope with such disasters used analogical reasoning and prophetic "revelations" in dreams, and resulted in the creation of major new cults around a new collective charm. These could then diffuse and turn into religious movements sweeping from village to village. By the late nineteenth century these movements were centered around charms of war to resist the colonial conquest or were millennial movements promising the eradication of witches. There is no direct evidence for such religious movements in earlier times. However, such dynamics and new cults have always been a crucial part of the worldview of the peoples of the forest.[90] Whether their aim was to find witches, to relieve epidemics, to avert or promote war, they were always similar in structure but novel in content, seeking new answers to cope with the major crises as they arose. Born out of novel thoughts about the crisis of the moment, they always involved attempts to eliminate major discrepancies between cognitive and physical reality.

Thus although the worldview in general underlay the very meaning of all institutions, it was itself constantly influenced by practical situations. Society and culture were part and parcel of a single dynamic system that, while true to its principles, ceaselessly altered the application and derivations of these principles, changing as situations and evolving experience dictated.

A HISTORICAL WATERSHED

In conclusion, attention must be drawn to a condition underlying the functioning of the whole set of interlocking institutions and their system of production, namely low population densities. The district was best demarcated from its neighbors and maintained a better level of internal solidarity in areas of low population density; village and Houses frequently moved from one place of settlement to another. Houses, and indeed individual men, freely chose their residences, and big man leadership was inherently a competition to attract more people to one's House. These institutional arrangements all presupposed the availability of unsettled open spaces and low population densities. Freewheeling competition was too destructive in confined quarters. Losers had to be given an "exit," a chance to settle out of range elsewhere.[91] The system of production in the ancestral tradition presupposed low population densities because of the needs for shifting cultivation and new lands for trapping, gathering, and hunting. Likewise, high individual mobility, following optimal ratios of return for work, functioned well only in conditions of similar densities.

At the outset low population densities were the norm and there was no conflict. In time, however, the very success of the ancestral tradition and the resulting growth in population were to create one. Critical population density was reached rather quickly, precisely because the provision of low density allowed for very extensive land use, which was, in turn, central to these societies. Relative overpopulation began in these systems when all the land was in use. Taking the shifting of villages into account, this occurred at a density of approximately four persons per square kilometer.[92] That was an upper limit, and people probably felt uneasy long before it was reached. Densities equal to or higher than four per square kilometer forced an adaptation of basic social institutions and of the system of production, and also led to a faster pace of change in most habitats.

The standard answer to such a situation was an internal social transformation in areas of high relative density, often accompanied by an outflow from relatively overpopulated areas. These dynamics first began to occur after the colonists had occupied the whole area, perhaps therefore in the second half of the first millennium A.D.

Such internal transformations could trigger chain reactions over vast distances, because all the communities in a continuously inhabited area formed a single social system. In its initial state, the system consisted of similar competing Houses aligned in similar antagonistic districts. The system was in a stable dynamic equilibrium, because all the Houses and districts were *similar:* equal in manpower, and hence in military strength. But the system was potentially chaotic: one small change could trigger vast, unforeseeable, albeit not random, consequences.

Once an innovation in a single House or district made it *dissimilar,* and raised its military potential (usually because it raised the efficiency of its internal cohesion in times of stress and hence the size of its available manpower in time of war), that district threatened all others. The equilibrium was broken. The now insecure, competing neighboring districts sought to increase their efficiency by adopting the innovation or by inventing an equivalent innovation. In doing so, they transferred the disequilibrium to districts farther out from the center. A chain reaction set in, which would stop only when it reached the limits of the system: either sparsely populated areas, where the demographic conditions of the system did not obtain, or districts of equal or superior strength, derived from an innovation stemming from another epicenter. At that point the system could return to its initial state. Usually it did not, because destabilization was followed by escalation. The effects of one successful innovation encouraged the further elaboration of its principles by a House or district, usually in or near the original epicenter.

In equatorial Africa such innovations seem to have been brought on by an increase in size of a successful House, which itself was often assisted by especially favorable environmental or trading conditions. The etymological connection between wealth and leadership points in that direction. But, as the evidence for economic growth is still unknown, its concrete role as a precipitator in the system cannot be assessed, and one must be content with the story of the institutional developments. In any case environment or economics cannot be seen as the root cause of such dynamics, because their effects were neither automatic nor necessary. Nor should one argue from such evidence that all these developments owed nothing to the ancestral tradition. To the contrary, all the social innovations which will be chronicled in the next chapters were but an elaboration of the social legacy of the ancestral tradition, as presented in this chapter.

Four

The Trail of the Leopard in the Inner Basin

How did the passage of time after A.D. 1000 transform the common and ancient institutional framework of society as sketched in the previous chapter? It is time to tell that story. The emphasis now lies on the plasticity of the tradition and on sociopolitical change. For even if their dynamics presuppose many an economic engine, sociopolitical institutions shaped society and culture. Moreover, from a comparative perspective, these institutions are a unique legacy to the diversity of political institutions in the world, because equatorial Africans grappled in an original way with the question of how to maintain local autonomy paramount, even while enlarging the scale of society. An institutional history is also fitting to refute the views, lingering even now, that there has not been any institutional change at all among the peoples studied. And finally, today more and earlier evidence is available about the sociopolitical past than there is about other varieties of history. This chapter tells the tale for the central core of the area, and the next two continue it for its western and eastern flanks, respectively.

The inner basin on both sides of the great fold of the Zaire, between the Sangha and the lower middle Zaire to the west and the Lualaba to the east, lies within the belt of rainforests (map 4.1). Its habitats consist of marsh and inundated forests of various sorts in its western half and of forests on dry land in the eastern half. A 25-mile-wide expansion of the Zaire near the summit of its main arch and another one below its confluence with the Ubangi created a set of rich riverside habitats of their own. Semideciduous, rather than evergreen, forests predominated in the south, where intercalary savannas were also especially important. No locality in the area was far from a navigable river, and the network of

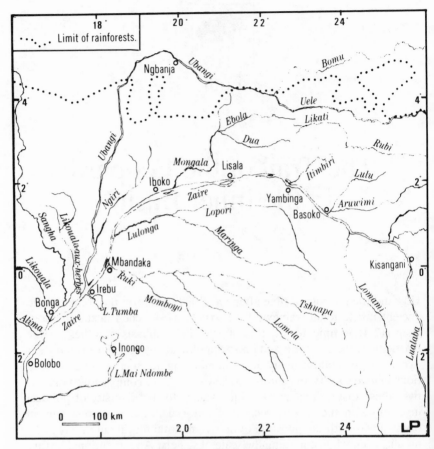

Map 4.1.   The inner basin

rivers facilitated travel over long distances. This accounts in part for the
huge area occupied by the closely related dialects or languages of the
Mongo group, which span the whole inner basin south of the great Zaire
bend. The network also created strategic locations near the confluence
of major river systems on the rare mounds that were high enough for
village settlement. Under such conditions it is not surprising that long
ago the population had specialized into fishing peoples, farmer trappers,
and hunter gatherers.[1]

   The archaeological finds recovered so far from the area come from
the sites along the rivers. A first set includes spectacular and beautiful
ceramics, dating to at least the thirteenth century, and labeled the
Bondongo horizon. This evolved into a later Nkile horizon perhaps by
the fourteenth century. Ceramics made in the nineteenth century were
further developments of Nkile ware. Bondongo pottery is found on the

banks of the Lulonga and Maringa rivers, on the Tshuapa, Momboyo, and Ruki rivers ranging over more than 900 km, and on the lower Ubangi as far upstream as Ngbanja, 225 km upriver as the crow flies. The data support the view that fishing folk expanded up the Tshuapa from the Ruki sometime before A.D. 1200 but continued to participate in a single network of communication.[2] Different ceramics of unknown age were found on the banks of the upper Tshuapa, and iron-smelting furnaces near Mbandaka date to between the fifteenth and eighteenth centuries.[3]

Recent research has traced other ceramic horizons along the banks of the Sangha and Likouala-aux-herbes rivers, as well as four different sets along the Congolese bank of the Zaire between the Malebo Pool and the Alima. None of these is as yet dated, but they attest to long-range communication by water because the same ceramics extend over hundreds of miles.[4]

On the eve of the onset of the major transformations to be discussed, social structure in the region still conformed in general to the common tradition, although numerous variations on the framework had appeared. A picture of the situation for the whole of the inner Zaire basin is not yet available, but one can catch glimpses of some local social structures by or just after A.D. 1000. Even a quick sketch of one of these gives one an appreciation for the degree of magnitude of change that had taken place since the days of settlement. Because the available information is best for the western Mongo near Mbandaka, their situation will be discussed.[5]

Innovations in terminology show that of the three interlocking institutions, the House had grown in importance at the expense of the village. It had kept its character as a bilateral "family" and was called *etúká*, "the hearth stone," over a large area ranging from the upper Ogooué to northern Maniema. Its leader, the big man, now had an important patrimony to manage.[6] He was still thought of as rich, but also—and this is new—as legitimate. *Nsomi* means "legitimate successor." In kinship terminology a major structural change had taken place to reflect a preference for marriage by bridewealth. The children of the man who had received a woman's bridewealth were treated as if they belonged to a lower generation than her children. This practice constitutes a Crow system of kinship terminology. For the Mongo, a woman was not quite of equivalent worth to the valuables given as bridewealth for her. Therefore the wife-giving House owed the House that had given the bridewealth. Hence the lower genealogical status. In this reasoning the new role of wealth in general, and of the patrimony in particular, is evident. The existence of a House treasure may have been the main cause for the appearance of a concept of legitimate succession, because untrammeled competition for the succession could dissipate the patrimony very quickly and ruin the House. At the same time it became easier for one candidate to acquire wealth concentrated in a single hoard of valuables, especially if he were designated ahead of time as the probable successor. Once invented, the concept of legitimate succession in turn reinforced the permanence of Houses over time.[7] The increasing role of bridewealth, which was even then paid in valuable commodities (mostly metals), fostered close links between trade and the power of each House. Given the archaeological evidence for communication along the rivers and the known rarity of iron ores in much of the sector, it is clear that trade included ore, raw metal, and metal objects. Insofar as "valuables" were metal objects, and metal was linked to bridewealth, and bridewealth was the dominant form of marriage, Houses better placed for trade grew faster than, and perhaps at the expense of, others.[8] Although this situation contrasted with the situation in ancestral times, especially with regard to the altered status of big men, the overall structures remained quite similar to the ancestral ones, especially in terms of conceptual reality. Conceptual change usually recognized and sanctioned ongoing changes in physical practice, giving them the status of permanence. In turn, however, they often provoked major readjustments in physical practice, as is evident from the two major chains of institutional change presented in this chapter.

INVENTING LINEAGES

The trail of the leopard is the trail of power.[9] Among all peoples of the rainforests without exception, the leopard was a major emblem of political power and apparently always had been.[10] Hence the disposition of the spoils of the leopard, from hunter to highest authority, is the best indicator of the political structure. To keep its spoils was to proclaim one's independence. To hand them over was to recognize a superior authority. The spoils of leopards went beyond most villages to the seat of a district head. Late-nineteenth-century evidence, in almost the whole inner basin, shows first that there were practically no situations left where the largest political unit was a district in which all villages were equal. Second, in part of the area the largest polities now encompassed thousands, sometimes tens of thousands of people, or as many as are found elsewhere in centralized chiefdoms. Society was more complex than earlier observers have believed. Third, there were a variety of political systems in the region. Hence the argument that there was no political history to recover in the area because the institutions of these peoples had never changed is patently wrong. Comparison soon shows that several major dynamics have been at work. In most cases decentralization was maintained, but district-level cooperation between Houses and settlements became more structured and was cast in a new cognitive mold. In some cases centralization became acceptable and chiefdoms or even kingdoms appeared.

Dominant Houses

The first cognitive innovation was a closer identification of all villagers with the founding House of a village, whether or not they were members. Long ago, perhaps in the eleventh or twelfth century, perhaps even earlier, this founding House became so identified with all the inhabitants of the village that they began to look at their social relations to other villages in the district as if they were members of the founding House. The relatives of the big man of the founding House became their relatives, his in-laws, their in-laws, his allies, their allies. The relations between villages were now thought of as relations between their two founding Houses. Allied villages had always formed a district, but now such an alliance came to be thought of as the relation of families linked by marriage. The linguistic evidence for this is the appearance of a new term, *noko,* a reciprocal term designating both mother's brother and sister's son, rather than the older "male mother" and "child of sister" terms. *Noko* actually meant "intermediary" in some languages.[11] Its use thus stressed the alliance aspect of the relationship and its equality, rather than the exact kinship relations involved. And the term was applied to whole villages. When a founding House contracted a marriage in another village, the two villages became *noko,* or "allies." Moreover, where a fraction of a founding House split off to found another settlement, the original settlement and its offshoot began to think of themselves as "brothers."

This identification of all the inhabitants with the leading House could happen only if the choice of Houses in general had become more limited, if villages stayed in the same general spot for a long time, thus escaping disintegration in their constituent Houses, and if the competition for leadership in the founding House on the death of its big man was sufficiently channeled to avoid a break-up. These conditions point to practices that had sprung up before the cognitive reality absorbed them. Mobility for Houses and villages could be restricted where suitable land for settlement was scarce. This was the case in inundated forests, and especially along most stretches at the bend of the Zaire River, where only rare headlands and mounds were adapted for situating a village. Villages could stay on the same site much longer if they made their living by fishing rather than by farming. Fishing villages needed to move only occasionally and over a very short distance whenever the actual village site became too dirty. Hence they did not need much land. For these reasons one suspects that the new cognitive attitudes occurred first in fishing settlements. Some of these sites were far more desirable than others, the ideal being a location commanding a node of commerce, especially at the confluence of a tributary with a mainstream. Basoko, for instance, was such a site. It was located near the confluence of the Aruwimi, the Lulu, and the Zaire, and not very far from the Lomami.[12] A founding House would not easily relinquish such excellent positions. Indeed the ruling House of Basoko had occupied the site continuously, at least since 1750. Sometimes people went to great lengths to occupy an ideal site. The locale of Bonga near the mouth of the two Likoualas and the Sangha was so desirable that a large town was built there on artificial mounds.[13]

Given the conditions of stability and desirability of a site, the cognitive innovation represented by the use of the term *noko* probably arose in an inundated forest and probably in fishing settlements. Its distribution all along the great fold of the Zaire supports this view, even though the term also extended well beyond the river to the north, northeast, and southeast.[14]

Lineage and District

A much bigger change was still in the offing. Villages within a district became physically unequal, and new military institutions and new weaponry appeared. In terms of cognitive reality a system of Omaha kinship terminology was invented, and later the patrilineage emerged to sanction, organize, and give meaning to the other innovations. To understand this further dramatic change, however, the context, even if not directly attested at this time, must be kept in mind. Villages and their leading Houses on favorable sites could expect attack by others who coveted their prosperous location. The better the location, the greater the security problem. Hence military innovation. At the same time more young men chose to live in a prosperous village with a higher standard of living and a more exciting life than elsewhere. This influx strengthened the defenses of such a village. Indeed the population of desirable regions as a whole must have risen through immigration for the same reasons. Finally the villages near the mouths of the Itimbiri, Aruwimi, and Lulu, especially, were in trading contact with the non-Bantu-speaking peoples of the savanna borders in the Uele Basin and derived new goods and ideas from there. To account for the major institutional changes that occurred, one postulates increased intensity of trade, trade over increasingly longer distances, the presence of much less mobile and larger villages, and much greater differences between the bigger and the smaller villages.

As more destructive wars began to be fought, increased insecurity was countered by changes in armament and tactics. Still, wars were apparently not frequent or bad enough yet to lead to the building of palisades and ditches outside the villages or of fortified places within them. The stabbing spear and shield became the main weapons. A curved and hooked scimitar came into fashion, which allowed one to hook an opponent's shield aside and leave him vulnerable (figure 4.1). This weapon was either borrowed from the savannas to the north or invented here from a throwing knife prototype.[15] Tactics were also altered. Spearmen were set up as a body, several ranks deep, aligned behind a wall of shields for fighting on village plazas. In the nineteenth century, ambushing the enemy en route was also common, and the tactic may have been quite old. In this case the warriors were strung out in one or two lines on both sides of the passage and often in several bodies.[16] On water huge war canoes were loaded with 40 and sometimes even twice that many spearmen. Such strategies required training and at least enough discipline among the soldiers not to break rank. Both of these conditions were observed in the late nineteenth century and must be as old as the armament and the tactics.[17] Military success also obviously depended on numerical superiority. A village of 100, containing perhaps 20 or 30 adult men, could not fight this way. The strategy presupposed either much larger settlements or district-wide cooperation in war. As this form of warfare developed, cooperation between the villages of a district had to become more efficient. Safety was sought in numbers, and larger settlements appeared. Once such a development was underway, the resulting growing inequality of settlement size required adaptations in the realm of cognitive reality.

The growth of unequal strength between villages was translated into cognitive terms when villages began no longer to be seen as equal *noko*, but either as superior "elder brother" and inferior "younger brother," if their founding Houses were related, or as superior "mother's brothers" and inferior "sister's sons," if their founding Houses were only allies.[18] The new principle that a House which gave a wife became superior to one which received a wife became firmly entrenched. The Omaha system of kinship terminology is based on this principle. It probably spread in the region of the Zaire from Kisangani to Basoko and in the lower Aruwimi basin at this time.[19] The typical features of the system were that kin on the mother's side, the givers of a wife, were elevated by a generation in relation to kin on the father's side, because the gift of a woman in marriage was felt to outweigh the matrimonial compensation. Only a countergift of a woman could even the score. This perception then is linked to the dominant form of marriage: delayed exchange by the use of matrimonial compensation or preferential rights over future marriages. This form raises the question of credit or debt, whereas direct exchange of one woman for another is of necessity an equal exchange. In the Crow system it was felt that compensation exceeded the value of the woman because matrimonial goods could potentially be used for other

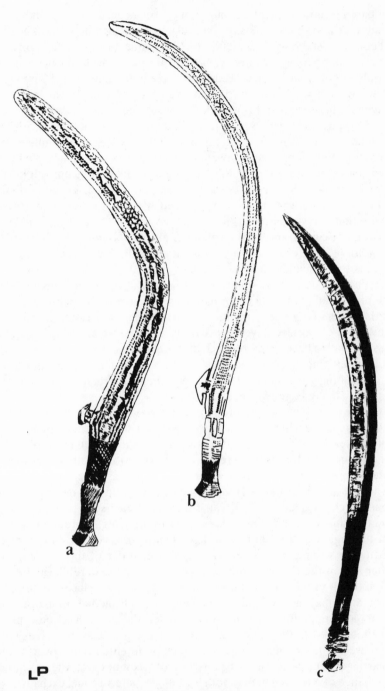

LP

Figure 4.1. Scimitars
a. Yambinga b. Aruwimi c. Wooden warclub, Ngando, Middle Tshuapa

purposes. In the Omaha case it was felt that the value of the goods could never equal the value of a woman, probably because of her potential offspring. Given the paramount importance of numbers of men in matters of defense, a woman's contribution to the reproduction of manpower in the settlement was felt to be crucial. Finally it follows, from the very fact that Omaha and Crow systems are contradictory in their assessments, that the superiority of "wife givers" is not "natural." It is a contingency of history.[20]

The adoption of the Omaha system of kinship terminology eventually led to a fundamental transformation of the cognitive reality of the House from a "family" into a "patrilineage." The Omaha terminology sets apart males linked to each other by descent through men only. That is why G. P. Murdock considered such systems to be distinctive of patrilineal societies.[21] But the adoption of this terminology merely facilitates a transition from an ideology of undifferentiated descent to a patrilineal ideology: it does not predicate it. Somewhere in the region people became conscious of this feature of the system and patrilinearity sprang into existence. Most likely it occurred in the general area of the mouth of the Aruwimi, rather than near the mouth of the Itimbiri, because the people there later did not use an Omaha system of terminology.

The innovation was so useful in the representation of the internal organization of the village, and especially of the district, that it rapidly spread and reinforced the physical reality of superior and inferior Houses and villages. The patrilineal image contains a detailed hierarchy of age and generation. Smaller Houses in a village could be perceived as descendants from younger brothers. Closely allied villages were supposedly descendants of elder or younger brothers. The former district, consisting of supposedly equal villages, now became a formal structure where every village retained its autonomy, yet occupied a precise position in a hierarchy as expressed by a common genealogy, where cognitive distinctions between senior and junior at each step corresponded to physical superiority or inferiority. A sign of the persistent autonomy of each village was the practice of all villages rallying to a common cause only in times of war, if they were attacked from the outside. Conflicts within the district did not trigger obligatory alliances, but they tended to be settled through mediation by the leaders of the senior village in the cluster.

As stated earlier, the new political organization was most clearly expressed by the trail of the leopard's spoils. Whereas the spoils used to go from the hunter to the head of his House, and to the head of the founding House in the village, they now went further, to the head of an elder village, and finally to the head of the founding House of the most senior village in the district. There the animal was skinned and cut up in a precise ceremony that involved the leaders of all the villages of the district, seated according to rank. The superiority of the most senior leader was indicated at all times by a sort of gibbet for leopards outside his home; simpler gibbets marked the residence of lesser leaders.[22] The division of the spoils of the python, eagle, and pangolin followed the same ritual route, but with much less pomp.[23] Occurring at least several times a year, the disposition of such spoils gave outward expression to the image of a lineage, thus strengthening the new structure of hierarchy. The new cognitive reality did wonders to define the concrete expression of solidarity between the villages of a district. Apart from the ceremonies dealing with the "noble" animals, the main occasion for manifestation of the hierarchy was of course war. After all, the increase of both the frequency of war and the size of military detachments had triggered the whole development in the first place. So the lineage hierarchy was applied to armies. The place of each contingent was determined by the place of its leader in the accepted common genealogy.[24] Conflicts between villages came to be settled by assemblies of village leaders arranged again in an accepted genealogical order.[25] In the fullness of time even the spatial location of villages came to express the patrilineal genealogy. Within a village, elders lived farther downstream than others. In the district, senior villages were located in the safest sites and the most junior were located in the most exposed sites, still taking into account the cardinal directions of downstream and upstream.[26]

Such institutional innovation was bound to bring linguistic innovation in its wake. This took the form of designating Houses, villages, and sometimes districts by the name of the supposedly patrilineal, ancestral founder, prefixed by *ya-*. The prefix means "the children of" or "the people of." Whatever the origin of this practice, in the region it was an innovation and one consistently linked with the new patrilineal institution.[27] It expressed the new vision in a powerful but economical way.

The transformation from loosely to tightly organized districts occurred in the lands near the mouth of the Aruwimi. Here were choice sites, large villages, and easy communication with the north from whence the *ya-* prefix perhaps came. By 1880 the highest population densities in the northern half of the region considered in this chapter were found here, and from here as far as the lands west of the lower Itimbiri. Their build-up may well have begun during this period, well before A.D. 1400. From here the notion of the patrilineage quickly spread to the environs of the mouth of the Itimbiri and the vicinity of the mouth of the Lomami. Given the sequence of components involved, it would be wrong to imagine that the whole process developed in a single village or even in a single district near the mouth of the Aruwimi. Rather, the whole region formed a single interacting zone where everything crystallized into a single new model of society.

Expansion and Counterinnovation

Districts that accepted patrilinearity became well-structured and coordinated entities, which gave them an inestimable advantage in war over their neighbors and competitors, until the latter too accepted the new institutions. It is therefore not surprising that the invention of patrilinearity, allied to the new ways of war, exerted a major and rather rapid impact over wide areas (map 4.2). To the south adventurous leaders used their spearmen to dominate the local people west of the lower Lomami, and then, farther south and west, carried the new political system with them and incorporated local big men in it. But the movement southward changed in character beyond 1° south. Population densities there were very low. Most of the area was still inhabited by nomadic hunters and gatherers. Some were of pygmy stock (the Jofe), and some were apparently the descendants of immigrant farmers or fishermen who had abandoned farming (Lokaló).[28] The new leaders brought with them immigrants and their languages, such as Yela or Ngando. They moved as far south as the lakes of Lonkonya in the Lukenie basin, a district blessed with good iron ore resources. There they clashed with denser farming populations in which an efficient district organization of another type, the *nkúmú* type, was expanding at that time. They could field as many warriors as the lancers from the north did, and although their armament was different (archers and swordsmen rather than spearmen), they were a match for the northerners. Oral traditions recall the clash as the battle of Bolongo Itoko. The invading lancers were stopped in their tracks. The iron ore district remained divided between the warring parties.[29] Westward the expansion petered out when local populations, such as the Bosaka between Tshuapa and Maringa, took over enough of the organization of their eastern neighbors to match their numbers and began to make efficient use of archers alongside spearmen.[30]

The evidence for the expansion is clear enough. The *ya-* toponyms south of the Zaire map it. The modern distribution of spearmen with long shields is a little larger, and that of scimitars, and imitations in wood, does not quite cover the area of the *ya-* names. The actual ceremonials for leopards and other "noble" animals, the cognitive military and spatial views, as well as the basic ideas about lineage, all correspond even though, here as in the heartland at that time, it was still a timid patrilinearity. The innovative character of the ideology is also evident from a number of linguistic innovations concerning the notions of lineage, larger lineage, and elder lineage, as one would expect. *Ndongo,* "oldest lineage in a group," for example, is a novel meaning of an old form. Earlier in this area it meant "harem." One sees how a system with senior and junior villages was still interpreted by the old family meta-

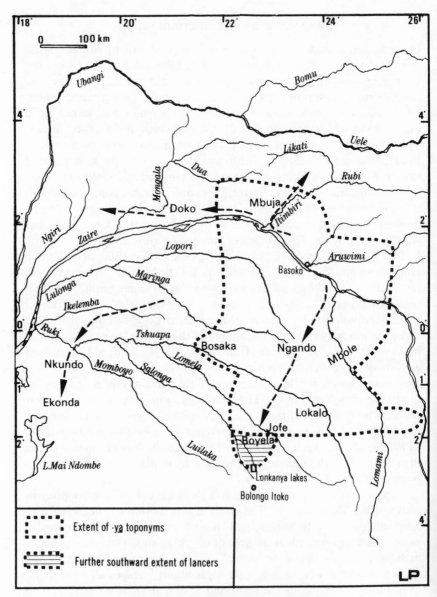

Map 4.2.   Early expansion in the inner basin

phor of a big man and his wives. Another nice touch is the borrowing by all the Mbole and the eastern Mongo of the term *bokenge* as far south as the upper Tshuapa. That term is a Soan innovation to designate "town" rather than small "village." It originated on the banks of the Zaire when larger settlements grew there and started the whole process of innovation discussed in this section. Lastly a number of fortuitous elements, such as the type of hand piano found among the eastern Mongo, also point to diffusion from the north.[31]

The clash at Bolongo Itoko can be approximately dated to before 1500.[32] A roughly estimated chronology for the onset of the *ya-* expansion can be derived from this by dead reckoning in centuries. The distance from the mouth of the Lomami to Bolongo Itoko is some 420 km as the crow flies. The expansion may well have taken the whole fifteenth century, and the original process by which lineages appeared was completed before c. 1400. This process by itself probably spanned several generations and may even have lasted a century or more. The adoption of the *noko* term for allies would then date at the latest from c. 1300.

The creation of each patrilineal district north of the river was also becoming a threat to its neighboring districts, just as was happening in the south. Most peoples there adopted the innovation. But one people on the northern bank of the Zaire, later known as the Doko, resisted this solution. After they adopted the *noko* system, their villages gradually became very large, perhaps as the result of increased trade, but certainly in part also as a defense against the pressure of patrilineal districts to the east, whose new ways of waging war they had adopted.[33] Such large villages or towns soon became strongly endogamous, because their size now allowed for more internal marriages. As the villages swelled to towns, the authority and prestige of the big man of the founding House increased concomitantly. This was attributed to supernatural support, and the village leader gradually acquired most of the attributes of sacred kingship. His harem also swelled, for he married often in order to attract followers and to ally himself directly to more Houses in his own and other settlements.[34] The succession to this office eventually became so crucial for the welfare and the security of the whole town and its district that it could no longer be left to the chance of an open competition. Surviving brothers had always been the foremost among competitors. But given the size of the harems, there were now many brothers. In such a situation, brothers of the same mother usually tended to group their forces and to be backed by the House of origin of their mother. Succession struggles became struggles between minor Houses in the town. To limit the succession to the issue of one woman was one obvious way to eliminate fights between the minor Houses and to channel succession struggles. Once people had become aware of the notion of unilineal descent as practiced by their troublesome neighbors to the east, this could and did lead to the adoption of matrilineal succession.

But the consequences of this cognitive revolution were just as important as those that had happened when patrilinearity had emerged to the east of the Doko. Relations within the town or the district were no longer perceived in terms of kinship at all because of the continuing practice for married women to settle in the Houses of their husbands. As a result, members of a matrilineage were dispersed among different Houses, and the leaders of the Houses of a single village could no longer claim to be even fictitious brothers. A founding House ruled because it had a right to the territory. Indeed its heroes became the nature spirits of the land,[35] and the founding House became a dynasty. In time this led to the notion of territorial chiefdom. By the nineteenth century the Bondongo lineage ruled the country.[36] The chiefdom thus replaced the district, or at least some districts. By the 1880s units containing several major towns are mentioned, but in some cases they seem to have been linked only by ties of alliance and not by a common dynasty.[37]

Meanwhile the combination of large settlements and matrilineal succession had been sufficient to hold off the advance of the patrilineal structure of districts from the east. In turn, the matrilineal system itself spread westward and was adopted by one district after another, to reduce the local imbalances of power. By the end of the eighteenth century the institution had reached the edge of the peoples of the Ngiri and was still expanding.[38] It was also practiced among those Doko who lived south of the Zaire bend in the Lopori Valley. The military organization of spearmen was taken over by the local Mongo population of the Lopori Valley. There may be some connection between this and the choice of matrilineal relatives as preferred successors in some bilateral northern Mongo groups.[39]

The expansion of patrilinearity or matrilinearity cannot yet be linked to a known conquest from the northwestern Mongo area. Here the people, later called Nkundo, left the lands of the middle Maringa and upper Ikelemba to conquer the lands west toward the lower Ruki and Momboyo. The earlier occupants of these lands in turn moved southward to an area northeast of Lake Mai Ndombe, where they settled perhaps by the sixteenth century.[40]

Continued Expansion

The new perception of districts, as the lands of segmentary patrilineages, had reached one group after another in the Itimbiri Valley as far upstream as the valleys of the Likati and the Rubi (map 4.3). By the sixteenth century this perception underwent a further change among the people of the upper Likati, who were partly Bantu and partly Ngbandi speakers. One presumably Ngbandi group there developed the notion of patrilineal succession to its logical conclusion, by restricting legitimate succession to only the first male born. Hitherto succession had always been legitimized as belonging to the eldest of the surviving brothers of the deceased. Hence a surfeit of legitimate candidates often appeared. A break in generations occurred only after the line of brothers had run

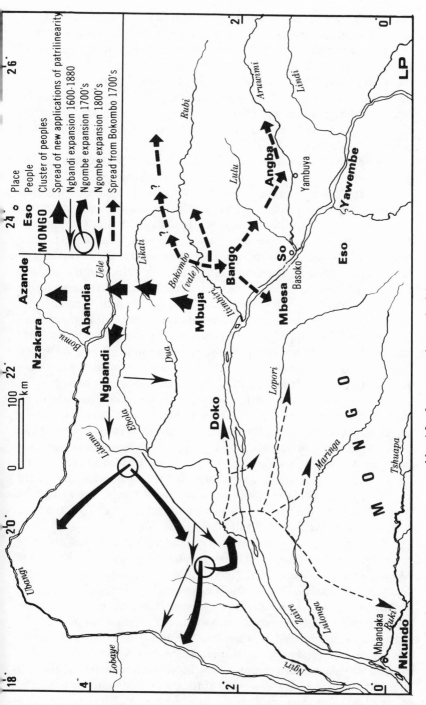

Map 4.3. Later expansion north of the equator

out of life. Then the oldest of their sons succeeded, to start a new generation of rule by successive brothers. But "oldest" was ambiguous. Whether it referred to absolute age or to the genealogical seniority of the father of the claimant was left in abeyance. Hence there was still plenty of leeway for quarrels. The simple new Ngbandi rule clearly identified a single successor. And although succession rules count for little in actual political struggles, legitimacy does bring supporters and makes it possible to build up bases for power long before the actual succession occurs.[41]

So this change in rule made a difference, and a spectacular one. The principle of the first-born allowed for the emergence of an oldest segment, a true dynasty, lording it over the other precisely labeled segments of a genealogy that included everyone. The strongest House became the dynasty, and its close allies turned their Houses into tight junior lineages to defend the influential positions their leaders had acquired. Real centralization resulted, and true segmentary lineages are an indication of it. Chiefdoms, and soon kingdoms, appeared. The effects in the savanna lands of the confluence of Uele and Bomu were the creation of the Nzakara kingdom and of smaller Abandia kingdoms with Ngbandi rulers around 1600.[42] By the eighteenth century the Azande principalities began to form, and by 1800 they began their famous sweep eastward, subjugating all the less cohesive political bodies in the Bomu Valley and in most of the lands north of the Uele. Azande armament and tactics were mainly those of the spearmen already described. The success of the Azande, however, had more to do with the new centralizing institutions than with their armament.[43] Meanwhile the Ngbandi fanned out along the Ubangi in the seventeenth and eighteenth centuries, subjugating and displacing people of various language groups as they went, especially between the Ubangi and the Dua rivers.[44] They founded chiefdoms with clear dynasties and subtle ceremonials for the disposition of leopard trophies, emphasizing seniority and rank to a nicety. From then on Ngbandi became the prestige language and culture of Ubangi and their warriors were feared by one and all.[45]

Among the groups met by the expanding Ngbandi was a Bantu-speaking population that lived in the Likame River basin and west of the Mongala River. Later called Ngombe or "Bushmen,"[46] they did not react to the Ngbandi threat by flight nor were they all absorbed. Like the Doko, they seem to have had stronger and larger villages in which the village chief already played an important role. They responded to the Ngbandi threat by further reinforcing their village structures and by increasing the cohesion of the district. At the district level stable confederations of villages were created. The villages within them were thought of as "brothers," a view that was expressed by a common genealogical framework. The term used shows that people thought in terms of a group of all the descendants from a common ancestor, that is, of a family and not of a lineage.[47] Similarly within each village the constituent Houses were now perceived as but junior counterparts to the dominant founding House, whose leader was the village speaker. The other Houses would no longer let any single House secede at will. The village was further strengthened as a unit by a high level of endogamy and by the presence of age groups (*kóla*), even though the House remained dominant in village affairs.[48]

The conception of a unified village was solidified even more by the invention of a village government separate from the leadership of the founding House. This consisted of the speaker, a military commander chosen for his achievements, and a village headman. The village headman was elected from among the men of the founding House by the leaders of all the Houses and was not usually its eldest member. Candidates in the nineteenth century were chosen for their wealth, their talents for arbitration, and their physical prowess in wrestling. The installation process included a human sacrifice by the hand of the candidate, recognition by other village headmen, a ritual seclusion to obtain the approval of the hero spirits, and then various initiation rituals, which recall practices of sacred kingship elsewhere in Africa. Village autonomy and the power of its chief were also expressed by the trail of the leopard's spoils. They went directly to this chief and never any further.[49]

Lastly, village exclusivity and esprit de corps were nicely expressed by the practice of naming villages as *boso,* + X, meaning "we + X." The younger Ngombe age groups, equipped with swords, throwing knives, and spears, underwent fairly intensive military training. The villages were bigger than was usual for agricultural settlements in the area under study. Hence they had to be more mobile, because depletion of both soil and game increases at almost the same rate as the population increases. Hunting may also have been practiced more here than elsewhere and have added to the mobility of the group.

But even in their confederation of villages, the Ngombe could not always hold out against the often larger forces of Ngbandi.[50] On the other hand they were more powerful than any of their southern and most of their western neighbors. Thus during the eighteenth century they expanded to the south and west, and reached the Ubangi and the Zaire rivers before 1800. In the Zaire bend they became slave raiders, selling their catch in the towns on the river banks. Some of them, thirsty for additional conquests and slaves, crossed the Zaire. They expanded in the basins of the Lulonga-Lopori-Maringa and Ikelemba, waged pitched battles against the Mongo of the area, and had wrested a large territory from them by the late 1880s.[51]

The Ngbandi armies proclaimed that they feared nothing except the war magic, and consequently the military force, of one group to their southeast.[52] There, and toward the lands west of the lower Itimbiri, lived the people later known as Mbuja and related groups. The patrilineal dispensation here received a new twist in the seventeenth century and augmented the internal cohesion of its districts. This occurred perhaps in part as a reaction to the invention of primogeniture on the upper Likati, and certainly also as a further development of the patrilineal ethos itself. It was now applied more broadly than merely to justify legitimacy of command and place of residence. Now religion and healing were drawn into the patrilineal ideology. A solemn and collective cult for the skulls and other relics of ancestral heroes was developed, and relics were incorporated into all powerful charms and medicines.[53] The lineage idea itself became rooted more and more deeply as villages in increasingly large clusters were thought of as patrilineal kin in clear genealogical relation to each other. This trend accompanied a further growth in size of armed forces. The Mbuja were gradually becoming a menace. Oral traditions from the Itimbiri Valley and eastward as far as the Lulu and the Aruwimi tell of a vale of Bokombo, west of the middle Itimbiri, in Mbuja land. A host of ethnic groups claim to have come from Bokombo.[54] Rather than the cradle for large-scale migration which the traditions make the vale out to be, Bokombo was probably a seventeenth-century land of innovation and prestige, from which the new military, political, and religious style spread out northward and eastward and to which leaders all over the area wanted to be linked. By genealogical counts, the spread of this new style began c. 1700 and was accompanied by local wars of conquest. This affected all the populations from the left bank of the Itimbiri to and beyond the Lulu, as well as those of the lower Aruwimi Valley. Even the Mbesa people, across the expanse of the Zaire upstream of the mouth of the Itimbiri, were affected.

Additional institutional refinements were invented. In the communities along the Aruwimi, leaders began to designate which of their sons would form senior branches of their dynasties in the future, and which ones would form branches subservient to each particular senior branch, irrespective of the rank order of the wives of the leader or the order of births of the sons. This strengthened the concept of a dynasty even more, so that by the eighteenth century only one House in each ethnic group was regarded as supreme. Centralization had not yet progressed to the point that all other Houses became tributary or that the senior villages always enjoyed military supremacy. The leopard still halted on its way to the supreme authority at the residence of each successive senior leader. But centralization was on the march.[55] From the first half of the eighteenth century onward, a single dynasty ruled all the 15,000 or 20,000 So (a people) of Basoko district. Ten thousand of these people lived in Basoko town around a ruler who received the leopard's spoils directly. The succession became matrilineal here, purportedly so that the main patrilineages in the country succeeded each other in turn, at least in theory. In practice the strongest House secured the chieftaincy.[56] Farther upstream near the lower Lomami, the Yawembe had united into a chiefdom by 1880; among their Eso neighbors, two Houses were in the process of building up sizable chiefdoms. The dynasties put one of their members as overseer in each village of the territory they claimed. When the first Zanzibari traders arrived around 1883 the bigger of the two dynasties began to force the 30 villages it controlled to pay tribute.[57] By then, under pressure from their northern neighbors, the Mbuja had grouped themselves into only three major stable confederations, each tens of thousands strong. A separate chiefly role and status had emerged at the apex of such units, and the confederations were solidifying into chiefdoms.[58]

The developments sketched in this section show that, in general, there was no concerted drive by the peoples of these vast lands to encompass larger numbers of people in each polity, to increase the scale of the spatial units, or to invent ever-more-centralized governments. But a concern with safety through better coordination of individual communities in times of stress is undeniable. Even so, in spite of everything else, these peoples strove to the last to safeguard the internal autonomy of each community, or each House. This underlies the invention of so many original political systems.

Once one innovation resulted in more efficient cooperation within a district, it upset the local balance of power and started a chain reaction. Each innovation had to be copied or matched by a counterinnovation. The result was an increase in the demographic and spatial scales of societies. The data refute the common idea that increase in size and complexity necessarily must lead to the formation of a kingdom or state, although this was still happening in certain instances. The next section relates the unfolding of a parallel chain of political change, occurring during the same centuries. It led to broadly similar outcomes, including the birth of some chiefdoms, and indeed kingdoms, but mostly it led to the emergence of new forms of association to safeguard the autonomy of the basic community in a time of expansion. And yet its starting point was totally different.

DIVIDING THE SACRED EMBLEMS

"Dividing the sacred emblems," or *bokapa ekopo,* is an expression which resonates in oral traditions about the origin of people or their political institutions throughout the southern Mongo world, from the Zaire and Lake Mai Ndombe to the upper Sankuru. In the beginning the expression meant "to divide the skin of the leopard," and referred to the practice already described, in which strips of the leopard skin were presented to big men as emblems of their authority.[59] But this is not what most later traditions refer to. They refer to a block of white kaolin, sometimes mixed with the earth of an anthill, materials from the abode of powerful nature spirits and imbued with their spiritual force, giving those who received them the power to rule. The traditions tell us about a novel legitimacy and about new institutions of government.

Nkúmú

On the eve of the colonial conquest Lake Mai Ndombe was surrounded by great chiefdoms and one kingdom, which all shared similar political institutions. The chief or king was called *nkúmú* or *nkúm*, a term which has come to designate this political system ever since the pioneering studies of E. Sulzmann and E. Müller. The *nkúmú* title was accompanied by a plethora of symbols and emblems, particular privileges and taboos, a special place of residence, and the attribution of honorific titles to dignitaries of his household.[60]

Court traditions, gathered at least from the early 1920s on, claim remarkable historical depths for this institution.[61] A genealogy of Bolia kings lists a succession of 38 kings; the other chiefdoms around the lake commonly list 20–23 reigns. Moreover they all claim a common origin and give precedence to the Bolia, who in the nineteenth century were the most prestigious power in the area.[62] Bolia traditions describe an Eden near a great river, not far from intercalary savannas in the forest, where people lived near the primordial anthill from which they had emerged. From this region came the horns of the *mangala* antelope, a major emblem still kept at the court in the 1880s.[63] The Eve of these traditions bore a series of twins who, in turn, procreated the people of the different chiefdoms around Lake Mai Ndombe, each with their special talents. Thus the Bolia were warriors, the Ntomba fishermen, the Jia rich in *nji* currency. They then all migrated from the cradle of their humanity with the Bolia in the vanguard. The relevant traditions are vague on the route of migration until the Bolia arrived on the upper Lokoro River not far from the present Lokolama. There the migrants were halted by Lotoko, chief of the "swarm of hornets of Bosanga" (*Nsese la Bosanga*), whose capital was Ibayima and who ruled the lands between the springs of the Lotoi and the Lokoro. But the Bolia defeated the Bosanga, took Lotoko's insignia, his drum, and his basket of cloth richly embroidered with exotic shells, and appropriated them for their leader. Their allies, the Ntomba, now of Lake Tumba, pursued and killed Lotoko and thus also became *nkúmú*. Then both groups continued on their way to the lands between Lakes Mai Ndombe and Tumba.

The Bolia subjugated the aboriginal population they found there. Later a group of Ntomba left Lake Tumba, destroyed the last remnants of the Nsese la Bosanga on Lake Mai Ndombe, and established themselves in their foe's capital at present-day Inongo. Meanwhile the Bolia expanded to the western hinterland of the lake and imposed the Sengele chiefdoms there on older populations.[64]

These traditions claim that the specific institution of the *nkúmú* with their *ekopo* were copied from the Bosanga of Lotoko, near the middle or upper Lokoro. A great intercalary savanna called Ila lies to the immediate south of the river. To people coming from the inundated forests to the north it must have been a wonderful sight.[65] The earlier traditions of the Bolia referring to the creation of the world derive from cosmological speculation, and describe an ideal life in a golden age. It would be an error to try to identify a real place with this Eden.[66] Was the middle Lokoro then the birthplace of the system? Perhaps, but one should remember that Ntomba traditions speak of the conquest of a chiefdom on Lake Mai Ndombe itself. Moreover, the location of the shrine of Mbomb'Ipoku, *the* spirit of the lake and the senior spirit of the whole region, may well reveal a clue as to the location of the first strong chiefdom, perhaps antedating the Bolia state. All that can be said until archaeologists identify a hierarchy of settlements is that the political system evolved in this general area.[67]

Some authors have dated the emergence of *nkúmú* chiefdoms to the end of the fifteenth century by using average lengths of reign or of generation. But, as Sulzmann observes, this procedure is not reliable. Still, she obviously believes that the phenomenon is ancient, because in her view the Boma kingdom, situated southwest of Lake Mai Ndombe and known from written sources c. 1650, derives from the Bolia kingdom.[68] One can also estimate a rough *terminus ante quem* by calculating backward from the known chronology of the Kuba kingdom, which is derived from the *nkúmú*-system and was founded in the first quarter of the seventeenth century. That yields an estimate of the end of the fourteenth century at the latest for a chiefdom on the middle Lokoro.[69]

The traditions do not tell us how the ideology of *nkúmú* arose. Thanks to a painstaking study by E. W. Müller, we know how the institution spread among the Ekonda, the eastern neighbors of the Bolia. When a rich big man wanted recognition by his peers as an exceptional achiever, he took the title *nkúmú* during a lavish feast to which the great leaders of the vicinity were invited, especially those who had already taken such a title. At this feast the candidate was given a bit of the sacred emblem of his colleagues and was then entitled to wear or display other emblems, plant special trees around his compound, and assume special etiquette and taboos. He also in turn gave honorific

titles, recognized by all, to some of his spouses, junior kin, and followers. Henceforth all would accept the leader's pretensions and honor him
as *nkúmú*. In some villages several *nkúmú* could coexist and their feasts
were less lavish than in other villages, where only one leader could be
nkúmú at any given time.[70]

It is very tempting to think that the process of the emergence of the
nkúmú institutional complex was similar to the dynamics described by
E. W. Müller. Such a view is supported by the extension of the meaning
of *ndóngó*, "harem," to include also "capital" among the Ntomba of
Lakes Tumba and Mai Ndombe and among the Mpama in accordance
with familiar imagery in the area: the lesser headmen are the wives of
the chief. The *nkúmú* innovation thus revolved around the status and
role of the big man in competition, a competition arbitrated by the *vox
populi* in the village and the district. Because some leaders had succeeded in building up Houses that were clearly larger than others, they
wanted recognition, perhaps out of vanity, but certainly also because
they knew that prestige breeds more power. The assumption of the title
nkúmú sanctioned this success, and itself served as a springboard for
further expansion. Public recognition of success attracted even more
dependents to the lucky House, and the various leaders who took the
title bolstered each other's prestige, even though they remained in competition with each other.

In time the membership of the strongest Houses became so large
that a single House occupied a whole village. And some still grew. They
then began to subjugate others, probably by threat of war. Eventually
the most successful Houses dominated small villages around their settlement, thus gradually building up a chiefdom. In the end Lotoko ruled
over a chiefdom and lived in a capital. As the size of successful houses
swelled, institutions surrounding the ideology of chieftaincy, the key to
the whole dynamic process, swelled as well, and in the end produced a
richly sacred kingship. Such an ideology explains the success of these
leaders and institutionalized their achievements and their succession, for
this growth of social scale could occur only if rules of succession prevented great Houses from collapsing during an interregnum. A most
original institution emerged to prevent just such collapses by channeling
competition for the succession. It consisted in the spectacular practice of
subjecting the challengers to a test destined to show who among them
was the choice of the nature spirits. They were asked to perform a
miracle. The one who did the most miraculous thing, and there was
always a purported miracle, was the choice of the nature spirits. In
addition, every test also strengthened the overall belief in the supernatural basis of the *nkúmú*'s authority and thus reinforced the whole institutional complex.[71]

Spread of the Nkúmú Complex

From its inception on the Lokoro the *nkúmú* complex spread (see map 4.4). We mentioned the traditions that tell of its expansion westward as far as Lakes Mai Ndombe and Tumba. From there chiefdoms were founded by conquest, as the Bolia did among the Sengele between Mai Ndombe and Zaire and, by imitation, as happened among the Mpama.[72] The title itself gradually disseminated farther without leading to the formation of chiefdoms, as was the case among the Ekonda, the Nkundó of the Ruki, and even the occasional Bobangi chief.[73]

Meanwhile the complex also spread southeast to the lands between Lokoro and the lower Kasai and even beyond. The traditions of the populations in these areas portray this diffusion as a migration from a place of *bokapa ekopo,* where the chief who had the sacred emblems shared them with others, who then moved away to new territory until they reached another place for *bokapa ekopo.* The use of a number of common toponyms in the traditions, such as Bolongo Mpo ("the harbor of Mpo"), show that, if nothing else, at least the same tales about the institution diffused everywhere. The traditions are also reinforced by the presence of the same specific titles for *nkúmú* over wide areas. Each *nkúmú* takes an individual title for his dynasty. Thus, for instance, *iyêli* is the title of the chief of Inongo on Lake Mai Ndombe and of the main Ngongó chief on the banks of the Sankuru farthest to the northeast of the Kuba kingdom. *Etóci* is the common Ndengese title for such chiefs on the middle Lukenie and *etóti* is the senior title among the Sengele, west of Lake Mai Ndombe. Considering this evidence, there is no doubt that the complex spread, but it did so by small parties, rather than by mass migration, and perhaps by modest conquests.[74]

A portion of Lotoko's own people, the Bosanga, were responsible for one expansion. They moved to the north of the middle Lukenie, upstream from the present town of Dekese. The leading House of the Ndengese still carries the name Bosanga. There a quarrel divided the Bosongo from the Ndengese. The Bosongo began to cross the Sankuru, where they gradually incorporated the older matrilineal settlers, elaborated a new society based on the matrilinearity, and formed the first Kuba chiefdoms. Two among these, the Bushong and Pyang, eventually subjugated most of the older settlers, became much larger than the others, and began a struggle for supremacy which ended only after a leader of foreign origin became chief of the Bushong c. 1625, subjugated the Pyang, and founded the large Kuba kingdom. During the next century the kingdom developed a complex of original centralized institutions.[75]

Meanwhile, near Bolongo Itoko, the Ndengese moving northeast met the *ya-* lancers expanding from the north. They fought each other to

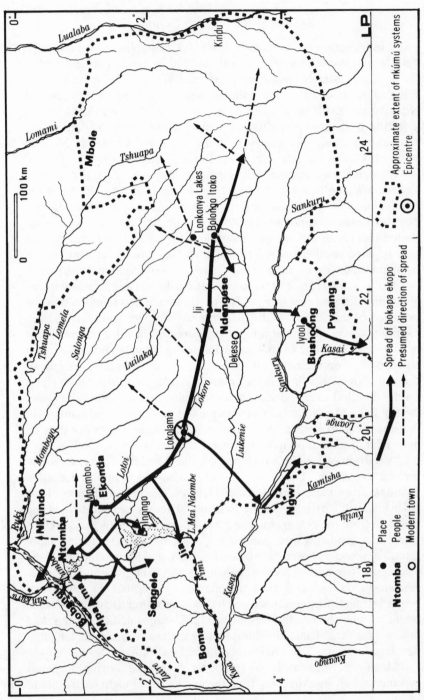

Map 4.4. Nkúmú expansion

a standstill. The Ndengese and their allies settled between Bolongo Itoko and the Lukenie. Later, *nkúmú* titles proliferated among them, and their *nkúmú* formed a titled association which acted as the supreme authority in this ethnic group.[76]

Between the lower Kasai and the Lukenie *nkúmú*, taking different titles, also multiplied, so that an honorific hierarchy of titles gradually emerged in every large village. But this proliferation did not occur in one such group, the Ngwi. They crossed the lower Kasai and formed two small kingdoms on its southern bank at an unknown date before 1750.[77]

From Bolongo Itoko the *nkúmú* institution continued to spread northeast and eastward under the name *nkúmí*, but with yet another new organizational twist. In the upper Lukenie basin and as far away as the Lualaba, there appeared the *nkúmí okanda* association. The *nkúmí* there were numerous. Each one was installed during a great potlatch between Houses linked by matrimonial alliance. Together the *nkúmí* formed a council and an association in each village. They built up an internal hierarchy of titles among themselves and moved up the ladder of prestige by giving payments to the higher-titled chiefs during lavish feasts.[78] The complex became ever more intricate and was finally transformed into government by association of a type practiced in the Lomami basin and to be described in chapter 6. This also happened to the *nkúmí* title among the Mbole, between Lomami and Lualaba. The *nkúmí* of the upper Tshuapa were somewhat different, but the scarce data do not allow one to say much about the specific institutions there except that, in one group at least, succession to the titles became matrilineal.[79]

The *nkúmú* institutional complex also spread north of the Lokoro, where it soon turned into a village association of big men, centered around dances and the wearing of emblems (the *ekopo,* or "majesty"). The scanty literature calls it the *ekofo* dance association. In most cases here it was added to the existing big man structure without altering it very much, and, in this guise, one finds it among all the Mongo south of the Tshuapa. Still it must have been more than just an association for dances and feasts with redistributions of wealth, but its role remains unknown. In one case at least, along the upper Salonga River, the full original *nkúmú* complex had diffused as well. The would-be titleholder arranged for a great feast, was installed, received emblems (among them the sacred kaolin), assumed taboos, and gave special titles to some of his wives and dependents. He became a sacred person. Much later in life he could accede to an even more exalted status by giving another feast, at which he announced that he was now dropping the taboos he had assumed. This is clearly the *nkúmú* institution, but it was not designated by that name. Perhaps there is a hint here of two successive introductions of institutions of prestige: first the association and later a fuller form.[80]

The preceding merely sketches the spread of the *nkúmú* complex, but does not detail its later transformations, especially in regions where chiefdoms or kingdoms appeared. Here complex structural changes continued and reached into all aspects of social and cultural life. One of these was the adoption of matrilinearity from the older settlers by the Ngwi and the Kuba, which destroyed the political importance of Houses and villages. The structure of chiefdoms was altered also when new social categories of nobles and patricians appeared, including one consisting of the sons and grandsons of chiefs.

The peaks of complexity of this type were reached by the Sengele and Ntomba chiefdoms and in the Boma kingdom around Lake Mai Ndombe. Their inhabitants explicitly or implicitly acknowledged both matri- and patrilinearity at the same time but for different purposes: successions, inheritance, questions of residence, and ritual memberships. They built up especially complex social stratifications as a result. The matrilineal component in all these cases was contributed by the autochthonous populations, who had already been influenced by earlier political innovations from the Kongo and Teke groups to the southwest. In all these cases, as indeed in the Mpama and Ntomba (Lake Tumba) chiefdoms, more institutional changes followed because of this increased stratification and because of the power struggles among the leading Houses of the land. Some of these innovations found inspiration in practices among their southern and southwestern neighbors, while in turn inspiring further institutional development among them. Such mutual influences grew predictably more intensive as the trade on the river Zaire increased after c. 1525, when that artery of commerce began to be linked with the Atlantic trade. Yet change in these kingdoms and chiefdoms was not mainly induced by outside influences. Most of their later institutional history, however complex, stemmed from unintended structural consequences of past choices, not least from the very elaboration and adoption of the *nkúmú* complex. In all these cases a chain of reactions fed continuous internal innovations. Outside innovations were accepted only insofar as they made sense in terms of existing structures.[81]

In this chapter the reader has encountered two major chains of transformations that ultimately derived from the original three interlocked social units and affected the whole inner basin of the area. The epicenters of both lay well within the area covered by rainforests, but on major ecotones: each epicenter covered several widely different habitats. This is as true for the region of the Lokoro, with its mix of inundated forests and nearby savannas, and perhaps the lacustrine environment of Mai Ndombe itself, as it is for the Aruwimi confluence. Will this hold for all other epicenters as well, and, if so, how should this correlation be explained? Second, it seems that physical change had to be transformed into cognitive change before a structural alteration could become permanent. Finally, the plasticity and the potential for transformation underlying the ancestral structure is already impressive, and the reader has yet to encounter the full range of transformations that arose out of that ancestral tradition. The previous chapter made clear that "ancestral tradition" is no fiction. But still, does it make sense to talk about the legacy of such a tradition when the possible legacies range from fragile temporary village communities to a confederation comprising tens of thousands of people and to a kingdom numbering over 100,000 subjects? Are the changes not of such a magnitude as to eclipse the common origin and render it of no moment? House, village, district, and big men as leaders never really went away, but how much does this matter in the face of the very different Houses, villages, districts, and leaders found by the mid-nineteenth century in different parts of the inner basin? Additional evidence will be brought to bear on these questions in the next chapters and will raise other issues about tradition as change.

Five

Between Ocean and Rivers

Geography and settlement made the lands between the Zaire, the Sangha, and the ocean much more diverse than the inner basin. From north to south one recognizes major differences between a small western Cameroon area roughly west of the Mungo, the island of Bioko, the lands north of the great Ogooué bend, and the lands south of the Ogooué. From west to east a succession of different habitats with different resources made for much variety from coast to coastal plains, mountains, forested plateaus, and then to marsh north of the equator and elevated sandy grasslands south of it. The ocean and the Zaire River system inland were highways; the mountain crest acted as a barrier to communication; the great marshes were insuperable obstacles to landlubbers but easy of access to water-people; and travel overland was not difficult on the plateaus, except where major rivers had to be crossed.[1]

The centers of the most influential and distinctive long-term historical innovations were located near the northern and southern edges of the area, as well as on the island of Bioko, rather than in the middle of the region, and their influence at first expanded predominantly on north to south axes, rather than east to west. Therefore the three sections of this chapter deal respectively with the northern half of the region, Bioko, and the region south of the Ogooué.

THE NORTHWEST

Of all the Bantu speakers the farmer trappers settled the northwest first, and there they may have first become metal users. Hence their history has much greater time-depth in this region than elsewhere, and the interaction of the peoples in this area has also been going on for many more centuries than elsewhere.[2] Moreover, this area has been the most open to later influences from Nigeria, from the grasslands, and even from the bend of the Ubangi River. In turn it has influenced the adjacent savanna regions. Because of the enormous historical time-depths—4,000 years or more—it is particularly difficult to discover and disentangle the successive historical developments that occurred since the days of the ancestral western Bantu–type of society.

Early Developments

In a remote past the village and the district substantially gained in internal cohesion by the adoption of separate secret associations for men and women. Such societies participated in most aspects of social life. Especially important for the social organization as a whole was their role in public government, the maintenance of order, and the reproduction of culture in initiation and similar rituals of induction. Such associations are found in practically the whole western area as well as in adjacent Nigeria and in the Cameroon grasslands.[3] The antiquity of this innovation is unknown and cannot be gathered from linguistic evidence now, for common terminology has long since given way to local or regional innovations, if only because such a set of associations is a very dynamic institutional whole.[4] In western Cameroon, along the Cameroon coast, and on Bioko there were also age categories in the nineteenth century then playing a role similar to a minor association.[5]

By the late nineteenth century the more or less compact village[6] was the dominant institution in western Cameroon, but not farther eastward. The nineteenth-century peoples north of the Sanaga and as far east as the Mbam River, peoples of the Saa group,[7] and the Mabea behind the southern coastal strip of Cameroon lived in dispersed settlements. The antiquity of this pattern can only be guessed at. The same people, except for the Mabea, then were organized into patrilineages and practiced succession by sons. Farther east the Sanaga-Ntem group,[8] the Makaa, and probably the Njem,[9] who lived in compact villages, recognized a hierarchy of segmentary patrilineages. Moreover, in the whole area of patrilineal groups and beyond, one communal building for men, called by reflexes of the common form *-bánjá,[10] was built for each House, rather than one per village as was common farther west and south (map 5.1). This is an unambiguous sign of the primacy of the House in relation to the village, even where villages were as large and strong as they were in southeastern Cameroon and in northeastern Gabon.[11]

Like the distribution of associations, these communal dwellings are the fruit of a long and ancient institutional history. The scenario that best accounts for the data posits that, following the example of people in the Cameroon grasslands and in the savanna, the inhabitants of the area

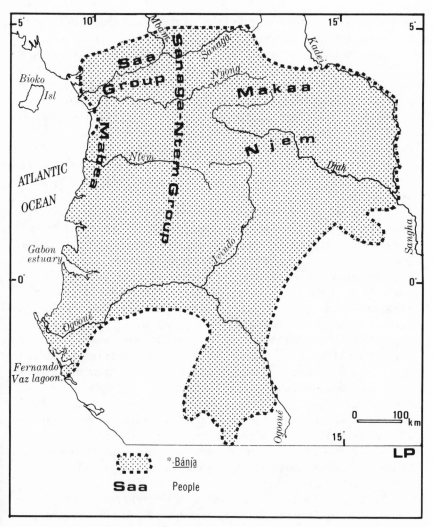

Map 5.1.   Communal building, *-bánjá*

north of the Sanaga adopted a mode of dispersed settlement, wherein each House built its own hamlet. Yet they continued the practice of erecting a communal building for men in each settlement. Earlier this had strengthened the esprit de corps in the village but it now reinforced the role of the House. Common associations continued to exist but now functioned at the district level. Some time later the peoples farther east also began to build communal buildings for each House, despite the fact that they continued to live in compact villages. All of this probably happened long before the principles of patrilineal descent appeared among the Bantu speakers north of the Sanaga.

The scenario is tempting, and an examination of the vocabulary related to the institutions involved neither contradicts nor confirms it, but unfortunately it remains inconclusive. The terminology for village (absent in the Saa group and north of the Sanaga) is not helpful. Everywhere else in the affected areas it is based on *-yadí (CS 1898, ps 483) and is older than any of the phenomena involved in the scenario.[12] The same is true for the most basic term to designate a "social category."[13] These terms merely substantiate that at one time these groups shared a village institution and a common representation of a large social group as a "family."

The one clear innovation in the terminology for social groups is a term derived from the ancestral form for "male," which refers to a lineage and is shared by all the patrilineal groups, except perhaps for the Njem (see map 5.2).[14] The Saa group and the Sanaga-Ntem group also share an innovation of meaning for CS 192–93, which no longer meant solely "home" but "territory" or "land" in the Saa group and "basic lineage" in the Sanaga-Ntem group.[15] Patrilinearity north of the Sanaga, both west and east of the lower Mbam, appeared in an area of high population density on the northern edge of the forest habitats from the bend of the Mbam River eastward north of the Sanaga. The density can be inferred from the present landscapes, which result from the destruction of former forests, and not merely from present population densities west of the Mbam or just south of the Sanaga. Yet this cluster of higher population was not a direct continuation of the relative large population clusters found on the Bamileke Plateau.[16] The high density of population meant that more cooperation was needed for defense than elsewhere.[17] The development of a patrilineal system in the area followed an ancient increase in population size.

Although all the peoples west of the Mbam adopted the principles of patrilinearity and showed some segmentation, the ideology achieved its greatest extent among speakers of the Saa languages, who all claimed a common ancestor and therefore also claimed to have come from a single place of origin called Ngok Lituba, an inselberg north of the Sanaga and west of the Mbam. From there, according to traditions, they spread westward as far as the Mungo and southward beyond the Nyong (see map 5.2).[18] There is good reason to doubt the historicity of this migration, because the languages of the different branches within the Saa group are so divergent. Thus the southernmost branch, the Elog Mpoo, shares only some 68 percent of its basic vocabulary with its neighbor Saa itself, which yields a glottochronological estimate of the eighth century A.D. for their separation. There is also botanical evidence for a relatively dense occupation of the hinterland of Douala before some three or four

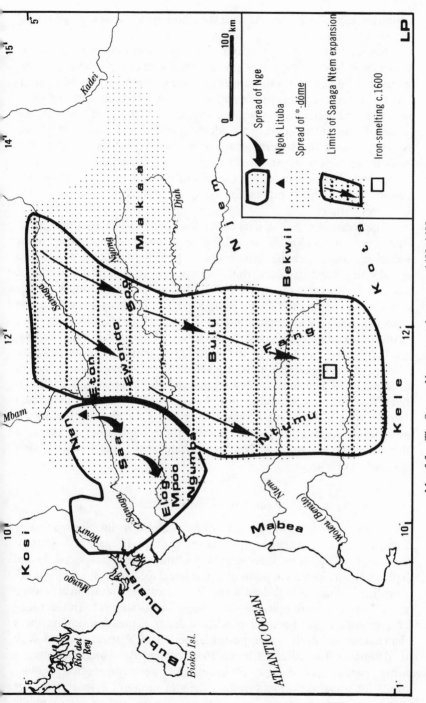

Map 5.2.   The Sanaga-Ntem expansion: c. A.D. 1400–1600

centuries ago, which conflicts with the claim for a recent immigration of the populations there.[19]

Rather than relating to any population movement, the oral traditions about Ngok Lituba seem to refer to the spread of the prestigious governing Nge association, a club of big men, or *mbombog,* which regulated relations between Houses and districts. A patrilineal master genealogy, some 10 generations deep and extending back to a single common ancestor, was at the heart of the ideology of Nge. The relics of heroes, which provided the supernatural sanction for each local Nge chapter, were those of persons who had places in this genealogy. The expansion from Ngok Lituba occurred at an unknown date before the eighteenth century (given the depth of the common genealogy), perhaps many centuries earlier.[20]

The creation of Nge and its expansion occurred well after the institution of patrilinearity in the area, because the latter is presupposed in the genealogy, and hence the diffusion of the term for "male" to designate a social group must be older. But it seems to have occurred at the same time or shortly after the invention of a full-fledged, segmentary lineage organization among the neighboring Sanaga-Ntem people, because one finds traces of a segmentary pattern in the Saa master genealogy. This expressed relative positions between different lineages, 8 or 10 generations deep, but without the development of a special terminology to distinguish segments at different levels of the genealogy, and hence of different sizes between the household and the largest lineage. Tentatively this leads one to assume that the creation of Nge in the lands near Ngok Lituba was a counterinnovation to offset the threat posed by the adoption of segmentary patrilineages by the Sanaga-Ntem speakers. In that case, the invention of Nge would date to the fourteenth or early fifteenth centuries.

The Sanaga-Ntem Expansion

The early Sanaga-Ntem speakers were localized in the Sanaga Valley from the Mbam confluence upstream to perhaps 13° east and north of the valley.[21] They were then neighbors of the eastern Saa speakers and had taken part in the adoption of a patrilineal ideology. But they did not stop there. They established a set of imbricated, hierarchical lineage units, from the household level to a large territorial level. The ideology of segmentary patrilinearity reached a fuller expression among them than among any of the other groups around them. A special terminology to designate five different levels (four among the Fang) of lineages arose, genealogies of up to 30 generations were constructed as blueprints for social coordination, and skulls of supposed lineage founders were kept and venerated. Associations occupied only a minor public role, either because they had been of minor importance before or because they had lost pride of place to the segmentary organization.[22] All the peoples in this cluster later claimed traditions of emigration from a savanna located on the northern side of a major river, probably the Sanaga, but they did not claim an origin from a single point, such as Ngok Lituba, or from a single ancestor. Given the various claims made by different scholars as to a "Fang" or "Pahouin" migration, and the case of Ngok Lituba where populations probably did not expand, it is wise to establish first whether such an expansion of population really occurred.[23]

The Sanaga-Ntem group expanded from the banks of the Sanagra to the valleys of the upper Ntem and Woleu rivers in northern Gabon and Rio Muni (see map 5.2). The reality of the expansion cannot be doubted because the linguistic evidence supporting it is so strong. Map 5.2 shows a broad gulf of Sanaga-Ntem languages splitting the languages of the southern Cameroon block, with a few remnants of a fishing population along the Nyong (the Soo) attesting to the earlier continuous distribution of that language group. Farther south, in northern Gabon, the gulf now splits the block of old northern Gabonese languages. This situation can result only from an expansion of the languages of the Sanaga-Ntem group, and a rather rapid one, since the languages within the gulf are closely related. The greatest differentiation within the Sanaga-Ntem group lies on both sides of the Sanaga, east of the Mbam confluence, and thus confirms that the cradle of the group lay in this area.[24]

The contrast between high densities of population in the cradle and low densities south of the Sanaga was especially great then and explains why the expansion took place. Even population density figures from the 1950s still place some four-fifths of the speakers of Sanaga-Ntem languages north of Yaounde. Indeed the present landscapes there result from the destruction of large areas of forest by long human occupation.[25]

The internal relationships of the Ewondo, Bane, Bulu, Ntumu, and Fang languages, which make up this southern expanse, show that the expansion occurred over a front with a western Ewondo-Ntumu and an eastern Bulu-Fang wing. South of the Ntem the Ntumu formed a new node of population growth, which led to deforestation there, perhaps in part as a result of intensive iron-smelting activities.[26] And although one cannot describe with any certainty the process of migration itself, several patterns from the nineteenth century and from this general area help us to visualize it. First scouts, hunters, or subordinate hunter gatherers identified good settlement sites. Then pioneers, probably younger people, settled there, to be joined by the main mass of the residential lineage *mvog* a year or two later.[27] An alternative pattern, documented from the Fang in the nineteenth century, may also have existed in earlier

times. In this process a settlement behind the one on the frontier by-
passed it and settled beyond it according to the normal rhythms of
drift.[28] The speed of the advance can be estimated as follows. New
settlements in the nineteenth century were founded some 20–30 km
from the old ones.[29] The distance between Sanaga and Ntem, as the
crow flies, is only 210 km or perhaps twice that on the ground, say 420
km. Normal drift every five years of some 20 km would bring the emigrants to the banks of the Ntem after about a century.

Given the very low population density of the area in which they
moved, the immigrants did not at first much disturb the earlier local
population. Later on, local people, living in less widely structured
groups than the immigrants, were culturally and linguistically absorbed
by the newcomers, as happened in the last century and a half during a
recent Fang migration. Some neighboring peoples efficiently blocked
further expansion because they had effective measures of social mobiliza-
tion on a sufficiently large scale. To the west the Nge association and
patrilinearity along with a higher population density kept the Sanaga-
Ntem people out of Saa-held lands. Elsewhere, however, the expanding
Sanaga-Ntem peoples met little resistance. In these areas of low densities many earlier settlers simply moved out of range, although some took
efficient defensive measures by temporarily congregating in large villages, such as are known from the Bekwil and Kota in the last century.
That seems to have happened among the Makaa on the northeastern
flank of the gulf.[30]

So far the only way to date this expansion is by glottochronological
dating. This dates the linguistic diversification following expansion in
the Ntumu-Ewondo-Bulu-Fang complex to between 1440 and 1620 and
allows us to estimate that the expansion took place in the fourteenth or
fifteenth century. The iron-smelting sites dated to c. 1600 in the upper
Ntem area are probably of Ntumu or Fang origin.[31] It follows from the
above that the adoption of patrilinearity and the first development of a
segmentary system in the Mbam-Sanaga area must be older still by a
century or so at least, and that the diffusion of patrilinearity in the Saa
group and among the Makaa speakers farther upstream and south of the
Sanaga was contemporary with the invention of the segmentary system
by the Sanaga-Ntem speakers, which occurred in the thirteenth or fourteenth century at the latest.

The Sanaga-Ntem expansion had a significant cultural and social
impact in the whole region. The very fact of their expansion carried
prestige. The Ngumba speakers and neighbors to the west of the gulf
and the Njem speakers to the east adopted patrilineal ideologies. A
number of novelties were brought by the newcomers, some of which
were adopted by the earlier inhabitants. The use of the crossbow for
hunting and as a weapon of war and the use of harps and xylophones are

examples of this.[32] In return some or all immigrants adopted local features from the previous settlers, such as hunting techniques, for example.[33] This interaction between old-timers and newcomers forms a major theme of the overall history of the area over the last four or five centuries and deserves future in-depth study.

This account of the Sanaga-Ntem expansion differs considerably from previous hypotheses. These are unsatisfactory because they have tended to weave the traditions from all the populations in the cluster together as a single account, as if they were all part of the same collective remembrance, and so have confused this expansion with the separate nineteenth-century migrations of the Bane, Bulu, and Fang (which all began after 1830), thus shortening the relevant chronology. Moreover, a later (seventeenth, eighteenth century?) conquest by Beti leaders over Bane and perhaps Ewondo is also submerged. In addition, ethnographic parallels have been used to claim remote and sometimes romantic origins for the whole cluster, despite known linguistic evidence to the contrary.[34]

BIOKO

Bioko is a small mountainous island of only 72 km at its longest by 35 km on average (see map 5.3). It counted perhaps as many as 30,000 people in the 1820s, at a density of 15 persons per square kilometer overall, which meant that effectively occupied land had densities as high as 30 persons per square kilometer.[35] Why then devote a whole section of this book to an account of its past? Because Bioko developed unusual institutions as the result of an unusual degree of isolation and because these institutions culminated in the formation of a kingdom which emerged at nearly the same moment that the British created the embryo of a colony in 1827 by establishing a naval base at Clarence (Malabo). Did this kingdom result as the inevitable logical conclusion of slowly progressing centralization? Did it result from overpopulation? Was it a defensive reflex against foreign intrusion? These lines of thought are the familiar ones many scholars have used to explain the appearance of kingdoms, and Bioko's past offers an unusual opportunity to test such arguments.

Despite its position near the mainland, despite its pattern of early settlement along the shorelines, despite later immigration from the mainland, despite the early European presence (1472) in this part of the Atlantic, Bioko remained isolated. This resulted in part from the adverse patterns of the prevailing winds and currents on its southern and eastern coasts, and in part from the volition of its inhabitants, the Bubi. By the early 1500s they had already earned the reputation of being "savage people," and they successfully refused to be drawn into the

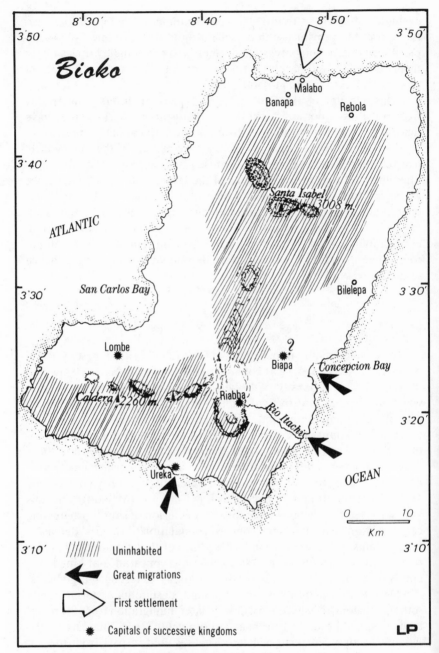

Map 5.3.   Bioko

138

slave trade. To counter kidnaping of slaves along the coast, they moved their settlements away from the shores to high and less accessible ground. Moreover, they succeeded in scuttling all attempted European settlement on their coasts until 1827.[36]

The extent of Bubi isolation can be gauged by linguistic and ethnographic evidence. Bubi is a single western Bantu language, which split off the main bulk in very early times. The language comprised several major dialects, but although neighboring dialects were mutually understandable from north to southwest to southeast, the most divergent dialects on the northern and the southeastern coasts were not. In part, this situation attests to a long linguistic development on the island itself, but in part it resulted from the effect of loans from languages of the mainland on the southern dialects.[37]

Even a cursory examination of Bubi society and culture, as recorded from the 1840s to the 1880s, documents both a high degree of originality compared with societies and cultures on the mainland and also common patterns and close interaction between all the settlements on the island. The relative isolation of the islanders has been evident to outsiders from the outset because of the Neolithic character of Bubi material culture. They were the only Bantu speakers who did not mine, smelt, or use metals until c. 1800.

By the late eighteenth century Bubi isolation was being breached. African traders coming in canoes from the Niger Delta, Calabar, the Rio del Rey, and Douala, as well as some slaving vessels, came both to the northern coast and to the Bay of San Carlos to buy yams. They began to sell bits of iron by 1800. In 1827 Clarence (Malabo) was founded on the northern coast, and there the British began to settle liberated slaves and Krumen, free laborers recruited on the coast of Liberia. This soon shattered the isolation of the island. By 1846 the coast was ringed by trading factories, and stone tools had virtually disappeared.[38]

Archaeological evidence attests to the early phases of settlement on Bioko. The earliest known sites lie on the northern coast. They reveal a Neolithic occupation without ceramics, which has not been dated. From the seventh century A.D. on, pottery appears. Compared with all other pottery styles in west-central Africa, this ceramic tradition is unique. The succeeding archaeological phases, as established from tool shapes and ceramics, exhibit an unbroken stylistic series to the ceramics of the nineteenth century, an impressive testimony to strong cultural continuity. By the eleventh century settlements began to move inland, and by the fourteenth century the population density increased, much of the rainforest began to be destroyed, and the peopling of the interior became more intensive.[39]

Some oral traditions about settlement reflect great antiquity when they claim that the first Bubi people issued from the crater of the Santa

Isabel peak, which dominates the northern half of the island. Most traditions, however, tell of a Great Migration comprising four waves of immigrants, who landed in the southern and southeastern portion of the island,
and then fanned away from this area to settle all over the island. Such
traditions are backed up by a series of objects, mostly paddles, canoes,
and sacred fires, which were used as emblems and palladia. Such practices
firmly linked the traditions of the Great Migration to the nobility ruling in
the nineteenth century. They suggest that the immigrants conquered the
earlier Bubi settlers. Nevertheless the archaeological and linguistic evidence makes it clear that, conquerors or not, the immigrants adopted the
language and the material culture of the aboriginal population.[40]

Where did these immigrants come from, and when did they arrive?
These questions are of interest to any institutional history of Bioko.
Some writers have speculated on superficial grounds that the immigrants
of the traditions came from the coasts of the southern Cameroons, or
Rio Muni, or Gabon. Only a thorough examination of loaning in the
southern Bubi dialects will eventually yield further evidence on this
point. The traditions make it clear, by referring to four waves of immigrants, that the process of migration lasted for some time. All authors
have dated its conclusion to the fifteenth century at the latest, just
before the arrival of Europeans in the area. The grounds given for this
chronology are not valid. Still, the reputation earned by the Bubi as
intractable and their successful eviction of a Portuguese settlement in the
1520s argue for the existence of a degree of institutional coordination,
which seems to have developed only after the conquest by the immigrants. The archaeological evidence in hand suggests that the Great
Migration ended in the fourteenth century, when there was a great
increase in settlements on the island.[41]

Before the arrival of these immigrants, and hence before the fourteenth century, the main outline of the social structure of the Bubi can
be sketched out as follows.[42] The original western Bantu district had
disappeared, and the original village had developed very novel features.
Villages were still composed of Houses, but the village site was inhabited for only part of the year. The members of the Houses lived in
hamlets on their own lands during the major farming seasons, and they,
not the village, owned the land. The village was used as a central rallying
point and its hub was the *rijata* (CS 47 *-dá,* "village") or *ritaka* (derivation of CS 457, "place of settling palavers"), the "palace" of the chief.
The village had become so similar, on a smaller scale, to the old district
that the western Bantu term for district was used to designate the central
village and its outlying hamlets.

Although the entire male adult population continued to settle together in Houses, a differentiation had occurred in two age-related categories, the older married men and the younger adult bachelors, each

group having its own formal leader. These were their spokesmen in general deliberations, in court palavers, and in directing collective hunts. The sense of generation was so strong that succession to the formalized leadership position as chief of the village or of the district was limited to uterine (and probably also agnatic) brothers, and apparently occurred without any ceremony. When the last of the brothers died, elections took place among the married men of the Houses in the village to choose a new chief.

The former western Bantu term for "chief" had been abandoned in favor of *etakio,* "ruler." This form is derived from *otaka,* "to rule," whose first meaning was "to settle disputes" (CS 475 *-dáka*). A set of other related Bubi terms, such as *botaki,* "subject, servant," and *ritaka* attests to the centrality of this notion. Chiefs had to be wealthy in yams and goats and they were polygynous. The extent to which they could use their wives to attract male clients, however, seems to have been small, because men had complete control over women only until the death of their first husbands. Once widowed or repudiated, a woman could choose her lover. Hence even poor men were not utterly dependent on their elders to acquire spouses.

The basic worldview of the Bubi had become quite different from that of the people on the mainland, especially in matters of religion. Among other beliefs, they were convinced of the existence of specific, male, ancestral guardian spirits, the *mmo,* who belonged to the generation preceding that of the oldest living men and who in the hierarchy of the spirit world belonged to the category of the older spirits. Every newborn baby had a specific *mmo* from the family of the husband as a personal guardian. This *mmo* had bought the baby's soul (personality) from the spirit who created the embryos, and it remained the guardian of the child during its lifetime. This created a strong link between father and child. But beyond this, patrilinearity was not strongly developed. Generational place was more important than the place occupied in line of descent, and generational place underlay the ideology of chieftaincy.

The legitimacy and the authority of the chiefs were linked to the backing of religious specialists who were both healers and mediums. Every district and village was thought to be protected by a spirit, whose wishes were made known directly to the head priest of the district or of the village. Annual festivals, linked to the planting of yams, and later to the cocoyam, expressed the supernatural dimension of chieftaincy.

Two types of war existed among the early Bubi, as among the western Bantu generally, but, even in wars of destruction, massive frontal attacks and the total destruction of enemy villages were apparently unknown. This is related to the weaponry then available. Bubi traditions say that their earliest weapons were sharpened stones, thrown with a sling, and knobkerries. Barbed spears with fire-hardened points, often dipped in poison, were used only for hunting. According to a well-known tale one specific chief began to use them in war and others followed suit. Whether this occurred before or after the Great Migration is not specified. Even then it seems that shields, which are essential for massive frontal attacks, were not in use.

There cannot be much doubt that the immigrants who landed during the Great Migration actually conquered the island.[43] This is especially clear in traditions about the Tete and the Bokoko, who supposedly formed the last wave of the Great Migration. Once they left the coast, they adopted a disposition of marching—with warriors (the Bokoko) in the vanguard, the leaders, women, and dependents in the middle, and another band of warriors (the Tete) in the rear—and they conquered many lands. The military advantage of the immigrants probably lay in their use of massed spearmen, whose first lines were protected by huge shields and cuirasses, and in their practice of fighting until the enemy surrendered unconditionally, so that the victors could destroy enemy settlements and disperse their inhabitants. Moreover, at least initially and for a few years thereafter, the immigrants certainly used the iron-tipped spears, and perhaps iron knives, which they brought with them.[44] These may well have been more efficient than the wooden javelins of their opponents. Finally, if the lesson drawn from all accounts of later wars holds for these times also, the immigrants must have mustered more men for each battle. Bubi dispositions for marching and for battle recall the practices of the spearmen of the inner basin and remind one that, here as there, massed spearmen imply the operation of new institutions making for tighter cooperation. Indeed, that holds true also for the logistics of the Great Migration itself, which required the planned transport over sea of a number of people, including women and children, and goods. Whatever the exact nature of these institutional arrangements once was, they soon fused with the institutional framework of the vanquished aborigines to give birth to a new institutional framework, probably by or before A.D. 1400.

The two main and interlocked political innovations that constituted this new framework were the creation of a sharply defined hereditary aristocracy, composed of the victors, and the emergence of districts, *nse*, encompassing several of the former *bese*,[45] in which the villages now paid tribute to the district chief, who also collected the fines meted out in courts. On this basis, complex sets of further innovations arose during the following four centuries.

The aristocracy was hereditary in the male line, and soon gave rise to two sharply separated classes: the aristocrats (*boita*) and the ordinary folk (*bobala*). They did not live in the same Houses or villages, they did not eat together, and they rarely intermarried. All the chiefs were aristocrats, as were most of the warriors with shields and cuirasses. In time servants became a third social class, and by the nineteenth century an incipient caste system had emerged, according to which fishermen, wine tappers, and hunters also became separate groups that were even buried apart. But heredity was not the only factor involved and social mobility was not absolutely frozen. One could still marry into another class. Even access to noble status by plebeians of sufficient valor and wealth was possible. Within the nobility, access to chiefly status or to various titles which developed at the district level had to be achieved. Competition for prestige was so great that even among chiefs the use of honorary titles to confer special distinction arose. Wealthy men and women approved by the spirits and men who had killed an enemy could acquire them. But such titles were not hereditary.[46]

The immigrants seem to have imported a novel designation for chiefs, *botuku* ("lord"), and with it a concept of chieftaincy in which valor and command over clients was added to the previous stress on wealth and arbitration.[47] Only nobles could succeed, but heredity was restricted to a set of uterine brothers. Whenever the ruling generation in a chiefdom had died out, the council, composed of all nobles in the area assisted perhaps by neighboring chiefs, chose another, usually unrelated, noble, and installed him or her with great pomp. Hence the different chiefdoms were not perceived as being linked to each other by fictive ties of kinship in one grand genealogy. There was nothing segmentary about the Bubi system. Wealth, derived from fines, loot, and tribute, became more and more crucial in the system, probably because it allowed a chief to increase the number of his dependents. By the eighteenth and nineteenth centuries, if not before, there were institutionalized feasts where chiefs showed and boasted of their wealth; crimes of theft (including adultery) were punished in an extremely harsh manner; and a currency for social and economic transactions had arisen. This currency consisted of strings of certain shells, formerly worn as jewelry and now both worn as a display of power and used for payments. Goats, which had been a major form of wealth before then, also became political emblems.

Chiefs had harems and struggled to control access to all virgin women. By the mid-1800s the richest held from 60 to 200 wives. The development of such harems led to such severe competition for young virgins that women were betrothed even before birth. The severity of sanctions for adultery may well be linked to the creation of harems, and the older opposition between the groups of married men and bachelors must have become more intense as the number of women available to all dwindled. The competition for women in first marriage also accounts for the emerging practice of considering that a deceased husband would still be the father of the first child or even the first three children born to a woman married to a later husband.[48]

The military and territorial positions of the new leaders were soon matched by appropriate religious ideology and practices. The official priest corresponding to each political level now claimed that all power came from a single source, a Creator God whose sacred fire he tended, a fire believed to be the descendant of that which the immigrants had brought with them. Thus, despite the competition and the many wars between chiefdoms, the principle of the unity of both chieftaincy and the nobility was maintained. This sense of unity was strengthened by the appearance of a new category of unofficial priests, all worshipping a common God. The spiritual legitimacy of chieftaincy was expressed by the growing complexity of the rituals for burial and succession, as well as in the growing number of annual rituals.[49]

The creation of chiefdoms led to the development of an assembly of councilors composed of the heads of the villages in the chiefdom and perhaps of other nobles, to the establishment of more precise procedures for trying court cases, and to the creation of a tiny central police force, composed of experienced noble warriors and relatives of the chief. Such innovations were accompanied by the creation of matching military and civilian titles to which local nobles could aspire. Bubi traditions recall the unceasing competition among chiefdoms in their struggle to increase in size and population. However, this did not lead to the appearance of principalities or to an increase in size and a decrease in number of chiefdoms. The Bubi claim that the frequent wars finally resulted in the creation of a single kingdom for the whole island under Moka, the chief of Riabba.[50]

The rise of Moka can be dated to approximately 1835–1845.[51] He is said to have been recognized by the 27 other chiefs as their overlord because he promised to do away with war. A small army of up to 300 of his noble retainers, armed with guns, enforced the peace. The chiefly institutions at this court now became "national," and his council was enlarged to include all the chiefs of the island. But the council met infrequently, and no central institution for gathering royal tribute or any judicial system of appeal beyond the chiefdom was ever developed. Centralization remained quite limited. In view of the position of Gil Delgado, who explains the rise of the kingdom as the result of the operation of a general law by which territorial scale and centralization gradually increase over time, it must be stressed that the kingdom arose directly out of many chiefdoms, each incorporating a handful of villages. Moreover, Moka was not the first chief to become king or attempt to do so. There are some indications that before him the chiefs of Ureka, in the far south, had claimed supreme authority; another tradition claims that it was a king's magic which foiled the attempted Spanish settlement at Concepción Bay in 1780; and the tradition about the spirit of the Lombe Lagoon in the southwest makes it clear that, even earlier, a chief of that area had toured the island and had fruitlessly attempted to be recognized as paramount by all the other chiefs. The rise of Moka was therefore preceded by other attempts to establish a kingdom. It is also good to note that the process did not involve conquest, but a claim based on supposed spiritual superiority allied to sufficient wealth and power. Wealth by itself did not suffice, for by the time Moka became king, other chiefs close to Clarence (Malabo) were much wealthier than he was and probably had more guns than he had.[52]

The isolation of Bioko began to crumble after c. 1750, when neighboring African groups and some European ships began to buy large quantities of yams in the Bays of Malabo and San Carlos. Iron began to trickle into the country and was turned into weapons, especially after 1820. By 1827 the foundation of Clarence signaled the start for a significant immigration by West Africans. By the 1840s external trade had become intensive, numerous African immigrants had settled, especially in the north, and missionaries began to spread the gospel. By the 1880s all these influences were still being incorporated piecemeal into the overarching worldview, value system, and institutional framework of the kingdom, at least in the south. By then, however, direct Spanish control was beginning to take hold in the north, and by 1904 Bubi autonomy had everywhere disappeared.[53]

The institutional history of Bioko shows how a basic configuration, the one that arose from the Great Migration, dictated all future developments, not only in isolation, but even for a century after that isolation ended. In this it represents the experience of all equatorial Africa. This history also illustrates the dangers of invoking the operation of "historical laws" or processes such as "overpopulation" or "defense" as automatic explanations. The high population density of Bioko was older than the kingdom. It had been commented on since before the seventeenth century.[54] A degree of pressure on land and the threat of war had been associated with it, but it had led neither to island-wide wars nor to famine. When Moka founded the kingdom, the population was falling as the result of new epidemics such as smallpox. Although it is true that the earliest known attempt to claim a paramountcy occurred in the most densely populated part of the island, San Carlos Bay, another one occurred at Ureka in the least densely populated area! As to defense: Moka never offered to unite the Bubi to drive out the colonial authorities around Malabo. Still, the traditions stress that chiefs accepted kingship to lessen the frequency of war. Yet why success in c. 1840 and not before? Wars had been equally frequent when the earlier attempts were made. No doubt both population density and insecurity played a role in the rise of the kingdom, but they were only background factors among others.

A kingdom could emerge out of the whole sociopolitical system when people had come to accept the idea of a supreme title as a desirable outcome to the dynamic drift of their political institutions. The idea had to arise and be tested for perhaps a century; and only then did Moka succeed. These are conclusions to bear in mind as the reader now turns to an account of the rise of states in the southwest.

THE SOUTHWEST: THE GROWTH OF STATES

The dominant process in the institutional history of this area has been one of increasing centralization leading to the emergence of first chiefdoms, then principalities, kingdoms, and finally three large kingdoms surrounded by a circle of smaller kingdoms and chiefdoms. Beginning with political units of 500 people each, one ends up with states 1,000-fold larger. How did this happen?

Chiefdoms Emerged

After the absorption of the immigrant eastern Bantu–speaking cereal farmers, perhaps around A.D. 500, the social organization of the area was still based on the House (*nzó'* [CS 946]), the village (*bulá* [CS 447])—with the special meaning "home," which implies possible choices of residence—and the district (*nsí* [CS 331]). Big men (*mfúmú, mpfõ* [CS 1263–65]) led the House and the village. The district had no single leader. Such groups were still thought of as bilateral families (*ibúúru* in Tio, *libóta* farther north [CS 208]), with the big man as the elder (*nkuluntu* in Kongo, *wookuru* in Tio [both from CS 1197, "old in age"]). The House included family members, some affines, clients (A21),[55] and, in many cases, local hunter gatherers (*babongo, mbakambaka*),[56] who had been drawn into relations of economic dependency. Friendship between unrelated persons of equal rank (A18) was relevant as well, because friends could settle with friends; commercial relations between big men, which bolstered their prestige within their Houses, were idealized as friendship too.[57] The big men needed wealth to attract followers and skill in its management. Equally important were their talents as arbiters to resolve conflicts between their followers within the House. Hence the palaver was a central institution.[58] Their followers attributed their success to supposed links with occult powers, especially to charms (*nkísi* [A114 and CS 1071–73]), or to a pact with nature spirits (*nkíra* [also A114]). Moreover, big men were seen as a special type of wizard.[59] Houses congregated in villages for security purposes, hence their defensive village charms (A7),[60] which were the main collective institution at this level. When a village was founded, its headman erected this charm with the collaboration of the heads of all the Houses that planned to settle with him there. The balance of forces in the system as a whole was extremely stable. Competition between big men, and the breakup of each House at the demise of its leader, prevented any House, however fortunate, from dominating a village, let alone a district, for very long. Only an improbable combination of circumstances of special access to wealth, the exceptional longevity of a leader, and the succession of several especially talented leaders could break the balance of power among Houses and villages. Yet in this area it happened.

The unfolding of a more complex economic system by or after the sixth century A.D. was responsible for a gradual destabilization of the old system in this area. It was rich in diverse resources, most of which were already being exploited before A.D. 500. By then the economy was based on a higher-yielding agricultural base, which allowed for the growth of trade and regional specialization.[61] An innovative verb, "to sell" (CS 1697), sprang up in the lower and middle Zaire area at an unknown time, but presumably before 1500. Its meaning is a derivation of CS 1698, "to set a trap"! In Kongo this is associated with the name Teke. This may well have arisen in conjunction with the early trade in copper in the lower and middle Zaire area.

Houses located in favorable locales grew wealthy, and their members eventually realized that succession struggles merely squandered the patrimony of the House and effectively destroyed it. The pressure grew on leaders to develop at least some principles of succession and legitimacy. The ideological model of the family was retained and the legitimate successor, therefore, should be a close kinsman of the leader, with some wealth in his own right and preferably of mature age.[62] Such principles still allowed for multiple competitors. Yet just limiting the number of contenders must have increased the number of Houses that successfully survived the transition from one leader to another.

The first trace of centralization is the appearance of the term *nkáni*[63] for "leader" (see map 5.4). Its distribution encompasses the whole region studied in this section. This noun is derived from an ancient verb which also yielded other derivations, such as the Kongo forms *kanu,* "to decide, to judge, to settle," and *mukanu,* "judgment." *Nkáni*'s semantic field encompasses the notions of wisdom, arbitration, wealth, founding a village, and having a great "family," that is, a House. In the chiefdoms of the upper Ogooué of the Alima-Likouala area and in southwestern Gabon the term also means "chief," and farther south in the principalities of various Teke groups it means "vassal chief." The term is evidence of a new role of arbitration between big men, and hence above them. The status associated with the rise of *nkáni* was that of headman or chief.

Its distribution does not allow us to pinpoint the first appearance of the term, but that is not really important. For once a single district

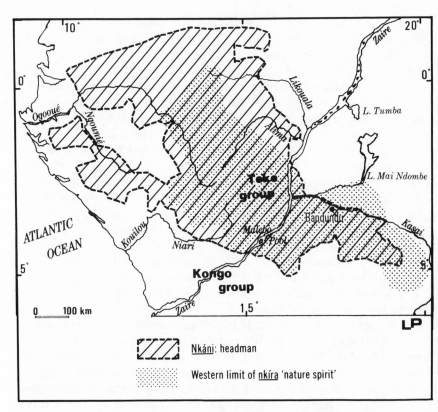

Map 5.4. The spread of the term *nkáni* meaning "chief"

turned into a chiefdom, it was bound to be imitated rapidly by its neighbors. Even the appearance of a single chiefdom broke the balance of power in the whole area. Its military potential exceeded that of neighboring, less well coordinated units. The insecurity of their inhabitants increased, and to restore the balance they too had to achieve a greater internal cohesion. For the sake of security such units were then ready to accept a chief. Moreover the first *nkáni* set a standard for other ambitious big men to emulate. Thus the creation of chieftaincy acted as a catalyst which transformed the basic institutions over a vast area. It is quite likely that the institution of chieftaincy with its rules of succession, its rituals, perquisites, and ideology was perfected in a competitive dialogue between districts over a large area. We may never know when this process began, but it would not be surprising if it had begun long before the end of the first millennium A.D.

The chief was the "master of the land" (*ngáánsi* in Kongo, *ngántsi* in Tio), a formulation that stresses the ideological character of "founder" and the link with nature spirits (Tio *nkíra*) or "charms of the land" (Kongo *nkísi ntsi*). This was expressed by his right to the noble animals—leopard, eagle, and python—and to a portion of other mammals hunted. The chief's village became a "capital."[64] The notions of authority, succession, court of justice, tribute, emblem, and government developed, along with some titled positions within the ruling House, which had become too large to remain internally undifferentiated. All this began to grow around the new role of chief. Such notions were to blossom once the principality appeared. For the first step on the road to centralization was followed by others. The very competition that had kept the early system in such a stable state now fueled an escalation of centralization.

Principalities Appeared

The next step in that process was the conquest and subordination of one chiefdom by another and the appearance of a new political role, that of paramount chief. Thus was the principality born. But in this area the principality is also characterized by a set of political titles consisting of two subsets: one attached to the House of the prince, and one territorial. The prince came to be called *mwéné* ("master of," "owner of")[65] followed by the name of his principality. A whole set of terms common to both the Kongo and the Teke portions of the area now appear. They include: *mpu*, "authority"; *mbáli* (Tio and others)/ *mbazi* "court of justice"; *mbanza* (Kongo and others)/*mbéé* (Tio), "capital"; and *nlunga* (Kongo)/*ōlua* (Tio), "copper ring of office."[66] Apart from *mpu* these are all old linguistic forms with a new meaning. They prove that the principality grew up in the area, and that this occurred in a few centers which mutually influenced each other. There must have been at least two centers, because other Kongo and Teke terms differ. These include "succession," "priest of the principality," "to govern," and "tribute." Titles were constructed using the particle *né-*, *ná-* (Kongo), or *mwé-*, *má-* (Loango)—a short form for *mwéné* in the Kongo world—or *ngá-* in the Teke world, where this particle is regularly used to designate "master of" or "owner."[67] In the realm of ideology a complex ritual of enthronement, a genuine initiation of the prince, developed in all principalities, although the terminology linked to it varied in different parts of the area. Only the principle of an initiation diffused over the whole area. Principalities arose in a few independent localities, but extensively borrowed innovations from one another. This innovation appeared at least once among the Kongo north of the lower Zaire, once among the Teke, and probably once along the lower Kasai (see map 5.5).

Because the first great principalities must have enjoyed great prestige over a large area and because their courts must have been arbiters of

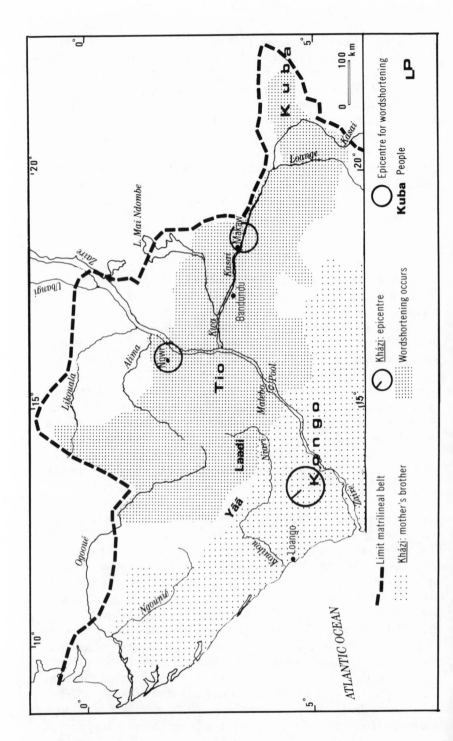

elegance everywhere, it is possible to link a specific linguistic fashion to the first Teke principalities. The phenomenon, of which speakers are quite conscious, consists in the practice of shortening words. In the most extreme case the second syllable of the root is dropped except for the tone, a lengthening of the final remaining vowel and nasalization of that vowel if a nasal consonant occurred in the last syllable.[68] Thus *masángu* ("millet") in Kongo becomes *āsā* in Tio. The centers where the shortest forms are found lie respectively in Teke country west of the Zaire River and in the lower Kasai Valley upstream of Bandundu. Between this core area and the area where shortening does not occur lie a series of languages with intermediate shortening: for example, "wild spinach" is *mfumbu* in Kongo, *pfúumbu* among the neighboring Yáā, *mpfuumo* among their neighbors, the Teke Láali, and *mpfūū* among the Tio. The phenomenon is of considerable extent and age. By 1583 there is a comment about this phenomenon for Tio,[69] and a Kuba extension occurred from the second quarter of the seventeenth century on.

The prestige that led to the diffusion of this fashion of speech was political among the Kuba, which is also the most likely cause for the main diffusion. One may even think that where the phenomenon is the most pronounced, there lies its heartland. This would have been the first truly large principality that appeared in the area. That reasoning points to Teke country west of the Zaire, and probably to the principality at Ngwi, north of Gamboma. Within the area of the spread of the linguistic fashion a second diffusion of terms also occurred. These designated single and twinned clapperless bells, which are emblems of authority wherever they occur and therefore an *assured* indication of political prestige.[70] The idea that the diffusion of the fashion of speech was due to political prestige, first suggested by the Kuba data, is reinforced by this set of data. In addition, the fact that the new linguistic fashion did not affect even relatively nearby Kongo lands indicates that these peoples marched to the sound of a different drummer. Kongo already had developed its own centers of prestige, probably one or several principalities in Mayombe.[71]

The diffusion of the bells yields a rough chronology which leads to a *terminus ante quem* for the appearance of the principality at Ngwi before A.D. 1200.[72] The new fashion of speech had appeared even earlier. From all of this one concludes that both Teke and Kongo principalities originated well before A.D. 1200.

The Teke principality consisted of a prince ruling over the *nkáni*, now "vassals." The idea or representation of principality was expressed by a repertory of court titles, a set of rituals, including the initiation ritual of the prince, a set of emblems, and an ideological link with a specific nature spirit, or *nkíra*. The prince was judge in the last instance and reserved the right to condemn to death, but he could not maintain a monopoly on small wars. Vendettas between villages continued as before. His revenue came from fines levied in court as well as from tribute and probably loot. Military forces were still probably limited to a few hundred men, and the military organization seems not to have been strongly developed. The rise of the principality was accompanied by greater social stratification. A distinction grew between aristocracy, "the people of the species of authority," and the plebeians (literally, "orphans": *antsaana* or *ankieri*), who included the leaders of Houses. Other social statuses included persons given in pawn, clients, dependents, persons paid to atone for the death of others, and perhaps prisoners of war. A special term to designate bought slaves did not exist. These statuses reflect the internal organization of successful Houses. These had by then achieved such a size that internal differentiation of this sort made sense. Yet in the collective imagination the House still remained a bilateral family.[73]

The Invention of Matrilinearity

Meanwhile, north of the lower Zaire and not far from the ocean, the first Kongo principalities were taking shape and a dramatic development took place there as part of this process. The Kongo of Mayombe invented the principle of matrilinearity, which was later to affect a great portion of central Africa. This is not to say that matrilinearity was invented only once. It has already been said that north of the great Zaire bend and in western Cameroon matrilinearity appeared independently. But when it was invented in Mayombe, it diffused far and wide.

One root of the process was the practice of paying matrimonial compensation, an old practice in the region.[74] Goods used for this purpose consisted of metal objects (copper especially) and perhaps squares of raffia. The leader of the House was, therefore, as elsewhere, the manager of the group's hoard of these goods. These could be used to acquire women, to pay compensation in witchcraft or murder cases, and to acquire dependents. The relative power of each House was a function of the size of its hoard. The inheritance of the treasury became crucial to the survival of the House. So vital were these goods to the health of the House that the Kongo and their neighbors in Gabon began to think that the goods exchanged for a woman in marriage were not really equivalent to the woman in value. The goods were worth more; therefore, the group receiving the goods became the debtor of the group receiving the woman. This vision was reflected in a new type of kinship terminology, whereby the creditors downgraded the debtors by a generation and debtors upgraded creditors by one generation. This is the Crow type of terminology in which descendants of the mother's brother of the speaker of the same generation as the speaker are addressed as children of the speaker, and those of the father's sister of the speaker are parents. The Kongo now called the mother's brother *ngwa nkhazi,* "my mother wife," to stress the debt he owed. This kind of terminology sets blocks of matrilineal relatives apart. As soon as they became conscious of the feature, matrilinearity was born. From this the next step is the formation of matrilineages.[75]

The Crow system did not by itself necessarily produce matrilinearity. It did not, for instance, do so among most Mongo speakers. Lineages in the Kongo area grew out of the earlier process of centralization itself, either at the chiefdom or, more likely, at the principality level. An effect of that process of centralization was to set up competition for the titles that were created at the courts, because they carried privileges and represented achieved positions of influence. This, once again, raised the question of succession. It is thus probable that matrilineages were invented to safeguard political rights and at the same time the right to inherit the House treasuries.[76]

As soon as the principle was imagined, it affected the internal structure of the village and of the chiefdom. Matrilineal descent in these matters did not alter the disposition that a married woman lived at the residence of her husband. Her children lived with her and hence away from their mother's brothers. There was therefore no congruence between residence and lineage, and members of the same lineage lived in different villages or quarters. Moreover, the village and chiefdom could no longer be seen as the residences of a single large family, but were now perceived as inhabited by a collection of different matrilineages. Chieftaincy now perforce rested on a claim of authority over territory alone, without any pretense of common descent. Such a claim flowed from the notion that the ruling lineage had founded the chiefdom, as if the chiefdom was but a village writ large. The village itself was ruled by the head of a matrilineage which also rested its claim on the grounds that it had founded the settlement and "owned" the land. The village council was no longer a forum for equals, but became merely consultative to its headman.

Matrilinearity spawned two new groups: the local matrilineage, or "belly" (*divumu*), and the clan, which took an old name for "House" (*dikanda*).[77] The House became a residential matrilineal section, with a kernel consisting of a few uterine brothers and some of their uterine nephews, who joined them after the death of their fathers. Succession to the leadership of the House was regulated by the order of birth. The clan grew naturally out of the lack of congruence between descent and residence. The spatial dispersion of matrilineal relatives constantly increased as a result of marriage. Soon small groups of matrilineal relatives knew only that they were somehow related, because of their common name and praise names. The creation of the position of head of the clan became inevitable, and it went to the head of the strongest known lineage. A clanhead legitimized this situation by claiming to be the head of the oldest lineage stemming from the oldest daughter of an original ancestral mother. The authority of a clanhead exceeded the territory of the village he headed himself. He tended to look upon the domains of all the villages controlled by a lineage of his clan as his lands. Because these places were dispersed in the landscape, the area under the authority of clanhead could not directly become a chiefdom. Indeed, clan ties cut across those that were claimed by heads of chiefdoms. The rise of matriclans tended therefore to weaken individual chiefdoms. Given these conditions, a principality could be created only through an alliance of all the clanheads in a given region. Oral tradition portrays the rise of the kingdom of Loango in just this way.[78] That picture, however, is quite unlikely to correspond to events in the past, given the large number of clanheads involved and the competition between them. The tradition merely seems to be a consequence of matrilineal ideologies. In practice, Kongo principalities also arose through conquest.

Matriclans did not create the Kongo principalities. Rather the reverse occurred. Lineages and clans represented both a defensive reflex for the autonomy of small groups against growing centralization and at the same time a mechanism to defend the advantageous positions gained through titles within such a structure. At the level of the principality, matriclans became an alternative way of visualizing political space. Thus with few exceptions, among which Loango stands out, Kongo principalities seem to have kept the principle of undifferentiated or bilateral succession within the ruling House, both for the supreme title, and for most of the major titles. Lineages and clans now merely strengthened the position of the title holders, who in physical reality held their positions as members of the single ruling House. This allowed the ruling House to co-opt a number of matrilineages.

As women married and went to live in foreign villages, matrilinearity spread far and wide, but not always with the Kongo terminology or with the same social field of application as among the Kongo. The designation "belly" spread as far away as the lower Ogooué, along with the "mother wife" designation for the mother's brother, but not the term *kanda*. The terms *kanda* and "belly" spread unevenly in the valleys of the lower Kasai and Kwilu, but not the designation for mother's brother. In the area of Mai Ndombe the local *nkúmú* eventually developed double descent, designating matrilineages and patrilineages respectively by terms referring to the reproductive organs. In the Kwango area and in Angola the matrilineal principle came to be extended further than it had been in Kongo society and led to the creation of new institutions.[79] In the center of the Teke world, among the Tio, matrilinearity achieved only a modest place. The clan did not develop, and the matrilineage took the name of "House." Thus in present terminology, "the group of birth" of the Teke is opposed to the "matrilineal clan" of the Kongo and the Teke "House" corresponds to the Kongo "belly."

Kingdoms Arose

At the outset the territory of the principality included only a few chiefdoms, and perhaps not even a hundredth of the population of the later kingdom of Kongo. As long as principalities or blocks of allied principalities were of equal strength, the situation remained stable. But over time certain principalities became stronger as a result of successful wars, trade, and small demographic or other advantages. They then absorbed weaker neighbors and eventually came to encompass tens of thousands of inhabitants. But without further institutional and ideological adaptation such a large principality no longer could rule its lands successfully from a single central place. Secession must have been as common as conquest was. This instigated the creation of yet another territorial level: the kingdom. In this process, war of conquest became important. Innovations in armament,[80] training, tactics, deployment in battle, and magic for war occurred. The former term for "pawn," *nkoli*,[81] acquired the new meaning of "prisoner of war," and with prisoners a form of slavery appeared.

The increase in size of the body politic brought with it further structuration of economic space, especially a flowering of trade. Tribute and fines from the whole territory flowed to the court of each principality. In turn the court acted as a locus for redistribution of such income to notables and courtiers, and became a focus for the consumption of luxury goods. As the size of capitals grew, so did the need to import and retail food. Given all this, it is no wonder that marketplaces arose there. With increased trade came a set of innovative commercial institutions such as market regulations, commercial law, the four-day week, which regulated the periodicity of markets, and a monetary system based on iron, copper, and raffia-square units. The copper belt north of the lower Zaire seems to have been a major focus for these innovations, although the major commercial centers were, no doubt, the political capitals as well as major nodes of commerce, as for example the relays around the Malebo Pool.[82] The fragmentary archaeological record extant today documents three major areas by the end of the fourteenth century: a coastal area north of the lower Zaire, an area on either side of the lower Zaire, and an area farther north. These corresponded respectively to the coastal states (the main one was to be Loango), the state of Kongo, and the Tio kingdom.[83]

The first kingdoms were no doubt relatively small. "King" in Tio is *ōkóo*, a derivation of **-kóko* (CS 1204, ps 309 [3:310]), whose older meaning was "ancestor," "grandparent." The etymology shows that the analogy between family and state still remained dominant in the Teke mind. In Kongo and in the coastal area the corresponding term *ntinu* derived from the verb "to cut" and its subsidiary meaning "to settle court cases." But a second term, *ntotila,* arose with the meaning "he who groups people around him," and it also has connotations of luck and wealth. Hence the king was still seen as a typical big man and as a judge.[84]

There seem to have been only two early cradles for the emergence of kingdoms: one north of the lower Zaire, where the greatest number of Kongo principalities were located before the kingdom arose,[85] and one on the northern or northwestern edge of the Tio kingdom (map 5.6). At first a set of constellations of small kingdoms developed, together covering all or most of the territories of the later major states, in which they usually survived as provinces. The three main kingdoms—Kongo, Loango, and Tio—all arose through the fusion of former principalities and smaller kingdoms. According to oral traditions the founder of the Kongo kingdom was a scion of the dynasty of the small Bungu monarchy, north of the lower Zaire. He crossed the river to "the hill of division," where he subjugated the local leader and priest and "divided the provinces." Other traditions make the path of conquest and of peaceful submission of the former principalities and states clear.[86] The traditions of Loango relate that their founding clan came from a small coastal kingdom to the south and also mention a connection with Bungu. The Tio tell of a northern origin in the principality at Ngwi, north of Gamboma, or simply from the north. Other indications confirm that the kingdom first developed on the plateau of Nsa, just south of Gamboma.[87]

Proposed dates for the emergence of the Kongo kingdom derive from an examination of the known list of kings in the seventeenth century. Most authors propose the fourteenth century or even 1400. They often accept dubious Kongo claims that Loango was at first but a province of Kongo, which broke away, perhaps as late as the 1570s. For me there is no doubt that this state may well be as old as Kongo itself, given the history of the acquisition of its provinces. An unsubstantiated claim that the Tio kingdom was older than the others dates from the seventeenth century. If so, it cannot have been much older than the Kongo kingdom; otherwise it would have influenced Kongo more than it did. In sum, one may think of the fourteenth century in connection with the rise of all three kingdoms until future excavations in the Kongo and first Loango capitals, in the princely cemetery in Bungu as well as on several old Tio sites, give us a more precise chronology.[88]

The three main kingdoms shared major common institutional structures, but also exhibited major differences. Two bodies of title holders existed everywhere: one lived at the court or at the palace; the other was

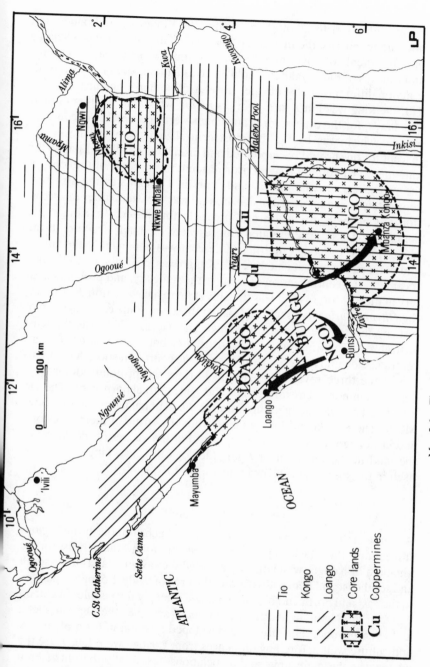

Map 5.6. The three main kingdoms: Kongo, Loango, Tio

comprised of territorial officials. Among the Kongo and in Loango, but not among the Tio, the first group was divided in two: officials in charge of departments of government such as justice, revenue, and the army, and officials of the royal household, such as a major-domo. This reveals a major difference between the Tio and the other kingdoms. For the Tio, the king was but a lord over his *nkáni,* who were masters in their own lands; for the others, lords and chiefs were accountable at court. In Kongo, which was by far the most centralized, provincial governors (except for one) could be appointed and dismissed at will. In Loango the king merely appointed a supervisor resident at the court of the lords of the provinces. On the other hand, only in Loango was the structure completely based on matrilineal clans and was the exact order of succession among heirs to the throne precisely formalized. In Kongo and among the Tio undifferentiated Houses were the main structure at the higher levels. In Kongo matrilineal descent was dominant at the village and perhaps the lowest chiefly level. Kongo was in a class by itself when it came to the centralization of tribute, the judiciary, and probably military matters. Moreover, it was the only state to have a national currency, the *Olivancillaria nana* shell. In Loango there was some centralization of justice, and tribute went to the king. The Tio kingdom was the least centralized. The king only received tribute, but there was no military centralization and not even a single supreme court of justice. A comparison of the three royal ideologies also brings out profound differences despite common ancestral features and some mutual borrowing. The Tio king ruled because he held the shrine of the national nature spirit, Nkwe Mbali. The Kongo and Loango kings ruled by virtue of their ancestors, and in Loango, by virtue of the approval of the keeper of the charm of the land in the kingdom of Ngoi. Ideologically each kingdom rooted itself in the specifics of its own religious history.[89]

North of the Kingdoms

As these states took shape they provoked much turmoil in the regions surrounding them (see map 5.7). One need not follow this process for the kingdom of Kongo, which mostly affected the savanna lands to its south and southeast and hence lies beyond the area of study. Loango expanded to the east and north and began to influence deeply the peoples of Gabon between the Ngounié and the ocean, as far away as the Ogooué Delta and even beyond. This area had developed a common form of society and culture well before any influences from Loango were felt. Here the village was the main unit, and associations—especially the *mwiri,* into which the boys were initiated, and a higher-level association for men backed by the approval of spirits—provided it with both government and an impressive esprit de corps.[90] So did the presence of a village temple, the *mbánjá* for the cult linked to the men's associations.[91] An expression of this commonality of structure and culture in the area was the use everywhere of the *nkendo* bell with bent handle and the skin of a wildcat as an emblem of authority and a means to call the attention of spirits and heroes.[92] The first influence from the south was the adoption of matrilinearity from about the twelfth century onward.[93] But these peoples put the notion of matriclan to a very specific use. They claimed that each local clan was equivalent to other clans elsewhere and derived from a common ancestor. Thus they built up a network of regional alliances by inventing lists of correspondences between the names of different clans. In this way they overcame the lack of common overarching institutions between districts and perhaps villages. Soon the whole area formed a single social whole, even while it remained strongly decentralized.[94]

The influence of the royal institutions of Loango is attested by 1600 along the coast in the nomenclature of titles and by some other terms and emblems as far north as the Gabon Estuary,[95] but we do not know exactly when it began. Mayumba, the southern portion of the area, had turned itself into a loose principality on the Loango model well before 1500 and had been incorporated into that kingdom by then, or during the sixteenth century. A representative of the king of Loango was stationed there and the local prince paid an occasional tribute of women to the king. As early as 1583, one author even claimed that the territory of Loango extended all the way to Cape Lopez. Sete Cama had a lord by 1600, probably subordinate to the prince at Mayumba.[96] Loango's commercial dominance by 1600 is certain, but there may not have been much economic control. For instance, it is not known when people from Loango built a post on the lower Ngounié named after their capital and created a small chiefdom and ethnic group there to which they gave their own name, Vili. Nor is it known whether this was a political outpost of the kingdom. One may only presume that this settlement was linked to the ivory trade, which by 1600 was already reaching deep inside the area.[97]

In the seventeenth century at the latest, a loose confederation of districts developed. The leaders of each district met to discuss matters of common concern and, as this happened more and more often, the practice became an alternative to chiefdoms everywhere in the Ngounié Valley.[98] By or before 1700 the Myene in the Ogooué Delta had created or were creating kingdoms obviously inspired by Loango; from 1600 onward, an impressive array of evidence documents a pervasive general influence from Loango into the area.[99] These developments are so intertwined with the Atlantic trade, however, that they will be considered in a later chapter.

The Tio kingdom, even though it was so decentralized that military campaigns were always organized by local princes, still had a discernible effect on its neighbors to the north and northeast (see map 5.8). There

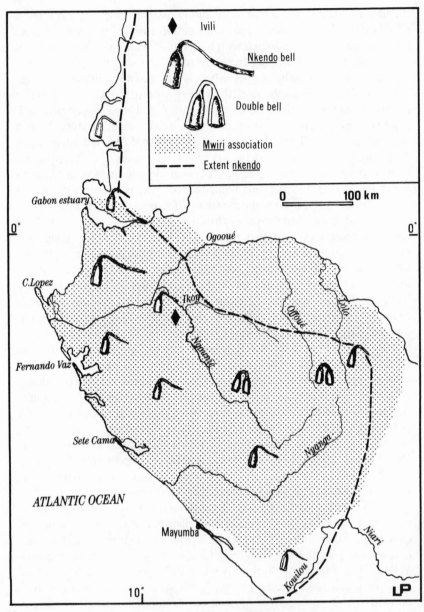

Map 5.7. Southern Gabon

160

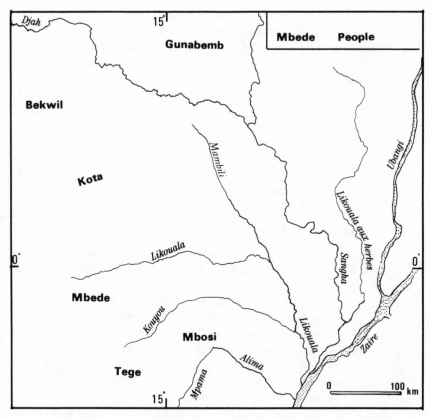

Map 5.8.   Northern Congo

the Mbede created a chiefdom, or *ngali,* and both the Mbede and the peoples of the Alima-Likouala invented an association of chiefs, the *onkáni,* to better coordinate a common defense. The title system of such chiefdoms found a weak echo in the Alima-Likouala area where the *nkwere* assisted the chief or *mwéné.* This degree of centralization proved to be quite sufficient. In the eighteenth and nineteenth centuries the local Tege, Mbede, and Mboshi groups frequently waged wars on each other, but were fairly evenly matched. By then, the dynamics of their further political history were also linked to the Atlantic slave trade, which reached them by both overland and river routes.[100]

Peoples beyond these groups reacted as follows. The Kota of northeastern Gabon, and others beyond, adopted the title of *nkáni* but merely to apply it to their big men. The Shake, the closest Kota group to the Mbede, accepted the institution of warleaders commanding several "clans," thus probably matching the manpower of a Mbede chiefdom.

The Kota themselves began to live in larger villages containing more Houses than hitherto, which increased local security. Their northern neighbors, the Bekwil, and perhaps others beyond, such as the Gunabemb, followed suit. The Kota, furthermore, strengthened the authority of the big men within their large villages by developing the *satsi* rituals of circumcision for the sons of their leading men. This in turn was adopted by the Mbede. As to the peoples north and east of the Likouala area, they were very little affected by developments there, in part because they lived in inundated forests and marshes. Still, titles were attractive and the practice spread northward, even beyond the upper Likoualaaux-herbes, but without much institutional effect, since the communities were so small and so scattered in this region.[101]

Original State Formations in the Lower Kasai Region

It is tempting to attribute all evidence of centralization east of the Tio kingdom, both north and south of the lower Kasai, to Tio influence. The lower Kasai area, as far away as the mouth of the Loange (see map 5.9), had been influenced by the fashions of speech in the early Teke principalities, and they had borrowed bells as emblems of authority and power. The matrilinearity of these regions, like the existence of markets, weeks, and currencies, can be traced to Kongo influence.[102] The exigencies of security and the impact of trade account for diffusions which reached from neighbor to neighbor over such distances. Tempting this might be, but it would also be misleading.

First, one must realize that ethnographic, linguistic, and oral traditional data from the area make clear that there have been other influences. Thus the Ngwi kingdoms belonged to the *nkúmú* tradition of the north, and influence from that quarter is evident everywhere north of the lower Kasai. It probably dates from the sixteenth century onward. Then there are eighteenth- and nineteenth-century influences from the Pende and Lunda worlds in the south, and there are renewed eighteenth-century influences from the Tio and the Kongo worlds.[103] It is therefore not easy to disentangle the institutional histories of these areas. Second, one should not overlook that there was a second epicenter where final syllables of words were shortened, along both banks of the lower Kasai in the area of Makaw. And the terminology for bells shows that the Tio terms were not accepted among the Boma and Saa, north of the lower Kasai. Rather they show influences from the Mai Ndombe area.[104]

The available ethnographic and linguistic evidence still does not suffice to warrant many firm conclusions. It suggests that there existed on the lower Kasai a center of original development focused on the Boma, Buma, Saa, and Yans groups. Much of the political terminology, especially in the first three groups, is quite original.[105] The evidence

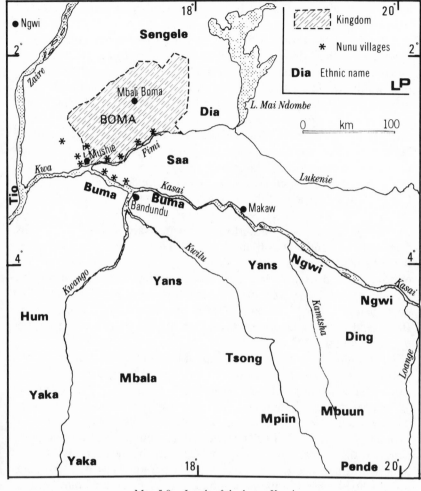

Map 5.9.   Lands of the lower Kasai

suggests that, after having been influenced by the new Teke fashion of
speech, people in the Makaw area took over as role models and innova-
tors and pursued their own more radical dynamic of shortening words.
Finally, there is the massive evidence that, at the very latest, by the mid-
seventeenth century a kingdom whose structures were on the whole
quite different and much more centralized than those of the Tio kingdom had arisen among the Boma north of the lower Kasai-Fimi.[106]
References to another kingdom, the monarchy of Mwenemoegi (*mwéné
Mushie*) or Nimeamaya, date from 1561 onward. They refer to the small
chiefdom of the Nunu of Mushie on the Kwa and make clear that central-

ized government was known in portions of this area by the sixteenth century.[107]

Chiefdoms and principalities obviously existed much earlier in this region. Both the oral tradition and the later organization of the Boma kingdom show that there were first small chiefdoms, then principalities, then a final conquest by the ruling dynasty of the Ngeliboma.[108] Teke influence is mainly apparent in the ideology of the charm referring to the national nature spirit. This is linked to the notion of *nkirá*, which is found in the whole area of lower Kasai, and undoubtedly stems from the Teke world. The designation for the common people as *monshyâ* or *nsân* (Saa) and *nsaan* (Yans) is also probably derived from the Tio. Such elements indicate influence by early Teke principalities. So does the use by the Nunu of Mushie of the common Kongo and Tio *mwéné*.

But among the Boma, Saa, Yans, and others, the designations for chiefs, princes, dynasty, authority, and territory are original[109] and indicate that Teke influences found already well-entrenched chiefdoms in the area. The Teke example may have given the impetus to the creation of both Saa and Boma principalities, but this impetus was mediated by local innovation. The area north of the lower Kasai therefore had chiefdoms before 1200. More centralized structures followed, which led to Boma and strong Saa principalities that were later influenced by the *nkúmú* tradition.[110]

The founders of the Boma kingdom could even have been *nkúmú* princes, but the preceding lords claim to be linked to the autochthons among the Sengele just to the north and the Buma group south of the Kasai near modern Bandundu. Such claims imply, however, that chiefdoms existed before then among the Buma and probably also among their neighbors, the Yans. The relevant vocabulary shows correspondences with the Saa terminology and supports the idea that the area of Makaw was a cradle for the invention of chiefdoms and perhaps small principalities. Oral traditions of groups farther upstream hold that the founders of their chiefdoms and principalities came from "downstream," but trace them no farther than below the confluence of the Kamtsha, that is, to this same Makaw area.[111] It certainly looks as if this area was the cradle for a political innovation that spread over the whole lower Kasai region and ultimately gave rise to the Boma kingdom.

The tale of relentless territorial centralization from big man to king that has been told in this section seems to confirm long-held and beloved stereotypes about the origin of the state. Many a reader may conclude that this is how social scale is enlarged, this is how complex societies necessarily arise. But that is simply not true, as the institutional history of all the other societies of people in the rainforests show. Nor should one attribute state formation necessarily to the open habitats or the presence of rich diversified resources and consequent trade in the region. Trade on a large scale and areas rich in diversified resources are not unknown elsewhere in equatorial Africa. The next chapter will show very different paths toward achieving greater social scale and will document yet two other pathways of development in the rise of kingdoms. The reader must therefore keep an open mind and perhaps wonder why the track of institutional change was so different in the southwestern quadrant, rather than dismiss the record in all the other parts of the area as indicative of arrested or abnormal development.

Six

The Eastern Uplands

The lands between the inner basin and the great mountain range bordering the Rift Valley (see map 6.1) were among the last to be settled by western Bantu farmers. This perhaps accounts for the presence in the nineteenth century of only a few high population densities in a sea of almost empty lands, in stark contrast to the very high population densities on the eastern side of the mountain crests. In these eastern uplands the population tended to cluster along the major waterways, such as the lower Lomami, the Lualaba, and the Aruwimi. By then three kernels of higher population densities existed in what had become exceptionally favorable natural habitats. One lay on the borderland between the rainforests and the northern savanna, from the middle Uele to the Aruwimi. Another, less-populated one stretched eastward of the Lualaba, north to south from Kindu to Kongolo, and thus also straddled the savanna forest boundary. A third, lesser pocket of higher population density abutted on the mountains in southern Maniema.[1] These kernels, visible residues of historical processes, corresponded to centers of past institutional developments.

Their location also draws attention to two other features typical of the eastern uplands. The first is the influence of outsiders on western Bantu speakers. This extended over the whole region and introduced elements extraneous to the earlier tradition of the forests. In the north the impact of southern central Sudanic speakers is evident on the Bantu languages as far as 1° 30' south. In the south, eastern Bantu speech strongly influenced the languages of Maniema. Linguistic influence from the languages of the great lakes was of little consequence, except that west and northwest of Lake Kivu two of these languages were actually spoken by people living in the rainforests.[2] The second feature is that the region contained two historical foci: one in the north and one in the

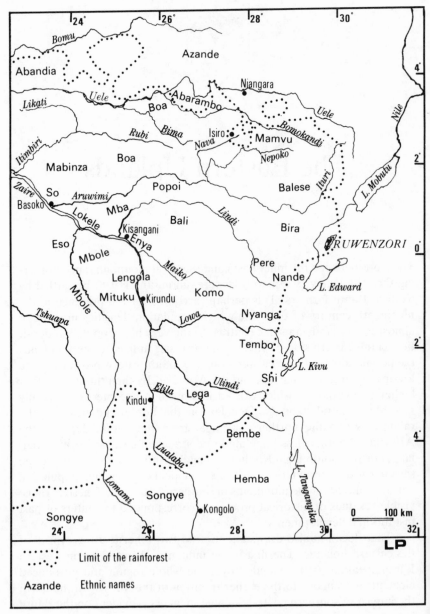

Map 6.1. The eastern uplands

south. This had been so ever since the first farmers settled the land, and it remained so for the whole period, despite mutual influences between north and south. This chapter is therefore divided into two sections, one for each of these foci.

UELE AND ITURI

The story in this section relates how farmers from diverse cultural backgrounds met in the same area, forged a new tradition there, and turned the lands of the middle Bomokandi–Nepoko into a hub for the whole region (see map 6.2).[3] Within this hub speakers of 28 languages of the three main language families of Africa are now lumped together in northeastern Zaire, as if people had immigrated to this area from every point of the compass.[4]

The boundary between the rainforest habitats to the south and the savannas to the north dissolves in these lands, which consist of a human-made gulf deep into the rainforests, where the landscape varies from evergreen rainforest to half-deciduous forest to a mosaic of woods and savanna with tall grasses to predominantly savanna. The first farmers created a bundle of ecotones here that yielded an impressive variety of different resources. Once this had been achieved, these lands became the cynosure for immigrants from the whole region.

A Congress of Traditions

The first farmers, probably Ubangian speakers, came from the west and brought a tradition of polished tools with them, among which the most remarkable were strong axes made of hematite with a very high content of iron. So sturdy were these axes that people continued to make them even as late as the seventeenth century.[5] Then followed Bantu speakers from the southwest, among them the ancestors of the Mabodo, who settled on the forest-savanna boundary near and beyond 3° north, and the ancestors of the Buan group, who began to diversify in the last centuries B.C. just south of the middle Bomokandi Valley, then solid rainforest. Meanwhile southern central Sudanic speakers were differentiating into several language groups in the highlands west of the Nile and Lake Mobutu.[6] Iron smelting came to be practiced here from about 300 B.C. onward, and the banana was probably adopted in the first centuries of our era.[7] This last development especially is to be linked to several population expansions that followed: the expansion of proto-Mamvu speakers deep into the Ituri forests east of longitude 28° east, where they influenced all Bantu speakers; the expansion of Buan speakers, north between Uele and Bomu but also south in the Aruwimi area; and per-

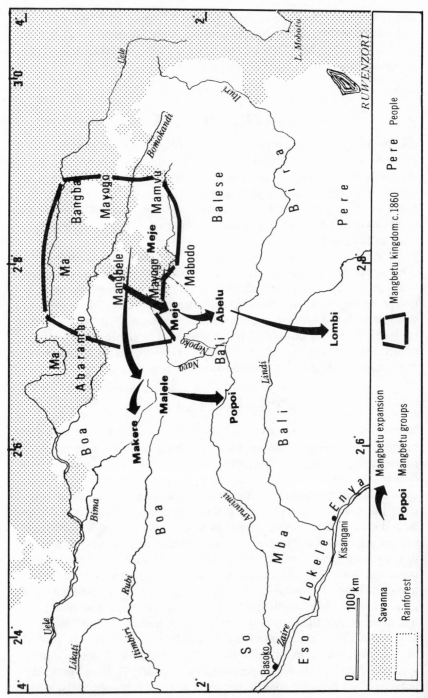

Savanna

Rainforest

Mangbetu expansion

Popoi Mangbetu groups

Mangbetu kingdom c.1860

Pere People

RUWENZORI

100 km

170

haps the expansion of the Ubangian language groups west toward the Ubangi as well as toward the Zaire bend.

Each of the three main immigrant groups had brought its own social heritage. Only a minority of proto-Ubangians were specialized fishermen. They settled along the Uele and other major rivers. Among the others hunting remained quite important, although they also grew yams. As a consequence, they were quite mobile and lived in dispersed settlements. Cooperation between families may have been similar to Abarambo practices in the late nineteenth century. For example, all the families that roamed the same river valley cooperated with each other in times of stress. The Abarambo spatial unit was a whole river valley.[8] The proto-Ubangians lacked an ideology of leadership, and it remains unclear whether even temporary leaders, for instance in war, were recognized beyond the level of the extended household. Integrative institutions between households seem to have been very weak. There was no complex initiation ritual for boys, and marriage was not, it seems, an occasion to build long-lasting ties among a wide set of households.[9]

The original southern central Sudanic culture had been one of herders and farmers living in dispersed settlements, where each household lived by itself without territorial leadership beyond the household. But age grades, and rituals of induction into them, provided a wider social setting. The proto-Mamvu had given up cattle as they entered the tsetse-infested areas of the savannas to the west of the rift. Goats then replaced cattle and farming grew in importance. At first the main crops were cereals; later yams and finally bananas came to predominate. The looseness of their social organization can be gauged by the fact that their preferred form of marriage was for two men to marry each other's sisters. Thus matrimonial alliances between extended households did not lead to lasting mutual obligations, because there existed no matrimonial debt or credit between them. Hence marital alliances were no basis for subsequent long-term alliances among several groups. Wealth was not involved with marriage either, and therefore matrimonial exchange could not be used by would-be big men to build up a core of followers. Thus marriage was not used to construct political entities. Circumcision was not practiced, and the former institution of age grades decayed. There was therefore very little organization in proto-Mamvu society beyond the extended household. There were Houses, but no villages, no districts, and no big men.[10]

Great was the contrast of these two traditions with the western Bantu tradition as inherited by the ancestors of the Mabodo and the Buans. They had districts, villages, Houses, big men, and elaborate circumcision rituals in the village, and at an early date they had adopted bridewealth as a major form of marriage, thus reinforcing the basis of authority for big men. Their economy was perfectly adapted to forest environments, and they also benefited a great deal from the adoption of the banana, both in saving labor and in obtaining an excess of production, which they traded for meat and honey with the aboriginal hunters and gatherers whom they slowly enticed to attach themselves to Buan and Mabodo villages.[11]

Birth of a New Tradition

The Ubangian Mayogo and Bangba, the southern central Sudanic Mamvu, and the Bantu Buans all mixed during the second half-millennium of our era in the middle Bomokandi and Nepoko area, and by A.D. 1000 their different heritages had fused into a new common tradition. This combined much of the Buan forest heritage with features from the Mamvu savanna way of life. The mix of technologies is evident in hunting and farming. The practice of large-scale hunting associated with the burning of grasslands, typical of the savanna, survived alongside hunting with nets, typical of the forest. The inventory of crops now included cereals and other savanna species, as well as forest crops. The association of crops, typical of the forests, now went along with crop rotations from the savannas. The length of time a field would lie fallow was reduced to accommodate the Mamvu habit of more intensive agriculture, but, when no new fertilizing techniques were used, soils were overworked, forests turned into savanna lands, and the ecotone between rainforest lands and savannas was pushed southward. In the social sphere the new tradition adopted compact settlement, but a village consisted of only a single House, itself larger and with a stronger internal cohesion and greater social stratification than any household had been in any of the previous traditions. Marriage with matrimonial compensation became prominent and allowed big men to use greater surpluses to build up sizable harems, attract more young men, increase the labor force, and extend a network of defensive alliances. Meanwhile wider community ties loosened as village and House became coterminous, as the district disappeared, and as older ideas about leadership were now transferred to big men.[12]

In addition, most of the Buan speakers were drifting slowly away from the lands of the middle Bomokandi to expand westward toward the upper Itimbiri and the Likati, and more Mamvu and Mayogo continued to drift into the middle Bomokandi–Nepoko area from the east. These were slow movements, spread out over centuries, and they did not prevent the common tradition from taking root. These movements culminated c. A.D. 1000 in the middle Bomokandi–Nepoko region of speakers with the arrival of another southern central Sudanic language group, the Mangbetu. They came from the higher and much drier lands where the present borders of Zaire, Sudan, and Uganda meet. When they arrived in these different climes, they came to be so heavily indebted to Bantu-speaking teachers that they borrowed almost their whole vocabulary relating to their new habitat from Bantu languages.

Once in the region, they migrated farther and began to split up into several language groups. During the next half-millennium Mangbetu speakers spread far and wide from 3° north to the equator from 26° east to 28° east. The ancestors of the Abelu and Lombi settled in the deep forests of the Lindi River valley and to the east of the lower Nepoko, respectively. They were followed by the forebears of the Meje, who occupied the edges of the forests of the Nepoko. Meanwhile the ancestors of the Makere and Malele moved southwest of the Bomokandi into the Bima Valley, and the Popoi went even farther south into those regions to settle on the banks of the Aruwimi. They all settled in interstices between lands exploited by others. Each of the resulting groups came to be acculturated by their neighbors, but they all kept to the basic proto-Mangbetu structural feature: one village, one House. In turn each of them, except for the Lombi, brought their neighbors into fresh contact with the new tradition of the middle Bomokandi–Nepoko as well.[13]

On balance more people immigrated into the core middle Bomokandi–Nepoko area than emigrated. The population density grew and, inevitably, so did the frequency and scale of conflict. This in turn led to new military dispositions, including, after A.D. 1000, a new standard formation for battle. Spearmen covered by body shields fought in serried ranks, a tactic that requires both discipline and a sizable number of men. Close-combat stabbing weapons were perfected. Spear and shield had been used in the area long before, but the curved knife, or *trombash,* used to hook an opponent's shield out of the way for a spear thrust to follow, was new. It developed out of the sickle, commonly used for reaping cereals in the east. Missile weaponry lost prestige, and the use of the bow in war became almost obsolete north of the middle Bomokandi Valley.[14]

The new tactics meant that more men were available and that a new type of House was being developed. Houses became larger and more efficient. They had more members, became internally more differentiated, and developed more efficient practices of succession. One surmises that the success of the Mangbetu expansion was at least facilitated by the increased size of their average House. In the heartland the process of enlarging the House continued to the point that, by the onset of the eighteenth century, the largest Houses encompassed several settlements and were well on the way to turn into House chiefdoms. By that time clients had become more numerous, slaves were procured by trade or as prisoners of war, harems became larger, and Houses used specialized semimercenary warriors, designated by special terms.[15] The vexing problem of an orderly succession of leadership was solved as follows. The leader of the House designated an official heir and gave him some responsibility. The field of legitimate contenders was limited to the sons of the incumbent, and the eldest son was often the designated heir. This strengthened the continuity of leadership, although it did not lead to a full-fledged patrilineal ideology and the formation of strict lineages.[16] Leadership continued to be thought of as an achieved status, not an inherited right. Strife and occasional takeovers of a House continued in the eighteenth century despite designation of an official heir. The story of the fugitive hunter Manziga, who was to forge the most famous of all Houses in the latter part of that century, attests to this. The inequalities between stronger and weaker Houses grew apace. The stronger Houses became more dominant. They justified their demands on the weaker ones by a claim of superiority either as givers of wives to them or, on the contrary, as receivers of wives from them, but receivers entitled to superiority by virtue of a joking relationship (i.e., a relationship in which partners were entitled to abuse each other freely without retaliation). Usually the inferior (junior, debtor) party was the more aggressive one. In this case the debtor happened to be the more powerful partner and perverted the intent of the institution.[17]

However, the gradual increase in scale of the House in the core area did not prevent the immigration of yet another group of people. Mabodo began to drift westward from the springs of the Nepoko and the Ituri to occupy territory in the middle Nepoko area, probably starting in the seventeenth century. Indeed for a while they became the political pacesetters in the region.[18] Even though their Houses were weaker and smaller than those in the middle Bomokandi–Nepoko tradition, they had maintained the old Bantu village and district organization. The cohesion within the districts had been further enhanced as they developed strong segmentary lineages, bolstered by a special institution and ideology, *embaa,* a term referring to the principle of legitimate patrilineal succession and also designating a set of rituals, charms, and emblems related to it.[19] Such objects were in the charge of a keeper who had special political status. And so, even though their Houses were weaker, the Mabodo still fielded as many or more warriors as any enemy could muster. Moreover, their armament may have been slightly superior, because in addition to massed spearmen they used archers shooting poisoned arrows.[20] Their lineages made such an impression that the Mangbetu groups began to designate their Houses by the compound prefix *Mava-*, in which *va-* was taken over from the *ba-* that prefixed Mabodo names of lineages. Another effect of their settlement in the area was to force the Meje and Abelu groups surrounding them to accelerate the increase in scale of the local Houses.

Not only was the Mabodo organization a match for their northern neighbors, it was also a menace to their southern neighbors, the Bali of the Aruwimi River. They reacted in the eighteenth century with an institutional innovation of their own: the *mambela*. This evolved in a district famous for its iron-smelting industry near the lower Nepoko, not far from the Mabodo. The Bali had long practiced collective initiations without circumcision for boys, called *mambela* at the village level. Now they began to link long strings of villages in a single *mambela* network. The ritual started in one village and then went from place to place in a set sequence, thus reinforcing and expanding cooperation at a district level.[21] The Bali also borrowed the position of warleader, *gama*, from the Mabodo, who themselves had it from the east. The term ultimately derives from eastern Bantu *mukama*, "king," in the northern great lakes. A single leader now directed the coalition of allied villages in war, a gain in military efficiency. The Bali further contained the Mabodo by relying on ambush by archers using poisoned arrows and by avoiding giving battle to massed spearmen in the open. Given the low density of population in their lands, this tactic proved to be quite effective.[22] Even more efficient in border areas was the use of terrorist murder by leopard men (*aniota*) sent out by the village leaders, as circumstances dictated, to assassinate unsuspecting victims, often women belonging to hostile villages.[23] Mabodo and Bali prestige grew as a result of institutional innovations, and their languages began to spread in the deep forests at the expense of the Lombi, Abelu, and several smaller Bantu languages in the upper Aruwimi and lower Ituri areas.

From Big Man to King

In the 1700s the spiral of innovation induced by the loss of equilibrium of military strength between average houses led to the appearance of embryonic and then strong House-chiefdoms in the area most under stress, just north and south of the new Mabodo settlements. Late in the century eight House-chiefdoms had come to dominate the area of high population density, the largest and most cohesive lying toward the Nepoko and its affluent, the Nava River. The Mabodo now trailed the Meje in prestige, even though their districts were still strong enough to resist aggression by any of the new House-chiefdoms.[24] Meanwhile the House-chiefdoms rapidly expanded toward the headwaters of the Bomokandi without effective opposition. The small local Mamvu Houses met the threat by settling on rocky outcrops for defense, but the measure was inefficient. The Mamvu lands became a raiding ground for slaves and other loot (mostly goats), and foreign adventurers began to establish House-chiefdoms of their own there.[25] In contrast to Meje superiority, Mangbetu speakers in the Bima Valley were on the defensive against Buan speakers. The Buans had adopted the highly efficient patrilineal segmentary organization to coordi-

nate military action over large districts, which had developed in the upper
Likati area from 1600 onward. The increase in the size of Makere Houses
barely sufficed to provide a balance of power in the region. Even so, they
were gradually losing ground to Buan settlements west of the Bima
River.[26] By and after 1750, the older populations near the lower
Bomokandi were also on the defensive, as they came under indirect pressure of the expanding Abandia and early Azande Avungura peoples. The
mobile Abarambo, who lived south of the Bomu River c. 1750, began to
retreat southward in the face of Azande attack, crossed the Uele, and
settled between the older inhabitants north of the Makere settlements.[27]

In this highly labile situation a single catalyst could transform the
whole political landscape. Manziga of the Mabiti group proved to be just
such a catalyst. A self-made man, he began his career as an adopted
client. After 1750 he took over the House of his master east of the lower
Nepoko in the Abelu area, enlarged it, moved to Meje lands, and successively overran several House-chiefdoms as far north as the Bomokandi
River. His son and heir, Nabiembali, undertook further conquests after
1800 to subjugate the whole middle Bomokandi–Nepoko area, except
for the main House-chiefdom of the Mayogo speakers and the Mabodo
lands.[28] In a mere generation a House-chiefdom had given rise to a
kingdom. As a sign of the transformation the name Mabiti was dropped
and Mangbetu became the official name for the new political unit.[29]
After 1815 Nabiembali launched conquests outside of these heartlands
to subjugate the area between the Uele in the north, the Makere Houses
in the west, and many of the Mamvu lands to the east, incorporating
people from many different ethnic and linguistic backgrounds into the
new Mangbetu state. This turned the kingdom into a very different
cultural entity. By 1820 Nabiembali was strong enough to defeat the first
Azande attacks from across the Uele, and thus bought time for the new
Mangbetu entity to grow roots.[30]

So rapid was the growth of Nabiembali's kingdom that the development of appropriate institutions for this new social formation did not
keep pace. Mangbetu political institutions remained those of the House-
chiefdom. Nabiembali continued to gather kin, wives, clients, and slaves
around him. Political relationships continued to be tagged with kinship
terms, and relations between House-chiefdoms within the state were still
thought of in matrimonial terms. Nabiembali gave local leaders women
to marry or married some of their women. In the first case, he was
mother's brother to the male children of the union, one of whom was
then put in charge of his mother's House-chiefdom. In the second case,
his sons were sister's sons to the leaders of their mother's group, and he
placed them as his representatives in those groups on the strength of that
tie. He chose his own advisors from among close kinsmen, faithful clients, and slaves utterly dependent on his personal patronage. The royal

ideology remained rooted in big man conceptions of talent, intelligence, and supernaturally induced luck. After 1850, when tension became apparent among the crowd of sons and nephews of Nabiembali, the *mapingo* oracle, which predicted success in war, became popular among the elite. As to royal insignia, they were ill-defined objects denoting exceptional prestige or exceptional wealth and remained but an index of the fortunes of the leader.[31]

Nabiembali also failed to create new judicial, military, or financial institutions. The core of the military remained the royal bodyguard comprising professional mercenaries, close relatives, and dependents of the king. Government revenues stemmed at first from loot, from food production by the women and slaves at the ruler's court, and probably from court fines. After the 1850s, income from tribute and trade became more important, but tribute was still explained in terms of gift giving. No centralized and hierarchical judiciary system developed at all. Thus the economic and judicial underpinnings of the state remained very weak indeed.[32]

As long as Nabiembali kept his sons in check the system worked. But when his eldest son Tuba rebelled and deposed him in 1859, the system collapsed. Tuba lacked both the military power and the prestige to align the other chiefs behind him. A series of civil wars followed and the last king, Mbunza, fell in battle in 1873. The kingdom broke up and was replaced by a number of smaller entities which began expanding into new lands shortly after Tuba took over.[33] By the 1870s, general unrest was extreme, because both Azande princes and slave traders from the Sudan became very active in the area. So serious was this situation that an older war charm, the *nebeli,* now evolved into a secret self-help association to protect its adherents against both outside enemies and chiefs.[34]

The history of the northeastern portions of the rainforests is one of the clearest examples of the impact institutional change can have on large areas by altering the equilibrium of forces between the units in a stable political "system." In this case the first impulse came from the birth of a new tradition (in the middle Bomokandi–Nepoko area), followed by the increasing attraction of this core area, and its consequent population build-up. The Mabodo provided a second impulse, whose ultimate origins lay in the faraway great lakes region beyond the mountains. Manziga's success was a result of these impulses, but also the beginning of a much more ambitious body politic: the kingdom.

THE SOUTHEAST: ASSOCIATIONS AND BROTHERHOODS

The southeastern quadrant of the rainforest area forms a cultural continuum (see map 6.3). The most distinguished ethnographer of the region attributes this to "cultural mixtures, transitional among larger entities. That kind of interlinkage makes an immense region in eastern Zaire a cultural continuum." Earlier sources also acknowledge general cultural connections among many populations, as well as specific ties, arising from voluntary associations. These voluntary associations showed "uniform structural, organizational, and ideological principles." Individual rituals and terminology can also be traced over considerable distances.[35] Various studies document interlocking distributions of vocabulary and practices, associated with such voluntary associations, in the whole area over four degrees of latitude from the equator southward and three to four degrees of longitude between 25° east and 29° east.[36]

Such cultural similarities have been held to be "not merely the result of local diffusion of cultural traits; they are also the product of common origins." A congeries of interrelated ethnic groups was believed to have migrated from the Ruwenzori range both westward and southward, already equipped with circumcision rites and the rudiments of *bwámi,* the overarching association among the Lega and Bembe of southeastern Maniema. They carried these institutions over the whole of Maniema in different varieties according to the vagaries of migrations and encounters. One major epicenter for further development lay on the banks of the Lualaba between the confluences of the Lowa and the Elila, and a second epicenter lay in the high mountains of Itombwe and the upper Lwindi, west-northwest of the head of Lake Tanganyika.[37]

Although the area has recently exhibited a definite cultural continuum, especially in institutions related to initiations and voluntary associations, the view that this was due to a common origin of the populations involved cannot be sustained. After all, the area was a last frontier for farmers from different origins bent on expansion. Settlers in this region came from different cultural backgrounds. Northern Maniema is inhabited by people from the Buan language family. They arrived there from the northwest in the last centuries B.C. Later they became so influenced by a southern central Sudanic tongue that their languages even lost much of the basic concord system typical of Bantu languages. Southern Maniema was settled in the first centuries A.D. from the south by speakers of the Maniema group of languages, carriers of a mixed western and eastern Bantu heritage, which was similar to the culture of the savanna peoples of southeastern Zaire.[38] Not much later, members of the linguistic and cultural group of the great lakes, itself a subdivision of eastern Bantu, drifted west of their mountain habitats into the nearby rainforests west and northwest of Lake Kivu.[39] Moreover, there is no evidence that any type of association was important in any of these traditions at the time of their immigration, although rituals of circumcision may have been. More recently, associations have also been a strong feature of the populations living in the savannas of southeastern Zaire,

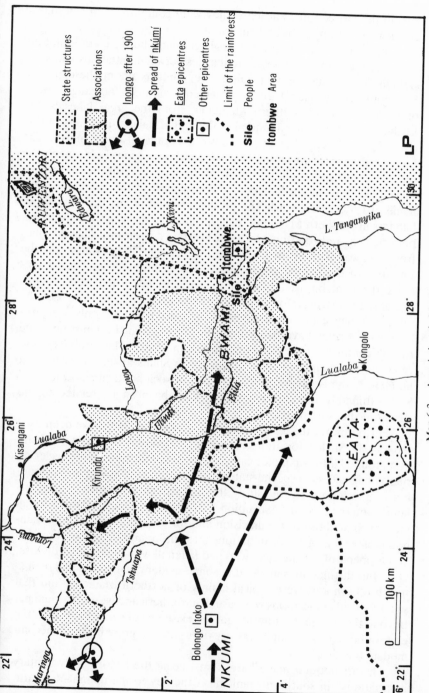

Map 6.3. Associations in Maniema

but, in the last centuries at least, they were combined with centralized government in kingdoms and chiefdoms.[40]

Under such circumstances a single common heritage could not account for the many undoubted similarities between initiations and associations. These must be the result of later contacts among these groups. Such contacts are evident. By the nineteenth century a far-flung network of trade existed in southern Maniema, from the great lakes to the Lualaba and the Lomami, and also along the Lualaba, and west of that river, from the savannas in the south to Kisangani in the north. The Lualaba River was the main artery of the whole region. Fishermen were the carriers of trade and, although of the most heterogeneous origins, they spoke a common language and answered to the common ethnic name of Enya or Genya.[41] The products traded reflect the diversity of habitats in southern Maniema: palm products, salt, iron, raffia squares, pottery, fish, redwood powder, and livestock. Even rare quartz stones from far-away Ruwenzori found their way, some 350 km south, into the treasures of the *bwámi* association of the Lega people.[42] The peoples along the Lualaba used a common currency, the *viringi*, consisting of bits of shell in strings, for social and other payments. The Lega used the same currency, called *musanga* here, for social payments only. Remarkably, such strings have been found in graves from the ninth until the twelfth centuries at the Sanga necropole in Shaba. That probably indicates the importance of social payments in Shaba at that time, but not necessarily the existence there and then of sociopolitical associations.[43] Still, ultimately the currency of the Lualaba must be related to the strings of shells at Sanga.

Furthermore, the term "voluntary association" may have been used too loosely. Such associations include a great variety of rituals which are best grouped into two major categories: rites of the normal life cycle and rites giving access to special status in an overarching governing sociopolitical association. In this study the first category is labeled "brotherhood" and the second "association." Brotherhoods include rituals for all men, such as those of circumcision and for induction into mature manhood, as well as a set of initiations into curing and divination brotherhoods open only to the elect who had fallen ill with a particular disease. Once this distinction is made, it becomes evident that curing and divination brotherhoods were typical mainly of northern Maniema and that sociopolitical associations were usual in southern and western Maniema. Beyond these, one must not forget the existence of small states near the eastern boundary. A single history of origin and growth cannot accommodate this diversity.

The assumption made here, that tracing the history of "voluntary associations" in southern Maniema is the key to the dominant institutional history of the area, is also partly shared by its inhabitants. The past was told here in terms of migrations and genealogies but also, and this is unusual, in terms of who achieved what within the dominant association and of how its rites and titles changed over time.[44] Both associations and the emergence of segmentary patrilinearity are a valid focus for the historian here. On the other hand, in much of northern Maniema the collective memory was very short as a result of an unusually minuscule scale of society: on most issues memory does not reach beyond a century. Yet rituals of initiation and healing were so central in their lives and thoughts that undoubtedly they were also the major focus of their past social history.[45] Since brotherhoods and associations are a proper focus for the institutional historian and since the origins of these phenomena are multiple, one can now discuss them in turn.

A Rule of Wealth and Wisdom

The lands of southern Maniema were rich in trade and probably contained nodes of sizable population density. This allowed wealth to be accumulated and rendered possible the emergence of an overarching hierarchical sociopolitical association.[46] Such associations were institutionalized rites of initiation to titles, which could be acquired in a fixed order from the lowest title over different grades to the highest rank of the highest level. Initiation to each grade was based on a series of ever more expensive rituals. In most societies the only criteria required to have access to the whole hierarchy of main titles were previous circumcision, wealth, male gender, and, for the higher grades, that the man be married. A wife was to keep step with the ranks of her husband in a parallel series of female initiations. Only in a few societies, all on the eastern rim of the area, were some of the higher positions restricted by birth to certain members of particular senior lineage segments. The grades were organized into two blocks of lower and higher ranks. The division into aristocrats and plebeians was quite explicit everywhere along the Lualaba, but less so for people in the Lega and Bembe groups, although the blocks existed there also. Members of the high ranks were called *mokota* there, as were members of the aristocracy along a portion of the Lualaba.[47] The prizes of high rank were elevated status, fame, power and authority, quasi-immunity from legal pursuit, and wealth derived from entrance fees. The ideology stressed that the meaning of the association was to allow the meritorious to increase their moral qualities and wisdom as they became privy to deeper and deeper truths and secrets. In fact the higher the rank, the more the initiation process involved wider and wider descent and neighborhood groups, so that the achievement of really high rank showed proven collective support of large groups of people. Decisions made collectively by members of the highest grade amounted to government decrees. For the Bembe and Lega, *bwámi* was government.[48]

The cradle of the block of lower ranks in these associations can be found along the Lualaba, perhaps near the confluence of the Lowa River. The Lega of the southeast claim that the basic ranks within their *bwámi* association originate there, because the Lega themselves claim to have come from there, and one also finds two of the three other major titling systems that share many features with *bwámi* in that area.[49] Here and farther south into the savanna country, a simpler early form of association, including some three or four ranks, and a rich succession of rites may have existed for many centuries. It probably mostly affected people living in the villages that made up a district, reinforcing their sense of commonality.

But the block of high ranks in such associations, the ranks specifically tied to political control, linked to an upper class, and destined to guide political competition between big men into less destructive channels,[50] may not have emerged there simply as an elaboration of the existing associations. The idea of high rank and of social classes seems to have been imported from the grasslands in the south and specifically from the *eata* political system. Long before the end of the eighteenth century, the eastern Songye groups north of the great Lomami bend had been organized into a rather unusual political structure: an aristocratic republican state, existing along with their overarching secret association, *bukishi*. The population was divided into the classes of rulers and ruled. A president was elected by his peers among the leaders of five or so groups of aristocrats for a term of three to five years. Upon his election he paid valuable gifts to the other leaders. A strict division between aristocratic eligibles and plebeians was crucial to its functioning. The president went to live near a sacred grove, called *eata*,[51] until his time was up. He could never be reelected, although one of his sons could become the president. *Eata* is an original variant on the more common pattern of centralized states, where several branches of the royal dynasty rule in succession for a lifetime each. By a rough estimate, the institution already existed in the fifteenth or sixteenth century. A number of *eata* groves survive, and so the trees can be dated and may one day yield a more precise chronology. After 1820 *eata* was ousted in part of the area by a novel political system, characterized by the *luhuna* throne of Luban origin.[52]

Eata's influence on the associations of the Lualaba is easily traced through the formal division between aristocrats and commoners and by the tales attached to this division.[53] The division of ranks in the associations into blocks of upper and lower ranks confirms it. Among the Metoko west of the river one report even specifically mentioned that "chiefs" could be removed.[54] The extant data are sufficient to indicate that the practice of a ruling association spread from the Lowa area northward along the river and between Lualaba and Lomami, first to the *bufumu* associations north of present-day Kasongo, then to the *nsubi*, the *esambo*, and the *lokengo* associations farther down the Lualaba,[55] and then to the *mokota* of the Lengola and Mituku people farther north, where various elements from northern Maniema were integrated. The *nkúmí* association from the inner basin had spread here and was now integrated into this association, but we do not know which of the two types of associations arrived first in the area. On the whole it is likely that *mokota* was earlier, at least in its lower grades, which are similar in many and varying ways with the Lega *bwámi, nsubi, esambo,* and *lokengo.*[56] In all these areas, one effect of the spread of the association was to increase the geographic scale of cooperation and common coordination among adherents of the highest ranks beyond the ancient district. The recorded tradition of a "king" of the Lengola may be an echo of this. There clearly never was such a king, but the ideal of the supreme centralization existed.[57]

The association, carrying some Mituku features, spread all the way to the Mbole on the Zaire downstream from Kisangani. The governing institutions of the Mbole were then those which the ya- lancers had brought from the river. The association adapted to it and even took the name *lilwá,* after the earlier name for the circumcision rituals of the peoples along the banks of the Zaire from Kisangani to Basoko.[58] In the nineteenth century the *lilwá* association of the Mbole was still gaining ground in the upper Tshuapa basin. The age-grade movement, *inongo,* which began spreading along the lower Lomami and south of the middle Tshuapa basin westward by 1900, may well be an offshoot of it.[59]

East of the river oral traditions allow one to trace the diffusion of the higher grades. According to tradition, a particular subgroup of the Lega, the Babongolo, bought the right to initiate to the *kindi,* the basic rank in this block, from the neighboring Kaluba, a fishermen's group along the Lualaba near the present town of Kirundu. The Lega later called the new type of *bwámi* that resulted "*bwámi* of the hat," because its supreme emblem was a hat. The Babongolo then moved to the southwestern part of Lega country and the "*bwámi* of the hat" spread from here north and eastward to the high mountains, to the very edge of the great lakes area.[60] Dispersed settlement, allied to a political tradition of centralization based on a sacred kingship, had been practiced there for many centuries. The sacred king was called *mwámi,* an ancient term from which the Lega and Bembe expression *bwámi* derives.[61] In this region and specifically near the Itombwe Plateau and on the upper Lwindi River, the "*bwámi* of the hat" came into contact with the great lakes tradition of sacred kingship. This example led to the invention of a still higher grade in the association, but a grade that could be occupied only by a single member at a time, the *mwámi*. Moreover, this title became hereditary, and was restricted to the eldest son of the first wife. Positional succession was introduced. This means that the successor took over the name and supposedly the identity of his predecessor. Princes of the royal line formed an aristocracy, the Baluci, existing outside and parallel to the *bwámi* title system. The association became the framework for a state. This occurred among the Sile, probably in the seventeenth century. It is there that the association acquired the name *bwámi*, which then diffused west again toward the Lualaba. Neighbors of the Sile, the Nyindu, who had earlier been organized into a miniature kingdom, now also adopted the "*bwámi* of the hat" and developed a new form of it called "the *bwámi* of the shell," because the shell was the emblem of its highest rank.[62] This acquired so much prestige that the founders of various dynasties west and south of Lake Kivu claim the upper Lwindi as the place of their origin.[63] Traditions about the *bwámi* associations, as well as their titles and rituals, tell us that during the whole period up to the twentieth century the association remained quite dynamic. New levels within ranks, and rituals, emblems, and teachings continued to be developed in many places, spreading by marriage relationships and by purchase. As part of this dynamic, names and ritual elements from associations of northern Maniema thus also seeped into the *bwámi* from the north.[64]

The impact of *bwámi* on the social organizations of the Lega and Bembe and vice versa deserves further study. Their political organization in the nineteenth century included Houses led by a *mokota*, or *gúmi*, whose patriline formed the core of the House, village, and district, in which one recognizes the three units of western Bantu tradition. The position of district leader was always attributed either to the highest-ranking person in *bwámi* or to another high-ranking individual. A major early source claims that the district leaders were "great chiefs" (i.e., they ruled over substantial numbers of villages), that abdication was common, and that chiefs left their office to a brother or son. The social organization has been described in terms of descent ideology of segmentary patrilineages, but affinal relations were very important, and consequently an Omaha system of terminology was adopted. The role of marriages in establishing a vast network of alliances was exceptional. In turn this network supported a complex system of exchange of goods, which produced wealth. Moreover, at almost all levels, large groups of unrelated people were incorporated into the patrilineages, so that, *de facto*, one is dealing with a set of territorial entities in which authority was justified by the ideology of segmentary lineages.[65]

The usual view is that the *bwámi* association modeled itself on existing complex segmentary patrilineages which had always been there. But it may well have been the contrary: patrilineages developed as the *bwámi* association developed. The exceptional importance of affinal groups and the degree of actual collaboration between bilateral relatives in the area lead one to think that, at first, the ideology in the area was one of undifferentiated groups around big men, which functioned as matrimonial groups. The next most likely scenario is that the western Lega adopted the *nkúmi* (*gúmi*) ideology. Over time, exchange through matrimonial gift and trade increased, treasuries were established, and problems of marital alliance had to be solved. The adoption of Omaha kinship terminology followed. This was succeeded by the discovery of patrilinearity, which turned matrimonial groups into patrilineages. When *bwámi* appeared, it channeled competition among big men, but also fostered the desire by Houses to retain the positions that their leaders had achieved and, if possible, to enlarge their overall posture in *bwámi*. Patrilineages became more complex as a result. In the eastern Lega country, meanwhile, small centralized states of great lakes area vintage already were patrilineal. By the seventeenth century and later, the adoption of the block of high ranks in the west and the continuing development of more titles strongly stimulated the growth and extension of vast segmentary lineages. The development of *bwámi* thus interacted with a segmentary lineage ideology. As one grew, so did the other. Therefore the number of people incorporated into a single *bwámi* association, the spatial extent of a single association, and the complexity of segmentary lineages covaried. As a result of the historical dynamics outlined, all these numbers, territories, and complexities rose considerably from west to east by 1900.[66]

Ministates in the Mountains

On the western slopes all along the mountains bordering the uplands of Maniema in the area west of Lakes Kivu and Edward, the forests harbored tiny principalities ruled by a *mwámi*. In the nineteenth century, going from north to south, they belonged to Pere, Nyanga, Tembo, and Nyindu speakers. These languages belong to the great lakes group, with the possible exception of Pere, which is little known and supposedly related to northern Maniema languages.[67] They strike us as theater-like states, because their minuscule size was matched by elaborate rules for succession, accession to the throne, and royal burial, by a complex titulature surrounding the royal office, and by intricate royal rituals and a plethora of emblems, as if these district-sized kingdoms were the equals of the great kingdoms that lay beyond the rift itself. These societies are in part involuted reminiscences of what others farther east had been before large states appeared in the great lakes area, in part imitations of these kingdoms, and in part quite original elaborations. Divine kingship, a rainmaking ritual as the legitimation par excellence of the monarchy, a stress on divination, and patrilineal clans were all ultimately part of the old great lakes heritage, although some details associated with them may, in fact, be relatively recent borrowings from farther east.[68]

These peoples are of interest here because of their own innovations and because of the influence they exercised to their west. The diffusion of the titles *mwámi* and *mukama* in northern Maniema are a proof of their prestige. The Nyanga had invented many different associations and brotherhoods (*mpa*) and their own details for the circumcision rituals for boys. At present there are only a few notes concerning their main hierarchical association, *mbuntsu*, and about the *mumbira* brotherhood for healing, despite the fact that almost every Nyanga House had its own association. All of these had grown out of their circumcision rituals, *mukumo*. Such inventions spread, and aspects of Nyanga ritual are found everywhere between their homeland and the lower Lindi.[69] Thus *mbuntsu* became a healing brotherhood in northern Maniema, and was integrated as a ritual in the *bwámi* farther south. The term *mumbira* is related to *mambela*, the Bali initiation for boys, and also appears as a technical term in the circumcision rituals of their neighbors, the Komo of northern Maniema. The Komo also claim that two of the styles of ninteenth-century circumcision rituals, the *gandjá ámondaa* and the *dokpo*, successively originated from their area bordering the Nyanga. However, despite the plethora of brotherhoods found among the Nyanga, the overall structure and dynamics of their rituals of healing are shared by all the peoples of northern Maniema. The Nyanga received as much as they gave, and their innovations form part of an area of continuous ritual innovation extending over the whole of northern Maniema.[70] And yet, at the same time, the Nyanga and related populations high in the mountains were firmly rooted in the foreign cultural world of the great lakes.

Brotherhoods in Northern Maniema

The social organization of the peoples of northern Maniema before 1870 differed significantly from that of peoples farther south. Indeed the structural pattern of their societies diverged more from the proto–western Bantu system than those of any other part of equatorial Africa. Their societies were more fragmented into tiny autonomous groups than anywhere else. This situation probably resulted from an early southern central Sudanic influence which so strongly marks the languages of the area. It had not always been so; the languages retain traces of a former participation in the House-village-district system of the inner basin.[71] Distributed very sparsely over the land, much more mobile, and much less involved in trade than others, by 1880 they were divided into a myriad of landholding Houses, each in its small village,[72] grouped in clusters and separated from each other by empty forests. The most striking feature of these societies then was their atomization. Each House was thought of as consisting of men descended from a common ancestor five generations before, all on equal footing, except for their relative age-statuses, as child, circumcised man, father, and, perhaps by then, father of a child of each sex. Here as among the fragmented Mamvu and others of the northeast, sister exchange was the expected form of marriage. Multiple marriages between the same Houses and the same set of "brothers and sisters" were favored, so that polygyny was possible. But still marriage was not used to build up alliances between Houses lasting for more than a generation or at most two. The rules of exogamy favored the maximum diversification of marriage alliances possible.[73] Because of these rules, however, big men could not easily contract multiple marriages to attract clients and build up power, and dependent statuses, such as clients, adopted persons, protected people, and serfs, did not exist in northern Maniema proper.[74]

Each House was perceived to be a part of a small cluster of segments belonging to one of the 80-odd clans, named after totemic animals or objects. Membership was inherited in the patrilineal line, through the acceptance of the clan's name, its totemic food interdiction, and related myth. Segments recognized others as belonging to their clan, because of their common totemic allegiance. But as a result of high mobility, especially in northern Maniema proper, such segments of the same clan could be found hundreds of kilometers from each other, and common clanship did not create a community larger than the House.[75]

The relationship between a physical reality with a structure of separate unrelated Houses and a cognitive reality based on the principle of patrilinearity makes little sense. Certainly gender distinctions were important and rooted in the physical reality of different occupations and careers, as well as in the cognitive reality of terminology. But gender and unilinearity are not coterminous. Patrilinearity did not seem to have any practical applications or impact, and that is puzzling. Why and since when was patrilinearity for descent practiced in these societies, even if only as a principle of clanship? Neither pressures to defend successions nor inheritance seems to have been involved. Functionally the ideology seems irrelevant. Was the patrilineal ideology of very recent vintage, did it date from the Zanzibari occupation of the 1880s when marriage with matrimonial compensation first became important, was it imposed by the colonial administration, or was it older? One suspects that it was recent, if only because the collective memory of these societies in these matters does not go beyond Zanzibari times, but the enigma remains.

Of all the nineteenth-century societies in the forest, these were the most egalitarian and the least differentiated socially. They lived in some of the least densely populated tracts of the whole area of study, where each House held huge stretches of forest as hunting territory. They were among the most mobile peoples in the rainforests, and their particularism was extreme. This held true especially for the populations south of the Ituri River, where hunting was the predominant activity and where the specialized hunter gatherers had been either driven out or absorbed. Near the Ituri River and northward, agriculture predominated, hunter gatherers provided products from the forest, and each of their groups stood in a dependent relation to a House of farmers. But even there mobility and local autonomy remained remarkably high.[76]

One may well wonder then, if, apart from clans and marriage alliances, these people had any institutions in common and whether the common cultures and languages maintained themselves merely by the great mobility of the Houses and the extreme dispersal of marriage alliances. It is in this context that the other outstanding feature of these cultures and peoples stands out: the presence of brotherhoods based on rituals of healing. These are the *esomba* rituals.[77] When someone fell ill, the diviner *aba nkunda* determined the nature of the illness. He attributed it to the presence of a noxious charm, which he found and destroyed. If the patient did not then recover, the illness was attributed either to a slighted ancestor or to *esomba*. The latter frequently happened. In that case the patient had to be initiated into the brotherhood appropriate to the disease, and into which all those who had been afflicted by this disease had been inducted. In the cognitive reality of these people, disease was always thought to be caused by collective action, and hence the treatment had to be collective as well. But it sometimes happened that the cognitive reality of disease and its physical reality were not congruent: the induction into the relevant brotherhood did not efficiently cure the stricken person. Hence, and because the cure had to be collective, a new healing ritual and a new brotherhood were then required. This explains the high frequency with which new ritual initiations replaced older treatments. The people in the area perceived these healing rites as rituals of initiation into a new status, that of a person who had the experience of a stated disease. These healing brotherhoods have been the inspiration and the source of the *úmbá* rituals of induction into mature manhood, which sprang up after Zanzibari domination had forced great changes in settlement patterns and leadership in the area. According to de Mahieu, they have also been the inspiration for the rituals accompanying circumcision which initiated boys into manhood. For him the rituals of healing and their brotherhoods were then the oldest pattern of ritual in the area. Yet each particular brotherhood was probably relatively new, given the dynamics of the replacement of older inefficient cults by presumably more efficient new cults. The dynamics involved are well documented by the succession of religious movements in colonial times.[78] Their activity in precolonial times is traced by the presence of common terminologies and associated ritual sequences often over the whole of northern Maniema and even beyond in southern Maniema and in the lands between the Lomami and the Lualaba.[79] This is most evident in the realm of circumcision rituals (see map 6.4). The practice of circumcision is undoubtedly old and, as the term *gandjá* indicates, may have been brought into the area by the first immigrant western Bantu farmers.[80] The structure of many of the associated rituals also shows numerous common features, from the mountain slopes to the Lomami and even beyond the lower Itimbiri, although these are probably only a few centuries old. There were fashions in ritual sequences as the terminologies show. Thus the *mambela* style, associated with the concept of an initiation bird, may have spread from the mountain rims to the lower Lindi. *Alútú* was a mid-nineteenth-century style, now still stretching from near Kisangani to near Lake Mobutu, but ousted over the rest of the area by a new *kentende* style, which spread from the savannas south of Maniema and perhaps even from Shaba.[81] By 1900 the *Lilwá* style was still common from the confluence of the Itimbiri to the lower Lindi, where it had been dominant since at least the eighteenth century.[82] The terminologies and what data exist about the rituals themselves reveal a continuous flux of innovation and borrowing over the whole of Maniema.

Each of these brotherhoods was comprised of ordinary members and the initiators, the masters of the rituals. The latter transcended individual villages to form a brotherhood. In the colonial era they were the true leaders in the societies of northern Maniema and were designated by the name *moáme*. In the middle of the nineteenth century such masters included the initiators of diviners into a special brotherhood; the leaders of each type of healing ritual; and the *mena gandjá*, the leaders of the rituals of circumcision—all of whom were initiated into their leadership roles by their peers.[83]

The brotherhoods constituted the larger framework for social and cultural interaction and played a crucial role of integration between the myriad small communities in northern Maniema. But this role did not consist of action by their leaders to mediate disputes, settle wars, or coordinate common activities by promulgating norms or laws. The brotherhoods did not act as common government. Rather, they were all-important, because they continuously created cognitive, social, and cultural realities. Thus, in the colonial period, the complexes of rituals of circumcision and induction into mature manhood created the notions of and gave meaning to the different age grades that then structured expectation, behavior, and personal aspiration in each village. These statuses were fully active only during the ritual performances themselves. Hence the internal articulation of society required frequent rituals to thrive.[84] Undoubtedly this was also the case in earlier times. Yet brotherhoods

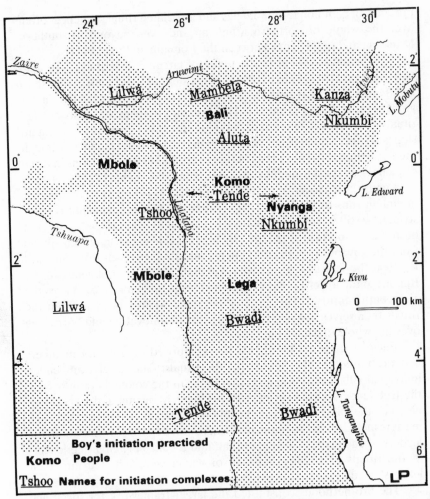

Map 6.4.　Circumcision rituals in Maniema

varied by the rank of their leaders. In the nineteenth century the holders of the circumcision and of the divining rituals had the most prestige and exercised the most influence in northern Maniema. But even while cognitively they created and maintained society, they did not rule.

Because healing and circumcision brotherhoods are found all over Maniema, and because circumcision as a practice seems to have reached the region with the farmers from the northwest, it is tempting to set up a sequence that starts with the circumcision rituals and places them at the arrival of the first settlers in northern Maniema. A brotherhood of initiators developed out of those rituals. Then rituals for the initiation of diviners followed this pattern. Next healing came to be understood as the practice of a new initiation, and the rituals were patterned after those of initiation. Finally the practice of continuing to initiate the initiators of the previous level led to˙ the appearance of several levels of initiation and the first form of *bwámi* on the Lualaba.

It is a logical, tempting, and even possible scenario. Yet there are . objections. First, there is no evidence at all about early circumcision rituals, if indeed circumcision was accompanied by much ritual in early times. Second, this view totally overlooks the fit between the circumcision and *esomba* rituals on the one hand and the general social profile of extreme decentralization in northern Maniema on the other. It is quite likely that the brotherhoods arose after the peoples in these lands had become thoroughly decentralized. That was itself the probable result of contact with the tradition of southern central Sudanic speakers. Once invented as therapy management, the rituals would then have flourished to maintain the sense of a wider society through their performances. Third, the *bwámi* type of association could just as well have adopted the rituals of healing brotherhoods after its own development had occurred, because they unified and enriched the overarching association itself. There can be little doubt that this has been the case in recent centuries.[85] It follows from such objections that one cannot simply conclude a historical sequence from a logical one.

The historical sequence is undoubtedly much more complex. Only the patient study of the details of ritual performances and their terminology in the whole area will allow the accurate seriation of influences and innovations and give access to a historical sequence. Meanwhile one must accept that the social history of northern Maniema cannot be reconstructed today beyond the middle of the nineteenth century. One knows only that, at some time after the first farmers settled there, their original heritage was transformed into a new society characterized by the most extreme egalitarian and decentralized way of life found in equatorial Africa. Later, but well before the nineteenth century, *esomba,* the brotherhoods of healing rituals, were invented and became the cultural hallmark of the region.

DYNAMICS OF TRADITION

The last three chapters have described how widely differing societies arose out of the single ancestral tradition by major transformations: a summary of some of the societies that came to differ most from the original one ranges from two kinds of segmentary lineage societies (northern inner basin and Sanaga-Ntem), to four kinds of associations (Ngounié, *nkúmú,* southern Maniema, and *esomba*), to five kinds of chiefdoms or kingdoms (*nkúmú*, Bioko, southwestern kingdoms, Bomokandi-Nepoko, and eastern Lega). In no case were there even approximately identical paths of transformation from the common ancestral tradition to the resulting society, even in situations where the same kind of society resulted. This is an impressive testimony to the inherent dynamic potential of the original tradition. The diversity of outcomes is equally remarkable. For instance: the Mangbetu kingdom grew out of a House; the Sile kingdom out of a hierarchy of associations; the Bolia, Kuba, and Ngwi kingdoms out of an uneven concentration of resources between Houses, accompanied by an ideological exaltation of the big man and some conquests; the Kongo and Tio kingdoms out of a persistent, slow process of centralization. In northern Maniema brotherhoods were multiple, an expression of extreme decentralization, and in southern Maniema a single, overarching, and ultimately centralizing association governed. Such results make it evident that one cannot predict the "evolution" of social institutions.

Internal innovations were the rule in the western two-thirds of the area. There transformations of the equatorial Bantu tradition occurred virtually within a closed system. Apart from minor seepage,[86] this area was practically insulated from outside influences. But that is not true for the peoples discussed in this chapter. External influences played a leading role in the northeastern quarter, as most of the Bantu speakers there adopted the basic institutions of an early southern central Sudanic tradition. But even there very different effects sometimes resulted. The same ancestral southern central Sudanic tradition, based on the House only, was the root both of the Mangbetu kingdom and of the diametrically opposed particularistic *esomba* system in northern Maniema. In southern Maniema interchange between peoples in the forests and their neighbors in the savannas and woodlands of southeastern Zaire remained lively, apparently ever since they first colonized the forests. Still, the people of the forests did not simply copy the ruling institutions from their neighbors: they were only inspired by them. The same holds true for contacts with peoples in the great lakes area. Their traditions of kingship did not affect the peoples of northern Maniema or Ituri in depth. The examples of the Sile and Nyindu kingdoms are impressive: the first belongs to the equatorial Bantu tradition, the second to the great lakes tradition. In the first, kingship was grafted onto a *bwámi* association as its last rung; in the second, *bwámi* was grafted onto a monarchy as an ideology and a title system. Or compare both with Nyanga chiefdoms, where the royal institutions were of the great lakes but the brotherhoods of northern Maniema. So although it is a truism to say that, in a situation of internal sovereignty, internal dynamics always remain determining because they decide which outside traditions are to inspire which innovations and how, still the amazing range of choices available to the carriers of a tradition is often underrated.

The diversity of the resulting kinds of societies may well lead some readers to wonder whether, in recent centuries, the equatorial tradition was still molding the societies that had developed from it. The answer is emphatically yes. The main terms of cognitive reality were still quite similar, and a good deal of the ancestral vocabulary remained to show it. Even in the realm of social institutions, the role of big men—often more institutionalized than it had been earlier, but with the same basic ideology of supernatural luck—continued to coexist with the egalitarian ideals implied in beliefs in witchcraft, even if in extreme cases they took on the coloring of sacred kingship. For instance, everywhere in the area ceremonies and rules for the disposition of the spoils of the leopard remained crucial, and everywhere leopard, python, and eagle remained the signs of authority. In most cases Houses, villages, and districts all survived, even though the relative weight of each with regard to the others shifted from society to society. In some cases Houses absorbed the village, as happened in the middle Bomokandi area, among the Saa peoples of Cameroon, among some of the Sanaga-Ntem peoples, and in northern Maniema. In a few cases, such as in southern Gabon and among the Ngombe, the village became the strongest unit. In the cases where chiefdoms, principalities, or kingdoms resulted, the district became the strongest unit, but usually in conjunction with a House. Many of the differences between the resulting societies, however, stemmed from the invention of new institutions which built on, rather than eliminated, the older basic groups.

Unique and unpredictable as the results of the transformations from the single ancestral societies have been, still the dynamics involved had much in common. The ancestral system was stable only as long as the different competing districts were in equilibrium with each other, and as long as different competing big men were about equally strong. As soon as that balance was broken by an innovation, diffusion of the innovation or a counterinnovation followed in a continuing attempt to restore stability.

The ancestral system had been well adapted to low densities of population and limited trade. When these conditions changed, innovation had to follow. The first case concerned the introduction of new resources such as the cultivation of bananas and the acquisition of metallurgy. Once adopted by all, these no longer disturbed the equilibrium, but during their introduction they undoubtedly did. Hunters and gathers did not adopt them and consequently became dependent on villagers. Second, there is the case of unequal access to resources. Societies across major ecotones had a greater diversity of resources than others. It was possible in such circumstances for the population density to grow faster, bringing with it a higher frequency of conflicts and leading to efforts to strengthen cooperation, especially within the district. Once trading exchanges became frequent in areas across ecotones with very different resource bases or over longer distances, using the waterways with their potential for cheap transport, certain localities became strategic spots for settlement. The Houses and villages which occupied them grew rich, attracting dependents and at the same time facing more challenges than others. This led to innovation. Then there is the invention of a new meaning for existing resources, a shift in cognitive reality. Once it became a practice to designate certain goods as fit for social payments, especially bridewealth, and the only goods that would do for such payments, the House developed a patrimony and with it the potential for greater longevity. Over time systematic inequality developed among Houses and their big men and led to innovation. The changing environmental and economic base clearly was crucial for the dynamics of innovation.

It would be dangerous, however, to reduce the dynamics of innovation to an environmental determinism of the sort that claims that kingdoms arose only in open landscapes with diversified resources, never in the forests. Chiefdoms and kingdoms did arise in landscapes such as the confluence of the Lomami and the Zaire, the confluence of the Aruwimi and the Zaire, and north of Lake Mai Ndombe; centralizing, overarching associations also arose in the rainforests of the Lualaba, *north* of the limit of the open grasslands. The only defensible generalization is that centralizing societies began in areas of rich resources. Even so, not all areas with rich resources provoked centralization. For one should never forget that the habitats of equatorial Africa—especially in its rainforests—were very diverse, and hence multiple ecotones were common. The correlation between centralizing innovations and areas rich in resources is only apparent and superficial. It takes no account of the fact that resources exist only in the eye of the beholder. Culture thus becomes crucial here, both as knowledge and technique and as a value system. Nothing dictates a priori that metal rings, anvils, or spears are to be good for social payments and matrimonial compensation, and hence that access to rich sources of metal would be a major asset beyond the availability of tools and weaponry. Environmental determinism also overlooks the importance of systems of exchange by which rich resources can be available far from the place where the raw materials are found. In the nineteenth century Basoko was a major center of metallurgy, even though it was hundreds of kilometers away from good iron ore.

Innovations responded to shifts in environmental bases and economics, but the latter do not wholly explain the phenomenon. Historical accident was important. A particularly attractive or effective personality, luck in trade or in war, a new tactic in battle, a particular incident during a ritual—all could happen by accident and provoke change. Yet although incidents in physical reality occurred all the time—the weather is never twice the same—innovation took root only when it moved from the physical realm to conscious acceptance in the cognitive realm. Hence not all historical accidents or physical change brought transformation. Usually, however, a physical change did last long enough to impress itself on cognitive reality. This holds true even for personalities. King Moka of Bioko ruled for half a century and his innovations became custom in his lifetime. As the physical norm changed, cognitive reality became conscious of this and accepted it. Once Omaha or Crow kinship terminology was adopted, for instance, and introduced a practical classification of kin in unilineal groups, the transition to unilinearity depended on the cognitive recognition of that fact. When that happened, a major transformation had taken place. To give another example, certain goods began to be appreciated more and more in particular marriage transitions, well before cognitive recognition of this took place. Once recognition occurred, however, a major transformation followed in matrimonial exchange and ultimately in the management and the structuring of the House.

Given the crucial role of cognitive reality, it follows that new ideas conceivably could precede and lead to a change in practice. In the absence of the relevant data this is particularly hard to prove, but lack of data should not blind us to the possibility that it happened. Indeed one suspects that, in the elaboration of ideologies and in ritual especially, new ideas and values enacted in performance may well have created new statuses and roles and stimulated change. The *esomba* brotherhoods testify to that.

The discussion of the dynamics of innovation so far still remains somewhat surrealistic, in that it treats innovation as discrete, as if it began at point A and terminated at point B. In reality innovations formed chains of change. New disparities constantly appeared between the physical and the conceptual reality, and the gap had to be closed by altering the accepted conceptual reality, which in turn provoked new changes in physical reality. It has been seen that this is precisely the dynamic behind the never-ending stream of new *esomba* rituals. Therefore the debate between materialists and idealists as to the priority of physical or conceptual reality makes little sense, because change is perpetual, forever yoked to continuity. During this process of innovation all the principles and the fundamental options inherited from the ancestral tradition remained a gyroscope in the voyage through time: they determined what was perceivable and imaginable as change.

The next chapter introduces a new element into the situation: an irruption from distant shores. The previous chapters told how the ancestral tradition of equatorial Africa was transformed and yet how, except in the northeast, the many societies that resulted still remained within its common ambit. But by 1500 the isolation of the area was shattered. The Atlantic trade issued a major challenge to the dominant tradition, precisely where it had hitherto been least affected by outside influences. The next chapter deals with its impact on the dynamics of the equatorial tradition. Would institutional change continue to be contained within the scope of the one common ancestral tradition, or would societies and cultures now emerge that departed from the foundations of the ancient tradition?

Seven

Challenge from the Atlantic

Portuguese caravels cleaving the waters between Bioko—the island they named Fernando Poo in 1472—and the mouth of the Zaire in 1483 were the first harbingers of a new era, heralding the emergence of a European world-economy in the lands of the Atlantic. From then right up until the conquest of central Africa, a growing portion of equatorial Africa was continually challenged by European commercial initiatives in the Atlantic. When Stanley descended the Zaire River in 1877, almost two-thirds of equatorial Africa had fallen into the orbit of the Atlantic trading system, and precisely the two-thirds that had hitherto been the most sheltered.

In the previous chapters the dynamics of changing social formations within the framework of the equatorial tradition have been told. It has also been repeatedly stressed that the impulse for political change must have stemmed in a large part from economic change, especially from changing patterns of trade. The appearance of a new trading system was not bound at first to affect the internal dynamics of the tradition very much, because regional trade had existed before. But the Atlantic trade soon outstripped the volume of transactions that had hitherto been common, even on the busiest arteries of local trade. One can judge the importance of this fact by remembering that the onset of the industrial revolution in Europe is measured by the sudden spurt in the volume of goods produced. Even if the growth of volume was less precipitous in equatorial Africa, still the Atlantic trade was a spur, equivalent to the industrial revolution. Its effects must have been equally impressive. However, unlike the industrial revolution, which was home-grown, the Atlantic trade was accompanied by foreign values, attitudes, and ideas. It therefore posed even more of a challenge to the old ways than the industrial revolution did in Europe.

Given this situation, did the ancestral tradition survive at all, and if so, at what cost? Was it predominantly the internal dynamics inherent in the tradition that continued to shape the changing societies and cultures? Or were the outside forces now unleashed so powerful, was the loss of local initiative so great, that they eliminated the internal dynamics? To answer these questions this chapter focuses on major institutional transformations and their main economic causes only, in line with the focus of the whole study so far. Thus the rich historical detail that now becomes available must be left aside, firmly albeit reluctantly.[1] Nor does the chapter focus, therefore, on the Atlantic trade as a system, but only on its impact in equatorial Africa.[2] Still, in order to understand the social and political history of the various societies involved, it is useful first to sketch the appearance and development of the trading system over space and time, as well as its major economic and demographic impacts. This brings with it the risk of making it appear as if all that happened for four centuries was but a passive "local" reaction to an expanding world system. That definitely was not so. Yet it is easier to grasp the sociopolitical evolution once the underlying general economic conditions are known. Indeed in previous chapters this pattern of exposition often has been followed for the same reason.

THE ATLANTIC TRADING SYSTEM IN EQUATORIAL AFRICA

The history of the Atlantic trade falls into three main phases between its inception just before 1500 and the conquest of equatorial Africa by European powers (see map 7.1). The formative phase, lasting from c. 1500 to c. 1660, saw the development of a system which came to rely for the most part on the export of slaves. Its main achievements were, first, to find which goods were so attractive to Africans that they were willing to export slaves in return for them and, second, to develop a mechanism that bridged the chasm between a European market economy, based on the value of precious metals, and equatorial economies, based on the use of currencies unrelated to precious metals. The second phase, from c. 1660 to c. 1830, was the heyday of the slave trade. The basic conditions and mechanisms for trading had been provided by then, and a continuous rise in the volume of trade was now possible. In consequence, the major demographic, economic, and social impacts of the system on the area occurred during the eighteenth century. After c. 1830 a major shift in the system took place. As a result of the industrial revolution, another huge rise occurred in the volume of trade, especially of imports, but now the first place in exports shifted from slaves to ivory and an assortment of raw materials for the factories in Europe.

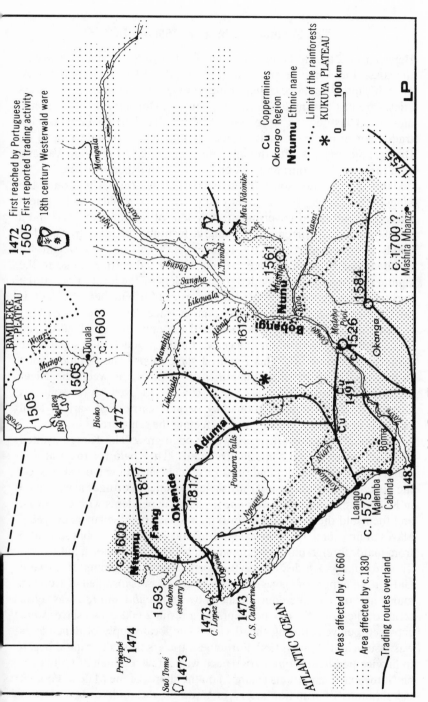

Map 7.1. The Atlantic trade before 1830

The Formative Phase: c. 1500–c. 1660

Between 1472 and 1483 the Portuguese tested various points of entry on the coast, but found no place north of the Zaire River where the prospects for more than occasional trade were good. The local coastal societies were just too small in terms of people and territory; their economic and social institutions were too undifferentiated to facilitate foreign trade. For example, no slave trade or other trade ever developed on Bioko, and contacts with the inhabitants near Cape Fernando Vaz and with those of the Wouri and Gabon estuaries remained sporadic.

But in 1483, just south of the estuary of the Zaire, they found the kingdom of Kongo, which could easily sustain systematic trade. There existed a centralized government, a system of rotating markets, and a standard national currency, the *nzimbu*. Institutions for the transport of goods overland were also well developed. Volume and weight for headloads had long since been standardized, and carriers to go to the capital of Kongo were provided to the traders by the local prince at the harbor. Caravans were modeled after parties of tribute bearers. All this facilitated contact and a relatively regular trade developed after 1491.[3]

In 1486 the Portuguese also settled the uninhabited island of Saō Tomé, intending to turn it into a center for the production of sugar, then a precious commodity. This required slave labor. The islanders soon turned to slaving in small quantities from points between the Niger Delta in the north and the Loango coast, and even as far south as Luanda Bay. But equally soon they became carriers of various local products in a modest coastal trade affecting the same area.[4]

From c. 1500 onward trade with Kongo grew. The Kongo wanted technical advisors and some luxury goods. They paid for them at first mainly in copper bangles and prestige objects, including ivory. But soon the Portuguese would accept only slaves. Resident Portuguese were paid in Kongo's shell currency (*nzimbu*), bought dependents with their fees, and then sold them to their countrymen for Portuguese currency (*reis*). Slaves at first came from the sale of such local dependents, but soon also from major foreign military campaigns (1514) and from local kidnaping. This provoked such disorder that, shortly after 1520, ground rules were laid for the export of slaves, a royal supervisor was installed at Kongo's major harbor, and the equivalence between *nzimbu* and *reis* was set in terms of the price for a dependent. As a result 2,000–3,000 slaves were exported per year during this decade. The local supply of dependents was insufficient, however, so Portuguese traders from the capital began to finance peddlers (*pombeiros*), each with a few retainers, to buy people at the existing markets (*pumbo*) on the shores of the Malebo Pool, at the terminus of a major artery of trade up the middle Zaire River. Hitherto a trade in slaves had not existed at the Malebo Pool. Proof of this lies in the fact that commercial slaves are still designated in Tio and other languages of the area as "person of *nzimbu*," "person acquired with Kongo shell money." But the insistent demand of *pombeiros* for slaves and the local thirst for European prestige goods led traders there to sell their dependents.[5] Thus it came to pass that it was the inner basin area, not the coastal lands of equatorial Africa, which were first and most deeply affected by the slave trade. By 1525 the system already included not only a port of entry but also caravan routes and relays, both at the capital and at the Malebo Pool.

Volume grew apace between the 1520s and the later 1560s to over 7,000 slaves per year, and most slaves were now exported to the Americas. A trade boycott initiated by the Kongo (1561) followed by a war with the Tio kings (1567), probably for control of the lucrative markets at the Malebo Pool, then disturbed the flow of trade. There followed the notorious Jaga invasion (1568), which almost destroyed the kingdom, flooded the coast with slaves, and was repelled by 1576 only because a Portuguese army assisted the king of Kongo. This was the first instance of an inland people attempting to gain wealth by cutting out middlemen along the trade routes.

Trade then began anew, but now the harbor of Kongo was no longer the main or even a major point of entry. It was eclipsed by Luanda. The Portuguese had used the confusion of the Jaga war to settle there on Kongo land and lay claim to a colony, Angola, in its hinterland. Luanda now became the hub of the slave trade, attracting slaves even from the Malebo Pool and from a new relay, Okango on the lower Kwango, at the head of a route going toward the lower middle Kwilu. The individual *pombeiro* peddler parties of yore had now become regular caravans when several *pombeiro* parties joined forces, mainly for safety against robbers. The larger parties, however, were still financed by the patrons of each of the participants, not by any single person.[6]

The next shift in the system came with the rise of the port of Loango, which because it was the capital of a kingdom had an extensive hinterland from the start. As in Kongo there were markets, and a general currency consisting of squares of raffia cloth was in use. The inhabitants had imported iron and copper from the region beyond Mayombe, probably ever since the town was established. To do this they used to travel in parties to the mining areas during the dry season and exploit the ore themselves. In this fashion an incipient caravan system had already taken shape before any Europeans arrived. As a result Europeans never became involved themselves with the inland trade from the Loango coast.[7]

The city of Loango had developed first as a major point in the coastal trade in the days of the Jaga invasion. It soon rose to a certain importance as an exporter of raffia cloth, which was then used as currency in Luanda. Only a few slaves were exported then. The city became a major point of entry for the Atlantic trade with the arrival of the Dutch (1593). The Dutch made it their main base, with secondary points of contact all along the coast from Rio del Rey to the Congo estuary. They bought ivory and redwood, not slaves. The slave trade took hold so slowly here that all the harbors on this coast combined exported only 300 slaves per year between 1630 and 1650, a figure that reached only about 1,000 by 1660. Still, the Dutch presence provided competition, and imports at Loango became of better quality and were less expensive than they were south of the estuary of the Zaire River.[8]

Spurred on by the Dutch trade, the caravan system became more organized and caravans roamed farther abroad. Traders agreed to travel together under the command of a common leader, who was not only an experienced guide but had also established formal relations of alliance with trading partners in various settlements along the major routes in the interior. Such trading friends were often related by marriage or by bloodbrotherhood. Caravaneers were called Vili, a name that soon was to be used as an ethnic name for all the people from the coastal provinces of the Loango kingdom. At the same time Loango's hinterland rapidly grew. It extended deep into southern Gabon (the source of ivory and redwood), toward the lands of the upper Ogooué (at first probably for ivory), and reached the Malebo Pool (for raffia cloth along the road and slaves at the pool). Because the Dutch sold guns and because their other commodities were lower in price and of higher quality than those of their Portuguese competitors, Vili traders soon penetrated the markets south of the Zaire River, traveling far into the savannas, even to the markets of the middle Kwango and the Cuanza in the very backyard of Luanda.[9]

Meanwhile the markets at the Malebo Pool remained major suppliers of slaves to the Luanda network and of ivory to the Loango network. These people and commodities were brought there by canoe from upstream. At first the traders were only fishermen who traded part-time, as had been their wont long before 1500. But under the growing impetus of the Atlantic trade some, such as the people later called Nunu, became professional carriers, and the routes stretched continually farther upstream of the Malebo Pool. The trade reached the environs of Lake Mai Ndombe even before the Jaga invasion and the wide stretch of river near the confluence of the Alima River before 1612.[10]

During this formative period the internal dynamics of the emerging slave-trading system already were becoming evident. Basically the system altered over time with the volume and character of imports accepted by the African customers and with the volume of the European demand for slaves. The slaves were to be sold in the Americas, and the demand for them depended on the need for labor there. European goods were first in demand as exotic luxury items, which African leaders used as instruments to increase their prestige, attract more clients and dependents, and hence increase their power. The demand for such imports was self-sustaining. These imported instruments of power upset the balance of regional power to a greater or lesser degree, so that leaders farther away from the coast also sought them to right the balance of power again. Among them textiles and guns were especially important.[11] The imported goods themselves thus exerted a pressure to expand the area affected by trade right from the start. Later, as the volume of imports rose, once-rare commodities became common and they lost their prestige value. But in the case of guns and gunpowder, their military and hence political value remained; in the case of textiles and some other objects, demand now came from lower strata of society imitating their betters of yesterday.

The area affected by the trade expanded in direct relation to the demand for slaves, who had to be procured from farther and farther away. The demand for imports—especially textiles, guns, and copper items—can be held to have been insatiable and hence was always responsive. The volume of the slave trade is therefore a good indicator of the whole system. That is true during periods of expansion, but during periods of falling demand there was no contraction of the area affected. The expansion of the trading area led to permanent change. The need of leaders for European imports as instruments of power accounts for this only in part. Permanent change resulted mainly from the fact that once commercial routes and relays had developed, they could also carry other goods for trade within the area itself. This is especially true for waterborne trade, where unused capacity on trips downriver allowed carriers to transport such other goods at virtually no extra cost.

The forward edge of the expanding trading area was usually a turbulent zone. In the early years slaves were kidnaped right near the coast. By the 1520s the practice was abandoned because the turmoil this caused hampered orderly trade and actually prevented growth. The edge of the area lay beyond the Malebo Pool by 1568, when the Jaga invasion produced the first of many incidents in which people who were out of reach of the orderly trading area attempted to overrun a relay to profit from the trade. So far no certain early cases are known of either slave-raiding or migration away from the forward edge of the trading area, although this occurred in the eighteenth century and was common in the nineteenth century. As soon as the front of the trading area moved forward, the turbulence moved with it: defined nodes or relays of commerce appeared in the former borderlands, stable zones of supply emerged, and well-defined routes developed. The region was absorbed into the lands of orderly trade.

The Heyday of the Slave Trade: c. 1660–c. 1830

The period of the most massive slave trade was heralded by the break-up of the Kongo kingdom after the battle of Ambwila (1665), which led to a total reorganization of the area and left the harbors of the Loango coast in a dominant position. French and English slave traders arrived soon thereafter, and the Dutch also turned to intensive slave trading. Between 1660 and 1793 the volume of slave exports kept soaring while the price per slave rose as the result of both absolute demand for slaves and competition. A first peak was reached on the Loango coast in 1685–1705 with an average of 6,000 slaves exported per year. It implies a strong advance of the leading edge of the area. The annual figure then dropped to 2,000 in the next decade, steadily climbed until it reached 5,000 by midcentury, and then soared to its absolute peak between 1755 and 1793 with an annual average of 13,500 slaves per year or over half a million in less than 40 years.[12] The system had then achieved its greatest extent, except for southern Cameroon (see map 7.1). On the Loango coast the European traders exploited the competition between the three main harbors there: Loango, Malemba, and Cabinda, each the capital of its own kingdom. Yet they were not able to stop the continual rise in prices for slaves. Over the period dominance in the trade shifted southward from Loango to Malemba, then to Cabinda, and after 1800 to Boma, well inside the Zaire Estuary. The number of secondary points of entry for the slave trade also increased. Thus, in the eighteenth century, slave trading came to the Gabon Estuary, which was a small importer of slaves in the seventeenth century, and to the Wouri Estuary, where a relatively important slave trade flourished especially after 1750. In the eighteenth century some slaves were also bought at Cape Lopez.[13] By the end of the period the trading area encompassed all of equatorial Africa south of a front running from the Ogooué Valley to Poubara Falls, the lower Mambili basin, the lower Ubangi, and the Mongala basin approximately as far as 22° east. North of the Ogooué, a network centered on Douala used the Mungo, Wouri, Dibamba, and lower Sanaga rivers as trade routes and tapped populations as far as the Bamileke Plateau.[14]

From 1660 to 1793 almost a million slaves were exported from the Loango coast. A substantial drop in exports after 1793, first caused by the Napoleonic wars and then by the formal abolition of the slave trade by Great Britain in 1807, did not have major effects beyond the fortunes of the coastal harbors, because Brazilian and some Spanish-Cuban traders moved in to take the places of the British and the French. By 1810 the slave trade was flourishing again; another 275,000 slaves were to be shipped from the Loango coast by Portuguese, Spanish, and American traders before 1835.[15]

By the end of the seventeenth century a series of institutions tied to the slave trade had been perfected. A mechanism for setting prices had developed at the ports of the Loango coast. The operation occurred in two phases. On the arrival of a ship an overall price was set in terms of a standard of value: the ideal slave or the ideal ivory tusk for a specified amount of goods, a "packet." It soon became conventional that the "packet" should be tripartite and consist of textiles, guns and powder (for the sale of a slave), and other goods, usually metal ones (brass being a preferred item), but also beads, shells, and other sundry items. This arrangement may well have followed existing norms for the payment of matrimonial compensations, which themselves later included an assortment of commercial goods in high demand. Once this price was agreed to, a second round of bargaining for the actual content of the exchange took place. A real slave or tusk was evaluated in relation to the ideal norm, and the actual composition of the "packet" was adjusted. By 1700 commercial law was well developed with regard to both procedures and substance. So was commercial practice.

On arrival the European trader began by paying "customs" in commodities. This was a payment to the local political leader to be allowed to trade. This usage had grown out of the older customary gift to the local king, but, in the eighteenth century, it was usually given to a special official appointed to deal with European traders, to oversee legal problems, and to represent them at court. The European trader then bargained with a general broker to set the standard of value first, and to conduct all subsequent price negotiations. Given the intricacies of the price-setting mechanism, brokers were indispensable to the system. Their role may well have grown out of the existing role of "landlord" on the inland markets. The landlord lodged foreign traders and, for a commission, brought them in contact with trading partners. Like landlords, brokers did not own any of the commodities or any slaves for sale. They therefore avoided most commercial risks and undoubtedly were the persons whom the trade profited the most. It is not surprising that by the eighteenth century most of them were persons of high rank and status.[16]

The place of trade at first was usually only a flimsy temporary shed on the beach, from which the Europeans returned to the ship every night. Already by 1600, however, the Dutch had built warehouses or "factories" north of the Loango coast. In the later eighteenth century such places of business became common in Loango, and they provoked the first cession of land, that is, a perpetual rent from the African point of view and a true sale of real estate from the European one. Labor needs for these establishments were first met by buying slaves, but later a rudimentary labor market developed, as Europeans rented slaves from African owners for the duration of their needs.[17]

As the volume of trade increased and slaves became the major export, caravans grew bigger, were better armed, and went farther for longer periods. They were still led by a single guide who enjoyed great authority. They enhanced their protection not just by increasing their size and by carrying guns, but even more by carrying special caravan *nkisi*, or charms, which were feared by local people inland far and wide. In contrast to the situation south of the Zaire Estuary, outfitting caravans did not involve the provision of credit by European traders to a large extent, but was realized on the profits of earlier expeditions. This was also true of travel by river. Here, however, each captain of a large trading canoe was independent and exercised full authority over his paddlers, usually slaves or dependents of the owner of the craft. Still, canoes often traveled in flotillas for safety's sake.[18] The continual rise in volume of the Atlantic trade, decade after decade, turned occasional carrying into a specialized occupation for more and more groups, especially along major arteries of commerce and especially by water. Inevitably such carriers began to be designated by special names which developed into ethnic labels, just as had happened to the Vili. The Nunu, Bobangi, Okande, and Aduma are the best known among them.[19]

Along with the expansion of the hinterlands the old cyclical markets also spread, especially on the overland routes. As the routes went ever farther and the hinterland was unified, they brought regions with different currencies into contact with each other. That provoked a complex specialization and exchange of financial instruments, especially at the Malebo Pool. The raffia currencies did not spread far, but Kongo's *nzimbu* currency was accepted along the river above the Malebo Pool as far as the Alima, on the Kwa, and on the lower Kasai. However, it was ousted, apparently in the eighteenth century, by the *ngele,* a copper rod that had been in use among the Tio. The *ngele* then became the universal standard of value for slaves and ivory in all the inner basin regions. In the trading area of the Gabon rivers, markets did not develop. North of the estuary, among the Fang and Ntumu peoples, competitive exchanges between big men, or *bilabi,* took their place. Goods from the interior were exchanged for goods from the coast at these potlatches. Here the currency for social payments, also used in matrimonial payments, was the iron rod, *bikie.* This became the standard of value in the trade of that area. Farther into southeastern Cameroon, away from any organized trade route, the only effect of the Atlantic trade well into the nineteenth century was the frequency with which ivory tusks were used for matrimonial and other social payments. Tusks had special value because they were in demand by western neighbors, who exchanged them through *bilabi* for goods from the coast.[20]

The practice of hoarding currency or staple commodities of the trade led to a new notion of wealth on the Loango coast and on the Zaire River, as commodities came to be used, not just as instruments to directly acquire dependents or wives, but also as a means of investment to obtain more commodities later.[21] Credit, debt in currency, and interest, all developed apace with the trade. In the absence of a market for labor and land, however, the effect of capital formation remained limited, and the ultimate goal in amassing wealth still remained the acquisition of dependents. Yet a larger amount of currencies was tied up in financing the trade, so that the sector of "mercantile capital" grew, a practice that facilitated the increased consumption of imports, especially textiles and guns, by most of the populations west of the Malebo Pool. Such commodities were no longer luxury items, but had become necessities.

The growth in European demand was met mostly by expanding the area affected by the Atlantic trade, not by extracting an ever greater number of slaves from the same region. At first sight, then, the only innovation induced by this process was the need to feed slaves en route to the coast, not the need for new ways to procure slaves. Persons were still first enslaved as prisoners of war or as pawns for debts, including court fines. But in practice, on the forward edge of the trading zone, kidnaping occurred and raids were started to capture slaves. Closer to the coast, existing legal processes were perverted to raise the supply of slaves. Defenseless people were condemned to slavery under the most trifling of pretexts, such as for breaking an imported dish. In many cases, death penalties were commuted to sale into slavery. A major institutional change also occurred within the trading zone because of the practice of selling slaves. This led to a new status division within the category of "slave" groups between slaves for sale and "household" slaves, who could not be sold. The multiplication of unequal social statuses was the most striking outward sign of a deeper change brought on by the slave trade. A variety of such statuses had existed before, but their number and the specialization of their roles greatly increased during this period.[22]

The continual expansion resulting from the great growth of the trade during the eighteenth century did not directly lead to major institutional innovations. But during that century it nevertheless transformed the economic geography of a great portion of equatorial Africa, and thus indirectly exercised a profound impact on the various social and political institutions of the equatorial tradition. Moreover, trading in people as if they were commodities directly affected older notions of humanity and older ideologies of social stratification.

The Industrial Age: c. 1830–1880

The full impact of the industrial revolution reached the coast in the last precolonial period (see map 7.2). Huge quantities of very cheap manufactured goods were now landed all along the shores of equatorial Africa

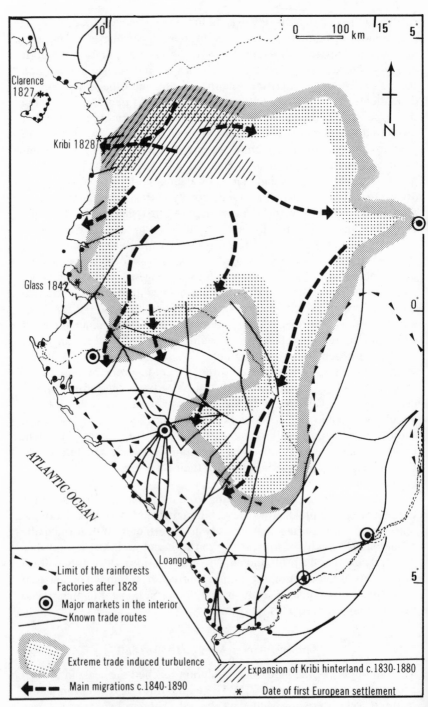

Map 7.2. The Atlantic trade: 1830–1880

208

and flowed inland from there. By midcentury the volume of these imports dwarfed the highest volume of imports of the eighteenth century into insignificance. From 1827 onward, points of entry multiplied on the coasts as commercial firms built "factories," which by the 1870s dotted the shores from Banana to Victoria. The most fateful of these was the foundation of such an establishment at Kribi on the southern coast of Cameroon in 1828. It led to the rapid creation of a new network of trade inland to central and eastern Cameroon, the only area that had hitherto not been drawn into the hinterland of the Atlantic trade.[23]

The increase in volume of imports and the multiplication of points of entry are the salient features of the new age, more so than the gradual suppression of the slave trade. Officially the slave trade was no longer the dominant trade and it was not the raison d'être for these commercial establishments. Trade in so-called legitimate products was. This expression refers especially to ivory, the most lucrative of all legitimate commodities and the mainstay of the trade throughout the whole period. Other legitimate products included palm oil, peanuts, lumber, and, after about 1870, rubber. However, their output in volume and value was low. Trade was possible only because the European cost-price of imports was now so cheap. The new demand led to more intensive elephant hunting, sometimes by specialists such as the Kele people in the hinterland of the Ogooué Delta and the Gabon Estuary. But in general the nature of production and trade did not change much. Only in the hinterlands of Douala and of the Loango coast is there evidence for adjustment to the new European demand. Palm oil and kernels were produced there in orchards tended by slaves. Groundnuts for sale were mainly cultivated by free Nzabi farmers, east of the upper Ngounié, and by slaves both on the Loango coast and among the Punu, near the upper Ngounié.[24]

Meanwhile the slave trade continued, although it had become clandestine in practice after about 1830, when British and French naval squadrons began to repress it, first north and later south of the equator. Traders now hid their operations by building barracoons or stockades to hold slaves in desolate and remote places, especially on the Gabonese coast and in the creeks along the estuary of the lower Zaire.[25] Figures on slave exports are contradictory. Forty-six hundred slaves were allegedly exported from the whole coast in 1841–1843, but for 1859–1860 alone one author cites an informed estimate of 30,000 slaves exported from just the Zaire Estuary.[26] Because the trade was by then illicit, discrepancies in figures reported should be expected. Still, a discrepancy of such magnitude merely indicates that the subject has not been well enough studied for the period. At least it is certain that some slaves were exported from the Zaire Estuary until well into the 1870s and from the delta of the Ogooué until 1900.

It is becoming clear that the legitimate trade by itself did not develop to the extent it did merely through the buying of ivory and the odd lots of palm oil or groundnuts. The legitimate traders sold an as yet unknown but considerable proportion of their commodities for cash to slave traders from the Americas. A good deal of their profits, therefore, still stemmed from the slave trade, but these were effectively hidden from view, and the merchants involved incurred none of the risks involved in the slave trade. Moreover legitimate factories continued to use slaves for labor. They often rented gangs of slaves from local dignitaries, for slavery on the coast was not abolished, and they also bought slaves. Slaveholding actually increased in the hinterland of Douala and perhaps in the hinterland of the Loango coast as well, because slaves were now put to use as agricultural producers.[27]

The deployment of factories along the coast changed the commercial geography there and rapidly brought much of southern Cameroon into the Atlantic sphere through the port of Kribi. By 1850 the forward edge of the trading area had reached the plateaus of south-central Cameroon and met the frontier of the West African trading area, along the Sanaga north of present-day Yaounde. By the 1880s it had reached the Sangha at Ouesso, and was merging there with the older trading area of the inner basin. South of Kribi, every new factory site along the coast became a point of entry on its own and produced new local trading routes. This led to the emergence of new middlemen groups in the hinterland, such as the Kele north of the Ogooué, the Nkomi west of the lower Ngounié, the Gisir and the Punu west of the upper Ngounié, and the Tsogho beyond that river. The situation produced major tensions and upheavals among the populations, throwing many local regions into great turmoil. Major migrations toward the coast occurred everywhere in the deep hinterland from Kribi to Loango.[28] To speak of a state of crisis is hardly an exaggeration, a crisis that by 1880 engulfed all of southern Cameroon, Gabon, and lower Congo.

However, the advent of trading posts was only a first step. The establishment of the English at Clarence on Bioko in 1827, and of the French on the Gabon Estuary in 1839, were the first toeholds of territorial colonies. In the early 1840s mission stations followed in Clarence, Douala, Victoria, Corisco, and Gabon. They launched a direct assault on the western Bantu worldview. Then in the late 1850s came the first "explorations" by men like Mackey and du Chaillu. These men often witnessed the first epidemics of smallpox and other foreign diseases. They in turn were followed in the 1860s by European traders, officers from the French navy, and others in a steady stream culminating in the fateful voyages of de Brazza (1875–1878) and Stanley (1877), who were the direct forerunners of the colonial conquest. Meanwhile European technology improved constantly throughout the century and continually widened the technological gap between equatorial Africa and Europe.

With every passing decade, Europe's military potential grew, and improved navigation brought that continent closer and closer to the African shores.[29] In the face of such a succession of onslaughts it looked as if the equatorial tradition might not be able to survive much longer. In the event, however, its conquerors would still need 40 years to destroy it.

Having sketched the main outlines of the challenge posed by the Atlantic trade, we need to sum up its overall economic impact on the societies of the region before we can examine whether and how the social systems of western equatorial Africa between 1500 and 1880 managed to cope with this trade which turned into an onslaught.

THE ECONOMIC IMPACT

The spread of the Atlantic trade created a single, integrated economic area in equatorial Africa that transcended in complexity any spatial ensemble which had hitherto existed there and dwarfed it in size (see map 7.3). By 1880 almost two-thirds of the whole area had been reorganized around a framework of trade routes leading to the coasts. The operation of those routes required and promoted the introduction of new processes of food production. After a new region had been tapped, significant population realignments could occur, and the region began to specialize in products and services complementary to the specialized production of others elsewhere in the wider area. But the creation of this huge economic entity exacted a high cost through the forced emigration of slaves, and hence significant loss of population.

Trade Routes and Agricultural Innovation

When the trading system began the coastal points of entry were able to supply merchant ships with the food required for their long voyages. But as soon as the slave trade began to bring hundreds and then thousands of slaves to the ports, the provision of foodstuffs for them, both before embarkation and to feed them during the Atlantic crossing, outran the usual resources. It became necessary for people at points of entry, relay stations, and even along the routes to increase food production. Even then the need soon exceeded the potential supply available through the usual methods of production. One solution, adopted in regions such as the capital of Kongo before 1665, the hinterlands of Loango, the Gabon Estuary, and Douala, and even the upper Mungo area, was to create slave villages and farms to boost food production. But this was expensive. As early as the mid-sixteenth century, the Portuguese attempted to alleviate the shortages by the introduction of new high-yielding American crops. They brought in maize, manioc, groundnuts, and lima beans.

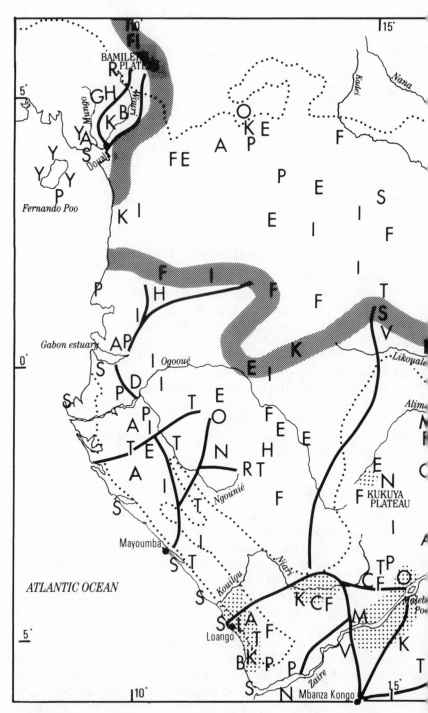

Map 7.3. Economic specialization in the Atlantic trading area. Key to products for export is given on page 214.

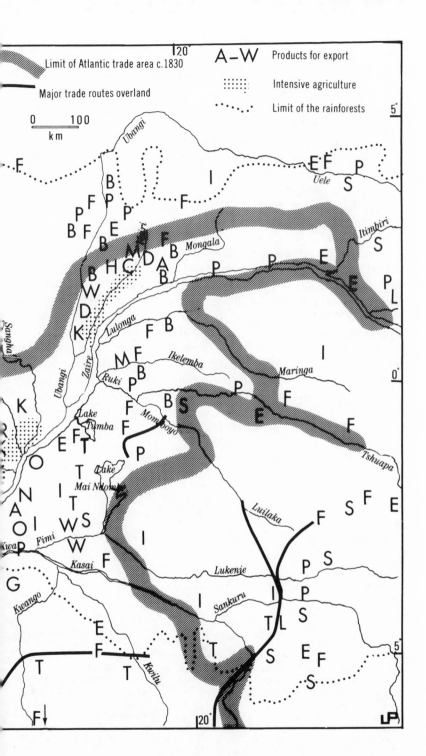

Chili peppers and tobacco also found their way to the area. All these crops were grown on the coast shortly after 1600, and spread from there, to be found by 1880 far beyond even the Atlantic trading area. Later, other plants were introduced, especially during the nineteenth century when foreigners associated with the factories and missions attempted to grow the vegetables and fruits to which they were accustomed. Whereas data are abundant for agriculture, information about livestock such as pigs, ducks, and sheep is scant.[30]

Of the crops, manioc was the best adapted to forest habitats, the highest yielding, and the most important for the slave trade itself, because it could be processed into "bread," which would preserve well for several months. It was therefore an ideal food to feed travelers and slaves. But its cultivation required more labor in the field than what was required for a similar yield of bananas, and its preparation into edible food required at least twice the amount of labor that other foods did. Almost all this extra labor had to be carried out by women or slaves.[31] This explains why cassava did not spread over all the rainforests equally, but was at first grown only along the major trade routes and in the immediate hinterland of the harbors. In the eighteenth and nineteenth centuries it spread over all the lower Zaire, Ogooué, and Kasai basins as well. Intensive cultivation for export had been organized by then near the major river routes; the fields along the Alima, the Ikelemba, and near the Malebo Pool are the best known.[32]

Key to Products for Export and Notes to Map 7.3.

A.	mats, basketry, nets	L.	jewelry, luxury products
B.	boatbuilding, boats	M.	manioc
C.	copper	N.	groundnuts
D.	bananas	O.	tobacco
E.	smithing, iron objects	P.	ceramics
	copper objects	R.	cattle
F.	iron smelting, raw iron	S.	salt
G.	goats	T.	textiles
H.	sheep	V.	pigs
I.	ivory	W.	beer, sugarcane wine
K.	palm products	Y.	yams

Notes: As fish was produced by specialists along all the major rivers along the coast, the product is not indicated here. Similarly, all forest areas near either the limit of the rainforests, or near areas where the product was lacking, exported redwood and this is not indicated on the map. Slave raiding and piracy on water or on land shifted so much over time that these activities have not been indicated.

Map 7.3 cannot be considered to be definitive. There are more reports about such exports for some areas than for others. For example, the western Cameroons are underreported, and the data for southwestern Gabon are probably complete. Despite this fact, however, the overall impression to be gained from this map is probably correct: specialization was much more developed within the Atlantic trade zone than outside it.

Maize, which has higher yields and withstands high humidity better than other cereals, did well in the moist savannas, but spread very unevenly in rainforests such as those of Gabon, where it was intercropped with bananas. In these habitats the crop required more clearing than was usual, and its yields were not spectacular because of the very high humidity. Hence maize was rather unimportant in the rainforests themselves, even though its cultivation led to sometimes dramatic increases in yields per acre on the margins of rainforests.[33] Groundnuts require open surfaces and sandy soils, which restricted their large-scale cultivation to suitable lands, usually in the savannas but also in a few favorable sets of habitats in southern Gabon, especially where the demand for this crop by nineteenth-century European traders spurred its cultivation. Elsewhere it remained a minor crop or was not adopted at all. Beans fitted in very well with the earlier varieties of Old World pulses and complemented or replaced these in many regions.[34]

Although not a foodcrop, tobacco became an indispensable plant because addiction to smoking spread rapidly. Tobacco thrives best on sandy soils, but will grow in very humid conditions anywhere. It therefore spread everywhere in *falga* gardens. Plantations geared toward large-scale export arose during the eighteenth and nineteenth centuries in the southwest, near the edges of rainforests, in the vicinity of major trade routes near the Malebo Pool, and near the northern edge of the Bateke plateaus, but also farther away and in rainforests among the Masango people of southern Gabon.[35]

For similar reasons more labor-intensive agricultural techniques appeared during these centuries. Some can be linked directly to the new crops. These include mounding, ridging, and extra weeding in relation to cassava. In addition, fertilizing with weeds, or the more efficient underground burning of weeds, became common in the lower Zaire basin, and on the Bateke plateaus, especially on the Kukuya Plateau, which probably acquired its high density of population during these centuries. Such techniques boosted yields, preserved nutrients, and permitted efficient rotation of crops. They also required the use of the hoe, so that this implement may have diffused widely during this era. Moreover, all this extra work fell on women. There may well be a connection between the adoption of such techniques and the availability of more female labor, either through purchases of slaves or as the result of the gender imbalance in purchases of slaves by Europeans, which left a greater ratio of women to men. The efficient practice of women's collective farming, or *kitemo*, in lower Zaire and Congo probably developed in the zones of intensive farming.[36]

The most exceptional agricultural development occurred in the marshes of the middle Ngiri, probably from the later eighteenth century onward. Here farmers built a square of retaining walls made with logs in the marsh, filled this coffer with earth, and used the resulting mounds of fertile soil for very high yield cultivation. Every year the mound had to be recharged with silt and the walls repaired. Because the labor input required was as spectacular as the returns, such agriculture would have been impossible without an intensive slave trade in which the free men of the area, fishermen and traders, also participated. Moreover, the different settlements in this small area specialized in growing different crops, including bananas, palm trees, water yams, and taro; others specialized in iron smelting and the production of goats.[37] The major nineteenth-century town of Bonga, the Venice of the Congo, was built on mounds, an inch or so above water level, at the confluence of the Sangha, Likouala, and Zaire. Methods similar to those practiced in the Ngiri Valley were also used at Bonga and in the surrounding country to produce the food.[38]

Complementary Regional Specialization

As the Atlantic trade grew, fueled by the demand for ivory, slaves, and European commodities, it tapped and integrated areas where regional and even longer-distance trade (along the Zaire River) had been established long before. The demands of the whole system did not prevent people from also transporting commodities other than those destined for the Atlantic markets. Indeed, the increase in size of the trading area stimulated trade in regional commodities as well. Goods which hitherto had been exchanged on a small scale could now be diffused more widely, and new specializations also arose. A few of these regional products, such as raffia squares, iron objects, and especially copper, were just as valuable as the imports were, and hence could bear the cost of being carried farther than had been customary. This was facilitated by the spare transport capacity on the downstream stretches of river, which resulted from the volume of slaves and ivory being much smaller than the volume of commodities bought with them. In addition, traffic by water used canoes, manned by only a few paddlers, which could carry up to three tons and made the exports of bulky low-value goods worthwhile. The highway between the Loango coast and the Malebo Pool, and probably other routes as well, also had excess capacity. On the trip to the pool, commodities were continually sold and bought along the route, and on the return trip the slaves could, if necessary, be pressed into porterage.

Thus special local products found a wider market. Further specialization along the routes and in the relays occurred because manpower was diverted from the labor-consuming tasks of food production to trading and carrying, thus creating markets for the sale of local food produce and for objects necessary to the carriers, such as baskets, mats, and rope.[39]

Specialized production existed for rare and valuable items, such as copper and raffia mats, well before 1600, but when the trade became intensive after 1700, the tendency to specialize production affected almost every commodity. The local manufacture of goods made with raw materials of indifferent quality and the manufacture of goods made under local conditions of especially labor-intensive production were abandoned when cheaper substitutes became available on the markets. Under such conditions even the production of certain foods was discontinued. Conversely, locally abundant resources that were rare elsewhere were now more intensively exploited in large quantities for sale on the markets. As a consequence individual communities lost some skills but perfected others. The single integrated system of production and distribution that resulted had grown to such an extent by the 1880s that Pecile compared the volume and intensity of the trade on the most-plied route to the traffic in the hinterland of Trieste, then the main outlet of the Austro-Hungarian Empire.[40] As map 7.3 indicates, regional commodities included fish, salt, goats, sheep, tobacco, manioc, groundnuts, yams, sugar cane wine, and other edibles; ceramics of all sorts; iron and iron objects; copper and copper objects; raffia squares; canoes; luxury products such as jewelry and charms; items for the local trade such as mats, baskets, and rope; and widely distributed products like camwood cosmetics (not listed on the map). Specialized services such as fishing, hunting, carrying, piracy, and slave raiding must be added to the specialties.[41]

The enlargement of the scale, complexity, and intensity also led to population realignment either in order to come closer to or to flee farther away from routes and relays. The Jaga movement of 1568 can be seen as the first of such realignments. It is not clear whether the Jaga went toward the coast because the wealth generated by the trade attracted them or because they were motivated by the desire to participate more directly in the Atlantic trade. In any event, during their occupation of Kongo a flood of slaves were sold. From that time on, similar population realignments became a recurrent feature in the history of the area. It is as if the creation of new routes generated a magnetic field that reoriented the settlement of the population around their axes. The process was most spectacular after c. 1840 in Cameroon and Gabon, as a result of the rapid multiplication of points of entry, each of which acted as a new lodestone for people from far-away lands.

The irruption of the Atlantic trading system exercised a major and growing impact on equatorial Africa. The large-scale dynamics of change in this era flowed from the growing commercial sector. But the procurement system itself was the impressive product of continuous local initiative and invention. This went far beyond a mere reaction to the exigencies of the Atlantic trade. New initiatives encompassing all economic life—from production or distribution to the procurement of labor—built on preexisting tendencies, at least in the southwestern quad-rant of the area. Regional trade, markets, currencies, some specialized production of minerals and ceramics, unequal statuses, the division of labor by age and gender—all were older than the advent of the Atlantic slave trade. The challenge posed by the Atlantic trade was met by speed-ing up tendencies already present in previous commercial developments.

The Atlantic Trade and Population Losses

The economic growth of equatorial Africa over four centuries was achieved at an appalling demographic cost. Its exact amplitude and its effects have been much discussed for over a generation, yet even now no detailed answers can be given. How many slaves were exported from equatorial Africa, and how much did this huge emigration affect the size of the population of the area? The best available total figures are 982,000 people between 1660 and 1793 and another 240,000 between 1810 to 1843, with margins of error of up to 20 percent. In all perhaps 1.5 million people were taken to the Americas between 1500 and 1900.[42] But such figures cannot be used directly to estimate the total population losses in equatorial Africa. First, many of the slaves exported through the Loango coast came from the savanna areas to the south, and some of those sold in the harbors of the savanna lands, especially before 1660, came from equatorial Africa. Also, exports from Douala after c. 1750 comprised a higher proportion of people from the Bamileke Plateau. Second, how does one estimate losses before slaves reached the coast? These include losses during slaving raids (but not all losses in any war), losses in transit, and losses at the points of embarkation. Indications exist for trade in Angola and in the southern savanna which lead to the conclusion that roughly half of the slaves captured died before they were exported.[43] But such figures cannot simply be transposed to equatorial Africa, where the financial structure and the general conditions of trade were very different. European credit played a lesser role here than in central Africa, and left the ownership of the slaves in the hands of the various carriers and middlemen; accordingly this meant that these trad-ers stood to lose more from the death of slaves in their care than did traders farther south. Therefore they may well have been much less callous. A large number of slaves traveled by canoe for a long portion of their voyage to the coast, which was faster and entailed much less hard-ship than overland travel. Moreover, fewer slaves were systematically captured in large-scale raiding and war than was the case in the large states of the south. Third, for lack of any documentary basis, losses relative to the whole population cannot be calculated with any pretense at precision. Lastly, the rate of natural increase of these populations is unknown. Although it is known that a third of the exports were women, there are no clear figures as to how many of these were of childbearing age.[44]

Under the circumstances one can indicate only some general parameters. The worst-case scenario first: The height of the trade occurred from 1660 to 1840; 1,222,000 were exported then. Losses before embarkation equaled this number; hence the loss of population was 2,444,000. The area affected was approximately 1 million square kilometers; at a population density of four persons per square kilometer, it yielded 4 million people at the outset of the period. The annual loss then was 13,577.77, or 0.3 percent of the population. Assuming a 0.5 percent rate of natural increase, the population still increased slowly. For the period of heaviest trading, 1756–1793, the result is different: 513,000 slaves were exported from the Loango coast. Rough proportions for slaves from central versus equatorial Africa are given by Degrandpré for the harbor of Loango in the 1770s and 1780s: 38.7 percent were "Kongo" (i.e., Kongo or bought by Kongo), from almost all of central Africa; 36.08 percent were "Mayombe," from Mayombe, southern Gabon, and upper Ogooué; 19.42 percent were "Teke" and "Mondonge" (i.e., Teke-related populations); and 5.55 percent were "Bobangi" (i.e., from upstream of the Malebo Pool).[45] Therefore 38.7 percent of the slaves coming from central Africa subtracted from the total leaves 314,469 slaves exported from equatorial Africa and 628,938 persons lost. This yields an annual loss of 16,998, or 0.42 percent of the population. There was still no depopulation.

These calculations exaggerate the losses of slaves from the point of capture to the boarding of ships. On the other hand it is conceivable that the annual natural increase was less than 0.5 percent. Still, there was no population loss unless that rate lay well below 0.4 percent. Nevertheless, the population stagnated during the worst periods before c. 1840.

Given the fact that only a third of the exports were women, and not all of them of childbearing age, the demographic effect was further cushioned. Thus in the worst period that meant an export of 5,666 women or, calculating generously, perhaps 5,000 fertile women per year out of a total of some 666,666 persons per year, or around 0.75 percent. This was a cumulative loss but probably not enough to affect the rate of natural increase so much as to lead to depopulation. The slave trade led to an increase in polygyny, because more than twice as many adult men as nubile women were lost each year (1.69 percent of all adult men). Polygyny meant less infant mortality, because births were more carefully spaced, thus making up for some of the lost fertility. But one must also consider a drop in natality stemming from the internal use of slaves. People such as the Bobangi traders imported slave women in large numbers, and such women often practiced abortion. On balance then, one must conclude that the external slave trade certainly prevented any growth in population during the eighteenth and early nineteenth centuries. This, added to the internal slave trade, may have resulted in some depopulation.[46]

EQUATORIAL SOCIETIES IN THE DAYS OF THE ATLANTIC TRADE

The preceding sections have presented the history of the Atlantic trade in western equatorial Africa and stressed its economic and demographic impact. Now one can directly address the two questions with which this chapter opened. Was it predominantly the internal dynamics inherent in the tradition that continued to shape the changing societies and cultures? And to what degree did the equatorial tradition survive in the affected areas?

The Fate of the Kingdoms

When the Portuguese arrived in Kongo their aim was not just to trade but to convert the inhabitants to the Catholic religion and, in general, to their own cultural heritage. The court of Kongo converted but flatly refused to consider the proposed institutional changes in the political structure, just as they also refused them, for instance, in matrimonial matters. They integrated the new religion into the ideology of kingship on their own terms, and the kings of Kongo remained firmly in control of their societies. The first genuine challenge came with the Jaga invasion. Even in that crisis, and despite their reliance on a Portuguese army, the Kongo elite succeeded in upholding their social and political system.[47] Yet the Atlantic trade system began to erode these structures in two ways. After the hub of the trade moved to Luanda, the financial strength of the court eroded: Kongo currency suffered from severe bouts of inflation. Second, the Kongo kings were unable to prevent the increase in military strength of the princes in the coastal province, who used their position in the trading network to convert wealth into armaments. By 1636 the coastal prince of Soyo had broken away from the state, and in later years the kings were unable to reduce him to submission. The Kongo state collapsed in 1665, when its king was killed in battle against a Portuguese army at Ambwila. During the strife over the succession after this event, the whole political system unraveled. The battle of Ambwila obviously was only a trigger. Historians still argue over to what extent the collapse resulted from the growing institutional inability to cope with the process of succession in the seventeenth century, because different factions appeared in the blocks of potential successors, or whether it was really an inevitable effect of the Atlantic trade.[48]

The façade of the kingdom was eventually restored after 40 years of strife, but the dominant sociopolitical structures had totally changed. The aristocracy had scattered from the capital to seek refuge in local districts and build up new foci of power there.. Part of the Kongo population moved north across the Zaire toward the copper belt and the prosperous regions astride the route from Loango to the Malebo Pool. After 1700 power fell into the hands of a few new big men among the former aristocracy, each ruling only over a district. Income from the slave trade was directly converted into power by buying a retinue of household slaves and attracting dependents. The new structures were large Houses, usually led in the eighteenth century by former aristocrats and later on by merchant princes who claimed aristocratic descent. Meanwhile matriclan ideology developed rapidly. Its idioms justified the whole gamut of dependent statuses as well as claims over territory. The core of each House was seen as a clan segment, and rule within it was legitimized in clan language, although legitimacy was still linked to the king and capital. The charter myths after 1700 were the traditions of how the clans had emigrated from the former Kongo capital, and how they were heirs to its rule. Besides the ideal of kingship, some of its emblems and its rituals survived. Some emigrants north of the river, such as the Nsundi clans, attempted to recreate the conceptual reality of kingship and chieftaincy roles in the eighteenth century. In memory of Kongo their Lilliputian states boasted overly complex titulatures and enacted rich rituals, but nevertheless they remained merely a collection of small chiefdoms.[49]

North of the Zaire the existing small but ancient states south of Loango maintained territorial control, but by 1700 they were also hollowed out from the inside. In the ports power gradually devolved into the hands of a few families, each of which was the center of a large House, led by a titled merchant, usually a powerful broker in the slave trade, and the ancient title system turned into a mechanism for the regulation of their competition. Kingship continued to exist and kings were sacralized rather more than in earlier days; in the eighteenth century this turned them into mere figureheads, almost figments of the collective imagination, just as the king of Kongo was by then. By the nineteenth century the only effective central sanction in each harbor town was provided by the regulatory *ndunga* association to which the big men belonged. Acting collectively in the association, they could bankrupt and, on occasion, even destroy any House that had become too ruthless in its dealings with others.[50]

In Loango itself matrilineal lineages had already formed the core of the ruling Houses by 1600. Centralized kingship, backed by the Houses of the major titleholders, whose heads were merchants or brokers in the slave trade, flourished for much of the first half of the seventeenth century. But by 1700 royalty was becoming weak. Two short generations later the royal matrilineal line died out. The ensuing crisis was resolved c. 1750 by abandoning real power to the merchant princes, who led the six factions that comprised the 27 major clans, in return for the acceptance of a new dynastic line. Merchant princes formed a crown council of their own in a capital. The new royal lineage was isolated in the old royal seat. Royal princes were barred from accumulating wealth, and the merchant princes stored their treasures for safekeeping in famous and feared shrines. Accession to kingship became a long and expensive process, insuring protracted regencies by the crown council. Then on the death of the first king of the new line in 1766, even his small royal House split into two parts. The royal capital was abandoned. As elsewhere in the region, from now on kings became mere figureheads. No new king was installed until 1773, and after he died in 1787 the throne remained vacant for much of the following century.[51]

By c. 1750 there is evidence for a territorial breakup in Loango provinces. Central authority dissolved there, to be replaced by coalitions led by merchants and justified by clanship. Just as had happened in neighboring Nsundi, the leaders of one such coalition, the Bumwele clan, attempted to construct a new kingdom on either side of the Kouilou River bend in the eighteenth and nineteenth centuries. But their leaders could not overcome competitors and never fully succeeded. In practice the region remained decentralized, its trade routes and market places controlled by shifting coalitions of big men.[52]

Meanwhile, along the main route from the Loango coast to the Malebo Pool, a whole new political structure appeared. The road was old and ran at first from Loango to the copper-mining district, then to the limit of Loango's realm. From this district another ancient route ran to the markets of the Malebo Pool, mostly through territory that at first owed allegiance to the Tio state. Most of the copper belt itself seems never to have been firmly in the orbit of any state. The route probably became unified with the growth of the slave trade after 1600, and it became a coveted area. By the 1620s new migrants, called "bandits," or Jaga by the older inhabitants, destroyed the kingdom of Bungu in this region and occupied part of the trade route for much of the seventeenth century. In the next century came the Kongo emigrant farmers and aristocrats, who slowly became preponderant along most of the road.[53]

In or near the copper-belt markets were old and hallowed institutions, among them matrilinearity, which predated the direct trade between Loango and the Malebo Pool (see map 7.4). As this trade grew, however, the Houses in the area acquired more dependents and legitimized this situation in the prevailing idiom of matrilinearity. Dependents were justified as "children" (hence not heirs), "grandchildren," and affines. At the same time the general insecurity of the region also grew because of increased internal competition between Houses and be-

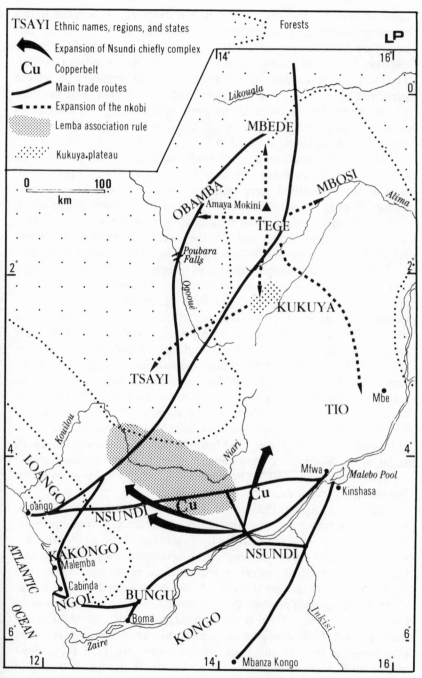

Map 7.4. *Lemba* and *Nkobi*

223

cause of Kongo immigration from south of the river. The solution to this situation was to turn markets into centers of regional cooperation. Markets were held in open spaces between villages and organized by the leaders of the participating villages acting in concert as judges (*nzonzi*). They settled commercial disputes and resolved all conflicts between the participating villages, often after these had led to fighting and a disruption of the market. In order to enjoy authority in their own settlements as well as elsewhere, such judges had to enjoy the trust of all. This they derived from the *lemba* association.

Lemba originated as a royal medicinal cult in Loango, and was probably brought by Loango traders. In the copper-belt variant, members of the association were initiated into a cult based on portable shrines, kept in boxes called *nkobe*. The initiation inducted them into a club of big men, proving that they had the right connections because they were allowed to join and that they were rich because they could afford the heavy payments to colleagues. The composition of the lodges made it clear that rulings imposed by a conclave of *lemba* members could be enforced. More than this, however, the power of the initiation and its shrines certified that they were peacemakers, and that their matrimonial alliances, which were so crucial in keeping competition between big men in the area within limits, would last, because their wives were also initiated into *lemba* and, once a husband and wife had been inducted, their marriage became indissoluble. Finally, *lemba* members acting in concert also provided the main healing rituals. Thus its members upheld not only the physical peace but the spiritual peace as well, because all disease was held to be an index of social disharmony. The prestigious ancestry of *lemba* explains its initial spread, but it acquired its full meaning, role, and function only after it spread eastward as far as the Malebo Pool and northeastward to the first relays beyond the Kouilou on the roads to Poubara Falls and to the Likouala basin. Westward it became established even in Haiti.[54]

The trade route to the upper Likouala basin led to further institutional developments in the principalities of that area, beyond the effective sway of the Tio kingdom. By the beginning of the eighteenth century some leaders grew rich there and developed a legitimacy of rule based on the spiritual powers of Me lo Kima, or Amaya Mokini, the highest mountain site on the Zaire-Ogooué watershed near 1° south. Claiming miraculous powers, they succeeded in being adopted as overlords by the western Teke, in the upper Ogooué area, on the Kukuya Plateau, and farther southwest almost to the Kouilou bend, thus strengthening the existing principalities there. By 1750 these now-mighty lords began to legitimize the power they derived from trading in a more concrete way. They claimed that their power stemmed from portable charms, which were named *nkobi* (after the boxes in which they were kept) and which they said they had received at the Me lo Kima site. In fact the first physical *nkobi* probably came along the trade routes from the *lemba* area as *lemba nkobe*. The *nkobi* movement affected all the lands around this site.

By the possession of a *nkobi*, the major lords in the northern part of the Tio kingdom, grown autonomous through trade, now claimed spiritual independence as well. This led to a series of wars in the kingdom, which resulted in a settlement only as late as 1840. The spiritual preeminence of the Tio king was maintained, but practically every great lord of the north had gained autonomy. Tio kingship and the major lordships now became concentrated in the hands of a small family. The system regained a new lease on life, but by 1880 that moment too had passed, and, as in Loango and Kongo, kingship survived because kings had become "but popes," as Guiral was to put it. The diffusion of *nkobi* to the north and to the east-southeast strengthened the authority of the chiefs in the Likouala basin and among the Tege lords of the upper Ogooué.[55]

The Mbede-Obamba, who were the main traders in the upper Ogooué area, also adopted the *nkobi* box, but not its contents. They translated the religious ideology of charms into their own religious idiom. Their *nkobi* held the bones of venerated ancestral heroes. The political effects of this adoption were much less spectacular than elsewhere. In this area the growth of the trade routes fueled the growth of military strength among the main leaders to such an extent, however, that in the region of Poubara Falls and farther south major warlords began extending their rule over lesser lords; by the late nineteenth century they were creating sizable centralized states of their own, each ruled jointly by a warlord and a peace lord.[56]

Firms and Towns in the Inner Basin

The impact of the Atlantic trade on the institutions of the peoples along the Zaire River upstream of the Malebo Pool was much less diversified than it was farther west (see map 7.5). Here large, centralized territorial polities had never existed. Structural change began when some groups of fishermen became traders and carriers. The best-known case was that of the Bobangi. Some fishing villages in the peninsula formed by the confluence of the Ubangi and the Zaire probably first entered the trade in the seventeenth century. Seeing lucrative opportunities, local big men emigrated to found new villages downstream, closer to the Malebo Pool, but were careful to preserve links not only with their village of origin but also with other colonies from that village by reciprocal hospitality, blood-brotherhood, and marriage.

By the mid- to late eighteenth century the Bobangi already operated

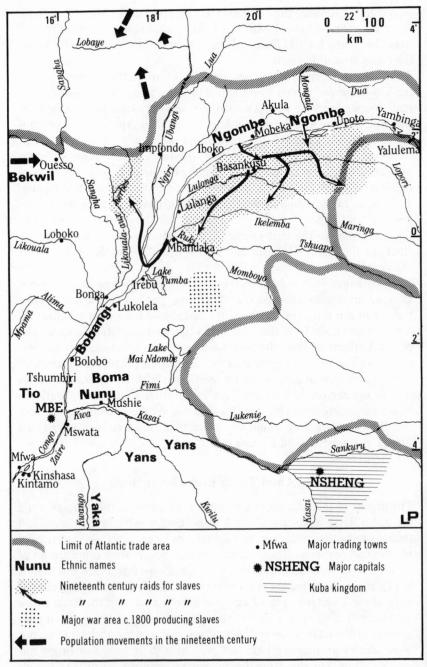

Map 7.5. The inner basin in the age of the slave trade

as far as the middle and upper Alima, and between c. 1820 and 1840 the Tio and Bobangi went to war for control of the stretch of river between the Malebo Pool and the confluence of the Kwa River. The Tio maintained control. Such fighting was not rare when different groups of carriers carved out commercial spheres for themselves. Thus the Nunu operated from the Kwa to Lake Mai Ndombe, the people of Irebu from Lake Tumba to beyond the confluence of the Lulonga, including the tributaries of the Zaire River, the Bangala from the Lulonga to near present Lisala, and the Poto from there to Yalulema, downstream of Basoko. Each of these groups with its network of far-flung villages came to be seen, and thought of itself, as an ethnic group.[57]

The trading Houses which formed the backbone of these networks soon became different from other Houses in the region by virtue of their size, their composition, a new internal division of labor, and a new ideology. Houses became business firms, and wealthy, successful firms were larger than other Houses. They included only a tiny nucleus of free people, but social status was fluid, because the talents of a man as a trader overrode any ascriptive status, including slavery. But the living conditions were so onerous for most women that they preferred to abort rather than raise children in such surroundings. The firms thus depended on foreign women and young male slaves to reproduce themselves, and constantly needed fresh recruits.[58]

As to size and composition, Mswata in 1882 was a typical successful firm. It counted 290 people but only 8 free men. The head, Chief Ngobila, had 85 wives. There were about 125 dependents, a majority of them men. This firm, like many others, was then about 10 times larger than an ordinary House.[59]

The internal division of labor was as follows: Women farmed to provide the surplus necessary for the trading expeditions and did the household chores. These included the lengthy and dreary job of processing cassava into loaves that could be preserved for months and taken on longer journeys. Most of these women belonged to the polygynous household of the big man himself. This household was often arranged in two bodies, each headed by a senior spouse. Younger wives were assigned to older women, and each of the women pawns and slaves was attached to a particular mistress. Male slaves assisted women. The ordinary rules of the division of labor by gender did not apply to them, and much of what they did was woman's work, such as fetching firewood and water or cultivating fields, which they also cleared. Slaves were used as paddlers, as providers of fish and game, as labor to maintain houses, boats, nets, or items needed in the trade, and as soldiers in war. Few among them were married, except for the more trusted ones, who became trading agents to collect goods in the interior and who assisted their master in his operations, either at home or on commercial trips. All slaves and women also constituted a reserve of capital to be used in bad times to settle debts. The few older free men were overseers of their own households; their young colleagues assisted the leader of the firm or, sometimes, replaced him on lesser trading ventures.

The firm was a unit well adapted to an expanding commercial system. Able men—and, very rarely, able women—rose to positions of responsibility, so that cases where slaves succeeded their master, or even the big man himself, were not at all uncommon. The most famous example is that of Ngaliema, a slave of the head of Kintamo, who succeeded as head of the firm and the town just before 1877, when he hosted Stanley. The measure of achievement was the ability to become wealthy. But in order to reach this goal men often had to assert themselves against others in violent ways. Aggressive personalities were quite common and big men were often physically strong men. The leader of the firm was obeyed only because of his wealth. He would lose his position, and could indeed even be sold as a slave himself, if he lost his wealth in war, in trade, or as the result of games of chance, which were the favorite pastime in such communities.[60]

The change in ideology and religion which took place in such communities expressed this climate of aggression. Witchcraft accusations were endemic and actual poisoning also may have been quite common. Suspicion was ever rife. When a free man died, an autopsy was performed to discover the witchcraft stuff in his belly, to establish whether he had been a witch or had been bewitched. Leaders relied on numerous, very expensive charms, often bought far away at great expense. Traders were supposed to be shielded by a guardian spirit who took the shape of a hippopotamus or crocodile. This was their *ezo,* which always traveled with them.[61]

Such firms were corrosive of other authority. Even in the eighteenth century, House leaders near present-day Mbandaka had to defend their preeminence by ruling out the possibility that local eminence could be achieved just by a display of wealth. This had hitherto been achieved by the practice of bestowing the *bolumbu* status on a wife or daughter during a lavish feast in which big men of the whole vicinity were entertained and given gifts. It was easy for the new traders to do this, so new rules had to be developed that stressed ascribed status. Only the high-born were allowed to have *bolumbu.*[62] An example from the upper Sangha, probably in the 1880s or 1890s, shows exactly how antagonistic the new commercial leadership was to older authority. The Bekwil lived in large villages, often composed of 10 or more Houses, under the leadership of a village headman respected for his talent for arbitration. At this time the eastern Bekwil had begun to participate in the trade on the Sangha River. They developed firms. The Houses within a village began to compete mercilessly with each other to corner the local trade. House leaders organized an association, the *ngon,* or gorilla dancing society, to express this struggle. Competing leaders attempted to force their rivals to submit themselves publicly to their leadership. Unable to keep the public peace, the local village leader lost all credit, and gradually the many Houses in such a village were reduced to a few firms.[63]

Firms obviously tended to occupy the choicest sites for trade, but these were limited around the major rivers. Hence it was not uncommon for several leaders of firms to settle together and form a town. The model for such towns was the great agglomeration, flourishing at the latest by the mid-seventeenth century, near the present Kinshasa. Often the firms recognized the leadership of the strongest among them, as if they were still Houses in a single village. This was the structure of Iboko in 1883, where the giant Mata Bwike, with his 70 wives, was the undisputed chief.[64] Even more commonly, firms settled alongside but some distance away from others, as was the case in nineteenth-century Bolobo or Kinshasa. In Kinshasa the Tio overlord of the 1660s had long since lost control. This situation resulted in a string of establishments without a single formally acknowledged leader—a town in size, but not in structure. Once in a while, a single firm became big enough to form a town all on its own. Thus Mswata in the 1880s was but the site of the firm of Ngobila.

Towns, unlike firms, were neither strong nor novel social units. In structure most were merely villages writ large; they existed only because strong firms jostled to occupy coveted locales and were held together by the need for a common defense. Nevertheless they were remarkable for their size. Many along the Zaire River counted over 5,000 inhabitants and perhaps five surpassed the 10,000 mark, a size otherwise known only from such places as the former capital of Kongo or the Kuba capital. The size of these towns indicates their central position in the economic organization of a far-reaching space.[65] The net result of the whole evolution was to transform the old bases of House and village into firm and town, respectively, and the old district disappeared.

In the nineteenth century, and perhaps earlier as well, slave-raiding parties provided many of the slaves in the inner basin. The people now living near present-day Mbandaka recollect that men who set out on hunting expeditions reached even the upper Likouala-aux-herbes. They, and probably men of Irebu as well, were the feared Nkasa, who ascended the Ruki and its affluents to raid for slaves. The peoples of the Lobaye River basin claim to have fled slave raiding in the lower Ubangi regions as early as c. 1800.[66] Traders also bought prisoners of war wherever possible, and in doing so actually encouraged warfare. Shortly after 1800 Ikenge's conquests in the lands of the Momboyo may well have yielded slaves for the Nkasa. Later, the Ngombe expanded across the

Zaire bend into the Lulonga, Lopori, and Maringa basins, and toward the Ikelemba, looking for land and loot. They captured many slaves and sold them to traders from Irebu along the Lulonga and Maringa rivers.[67] By 1880 insecurity was so great in the lands from the lower Ubangi to the Lopori that elaborate new sorts of fortifications, armaments, and ambush tactics appeared.[68] Such phenomena, as well as the swelling of the towns with immigrants from their rural environs and with purchased slaves, led to a significant redistribution of the population in these areas.

In the lower Kasai River area the trade did not lead to the collapse of the existing political structures. The Boma kingdom lost control over Mushie, the main base for the Nunu carriers on the Kwa, probably before 1560. However, except for some eighteenth-century raids by their northern neighbors intending to capture slaves for sale, that was the extent of their loss. South of the river, new Yans principalities were founded by fresh arrivals from the Teke plateaus in the eighteenth century, apparently on conventional lines. The impact of the slave trade began here with the rise of the slave-trading state of the Yaka, which was linked both to the Luanda and to the Loango coast networks. By 1800 Yaka raids caused many to migrate out of reach toward the east and north, thus putting pressure on the already settled peoples of the lower Kasai, but not enough to cause major change there. The influx of refugees and the prestige of the Yaka merely led to the adoption of some new honorific titles and emblems there.[69]

The greatest upheaval in this sector was the creation of the Kuba kingdom by an early-seventeenth-century founder, who came from the Kwilu River basin and may have been a trader. But if trade played a role there, it acted merely as a stimulus. The state developed without any outside interference. Its later structures, some of which find no parallels in any other political system, were due to local inventions, and grew out of preexisting institutions. The Kuba remained on the extreme edge of the Atlantic trading area from c. 1750 onward. This allowed their kings to maintain firm central control over the activities of long-distance slave traders from Angola. They imported slaves, exported ivory, and derived great wealth from such operations, especially after 1880.[70]

The Northern Coasts

Little is known about the northern coasts, except that societies there were organized on a very small scale, and commercial contacts along most of these coasts remained sporadic (see map 7.6). By 1600 the peoples from the Rio Muni area and around the Gabon Estuary seem to have lived in typical Houses and villages. When the Dutch reached the estuary, they found three chiefs there, one on each bank of the lower estuary, and a chief called Pongo, on an island also called Pongo. The

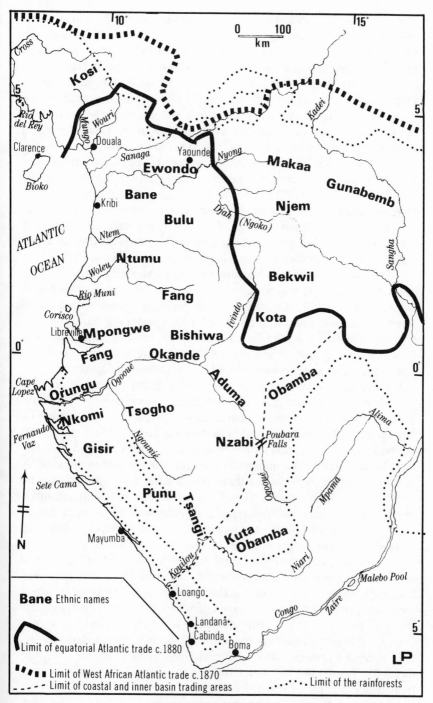

Map 7.6.   Western equatorial Africa: 1830–1880

231

chief and his counterpart north of the estuary, were allied against the third one, who seems to have been allied in turn to leaders in the Ogooué Delta farther south. Yet the people of the estuary were even then strong enough and interested enough in the Atlantic trade to destroy an early Dutch settlement on Corisco Island. Later on, one of the three chiefs on the estuary became more powerful than the others but no central court, not even a full-fledged title system, seems to have developed there despite the facts that the principles of the Loango political system were known there and that a formal dance, *ivanga*, in which the roles of these titles were acted out was adopted. The chiefs met together to discuss matters of common interest and to plan common activities, such as raids along the Cameroon coast or against the inhabitants of the Ogooué Delta. The existence at all times of a common political secret association is very likely, but not directly documented. This period of cooperation ended with the Dutch punitive expedition against the major leader in 1698. The then-leading House or clan was destroyed.[71]

The place most visited by ships from the sixteenth century onward was Cape Lopez. It was a victualing point on the routes to and from Europe and South America. Even ships plying the Asian routes would often take on water and fruit there. In that context trade was secondary. By 1600 there was a ruler in the area living in an inland court with Kongo-sounding names, and there may well have been titled officials. The influence of Loango was strong here, as is shown by a vocabulary of that time. But because much of the Ogooué Delta consists of marshes and, then as now, harbored a tiny population, any embryonic kingdom, if one existed, must have remained largely a realm of the mind. The same holds for the rarely visited Fernando Vaz Lagoon where the Nkomi dwelled, although the population here was more concentrated.[72]

Shortly after 1700 a minor trade in slaves developed in the area. A number of Mpongwe Houses then moved from the hinterland to the nearby shores of the estuary. They formed several strong and centralized districts with leaders who claimed legitimacy and were given formal status as clan heads. Such units formed fugitive coalitions and began to jockey for the best position along the estuary to attract the trade. Some succeeded and gradually forced weaker clans into subordinate positions. By the 1830s three main clan heads still ruled, and Mpongwe clans were becoming patrilineal. But their authority was challenged by at least two merchant princes who had organized their own firms, trading, transporting, and producing food. This challenge was then probably of recent vintage, because the ideology of ascribed status still remained the universally accepted cement of local authority. Between 1839 and 1842, the three clan heads, not the merchant princes, were the ones who signed treaties and accepted French sovereignty.[73]

At Cape Lopez the wealth that now accrued to the local leader from a modest trade in slaves allowed him to become a powerful king. The kingdom of the Orungu reached its zenith between 1790 and 1850, and the inhabitants of the Fernando Vaz Lagoon area, threatened by this development, also created a strong kingdom. The Orungu traded up the river and the inhabitants of Fernando Vaz traded overland to the lower Ngounié. The inhabitants of the hinterland did not react swiftly to this build-up of power. Their organization in a coalition of districts whose chiefs met to coordinate affairs of common interest, as they still did in the mid-nineteenth century, apparently sufficed for security. And yet in this area slave traders did create real pressures, because the traditions of some inland groups tell that they fled the coast to avoid the "kidnaping birds of prey."[74]

Very little is known about the coastal societies of Cameroon before the establishment of the Duala on the coast around 1650, and trade was little organized there. The main place of trade lay on the shores of the Rio del Rey.[75] The Duala moved from a nearby home inland to settle on the site of Douala. They attacked and destroyed the trading post at the Rio del Rey, many of whose inhabitants apparently migrated to New Calabar and founded a major emporium there. Duala oral traditions represent the group as a single lineage, which grew and later divided into sublineages. But, probably from the outset, associations were also important in town. Moreover, it is likely that very soon after settlement the town grew through voluntary immigration, as other Houses joined the founding House—all of which is hidden or omitted from the streamlined genealogy. After 1700, and especially after 1750, Douala became the hub for a thriving slave trade. Although no direct eighteenth-century report about its society is known, the rise of men of modest condition and the fact that different "sublineages" had reserved the rights to different trade and slaving routes suggest that in the eighteenth century Douala became a coalition of firms acknowledging the leadership of the strongest, justified by the ideologies of descent from a common ancestor and of first occupancy. The presence of common secret associations also helped to maintain sufficient social cohesion. As the eighteenth century progressed and trade grew, the founding firm began to lose its grip and other leading firms in the coalition grew stronger. Although for most of the eighteenth century the big men who competed with the king were forced out of town and left to try their fortunes on the coast toward the Rio del Rey, by 1800 they could remain in town and compete there.[76]

After 1830 the whole picture on the northern coasts changed dramatically. Previously unheard-of mountains of riches, the wellspring of much more potential power than firearms could provide, washed ashore in torrents even while the slave trade, with slaves now for resale within the area itself, continued unabated in the interior. The availability of foreign goods in such quantities seems to have unleashed a paroxysm of

violence inland. Some peoples moved to stake a share in the riches to be
had along the major routes and in the trading towns along the major
rivers. Others, to the contrary, moved away from relays, routes, and
supply areas for fear of decimation. Perhaps the most spectacular population movements were those of the Sanaga-Ntem peoples. Barely a decade after Kribi was founded, the Bane and Bulu began to race west
from the central reaches of the Nyong toward the coast, and the Bulu
also expanded south and east toward the bend of the Dja in search of
ivory, slaves, and loot.[77] Farther south, major Fang and Ntumu migrations from the Woleu and Ntem rivers began by 1840; they proceeded in
the direction of the coast, to the middle Ogooué and to the confluence of
the Ngounié and the Ogooué. They had been preceded two decades
earlier by a movement from the Bakele inland of the estuary toward the
coast and by the Bichiwa of the right bank of the upper Ivindo toward
the confluence of the Ivindo.[78] South of the Ogooué, meanwhile, a much
slower but massive drift brought the Nzabi and Tsangi south and west of
their earlier seats, to new lands with better access to the trade routes.
Earlier, by 1800, people from northeastern Gabon, attracted by the
overland trade route to Loango, had begun to cross the upper Ogooué
near Poubara Falls and moved south and then southwestward. Village
after village moved farther coastward along the commercial routes to
establish themselves as traders or as pirates who would raid the major
caravan route from Poubara to Loango. A series of major wars in the
lands of the upper Likouala basin may also have been related to the
increase in the volume of overland trade.[79]

The relatively sudden appearance of a massive zone of turbulence in
Cameroon and Gabon was not accompanied by novel institutions, only
by a swelling of membership in the patrilineages of the north, as people
raced to the coast and the Ogooué. Meanwhile on the coast itself deep
changes were occurring. On the estuary, existing strains between major
clan leaders allowed the French to settle at the site of Libreville, and an
American Presbyterian mission settled nearby under the protection of
Ntoko, a leading merchant prince. The whole of Mpongwe society
quickly turned into true firms, incorporating the ruthless ideology of
achievement and the finest gradations of status as expressed in dress and
comportment. Indeed the first big borrowing of French culture served to
create and uphold such status differences. The French post protected the
older style of leadership well enough to maintain an outward status quo,
but it turned the clan chiefs into hostages.[80]

Beyond the Orungu kingdom in the Ogooué a number of societies,
as far upstream as the Ngounié confluence, now turned into kingdoms,
more or less following the Orungu model. The most original of these was
that of the Okande carriers, who dominated the tract of the Ogooué
between the Ngounié and the Ivindo. They developed a dual leadership

with a religious and a secular leader, who derived their revenues from their control of the trade on the river. Meanwhile the Orungu king could no longer channel all the incoming wealth through his office, and lesser men built up their own power. His kingdom decayed.[81] In Douala a similar story unfolded. The termination of the slave trade at Douala around 1840 did not end slavery. Far from it. Slaves were now employed on plantations and in town to produce and carry the commodities required by the legitimate trade. At the same time the respective importance of the different leading firms in the hinterlands shifted. The founding firm was no longer the strongest, and even the associations were not able to prevent internal strife. The slaves began to form their own secret associations, whose prestige stemmed from the societies of the Bamileke Plateau. These they used to resist the ever-increasing demands for labor from their masters. The situation slowly deteriorated. Recent Duala traditions have it that a new institution, the *ngondo,* or collective council, developed in the 1840s to put an end to the strife between the major firms, but at least one historian disputes that this really happened. By 1845 the king was no longer strong enough to forbid the establishment of a Baptist mission, invited by a rival leader. Strife became so bad that by 1856 the main firms accepted arbitration by the British consul stationed at Clarence. The relations between the social classes steadily continued to worsen as well. By 1858 one of the older associations of free men, which some slaves were allowed to join and which was led by a royal prince, turned into an instrument of repression. The slave societies answered with a very effective boycott, and once again the British consul had to mediate. In the succeeding years social chaos steadily worsened to the point that in 1877 and succeeding years the chiefs of Douala, perhaps fearful of being overthrown by the slave class, took the spectacular step of petitioning Queen Victoria to extend British rule to their city.[82]

In the case of the Duala, the network of dominant social institutions regulating society had collapsed. The heritage of the western Bantu tradition had proved to be inadequate. This collapse was no doubt due in the first instance to the strains generated by the Atlantic trade, but the role of the first Christian mission should not be underrated either. Ever since 1845 its teaching had been undermining the collective certainties of conceptual reality, thus piling mental uncertainty on top of the growing physical insecurity.[83]

CONCLUSION: TRADITION UNDER STRESS

There can be no doubt that the impact of the Atlantic trade on the societies of the region was marked. After having strengthened them at first, trade overwhelmed kingdoms such as Kongo, Loango, and those of the Tio and of the Orungu. The exigencies of trade played a leading role in the setting up of *lemba* or of firms. Yet every time a structure was destroyed, the innovation to replace it—be it the matriclan, the House, or an association—was drawn from the wellsprings of the equatorial tradition. Only in the final days of Douala was the tradition unable to adapt, and even that exception sets off the magnitude of the achievement elsewhere. Still there was a difference between situations where such innovations were "crisis" inventions, forced by the outside, and where they were "natural," internal developments. Consider, for instance, the contrast between the Kuba kingdom and the people on the copper belt of the lower Congo. In the first case, the internal dynamics produced a set of very novel administrative and judicial institutions in the eighteenth century, institutions that were called for by the very success of the creation of the kingdom a century earlier. The continuity was total. In the second case, the *lemba* solution was also derived from previously known institutions, but it was not in continuity with the previous experience of the peoples of the copper belt. It was, as it were, an emergency solution to cope with an externally induced crisis. The discontinuity was glaring. Clearly in such situations the equatorial tradition was very much on the defensive.

But the tradition was not defeated. It adapted. It invented new structures which in practice fell outside of its own parameters. The firm was an organization which traded for trade's sake, something absolutely foreign to the old tradition. The ideology of its leadership rested on wealth and violence only, in contrast with ancient leading roles. Yet superficially it was still a House, and its members still used the old kinship terminology. The need to institutionalize trust between trading partners created the custom of bloodbrotherhood, a way to accommodate the new role by making it kinship and hence traditional. In the cases of the *nkobi* lords, *lemba*, and new titles in the coastal kingdoms, orthodox ideology was pressed into service to justify attitudes and aspirations which fell outside the realm of previously accepted practice. In all these instances the tradition denied what was happening and recast it in terms of its own cognitive realm. In the physical world the impact of the Atlantic trade might be predominant, yet in the cognitive world the old tradition firmly held the reins.

Seen from this angle, the integrity with which the tradition was maintained is most impressive. With an awe-inspiring finality, Kongo dismissed most of the Portuguese civilization that was pressed on it and accepted a Christianity refashioned in its own terms. No part of equatorial Africa saw the equal of the Ambaquista communities in Angola, with their total assumption of European worldviews, values, aspirations, and ways of life. Despite the new ways of living brought in the wake of

Atlantic trading, no foreign ideals or basic concepts were accepted and not even much of a dent was made in the aspirations of individuals. For all that wealth was sought by traders, wealth for its own sake did not acquire followers. The spirit of capitalism made no genuine inroads. Wealth remained what it had always been: a crucial avenue to authority and power in equatorial Africa. Before 1880, no one would have said what the Kuba king said in 1953: "If you are a man who seeks money, you are a man for whom people do not count," although they might have agreed that "money makes the proud man, poverty is the place for flattery."[84]

In the final analysis, the tradition retained its ability to determine the future, to reject unwanted innovations, and to invent institutions, ideologies, values, and concepts to cope with its new environment. It maintained its own criteria of significance. Nowhere is this more evident than in its retention of the cherished principle of local autonomy and decentralization, even while creating the institutions necessary to accommodate the rise of a single huge economic space around an integrated system of distribution. This feature cannot just be dismissed by pleading the corrosive effects of the Atlantic trade on centralizing authority.[85] This remarkable achievement again emphasizes that the ability to refuse centralization while maintaining the necessary cohesion among a myriad of autonomous units has been the most original contribution of western Bantu tradition to the institutional history of the world.

Eight

Death of a Tradition

As told by most history books, the colonial scramble for equatorial Africa began with the arrival of H. M. Stanley at Banana on the Zaire River in 1879 and the signing of a treaty with the Tio king Makoko by S. P. de Brazza in 1880. The Act of Berlin in 1885 laid down the conditions for valid colonial claims. Stable boundaries between colonies in the area of the rainforests were soon attained, except for the border of German Kamerun and the French territories, which became definitive only during the First World War. It thus seems as if colonies sprang up complete in all details like mushrooms after a rainstorm. This view obscures the most important process that actually occurred: the conquest of equatorial Africa. It obscures its most important fact: that the conquest took 40 years to complete, that is, 40 years to destroy the equatorial tradition. It passes over the violence of an apocalyptic conquest. A combination of war, destruction by fire, disease, and hunger finally succeeded in breaking overt African resistance by 1920, at the cost of an estimated half of the total population of the area.[1]

Even while they were conquering the area, the Europeans were implementing their concept of a modern state with its centralized bureaucratic and, in the colonies, autocratic government. They justified the conquest in the name of a "civilizing mission." Colonial agents and missionaries continually invoked this principle to destroy most outward manifestations of the old tradition. At the same time they first built their own cognitive view of rural African society and then imposed it on daily life before or during the 1920s. The only concession to the equatorial way of life was to preserve some cultural flotsam and jetsam, and to erect a structure labeled customary law, which was utterly foreign to the spirit of the former tradition. Customary law was the headstone on its grave.

CONQUEST AND THE FOUR HORSEMEN

The growth of the world industrial economy at first fostered a powerful commercial expansion by proxy in the Nile Valley and in the Indian Ocean from bases in Khartoum and Zanzibar. This took the form of armed expeditions of traders raiding for slaves and ivory. Sudanese and Zanzibari raiding parties appeared in the eastern part of equatorial Africa in 1865 and 1869, respectively (see map 8.1). The Sudanese parties were at first defeated, but later gained local allies with whose help they fared better. The Mangbetu king Mbunza died in 1873 in battle against enemies backed by the Sudanese. The kingdom broke up, and the Sudanese raiders now dominated the scene. By 1880 the Egyptian government began the incorporation of the area into its Equatoria Province. But faced by the insurrection of the Mahdi, its officials evacuated these lands by 1885. Local Mangbetu and Azande rulers enjoyed only two years of respite before Zanzibari raiding parties arrived from the south. They allied with Azande princes and helped them to gain more lands in the forest, until a large military column of the Independent Congo State broke their power in 1891. At first Congo state agents also had to rely on local alliances with strong rulers. Later they gradually destroyed the power of one ruler after the other, until the last one was defeated in 1916.[2]

Meanwhile a coalition of Zanzibari raiders and traders had founded Nyangwe in 1869 on the Lualaba River as a base for their operations. Five years later they accepted the primacy of Tippo Tib, who had laid the basis for a territorial organization in an area farther west, just south of the forests. Tippo Tib accompanied Stanley part of the way down the river late in 1876. Soon Zanzibari raids and then territorial occupation followed in that direction, but not before Tippo Tib had incorporated into his bands local soldiers knowledgeable about rainforest environments. These, the people of the Matampa country, or Matambatamba as they were known to their victims, allowed the Zanzibari to expand the area they controlled. By 1887 their raids were reaching the Uele, Ituri, upper Lopori, and upper Tshuapa valleys. After minor clashes with Congo state troops over stocks of ivory, war broke out between the state and the Zanzibari in 1892. The Zanzibari were defeated by 1894, but most of their officials and merchants were left in place and recruited as auxiliaries. The last Zanzibari officials were not dismissed until c. 1920, which explains why the Zanzibari, unlike the Sudanese in the north, left a strong cultural mark on the lands they had occupied.[3]

Sudanese and Zanzibari conquests succeeded not just by military superiority in armament but also because they were able to ally themselves to local rulers, such as Azande princes on the lookout for confederates in their local wars, or at least to co-opt large numbers of local

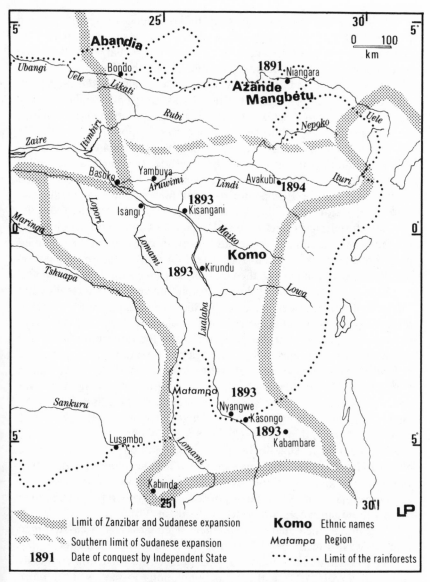

Map 8.1.   Sudanese and Zanzibari trading area: 1869–1894

Houses, whose leaders were eager for loot. In some regions the territorial restructuring of the Zanzibari left a marked impact on local institutions. All along the Lualaba and in the lower Lomami area, some of the
mokota, the titleholders of the local overarching associations, were recognized as chiefs and began to act as such. In northern Maniema the

Zanzibari forced populations to settle in large villages, appointed young local big men as headmen, called *sultani,* and assisted them to gain genuine power. To cope with this novel pattern of larger settlements, and to reassert the hierarchical principle of age, the Komo developed a new brotherhood, the *úmbá,* whose complex rituals marked the transition for males from adulthood to fatherhood. *Umbá* provided the means to coordinate the interaction of elders in the larger settlements, and thus provide a collective counterweight to the *sultani's* power.[4]

The European imperial expansion followed the Sudanese and Zanzibari irruption in equatorial Africa by a decade (see map 8.2). It started quite suddenly once the issue of African colonies had become embroiled in the politics of the European balance of power. European claims and settlement before 1879 had been quite limited. As late as 1883 the British refused the protectorate of Douala. In Gabon and on Bioko no real attempts were made to expand European rule beyond the occupied harbor town. Indeed, even in 1885, the Bubi still saw the Spanish governor as a chief among many, the chief of the Europeans in Santa Isabel.[5]

During the first years of the expansion, the need to sign treaties and the limited size of armed forces at the disposal of Europeans prevented major disturbances. They were usually tolerated, because they were perceived as just another trading outfit. After the ratification of the Act of Berlin, however, acts of violence against African villagers increased around European posts and related highways. An affray in Douala in December 1884, to clear part of the city for European settlement, was the first and perhaps the biggest of such early clashes. Systematic conquest came later, after local armies had been organized. The Force publique of the Independent Congo State was the first. A large army column was sent to Uele in 1890 and sizable military operations in the equatorial part of the country followed. These included the Zanzibari war and then an expedition against the Sudanese Mahdi. At the outset of that campaign in 1897 a large portion of the army rebelled. Fighting against these mutineers was concluded only in 1901.[6]

The major incitement to violence in equatorial Africa stemmed from its wealth in rubber. Rubber fetched high prices. Agents for the rubber companies or the Congo state pursued its collection ruthlessly and used terror to force the local populations to harvest ever more rubber. The people resisted and local fighting broke out, which soon escalated beyond the coercive power of the local rubber companies so that they had to appeal to the state's army. Sometimes sizable contingents of troops were then deployed to crush "rebellions." The rubber wars lasted from 1893 to about 1910 in the Congo state portion of the rainforests.[7]

In French Equatorial Africa the first battalion of colonial soldiers was created in 1883, but fighting in Congo and Gabon began only after

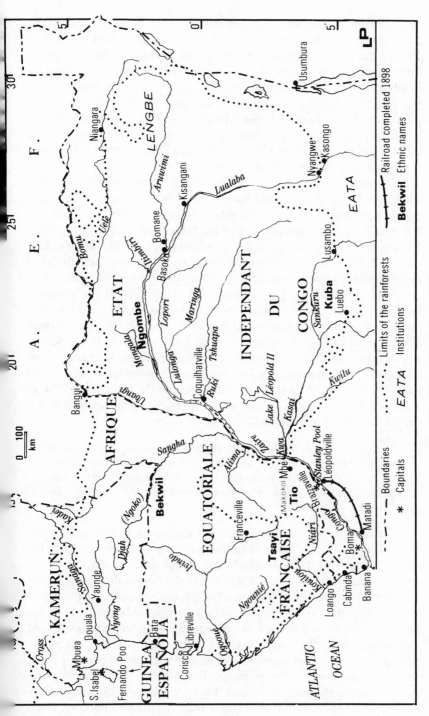

Map 8.2. Equatorial Africa in 1910

1902 and the conclusion of major military operations in Chad. Here, too, rubber was the trigger to violence. Such rubber wars lasted until 1920 in the border areas of Cameroon.[8] In German Kamerun a police force, the Polizeitruppe, was formed in 1891, and immediately became involved in fighting the population defending their trading monopoly on the roads from Douala toward the interior. By December 1893 the police rebelled and an army, the Schutztruppe, was created in 1895. The Schutztruppe was in action from the moment of its creation until the outbreak of the First World War. In southern Cameroon the rubber rush was responsible for most of its operations.[9]

The violence and utter destructiveness of such colonial wars is often still misunderstood. Routinely village after village was burned down and people fled, sometimes for years, into deep forests where they built only the flimsiest of shelters and depended largely on gathering for food. During the fighting and immediately afterward, casualties among Africans were high, but even more died later from the combined effects of malnutrition, overwork, and epidemics such as smallpox, measles, dysentery, and above all sleeping sickness. In some districts the conquest lasted for years. The Bekwil in Gabon and Congo confronted a sizable number of French colonial troops from 1907 to 1912, then the German Schutztruppe in 1912–1914, and then the French again in 1919–1920. It is a wonder that they survived at all.[10] The despair engendered by the conquest is evident in many a document similar to the following entry in a diary. This incident took place on the banks of the Aruwimi in 1894, in a district where countless unrecorded tragedies similar to this one recurred, as war raged back and forth for 20 years.

> *22 June 1895—*. . . A man from Baumaneh scouring the forest and loudly shouting for his wife and child who had lost their way there, comes too close to our camp and is shot by a bullet of one of our sentries. They bring us his head. Never have I seen such an expression of despair, of terror.[11]

The ultimate toll of war, hunger, and disease was terrifying. The fate of the Tsayi in Congo has perhaps been among the harshest. After the conquest was over, only 3 villages out of 135 survived and the ethnic group virtually disappeared.[12] Or consider the fate of the people in the lower valley of the Kwa. Late in 1890 the Catholic mission there witnessed the arrival of the first large military expedition of the Congo state, pillaging its way to the Uele and kidnaping people as prisoners. At that time Ebeke, the local leader of some eight villages, called the missionary to a district meeting to consider what to do about the fact that, in the last few months, 80 people had died and the 81st person was dying. Sleeping sickness had struck. These people were Bobangi traders and they may have carried the disease from the Malebo Pool, or, given the timing, perhaps the expedition introduced the disease. It would not be the first time that the military left epidemic disease in their wake. Ten years later, by 1900, the mission was abandoned because four-fifths of the local population had died.[13]

THE NEW RURAL COLONIAL SOCIETY

The familiar old ways of life were reeling under such novel calamities. The peoples in and around the rainforests had lost political control and, with it, the initiative to create institutions for coping with the new order. Furthermore, the hitherto unexpected events and disasters also opened up a tragic chasm between the physical and cognitive realities, which required new explanations and major adjustments of the equatorial tradition. The meeting called by Ebeke of the Kwa was assembled precisely to consider whether the epidemic could be halted by sending for a famous witch finder. The missionary instead sowed doubts about the efficacy of diviners and advised them to rely on God. But this was 1891, and people could still call a diviner to the rescue if they felt inclined to do so. By 1920 that was no longer easy. Such diviners were outlawed by then and prosecuted as confidence men and dangerous agitators.[14]

Missionaries directly inveighed against the old tradition in all its manifestations. They attempted to rally the youth and to use their grievances against their elders to abolish most public expressions of religion. In a number of cases this led to open clashes with local leaders, as occurred in the struggle between the Presbyterian missionaries in Gabon, on Corisco Island, and on the coast of southern Cameroon against the dominant association in the 1860s and 1870s. Missionaries, even then, found eloquent followers among the youth, who strove for an alliance of the old and the new, to discard what was "bad" and retain the "good." In other words, the enlightened youths now presumed to evaluate the core of their own tradition by the criteria of a foreign biblical tradition.[15] Local leaders sought to fight back. Where collective initiations existed, they used these as weapons to defend the tradition. Thus a struggle between a mission near Kisangani and the local *lilwá* initiators lasted for decades before the missionaries succeeded in breaking this alliance between the old and the young. By the 1930s many initiations of this sort had come to be outlawed in Zaire under one pretext or another, often because they supposedly harmed production quotas set for the rural population. Some initiations survived, but the time devoted to instruction was radically reduced. The campaign against initiations was particularly significant because it directly attacked the formal transmission of the old tradition's essence.[16]

Missions ridiculed and opposed nearly all expressions of the tradition, from "immoral" dances to worship of ancestors and nature spirits. Whenever they could, they invoked secular power to suppress institutions contrary to their ideas of "natural morality" and "law and order." State agents everywhere outlawed public divining, poison ordeals, many healing rituals, and human sacrifice at funerals, often without any idea of the consequences. In the minds of many Africans the first two measures meant that witchcraft now ran unchecked and that public health was ruined. In reaction, new healing and witchfinding cults sprang up to defend social and somatic harmony.[17] The degree to which crusading missionaries abhorred the old dispensation is evident from comments like "atavistically depraved" and "a morbid haunting by their ancestral spirits and occult forces that will leave them no respite." Such statements manifest the depth of their convictions and the heat of their battle against the core of the old tradition.[18]

During the first generation of conquest the conquerors expended considerable effort to "understand" local societies and cultures. Reams of ethnographic and legal questionnaires provided a stream of information. But from the outset these incorporated an abstract view of what such societies and their laws should be like.[19] Such efforts soon resulted in the creation of a conscious model of what societies in equatorial Africa were and should be. As early as 1909, the ethnography of de Calonne-Beaufaict, a disciple of Durkheim, provided the blueprint of a spurious, segmentary, hierarchized, patrilineal society for use in the Belgian Congo. This allowed the government to build up a practical administrative line of command. By 1920 agents in the colony were enjoined to "discover" this model wherever states did not exist, and the population was physically regrouped to conform to it. Dependent status did not exist in the model, so all dependent statuses from client or pawn to slave were gradually abolished. Leaders became mere "patriarchs," bereft of any source of power that did not directly derive from the colonial administration. So when in the 1950s an anthropologist found the Ngombe to be perfect examples of an egalitarian segmentary patrilineal society, he was unwittingly writing a testimonial to the efficiency of administrative action.[20]

In the territories ruled by France a slightly different model prevailed. Local peoples were perceived as families, grouped into villages only. The village became the new administrative unit. For the convenience of administration smaller villages were then united in artificial administrative villages, which in turn were grouped in cantons led by government appointees, except for a few cases in which former chiefdoms or kingdoms were involved. There a hereditary government chief could become *chef de canton*.[21]

These blueprints so blinded the Europeans to precolonial practice that they did not accept or even recognize institutions with which they were perfectly familiar at home. Tio kingship had been inherited bilaterally as inheritance is in France. Now it had to be matrilineal only. In eastern Kasai the rotating "presidency" of local political units was recognized but soon replaced by a hereditary chieftaincy to conform to standard practice elsewhere.[22] European conceptions of law also played a major role. Thus there could be only a single form of legal marriage, and marriage with the payment of bridewealth was deemed to be the closest to the European norms. Marriage by exchange, *lengbe* in northeastern Zaire, was held to be contrary to public morality—even though it was the dominant form of marriage there—on the grounds that it supposedly coerced the women involved. Succession and inheritance were standardized according to European practices, and wherever possible primogeniture was imposed. The very notion of customary law was a creation of Napoleonic law. Both procedural and substantive law had to pass the acid test of acceptance by European legal experts, as the cases of marriage and inheritance show. So even in the Belgian Congo, where officials prided themselves on the preservation of traditional customs and culture, they substituted their own constructions in order to preserve an old façade for a new order. A body of urban customary law even evolved for the Africans in the new colonial cities.[23]

The equatorial tradition finally died in the 1920s, killed by two simultaneous developments. First, in the realm of physical reality, the conquest prevented the tradition from inventing new structures to cope with a new situation. Instead the colonial government invented them. Its agents preserved some old practices, but the whole structure made sense only in the cognitive realm of the Europeans, not in the equatorial tradition. This process was just the opposite of the dynamics current in the previous period, when novel foreign practices were justified in terms of the old tradition. Second, the unforeseen and hitherto unimaginable events of the colonial conquest had created a gulf between the physical and the cognitive reality in the equatorial tradition at the very time that its cognitive reality was directly challenged by foreigners, whose own success seemed to bolster their claims to cognitive superiority. As a result, the cognitive part of the old tradition, its very core, went into an irreversible crisis. The peoples of the rainforests began first to doubt their own legacies and then to adopt portions of the foreign heritage. But they clung to their own languages and to much of the older cognitive content carried by them. Thus they turned into cultural schizophrenics, striving for a new synthesis which could not be achieved as long as freedom of action was denied them.

When independence loomed, insecurity exploded. The rural populations sensed that there was no turning back to an unsullied age of ancient tradition. What was the future then to bring? So violent was this insecurity among the central Kuba that, within a few months in 1959, they administered the poison ordeal to 500 suspected witches, in the hope of cleansing the social system of its colonial past and entering a happy millennium.[24] But this was the last desperate action of an ancient order. At the same time, variants of neo-African tradition were gestating in cities and the countryside. The transition to independence occurred, however, without the guidance of a basic new common tradition. Today that is still the situation, and the people of equatorial Africa are still bereft of a common mind and purpose.

Nine

On History and Tradition

It has been argued in this book that a single tradition flourished for millennia in equatorial Africa and a reconstruction of the political institutions of the peoples in the region has been proposed. The time has come to reflect on the findings. Our concluding remarks will be arranged on four main levels. First some thoughts about the validity of the proposed reconstruction. Only if the validity of this tale is high enough is it worthwhile to ponder its content. Moreover, if the methodology is valid in this case, it should be universally applicable to other areas with a similar mix of sources, and there are many of these in the world. At a second level follow some comments about the forces that have been involved in molding the past of the area itself. At yet a third level, considerations will be raised about tradition in general: what are the characteristics of all cultural traditions? Finally, how can the study of traditions contribute to the overall agenda of anthropology and history? Remarks about tradition in general and the value of its study must remain tentative jottings, for the intent of this book is to be but an introduction and a contribution to our substantive knowledge about the past of equatorial Africa. This is not a finished theoretical essay but only a prolegomenon to such an endeavor. Comments at the more general levels are intended then merely to offer a vista of intellectual landscapes in the hazy distance, as an invitation to lure future travelers.

THE PROBABLE PAST

The main goal of this study has been not only to show that a history of the peoples of equatorial Africa is possible but also to indicate how to reconstruct the probable past. The reader can judge how convincing the use of various techniques and sources has been. I hope at least to have demonstrated how wrong the positions are that there was no change in the lives of the inhabitants of the rainforests in equatorial Africa or that all traces of their past are hopelessly lost. But beyond the validity of using this or that source or technique there still lies the question of how valid the reconstruction as a whole should be held to be. Is this but one of very many possible reconstructions, or is it the most probable among very few alternatives? How probable is this proposed past?

The reconstruction as a whole consists of a set of interconnected propositions forming a complex hypothesis. It is a valid hypothesis insofar as it can be "falsified," as the philosophers call the process of testing. Insofar as the claims made here are predictive, in that they can be tested in the future, and because they are based on data, they constitute a hypothesis and are not mere speculation. Archaeological excavations are but the most obvious avenue to testing it. Indications have been given as to what should be found where and when, precisely to strengthen the validity of the hypothesis. Further work with any other new sources—be they written, oral, linguistic, biological, or based on the analysis of technology and style—will also allow the propositions made here to be tested. The "words and things" technique in particular is so rich and powerful in potential applications, by itself or in conjunction with other data,[1] that it will eventually test every part of the hypothesis.

This stance does not mean that I lack confidence in the propositions made in this book. To the contrary! They achieve a high order of validity because they are interconnected (the relation to the ancestral tradition) and because they claim to account for many data. The quality of a hypothesis varies with the density of the interconnections between its parts and with the number of the elements it attempts to explain. The more features it addresses, the higher the quality of the hypothesis, because the number of potential alternative hypotheses decreases with the number of features which have to be accounted for. This is why the dominant hypotheses in physics are so convincing: they address a multitude of disparate data by a single integrated hypothesis. The chances for a potential alternative solution become infinitesimally small. The main hypothesis laid out in this book is complex enough to induce confidence, even though the interconnection of its various component propositions often remains loose. An alternate overall hypothesis to account for all the data is possible but unlikely. On the other hand, many individual propositions will certainly be amended and recast, and once fresh data become available, some may even be abandoned. So, while there is a high degree of probability to the overall vision of the reconstructed past, it still remains true that this book constitutes but an agenda and stimulus for vigorous future inquiries.

HISTORY, HABITAT, EVOLUTION

Bantu-speaking immigrants brought a single ancestral western Bantu tradition into these lands, a tradition that then further crystallized as the result of a series of interactions between these farmers and their new habitats. A sketch of the main concrete features of this ancestral tradition provides us with a sense of long-term continuities which lasted here for millennia, a very long time perspective indeed. The necessary counterpoint of transformation and ceaseless change was then introduced to document the position that a tradition is a process: it lives only while it changes. Such transformations occurred in what was essentially a closed situation. On the whole the effect of other neighboring traditions on the equatorial Bantu tradition remained superficial, except for the peoples in the eastern reaches of the area. Later, under open conditions, this tradition still held its own, even when forcefully challenged by a tradition as different and foreign as the Christian European tradition, and new needs were met by innovation rather than through borrowing. The tradition did borrow tools, such as the gun, and new crops, and then adapted them to its own technological system,[2] but the stubbornness with which it held to its own concepts, values, institutions, and tools is much more remarkable. For instance, after centuries of trading, goods still retained their value as items for use rather than for exchange. Whenever possible, wealth in goods was still converted into followers. The principles underlying markets for land and labor were still rejected. The people carrying the tradition of the rainforests met challenges by innovating as the need arose, transforming the old into the new, as their institutional history at that time demonstrates. The tradition collapsed only when its bearers were conquered after 40 years of war and lost their independence of action with their self-determination.

This historical reconstruction has focused on political history, more specifically on the history of institutions. This choice was made on several grounds. First, a choice had to be made: the reconstruction of all facets of history is an impossibility, both in theory—histories are built around itineraries and arguments—and in practice. Second, the possibility of institutional change specifically was denied by earlier authors and their metaphors of unchanging amoebae, so it was worthwhile to study this history first. Third, political history is no mere epiphenomenon or dependent variable. The reader will have noticed over and over again how institutional innovations led to vast territorial expansion. Finally, a chronological framework, however tentative, can be proposed for many of these transformations, and thereby yields a concrete anchorage in time for this history of political institutions, even if the anchors sometimes prove to be less than steadfast.

The basic dynamic of these political institutions from the outset has been a tension between the desire for local autonomy and the need for security. In the ancestral situation, the internal cohesion within districts resulted from the interaction between Houses, especially leading Houses in a village, engaging in matrimonial alliances and exchanging special resources. The fluidity of residence in various villages and membership in various Houses for men was an outcome of the cognitive views concerning an undifferentiated or bilateral kinship system. The community of each person was thought of as that person's relatives, not as a closed descent group incorporating only and all the descendants of So-and-So. At the same time the residential flux of men and women tended to redistribute labor in optimal ways for production and standards of living. The resulting districts were all approximately equally powerful, so that a state of dynamic equilibrium prevailed over very large regions. Certainly the accidents of demography and the presence of special resources or a richer mix of resources produced some inequalities, and hence threats that could upset the balance of power, but many such advantages were but temporary and the threatened groups could move away. Very low population densities were therefore an integral part of the system. The decentralized system and its dynamic equilibrium were extremely stable, given the competition between big men and the movement of people between Houses.

Despite this stability, and in the very long run, one sees time and time again a breakdown of regional equilibria when one or another society became more powerful than its neighbors because it could mobilize more people more often or because it incorporated more people than its neighbors. No wonder that, even at the height of the Atlantic trade, equatorial Africans still thought of people as wealth, power, and mutual security. This superiority in manpower was achieved by strengthening internal institutions of cooperation within a district or a wider area and by adapting the cognitive representations of its inhabitants to this new situation. The circumstances for doing so required the conjunction of an exceptional and long-lived personality occurring among the big men and a simultaneous change in the local economic conditions, which allowed some big men with more wealth than others to attract more women and clients. Such men could then work in alliance with some of their peers to promote the status and power of all the members in the group or to better their own relative position. Alternatively it is possible that a talented individual used his renown as an arbitrator, a diviner, or a warrior to achieve a durable advantage. But there is very little evidence for these latter pathways to preeminence in equatorial Africa, with the exception of arbitrators, whereas the direct ties between economic well-being and success are constantly stressed. The history of political institutions is fully interwoven with the history of economic production and distribution, but the history of strong personalities is equally important. Alas, accounts of their lives unfortunately can no longer be recovered.

Once the equilibrium was broken on one point in a given area, people in the neighboring districts experienced considerable insecurity and had to react, either by adopting the structural innovations of the successful group or by inventing new institutions of their own that would restore the balance of power or give them an advantage. This sequence of innovation and counterinnovation destabilized the overall regional political system and produced in some regions an acceleration over time in the growth of the scale of political societies. To cite the most extreme case: in the southwest, Kongo societies passed from groupings of perhaps 500 inhabitants by A.D. 500 to 500,000 by 1400, a 1,000-fold growth in less than a millennium. Here one sees the effect of a drive toward centralization in the name of peace and security, but always at the expense of local autonomy.

More striking than this case are the myriad societies everywhere that refused to follow this path. Despite the threat to security entailed by decentralization, local leaders insisted on autonomy to the point of limiting cooperation at higher levels to such specific endeavors as trade, the preservation of health, or occasional military assistance. One must admire the ingenious solutions found to allow for both almost total local autonomy and cooperation where needed. That is the distinctive contribution and the special lesson to be learned from equatorial Africa in the world's panoply of political institutions. The inexorable march forward from local community to chiefdom, to principality, to kingdom or state, proposed by unilineal social evolutionists was not the only possible option.

The development of political institutions in equatorial Africa is perhaps the most impressive illustration of the power of a tradition to shape its future. Right from the outset two ideologies coexisted: one that extolled and explained the success of big men and one that stressed the ideal equality of all, which underlies the suspicion of witchcraft. In the southern savannas the first ideology developed into the so-called divine kingship so familiar in African anthropology. The second prevailed in equatorial Africa. Yet even in the states to the south, autonomy was still so prized that state control over the villages remained limited to a few activities, sometimes only to the payment of tribute.[3]

Given these dynamics of political history, as even superficial observation shows, there has been an acceleration of change over time in equatorial Africa. Except in the southwestern portion of the area, the first documented innovations occur after A.D. 1000, one—and, in some regions, two and almost three—millennia after Bantu speakers settled there. A more careful look at the data shows that these are not the first

changes. One perceives earlier innovations, but further in-depth research is needed to establish them firmly. The further one upstreams
into the past, the fainter the traces of the past become. But granting this,
the fact remains that almost everywhere by A.D. 1000 the scale of society
was still that of a district composed of four or five villages. One also
perceives that even in the second half of the first millennium A.D. communities provided with bananas were still colonizing empty lands. The
dynamics of escalation did not yet apply. It was just as easy and often
more attractive to move out of range, to restore security by increasing
distance.[4] The dynamics of escalation probably began toward the end of
the first millennium. As the evidence stands, a steady succession of
changes occurred in the inner basin and in the southeastern and southwestern parts of equatorial Africa. But as new equilibria were achieved,
breaks in the diffusion of innovations occurred—for example, after the
Sanaga-Ntem expansion or between western and eastern Mongo after
the *ya*-expansion—and there was never much speeding up in northern
Maniema and Ituri, although it did occur in southern Maniema and in
the southwestern quadrant. Evidently acceleration was not universal.
One has also seen increasing economic growth in the expanding area
that became involved with the Atlantic trade. It may be tempting to tie
the phenomenon of the speeding up of political change, where it occurred, to the outside impact of the European world-system, but this will
not account for acceleration in southern Maniema. Moreover, it must be
emphasized that, once firms had arisen and towns grew, there is no
further institutional acceleration linked to the Atlantic trade in the inner
basin, despite the large-scale turbulence and military innovation in the
later nineteenth century. Economic development did not automatically
trigger the appearance of larger-scale political societies, and acceleration, where it occurred, is part of a specific historical record and not a
property of political history everywhere in the region.

This conclusion is as relevant to social evolutionary theory as the
stress on autonomy is. Evolutionary theory can cope with either of these
phenomena only by enlarging its spatial scale to the scale of the world,
and by denying the relevance of innovations which do not point to
increased complexity and growth of scale.[5] Thus all this institutional
history, except for the southwestern quadrant, merely becomes peristal-
tic movement, in other words, stagnation. The flow of time is ignored,
except where the process postulated occurs. One may well suspect that
social evolutionary theory starts from the undoubted preponderance in
the world of a few, very large recent empires, to explain the past merely
as a set of preordained steps leading up to them. This theory mimics
biological evolutionary theory, but its actual subject matter, procedures,
and hypotheses are fundamentally different. It does not, therefore, par-

take of the high degree of validity rightly attached to biological evolutionary theory.

Most previous authors have accepted that the social condition of people in equatorial Africa was determined by their habitat: the equatorial forest. Although the diversity of the actual habitats has been pointed out and crude determinism is rejected by all, one can still wonder to what extent habitats actually determined the unfolding of the past in this region dominated by varieties of rainforests. One can argue that, after all, the role of economics in political history has been of great, perhaps even of primordial, importance, and does not economics include the availability of natural resources and their distribution? So is there not a determinism after all and if not, why not? First, a landscape is not a variable independent from the people who inhabit it. Both people and their habitats are part of a single reciprocal system. People and their natural environment constantly influence each other. Thus a natural disaster, such as a severe drought along the Loango coast or a devastating tornado or an outbreak of sleeping sickness, could force populations to abandon a locality or a district. But people could also change landscapes. Thus the ecotone of savanna and forest environments in the middle Bomokandi–Nepoko area attracted immigrants, but the population cut much of the forests, pushed the main ecotone farther south over the years, and created a parklike landscape that had not existed before. The fishermen of the floating meadows and marshes north of Bolobo managed their environment by draining, canalizing, and damming the flow of water, so as to create a huge, single fish-farming system and, in doing so, also changed the composition of the vegetation and fauna in various portions of the region.[6] Any one-way model of this constant, dynamic, and complex ecological interrelationship oversimplifies the picture. One-way models also distort the interface between physical habitats and communities, because the relation between them was mediated by the cognitive reality of the habitats in the people's minds, by their technological choices, by the strategies of labor they used, and by their perceived material, social, and ritual needs.

The extent and character of knowledge of equatorial Africans about their natural habitats have been grossly underrated, if only because most observers were not trained naturalists. The few extant inventories which list local names and uses of plants suffice to make this point and more. They show that local communities knew much more about their habitats than they needed to know for utilitarian purposes.[7] Precisely because the cognitive inventory of their environment practically matched the wealth of the physical reality around them, the inhabitants of these habitats had a wide range of choices. This knowledge allowed them to adopt a chosen strategy of resource exploitation, not have one forced upon them. They could always tap new raw materials for making tools, medicine, and food, or abandon some older resources and technologies when sociocultural goals or technology changed. Moreover, here as in other realms of life, physical and cognitive realities stood in a dynamic interrelationship. Women tested new plants, hunters tried different types of rope or different sizes of meshes for nets intended to capture animals, physicians experimented with novel medicines, and so on. This constant striving to match both realities is the essence of science, and in that sense science was practiced.

For even if the bulk of this knowledge was traditional, it was far from static. The reader will recall that the notion of optimal returns was deeply engrained in this tradition. Wherever a strategy made it possible to achieve a higher return per participant for a lower input, it was adopted, regardless of whether the returns were material or social. This constituted a strong force for constant trial-and-error methods of innovation. Right from the outset, total autarchy within any community was rejected as wasteful. Long before any Bantu-speaking farmers set foot there, the hunters and gatherers near Mbandaka received the raw materials for their stone tools from the confluence of the Kwa River 250 km away. By extending the space from which one drew raw materials and thus indirectly tapping many more habitats, individual communities overcame "limitations" imposed by the distribution of natural resources, and hence some of the "limitations" of their natural environment.[8]

But are there not richer and poorer environments, habitats where people flourished and others where they barely got by? Is it, for instance, not true that sizable states did not flourish in these rainforests? The correlation is true enough, but even a cursory comparison with rainforests in West Africa, in Yucatán, and in mainland Southeast Asia shows that such environments do not preclude the formation of large states such as those of the Bini, Akan, Maya, and Khmer. The distaste for centralized government lay in the dominant tradition, not in the natural environment.

Even so, one cannot help but be struck by the fact that most of the cradles of primary political innovation in equatorial Africa lay in zones blessed with especially diversified resources, on the borders or ecotones of several major types of habitat. The cradles in the inner basin, the southwestern quadrant, the northeast, southern Maniema, the island of Bioko, and the cradle on the Sanaga all appear to lie in zones rich in ecotones. In many of these cases considerable population densities, at least compared with neighboring areas, seem to have built up, and some triggered expansions. The image of a rich environment in which population booms and which leads to structural innovation and/or expansion is a tempting one. Indeed it has been used to explain the Bantu migrations themselves. And yet it will not work. Such a view underrates the choices communities have regarding population. Conscious demographic policies were followed in equatorial Africa, and population was controlled.[9] Hence a growth in population density was not an accident. Increased tensions and conflicts resulted from higher population densities, yes, but they may just as well have preceded the build-up of population, and they explain why competing groups strove to increase their memberships to the highest levels in the first place. And there was always the option to leave congested areas and move to low-density areas, thus evening out overall population densities. Evidently this did not happen on the banks of the middle Sanaga around 1400, no doubt because, despite the increase in population, the standards of living there were still more attractive than elsewhere. When emigration occurred in such cases, it means that something had changed in the equations within the homeland. Suddenly emigration became preferable to a continued life as a perpetual junior in an overcrowded homeland. Cognitive reality had changed, and certain local events, now unknown to us, made them change. These events may have been changes in the physical habitats, such as impoverishment of soil or game, but they may just as well have been social events, such as attempts at hegemony or increased exploitation of juniors. The correlation between political innovation and rich ecotones is not so easy to explain. Moreover, it may be only apparent, for not all rich ecotones gave rise to political innovations. They did not, for instance, in Ubangi. Obversely, not all places where ecotones were unremarkable lacked innovation. In northern Maniema, brotherhoods, adapted to very low population densities and an unusually mobile way of life, were developed. Finally, the correlations may in part be spurious. For, given the nature of rainforests and of the orography and hydrography of the area, the complexity of habitats is immense and ecotones occur everywhere, as was shown in chapter 2.[10] So whoever wants to find an ecotone will find one.

The study of the interrelationships between natural habitats and human communities is fascinating precisely because of the complexities involved and can be much furthered both by intensive local study and by comparative work. The study of similar sets of habitats outside of equatorial Africa—in the Amazon or in Southeast Asia, for instance—is perhaps the most promising avenue, provided sufficient care is given to the historical developments and the impact of tradition there.[11]

PROPERTIES OF TRADITION

Traditions are historical phenomena which occur everywhere. Historians, however, have tended to shy away from them for several reasons. The popular use of the term in the sense of "lack of change" irritates historians whose avocation is to discover change. They rightly feel that the term has been used in this sense as an excuse to state a historical claim without analyzing its validity. In addition, "tradition" is often invoked to designate the historical consciousness of a particular group, and more often than not the term is just a flag of convenience to legitimate a position held on other grounds.[12] Historians also often felt poorly equipped to cope with the enormous time-depths involved in such phenomena, and the often hopelessly vague, romantic, and emotion-laden description of their content discouraged scholars from subjecting them to close scrutiny.[13]

But traditions, as fundamental continuities which shape the futures of those who hold them, are not just in the minds of observers. They are "out there." They are phenomena with their own characteristics. This study of the equatorial tradition makes it possible to list some of these. First, there is the fundamental continuity of a concrete set of basic cognitive patterns and concepts in tradition. This can be seen in the use of a canon of scriptures in such traditions as the Confucian, Buddhist, and Judaeo-Muslim-Christian. The semantic data used in chapter 3 document this in the case of the western Bantu, as semantic data also do in the Polynesian case.[14] Some basic patterns in physical reality—for example, principles in the techniques of farming or seafaring—also belong to the tradition.

Second, traditions are processes. They must continually change to remain alive. Their relevance and central position can be assessed by their capacity for periodic renewal. The history of schisms and schools in the universalistic religions is a perfect example of this feature. So are the institutional transformations sketched in chapters 4 to 6. A tension always exists between the two realities people can be aware of: the cognitive reality, which predicts, and the physical reality, which then happens. When the discrepancies between them become too great or when people become aware of regularities in physical reality that do not exist in cognitive reality, the two realities have to be readjusted. The readjustment is the point where permanent change occurs. Because there are always discrepancies and attempts to bridge them are always made, a living tradition changes. Therefore tradition is a moving continuity.

Third, the relation between continuity and change within a tradition is one of unique developments flowing out of static basic principles. Continuity concerns basic choices, which, once made, are never again put into question. Basic views about ultimate reality, such as the existence of a single God and the central role witches play in disease, are examples. But so are the adoption of agriculture as the mainstay of food production and the organization of a House. These fundamental acquisitions then act as a touchstone for proposed innovations, whether from within or from without.[15] The tradition accepts, rejects, or molds borrowings to fit. It transforms even its dominant institutions while leaving its principles unquestioned. In hindsight the course of later history is perfectly clear. It is the unfolding of the consequences of the ancestral decisions or their concrete adaptation in the face of new circumstances. But the pathways of change can never be predicted. It is enough to chart the pathways by which the triad House-village-district was transmuted into later social structures, to realize that each case was different from all the others. Yet, in several cases, the same pathways were followed for a while. Thus the Omaha system of kinship nomenclature often arose out of matrimonial strategies and in turn often led to patrilinearity. The uniqueness can be attributed to historical accident, a factor as random as mutation is in the genetic heritage of a population. The dynamic similarities are the product of tendencies inherent in the basic common heritage. But one cannot know what they are before they manifest themselves, because they do not appear in all cases, as the history of equatorial African institutions shows. In short then, a tradition chooses its own future: the basic choices are followed by subsidiary choices, which close certain options for the future and leave other options open.

Fourth, because traditions are processes, the specific definition of a tradition is partly in the mind of the beholder. Traditions are massive phenomena lasting for millennia. They have no beginning, although they do come to an end. It is the observer who determines when a tradition begins, that is, when its basic principles have become sufficiently different from the tradition out of which it grew and have become sufficiently unquestioned to be accepted as the start of the phenomenon studied. Thus one speaks of a Judaeo-Christian-Muslim tradition, but one also speaks of separate Christian and Muslim traditions. One can speak of Buddhist tradition, but one can also speak of Tibetan or Japanese traditions. In central Africa one can speak of a western Bantu tradition in general or of an equatorial tradition of the forest as it differentiated from its sister tradition in the savanna. Because traditions grow only out of traditions, a subjective element is of necessity always injected by the observer.

Fifth, traditions need autonomy. The peoples who carry them must have the power of self-determination. A tradition is maimed when autonomy is lost. Given its capacity to accept, reject, or modify innovation, a tradition will not be overwhelmed by another major tradition as long as its carriers still retain enough liberty of choice. As the case of the Muslim tradition in the colonies in North Africa shows, sovereignty can be lost and yet a tradition be maintained, if at least the liberty of worship and education is preserved, so that the core of the tradition can be kept and transmitted.

In sum then traditions are self-regulating processes. They consist of a changing, inherited, collective body of cognitive and physical representations shared by their members. The cognitive representations are the core. They inform the understanding of the physical world and develop innovations to give meaning to changing circumstances in the physical realm, and do so in terms of the guiding principles of the tradition. Such innovations in turn alter the substance of the cognitive world itself. A tradition is harmed when it loses its ability to innovate efficiently. If the situation perdures, it will die. A tradition dies when its carriers abandon its fundamental principles to adopt those of another tradition. This happens only after a society has become aware of a state of major incongruence between the cognitive and the physical worlds of its tradition, and is also aware of an alternative paradigm. Doubts about the reality of its cognitive world can then paralyze any attempt to repair the incongruence. As the demise of the equatorial tradition shows, this does not necessarily entail that the alternative paradigm will take its place. The people involved may strive to develop a new tradition based on parts of the old cognitive views, views derived from elsewhere, and novel views originating with a single person at first, and later gradually accepted by that person's community.

The characteristics cited are probably only the most obvious features common to all traditions. Because this is not a work of theory they are not systematically pursued in depth. Still the scholar cannot help but be struck by the appearance here of the familiar conundrum about the relationship of regularity and historical accident, of event and structure, of change and continuity.[16] This should not be surprising because traditions are so massive and long-lived that they carry along and leave their imprint on huge segments of history.

COMPARATIVE ANTHROPOLOGY AND TRADITION

At heart anthropology is the comparative study of cultures. Yet when measured against both ethnography and theory formation, comparative anthropology stagnates. The reasons for this situation are well known. The methodology for systematic controlled comparison is deficient. In practice three different strategies have been used. The most common and oldest practice is to compare the case studied with similar cases known from other anthropological monographs elsewhere in the world. There is no search to find all the relevant cases around the world. Moreover, some authors still commit the fatal error of wrenching the features under scrutiny from their cultural and social context. The second strategy relies on one of the cross-cultural surveys. One uses all known cases, or one uses a sample. Often the hypothesis chosen is "proved" by statistical correlations. The fatal flaw here is the drastic oversimplification entailed by, and the biases inherent in, the master code used in compiling the chosen cross-cultural inventory. The lack of systematic assessment of the degree of independence among the units in the universe chosen (Galton's problem) is just as bad. Some authors ignore this variable, and therefore risk spurious correlations. Others sample on the basis of a classification of cases by culture area. A culture area groups all the units among which historical interconnections are known or suspected. But because the history of many cultures has not been studied, the connection, if any, for a given feature or sets of features is not known, and in practice geographical proximity and overall degree of similarity in the features studied decide the issue. Wrenching from their cultural and social contexts the features to be compared is especially common in this case. The third approach is informed by socio-cultural evolutionary theory. It seriates societies or cultures by measures of complexity, arrays them in sets or steps from simple to complex, and explains them as stages in a logical developmental series. This too will not do. I have already argued that the theory is not valid, and the reader will recall that a *logical* sequence does not necessarily correspond to a *historical* sequence. In particular too many cases, like that of the kingdom of Kongo, are known where regression, at least in the size of the polity, has occurred. This example also highlights another difficulty with the notion of "complexity": it is always selective. Hunters and gatherers may have very complex matrimonial systems, as in Australia, or hold very complex bodies of myth, as among the San, and yet will be placed at the bottom of the ladder by most indexes, which use features of social and political complexity.

Thus the usual methods of comparative anthropology are flawed, if not bankrupt. In all the approaches used, the status of the units of comparison remains unclear. It is not clear what analogies or correlations actually prove, or which similarities are homologies and which are analogies. It is unclear what degree of validity the findings have: are they universal laws, do they hold regionally, or are they similar in the mind of the observer only? Finally, these methods are all based on synchronic data, and the first two still build on the mythical ethnographic present.

The study of cultural tradition can change this situation and make the dream of controlled comparison come true. After all, this book is a comparative exercise: it compares and claims to account for the political institutions of approximately 200 different peoples. It does so by following the historical course of a single tradition; it does so without having to declare that this or that group is a valid unit of comparison; it includes all cases; it seeks out homologies first, but is not blind to analogy; it privileges the whole context of each of the cases included; and the precise status of the validity claimed for its findings is clear. Finally, and perhaps most important, it draws the historical record into comparison. This makes it as different from other approaches as a study of *in vitro* is from a study *in vivo*. Moreover, this approach is flexible. Nothing prevents it from being enlarged. In the equatorial African context one can focus on more specific comparisons, for instance, concerning initiation rituals into manhood, healing cults, weaponry, or forms of marriage. One can sort out the homologies first and then study the analogies. One can then further test whether the latter are the result of convergence or are the product of similar constraints and, if so, which ones.

The study of a single tradition is a type of comparison which remains relatively modest in geographical scope, but a good knowledge of the substance, the history, and the extent of a given tradition is still valuable to many other studies. A regional cultural perspective is necessary for any kind of local study, and research on local communities and cultures is the bread and butter of social and cultural anthropology. Even a functionalist, synchronic study of a given community needs this approach to clarify whether the functions discerned exist only in the eye of the beholder or represent conscious or unconscious systemic links.[17] Such a perspective is even more necessary for any other kind of study. For example, in a stimulating recent book about internal frontier processes in Africa, I. Kopytoff speaks of a single sub-Saharan "ecumene," a "fundamental cultural unity," "pan-African cultural principles" "over the past couple of millennia": in other words, a pan-African tradition.[18] He hastens to add that its precise dimensions remain largely unexplored. Still, in order to pursue his examination, he must revert time and again to some of its intuitively presumed features. The lack of exact knowledge about the precise dimensions of this tradition clearly hampers a full exploration of the topic. The evidential status of the generalizations remains ambiguous because their relation to traditions remains unclear. Is the "relative indifference to rootedness of Africans to physical space"[19] a statement about an accidental similarity? Does it result from an inherited common African cognitive pattern? Or from convergence due to similarities in the environments? Or is it a mirage, culled from the reports of writers who portrayed the African of their preconceptions rather than documented careful observations?

The study of a single tradition is easily enlarged by extension into related traditions. For instance, the fundamental institutions of society in the eastern Bantu tradition can be studied and compared with those of the western Bantu speakers, thus extending the area of research over most of a subcontinent. Or one can move to a systematic comparison of thematic issues across all the relevant traditions in the world, provided their internal history has first been reconstructed. If one wants to reach definitive conclusions about the interaction between humans and tropical rainforests, one compares the traditions of all the areas in the world past and present covered by rainforests. The impact of literacy on religion, the consequences of the adoption of the plow, the practice of genital mutilation, or what have you, can be studied in a definitive fashion in a similar way.

Obviously the requirements for such a program are staggering. Not only does a single scholar take a decade to arrive at a presentation of the main outlines of a single tradition, but also a thorough knowledge of even a single tradition calls on the minds of many individuals over a long time period. And this effort must be repeated all over the world before truly satisfying conditions for global comparison become possible. It will require a generation or two of much collaborative work to achieve such conditions. But then scholarship is a collective endeavor and the goal after all is the central issue of a whole discipline. In this arena it does no good to use shortcuts. Shortcuts in comparative anthropology merely produce shoddy results or are but the precipitation of intuitive opinion. The danger in either case is that the unknown is mistakenly believed to be known and further inquiry is stifled.

Meanwhile the comparative study of tradition as a phenomenon in its own right promises to address some fundamental issues in anthropology. Are the characteristics of tradition listed above universal? Are there others, and what are the precise links between these characteristics? Are the means by which traditions shape their futures the same? Are they reproduced by the same mechanisms in different societies? How are they linked, or not, as the case may be, to language and its semantic master code, or, for that matter, to the working of the human mind in general? What does the phenomenon of tradition have to say about regularity in history or about structure and event? What do traditions tell us about the human condition?

We stand then at the threshold of a road to be traveled to very distant lands. This study has been a prolegomenon, a preliminary observation, an invitation to journey. May its substantive hypothesis be checked and expanded, other traditions be studied, the phenomenon of tradition itself be given close scrutiny, and the comparative approach suggested actually be practiced.

Appendix
Notes
Works Cited
Index

Appendix

Comparative Lexical Data

This appendix provides a list of selected lexical items of great antiquity found in equatorial Bantu languages. It includes mainly items that have been used in this work, especially in chapter 3. Therefore the appendix constitutes by no means a full inventory of all common items, as even a glance at the semantic index in M. Guthrie's *Comparative Bantu* (2:176–80) will show. That index is itself becoming out-of-date as research progresses. The sources for the words compared are disparate. They include published dictionaries and vocabularies listed in Y. Bastin, *Bibliographie bantoue sélective,* dictionaries and vocabularies mostly published after 1974, and items culled from a host of ethnographic and grammatical studies. In this way data for some 147 languages have been assembled, out of an estimated total of fewer than 200. For most words, therefore, one can rely on a fine comparative grid.

The entries are arranged by meaning and numbered consecutively. The material is divided into nine rubrics: A. Social units; B. Social status; C. Social activities; D. Food production: Techniques and Tools; E. Domestic plants and animals; F. Industries: Techniques and tools; G. Exchange; H. Spirits and forces; I. Religious experts and activities. The rubrics are subsumed under two parts. In the first part the meaning for each entry is followed by the relevant forms. For each form, class is given where relevant, and the relevant entry in Guthrie cited. The distribution of reflexes is indicated by citing languages in which they occur. All variant meanings are indicated, but often not all the relevant languages are listed, although one or more for each relevant genetic grouping are given. The reflex form for each language is not provided. Skewing is indicated only when it throws light on the history of the form. After this material follow the proposed etymology and a concluding comment. Part 2, dealing with the rubrics D–I, groups shorter notes in the same order.

Linguists may object that the poor transcriptions of so many sources do not really allow one to propose secure reconstructions. However, practice has shown that such sources in fact rarely mislead, as is repeatedly evident in examples from H. A. Johnston's *A Comparative Study of the Bantu and Semi-Bantu Languages*. Moreover, in almost all cases perfect transcriptions exist for a few languages widely separated in space.

PART I. SOCIETY

A. Social Units

1. Large social group: *-dɔngɔ* 5/6, 7/8, CS 665, glossed by Guthrie as "kinship"; *-dongɔ* 5/6, CS 714, glossed as "tribe." Guthrie gives no cases from the area of study for CS 665 and two for 714, but also cites Tiv. Yet the form is common; see Mpongwe, Nkomi, Londo, Saa, Nen, Kundu, Kosi, Kombe, Fia, Yambassa, Ewondo, Fang, Tsogo, Kele, Kota, Duma, Mongo, Eso, Ngengele, Lega, Pende, Mbuun, Yans, and Buma. Bushong, Lele, and Ndengese have a strongly skewed form, *-donji*.

Etymology: The meaning is related to CS 664, same form, 3/4, 11/10, "line of objects," and both seem to be derived from CS 657–59 *-dɔ́ng-*, "to arrange," "to heap up," "to pack carefully," which is clearly proto-Bantu.

Comment: The term is at least proto-Bantu and meant at that time "large social group," perhaps "ethnic group." The connotation "kinship" is derived, but it establishes that even in those remote times common kinship was the justification for such social groups.

2. House: *-gandá,* 5/6, CS 779. Guthrie gives the meaning "clan." Aka, Poto, and Ngombe: "kingroup," "village"; Kako, Nyanga, and Tembo: "patrilineage"; Mbosi, Kongo, Mbala, and Tsong: "matriclan."

Etymology: The same form in classes 9/6, CS 780, occurs just as often with the meaning "village"; see Yáá, Yombe, Mbala, Bushong, Ngombe, and Mbuja. In Woyo and Tetela the form in class 9 means "the enclosure of a leader"; in Tio *kaaná* 9 means "quarter of a village" and hence *bamukaaná,* "those from within the quarter X," designates members of a House. And Angba has the meaning "surrounding of the village." The same form as CS 781, 9/10, "house" is attested to in Bongiri with that meaning. In addition, *-gandá* 9/10 means "camp" in Mbosi, Koyo,

Leka, Bobangi, Ekonda, Ntomba, Lia, Mongo, Lwankamba, and Lalia. Guthrie postulates that the primary meaning was "chief's enclosure." However, the distribution of the meaning "social group" is wider. It is also more central to the whole semantic field. So is the closely related meaning "quarter inhabited by a House."

Comment: The form is proto-Bantu, with the meaning "House" or "settlement inhabited by a House." It may be the oldest form designating this social unit still in existence.

*-cúká, 5/6, no CS. In the whole Mongo group, and in Wumbu, Bobangi, Mpama, Lingala, Libinza, Mbole, Tetela, Ngombe, Eso, Bushong, and Lega. Komo *etúgé* and Nzabi *tsuku,* "member of the matrilineage," are perhaps related. The large distribution is centered on the central inner basin and contiguous except for Wumbu.

Etymology: From the same form, class "anthill sp.," which in the central inner basin refers to a specific type of anthill used as a support for cooking pots. It is a metaphor for "hearth" and hence for "House."

Comment: This is an innovative metaphor going back to the period when the northern Zaire languages were still united with the southwestern group, as the Wumbu form indicates. The form was lost everywhere else but flourished in the inner basin.

*-bóta, 5/6, ps 50 (3:67). In Punu, Nzabi, Mbede, Tio, Mfinu, Mbosi, Mongo, Ntomba, Tetela, Ngwi, Bobangi, Mpama, Ngombe, Mbuja, and Eso; Tsogo, Sakata, and Dja: "matriclan."

Etymology: From CS 208 **-bót-,* "to give birth to" (extremely widespread in Bantu), itself probably derived from CS 211 **-bóto,* "seed," 9/10 or 11/10 (many languages including Tiv). Another derivation of the verb is CS 210.5 **-bóto,* "relative," 3/4, 5/6, 7/8: Kongo, Tio, Bobangi, Tetela, and Lega. Kota: "clan head."

Comment: The meaning "social group" is somewhat later than the emergence of western Bantu, since the verb from which it derives appeared only when the first splits had occurred in western Bantu. It is not found in northwest Bantu languages but is very common elsewhere. It can be applied to a House or a larger group. Despite the Sakata and Dja forms, it designates an undifferentiated kingroup—at the House level, not a lineage—and is as old as **-cuka.* It flourished because of its connection to a semantic field of such emotional and cognitive importance.

*-jó, 9/10, "matrilineage." Reflexes occur among the Nzabi, Duma, Mbede, Tsayi, Kukuya, Tio, Mfinu, Kunyi, the northernmost Kongo, Vans, Mpur, and Ding.

Etymology: From CS 946, 9/6, "house," for the same languages.

Comment: An innovation that occurred in the southwest, probably in the Nzabi or Teke groups. It is derived from the meaning "house," perhaps as late as c. A.D. 1200. Other examples of this semantic transfer occur in the northwestern Bantu languages.

-vumu, 5/6. Kongo, Boma, Yans, and Ding: "matrilineage."

Etymology: From CS 229, 5/6, "belly," "pregnancy," a meaning it has retained in the same languages.

Comment: Innovation. See next entry.

-kundu, 5/6, no CS. In Mongo, Lia, and Tetela; Ndumbu, Mbede, Tege, Ngwi, Sakata, Ntomba, and Bushoong: "matrilineage"; Mbosi: "familial domain."

Etymology: Also means "belly," "pregnancy," everywhere.

Comment: Innovation. The combined distribution of both *-kundu* and *-vumu* ranges from the Kongo group of languages to the Mongo group of languages and is continuous now. But that may well be accidental. The semantic extension from "pregnancy" to the "House core group" probably occurred first in *-kundu.* That distribution is discontinuous. It is not yet possible to estimate whether it first occurred in the Mongo or in the Mbede group.

3. Village: *-gi,* 3/4, CS 818. In Londo, Bubi, Vili Mbuja, Eso, Olombo, Angba Bali, Boa, Bati, Bira, Lega, Nyanga, and Tembo.

Etymology: Unknown. CS 936 *-je,* 3/4, is obviously a variant in eastern Bantu.

Comment: Proto-Bantu. Reflexes occur in a continuous large block in Uele, Ituri, and Maniema, in western Cameroon and Bioko, and on the Loango coast. Elsewhere within the area of study the form was replaced by other terms.

-bóga, 9/10, CS 192. In Noho, Benga, Aka, Ngando, Pande, Yakinga, Kabonga, Leke, Kele, Kota, Mboshi, Koyo, Mbede, Bobangi, Lingala, Libinza, Ngombe, Bembe, and class 7/8 Bongom; Ewondo, Bulu, Fang, and Ntumu: "the lineage inhabiting a village and the settlement"; Duala, Bulu and Foto: "home"; Mpongwe: "abandoned village."

Etymology: Unknown. Just possibly derived from ps 45 (3:62) *-bóg-,* "to plaster," "to dig foundations" (Duala, Bulu, and Bobangi) and "to mold pots" (Tio). The same form, 9/10, CS 193 ("path")—found in Bekwil, in the Mongo group, Tetela, Bushong, and Mbole—is related and derived from the meaning "village." Foto has the two meanings "home" and "road." Lega *mbuga,* 9/10, "inhabited place," is another derivation.

Comment: The area of distribution is solid, stretching from the southern Cameroon coast to northern Congo and the Mongala River, and also occurs in western Cameroon. The associated meanings cover the whole inner basin as well. The form is obviously younger than *-gi*. For further discussion, see next entry. The primary meaning may well have stressed the village plaza, which would explain the semantic shifts around the main area of distribution.

4. Home (my village, natal village): *-dá,* 14/6, CS 447, and *-yadí,* ps 483 (3:142). In Sekiani, Kosi, Mkako, Kaka, Gunabemb, Mpōmpō, Bekwil, Mpiemo, Ewondo, Bulu, Fang, Duma, Mbede, Kukuya, Tege, Tsayi, Tio, North Kongo, Vili, Kunyi, Yāā, Boma, Buma, Yans, Tsong, Mbuun, Ding, and Sakata. With a prefix of location *-ku,* it is found in Ngumba, Mabea, Bikele, and Njem. Kele, Kota, Kuta, and Ndasa have a form *akuli* that may be an even further elaboration of *-ku + yadí.* The whole Mongo group (except class 3/4) and Bushong have it as "natal village"; Luba has it as "interior of village."

Etymology: Unknown. Possibly from the dependent nominal (adjective) CS 448 "that, those," used with class 14 prefix to create an abstract noun.

Comment: The distribution of the form with the meaning "home," often with the additional connotation "village," stretches from the Loango and Gabonese coasts to the Lualaba near Kindu and from the southern margins of the study area to Franceville, the mouth of the Nkeni River, and the Maringa River. Moreover, reflexes are also found in western Cameroon, in the Sanaga-Ntem group, in Sekiani, west of the upper Sangha, and at least once between Sangha and Ubangi. The shape of the distribution and the languages included indicate great time-depth, but not proto–western Bantu. The stress on "my village (of choice)" or "my village (of birth)" makes sense, especially where kinship was undifferentiated and where men could choose to settle in one of several villages. The situation strongly suggests that unilinearity did not then exist. Both *-bóga* and *-dá* coexisted with *-gi* at first, stressing "my village" and "village plaza," respectively. They then drove *-gi* out from the western two-thirds of the area of study, probably just after the southwestern group of languages and the northern Zairian languages split. Later on *-bóga* displaced *-dá* in the areas where it now predominates. Although the historical significance of these processes for a social history is evident, their exact significance remains as yet unclear.

5. Place of authority: *-bánjá,* 5/6, 7/8, 11/10, CS 55 ("courtyard"). Guthrie's entry misleads as to the meaning and the claim that reflexes are absent in the rainforest areas. They are practically universal in the western two-thirds of those areas. North of the Ogooué the meaning is "men's public house," and there was one per House. Among the Tsogo and Pinji it designates the village temple. In the Kongo and Teke world it designates a capital. In Bushong it refers to the public plaza in the capital. In Ndengese it means "village." In the Mongo group of the inner basin, in Tetela, in Luba (Kasai and Shaba), and in Nande the term refers to the courtyard of each House. In Nande, Kirundi, and other languages of the great lakes area the term in class 7/8 means "yard, place to build," and in class 5/6 or 11/10, "palaver." The term has this latter meaning in Bobangi, Mongo, Lega, Tembo, and Nyanga. In Mongo, Bolia, and Luba the term is also applied to the House. In Enya *ko* + *ánjá,* a normal reflex with a locative prefix, means "outside," "in the village."

Etymology: Unknown.

Comment: The form is clearly proto-Bantu. Its semantic field is discussed by C. Grégoire, "Le champ sémantique du thème bantou *-bánjá.*" She concludes that "yard prepared to build a house" was the first meaning. But she lacked the historically important reflexes from the northwest and west which make clear that, in western Bantu at least, the primary meaning seems to have been "politically central place," at first probably a portion of the village plaza. The semantic evolution diverged. In one direction it led to the designation of communal buildings, capitals, and even a cemetery (in Kongo). In another it stressed the function of the place "palaver" and even the result "debt" (in Kongo). In yet another direction, the semantic evolution stressed the spatial character of the notion to yield "building site." The semantic history, especially in the western part of the area, reflects political processes of both decentralization and centralization.

6. Main village: *cɛngɛ,* 3/4, no CS. In Nkomi, Mboshi, Punu, Mongo, Tetela, Bushong, Nunu, Sakata, Ding, Songye, and many toponyms in the Kwilu area; Mpongwe, Ewondo, Bulu, Fang, Aka, and Bobangi: "village plaza"; Tio: "hunting camp"; Buma: "the villagers"; Tetela: "rich man"; Ombo "village"; Lega: "inhabited place."

Etymology: Innovation from **-cɛnga,* "sand," all singular classes, CS 325, and the derived CS 324 "grain" and ps 94 (3:96), "sandbank, island" (attested in most classes). Guthrie attests Mpongwe, Vili, Ngungulu, Mfinu Ntomba, Bolia, and Bushong; also Duala and Bulu: "pebble." One can add "sand," Mbosi "earth," and Mongo "rough surface." All the western Bantu forms end with -ɛ, not -a. The original form is proto-western Bantu. An evolution occurred from "sand" to "village plaza" to "main village."

Comment: The unbroken distribution of the innovation, except for Nkomi, points to a late innovation from an earlier meaning, "village plaza," itself derived from "sand." With the meaning "village plaza," the form is proto–western Bantu. The Nkomi, Punu, and inner basin usages meaning "main village" are later independent developments. Part of the diffusion in the inner basin may be associated with the expansion of the *nkúmú.*

-páta, 5/6, CS 1455, "village." In Kongo, Tetela, and Hungaan. The term means "capital" in the Luba languages including Songye *eata.* Guthrie errs in giving *-pata* with low tone, as the Luba data indicate.

Etymology: Derived from *-páta,* 3/4, 5/6, 9/10, CS 1456 ("tract of land"), which Guthrie gives as "valley." The Luba and Lunda forms refer to tracts of savanna, Kele to "land" or "country," and Bubi has "farm." With this meaning the form may well have developed early in western Bantu.

Comment: The passage from "tract of land" to the village occupying the tract occurred in Shaba and spread from there to Kongo. Later in Shaba and Kasai the Luba term evolved to mean "capital" and "court."

7. Village charm: *-kíndá,* 9/10, no CS. In Nkomi, Gisir, Lumbu, Mongo, Ntomba, Yajima, Bushong, Sakata, Mbosi, Tio, Yaka, and Ding. Mpongwe has "ancestor."

Etymology: Unknown.

Comment: There is a sizable distribution in the southwestern and central parts of the area of study.

8. To build: *-tóng-,* CS 1848, 1848y. In Duala, Saa, Ngumba, Fang, Kele, Nzabi, Tsangi, Mbede, Tio, Mfinu, Yans, Bobangi, Kongo, Hungaan, Ding, Mongo, and Bushoong.

Etymology: From CS 1847 "to sew." Guthrie lists many of the same languages (e.g., Ngumba, Nzabi, Tsangi, Mbede, Bobangi, Kongo, and Hungaan) and others such as Luba Kasai.

Comment: The term is proto–western Bantu. It is cited as an instance of information useful to archaeologists. Houses in these areas were usually built in whole or in part out of panels. At least the roof panels, and often wall panels, were woven out of plant material. Similarly the less well documented *-tóndɔ,* 3/4, CS 1790 ("ridgepole") and *-búngá,* 3/4, 9/10, ps 49 (3:66) indicate that such houses were rectangular with sloping roof panels.

9. District territory: *-cé,* 3/4,and variant *-cí,* CS 331. The distribution is practically universal.

Etymology: Derived from CS 330, same form, class 9, and includes an Ekoid language. In many languages the same term still means both "territory" and "ground."

Comment: proto–western Bantu, and note the stability of the notion of district.

10. Inhabitant of: rendered as *-cí,* 1/2, plus personal name, CS 343. In Nzebi, Tio, Bobangi, Mongo, Ntomba, Bushong, Tetela, and Kongo.

Etymology: May well be derived from the previous item. Innovation in the southwestern group of languages. In Kongo, and in the savanna to the south, CS 1167 *-kwá,* 1, 2, arose later and replaced *-cí* in many languages there.

Comment: This term dates from the split of the southwestern language group and expresses ethnicity. Other similar terms have a very limited distribution.

NOTE: For clan, see items 1 and 2.

B. Social Status and Noble Animals

11. Leader, big man: *-kúmú,* 1a/2, CS 1265. See Vansina, "Deep Down Time," map 2, for a distribution. Reflexes occur everywhere except in the Saa group of languages, in north Congo, and in northern Maniema. In the Myene group of languages and in Lele the meaning has shifted to "master." This is also a subsidiary meaning in the Kongo languages. Add to the distribution map *-gúmí,* 1/2 ("rich person"), in Lega and some related languages. Not indicated is the shift from *-kúmú* to *-kúmí,* which occurred among Nkucu and Tetela speakers of north Kasai and spread from there to the Mbole in the north and as far as the Lega in the east.

Etymology: Unknown. CS 1263 and 1263a *-kúm-,* "to become honored" (become rich), and its derivation CS 1264 *-kúmo,* "fame," are both derived from CS 1265 as the distributions show. The verbal derivation may have occurred independently several times.

Comment: Proto-Bantu. In western Bantu the link with wealth is very strong, e.g., in the Sanaga-Ntem languages and in Lega, and the first meaning of the verbs CS 1263 and 1263a is clearly "to become rich." This points to the importance of economics for the position of big men. The shifts of meaning in coastal regions are an effect of the slave trade; the Lele shift is part of a shift in the paired semantic fields of this form and of *kolomo,* 1a/2, which went from "chief elder" to "master of pawn" as Lele society innovated new basic institutions. The shape of *-kúmí* forms is that of a nominal derivation from a verb reflex of CS 1265 indicating the agent.

-kɔta, 1/2, no CS ("leader"). In Zimba, Binja, Lega, Mituku, Lengola, and Enya; in class 5/6, the meaning is "elder" in Kimbundu and "elder brother" in Ovimbundu.

Etymology: Derived from CS 1158 *-kɔt-,* "to become aged."

Comment: There were two independent innovations, one in Maniema and one in Angola. The distribution is greater than indicated north of Kisangani, the result of the use of this term by the Zanzibari to designate the chiefs they appointed as far downstream as the confluence of the Lomami. The innovation in Maniema consisted of a shift in meaning from "elder" to "leader" as the associated elders collectively became rulers.

-cángó or *-cángɔ́,* 1a/2, ps 76 and ps 77 (3:87). "His father," "leader"; Kosi, Kpe, Duala, Noho, Benga, Basaa, Sekiani, Mabea, Ngumba, Bongom, Mpiemo, Pande, Ngondi, Kaka, Bomwali, Njem, Bomam, Gunabemb, Kota, Bobangi, Mpama, Lingala, Ngombe, Doko, Poto, Mbuja, Lokele; Londo has a reflex of *-cángɛ́,* 1a/2, "his father." It does not occur north of the Sanaga, south of the Gabon Estuary, the middle Ogooué, and the Alima, or in the inner basin. It does not occur eastward beyond the Itimbiri, except for Lokele. The break in the distribution in Cameroon is only apparent.

Etymology: *-cí* + *-angó,* CS 334 + CS 864, "father of me." The honorific "*shá* + man's name" in the Luba languages, as well as in Cokwe and Ruund, is a derivation from ps 76 or ps 77.

Comment: Early innovation after the Myene split. The *shá-* forms rule out a later date. The presence of the parallel *nyangó, nyangɔ́,* 1a/2, CS 1389 ("mother") in Fang, Mbosi, Mongo, Tetela, Bushong (archaic), and Olombo also points to a wider earlier distribution. This is only one of the forms for "father," and an unusual one. It is cited because, wherever it occurs, it also is used as a title for the head of a House. The distribution is unusual but not unique. The distribution supports the view that the expression became rare by the time the northern Zairian languages split off, since Aka and Mbati (Isongo) lack it. The waxing and waning of this expression in very early times left a tantalizing whiff of the dynamics surrounding the ideology of the House many centuries B.C. ago.

12. Mother's brother (leader): *-kádi,* 1a/2, no CS. In Kongo, Vili, Lumbu, Gisir, Tsogo, Sangu, Punu, and Yombe.

Etymology: Same form as CS 986, "wife, woman," which is proto-Bantu.

Comment: Innovation, linked to the notion of matrilinearity. Because the full form *ngwakhazi* occurs only in northern Kongo (Yombe and Manianga region), this probably was its epicenter.

13. Headman: *-káni*, 1a/2, no CS. In Punu, Gisir, Kele, Bongom, Wumbu, Mbamwe, Ndasa, Wanji, Mbede and Ndumu (connotation: "rich"), Mbosi, Makwa, Tege, Tsayi, and Yãã; Shake and Kota: "judge," "notable," "wise person," "old person"; Kukuya, Tio, Mfinu, Boma, and Hum: "vassal chief"; Sakata, class 5/6: "court of chief"; Yans: "judge"; upper Ngiri: "member of warrior association."

Etymology: This is a noun derived from a verb. The verb should be *-gán-* but is unknown. There is a form *-gán-* CS 72 ("to think"), and same form CS 773 ("to tell a tale"), which are proto-Bantu, as are derivation CS 775 *-ganɔ*, class 6 ("wisdom"), and the same form 7/8, 9/ 10, 11/10 ("tale"). The meaning of *-gan-* is very close to the expected meaning for *-gán-*, and it is impossible, in Kongo, for instance, to know without better tonal data whether items such as *-kana* ("to decide," "to judge," "to arbitrate") and its derivations, *-kanu* (11/10, "courtcase"), *-kani* (14, "wisdom"), and *-kanu* (5, "wisdom"), belong to one root or the other. And one cannot but suspect that somehow *-gán-* is derived from *-gan-*.

Comment: Innovation in the southwest from a verbal form "arbitrator," later "chief," and later "vassal chief," in areas where principalities arose.

14. Lord: *-yéné*, 1/2, CS 1971, meaning (ii), "chief": Kongo, Vili, Tio, Boma, and Mbosi.

Etymology: Derivation of CS 1970 "self," the dependent nominal (adjective) of the same form which is proto-Bantu. Also note CS 1971, meaning (i), "owner."

Comment: There is a tight distribution in the southwest, and innovation in the Kongo or Teke group of languages.

15. To rule over: *-béád-*, CS 100: In Tsangi, Tio, Mfinu, and Kongo.

Etymology: Unknown.

Comment: Innovation in the Kongo or Teke group of languages.

16. Leopard: *-gɔyi*, 1a/2, 9/10 CS 862, and *-gɔ*, 1a/2, 9/10, CS 834. Universal distribution except for Ngombe, Doko, Lengola, Komo, Bira, Bali, and Tembo.

Etymology: Unknown.

Comment: Proto-Bantu. The leopard is thoroughly identified with political leadership. The cult for its relics is greatest where the term is missing. The proto-Bantu term was replaced there by a praise name.

17. Pangolin, sp.: **-ká,* 9/10, CS 991 has **-káka.* In Mpongwe, Duala, Saa, Fang, Mbede, Ndumu, Yans, Ding ("hedgehog"!), Bushong, Lele, Tetela, Ngombe, Luba Kasai, Kongo, and Lega. The rubric is absent in many vocabularies.

Etymology: Unknown. Some reflexes reduplicate the stem yielding the form Guthrie gives, but the nonterritorial distribution of the simple form from Duala to Komo indicates that the short form is the original one.

Comment: Proto-Bantu. One species of this animal (not always *Manis tricuspis*) played a major role in symbolic thought and in political privilege among several peoples in the area, including the Lega, Komo, and Lele. The preservation of so many reflexes may be indicative of the antiquity of its symbolic and political position.

18. Friend: **-dogó,* 1/2, CS 692, and **-dego,* ps 170 (3:187). In Mpongwe, Sekiani,Bekwil, Nzabi, Mbede, Yãã, Laadi, Kukuya, Tio, Ngungwel, Kongo, Vili, Bobangi, Lingala, and Mongo. There are many skewed forms. Because the second consonant in most reflexes is *k* and there is much evidence of skewing, the forms could well be **dokó* and **-deko.*

Etymology: CS 692 seems to be derived from CS 694 **-dok-* ("to name"), just as **-dokí* ("namesake") is. The form is possibly proto-Bantu.

Comment: Innovation probably from the Loango coast for the first form. The second one could originate in Mpongwe as a skewed loan from Vili and then spread to the upper Ogooué. The distribution (only along major trade routes) and the frequent skewing strongly suggest that in western Bantu the term began to spread with the Atlantic trade and was specifically applied to "trading partners." Guthrie tentatively attributes the form to proto-Bantu, because of the presence of reflexes in a contiguous area of Kenya, Uganda, and northern Tanzania, as well as the above. Given the known data this view cannot be sustained.

19. Namesake: **-dokí,* 1/2, ps 192 (3:187). In Bubi, Tio, Ngungwel, Bobangi, Ngombe, Mongo, Lia, Tetela, Bushong, Angba, Kongo, and Mbala; Lele: "warrior."

Etymology: Innovation from CS 694 **-dok-* ("to name"), which is possibly proto-Bantu.

Comment: The known distribution of this nominal derivation suggests two innovations—one in Bubi and one elsewhere—but the evidence does not allow dating of the second innovation to a time prior to the split of the northern Zairian and the southwestern languages, because there are no reflexes in the savannas to the south. Homonyms were held to share a single social identity to a great degree in certain of these societies, such as among the Angba. Hence the importance of the term.

-bɔ́mbɔ, 9/10, no CS. In Kpe, Nen, Tanga, Basaa, Elog Mpoo, Ewondo, and Fang.

Etymology: Unknown.

Comment: Innovation from an as yet unknown age, preceding the Sanaga-Ntem expansion in the northwest. Homonyms in this area also were thought to share a single social identity.

20. Age group, age mate: *-kóda,* 9/10, CS 1194 (1196–98). In Mpongwe, Kosi, Fang, Mongo, upper Ngiri, and Ngombe.

Etymology: Innovation from CS 1190 *-kúd-* ("to grow up"), which is proto-Bantu.

Comment: The term is proto–western Bantu. An age-grade organization may have existed at that time and spread with the migrants, as reflexes in Ovimbundu and Herero indicate. Later most societies abandoned the emphasis on relative age.

-báki, 1a/2, no CS. In Duma, Punu, Buma, Mongo, Bushong, Lele, Luba, Pende, and Mbala; Mbosi and Ruund: "friend," "colleague"; Ngombe? (*mbái,* 1/2).

Etymology: Unknown. The form is a deverbative nominal.

Comment: The distribution is sizable. Yet another indication of the past importance of age grades.

21. Dependent: *-peka,* 1/2, CS 1517, glossed as "slave." For the distribution of reflexes, see J. Vansina, "Deep Down Time," map 3. Nzabi, Mbede, Tsogo, and the neighboring Gabonese attestations postulate *-peka.* The Luba and Kongo reflexes also allow *-pika.* So does Bobangi, which has a skewed form, probably of Kongo origin. Since the Gabonese forms lie in the orbit of a major slave-trading route, one may wonder whether they did not borrow from Kongo or Punu and skewed *i* for *e.*

Etymology: If one reconstructs *-pika,* the noun is an innovation from CS 1550 *-pik-,* "to arrive," and at first meant "new settler" or "stranger." Otherwise the etymology is unknown.

Comment: The reflexes in the Luba languages, besides those that fan out from lower Congo along the trade routes, indicate that the term was not limited to Kongo (where it meant "servant") before 1500.

22. Serf: *-*tóá*, 1/2, CS 1804–5, "pygmy," "small hunter gatherer," "bushdweller." It has a connotation of "autochthon." Distribution is Tio, Lingala, Bobangi, Mongo, Bushong, Tetela, Luba, Bali, Mangbetu (as a loanword from Bali), Bodo, Nyanga, and Tembo; Zimba *twabantu*, class 10 (plural, no tone): "dwarf," literally "Twa people." Mangbetu *Aswa* is a loanword from the Bodo *ōcwá*, 1 (singular).

Etymology: Unknown. Ps 467 (4:123), "chief," with the same form and classes, is derived from CS 1894 "autochthon."

Comment: Proto-Bantu. In western Bantu the term designates only pygmies in the inner basin south of the Zaire bend, and both in Bali and in Bodo. Everywhere else it has been replaced by specific terms such as -*mbóté* (1/2,"pygmy") in Ituri and Maniema and -*bongo* in southern Gabon. See W. Dupré, "Die Babinga-Pygmäen," 29–38. Of these forms, *-*yaga*, *-*yagwa*, 1/2, in some languages of Ituri, and as "self-determination" in northern Congo and nearby southeastern Cameroon, are the most widespread and could be old in western Bantu with the meaning "savage." The first meaning of proto-Bantu *-*tóá* was "autochthon," hence "bushdweller" and "pygmy," with a further connotation of "dwarf."

23. Captive: *-*kɔ́dɛ*, 1a/2, 9/10, CS 1110, ps 304. In Kongo, Tio, Bobangi, and perhaps Zimba (*kola:* "war captive"); Mongo only possibly as an ethnonym for dependent groups.

Etymology: Unclear. Given its limited distribution, CS 1105 *-*kɔ́d*- ("work") in the great lakes area is derived from this root rather than being its source.

Comment: The total distribution of the reflexes allows one to reconstruct the form as proto-Bantu. The known distribution in western Bantu is limited to the lower Congo and lower Zaire and to the Zimba entry. Possibly an isolated Kongo or Tio item spread again with the meaning "war captive" when the principalities began to expand in lower Congo.

C. Social activities

24. Palaver: *-*gambo*, 5/6, 7/8, CS 771, and *-*yambo*, 5/6, 7/8, CS 1919. In Duala, Oli, Fang, Bongom, Lumbu, Kongo, Nzabi, Mbede, Sakata, Kongo, Koyo, Lingala, Bobangi, Ngombe, Mongo, Ntomba, Bushong, and Tetela.

Etymology: Proto-Bantu. Derived from CS 770 *-*gamb*- ("to speak," "to slander") and CS 1912 *-*yamb*- ("to speak"); same form as CS 1913 "to slander." All these constitute a single proto-form. CS 1912, 1913, and 1919 have been created merely to list reflexes which have lost the initial *k*.

Comment: This is the usual term in the region. It was replaced in the eastern part of the study area by various terms. In the west "palaver" is rendered in Mpongwe, Benga, Vãã, Tio, Mfinu, Mbundu, and Pende by reflexes of "palaver": *-dáka*, 9/6, 9/10. The same shape in other classes (CS 472–74) means "tongue," "throat," and "voice." The item is proto-Bantu for "throat," according to Guthrie.

25. To pay a fine: *-put-*, CS 1624. In Kongo, Nzabi, Punu, Mbaghi, Mbede, Ndumu, Tio, Tege, Ngando, Koyo, Bobangi (first meaning "to add together"), Lingala, Leke, Ngombe, Poto, Mbuja, Mongo, Bolia, Ntomba, Luba Kasai, and Luba Shaba.

Etymology: The meaning may have shifted from "to add together, to heap up" (the first meaning in Bobangi) to "to pay." CS 1628 *-putɔ*, 5/6 ("payment"), is a regular derivation.

Comment: Guthrie suggests proto–western Bantu. This is not likely. The distribution reflects colonial dynamics, when the meaning became "to pay in money" and spread with the monetary economy. Thus the Mongo, Bolia, and Ntomba skewed forms are of Lingala origin; one suspects the same for Koyo, Leke, Ngombe, Poto, and Mbuja. Lingala itself could well have borrowed the form from Bobangi. In precolonial times the item may have been well established in the southern savanna languages and in the Kongo, and perhaps in the Teke groups. The verb now relates to justice, to payments for joining an association, to bridewealth payments, and to commercial payments. It is unclear whether it referred only to fines, as Guthrie has it, or to other social payments as well.

26. Boy's initiation: *(i)* *-gandá*, (ii) *gandjá*, 3/4, no CS. Form (i): Yaka, Pende, Mbuun, Ruund, Cokwe, and Bushong; form (ii): Komo, Bira, Bali, Amba, Gbaya (*gaza*, loanword?), Ngombe and Moswea (*gaja*); Ngbandi with the meaning "castrated," as a loanword: Pende *-nganji* (no tone, 3/4): "circumcision mask"; and Bushong *ngyɛɛncy*, 9/10: "initiation wand."

Etymology: kánda, 3/4, "skin," in western Bantu. CS 1003 would be possible were it not for the opposed tonal pattern and the initial *k*.

Comment: Proto–western Bantu possible. The known distribution extends for form (i) in the south from the Kwango River to the Bushong. For form (ii) it extends in the south to Pende and Bushong, in the east to the peoples of northern Maniema, and in the north mainly to non-Bantu speakers of the Ubangi bend. Still the total absence of reflexes in the northwest prevents a firm reconstruction.

-yénd-/-bénd,* "to circumcise," no CS. Known reflexes: Duala *-énda,* "circumcise," and *bwende,* class 14, "circumcision"; Kete *-bindi,* 1/2, "initiate"; Bushoong *-byéén,* 1/2, "initiate."

Etymology: Unknown. Luba "uncivilized person," i.e., "uncircumcised," is a loan from Kete.

Comments: The distribution, slender as it is, still supports the notion of great antiquity for circumcision. It may be proto–western Bantu. Further research is indicated.

Other widespread terms relating to initiation include nominal derivations from the verb *-ténd-,* "to cut" (CS 1709, 1711): as agents (class 1/2, final vowel *i*): "circumcisers" (class 1/2, final back vowel); as objects: "initiates", and as action (class 7/8): "initiation." The root and the rules involved are proto-Bantu, but the reflexes in the northwest, in the northeast, and south of the area studied, as well as beyond, may have evolved independently. They do not by themselves prove that the ancestral western Bantu had circumcision rituals.

The term *-yadi,* class 14 ("initiation") extends from Bushong (loanword there from Kete) over Luba and Songye to Binja and Lega. It occurs in a single block of distribution, and the Bushong reflex is skewed. This may be due to a single expansion, probably from Kete outward.

27. War (restricted): *-bitá,* 5/6, 9/10, CS 151, and *-tá,* 5, 7/8, CS 1630. Note that CS 151 is CS 1630 plus a frozen class 8 prefix. Distribution is almost universal and includes Tiv.

Etymology: Derivation from *-tá-* 1633–34, of which the original meaning was "to throw" or "to shoot" (in Tiv), with its own derivations of "to call," "to name," "to say," and perhaps Guthrie's CS 1633 "to set a trap," "to play a game," and even "to do."

Comment: Proto-Bantu in the shape of CS 1630. The retention of the term almost everywhere could be due in part to the frequency of this type of war. Original war involved both missiles and teamwork. Hence "game." Despite the meaning of this root in other classes as "bow," one cannot conclude that bows were the preferred weapon. See items 30 and 31.

28. War (destructive): *-tumba,* 5/6, 9/10, CS 1872. In Mpongwe, Fang, Kele, Bekwil, Aka, Lingala, Leke, Koyo, Mbosi, Bobangi, Mpama, Ngombe, and Mongo languages; Bushong; "a fight." Kpe, Kundu, and Kosi, *njumá,* and Noho *edua,* "war," are perhaps skewed forms.

Etymology: Derived from CS 1870 *-tumb- ("to burn"), which is proto–western Bantu.

Comment: Innovation and consistent distribution over a wide area. If the items from western Cameroon are not related, eastern Cameroon could be the epicenter. This type of war involved the burning of the opponent's settlements.

-jɔmbí, 5/6, no CS. In Mpongwe, Nkomi, Bikele, Jue, Bekwil, Makaa, Mkako, Kweso (Pomo), and Bubi.

Etymology: Unknown. The same form occurs in class 7/8, "war camp," in central and southern Angola.

Comment: The spread of the four independent occurrences indicates great age, perhaps of proto–western Bantu status. See also item 29.

29. War specialist: *-dombé,* 7/8, no CS. In Ngombe, Mbuja, Poto, and Lebeo; Mongo: "intrepid person," "judge"; Lia, Ntomba, and Eso: "notable"; Bushoong, Lele, and Ooli: "war diviner"; and Luba Kasai: "cause to judge."

Etymology: This could be a skewed form of *-jɔmbí,* but there is no evidence for this view beyond the similarity of form and meaning. The forms do not occur together in adjacent languages.

Comment: The extent of the diffusion suggests that it is older than the last few centuries. The form spread from a single epicenter, perhaps in eastern Cameroon. Even the notorious Ngbandi warriors borrowed it from their Bantu-speaking neighbors as *lombé,* "forefighter."

30. Shield: *-guba,* 9/10, CS 906. Very widespread: Mpongwe, Tsogo, Bubi, Nen, Kundu, Nkosi, Duala, Noho, Benga, Kele, Bongom, Kota, Duma, Punu, Mbede, Tio, Tiene, Yans, Mbuun, Bobangi, Lingala, Poto, Ngombe, Mbuja, Mabinza, Bati, Benge, Bwa, Angba, Bali, Amba, Bira, So, Eso, Lokele, Mbole, Mongo, Tetela, and Kongo. CS 756 *-gabu,* 9/10 is found in Enya, Lengola, Mituku, Binja north, Lega, and Bangobango.

Etymology: Proto-Bantu for the two forms combined; the changes would be due to metathesis. Could it be derived from CS 908 *-gubó,* "hippopotamus," despite the differences in form?

Comment: In recent times shields were used with spears, not with bows. Given the existence of a proto–western Bantu item for "spear," this could also have been so in early times.

31. Bow: *-tá,* 3/4, 14/6, CS 1631. See J. Vansina, "Deep Down Time," map 1, for the distribution. The form is absent in most of Cameroon.

Along the coast of Cameroon other forms are used. In the Myene languages the meaning has shifted to designate a toy and a musical bow; in the interior of Cameroon and a portion of north Congo the crossbow has replaced the bow. The crossbow is designated by a term meaning "arrowshaft" in eastern Bantu (*-banɔ́*, 5/6,CS 45). In Uele, where the crossbow was also known, more complex forms are derived from *-tá*, CS1633–34. The form is absent in Bodo.

Etymology: Proto-Bantu derived from *tá*, "to throw," from which item 27 is also derived.

Comment: Proto-Bantu.

32. Spear: *-gɔngá*, 5/6, CS 857, and *-yɔngá*, 5/6, CS 2130. Distribution is almost universal in the study area including Tiv and elsewhere in western Bantu except for Ituri and Maniema. See J. Vansina, "Do Pygmies Have a History?" map 2.

Etymology: Unknown. Again the second form is identical to the first except for the loss of the initial consonant.

Comment: Proto-Bantu. The shapes of the spears are similar over large portions of the study area. Most were used for stabbing.

-túmo, *-túmo*, *-túmɔ*, 5/6, CS 1867, 1868. Almost universal in eastern Bantu and in Maniema. See J. Vansina, "Do Pygmies Have a History?" map 2.

Etymology: From CS 1866 *-túm* ("to stab"), which is proto-Bantu and includes Tiv ("to hit with a missile"). Despite the etymology, most of these spears were missiles.

Comment: Proto–eastern Bantu.

33. To marry: *-bád-*, CS 11. In Nen, Bubi, Tsogo, Lue, Duala, Kombe, Ngumba, Bikele, Njem, Bekwil, Kele, Bongom, Ngungwel, Tio, Tyene, Boma, Yans, Lwel, Bobangi, Lingala, Poto, Mbuja, Bati, Boa, Angba, and Bira; Kongo: "to copulate."

Etymology: Just possibly the same shape as CS 13 "to begin," which is probably proto-Bantu.

Comment: Proto–western Bantu.

-kóéd-, CS 1175. In Kongo, Vili, Punu, Lumbu, Nzabi, Tsayi, Ding, Lingala, Ngombe, Holoholo, and Tembo.

Etymology: *-kɔ́*, 1/2, CS 1091 (item 37) and verbal extension *-éd-* (CS 2188). Guthrie's comment on its etymology is not acceptable. The same shape with the meaning "to copulate" (CS 1177) is derived from this form, not the reverse. Item 35 is a later extension of this meaning.

Comment: Guthrie does not assess the antiquity of the item, "since the distribution is not very clear." With the additional entries given here, and for the same form under other meanings, there is no doubt that this verbal form is proto-Bantu. The first meaning was clearly "to marry." Later this meaning independently produced "to give bridewealth" (item 35), "marriage" (item 34), "bridewealth" (item 36), and "in-law" (item 37).

34. Marriage: *-báda, 3/4, 5/6, CS 17. In Nen, Tsogo, Bubi, Duala, Noho, Benga, Kombe, Ewondo, Ngumba, Bikele, Njem, Bekwil, Duma, Mbede, Tiene, Boma, Bobangi, Lingala, Mbuja, Mongo, Tetela, and Sakata; Saa, 1/2: "wife," Seki, 1/2: "son-in-law."

Etymology: Derived from CS 11 *-bád- ("to marry").

Comment: Proto-Bantu. This is the most common form for marriage but, given the existence of several types of marriage, rarely the only one.

-kéd-, class 14, no CS. In Vili, Nzabi, Punu, Ding, Ngombe, and Tembo. See Meeussen 5:3.

Etymology: See item 33. Item 36 is a later extension of meaning.

Comment: Several independent innovations.

35. To give bridewealth: *-kɔ́éd-, no CS. In Mpongwe, Kweso (Pomo), Mbede, and Tembo. See Meeussen 5:3.

Etymology: See item 33.

Comment: Independent innovations of unknown age.

36. Bridewealth: *-kɔ́, various classes, no CS. In Bubi (11/10?), Londo (19/11), and Bira (14/6).

-kɔ́éd-, various classes, no CS. In Mpongwe (5/6), Mkako, and Lega (7/8); in Nzabi (11/10) it refers to the first part of the bridewealth only.

Etymology: See item 33.

Comment: Several independent innovations of unknown age.

37. In-law: *-kɔ́, 1/2, 14/6, CS 1092. In Duala, Fia, Vili, Kongo, Hungaan, Yáá, Nzabi, Mbede, Kukuya, Tio, Yans, Ding, Mbuun, Bushong, Ngombe, Enya, Lega, Bodo, and Tembo; Boma: "son-in-law"; Njem: "brother-in-law"; Nen: "husband"; Tege: "brother"; Kweso (Pomo): "bachelor."

Etymology: Meaning derived from same form, CS 1091, "you." This must be understood to be "you" singular in address with the connotation that the person addressed is an outsider. See Guthrie's comment on CS 1165. CS 64 "you" referred to a person and CS 1091 "you" addressed a person. *-kóéd-,* "to marry" and "bridewealth," is derived from this. *Comment:* Possibly proto–western Bantu. At the latest the innovation occurred after the Bubi and Myene splits, and was then the usual form until ousted in many languages by *-gido.*

-kɔ́i, 1/2, CS 1174. In Bubi, Mpongwe, Nkomi, Tsogo, Tiene, Koyo, and Bobangi; Punu, Leke, and Tetela: "brother-in-law"; Boma: "daughter's husband." There are many other eastern Bantu reflexes. See Meeussen 5:3.

Etymology: Nominal derivation from item 36. Guthrie's form is incorrect.

Comment: Proto–western Bantu or earlier. The first meaning may have been "son-in-law."

-kɔ́éd-, 1/2, no CS. In Vili, Ngombe, and Yãã; Njem: "wife's brother"; Tege: "brother." See Meeussen 5:3.

Etymology: Nominal derivation of item 33 occurred several times independently.

-gidɔ, 14/6, no CS. In Nen, Kpe, Benga, Kombe, Saa, Elog Mpoo, Fia, Ewondo, Njem, Bekwil, Mpiemo, Mkako, Aka, Buma, Mongo, Tetela, Ngwi, Lingala, Angba, Komo, Bira, Lokele, Zimba, and others in eastern Bantu; Ding: "mother-in-law" only.

Etymology: From CS 822 *-gid-* ("to prohibit"). CS 826 *-gidɔ,* 3/4 ("taboo"), was a parallel development.

Comment: Innovation, younger than *-kɔ́-.* As Ding shows, this innovation, prompted by the avoidance behavior associated with this status, may have occurred independently at various times.

38. Husband: *-dómɛ,* 1/2, CS 697. In Tsogo, Londo, Duala, Saa, Yambasa, Bulu, Fang, Nzabi, Bongom, Ngungwel, Tio, Lokele, Mongo, Ntomba, Kongo, Luba Kasai, Zimba, and Lega. The distribution also includes Tiv and two Ekoid languages.

Etymology: The same form is also used as a dependent nominal (adjective) meaning "male" (same CS). However, Guthrie thinks that this is derived from the meaning "husband" and not the reverse.

Comment: Proto-Bantu for both "husband" and "male." Only in Cameroon do we find this root used to designate a type of lineage which is prima facie evidence for the development of a patrilineal ideology and perhaps a sentiment of patriarchy there. CS 698, same shape, "mother's brother," should be linked to the form "male mother," which is the most common designation for this status elsewhere and the counterpart of "female father" for father's sister.

PART 2. SHORTER NOTES

D. Food Production: Tools and Techniques

39. Field: *-gonda, 3/4, 5/6,9/10, CS 897. Proto-Bantu. The extensions of meaning of the term in various western Bantu languages show that it refers to a field cut out in the forest.

40. To work on a field: *-cád-, CS 247, and the derived *-cáda, 5/6, ps 60 (3:76), "field." Proto–western Bantu. Contrary to Guthrie, the association with working in agriculture is strong. CS 254, the nominal derived from this stem refers to agricultural work. Guthrie's CS 568 is unrelated; it is eastern Bantu and associated with hoeing.

41. To plant: *-kón-. CS 1217. Proto-Bantu.

42. To bury: *-kund-, CS 1269, and *-kundod-, CS 1269a ("to disinter"). Both are proto-Bantu and refer to root cultivation.

43. To poke and ram in (i.e., to use a digging stick): *-cɔk-, CS 371, and its reverse, "to poke out" (i.e., to disinter with a digging stick). Could be proto-Bantu. Guthrie gives few forest reflexes (Bulu and Mongo) and has more for *-cɔm-, CS 375, which has the same meaning (Bulu, Nzabi, Ngungwel, Tio, Kongo, and the reverse for Kongo and Tetela). CS 375 seems to have been gaining at the expense of CS 371.

44. Axe: *-témɔ, 5/6, 7/8, CS 1705, 1706. Guthrie has "hoe" for CS 1705 and "axe" for CS 1706 (hoe). Proto-Bantu. The first meaning in western Bantu was "axe." The meaning "hoe" was later acquired in the southwest under eastern Bantu influence.

*-bagɔ, 5/6, 7/8, 9/10, ps 6 (3:24). In Mpongwe; Benga: "adze." Duala, Bulu, Ngumba, Njem, and Makaa Kwakum have the meaning "hoe," which must be derived. It is of uncertain age, and it is not clear to what tool the form originally referred.

45. Digging stick: *-cɔká, 5/6. Proto-Bantu. Derived from CS 371. Guthrie gives the meaning "axe," which is the present meaning. The semantic derivation makes it clear that the item must have designated a digging stick, a by-now archaic object that has escaped the attention of most observers.

46. Hoe: *-góngo,* various classes, Guthrie CS 901 and ps 327 (3:237). In Oli, Abo, Kaalong, Nzabi, Mbede, Bobangi, Lingala, and Tetela. Innovation within western Bantu. But because hoes were unknown in early farming, the item may refer to an as yet unknown tool. Most present-day designations for hoes are derived from terms for "axe."

47. Platform in field on which to put loads and drying crops: *-táda,* most classes, CS 1640. Proto-Bantu. Guthrie gives few western Bantu forms. They include Mpongwe, Duala, Ntomba, and add Bushong. The eastern Bantu forms refer to granaries. The original meaning may have been "lookout," because the item seems to be derived from CS 1638 *-tád-,* "to look."

48. To set a trap: *-tég-,* CS 1698, and trap, *-támbɔ,* 3/4, CS 1661. Both forms are proto-Bantu. CS 1661 is derived from CS 1657 *-támb-* ("to walk," "to travel").

49. Safu (plum; *Pachylobis edulis):* *-sáfú,* 11/10, no CS. In Nkomi, Orungu, Kosi, Duala, Ewondo, Gisir, Punu, Wumbu, Vili, Kongo, Mongo, and Ngombe; Angba: "black banana sp." Could be proto–western Bantu. The distribution is badly known, since many authors do not report the item. This is typical for many gathered fruits. Future research can be expected to yield several proto–western Bantu terms.

50. To hunt: *-beng-,* CS 129. Proto-Bantu.

51. Hunting net: *-kida,* 14/6, no CS, and *-tái,* 14/6, no CS. For the distribution, see J. Vansina, "Do Pygmies Have a History?" map 3. Ancient innovation, given the complexities of the diffusion of both terms. Hunting nets were probably not proto-Bantu, but were invented in the western portion of the study area at an early date.

52. Dog bell: *-debo/dibɔ,* 5/6, CS 560. Proto–western Bantu. Such bells were made out of wood or the dried shells of fruits. Guthrie's assertion that the term did not occur in the rainforests is wrong. The distribution includes Bubi and the Mongo languages and the practice is universal. The tone of the second vowel of the ancestral form may have been high.

53. Arrow: *-banja,* 11/10, and *-banji,* 7/8, 11/10, CS 545, 57. Proto-Bantu or proto-western Bantu. The meaning is derived from "midrib of palm frond" with the same form. Such arrows were commonly poisoned and at first had wooden points. The distribution includes Tiv and an Ekoid language and covers much of the western two-thirds of the forest area. "Arrowshaft," *-banɔ,* 5/6, CS 45, which includes the meaning "crossbow" and is found from Uele to the Sanaga, is probably related to this form (as Nkim shows) and may well be its origin.

54. To fish with line: *-dɔ́b-*, CS 638. Proto-Bantu.

55. To fish with a basket: *-dub-*, CS 731. Proto-Bantu. The precise meaning is established by the same form CS 732, "to dip," which is derived from CS 731.

56. Fish: *-cú*, 9/10, CS 427, and *-cúé/cúí*, 9/6, 9/10, CS 429. Proto-Bantu. The original form is CS 427, which has a Tiv reflex. See Guthrie 1:118–19.

57. Canoe: *-yátɔ*, 14/6, 5/6, CS 1949. Proto-Bantu.

58. Paddle: *-gápí*, 9/10,and *-kápi* 9/10, CS 790. Proto-Bantu.

59. To row: *dug-*, CS 735. Proto-Bantu.

60. Fishhook: *-dɔ́bɔ*, many classes, CS 640. Proto-Bantu and derived from item 52. Contrary to Guthrie, early fishhooks were certainly not made from iron wire, iron being then unknown.

NOTE: Fishing was clearly a major occupation for the ancestral western Bantu. Further research may yet uncover other roots related to fishing tools such as traps, baskets, and perhaps types of nets.

E. Domestic Plants and Animals

61. Oil palm: *-bá*, 5/6, CS 1 and *-bída*, 5/6, CS 140. Proto-Bantu. CS 140 was the earliest form and includes Tiv.

62. Palm nut: *-gadí*, 9/10, 11/10, CS 768; *-bída*, 9/10, 11/10, CS 140 (Duala and Bobangi); and *-bá*, 11/10, CS 1 (Tetela). The forms are so variable that it is not possible to be certain which of CS 1 or 768 related in proto-Bantu times to the palm nut.

63. Oil: *-gúta*, class 6, CS 914, and *-kúta*, class 6, CS 1278. Proto-Bantu.

64. Palm oil: *-yadí,*class 6, CS 1898. Early western Bantu, replacing CS 1278 and CS 914.

65. Raffia palm: *-bɔɔndɔ*, 5/6, no CS: Duala, Jue, Bira, Balese (non-Bantu), Bushong, Luba languages, Lokele, and Nyanga; Aka?, *-pɔ́ndɔ:*

"raffia tree sp."; Tio, Nkucu, and Tetela: "raffia cloth"; Yombe *-bɔnde, 5/6: "orchard of palm trees." Early western Bantu.

66. Yam: *-koá, 7/8, CS 1166. Proto-Bantu. Probably *Dioscorea cayenensis.* A reflex in an Ekoid language is known.

67. Bean (pulse): *-kɔndɛ́, 5/6, 9/10, 11/10, CS 1222. Proto-Bantu.

68. Calabash: *-béndá, 9/10, CS 128. Perhaps proto–western Bantu. Proto-Bantu for "container." See J. Vansina, *The Children of Woot,* 263, item 30.

69. Calabash bottle: *-copa, 9/10, CS 426. This meaning occurs only in western Bantu. In early Bantu, it is "jar." Proto–western Bantu.

70. Gourd (*Cucumerops edulis*): *-ngɔndɔ́, 9/10. In Mpongwe, Benga, Fang, Kele, Ngove, Bushong, and Mongo; Duala: "gourd seeds," "groundnut." Early western Bantu or proto–western Bantu. This plant, cultivated for its oil, was a major crop in the forest areas.

71. Groundnut (*Voandzeia* spp.): *-jogó, 9/10, 11/10, CS 961, and *-jokó, ps 265 (3:255). Proto-Bantu. Many languages borrowed the name for the American groundnut (*Arachis hypogaea*) when this was introduced. As Duala shows (item 70), other names for the groundnut were derived from other competing oil-bearing plants.

72. Banana (AAB plantain): kɔndɛ, kɔndɔ, kɔ, 5/6, CS 1144, 1146, 1090. For the distribution, see map 2.11. Early innovation, probably from the southeast, replacing an earlier *bugo,* 5/6, itself a loanword.

73. Sugar cane: *-koogó, 3/4, CS 1201. The distribution covers the northwestern portion of the area of study as far as the Ubangi, as far south as the Alima (Mbosi, Mpama, and Bobangi), and beyond the middle Ogooué (Tsogo, Simba, and Pindji). It includes a good portion of the Mongo languages. This form may be the old one for "elephant grass" (*Panicum plicatum* and similar grasses), transferred in a different pair of classes to the new crop. It is well worth noting that *ngáakóo* is the common term in Ngbaka and Monzombo, *ngángúlû* in Mondunga and Aka, and *mongáú,* 3/4, in Ngombe and as far east as Amadi, where it is *angau.* The data are too incomplete to conclude at this point.

This is the most widespread term for sugar cane in the study area. Two major other roots—*-congo, 3/4 (southern Gabon, Teke country, and Mongo), and *céngé, 3/4 (all along the southern fringe of the forest and in southern Maniema)—should also be mentioned. These two may well be older terms for older grasses also, because their distribution largely agrees with genetic groupings. In addition a number of isolated forms appear here and there. The whole situation is typical of many of the introduced crops.

74. Pepper: *dongo,* 9/10, 11/10, CS 718. The form is proto–western Bantu; the meaning is not. It now refers to the *Capsicum frutescens* imports from the Americas. A transfer of meaning from an older "pepper" plant has occurred, but from which plant exactly remains unknown.

75. Dog: *-bóa,* 9/10, CS 174. Proto-Bantu.

76. Goat: *-bódi,* 9/10, CS 185. Proto-Bantu.

77. Fowl: *-kɔ́kɔ,* 9/10, CS 1126 (CS 1121, 1126, and 1203 are skewed items), and *-cócó,* 9/10, CS 402. Early loanword. See Guthrie 1:123–24, topogram 24. The animal was introduced from the east. Hence the greater diversity of terms in western Bantu is not surprising. In addition to the above, one finds reflexes of two completely different roots: *-kúba,* CS 1257, in the northwest, and *-combe,* 12/13, CS 415, in the savanna, which also is not surprising. These may well be forms once applied to designate another bird, e.g., a species of pigeon, and then transferred to domestic fowl.

78. Pig: *-godó,* 9/10, CS 887, is the basic form. All the reflexes given are western Bantu and Tiv. The basic form is proto-Bantu, since it includes a reflex from Tiv, but the meaning may be a type of warthog as in Bulu, not the domestic pig. "Warthog" (*Potamochoerus*) in many western Bantu languages is now rendered by a variant: *-goyá,* 9/10, CS 902. *-godobɛ,* 9/10, CS 888, is a longer eastern Bantu form referring to warthog. It is still not clear whether the domestic pig was ancient in the area of study. The balance of its distribution and of the ethnographic data suggests that it was not. The domestic pig was probably introduced by the Portuguese on the Atlantic Coast. This form is, moreover, not the only proto-Bantu one referring to warthogs; see *-coombo,* 9/10, no CS, in Tiv, Mongo, and Bushong.

79. Bee and honey: *-jóke,* 9/10, 11/10 bee, 14 honey, CS 962. Proto-Bantu. See Guthrie 1:124–25, topograms 28 and 29. Hunter gatherers and farmers alike greatly prized honey. Yet most peoples did not install beehives themselves.

F. Industries: Tools and Techniques

80. Salt: *-ngóá*, 3, CS 2176. Proto–western Bantu. This term designated sea salt as well as vegetal salt.

-kédɛ, class 3, CS 1031, derived from CS 1030 *-kɛ́d-* ("to filter"). This form designated vegetal salt. Most reflexes refer to savanna people.

81. Wine: *-dɔgu*, class 6, CS 649. The reflexes include Tiv in a skewed form. Proto–western Bantu or earlier. Guthrie's gloss "beer" is not correct. The lack of cereal agriculture meant that in early times no beer was brewed. In recent times the term referred primarily to palm wine and sugar cane wine.

-kana, class 6 (most reflexes: *-ana*, 6), no CS. In Duala, Ngumba, Ewondo, Ngombe, Poto, Mbuja, Boa, Benge, Bali, Eso, Lokele, Enya, Mbole, Tetela, Boyela, Ntomba, Bushong, Mbala, Yaka, Yans, Boma, Ding, and Mbuun. The form specifically refers to palm wine. It is ancient in the forest area, but conclusions must await further study.

82. Kaolin: *pémba*, class 9/11, and *pémbɛ́*, 9/11, CS 1477. Proto-Bantu. Kaolin was of great ritual importance and was used by some as potting clay.

83. Cosmetic powder made from the redwood (*Pterocarpus soyauxii*): *-góda*, 9/12 (often 11/10 for the tree), CS 877, *-kóda*, 9, CS 1193. The distribution includes Tiv, Aka, Ngbaka (Ubangian language loaned it), Ngando, Mbati, Bobangi, Lingala, Leke, Pande, Kaka, Ngombe, Bwa, Komo, Mbosi, Mongo languages, Tetela, Bushong, Kongo, Vili, Laadi, Masango, Ivea, Tio, Buma, Sakata, and Nande; Duala, 5: "red." Proto–western Bantu with the meanings "red" and "redwood powder," and perhaps even "redwood tree." The semantic evolution seems to have gone from the redwood to the color, and not the reverse as Guthrie states. Redwood powder was in great demand and the object of extensive trade. Hence an unusual number of skewed items.

84. To mold a pot: *-bómb-*, CS 199. Proto-Bantu.

85. Clay for pottery: *-bómba*, class 5, CS 200. Proto-Bantu derived from item 84.

-yegá, CS 1996. Reflexes are attested only in Duala (9), Bulu (19), and Bobangi (5). Still, an early western Bantu date is just possible.

86. Kitchen pot: *-dongó*, 9/10, CS 669; *-jongó*, ps 267 (3:267); *-nyengó*, CS 2084; and *-nyongó*, CS 2173a. These forms all descend from a common proto-Bantu form probably in the shape of *-(j)ongó* (see Meeussen 6:2). A number of other terms for pottery vessels refer to smaller cooking pots and water jars but do not have an ancestral western Bantu origin.

87. To plait: *-dok-*, CS 693. Proto-Bantu, but there are few reflexes in western Bantu.

-tóóng-, CS 1848. Also "to build." Proto-Bantu. Guthrie's gloss for CS 1847, "to sew," relates to the same activity. CS 1849 *-tongá*, 7/8 ("basket"), could be derived from this item, despite the tonal difference.

88. To sew: *-túm-*, CS 1865. Proto-Bantu. Derived from *-túm-* "to stab."

89. Raffia: *-péké*, 5/6, 11/10, no CS. In Tsogo, Ngombe, Mongo, Tetela, Bushong, Lega, and Luba languages; Tsogo, Pindji, Vove, Simba, Masango, Vili, Duma, Ndumu, and Mbede: "raffia tree"; Angba, Boa, and Songye: "raffia fiber"; Tetela, Nkucu, and Boyela: "cloth." The Tsogho reflex seems to have been borrowed. If so, the term is attested to just before the split between the northern Zairian and southwestern groups of languages.

90. Raffia fiber: *-pucu*, 9/10, 11/10, no CS. In Fang? (*-sví*, 3/4), Kongo, Mbala, Pende, Nzebi, Kukuya, and Buma; Yaka, Mbala, and Hungaan, all 7/8; Nyanga, 10, "cloth"; Kele, Kota, Tio, and Yans: "raffia tree"; Tsogo: "worked raffia fiber." The item is derived from the same form, CS 1587, "skin." Hence it once designated cloth; only later did it refer to the fiber and the tree. The Tsogho reflex seems to have been borrowed. If so, the term is attested to just before the split of the northern Zairian and southwestern groups of languages.

91. Loom: *-jánga*, 14/9, no CS. In Nen and Bushong; Saa: "raffia tree"; Vili and Kongo: "raffia cloth"; Pende: "weaver." The form is proto–western Bantu, but the meaning "loom" needs to be better attested.

92. Raffia cloth: *-báda*, 9/10, no CS. In Nkomi, Nen, Lombi, Lue, Lung, Kosi, Kpe, Duala, Saa, Bongkeng, Kongo, and Bushong. Variants in the final vowel are *e*, *o*, and *u*. Proto–western Bantu. Guthrie's CS 21 *-báde*, 9/10 ("palm frond"), is proto–western Bantu, and may be the origin of the term for raffia cloth or the reverse. Both "cloth" and "palm frond" occur in Nen. The frond is used to extract the raffia thread. On forms for cloth, see Guthrie 1:122 and topogram 18. In a number of languages the terms for clothing are derived from terms for skin (CS 873 and 1241).

-dambá, 7/8, CS 487. Proto–western Bantu, possibly derived from CS 483 *damb-,* ("to sprawl"), which is proto-Bantu. Note that CS 484, *damb-* ("to pay tribute"), and *-dambú,* 3/4 ("tribute"), are derived from this item. This underscores the value of raffia cloth in the kingdoms of the central African savanna.

-bóngɔ, 5/6, 11/10, no CS. In Mpongwe, Vili, Kongo, Lese, Huku, and Bira; Duma, Kele, and Ndumu: *Raphia humilis.* On the Loango coast and in Kongo it also meant "wealth." The distribution is strange. Reflexes are found in a portion of the southwestern quadrant and in the far northeast only. This could argue either for two recent independent innovations or for great antiquity, if the forms in both areas are indeed identical. Further research is needed.

-déd, 3/4, CS 516. In Kongo, Bushong, Pende, Bulu, Kwakum, and Kwanyama. Despite its spread this is a recent innovation stemming from Kongo, perhaps in the sixteenth century. The item is derived from *-ndédé,* 3/4, CS 517 ("European"), which itself may be derived from the same form with the meaning "whale."

93. Bark cloth tree *(Ficus thonningii* or *Ficus erystogmata* spp.): *-túlú,* 9/10, no CS (Mbati and Aka) and *-tóla,* 9/10, 11/10, 5/6, no CS (Mongo, So, Eso, Mbole, Enya, Tetela, Angba, and Mangbetu [loanword]). This also designates bark cloth in the Zairian cases. If the forms are related, the term could be of great antiquity.

94. Bark cloth: *-tɔngɔ,* 9/10, 7/8, no CS. In Nkomi, Galwa, Fang, Aka, Ngando, Mbati, Gisir, Ndzabi, Ndumu, and Mbede. The cloth was often named after the fig tree from which it was made. Of uncertain antiquity.

-gándá. 3/4, CS 782. Add Guthrie 1:122, who claims that this refers to skin worn as garment, but gives no evidence. The relevant term is CS 1003 *-kándá.* However, the last tone differs. Of the reflexes given, only Bekwil, Mpiemo, Kota, Tsogo, and Koyo are valid and the distribution area forms one block. This may be a late mutation and probably refers to bark cloth rather than to woven cloth, because bark cloth was the common clothing in these regions. The distribution may be more extensive if the Lumbu, Punu, Vungu, Varama, and Ngowe forms of *-katu* (9/10, no tone "bark cloth") were related.

95. Basket: *-tóndo,* 7/8, 9/10, CS 1844. Possibly proto-Bantu.

-tongá, 7/8, CS 1849. Possibly proto-Bantu.

96. Box: *-kɔbé,* 11/10, CS 1097.5. In Duala, Kongo, Tio (*nkobi*), Mbosi, Mbede, Bobangi, Mongo (*-kɔfɔ,* 9/10), and Bushong (*-kɔ́pi,* 5/6). The Duala reflex calls for a very early innovation, but active diffusion in the southwestern quadrant area occurred during the seventeenth and eighteenth centuries, starting from Kongo.

97. Iron ore: **-tádɛ,* 6/14, CS 1643. Bushong and Ambo are the only certain West African reflexes. It is derived from the same form, class 5/6, "stone," which is proto-Bantu. See Guthrie 1:124 and topogram 26. The original form meant "stone," not "iron ore."

98. Iron: **-tádɛ,* 7/14, CS 1644. In Nzabi, Kongo, Ovimbundu, and eastern Bantu. The root occurs in various iron objects. Guthrie lists Bulu, Tio, and Bobangi as cases. These are all innovations from item 97 with the meaning "stone."

  *-gɛda, 7, CS 800, "knife"; **yɛda,* ps 500 (3:212); **yɛdɛ́,* 3/4, 12/13, CS 1962 (add Tio, 7/8, "slag"); and **-bɛɛdí,* 9/10, CS 78, "knife," all belong together. This is an ancient loanword but spread over much of the Bantu-speaking area. See Guthrie 1:138, topogram 25.

99. To forge: **-túd-* CS 1861. The form is proto-Bantu, the meaning is an innovation. The older meaning probably was "to pound" or even "to fashion stone tools." See Guthrie 1:122 and topogram 19. The massive area of reflexes shows that the innovation reached all the western Bantu from the same single source.

100. Smith: **-túdi,* 1/2, no CS. Normal nominal derivation from item 99 and equally widespread with the same historical significance.

101. Smithy: **-guba,* class 5 or 14, CS 905 (ii). There are a number of reflexes in the northwestern portion of the study area from western Cameroon to Bulu and as far south as Tege, Mbosi, Bobangi, and Tiene including a Kongo skewed form, *-uvu,* class 11. Elsewhere a derivation of item 99 often occurs. Innovation. It is intriguing that the same form, same CS, refers to "bellows" in the great lakes area and elsewhere in eastern Africa.

102. Hammer: **-dondɔ,* 9/10, CS 706; **-jondɔ,* 9/10, CS 965; **-yondɔ/ nyondɔ,* 9/10, CS 2171. These are all variants of a common form. The presence of Tiv (a reflex of CS 706) indicates that the form is proto-

Bantu. But the meaning "iron hammer" is an innovation. The item refers to a heavy iron hammer.

103. Anvil: *-jondɔ/*-jondo, 9/10, CS 965.5. Guthrie lists Kombe, Bobangi, and Kongo. One should add Bali, Bodo, and Bira. This form is derived from item 102, among whose reflexes in the area many also mean "anvil," usually in class 10. It is noteworthy that anvils were stores of value and standards of value, e.g., in southern Gabon and in the Aruwimi-Nepoko area.

G. Exchange

104. To give: *pá, CS 1404. Proto-Bantu, often with the meaning "to hand over."

105. To divide: *-gab-, CS 754. It also means "to give away" (CS 755). Proto-Bantu with the nuance "to distribute." This was an important political activity. Many oral traditions, e.g., among the Kongo and Mongo groups, use this verb to describe the distribution of power, and some derivations attest to this meaning. The verbal derivation *gabed- (CS 755a) may be proto-Bantu, and specifically referred to patron-client relations both in the northwest and in the great lakes area. *-gabo/gabɔ, 5/6, CS 757 ("gift" and "generosity"), also had political connotations. To divide well was an art of big men.

106. To buy: *-dand-, CS 490. Add Nen to the distribution. Perhaps proto–western Bantu innovation.

*-cómb-, CS 414. The most common form in the study area. Despite Guthrie's comment, this is not a later innovation than *dand-, since both occur mixed in the far northwest (Bonkeng has -somb-, Long *-yan-). But the area covered by the reflexes of *-comb- was greatly extended by the expansion of the Atlantic trade system and later by the colonial conquest.

*-god-, CS 876, and the variant *-yud-, CS 2149. Proto-Bantu with the nuance "to barter." Also occurs in Ekoid languages.

107. To exchange: *-cɔ́b-, CS 364. The item may be proto–western Bantu but the meaning is unclear. It could be "to alternate."

108. To sell: *-tég-, CS 1697. In Kongo, Fumu, Tio, Ngungwel, Kukuya, Tege, Mbede, Tiene, Buma, Boma, Yans, Bobangi, Mongo, Ntomba Mai Ndombe, Ntomba Ntumba, Bolia, Lingala, Leke, Aka, and Bati. The form is an innovation, perhaps from the homophonous "to set a trap" (CS 1698). It probably developed in the southwest, perhaps in the copper-belt area, given the skewed forms, and spread upstream of the Malebo Pool as far as the Lobaye. Part of the expansion may date from colonial times.

Other items with this meaning are derived from causative common Bantu forms for "to buy," "to barter" (item 106), "to divide" (item 105), and even "to inherit." Often individual languages used several terms, which indicates that, in many parts of the area and in early days, selling was not an activity that was very distinct from gift giving and buying.

109. Market: *-mbombo,* 5/6. In Ndengese, Bushong, Nzali, Saa, and Elog Mpoo; Ding, same form: "market day"; Kele, same form: "money." The same form meaning "to sell" in Mbaghi, Leumbu, and Njem, and "to buy" in Mpiemo and Kaka, may be related. The noun with the meaning "market" would be merely a restricted innovation around the Kuba area, dating perhaps to the eighteenth or even nineteenth century, were it not for the reflexes in the Saa group. It may well be that the nouns are independent innovations derived from a much older verb "to buy" or "to barter" which just could be proto–western Bantu.

-bóngo, 5/6, no CS. In Lingala, Poto, Mbuja, Mabinza, So, Lokele, Enya, Angba, Lwel, and perhaps Bulu and Fang. Apart from the possible Bulu and Fang forms, the innovation is restricted to the great bend of the Zaire. Derived from the homophone CS 205 "beach," which was the site where markets were held. CS 205 is proto-Bantu.

-jándo, 5/6, no CS. In Kongo, Ngungwel, Koyo, Ding, Yans, Lingala, Leke, Ntomba Mai Ndombe, Ntomba Tumba, Bolia, Mongo, Bati, and Boa. The form may well be the origin of the following forms, all in the Teke group: *zú,* *-zó,* *-yú,* *-yó,* all 5/6, as in Fumu, Kukuya, Mbosi, Tio, Sakata, Yans, Ding, and Mbuun. *-jándo* is a late northeastern Kongo innovation attested by 1650. It probably originated in the copper belt and was borrowed by some of its neighbors in the Teke group, where the short form originated through elision of the -nd- and fusion of the vowels. This short form was used in the great markets of the Malebo Pool. It spread from there up both the Kasai and the Zaire, presumably as the Atlantic trade developed. Yet Bobangi does not use this term. The *-jándo* variant also spread upriver, but probably only in early colonial times. Thus the oldest form spread farthest, but last!

-kaca, 5/6, no CS. In Mpongwe, Tsogo, Seki, Kele, Punu, Nzabi, and Mbede. The term may have spread in southern Gabon from the Ogooué Delta and the Gabon Estuary into the Ngounié Valley as the Atlantic trade spread. If so, the spread is likely to date from the eighteenth or nineteenth century.

NOTE. The terms for market given here are only the most widespread of many different synonyms that occur in many languages. As the evidence indicates, markets—whether on the beach, in a village, or between villages—were poorly developed institutions until well into the present millennium.

110. Valuable good: *-yóma,* 7/8, CS 2164. Distribution in western Bantu and Ekoid. Proto-Bantu. The eastern Bantu reflexes (CS 2162, and ps 542 [4:206]) now all refer to iron. See Guthrie 1:124 and topogram 27.

111. To inherit: *cangod-,* ps 78 (1:87). Guthrie lists Duala and Tetela only and claims that the form may be proto-Bantu. Independent innovation from *-cang-,* possibly CS 284 ("to meet someone"), with a reversive active radical extension *-od-* (CS 2195).

112. Inheritance: *-kúá,* 5/6, CS 1253. In Ngombe, Kongo, and Herero. Guthrie postulates a proto–western Bantu origin. The form is obviously derived from *kú,* CS 1247, 1248, and 1249 ("to die," "death," "dead person"), which is proto-Bantu and whose reflexes are almost universal. Several independent innovations for item 112 are more likely than a remote common origin.

H. Spiritual Entities

113. Hero: *-dímo,* 3/4, 7/8, CS 619, "spirit" (ogre). The primary meaning is "spirit of a dead person" or "ancestral spirit": Mbote (hunter gatherers of Ituri) and Bira, *Molimo,* 1, "God." A Ngbandi reflex is a loan. The form is derived from CS 617 *dím-* ("to extinguish," "to become extinguished"). The link to the notion of a hero is "a person who became extinguished" or, as the derivation CS 618a *-dimed-* has it, "who got lost." None of the living had known him or her alive. Proto-Bantu. Originally the item referred to the spirits of long-deceased persons.

114. Nature spirit: *kéti,* *-kéta,* 3/4, CS 1073, and same form, CS 1072, with the meaning charm. In some languages the meaning of the term encompasses the "spirit" and its "shrine" or "charm." Doko *keta* (no tone), 1/2 ("the recent dead") should be included. Given the relative rarity of the reflexes for CS 1071 *-két* ("to do"), it is probably derived from CS 1072–73, not the reverse. Guthrie hazards a proto-Bantu diagnosis, but the distribution suggests an innovation before the split of the northern Zairian and southwestern groups of languages.

115. Ancestral spirit: *-gádi,* 1/2, no CS. In Aka, Ngombe, Mongo, Ntomba, Lele, and Bushong; Duala: "religion"; Kosi: "ancestral statue." The connotation was that such spirits were troublesome and bad. Derived from CS 759 *-gád-* ("to turn") and CS 760 ("to alter"), which is proto-Bantu. Item 115 is proto–western Bantu or arose early in western Bantu.

116. God: *-yambé,* 1a/2, CS 1917, and CS 925 *-jambé* are both variants of a single ancestral form. For the distribution, see A. Kagame, *La philosophie bantoue comparée,* map 3. The distribution of this form has been greatly extended by missionary teaching. Nevertheless before 1880 the forms *Nyambe(i)* and *Nzambi(e)* still covered much of the western third of the area of the study. Yet even before then, it had been expanded from Kongo eastward, probably as an effect of early missionary efforts and of political prestige (see J. Vansina, "The History of God among the Kuba," 17–39). Such expansions account for the many skewed forms. Finally, even *Nyame,* "God" in Twi (Ghana), may be relevant. All in all one may postulate a single innovation well before A.D. 1500 with the meaning "first spirit."

117. Charm: *bwanga,* class 14, CS 787. Probably derived from CS 785 *-gang-* ("to tie up") and its variant CS 1007. Proto-Bantu. The notion "root," *-ganga,* 3/4, CS 788, is derived from this form, because many medicines are made from roots.

118. Charm medicine: *-té,* 3/4, 14, CS 1730. Derived from *-té,* 3/4, 7/8, "tree." Both items are proto-Bantu. Most medicines were herbal remedies.

119. Charm, religious statue, omen: *-pengo,* 9/10, 11/10, CS 1534 (see Meeussen 2:1). Uele's *mapingo* oracle is a reflex. Possibly proto-Bantu, although there are no reflexes from the area of study, except in the northeastern and south-central sections, so that an eastern Bantu origin is not inconceivable. "Religious statue" may have been the primary meaning.

I. Religious Experts and Activities

120. Religious expert: *-ganga,* 1/2, 3/4, 9/10, CS 786. Practically universal distribution. Probably derived from CS 785 *-gang-* ("to tie up") and its variant CS 1007. Proto-Bantu. Same form as item 117.

121. To abstain: *-gíd-,* CS 822. Nearly universal distribution. Proto-Bantu.

122. Taboo: *-gído,* CS 826. Proto–western Bantu. Derived from item 121.

123. To bewitch: *-dog-,* CS 644. Nearly universal distribution. Proto-Bantu.

124. Witch: *dogi,* 1/2, no CS. Same form, class 14, CS 646, and *-dogo,* class 9, CS 647, both mean "witchcraft." Very widespread distributions. Derived from item 123. The forms are proto-Bantu. *-dogi,* CS 646 and CS 647, are also proto-Bantu.

125. Witch substance: *-jemba,* 5, 6, no CS. In Mpongwe and other Myene languages, Bubi, Londo, Kundu, Kosi, Kpe, Duala, Sekiani, Mabea, Bulu, Fang, Njem, Mpiemo, Ngondi, Ngombe, Bati, Bwa, Angba, Komo, and Bira. Same form, same class, "witchcraft": Bangangte (Bamileke Plateau), Mpongwe, Nkomi, Londo, Ngolo, Kpe, Kosi, Subu, Sekiani, Benga, Njem, Bobangi, Ngombe, Mbuja, Angba, Komo, Bira, Amba, northern Mongo languages, Kele, Bongom, Nzabi, Masango, Gisir, Mbede, and perhaps Yaka (*hempa*). The distributions run from the Ekoid languages to Lake Mobutu and reach southward to include much of southern Gabon, the Likwala, Lulonga, and lower Lomami basins, and northern Maniema to the Ruwenzori. There would be no doubt that the form was proto–western Bantu if it were not for the almost total absence of reflexes elsewhere. It could therefore be an ancient loanword. On balance, the term seems to have been suppressed elsewhere when beliefs in witchcraft substances changed. The surviving reflexes suggest that the first meaning was "witchcraft substance" rather than "witchcraft" itself. The ethnography suggests that this substance was closely linked to the power of big men.

-kundú, 5/6, no CS. In Ngondi, Bobangi, Lingala, Poto, Bati, Boa, So, Lokele, Mongo, Sakata, Kongo, and Yombe; Mangbetu and Mamvu languages borrowed the term. Innovation from "belly," ps 252 (3:240). The gloss should be "stomach" and the field of distribution is wider than indicated. It also includes the Mongo languages and Ngombe. The witchcraft organ was supposed to be in the stomach. The distributions of this meaning and the autopsy associated with it suggest that the item was an old innovation in the lower Congo and lower Zaire areas, because elsewhere another word for witch substance was abandoned. The term reached the most remote corners of both the Sangha and Ituri areas as a result, first, of the spread of the Atlantic trade and, later, of the spread of the colonial powers. Both these processes were accompanied by exceptional stress. See H. Baumann, "Likundu: Die Sektion der Zauberkraft," 73–85.

126. To divine: *-bók-*, CS 195. The reflexes are western Bantu of the savanna and two Ekoid languages. In between the two, the same form means "to cure," an innovation from this meaning. Proto–western Bantu.

127. Oracle: *-gámbí*, class 9, no CS. In Londo, Duala, Pongo, Subu, Bongkeng, Nkong, Yabasi, Saa, Elog Mpoo, Nen, Fia, Dibom, Nyokon, Bandem, Ewondo, Bulu, Mbang, Kosi, Batongtu, and others on the Bamileke Plateau. The name is often also the name of a spider (*Mygalidae* spp.) used in an oracle. It is an innovation of the recent past, despite the presence of reflexes in non-Bantu but related languages.

The situation is typical of the terminology of divination in general. Regional terms abound and usually represent linguistically recent innovations, indicating how dynamic the beliefs and practices were in this domain.

128. Poison oracle: *-kaca*, 9/10, also *Strychnos icaja* B., the vine from which the poison was made. In Mpongwe, Benga, Sekiani, and Kele. Also *Erythrophleum guineense* G.: Kongo, Vili, Yombe, Laadi, Ndumbu, Mbede, Ndasa, Tio, Bobangi, Leke, and Bongiri. Duala, Kosi, and Kpe: *kwa*, 9/10 ("poison oracle" and "*Erythrophleum guineense*," or sasswood), just might be related.

-bondó, 9/10, also for the *Strychnos icaja* B. vine. In Galwa, Nkomi, Orungu, Fang, Ngove, Gisir, Vungu, Punu, Lumbu, Vili, Laadi, Laali, Pinji, Duma, Nzabi, Masango, Ndumu, Ivea, Ivili, Vove, Kota, Mbosi, Bobangi, Lingala, Tiene, Mpama, and borrowed in the Ubangian languages Monzombo and Gbaya; Mbede, Ndumu, Ngombe (where the plant was *Strychnos dewevrii* G.), Mbuja, Poto, and Bwa: "ordeal" and "shrub from which the poison is obtained"; Mongo: "ordeal" and "*Pyrebacantha staudtii* H. vine."

-pomi, 5/6, also for *Erythrophleum guineense*. In Mongo, Boyela, Bushong, Lele, Mbuun, Pende, Cokwe, Tabwa, and Holoholo.

-yábi, class 3 or 12, CS 1884. In Songye, Lega, Binja North, Komo, Tembo, Nyanga, and Bira. The distribution covers most of Maniema and Ituri, the southeastern savanna of Central Africa, and a portion of the great lakes area. See H. Baumann, "Die Sambesi-Angola-Provinz," in his *Die Völker Afrikas und ihre traditionellen Kulturen* 1:633, map 34.

NOTE. The first three terms are interconnected, and hence the words fall into two groups. The interconnected words now usually designate the poison ordeal and the plant involved. But earlier the three terms may have referred to three separate items: (1) the ordeal, (2) the *Strychnos* plants, and (3) *Erythrophleum guineense*. All three could well be proto–western Bantu, even though one cannot now attribute the precise meanings 1–3 to a specific form. *-yábi* may well be proto–eastern Bantu, as Guthrie surmises.

129. To cure: *-bók-,* CS 195. All the reflexes are western Bantu including Boan. Proto-Bantu form because the same form, CS 196, "to divine," has the eastern Bantu reflexes. Proto–western Bantu innovated the meaning from item 126. The ps 47 (3:64), "doctor," is a regular derivation in Kongo, Yáá, and Tio. *-bóké* (not *bógí*), 5/6, ps 46 (3:63), "bundle," is derived from this root and first referred to "medicine bundles."

Notes

Chapter One: Voids and Blinders, Words and Things

1. R. Cornevin, *Histoire de l'Afrique* 2:26: "Thus appeared to us a first province which we call central equatorial Africa and which could be called the ahistorical region of black Africa, for no important state developed there."

2. Basic ethnographic summaries can be found in H. Baumann, ed., *Die Völker Afrikas und ihre traditionellen Kulturen* 1:685–784, and H. Baumann and D. Westermann, *Les peuples et les civilisations de l'Afrique*, 191–214, which posits two culture circles: pygmy and forest people. G. P. Murdock, *Africa: Its Peoples and Their Culture History,* instead distinguishes several cultural historical groups, namely: pygmies (48–51), northwestern Bantu (271–78), equatorial Bantu (278–84), and "Mongo and Luba" (284–90). The number of ethnic groups is derived from these sources; about 150 distinct languages are spoken in the area. Total population is estimated from recent figures for Gabon, Congo, Equatorial Guinea, the relevant *régions* of Zaire, and estimates for southern and southwestern Cameroon.

3. R. Cornevin, *Histoire de l'Afrique* 2:29 (quote). For the hostile milieu argument, see 28–29, where the horrors of Stanley's expedition to rescue Emin Pasha are cited as evidence; for the result, see 1:11: "They have preserved prehistoric civilisations until this very day." See idem, *Histoire du Congo Leo,* 29, for explicit environmental determinism, the assertion that no society "going beyond" clan structure can exist there, and the pronouncement, "These societies . . . have remained outside history." A similar but Marxist view is J. Suret Canale's in *Afrique noire* 1:44–45: "As long as mankind has not reached the stage that it can destroy or manage the forest . . . , that forest . . . acts as a brake on social evolution."

4. For example, J. Cornet, "Art Pygmée," 97–99. The fascination with pygmies, largely motivated by such views, has not abated in recent years, despite the abundance of publications. By 1970 the first specialized bibliographies appeared: cf. M. Liniger Goumaz, *Pygmées et autres races de petite taille: Bibliographie générale;* F. Plisnier-Ladame, *Les Pygmées.* In the 1980s the rate of research and publication is actually increasing, and at least one doctoral dissertation on the subject appears each year.

5. H. Deschamps, *Traditions orales et archives au Gabon,* 13. English authors use the expression "segmentary societies."

6. A. de Calonne-Beaufaict, *Les Ababua,* 60–65 (metaphor of the amoeba, 64); G. Hulstaert, *Les Mongo: Aperçu général,* 36–37.

7. As is explicit in J. Maes, "Les Warumbi," 628: "They do not know anything about the history of the tribe, ignore its origin, its migrations and the period when it arrived in the region where it is now settled." That was also all there was to history for the three most influential colonial syntheses: R. Avelot, "Recherches sur l'histoire des migrations dans le bassin de l'Ogooué et la région adjacente"; G. Van der Kerken, *L'Ethnie Mongo;* A. Moeller, *Les grandes lignes des migrations des Bantous de la province orientale du Congo Belge.*

8. H. Baumann and D. Westermann, *Les peuples:* "cercle congolais du nord"; H. Baumann, ed., *Die Völker Afrikas,* 685–91. For the seeming uniformity of the forest, see M. Kingsley, *Travels in West Africa,* 101.

9. A very widespread cliché. See, for instance, a 1959 citation in M. C. Reed, "An Ethnohistorical Study of the Political Economy of Ndjole, Gabon," 93 n. 20: "the broken and degenerate races, driven into the forests and malarial swamps by the war tribes," a view he still heard in Libreville in 1984.

10. These include approximately 60 professionals from 1875 to 1985, many fewer than anywhere else in Africa. The figure includes approximately 25 historians and 35 anthropologists, and excludes another 30 anthropologists working on pygmies.

11. See map 1.4 and chapter 2.

12. A. Kroeber, *Anthropology,* 253–54, 411; J. Steward, *Theory of Culture Change,* 37; G. R. Willey, *Archaeological Theories and Interpretations,* 373–74.

13. For the methodology concerning the written sources see B. Heintze and A. Jones, eds., "European Sources for Sub-Saharan Africa." For the methodology of oral tradition see J. Vansina, *Oral Tradition as History.* The statement about their chronological depth is based on the examination of the traditions that are extant in writing. For the archaeological situation see F. Van Noten, ed., *The Archaeology of Central Africa.* Since then (1982) intensive research has been underway in Gabon and surveys undertaken in Cameroon, Congo, Gabon, and parts of Zaire. Cf. articles in *Muntu, Nsi* (also current bibliography), and *Nyame Akuma.*

14. H. Brunschwig, "Une histoire de l'Afrique noire est-elle possible?" 2:85.

15. In general, see C. A. Schmitz, ed., *Historische Völkerkunde.* For the central European school, see F. Gräbner, *Methode der Ethnologie;* W. Schmidt, *The Culture Historical Method of Ethnology.* For the American school, see A. Kroeber, *Anthropology,* and more recently the journal *Ethnohistory* (1953–).

16. Recent manuals include R. Anttila, *An Introduction to Historical and Comparative Linguistics;* T. Bynon, *Historical Linguistics;* H. H. Hock, *Principles of Historical Linguistics;* W. Lehmann, *Historical Linguistics: An Introduction;* and the multiple book review "Archaeology and Language," *Current Anthropology* 29 (1988): esp. 445–47 (P. Baldi) and 449–53 (R. Coleman). The classic application to culture history remains E. Sapir, *Time Perspective in Aboriginal American Culture: A Study in Method.*

17. W. H. I. Bleek established the language family in 1851 and baptized it *Bantu* in 1869. C. Meinhof, "Grundriss einer Lautlehre der Bantusprachen," gave phonetic proof in 1899. In 1906 he published the first basic grammar of "common Bantu," *Grundzüge einer vergleichenden Grammatik der Bantusprachen.*

18. B. Heine, H. Hoff, and R. Vossen, "Neuere Ergebnisse zur Territorialgeschichte der Bantu"; Y. Bastin, A. Coupez, and B. de Halleux, "Classification lexicostatistique des langues bantoues"; Y. Bastin and A. Coupez, pers. com. 1985.

19. M. Swadesh, "Lexicostatistical Dating of Prehistoric Ethnic Contacts"; idem, "Towards Greater Accuracy in Lexicostatistical Dating."

20. D. H. Hymes, "Lexicostatistics So Far"; C. D. Chrétien, "The Mathematical Models of Glottochronology"; see also n. 16 above.

21. R. Anttila, *Historical and Comparative Linguistics:* in general, 133–53; for *Wörter und Sachen* (words and things) as a combination of linguistic and ethnographic data, 291–92. See also T. Bynon, *Historical Linguistics,* 62–63.

22. M. Guthrie, *Comparative Bantu,* to be checked with E. Meeussen, *Bantu Lexical Reconstructions.* Further discussion of Guthrie can be found in J. Vansina, "Deep Down Time."

23. "CS" stands for "comparative series" and "ps" for "partial series." Guthrie arranged his entries by CS and the number refers to the entry. But his "ps" are not always arranged under a number. Hence a page reference is given here. The vowel renderings for the CS in the text do not include the cedilla under *i* and *u,* which distinguishes vowels of first and second degree. These are therefore not differentiated in the text. For an exact rendering, see Guthrie's *Comparative Bantu.*

24. See discussion in R. Coleman, "Archaeology and Language," *Current Anthropology* (1988): 437–68, contra C. Renfrew. Starred items are as much "hard data" as archaeological sites are.

25. J. Vansina, *The Children of Woot,* 293, 297 (cf. Lele *ngal).*

26. Another example is the Tio fishing technique called *unteku.* It is a loanword because Tio never has a *k* as a second consonant of the root (-*teku).* Upriver the Likwala call the technique *muteku,* normal form in their language. The Tio borrowed it from them or from one of the other related groups of fishermen on the Zaire River. The anomaly of the form indicates that the loan is fairly recent. Otherwise the Tio speakers would have nativized it by dropping *k.* J. Vansina, *The Tio Kingdom of the Middle Congo: 1880–1892,* 136.

27. See chapter 5 and the discussion of *kazi katsi* (map 5.5; pp. 153–55).

28. M. McMaster, "Patterns of Interaction," chap. 7, e.g., fig. 7.11.

29. D. Cordell, "Throwing Knives in Equatorial Africa"; P. McNaughton, "The Throwing Knife in African History." The throwing knife is also found in seventeenth-century Loango: S. Brun, *Schiffarten,* 11. Compare also *osere, osele,* "throwing knife" in the Ivindo Valley, and *oshele* in the middle Lukenie Valley over 1,000 km away.

30. J. Vansina, "Deep Down Time," map showing -*kaya* "tobacco"; and idem, *Art History in Africa,* 168–73.

31. Skewing is the preservation of a borrowed form which is otherwise irregular in language. Skewed forms indicate borrowing rather than common descent. They are so indicated by M. Guthrie. The contrary does not rule out borrowing at all, for there are strong tendencies to adjust loans to usual patterns of "phonological nativization." Cf. H. H. Hock, *Principles of Historical Linguistics,* 90–97.

32. M. Swadesh, "Towards Greater Accuracy," 123, using a 85.4 percent retention rate per millennium as the constant (130).

33. R. Anttila, *Historical and Comparative Linguistics,* 396–98; T. Bynon *Historical Linguistics,* 266–72. For a strong negative reaction, cf. R. Coleman, "Archaeology and Language," 450.

34. A. Jones and B. Heintze, eds., "European Sources for Sub-Saharan Africa before 1900: Use and Abuse," esp. 1–17; J. Koponen, "Written Ethnographic Sources and Some Problems Concerned with Their Use in African Historiography," 55–69; R. Thornton, "Narrative Ethnography in Africa, 1850–1920," 503–20.

35. J. Vansina, "The Ethnographic Account as a Genre in Central Africa," 439, for examples of plagiarism by administrators. For the case of Trilles' work on pygmies, see K. Piskaty "Ist das Pygmäenwerk von Henri Trilles ein zuverlässige Quelle?"

36. Affonso Mvemba Nzinga and later kings of Kongo are inside sources but they are too far south. Cf. L. Jadin and M. Dicorato, *Correspondance de Dom Afonso roi du Congo: 1508–1543.*

37. J. Vansina, "Ethnographic Account."

38. E. Bassani has made a special study of ancient objects and iconography. See, for instance, his "I disegni dei Manoscritti Araldi del Padre Giovanni Antonio Cavazzi da Montecucolo."

39. C. Geary, "Photographs as Materials for African History."

40. F. Van Noten, *Archaeology of Central Africa,* 11.

41. E. Meeussen, "Het aanleggen van kollekties met geluidsopnemingen," 19.

42. W. J. Samarin, "Bondjo Ethnicity and Colonial Imagination," 345–65.

43. The discussion shows the administrative importance of "tribes." This case affected two provinces and the "ethnic" justification for their boundaries. Cf. J. Maes, "Note sur les populations Lalia et Yasayama du territoire des Dzalia," 175 (citing Stryckmans and Mazy); Van de Capelle, "Populations de Mondombe et Yolombo"; idem, "Note and Map"; A. Moeller, *Grands lignes,* 194–95; versus the authorities cited by M. De Ryck, *Les Lalia-Ngolu,* 21–22, and G. Van der Kerken, *L'Ethnie Mongo,* 54–55, 64, 75; These include Catholic missionary leaders fostering a "greater Mongo" consciousness. By 1935 the issue was administratively decided in favor of an inclusion in the Mongo group. Protes-

tant missionaries in the region maintained a separate Ngando "tribe" well after that date.

44. P. Van Leynseele, "Les Libinza de la Ngiri," iv, 30–35.

45. R. Harms, "Oral Tradition and Ethnicity."

46. T. E. Bowdich, *Mission from Cape Coast Castle to Ashantee*, 422–34; G. A. Robertson, *Notes on Africa*, 340; S. Koelle, *Polyglotta Africana:* itineraries. For a dicussion of ethnicity in Gabon, see L. Biffot, "Contribution à la connaissance et compréhension des populations rurales du nord-est du Gabon," 16–59.

47. G. Brausch, " 'Polyandrie' et 'mariage classique' chez les Bashi Lele"; M. Douglas, "A Form of Polyandry among the Lele of Kasai."

48. Field data for Kuba groups; J. Mertens, *Les Ba Dzing de la Kamtsha* 1:207–8. For cases involving objects, see J. Vansina, *Art History in Africa*, 31–33, 165.

49. P. Laburthe Tolra, *Les seigneurs de la forêt*, 422 n. 6 (a village near Yaounde moved 42 km at once in 1891); R. Letouzey, *Contribution de la botanique au problème d'une éventuelle langue pygmée*, 31 n. 15 (Baka hunters in eastern Cameroon moved over a 50-km radius); C. Amat, "Ngovayang II. Une village du sud-Cameroun," 61, 92, map 6 (200-km movement of a village in a generation); G. Hulstaert, *Les Mongo*, 16 (marriage up to 50 km away from birthplace), taking local variability in spatial mobility into account. For instance, in areas of very low population densities people moved farther and in areas of high population density distances were shorter.

50. Goebel, "Carte ethnographique de la zône Uere-Bili." Thus a set of maps of Uele already indicated ethnicity village by village in November and December 1908.

51. Uninhabited (*Unbewohnt*) or even *Tote Zone* ("dead area") occurs often in German reports and maps of southeastern Cameroon. Cf. F. Von Stein, "Expedition des Freiherrn von Stein," 185–86, and map by M. Moisel, "Skizze," 42–43. For population distributions in Gabon and Congo see G. Sautter, *De l'Atlantique au fleuve Congo*, vol. 2: *in fine;* for Zaire, see P. Gourou, "Notice de la carte de densité de la population au Congo Belge et au Ruanda-Urundi."

52. For the Independent Congo State, Congo, portions of Gabon, and Cameroon see routes on the map of J. Du Fief, "Carte de l'Etat Independant du Congo." All the rivers navigable by small boat were also reconnoitered; cross-checking information of the 50-km radius grid with reported ethnic groups shows that I could not find data specifically referring to the Babole of the lower Likouala-aux-herbes (but there are descriptions of the villages along the river) or to the Mbuli, Langa, and Kuti villages of the upper Tshuapa–Lomami area. Each "ethnic group" involved fewer than 1,000 inhabitants.

53. Occasionally one finds out-and-out fakes. Thus postcards from the 1930s showed nude Kuba women. In this area, however, men and women were always dressed.

54. E. Pechuel Loesche, *Volkskunde von Loango;* W. de Mahieu, *Structures et symboles;* idem, *Qui a obstrué la cascade?*

55. The major ones are M. Denis, *Histoire militaire de l'Afrique équatoriale française;* A. Lejeune-Choquet, *Histoire militaire du Congo* (Zaire); *La Force Publique de sa naissance à 1914* (Zaire). For German Kamerun see reports in *Deutsches Kolonialblatt.* Dates of colonial conquest are also often cited in local documents. The political register of each post in the Congo Independent State and in the Belgian Congo was kept from the date when the post was established and colonial rule began. Many of these registers still exist.

56. W. H. Sheppard, *Presbyterian Pioneers;* E. Torday and T. A. Joyce, *Notes ethnographiques . . . Les Bushongo;* H. Bucher, "The Mpongwe of the Gabon Estuary: A History to 1860."

57. G. Le Testu, "Les coutumes indigènes de la circonscription de la Nyanga (Gabon)"; idem, "La soumission des Bawanji"; C. Coquery Vidrovitch, *Le Congo au temps des grandes compagnies concessionnaires, 1898–1930,* 212–19.

58. J. Vansina, *Geschiedenis van de Kuba van ongeveer 1500 tot 1904,* 350–53, for an inquiry on the spot about the informants and information given to E. Torday for his *Bushongo.*

59. E. Zorzi, *Al Congo con Brazza.*

60. Among others, M. Douglas (Zaire) and M.-C. Dupré (Congo) both reported this. Still, Dupré was a mother of twins, recognized as such, and initiated in the arcana of twin lore. Douglas was an "honorary man," yet her gender prevented her from learning much about the senior men's society. It is clear that in fact gender roles in such circumstances become negotiable.

61. G. Van Bulck, *Les recherches linguistiques au Congo Belge;* Y. Bastin, *Bibliographie bantoue sélective.* After an initial period of trial and error, missions usually adopted a single language for the whole mission area rather than attempting to preach and teach in all the languages. Hence good records exist only for a minority of languages. On this question, cf. G. Van Bulck, *Les deux cartes linguistiques du Congo Belge,* and the rebuttal by G. Hulstaert, *Au sujet de deux cartes linguistiques du Congo belge.*

62. Cf. H. Scheub, *African Oral Narratives, Proverbs, Riddles, Poetry and Song: An Annotated Bibliography.* For an example, see T. Obenga, *Littérature traditionelle des Mbochi.*

63. E. Van de Woude, "Documents pour servir à la connaissance des populations du Congo Belge, 6–62, esp. 20–45; B. Jewsiewicki, "Etude analytique des archives administratives zairoises."

64. G. Van Bulck, *Deux cartes linguistiques,* and Y. Bastin, *Bibliographie bantoue selective,* are now supplemented by K. Kadima et al., *Atlas linguistique du Zaire: Inventaire préliminaire.* This is part of the projected linguistic atlas of all central Africa (Alac). The first systematic survey in equatorial Africa was the linguistic survey of the northern Bantu borderland (1949–52), but the whereabouts of the hundreds of standard general vocabularies gathered by Van Bulck are unknown. See G. Van Bulck, *Mission linguistique, 1949–1951,* 17–60. From

the 1970s onward such surveys have been undertaken again in Cameroon, Gabon, and Zaire.

65. H. A. Johnston, *A Comparative Study of the Bantu and Semi-Bantu Languages,* and others in his bibliography, 785–815. Other vocabularies have been published since, and a few earlier ones escaped even Johnston's attention.

66. Cultural vocabularies comprising from 110 to 500 items are now being compiled for some 150 languages in the area, sometimes from the most heterogeneous sources. Only the items dealing with the main social and political institutions have been used for this book.

67. These are A. Moeller, *Grandes lignes,* and G. Van der Kerken, *L'Ethnie Mongo.* On the latter, see G. Hulstaert, "Une lecture critique de *L'Ethnie Mongo* de G. Van der Kerken."

68. See J. Jacobs and J. Vansina, "Nshoong atoot: Het koninklijk epos der Bushoong," for a conscious historical tradition. See also A. De Rop and E. Boelaert, *Versions et fragments de l'épopée Mongo: Nsong'a Lianja* (and previously published versions); D. Biebuyck and K. Mateene, *The Mwindo Epic from the Banyanga (Congo Republic);* H. Pepper and P. De Wolf, *Un mvet de Zwè Nguéma,* for epics.

69. A list appears in E. Van de Woude, *Documents,* 13–17, 53–62; J. Vansina, "Ethnographic Account," 434–35.

70. Cf. n. 4. *Les racines du ciel* is the title of a novel dealing with pygmies. But even a serious account such as N. Ballif's came with the title *Les danseurs de Dieu: Chez les pygmées de la Sangha* ("The Dancers of God: Among the Pygmies of the Sangha"), an allusion to the dwarf of Pharao Pepi II of the Sixth Dynasty.

71. L. L. Cavalli-Sforza, *African Pygmies,* contains good examples of such preconceptions. Some modern studies take their cue more from the methodology of primate behavioral study than from the humanities, as in the title "The Relation between Exploration and Mating Range in Aka Pygmies," which is a contribution to Cavalli-Sforza's book.

72. W. N. Fenton coined the term. See "Ethnohistory and Its Problems."

Chapter Two: The Land and Its Settlement

1. P. T. White, "Tropical Rainforests," 2–46, on the vulnerability of these milieux.

2. Cf. FAO, UNESCO, *Soil Map of the World;* G. Laclavère, ed., *Atlas de la république Unie du Cameroun,* 25–27; R. Walter and J. Barret, eds., *Géographie et cartographie du Gabon,* 30–33; P. Vennetier, *Atlas de la République populaire du Congo,* 18–19.

3. G. Laclavère, *Atlas,* 16–19; R. Walter and J. Barret, *Géographie et cartographie,* 22–25; P. Vennetier, *Atlas,* 10–15.

4. See n. 3 and F. Bultot, "Notice de la carte des zones climatiques du Congo Belge et du Ruanda-Urundi."

5. F. Bultot, "Notice"; P. Vennetier, *Atlas,* 14 (Owando); G. Laclavère, *Atlas,* 19; R. Walter and J. Barret, *Géographie et cartographie,* 25.

6. The date varies from year to year. For Zaire, F. Bultot, "Notice," 7 (maps); idem, "Saisons et périodes sèches et pluvieuses au Congo belge et au Ruanda-Urundi." Bultot lists the usual dates for the onset of the dry season as well as the dates at which dry seasons began in abnormal years.

7. For the common view of pygmies as living fossils in the 1950s: R. Hartweg, *La vie secrète des pygmées,* 27: "They are a living prehistoric museum"; also 117. In the 1980s K. Duffy, *Children of the Forest,* vii–viii, 176–77: "a prehistoric group of hunters and gatherers who survived into the twentieth century" and "prestone age" (viii); ". . . the living spirits of our not so distant hunting and gathering ancestors" (177) and frontispiece: "An Egyptian dwarf about 2000 B.C." "Children" and "live in the present" (176), "harmony with the ecosystem" (176), and "innocent age" (177) round off the stereotype, unchanged since the Hellenistic pygmies in the land of the lotus eaters.

8. Sources cited in M. Reed, "An Ethnohistorical Study of the Political Economy of Ndjole, Gabon," 96.

9. The earliest exposition of the stereotype of the forest in H. M. Stanley, *Through the Dark Continent,* 408–9, begins with: "On the 6th of November [1876] we drew nearer to the dreaded black and chill forest called Mitamba, and at last, bidding farewell to sunshine and brightness entered it." For the full elaboration, see idem, *In Darkest Africa,* 134–292, esp. 138; T. H. Parke, *My Personal Experiences in Equatorial Africa,* 71–358; and other sources listed in R. Jones, *The Rescue of Emin Pasha.* It usually escapes readers that the terrors of the forest were described in order to excuse major errors of judgment made during the expedition.

10. P. Richards, "The Tropical Rain Forest"; K. A. Longman and J. Jenik, *Tropical Forest and Its Environment;* F. Fournier and A. Sasson, *Ecosystèmes forestiers tropicaux d'Afrique,* 92; W. Robyns, *Contribution à l'étude des formations herbeuses du district forestier central du Congo belge;* J. Vansina, "Peoples of the Forest," 77 n. 1 (further references). For maps, see F. White, *The Vegetation of Africa;* G. Laclavère; *Atlas,* 20–24; R. Walter and J. Barret, *Géographie et cartographie,* 34–37; P. Vennetier, *Atlas,* 16–17; and L. Peeters, *Les limites forêt-savane dans le nord du Congo en relation avec le milieu géographique.* For a general discussion of human-habitat interaction, see J. Vansina, "L'homme, les forêts et le passé en Afrique."

11. R. Harako, "The Mbuti as Hunters," and map by F. White, *Vegetation of Africa,* versus C. Turnbull, "Forest Hunters and Gatherers: The Mbuti Pygmies," 41. For further discussion see T. B. Hart, "The Ecology of a Single Species-Dominant Forest and Mixed Forest in Zaire."

12. Evidence for high human activity of long ago is discussed in chapters 5 and 6. Indicators for higher population densities followed by lower densities are the frequency of certain trees such as *Lophira alata* and the *Aucoumea.* At the

other extreme, stands of *Gilbertiodendron dewevrei* indicate low population densities for the last half millennium or more.

13. G. Laclavère, *Atlas*, 22–23.

14. G. Sautter, *De l'Atlantique au fleuve Congo*, 2:947–76. P. Gourou, *Les pays tropicaux*, 10–19, is less sanguine.

15. The "pygmies" are the celebrated case in this connection. Cf. J. Hiernaux, *The People of Africa*, 113–49; idem, "Long-term Biological Effects of Human Migration from the African Savanna to the Equatorial Forest." But more recently R. C. Bailey, "The Socioecology of Efe Pygmy Men in the Ituri Forest," 26–27, disputes this stand and points out that the present habitat of pygmies in the Ituri was savanna until c. 900 B.C. or possibly as late as A.D. 1200! The question needs further study.

16. P. Gourou, *La densité de la population rurale au Congo belge*, 116.

17. J. Maley, "Fragmentation de la forêt dense," 310, for a map and the link between amount of rainfall and the Benguela current; F. Van Noten, ed., *The Archaeology of Central Africa*, 22–25; J. Flenley, *The Equatorial Rain Forest: A Geological History*, 29–54, and human influence, 116–18.

18. F. Van Noten, *Archaeology*, 25. Elsewhere the forest was receding then. In the same area cf. M. C. Van Grunderbeek, E. Roche, and H. Doutrelepont, "L'âge du fer ancien au Rwanda et au Burundi," 46–48.

19. L. Demesse, *Techniques et économie des pygmées babinga*, 7, 28.

20. G. Laclavère, *Atlas*, 20–24; R. Walter and J. Barret, *Géographie et cartographie*, 34–37; P. Vennetier, *Atlas* 36–37. For savannas in the Late Stone Age, see R. Deschamps, R. Lanfranchi, A. Le Cocq, and D. Schwartz, "Reconstitution d'environnements quaternaires par l'étude de macrorestes végétaux (Pays Bateke, R. P. du Congo)."

21. F. Van Noten, ed., *The Archaeology of Central Africa;* F. Van Noten et al., "The Prehistory of Central Africa, Part 2"; R. Bayle des Hermens, "The Prehistory of Central Africa, Part 1" and references there. Archaeological activity has increased since then, however, and readers should consult the journals *Nyame Akuma, Nsi, Muntu,* and the *African Archaeological Review.*

22. F. Van Noten, ed., *Archaeology*, 29–30; L. Fiedler and J. Preuss, "Stone Tools from the Inner Zaire Basin"; B. Peyrot and R. Olisly, "Paleoenvironnement et archéologie au Gabon," 14–15; R. Lanfranchi, "Recherches préhistoriques en République populaire du Congo," 7.

23. But see R. C. Bailey, "Socioecology," 26–27, for some implicit doubts.

24. J. Hiernaux, *The People of Africa*, fig. 19, table 25. It follows from the palaeogeography that if Hiernaux's view on biological adaptation is accepted, then the clusters probably represent pygmy groups issuing from the different forest refuges, as indicated in J. Maley, "Fragmentation," 310.

25. On survivals of "pygmy" languages, see S. Seitz, *Die zentralafrikanischen Wildbeuterkulturen*, 19–23; J. M. C. Thomas, "Emprunt ou parenté?" 160–61; R. Letouzey, "Contribution de la botanique au problème d'une éventuelle

langue pygmée"; and A. Vorbichler, "Die Sprachliche Beziehungen zwischen den Waldnegern und Pygmäen in der Republik Kongo-Leo"; idem, "Zu dem Problem der Klasseneinteilung in Lebendiges und Lebloses in den Pygmäen- und Waldnegerdialekten des Ituri, Congo."

26. This already before the Neolithic: L. Fiedler and J. Preuss, "Stone Tools," 179, 182. B. Clist, "Un nouvel ensemble néolithique en Afrique centrale: Le groupe d'Okala au Gabon," 45, shows that stone axes in the Ogooué Delta came from about 300–350 km upstream.

27. A Gabonese informant cited by H. Deschamps, *Traditions orales et archives au Gabon,* 25.

28. Y. Bastin, A. Coupez, and B. de Halleux, "Classification lexicostatistique des langues bantoues (214 relevés)" and Bastin's 1983 communication about a larger set of western Bantu languages; P. B. Bennett and J. P. Sterk, "South Central Niger-Congo: A Reclassification"; and more recently T. C. Schadeberg, "The Lexicostatistic Base of Bennett and Sterk's Reclassification of Niger-Congo with Particular Reference to the Cohesion of Bantu." The group of Y. Bastin and A. Coupez is still at work on providing a complete genetic tree of the Bantu languages.

29. M. Guthrie, *Comparative Bantu:* index, 2:177, 178; J. Vansina, "Western Bantu Expansion," 132, 138, map 139. For details see chapter 3.

30. F. Nsuka and P. De Maret, "History of Bantu Metallurgy: Some Linguistic Aspects."

31. Exactly why some splinter groups did not expand farther promises to be a rewarding topic for future study. The scissions of the Yambasa-Nen, of the Myene-Tsogo, and of the Aka-Mbati small groups are of this type. The expected situation is exemplified by the split between the northern Zairian languages and the southwestern group. According to Hock, *Principles of Historical Linguistics,* 449, the presence of "flat tree diagrams" with mainly binary branchings are indicative of the spread of innovations in a dialect continuum in large ensembles of dialects; furthermore, the group average method used to find splits favors only two-way splits. Finally, historians will remember that a split represents a time period, not a moment, and a region, not a spot, and that the dates refer to language differences which took hold *after* separation.

32. According to the principle of Ockham's razor. The suggested routes are based on placing the locale of dispersals at the boundary of the resulting groups. The more branches disperse at once, the easier it is to fix such a locale. In this situation, however, only two-way splits occur but for one case. Specific environmental barriers such as the great swamps, the arid Bateke plateaus, and the inhospitable Du Chaillu massif have been taken into account as well. In the end, however, only archaeology will provide more than general directions of expansion.

33. M. McMaster, "Patterns of Interaction," chap. 2 for Buan. The label Soan is suggested here for the neighboring branch. The name is derived by

analogy from the "So" and "Eso" languages, which, among others, belong to this group.

34. P. De Maret, "Résultats des premières fouilles dans les abris de Shum Laka et d'Abeke au nord-ouest du Cameroun: Belgian archaeological project in Cameroon" (Obobogo); idem, "Recent Archaeological Research and Dates from Central Africa," 134–35 (Obobogo); idem, "The Ngovo Group: An Industry with Polished Stone Tools and Pottery in Lower Zaire," 127 (dates for Ngovo and Sakuzi); J. Denbow, A. Manima-Moubouha and N. Sanviti, "Archaeological Excavations along the Loango Coast Congo," 37–38 (Tchissanga); M. Eggert, "Imbonga and Batalimo: Ceramic Evidence for Early Settlement of the Equatorial Rain Forest," 133 (Imbonga; rejecting the Hanover dates still leaves samples 3, 7, and 9 and dates 310, 340, and 320 B.C.), 139–41 (Batalimo-Maluba; one date is at least 190 B.C. and two others 40 B.C. and A.D. 20); idem, "Archäologische Forschungen im zentralafrikanischen Regenwald," map 3223 (Imbonga and Batalimo-Maluba).

35. B. Clist, "Travaux archéologiques récents en République du Gabon, 1985–1986," 10, and pers. com. 1988. Ibid., 9, also gives 2920 +/−90 B.C. and 2450 +/−70 B.C. for different and earlier ceramics in this area, which have so far not been confirmed. If they are indeed associated with ceramics one would have to dissociate the spread of ceramics (earlier) from that of a food-producing economy, the latter being associated only with the expansion of the western Bantu languages.

36. M. McMaster, "Patterns of Interaction," chap. 2 for internal Buan divisions. This relates to the Zaire bend and the northeast, not to the Ubangi Valley where the Batalimo-Maluba types date to the last two centuries B.C. only.

37. The first case is calculated on carbon dates, the others are based on estimated loci of dispersal and glottochronological estimates. The first two cases should be compared with the speed of movement between the same Congo panhandle and the Niari Valley where the Kongo–Congo-Gabon groups split. That yields 600 km (1,200 double) in a mere 170 years, or 70 km/decade, which is suspiciously high. Despite the vagueness of dating estimates and of localities inherent in the calculation, the results remain suggestive of considerable variability in the rates of migration. In the examples above, the seceding northern Zaire speakers went slowly at first because they had to master the watery and marshy environments of the great swamps. Once at home on the waters, however, they raced.

38. S. Seitz, Zentralafrikanischen Wildbeuterkulturen, 22; W. Dupré, "Die Babinga-Pygmäen," 29–38. It is likely that the original term for pygmy specifically was *-yaka.

39. For example, S. Bahuchet and H. Guillaume, "Relations entre chasseurs-collecteurs pygmées et agriculteurs de la forêt du nord-ouest du bassin congolais," 111–17.

40. This stance conveniently denied rights from first occupation to the hunters and gatherers by essentially claiming that they were not fully human.

41. On fishing, see chapter 3. The rarity of suitable settlement sites along many rivers made clashes even more likely.

42. Future biological research would help to frame such questions better. Meanwhile, analogies with the decimation by disease of the autochthons in the New World should be distrusted. This was no invasion by organisms from another continent, but probably more a question of the relative prevalence of certain diseases in certain habitats.

43. D. Calvocoressi and N. David, "A New Survey of Radiocarbon and Thermoluminescence Dates for West Africa," 10 (Taruga), gives a ninth-century date for Taruga; L. Digombe et al., "Early Iron Age Prehistory in Gabon," 183. See also M. C. Van Grunderbeek, E. Roche, and H. Doutrelepont, *Le premier âge du fer au Rwanda et au Burundi,* 48–50 (great lakes).

44. In Gabon the situation is evolving rapidly with an active archaeological program. Cf. L. Digombe et al., "Early Iron Age Prehistory"; B. Clist, "Early Bantu Settlements in West-Central Africa," 380–82. Contrast this with the older data by P. De Maret, "Ngovo Group," 129–48, and more recent information in B. Clist, "La fin de l'âge de la pierre et les débuts de la métallurgie du fer au Gabon," 24–28, 29; L. Digombe et al., "Recherches archéologiques au Gabon: Année académique 1986–1987." Most recently B. Clist, "Un nouvel ensemble," 47–48, urges caution, which is reflected on map 2.10.

45. M. Eggert, "Archäologische Forschungen," 3234–35; idem, "Imbonga and Batalimo," 134, 141.

46. F. Van Noten, "The Early Iron Age in the Interlacustrine Region," 62, 65, 67.

47. M. McMaster, "Patterns of Interaction," chap. 4 and table 4.3.

48. F. Nsuka-Nkutsi and P. De Maret, "Etude comparative de quelques terme métallurgiques dans les langues bantoues," 731–42; M. Guthrie, *Comparative Bantu,* 1:132, 138–40 (see Appendix items 97–103); C. P. Blakney, "On 'Banana' and 'Iron'," 85–118. Distinctions between western and eastern Bantu must be added to these sources.

49. Such as C. Wrigley, "Speculations on the Economic Prehistory of Africa," 201–2 (iron spear). Copper and lead in lower Congo were probably smelted as early as iron. Cf. J. Denbow, A. Manima-Moubouha, N. Sanviti, "Archaeological Excavation," 39, who locate such smelting activity at Madingo-Kayes in the second or third century A.D.

50. E. Perrot and E. Vogt, *Les poisons de flèches et les poisons de l'épreuve des indigènes de l'Afrique,* 58–80. On the inferiority of wooden or horned tip spears, Bosékônsombo (Nkúmônsombo) correspondence to Hulstaert: supplement to his 19 February 1971.

51. A prehistoric ore center at Lebombi in Haut Ogooué Province lasted for half a millennium in a region where iron smelting was still a specialty in 1900; see P. R. Schmidt, L. Digombe et al., 17. The region of Abala was a major iron-smelting center as well, probably before the eighteenth century. M.-D. Dupré, "Pour une histoire des productions de la metallurgie du fer chez les Téké,

Ngungulu, Tio, Tsayi," 201–7; and R. Lanfranchi, "Esquisse archéologique des régions Teke," 83.

52. On the botanical characteristics, see G. Rossel, "Gewasinnovaties in Gabon," 25–49; E. De Langhe, "Bananas *Musa* spp.," 53–78; N. W. Simmonds, *Bananas;* R. M. Eggert, *Das Wirtschaftssystem der Mongo am Vorabend der Kolonisation,* 7–11; P. T. Perrault, "Banana-Manioc Farming Systems of the Tropical Forest," 6–28, 116–142; A. Raponda-Walker and R. Sillans, *Les plantes utiles du Gabon,* 447–54.

53. E. De Langhe, "La taxonomie du bananier plantain en Afrique équatoriale," 417–49; G. Rossel, "Gewasinnovaties," 28, 29; N. W. Simmonds, *Bananas.*

54. D. N. McMaster, "Speculations on Coming of the Banana to Uganda," 57–69, favors the East African route, perhaps via the Zambezi. J. Barrau, as cited by J. Bouquiaux and J. Thomas, "Le peuplement oubanguien," 3:816, favors the upper Nile. For E. De Langhe's views as interpreted by P. T. Perrault, see "Banana-Manioc Farming Systems," 121–22, and his "La taxonomie," 447–49. Argument based on varieties in J. Vansina, "Esquisse historique de l'agriculture en milieu forestier," 21–24 nn. 32–35.

55. G. Rossel, "Gewasinnovaties," 31–38; C. P. Blakney, "On 'Banana' and 'Iron'," 54–78; W. J. Möhlig, "Lehnwortforschung und Ethnohistorie," 7–20, map 18; E. Bylin, *Basakata: Le peuple du pays de l'entre-fleuves Lukenye-Kasai,* 98. -*bugu* and *bugugu: Bu-* is not a prefix class 14, which in Tsogo is *bo-*, and even if it were, *bugugu* could still be a reflex of -*bugu;* see A. Raponda-Walker and R. Sillans, *Plantes utiles,* 305.

56. For -*toto,* see C. P. Blakney "On 'Banana' and 'Iron'," 78. For Gabon, see A. Raponda-Walker and R. Sillans, *Plantes utiles,* 305; and for Bekwil, Gabon, and Cameroon, see G. Rossel, "Gewasinnovaties," 32; -*poko/poku/ bogo* as "banana tree" or "banana grove" occurs in Huku (Amba), Nyanga, Lega, Boa and related languages, Bira, Komo, Bali, So, Heso, Enya, Lengola, Metoko, Mongo and closely related languages, Sengele, Benga, and probably elsewhere. Other generic terms for "banana," such as *fondo, ndoo, -kube, -bō, gbede/kede* in the north from the Ubangi to Douala and the Cross River, as well as -*koma* and -*doso* in southern Maniema, indicate that only the major outlines of a linguistic study are known so far and that the full history of the banana in the area will be much more complex than had been imagined.

57. G. Rossel, "Gewasinnovaties," 26–31; G. A. Wainwright, "The Coming of the Banana to Uganda," 145–47; S. Munro Hay, "The Foreign Trade of the Aksumite Port of Adulis," 107–25. The banana was not such an exotic plant for the Axumites, who cultivated *ensete,* a relative of the banana; M. McMaster, "Patterns of Interaction," fig. 5.3. Using semantic evidence McMaster concluded that bananas spread among the Buans then living near the middle Bomokandi after A.D. 170 by glottochronological estimate, but ancient diffusion may well be indistinguishable from common origin here. The evidence assembled by M. Watson, *Agricultural Innovation in the Early Islamic World: The*

Diffusion of Crops and Farming Techniques, 700–1100, who argues for a late Muslim introduction, would best fit the high-yielding AAA cultivars.

58. Certainly before A.D. 1000. The introduction of the common fowl parallels the diffusion of the banana. To date, chicken bones are attested in Rwanda and southern Shaba by A.D. 1000. J. Vansina, "Esquisse historique de l'agriculture," 25.

59. See n. 25.

60. L. Bouquiaux and J. M. C. Thomas, "Le peuplement oubanguien," 807–24, includes Gbaya; D. E. Saxon, "Linguistic Evidence for the Eastward Spread of Ubangian Peoples," 66–77, excludes Gbaya as P. Bennett (ms. communication) does also. Thomas and Bouquiaux are unreliable on chronology and on postulated migrations. The dates are not based on any calculations. Tentative glottochronological dating is so early that the proposed Ngbaka and Gbanzili migration from Uele, rather than from farther northwest in the Central African Republic, is doubtful. The account of their migration on maps 3, 4, 6, and 7 and text 810–12 is incorrect in postulating late migrations up and down the lowermost Ubangi as far as Lake Tumba. Local oral traditions have a depth of three to four centuries here and do not remember anything but Bantu speakers in these areas.

61. The terminology for this group is still variable. The terms Moru-Madi (Tucker and Bryan) are still used, though Ehret labels the group east-central Sudanic. However, south-central Sudanic agrees best with the overall linguistic classifications. For the group, cf. A. N. Tucker and M. A. Bryan, *The Non-Bantu Languages of North-Eastern Africa,* 1–9; C. Ehret et al., "Some Thoughts on the Early history of the Nile-Congo Watershed," 85–112; A. Vorbichler, "Linguistische Bemerkungen zur Herkunft der Mamvu-Balese," 1145–54; idem, *Die Phonologie und Morphologie des Balese,* 9–12; idem, *Die Sprache der Mamvu,* 29–31, whose late chronology (after A.D. 1000) cannot be accepted given M. McMaster, "Patterns of Interaction," chap. 2, in which she proposes "before 440 B.C." for the proto-Mamvu subgroup in Uele; N. David, "Prehistory and Historical Linguistics in Central Africa," 80–81, would see their area of origin as far as 10° north rather than the 4° north proposed by Ehret.

62. These are the Nyanga and Tembo, who both speak languages of the great lakes. Western Bantu farmers began to occupy northern Maniema only in the last three centuries B.C. (M. McMaster, "Patterns of Interaction," table 1.4: 380–180 B.C. for the Bira split), so that a spread of Nyanga by an estimated c. A.D. 220 (split between Nyanga and other great lakes) is entirely plausible. The Tembo followed one or more centuries later.

63. See J. Vansina, "Western Bantu Expansion," 139–40. Although the agricultural innovations are evident, the extent of social and political elements remains unclear. Further research in the eastern vocabulary present in the western Bantu savanna languages is needed.

64. The Ngbandi movement is based on M. McMaster, "Patterns of Interaction," chap. 5, which according to her follow the Mba and Mondunga migrations. See her table 5.3 for the earliest Ngbandi influences in Uele.

65. For Ngbandi some evidence of mutual influence is shown in G. Hulstaert, "Lomongo en Ngbandi." Ngbandi influence is strong in various groups of Apagibeti, where it mingles with influences of Mondunga-Mba on a Bantu base. See, for instance, A. Van Houteghem, "Overzicht der Bantu dialekten van het gewest Lisala," 42–43, 49; H. Nzenze, "Note sur les Pagabete," 137. The languages of the Boa group also show some influence from this group (e.g., the use of *-le* suffix).

66. For the late date of the Balese split, see A. Vorbichler, *Sprache der Mamvu*, 29, for a 93 percent correspondence between Mamvu and Balese, which gives an A.D. 1720 date. For southern central Sudanic influences on Bantu, see M. McMaster, "Patterns of Interaction," chap. 4, tables 4.1, 4.2, and 4.3, for Bali. The influence of this Mamvu group on Komo or Bira is as evident as on Bali. These languages even abandoned their prefix classes. Southern central Sudanic influence on phonetics and on vocabulary are seen throughout the northeastern Bantu languages.

67. The only available chronological estimate places the onset of the Ngbandi migration along the Uele at A.D. 280. M. McMaster, "Patterns of Interaction," chap. 5, table 5.3, shows the earliest Ngbandi influence from c. A.D. 170 or shortly thereafter.

68. J. M. C. Thomas and L. Gouquiaux, "Le peuple oubanguien," 816, citing Barrau, merely state that the diffusion of the banana paralleled the migration of the Ngbaka Mabo. As to the generic terms, *fondo* in Ngbandi and the related *ndoo* in the Ngbaka Mabo–Gbanzili group do not seem to have congeners farther eastward. In the equatorial subgroup *poongo-* (*le*) in Mondunga and *bo-* (*le*) in Mba differ from each other. Yet M. McMaster, "Patterns of Interaction," chap. 5, argues that at the time of migration from the east, bananas there were already called *-bugu*.

69. By A.D. 500 (63 percent correspondence) we are at the level of minor linguistic subgroups and separate just under two-thirds of all languages listed for the area in the Tervuren survey. By A.D. 1000 (74 percent correspondence) we are at the level of individual languages with nearly three-fourths of all languages listed. With the exception of the Sanaga-Ntem area no major disjunctions, indicative of late massive migrations, occur on the linguistic maps. For the Sanaga-Ntem expansion, see chapter 5.

70. In his survey work, M. Eggert, "Imbonga and Batalimo," 3234–35, recognized a new ceramic, labeled Bondongo in the inner Zaire basin, starting from the thirteenth century. The distribution suggests a spread of fishermen from the lower Ubangi to the Ruki up the Tshuapa and the Maringa, but site excavations are needed.

71. For population densities, see F. Goffart, *Le Congo,* 94; E. V. Thevoz, "Kamerun Eisenbahn-Erkundungs-Expedition Bevölkerungsdichte"; G. Sautter, *De l'Atlantique,* vol. 2, endmaps; P. Gourou, *Pays tropicaux;* A. Annaert-Bruder "La densité de la population du Congo-Kinshasa," 161; J. Vansina, "Peoples of the Forest," 110.

Vegetation can reflect low or high densities in the past, but not in the very remote past: P. Foury, "Indications données par l'état actuel de la végétation sur la répartition ancienne des groupements humains," gives examples of vegetation following a high level of farming activity some three to four centuries ago. R. Letouzey, *Etude phytogéographique du Cameroun*, 142–45, confirms for *Lophira alata.* Stands of *Gilbertiodendron dewevrei* (ibid., 252), an evergreen forest climax habitat, point to undisturbed conditions for the last half millennium or more. But vegetation can probably not attest to the situation a millennium ago, and, at present, estimates about the time a given habitat needs to establish itself remain approximate. Still for the last half millennium forested habitats could tell us much about the distribution and the relative intensity of farming and farmers.

72. W. De Craemer, J. Vansina, and R. Fox, "Religious Movements in Central Africa," 463–65.

Chapter Three: Tradition: Ancient and Common

1. "A" stands for Appendix: Comparative Lexical Data. "CS" stands for Comparative Series and the reference number in M. Guthrie's *Comparative Bantu*, vols. 3 and 4. For the form of the CS and the evidence where no CS form is given, see Appendix.

2. Villages disappeared only among the Nen, Fia, Saa, and Mvumbo (Ngumba) peoples in Cameroon. The hamlet also was the normal settlement near the middle Uele, but there mostly among non-Bantu speakers. The district very rarely became coterminous with the village. On the upper Ngiri there were no districts in the area in precolonial days. Libinza is a modern ethnic name derived from the name for a village (P. Van Leynseele, "Les Libinza de la Ngiri," 32–33). I do not know of any recorded disappearance anywhere of the House.

3. J. A. Barnes, "African Models in the New Guinea Highlands,"; P. Van Leynseele, "Les Libinza," additional thesis no. 1. For general descriptions, cf. A. Cureau, *Les sociétés primitives de l'Afrique équatoriale*, 324–38, or I. Dugast, *Monographie de la tribu des Ndiki*, 2:451–53. For a portrait of a "big man" (Pando of the Gunabemb in southeastern Cameroon), see C. W. H. Koch, *Das Lied des Landes*, 78–82, and 72–74, 91–93; Kota and Nen are languages in which the term for leader literally means "big man" (*-nen*).

4. H. Koch, *Magie et chasse dans la forêt camerounaise*, 46.

5. Ibid., 48.

6. "Rich," "famous," *kúm*, reflex of CS 1263–64 derived from CS 1265 "big man." For a distribution map of CS 165, see J. Vansina, "Deep Down Time."

7. This was true in the later common culture. The trophies of these animals belonged to leaders who wore them. To appropriate a trophy was a formal declaration of insurgence. Leopard and python flesh were consumed only by a few persons in formal communion rites presided over by the leader. A special term for such "animals of leadership" exists in most languages. This custom does not imply that at one time these people were primarily hunters. It derives from

the notion of "living being," which includes only organisms that move. The "kings" of several classes of animals are the animals of leadership. Funeral rites for slain leopards were especially linked to leadership. Compare, for instance, Loango c. 1640–1668 in O. Dapper, *Naukeurige Beschrijvinge der Afrikaensche gewesten*, 542–43; and c. 1700 in N. Uring, *The Voyages and Travels of Captain Nathaniel Uring*, 36–37, who mentions "the gallows," as do A. Raponda-Walker and R. Sillans, *Rites et croyances des peuples du Gabon*, 235–36, for an Ivea village in 1907, which in turn recalls similar rites all over northern Zaire.

8. W. MacGaffey, "The Religious Commissions of the BaKongo." On the egalitarian ethic embedded in witchcraft generally, see J. Vansina, *The Tio Kingdom*, 240–41. Ethnographic comments on the notion of "luck" also fit this type of leadership. Because the notion "luck" is not recorded in most dictionaries, the potential proto–western Bantu is still unknown. See, for instance, G. Teßman, *Die Bubi auf Fernando Po*, 130–39. On the pangolin, cf. M. Douglas, "Animals in Lele Religious Symbolism," 50–56; D. Biebuyck, "Répartition et droits du pangolin chez les Balega"; W. de Mahieu, *Structures et symboles*, 38–40. Its unusual behavior and the taxonomic difficulties it presents have made it the emblem of this type of authority.

9. T. Irstam, *The King of Ganda*. For a list of "traits" of "divine kingship," see J. Vansina, *Le royaume kuba*, 98–103; F. Hagenbucher Sacripanti, *Les fondements spirituels du pouvoir au royaume de Loango*, 78–87; A. Aymemi, *Los Bubis en Fernando Poo*, 57–69.

10. Only larger-scale excavations will allow archaeologists to find and estimate respective sizes of House residential quarters.

11. House space was indicated by ditches across the village street (Foma: B. Crine, *La structure sociale des Foma*, 19), separate plazas (Boa: Védy, "Les Ababuas," 200–202), open spaces between the "hamlets" corresponding to the quarters (Tio: J. Vansina, *Tio Kingdom*, 506), or by communal houses for each House in the village street (Bekwil: A. Cureau, *Les sociétés primitives*, 242).

12. To use a felicitous adjective of C. Lévi-Strauss without evolutionary implications.

13. For instance, by the Myene forms: Mpongwe *obóta*, "parent"; Tsogo *obóta*, "clan"; and northwestern Bantu as Kosi *ebóa*, "House plaza," and Eso *liotsi*, "House." The form is universal with the meaning "House" in the inner basin block of languages (Mongo).

14. J. Vansina, "Lignage, idéologie et histoire en Afrique équatoriale," 140–48. The etymology of terms for "House" does not usually refer to gender, as one would expect in unilineal descent situations. The etymologies found refer to: "house," "bed," "hearth," "hearthstones," "plaza of authority," "offspring of," "grandchildren of," "species," "root," "shield," and "communal shed." Contrast this with "belly/female sex" in matrilineal groups of lower Zaire and the lower Kasai areas, and "sister" among matrilineal Myene and present-day patrilineal Mpongwe. Contrast also with "male" in the now strongly patrilineal groups of south-central Cameroon and "penis"/"vagina" around Lake Mai Ndombe, where there is now a double descent system.

15. The meaning of some reflexes given by M. Guthrie needs correction, e.g., G. Hulstaert, "Notes sur la langue des Bafóto," 129, *mbóa:* "road," "at home," "home village." Also add ps 482 to CS 447. In this connection see CS 694 "to name" and ps 192 (3:187) "namesake." Namesakes were a way to integrate outsiders among some hunting and gathering groups with high mobility, including the Mbuti of Ituri. Cf. R. Mc. Netting, *Cultural Ecology*, 15. The form is ancient but not western Bantu. Still, it includes more western reflexes than Guthrie has, for instance, for Bira.

16. G. Laumanns, *Verwandtschaftsnamen und Verwandtschaftsordnungen im Bantugebiet;* update with M. Guthrie, *Comparative Bantu*, 2:178d. Because kinship terms form a coherent system, two different comparisons are involved: one for the form and meaning of each term, one for the whole system. For an instance, see J. Vansina, *Children of Woot*, 105–6, 108–9, 291–95.

17. Although the original for "grandparent" may well have been CS 1204 in form, ps 309, cited with CS 1204, is probably the same. It is not just eastern Bantu as claimed by Guthrie, because many reflexes are found in Gabon and in the inner basin. CS 992 is probably proto–western Bantu and an innovation with respect to CS 1204. A variety of other terms also occurs, some with shared etymologies for "close ancestor." Note the reduplicated shape of the form as for "my" father and mother, forms due to baby talk.

18. G. P. Murdock, *Africa: Its Peoples and Their Culture History*, 29–30, after idem, *Social Structure*, 184–259, where the supposedly evolutionary development is given.

19. J. Vansina, "Peoples of the Forest," 88 n. 46 for Fang, Mongo, and Komo, respectively with four, eight, and three main forms of marriage. P. Laburthe Tolra, *Les seigneurs de la forêt*, 239–45, for the Bane, also with eight or nine primary forms. Cicisbeism was particularly widespread, since it was a mechanism to attract young men to one's House. As G. Dupré, *Un ordre et sa destruction*, 148–49, has argued, in general various forms of marriage were products of political decisions and not unworldly systems exchanging women automatically. The error in anthropological theory stems from the fact that for Europeans there could be only one valid marriage form at a time. Early on in the colonial period lawyers, administrators, and missionaries chose the form which they felt was "the only valid one."

20. E. Meeussen, *Bantu Lexical Reconstructions*, 5: 3.

21. Village size for 111 villages in southeastern Cameroon (1910–1912) yields 104.8 on average with 49.16 for the smallest average per ethnic group and 325 for the highest (on the margins of the grasslands in a war-torn situation). Extremes go from 5 or, if discounted, 12, to 787 or, if discounted, 462, with a clustering around 100; see C. W. H. Koch, "Die Stämme des Bezirks Molundu," 286–304. Early impressionistic figures elsewhere, or numbers for single villages elsewhere in the area, tend to confirm these results.

22. For instance, P. De Maret, "The Ngovo Group," 120–21, or for the sites near Loango, J. Denbow et al., "Archaeological Excavations," 37–42.

23. A. Cureau, *Sociétés primitives*, 218–44; J. Annaert, *Contribution à l'étude géoraphique de l'habitat et de l'habitation indigènes en milieu rural dans les provinces orientale et du Kivu.*

24. But in some languages such as Jofe or Foto the term means "path," clearly outside the village, and yet also "our village." Cf. n. 15.

25. Contrary to A. Cureau, *Sociétés primitives*, 214, who defines the village as "created by one man, for one man."

26. G. Dupré, *Un ordre et sa destruction*, 117–22.

27. From CS 1003 such terms as *nkaan*, "initiation," in southern Zaire, including some Kongo and Kuba. From CS 1709, 1711: *-téénde*, "an initiate." The distribution includes Maniema and portions of the north and the northwest. Also *-yénde*, "an initiand" (cf. Bushong *-byéén*, Kete *-bende*, Nen *-yindi*, Duala *-énda*, "to circumcise," and *bwende*, "initiation").

28. Boy's initiations have often been described. For example, cf. W. de Mahieu, *Qui a obstrué la cascade?*; A. Droogers, *The Dangerous Journey*; L. Perrois, "La circoncision Bakota (Gabon)" (children of high status); H. Van Geluwe, *Les Bali et les peuplades apparentées*, 64–67 (no circumcision then); J. Vansina, "Initiation Rituals of the Bushong" (also without circumcision); H. Van Geluwe, *Mamvu-Mangutu et Balese-Mvuba*, 70–72, for the middle Bomokandi, and 158–60 for Ituri. Unlike the practice of all other peoples, neither initiation nor circumcision was common among most peoples (Mongo group) of the inner Congo Basin.

29. Mumbanza mwa Bamwele, "Histoire des peuples riverains de l'entre Zaire-Ubangi," 163 and 155–73; A. Wolfe, *In the Ngombe Tradition*, 51. The term used is *kola*, a reflex of CS 1194. The Duala and Kpe age groups used another term (E. Ardener, *Coastal Bantu of the Cameroons*, 70–71); the Lele and Mongo term was derived from CS 664, "row." For the Lele, see M. Douglas, *The Lele of Kasai*, 68–84; for the Mongo, see R. Philippe, *Inongo: Les classes d'âge en région de la Lwafa (Tshuapa).*

30. See discussions in chapters 5 (Kongo, Loango, Cameroon, and Gabon) and 6 (Maniema). For minor associations, e.g., of elephant hunters along the Lokenye, see J. Cornet, "La société des chasseurs d'éléphants chez les Ipanga," also known among the Kuba.

31. P. Laburthe Tolra, *Seigneurs de la forêt*, 318–51; G. Hulstaert, *Les Mongo*, 43–46; J. Vansina, "Vers une histoire des sociétés Mongo," 18–20 and references; idem, *The Tio Kingdom*, 359–65. Quarrels within a village were even more restricted. Fighting of this sort went by a special term (CS 675), and usually no weapons more lethal than sticks were allowed.

32. CS 1872 may not have been quite proto–western Bantu according to Guthrie. But in addition to his references one can add many from the language groups he mentions or others close by (e.g., A80, C 30, C 60). One should add Basaa *-tumb*, "to hit strongly," and *tumbna*, "to hit each other ferociously," which not only expands the distribution of the term considerably but also pro-

vides good reason for assuming that the term derived from the verb "to burn" at
a very early date in western Bantu history.

33. For instance, F. Autenrieth, *Ins Inner-Hochland von Kamerun,* 105–9,
for a minor trade war; E. Sulzmann, "La soumission des Ekonda par les
Bombomba," for the war of conquest by Ikenge north of Lake Mai Ndombe or
the famous war of Pupu in northern Gabon c. 1880. Cf. A. Meyamm, "Zog Djo:
Un puissant sorcier, un chef et une divinité bakwelé," 17–21. Pupu is mentioned
by Pecile as an ethnic group in 1885: E. Zorzi, *Al Congo con Brazza,* 563, and
557–63 for local wars. See also L. Perrois, *Chroniques du pays kota,* 33–48; R.
Deschamps, *Traditions orales et archives au Gabon,* 66, 75.

34. The term is found from the Gabon coast (Nkomi) and the Kongo coast
to the Kuba in the southeast and as far as the Mongo and Ngombe languages in
the northeast (J. Vansina, *Children of Woot,* 314 n. 7, for part of the distribution). "Village charm" is the meaning everywhere, except in Nkomi, where it is
"hero, ancestor." Were it not that the distribution is continuous, and that so far
no Cameroonian reflexes have been found, one would conclude proto-western
status. This does not seem to be the case. An innovation in the southwestern
block of languages after their split from northern Zairian languages, followed by
diffusion to the inner basin, fits the known data well.

35. See Appendix.

36. H. M. Stanley, *In Darkest Africa* 1:141, for the quote. For "dead
zones" in southeastern Cameroon, for instance, see B. Förster, "Aus dem
Südostwinkel Kameruns," 158; A. Schulze, "German Congo and South Cameroons," 129, 132, 141–42, 157–61, and the 1902 map by M. Moisel ("Unbewohnt"
"Tote Zone").

37. L. Fiévez, "Le district de l'Equateur" (each district has its tattoos); A.
Engels, *Les Wangata,* 17–18; A. Verstraeten, "Les tatouages." Administrative
inquiries for the purpose of identification were made as late as 1930; see Jorissen, "Documentation ethnique: Tatouages," 1–2.

38. Although Guthrie has no CS, *-cenge* (village plaza," "capital") is undoubtedly of hoary antiquity. It is common from the Ogooué Delta to the Zaire
bend and beyond. Aka and Bobangi have "village plaza." Saa *nseng,* "plaine,
plateau, terrain plat," has the most general sense. The form occurs in all the
branches of western Bantu in the equatorial region, except for northwestern
Cameroon, the Nen-Yambasa group, and Bioko. The form is probably proto–
western Bantu, but the meaning "central village" is an innovation. Because it
occurs in Myene, in the southwestern group of languages, in the western part of
the northern Zaire languages, and in the inner basin, this may well have arisen
before the secession of the northern Zaire languages.

39. There are many more reflexes of CS 714 in western Bantu. CS 714 is
formally linked to CS 709 "to join by tying" and CS 711b "to go straight." CS 709
may well have been the source item for the others.

CS 665 has the same form as CS 664 meaning "line of objects" and often, in
the central Zaire basin, "age grade," but it may not have the same origin. The
form of CS 665 is thought to derive from CS 714 through a vowel change. This
new form corresponds to that of a set of terms meaning "to arrange" (CS 657),

"to heap up" (CS 658), which cannot be taken as the root of the etymology for "clan," although the existence of this allied form helps to understand the vowel change in CS 665, since the semantic fields are so close.

The item listed by Guthrie as "clan" (CS 779) derives from "village quarter." Guthrie's claim that there is no "synonymous CS" for "clan" is spurious given the vague character of the terms "clan," "tribe," and even "race" and "family." Terms for "clan" are also often used to designate "species."

40. J. Vansina, "Lignage, idéologie et histoire," 138–40, and chapter 5 (southern Gabon) for cases of obvious clan expansion and contraction in the nineteenth and twentieth centuries. Clan solidarity is expressed by the same terminology used for membership in a district.

41. J. Vansina, "Esquisse historique de l'agriculture en milieu forestier."

42. The earliest of these is Obobogo; see P. De Maret, "Recent Archaeological Research," 134.

43. *Cucumerops edulis* was found everywhere in the area as an important secondary crop. One term for it (*-gondo*) is perhaps even proto–western Bantu. For archaeological evidence of greens such as *Vernonia*, see J. Vansina, "Esquisse historique," 17.

44. P. De Maret, "Recent Archaeological Research," 134. Once again Obobogo is the earliest site. No western Bantu terms have been found as yet for any of these trees, although some terms are regionally widespread. Thus *nsafu* for *Pachylobus* is found from the Kongo coast to the lower Lomami at least. For other cases, see A. Bouquet and A. Jacquot, "Essai de géographie linguistique sur quelques plantes médicinales du Congo Brazzaville." Also see n. 57 below. The complex terminology for raffia palms and their products may well yield more proto–western Bantu terms.

45. M. Miracle, *Agriculture in the Congo Basin*, 31–175; J. Vansina, "Esquisse historique," 7–10. On the shifting of villages, G. Dupré, *Un ordre*, 108–13, asserts that in most cases this occurred before soil exhaustion would have been the main cause.

46. On *falga*, see L. Biffot, "Contribution," 69–74. There are very few actual descriptions of dawn gardens; see G. Le Testu, "Notes sur les cultures indigènes dans l'intérieur du Gabon," 542–44.

47. CS 2176 proto–western Bantu. On the southern margins, reflexes of this term meant "sea salt," and "salt from grasses" was designated by a reflex of CS 1031, itself derived from CS 1030, meaning "to filter," because salt was obtained by filtration of the ashes. For an example of the technique, see the illustration in E. Torday and T. A. Joyce, *Notes ethnographiques . . . Les Bushongo*, 22, 134, plate 17; for a case of restricted access to the famous salt pans of Odzala, see E. Zorzi, *Al Congo con Brazzo*, 567–69.

48. Comparative material with other rainforest areas in the world supports this conclusion. For instance, the Hmong of Thailand could cut all vegetation and burn it during the dry season without any collective labor, because the season was long enough. See R. Mischung, "Seßhaftigkeit und Intensivierung beim Brandrodungsfeldbau," 241–55.

49. M. Miracle, *Agriculture*, 43–61; P. T. Perrault, "Banana-Manioc Farming Systems of the Tropical Forest," 236–40. Burning was not practiced in late-nineteenth-century Bioko (G. Teßmann; *Die Bubi auf Fernando Poo*, 46–49) or among the Nyanga of Maniema (D. Biebuyck, *Rights in Land and Its Resources among the Nyanga*, 21–25).

50. Cf. chapter 2; also M. Watson, *Agricultural Innovation;* 51–54.

51. M. Watson, *Agricultural Innovation:* "sugar cane," 24–30; "citrus fruits," 42–50; "eggplant," 70–71. For eggplant in the crop rotation, see G. Dupré, *Un ordre*, 77–78; S. Jean, *Les jachères en Afrique tropicale*, 52. For sugar cane wine, see M. Miracle, *Agriculture*, 203–5, compared with 201–3 (palm wine).

52. M. Watson, *Agricultural Innovation*, 66–69; J. Vansina, "Esquisse historique," 25; the *zanj* name in southern Arabia suggests an introduction from East Africa, not the reverse, before A.D. 950.

53. M. Miracle, *Agriculture*, 137–42 (lower Congo, lower Zaire); T. Obenga, *La cuvette congolaise*, 78–79 (Likouala Basin); I. Dugast, *Monographie de la tribu des Ndiki* 1:114–21 (Nen country); G. Teßmann, *Die Bubi*, (green compost on Bioko); G. Sautter, *De l'Atlantique au fleuve Congo*, 262–64 (Alima-Sangha); P. Van Leynseele, "Les Libinza," 55–56; Mumbanza mwa Bamwele, "Histoire," 219–22, 254–58, 312–14, 319–26 (Ngiri). For an older account, see S. Brun, *Schiffarten*, 15 (Loango: knee-deep ditching). Much of this intensification was due to new commercial conditions accompanying the growth of the Atlantic trade and to the introduction of cassava in that context.

54. M. Miracle, *Agriculture*, 61–72, 74–87 (two field systems in the south), 87–103, 104–7 (Sudanese agriculture).

55. G. Hulstaert, "Nordkongo: Der zentrale Teil," 1:724, about the northwestern Mongo of the Ruki area.

56. S. Bahuchet, *Les pygmées aka de la forêt centrafricaine*, 189–226; idem, Étude écologique d'un campement de pygmées babinga," 526–32, 547–49; G. Bibeau, "De la maladie à la guérison: Essai d'analyse systémique de la médecine des Angbandi du Zaire," 96–97. The Ekonda know some 50 different edible mushrooms, according to D. Van Groenweghe, *Bobongo:* 260 n. 5. "The nutritional state of the forest dwellers is in general at least as good as that of the savanna dwellers, this being especially the case for the Pygmies and Pygmoids" (J. Hiernaux, "Long-term Biological Effects of Human Migration from the African Savanna to the Equatorial Forest," 214).

57. A. Chevalier, "Les rapports des Noirs avec la nature." In general, cf. A. Raponda-Walker and R. Sillans, *Les plantes utiles du Gabon* (includes comparative terminology); G. Hulstaert, *Notes de botanique mongo* (includes terminology); A. Bouquet, *Féticheurs et médecines traditionelles du Congo;* A. Bouquet and A. Jacquot, "Essai de géographie linguistique" (comparative terminology); E. Motte, *Les plantes chez les pygmées aka et les Monzombo de la Lobaye.*

58. See J. Vansina, "Habitat, Economy, and Society in Equatorial Africa," for the reasons why.

59. Especially S. Bahuchet, 'Étude écologique," 529–30, 547–49, for substitution; and G. Le Testu, "Notes sur les cultures indigènes dans l'interieur du Gabon," 547–48; P. L. Martrou, "Le nomadisme des Fangs," 512–13; and M. De Ryck, "La chasse chez les 'Lolia-Ngolu,' " 233, for seasons.

60. Reflexes of *-támb-*, "to set a trap," and *-támbo*, "trap" (CS 1659), which Guthrie holds to be the common Bantu form, are quite common in the portion of the area west of the Zaire, including Kongo and Ubangi. The later eastern Bantu form *-tég-*, "to set a trap" (CS 1699), also occurs in Kongo and is also reported in Nzabi, Metuku, and Tembo. The northern and central portions of the area use several other and fairly old terms, showing something of the dynamics in the technology of trapping. On traps, see G. Lindblom, *Jakt- och Fangstmetoder bland afrikanska folk.*

61. For some common terms for fauna, see M. Guthrie, *Comparative Bantu,* 2:176–77. Common terms for game such as warthogs, water antelopes, *bongo*, monkeys, elephants, and even leopards are reflexes of proto–western Bantu and stress the importance of hunting among them. In addition, the common western Bantu term meaning "to chase game" (CS 129) refers to the drive hunt (with or without nets). Yet it is possible that some other terms are ancient loans from an autochthonous language. Because these languages are extinct, this can be proved only by showing (a) that the terms are innovations in western Bantu and, perhaps, (b) that their shape shows some features which are aberrant. The "A" reflexes of CS 904 "to hunt" would be such a possible form.

62. Descriptions in H. Koch, *Magie et chasse,* 177–229 (Djue); G. Dupré, *Un ordre,* 49–53 (Nzabi), M. De Ryck "La chasse," 233–36 (Lalia). For terms for spear and hunting net, see J. Vansina, "Do Pygmies Have a History?" 438–42; for "bow" and "crossbow," see idem, "Deep Down Time." On hunting as a barometer, see e.g., M. Douglas, *Lele of Kasai,* 207–8, 215–18, 251–56.

63. G. Sautter, "Le plateau de Mbe," 27–30.

64. The Kele of Gabon were perhaps such a group in the nineteenth century, although they were also passionate traders (P. du Chaillu, *Voyages et aventures dans l'Afrique équatoriale,* 433–40; also R. Avelot, "Notice historique sur les Ba-Kalé," despite its unsubstantiated conjectures). For peoples in northern Maniema, see W. de Mahieu, *Qui a obstrué la cascade?* 12–15 and index "chasse"; D. Biebuyck, *Rights in Land,* 14–26.

65. CS 1949 "dug out canoe," CS 735 "to paddle," CS 790 and 1014 "paddle," CS 638 "to fish with a line," and the derived CS 640 "fish hook." CS 333, 427, 429 and 1858, all interconnected forms, "fish." CS 731 meaning "to dip" in the western part of the area may have a connection with CS 732 "to fish with a basket or net," which for Guthrie is proto-Bantu. But more attestations of the form are needed. As the vocabulary for fishing and its tools is further explored more terms may appear. For this potential, see Y. Ankei, "Connaissance populaire du poisson chez les Songola et les Bwari." But most of the similarities in terminology or in technology (e.g., the *brasero*) are probably due to multiple diffusion, because fishermen were also highly mobile traders at all periods.

66. For instance, in the Soan group the splits between So (fishermen) and Mbesa (landlubbers) and Lokele (fishermen) and Eso (landlubbers), or in the "Ngombe group" the split between the "water people" and the "landlubbers."

67. This history remains unresearched, or rather the detailed research done by social science scholars is generally not deemed of enough interest to be published at length. General monographs of the type of A. Goffin, *Les pêcheries et les poissons du Congo,* are incomplete and old. For the potential see for example: J. P. Gosse, "Les méthodes et engins de pêche des Lokele," or Y. Ankei, "Connaissance populaire du poisson."

68. J. Vansina, "Esquisse historique," 25 n. 46.

69. For the terminology of sheep, see C. Ehret, "Sheep and Central Sudanic Peoples in Southern Africa," but also J. Vansina, "Esquisse historique," 19 n. 28. All the terms in forest areas are also common in neighboring savanna areas, and none stretch right across the rainforests. Nineteenth-century evidence for trade showed trade in sheep from the margins of the savanna into the forest areas. As to pigs, CS 887–88 refer to "warthog" here and "pig" there. The meaning "pig" is clearly an innovation. By 1900 pigs were found only in the northwestern part of the area studied and on its southwestern and southern margins.

70. See the Appendix for terminology. Ceramics are directly attested on most sites. For specific industries and technologies, see E. Coart and A. De Hauleville, *La céramique;* E. Coart, *Les nattes;* H. Loir, *Le tissage du raphia au Congo belge.* Published inventories of collections held by museums are also a rich source of information, especially on carved items and on metalwork.

71. N. Van der Merwe, "The Advent of Iron in Africa," 485–501. For distributions, see E. Cline, *Mining and Metallurgy in Negro Africa;* L. Frobenius and L. Ritter van Wilm, *Atlas africanus;* E. Maquet, *Outils de forge du Congo, du Rwanda et du Burundi.*

72. H. Koch, *Magie et chasse,* 164–71.

73. For a fourth form meaning "to sell" (CS 1697), an innovation from CS 1698–99 "to set a trap"(!) in the lower and middle Zaire area, see chapter 5 (p. 147).

74. J. Denbow et al., "Archaeological Excavations," 39 (Loango); B. Clist, "Un nouvel ensemble," 45 (Gabon); L. Fiedler and J. Preuss, "Stone Tools from the Inner Zaire Basin," 179–82 (Lake Tumba).

75. P. De Maret, "The Ngovo Group," 116.

76. See L. Sundstrom, *The Exchange Economy of Pre-Colonial Africa,* for a general ethnographic overview. See also A. Thonnar, *Essai sur le système économique des primitifs d'après les populations de l'Etat Indépendent du Congo,* 82–114.

77. H. Tegnaeus, *Blood-brothers,* 103–18, 132–33.

78. M. Eggert and M. Kanimba, "Recherches archéologiques et ethnographiques dans les régions de l'Equateur (Zaire), de la Cuvette de la Sangha et de la Likouala (Congo)" (Sangha, Djah, and Likouala-aux-herbes); R. Lan-

franchi and B. Pinçon, "Résultats préliminaires des prospections archéologiques récentes sur les plateaux et collines Teke en R.P. du Congo," 25–27 (Malebo Pool to Alima).

79. W. MacGaffey, *Religion and Society in Central Africa*, 1–18; L. Mallart-Guimera, *Ni dos, ni ventre*, 23–101, 217–19, among others argues, however, for the existence of a single "symbolic system." This may well exist, but then it does so at an unconscious, undogmatic level.

80. C. Turnbull's description of monotheistic pygmies venerating "the forest" as Molimo by playing on trumpets is to be treated with caution (*Wayward Servants*, 76–80, 251–67; idem, "The *Molimo*: A Men's Religious Association among the Ituri Bambuti"). The term is a common reflex of CS 619. It may well have been used by one or another Christian group to signify "God." It was used as a borrowed term in that sense by Ngbandi in the 1970s for the name of a new religious movement (G. Bibeau, "De la maladie," 169–74).

81. Linked to CS 621 "to get lost" and CS 620 *-kudímba*, "to forget."

82. The use of the term *nkisi/ngesi* in the forests of Gabon, southern Congo, and portions of its southern rim in Zaire, as well as in all the southern savannas, is typical. It refers to a charm and to the entity activating it: in the forest, a nature spirit; in the savanna, a hero.

83. Supplement Guthrie with A. Kagame, *La philosophie Bantu comparée*, map 3.

84. As J. F. Thiel, *Ahnen, Geister, Höchste Wesen*, 169–77; for a discussion of "Nzambi," see ibid., 38–58.

85. A. Kagame *Philosophie Bantu comparée* 149–50, E. Andersson, *Contribution à l'ethnographie des Kuta* 2:23–31; J. Ittmann, *Volkskundliche und religiöse Begriffe im Nördlichen Waldland von Kamerun-Afrika und Uebersee*, 30–32; E. Ardener, *Coastal Bantu*, 92, for "sky" and "God" in Kpe and Duala; P. Wurm, *Die Religion der Küstenstämme in Kamerun*, 32–34.

86. W. MacGaffey, "The Religious Commissions of the BaKongo." His observations seem to hold throughout equatorial Africa.

87. Distribution of poison ordeals is in H. Baumann, *Die Völker Afrikas* 1:633, map 34; and W. Schilde, *Orakel und Gottesurteile in Afrika*, 229–61, esp. 247–58. The common names in the area are *-kasa* and *-bundu* in the western half and often together, *-ipomi* in the south, and *-avi* in the southeast and east. The trees used for the poison in most of the area were *Strychnos* species and *Erythrophleum guineense;* E. Perrot and E. Vogt, *Poisons des flèches*, 81–96, 157. The arrow poisons used, on the other hand, were often *Strophantes* spp. or cadaveric fluids.

88. "Abnormality" is not often included in dictionaries. Nor is "misfortune" or "good fortune." Good fortune corresponds to "strength" (CS 840). See also CS 909 and ps 249 (3:239).

89. Because the specific terminology for the tools and practice of medicine has not yet been gathered in enough detail, it is still too early to distinguish clearly between ancestral, later common, and still later innovative practices.

Even a discussion of the notions of health, illness, personhood, and individuality, although germane here, has been reluctantly omitted for the sake of concision. The notion of health implies "wholeness," and illness was a deficiency upon which the patient could act. The theory of personhood was complex. But to date none of these notions has been documented enough from different parts of the area to conclude anything further. Terms such as "dancing" or "drum," which are proto–western Bantu and were often used as shorthand for "performance," religious or not, should not be considered as specific evidence for the practice of medicine.

90. W. De Craemer et al., *Religious Movements,* 472–74.

91. The importance of an "exit" option and hence "empty" space has been brought home to me by M. Schatzberg. For example, see his *The Dialectics of Oppression in Zaire,* 137–38.

92. On 4 per km^2, cf. J. Vansina, "Le régime foncier dans la société kuba"; idem, "The Peoples of the Forest," 79, for an estimate of 3.75 per km^2 c. 1880, and 110 for map.

Chapter Four: The Trail of the Leopard in the Inner Basin

1. See chapter 3, n. 66. A common term, *elinga* or *balinga,* designates fishermen south of the great bend of the Zaire from the confluence of the Ubangi to the middle Lomami. By 1900 the hunter gatherers had disappeared from the region north of the Zaire River bend and for the most part had been absorbed by the farmer trappers in most forest areas on dry soils of the eastern half of the inner basin.

2. M. Eggert, "Archäologische Forschungen," 3223–25; idem, "Remarks on Exploring Archaeologically Unknown Rain Forest Territory," 286–91 and 320, for the few dates available. Although the eponymous site of Bondongo itself lies inland well east of Lake Tumba, its ceramics stemmed from the clay banks of the Ruki or the Momboyo; idem, "Der Keramikfund von Bondongo-Losombo"; E. Sulzmann, "Zentralafrikanische Keramik aus voreuropäischer Zeit."

3. M. Eggert, "Remarks," 312. For iron, see idem, "Archäologische Forschungen," 3235–37.

4. See chapter 3, n. 78.

5. The evidence about the western Mongo is the richest of all data in the inner basin. For lack of data and research data, see map 1.3; the amount of data needed for upstreaming becomes greater and needs to be more precise the further one moves back through time. With future intensive local research on "words and things" one can hope to obtain a complete picture of the situation c. A.D. 1000 and even earlier.

6. For detail, see J. Vansina, "Vers une histoire des sociétés mongo," 12–25, for the situation in the nineteenth century and earlier history. *Etúká* strictly meant "an anthill used as a stone for the hearth." The term *lokutu,* "patrimony,"

is derived from *nkutu*, "corpse," but is itself the source of *bokutu* (dialect: *bokutsu*), "rich person," from which many ethnonyms are derived all over the basin of the Lukenie, including *okusu* on the middle Lomami.

7. On the terminology itself, see E. Boelaert, "Terminologie classificatoire des Nkundó"; for Mongo explanations of their *nkóló/nkita* ("mistress"/"profit") system and the Crow terminology, see G. Hulstaert, *Le mariage des Nkundo*, 164–72; on the importance of valuables and bridewealth, see ibid., 105–230. *Nsomi* was later borrowed by the Mpama, in Ngenge, and in Lingala as "important person, free person" and as *ncomi,* "free man," in Bobangi.

8. However, iron smelting was practiced in the area as late as the eighteenth century by the "Losakanyi" (near Ingende and later west of Lake Tumba); see n. 3. The term *konga,* for copper bangles which formed the core of matrimonial compensation, in recent times refers to the Kongo people. Copper came from the mines of lower Congo, perhaps for many centuries. The dating of more hoards of valuables, as well as of the appearance of copper in the area, should strengthen this reconstruction.

9. See chapter 3, n. 7. Apart from the common noun for the leopard, the animal often was respectfully referred to in a circumlocutory way by a praise name. North of the Zaire bend and east of the Lualaba this practice became so usual that the common western Bantu noun was lost.

10. As the Belgian colonial administration realized. Early instructions to its political agents exhorted them to follow this trail to establish the hierarchy of "traditional" chiefs. Especially in the Oriental Province it was quite common to justify the proposed structure of a political hierarchy by referring to the trail of the spoils of the leopard. See, for instance, A. Bertrand, "Quelques notes sur la vie politique, le développement, la décadence des petites sociétés du bassin central du Congo," 81–82.

11. See, for instance, N. Rood, *Ngombe-Nederlands-Frans woordenboek,* 350.

12. And indeed in 1877 Stanley fought a large fleet at Basoko. H. M. Stanley, *Through the Dark Continent,* 497–501. He gives several other versions elsewhere, but they all extol the size of the enemy fleet and his own bravery.

13. G. Sautter, *De l'Atlantique,* 244; 259–60 and 261 for Bonga as the "Venice of Africa." In this sector Lukolela was on higher ground but less favorably located to control traffic from the affluents. Some other sites controlling confluences were: Bolobo (Alima), Irebu (Lake Tumba), Mbandaka (Ruki), Mobeka (Mongala). But note that Lisala, a major town in the nineteenth century, had only the advantage of lying on a headland. Iboko, where Stanley also fought a major battle in 1877, was not near any confluence.

14. The term is found in Aka, Lingala, Ngombe, Doko, Mbudza, Bati, Boa, and Komo in Maniema. It does not occur in Soan.

15. J. Maes, "Les sabres et massues des populations du Congo Belge," for the distribution of sabers; H. A. Johnston, *George Grenfell and the Congo* 2:766, 775, for pictures. Perhaps at first throwing knives had been used for this purpose

in the forest areas. On the throwing knife, cf. J. Maes, "Armes de jet des populations du Congo Belge"; J. Vansina, *Art History in Africa*, 168–70, and add Loango c. 1610 to the map there.

16. See, for example, A. Lejeune-Choquet, *Histoire militaire*, 191–200, 209–23. G. Burrows, *The Curse of Central Africa*, 241–44; P. Salmon, "Les carnets de campagne de Louis Leclercq," 268–69, for a comparison of nineteenth-century warfare north of the Zaire bend and in Mongo country.

17. G. Burrows, *Curse of Central Africa*, 236–37, describes Bango military training performed as a war dance.

18. For instance, among the Bangba; M. Fernandez-Fernandez, "Le rite et l'expérience," 47–69, and esp. 69–71. In addition they had a dependent of "brother-in-law." The ancestor was supposed to have come to live in the village as a dependent of his wife.

19. For a description of the Omaha system, see L. De Sousberghe and J. Ndembe, "La parenté chez les Lokele," 734–40; B. Crine, *La structure sociale des Foma*, 23–35.

20. See F. Héritier, *L'exercice de la parenté*, for a structuralist analysis of Omaha, Crow, and related systems of kinship. She stresses the links between such nomenclatures and patterns of marriages.

21. G. P. Murdock, *Social Structure*, 239–41, shows a 100 percent correlation between Omaha and "patrilineal descent" but not the reverse. F. Héritier, *L'Exercice de la parenté*, 30 and 68 n. 7, correctly concludes that Omaha is therefore not a necessary terminology for patrilinearity. Moreover, Crow and Omaha terminologies do exist in undifferentiated or bilateral descent systems.

22. J. Vansina, "Vers une histoire," 18, 29; F. Réquier, "Rapport d'enquête: Chefferie des Nkole nki Yamba," 20–22, for rich details on the various types of gibbets; M. Fernandez-Fernandez, "Le rite et l'Expérience," 57, for a symbolic use of such a gibbet.

23. For the python (*nguma*), for instance, cf. J. Soupart, "Les tatouages chez les Budja," 323; M. Fernandez-Fernandez, "Le rite et l'expérience," 48.

24. The most senior ones were usually in the center or brought up the rear. See, e.g., J. Vansina, "Vers une histoire," 18, 28–29; M. Fernandez-Fernandez, "Le rite et l'expérience," 41, 42, 69; J. Réquier, "Rapport d'enquête," 18–20.

25. J. Vansina, "Vers une histoire," 18. Colonial officials streamlined such assemblies and their hierarchies, but did not create them.

26. M. Fernandez-Fernandez, "Le rite et l'expérience," 14; J. Réquier, "Rapport d'enquête," 18.

27. It is a linguistic innovation in the Bantu languages of this area. Although it occurs in a number of Ubangian languages, it would be rash to claim that the Bantu speakers borrowed it from there. The closest of the Ubangian languages to the region is Ngbandi, where *ya*-occurs with the same meaning, but not as a prefix. Monzombo (of the Gbanziri group), now spoken on the Ubangi below Bangui, uses it in exactly the same way as the Bantu speakers do. See J. Vansina, "Vers une histoire," 27–28, 50–51, nn. 100 and 101.

28. For the divergence of opinion as to whether the Lokaló hunters and gatherers were pgymy or not, see Bosékônsombo, letter 19 February 1971, 5; G. Hulstaert, "Petite monographie des Bondombe," 37–45, 84–85; idem, *Eléments pour l'histoire Móngo ancienne:* 40; G. Hulstaert and Nakasa Bosékônsombo, "Encore Bondombe" 196–97, 198–200, 209–10, 212–17.

29. J. Vansina, "Vers une histoire," 26, 30, and nn. 84, 89, 115, 116; A. Bertrand, "Le problème Mongandu."

30. J. Vansina, "Vers une histoire," 31 and n. 122. Along the Tshuapa River near Bondombe (Mondombe) and farther west, the spearmen were stopped by efficient archery.

31. J. Réquier, "Rapport d'enquête," 22, for *nongo/ndongo* as "oldest lineage." Mpama and Ntomba of Mai Ndombe have *ndongo*, "capital" (the meaning of the modern town Inongo), and Bushoong *ndweengy*, "harem." G. Hulstaert, *Dictionnaire lomongo-français*, has *ndongó*, "harem" and later "political capital." On sabers and on the hand piano, see J. Maes, "Sabres et massues," 358–60, 364.

32. J. Vansina, "Vers une histoire," 27. This date is derived from "dead reckoning" backward in Kuba history. Kuba chiefdoms began to appear a century or more before the unification of the state c. 1625. The battle occurred before the first Kuba villages crossed the Sankuru. An "at the latest 1500" date fits well with estimates given for the onset of the *nkúmú* expansion.

33. F. E. Dhanis, "Le district d'Upoto et la fondation du camp de l'Arouwimi," 15–17, 26, 27–28; D. Wijnant, "Het Doko volk in hun handel en wandel," 593; idem, "De Doko's," 422.

34. D. Wijnant, "De Doko's," 410–15 (sacred kingship and officials); idem, "Het Doko volk," 211–13; F. E. Dhanis, "District d'Upoto," 31 (harem and dependents).

35. D. Wijnant, "De Doko's," 419.

36. D. Wijnant, "Het Doko volk," 206–7 (the six main matrilineages); idem, "De Doko's" 410 (Bondongo dynasty); idem, "Eene bladzijde uit de geschiedenis van Boela," 605–8 (the dynamics of succession and secession).

37. This spread was assisted in part by the dynamics of marriage. Married women continued to follow their husbands to the latters' places of residence, and despite the prevailing endogamy eventually lineages spread beyond each town; see D. Wijnant, "Het Doko volk," 210. For districts, see F. E. Dhanis, "District d'Upoto," 15–17, 26; D. Wijnant, "Eene bladzijde," 605–8.

38. Mumbanza mwa Bamwele, "Histoire," 105–16, notes that the Jando, Bamwe, and Ndolo remember the adoption of the matrilineal norms (107) which diffused (107–9). He erroneously thinks that the phenomenon was an original innovation stemming from the economic importance of women and the general poverty that did not allow for marriages with matrimonial compensation (110–16). Some of these groups bordered on Doko before the Ngombe expansion of the eighteenth century (45, and indeed the Bolondo were of Doko orgin). Hence it is most likely that matrilinearity spread from the Doko into the area during the eighteenth century.

39. D. Wijnant, "Het Doko volk," 207–8; idem, "Het Doko volk in hun handel," 584 n. 1. Doko crossed to the left bank before the Ngombe did. They were matrilineal, but later adopted the Ngombe language and by 1920 were "losing" their matrilinearity. But for matrilinearity in residence and in bridewealth as late as 1960, see N. Rood, "Lidoko et Mowea," 126. For the northern Mongo groups, see G. Van der Kerken, *L'ethnie Mongo,* 569–71, 573; De Coster, "Coutume mongo," 89/1 (division leopard, succession: matrilineal after "brothers"); L. De Sousberghe, *Don et contredon de la vie,* 125–26, 138 (bilateral for descent but matrilineal for succession after brothers).

40. J. Vansina, *Art History,* 32; E. Sulzmann, "La soumission des Ekonda par les Bombomba," 1–5. The organization of these peoples shows a few features that recall institutions of the patrilineal spearmen farther east. To resolve the question, more in-depth study is needed of the Mongo populations of the Maringa and Lopori.

41. The process described in this paragraph is suggested by the distribution of patrilineal succession by brothers as opposed to patrilineal succession by sons. Primogeniture was a known Ngbandi practice of succession; see B. Tanghe, *De Ngbandi naar het leven geschetst,* iii–iv, 82. The ambiguous meaning of "oldest" was and still is common in many patrilineal systems in general. Localization of the process derived from the tradition that the first Abandia chiefs spoke Ngbandi. Suggested chronology is arrived at by "dead reckoning" backward from the Nzakara and Abandia chronologies (n. 42). For the Ngbandi practices in the nineteenth century, see n. 45.

42. E. de Dampierre, *Un ancien royaume bandia du Haut-Oubangui,* 157–81; A. Hutereau, *Histoire des peuplades de l'Uele et de l'Ubangi,* 61–137.

43. A. de Calonne-Beaufaict, *Les Azande;* A. Hutereau, *Histoire,* 140–246; H. Vanden Plas, "La langue des Azande," 1:38–60; E. E. Evans Pritchard, *The Azande,* 267–83.

44. B. Tanghe, *De Ngbandi naar het leven,* 87–88 (historian), 107–10, 139–52 (war); idem, *De Ngbandi: Geschiedkundige bijdragen* (history); G. Bibeau, "De la maladie," 82–88, 92–93, 98–102.

45. On leopards, see B. Tanghe, *De Ngbandi naar het leven,* 6–7, 8–9, 67–69, 73, 131, 141, 154, 248–55. On Ngbandi prestige, see G. Hulstaert, "Nordkongo–Der zentrale Teil," 738; L. A. Almquist, "Symbolic Consensus in Ritual Practice," 74–75.

46. Various groups should be distinguished. Those of Bosobolo in the far north have been strongly influenced by the Ngbaka (A. Wolfe, *In the Ngombe Tradition,* 135–43; R. Mortier, "Ubangi onder linguistisch opzicht," 108–9). The Ngombe-Mbati of the lower Ubangi are acculturated by the Monzombo (R. Mortier, "Ubangi," 108–9). Many of the Bobo (Ngombe of Budjala) were clients of the Ngbandi (A. Verdcourt, "Organisation coutumière des juridictions indigènes dans le territoire de Bomboma," 17; M. Francart, "Note sur les institutions primitives des indigènes du territoire de Budjala," and farther south some were strongly influenced by the peoples of the upper Ngiri (A. Verdcourt, "Organisation coutumière," 19). The two other blocks of the Likime-Bango and south of the Zaire bend dominated their areas and seem to

represent best the original institutions on the Likame (A. Wolfe, *Ngombe Tradition*, 135–43). The "Ngombe" are a telling example of the creation of a "tribe" in colonial times, and show that no ethnographer or historian should trust "ethnic groups." See Mumbanza mwa Bamwele, "Les Ngombe de l'Equateur: Historique d'une identité."

47. The term was *libota* (A. Wolfe, *Ngombe Tradition*, 23; N. Rood, "Lidoko et Moweo": *libóta*, birth, *libóti*, "birthplace" and "family in the wider sense," which stresses bilaterality and territoriality). A. Wolfe, "The Dynamics of the Ngombe Segmentary System," 169, states that only this term is used, because in the Ngombe mind all the different types of lineages—whether ethnic, major, village, quarter, extended, or restricted family—are only stages of the same entity. Other evidence including the naming of all groups by *boso*-X, "we of X," which includes descendants and dependents, points to the same conclusion. However, evidence for strict unilineal ideas and practices is meager. Kinship terminology and rules of exogamy were bilateral, as was the distribution of spiritual power over kin; residence with the mother's brother was not rare even in the 1950s; and a cult for the father and the father's father may be patrifilial rather than expressing a concept of patrilinearity. Hence Wolfe's analysis in terms of segmentary lineages does not hold up, especially before c. 1920.

48. N. Rood, "Lidoko et Mowea": "age group"; A. Wolfe, *In the Ngombe Tradition*, 35, for the difficulty of seceding from a village. A new village could obtain a chief (*kúmú*) only with the blessing of the chief of its parent villages and the chiefs of other villages in the area.

49. A. Wolfe, *In the Ngombe Tradition*, 32–34, for the status and role of chiefs and for village government; terms in N. Rood, "Lidoko et Mowea": *elombé*, "leader," and *mowe*, "speaker"; cf. also F. E. Dhanis, "District d'Upoto," 16, 26–27 (*elombé*); Colle, "Les Gombe de l'Equateur," 155–57 (chief's status and investiture) and 149 (limited polygamy of chiefs). On the whole the "Ngombe" chief was more comparable to his Doko counterpart than to the Ngbandi chief.

50. A. Verdcourt, "Organisation coutumière," 171: "Their social and political constitution was much more anarchic than that of the Mongwandi and did not allow them to resist the Mongwandi." Nor were any people in the whole area a pushover. The obstinacy of their resistance to aggression is evident in the development of extensive fortifications in the whole area; see M. Eggert, "Archäologische Forschungen," 3238–40, for remnants of northern Mongo ditches and walls.

51. Colle, "Les Gombe de l'Equateur," 141–47, 157–60, 162–69. South of the Zaire the Ngombe sold slaves to traders coming to the main towns on the Lulonga and Lopori. The dominant place of war in the nineteenth century is attested by numerous personal names alluding to circumstances surrounding birth such as "war" and "civil war"; special expressions for "civil war," "trench warfare," "fight to the finish," and "flight from war" were frequent (M. Guilmin, "Proverbes des Ngombe"). Gruesome tales about training with throwing knives (Colle, "Les Gombe de l'Equateur," 144–45) also show how much war permeated Ngombe culture in the nineteenth century. No wonder that the

riverine people called them "the warriors" in 1889 (F. E. Dhanis, "District d'Upoto," 26–27).

52. On the *mono* charm, see E. Canisius, "A Campaign amongst Cannibals," 120–21.

53. The most detailed data concerning the Bobango are in the works of J. Fräßle. The conceptual underpinning of patrilinearity in the ideas about personality is detailed in his *Negerpsyche im Urwald am Lohali*, 14–17, 52–96, 141–44. For the Mbuja, H. Soupart, "Les coutumes budja," is the major source of information. For their manpower; see A. Lejeune-Choquet, *Histoire militaire*, map 192, text 191–200. In one battle no fewer than 1,800 shields were gathered on the battlefield, which presumes well over 2,000 combatants (192).

54. These include the Bobango, Mbesa, and all "Bangelima" in general. Cf., for instance, M. Fernandez-Fernandez, "Le rite et l'expérience," 32–36, 40–41, 287, for the Angba; V. Rouvroy, "Historique des Bobango et de quelques tribu voisines," 2.

55. M. Fernandez-Fernandez, "Le rite et l'expérience," 42–45, 51–58, for the Angba; J. Fräßle, *Negerpsyche*, 129, 134.

56. J. Fräßle, *Meiner Urwaldneger Denken und Handeln*, 51, 54; idem, *Fünf Jahre als Missionar im Herzen Afrikas*, 16 ("150 years ago" and Moyimba was chief when Stanley passed through the area in 1877. Moyimba died in 1911); Henrotin, "Historique des Basoo," 3–4, and genealogy annexed; De Bock, "Note concernant la constitution politique des Basoo," 4, dates the earliest chief to 1725 (six generations before Moyimba at 25 years each yields 150 years subtracted from c. 1875, when Moyimba became chief). On succession, see Fräßle, *Negerpsyche*, 134–36.

57. E. Torday, "Der Tofoke," 189–90, erroneously reports that all Eso recognized one supreme chief and that all village headmen were his kin. His remarks apply only to the Kombe group (perhaps 30 villages by 1883): L. Appermans, "Chefferie Kombe," 62–74, esp. 66, 67, 69, and 73. Another chiefdom in the making was that of the Bambelota. A. Bertrand, "Quelques notes," deals with the Yawembe chiefdom.

58. See n. 53 and E. Canisius, *Campaign amongst Cannibals*, 90, 97–98, 120–21, 403. This is not surprising at a time when the large trading towns on the Zaire River numbered as many as 10,000—including perhaps Yambinga, a Mbuja settlement—and at a time when large military forces from the north raided the Itimbiri Valley.

59. *Ekopo* means "skin" in the languages around Mai Ndombe, and "majestic authority" among the Nkundo. The form occurs without final vowel as *ekub* or *ekop* along the lower Kasai and among the Kuba. The emblems were lumps of kaolin everywhere, earth from an anthill in the Mai Ndombe area, a gigantic three-foot double bell, and a whole treasure of other objects kept by *muyum* among the Kuba.

60. E. Sulzmann, "Die bokopo-Herrschaft der Bolia"; E. W. Müller, "Das Fürstentum bei den Südwest-Mongo"; N. Van Everbroeck, *Mbomb'Ipoku: Le*

seigneur à l'abîme, 133–60; L. Gilliard, "Les Bolia: Mort et intronisation d'un grand chef"; A. Scohy, "A propos des Nkumu du lac Tumba"; H. D. Brown, "The Nkumu of the Tumba"; J. B. Stas, "Le nkumu chez les Ntomba de Bikoro"; Mpase Nselenge Mpeti, *L'évolution de la solidarité traditionelle en milieu rural et urbain du Zaire,* 104–12; Cordemans, "Les Pama," 6–41; A. Windels, "Chefferie des Pama-Bakutu," 32–70; J. Vansina, "Vers une histoire," 47–48 n. 85.

61. E. Sulzmann, "Orale Tradition und Chronologie," 553–58, 561–68.

62. Since their spirit Mbomb'Ipoku was considered to be the most powerful and senior "national" spirit; E. Sulzmann, "Die bokopo-Herrschaft," 404–5.

63. Or *mbangala,* a large savanna antelope. The place was called Mondombe. Most commentators have identified it with Bondombe on the middle Tshuapa River, but (a) there may be other "Mondombe" and (b) it is not clear that this name really belongs to the traditions.

64. N. Van Everbroeck, *Mbomb'Ipoku,* 6–50, who summarizes archival sources dating from the 1920s; E. Sulzmann, "Orale Tradition," 555–58, and citation of crucial earlier manuscript sources, 561–63; Vermassen, "La chefferie des Basengere," 1–3.

65. The usual localization of Mondombe at Bondombe on the Tshuapa will not fit. The nearest intercalary savanna lies north of the Zaire near the mouth of the Itimbiri. Savanna antelopes may well have roamed the vast savanna at Ila.

66. As no authors have made the point hitherto, it is worth stressing that these traditions do not refer to mass migration, but to the movements of leaders and their followers who established their rule over or allied themselves to aborigines.

67. *Contra* J. Vansina, "Peoples of the Forest," 94, which gave undue prominence to Mpama tradition.

68. E. Sulzmann, "Orale Tradition," 527–28, n. 4, and comment on the map by Vossius (1666) showing the Boma kingdom. Pages 561–63 are a discussion of the chronology of Van Everbroeck based on generations and yielding 1550 for the arrival of the first king in Bolia country. She accepts the notion that Bolia inhabited the area by c. 1300, because Bondongo ceramics are found in this area. With a list of 40 remembered names of kings a deep time-depth can be expected.

69. J. Vansina, *Children of Woot,* 245, 123–26.

70. E. W. Müller, "Das Fürstentum."

71. N. Van Everbroeck, *Mbomp'Ipoku,* 149–53; E. Sulzmann, "Die Bokopo-Herrschaft," 404–6; L. Gillard, "Les Bolia," 229–35; J. Vansina, *Children of Woot,* 49–51.

72. See n. 64; A. Windels, "Chefferie des Pama-Bakutu," 2–5; Cordemans, "Les Pama," 10–11.

73. E. W. Müller, "Das Fürstentum," (Ekonda); G. Hulstaert, *Dictionnaire: nkúm* (Mongo); E. Sulzmann, "Orale Tradition," 554 (Bobangi), 557 (Ekonda, Iyembe).

74. *Bokapa ekopo* occurs in traditions from the Mpama to the Kuba; Bolongo Mpo from the Ngwi kingdoms at least to the Kuba. For titles, see, e.g., N. Van Everbroeck, *Mbomp'Ipoku*, 27 (*iyêli*), 32 (*etóti*), J. Vansina, *Geschiedenis van de Kuba*, 161–62. *Iyêli* was the title of the Ngongó *nkúm* of Idanga.

75. E. Sulzmann, "Orale Tradition," 578 n. 51 (Bosanga which was also the name of their first "capital" in the area); J. Vansina, *Children of Woot*, 41–63; 113–15, 123–25 (Kuba).

76. E. Sulzmann, "Orale Tradition," 574–75 n. 26; J. Cornet "A propos des statues ndengese"; G. Van der Kerken, *L'ethnie Mongo* 1:341–44, 2:658–74. On Bolongo Itoko, see note 29 and J. Vansina, *Geschiedenis*, 169.

77. S. et J.Comhaire-Sylvain, "Les populations de Mai Ndombe," 24–26; G. Van der Kerken *L'ethnie Mongo*, 653–54; J. Vansina, *Geschiedenis*, 48 nn. 86–87; Ndaywell, "Organisation sociale et histoire," 158–92 (Ngwi political organization), 325–50 (Ngwi history), 375 (Ngwi chronology). The estimated date for their crossing of the Kasai is 1650–1742. This chronology rests on reign lengths and an uncertain Kuba tie-in seems particularly precarious.

78. G. Brausch, "La société N'Kutschu," 50–59; L. De Heusch, "Eléments de potlatch chez les Hamba," 337–48 (*nkúmi okanda*); Dimandja Luhaka, "Le pays de Katako-Kombe à l'époque coloniale," 25–28.

79. L. De Heusch, "Un système de parenté insolite," 1012–27 (Jonga in upper Tshuapa); A. Moeller, *Les grandes lignes des migrations*, 540–41, 567 index: *nkúmi* indicates a possible diffusion among the Mituku, as does the Lega form *ngúmi*. See also chapter 6.

80. J. Vansina, "Vers une histoire," 26–27, and nn. 88, 94; G. Hulstaert, "Over de volkstammen van de Lomela," 21, 29, 33, 39, 42; G. Van der Kerken, *L'Ethnie Mongo*, index: *ekofo*. For the complex case, see A. Bengala, "Le noble des Booli," 105–11. The title was *kokókokó*, an intensive form of "elder."

81. These internal histories have so far been worked out for only some societies. See Ndaywell, "Organisation" (Ngwi), and R. Tonnoir, *Giribuma*, but also see the critique by E. Sulzmann "Orale Tradition," and J. Vansina, *Children of Woot*. Much additional research is sorely needed. For instance, the processes by which the title system was developed into a system of territorial control by the societies around Lake Mai Ndombe and the process by which a system of double descent for succession was developed among the Ntomba and Sengele still need to be studied. Even the detailed organization of the *nkúmú* system among the populations of the Lukenie and of the *ekopo* south of the Tshuapa is still unknown.

Chapter Five: Between Ocean and Rivers

1. Thus early settlement occurred both by sea and over land. See map 2.8. The spread of iron smelting seems to have occurred on the plateau first and then

to have reached the coast later via the Ogooué Valley; the distribution of a variety of features indicates communication over the plateaus as well as along the rivers. Cf., for instance, the diffusion of throwing knives diagonally from the great Ubangi bend to the Gabon Estuary and to Loango.

2. See map 2.10.

3. K. Born, "Nordkongo—Der Westen," 712–13; for connections with adjacent West Africa, see P. A. Talbot, *The Peoples of Southern Nigeria*, vols. 2–3. (e.g., 3:754–801, "Societies and Clubs"); W. Hirschberg, "Das Crossflußgebiet und das Kameruner Grasland," 2:355–72.

4. As an introduction to associations, see, for Gabon, A. Raponda-Walker and R. Sillans, *Rites et croyances*, 171–293. The earliest reference is A. Battell, *The Strange Adventures of Andrew Battell*, 56–57, 82–83; the tattoo he describes on p. 56 corresponds to a *mwiri* tattoo in the same area mentioned by Raponda-Walker and Sillans, p. 230. For northern Gabon and southern Cameroon, see R. H. Nassau, *Fetichism in West Africa*, 138–55. For Cameroon, see H. Nicod, *La Vie mystérieuse de l'Afrique noire*, 91–122; C. Dikoume, "Etude concrète d'une société traditionnelle: Les Elog-Mpoo," 113–32; J. Rusillon, "Le rôle social d'une société secrète d'Afrique équatoriale"; J. Perono, "Les Basa," 103–5.; P. Wurm, *Die Religion der Küstenstämme in Kamerun*, 12–53; P. Valentin, *Jujus of the Forest Areas of West Cameroon*. For an in-depth study (among the Kosi), see H. Balz, *Where the Faith Has to Live*, 184–318.

5. **-kuda.* For Bubi, see n. 48. In Abo country the adolescent age group was politically represented by a leader at village level: F. Autenrieth, *Ins Inner-Hochland von Kamerun*. For Elog Mpoo, see C. Dikoume, "Les Elog-Mpoo," 133–34. Only coastal age groups under Duala or Malimba influence formed an association. For Duala, see M. Bekombo-Priso, "Les classes d'âge chez les Dwala," 289–307.

6. H. Balz, *Where the Faith Has to Live*, 37–43, discusses the differences between the Kosi-Mbo group and the Kpe group, where according to him villages were much less compact, although they were still fenced in.

7. I. Dugast, "Banen, Bafia, Balom," 141–42, 160, 166–67 (the reference to "village" is to a French colonial administrative unit); J. Champaud, *Mom: terroir Bassa*, 15. Still, L. M.Pouka, "Les Bassa du Cameroun," 158, states that the size of a village varied according to the size of the families settled there; E. Von Skopp, "Sitten und Gebräuche der Bakoko in Kamerun," 485, who gives a size from 3 to over 50 houses, substantiates this; see also G. Zenker, "Die Mabea," 2–3. However, the neighboring Ngumba lived in villages; cf. L. Conradt, "Die Ngúmba in Südkamerun," 333.

8. The A 70 speakers form a coherent group called "Pahouin" or even "Fang" in the literature. But P. Laburthe Tolra, *Les seigneurs de la forêt*, 18–19, rightly denounces the terminology because it unduly generalized from one observation in one ethnic group to all the others. To avoid a dubious ethnic name as well as the clumsy A 70 designation, derived from the partly outmoded classification by M. Guthrie, the group is labeled here as the Sanaga-Ntem group.

9. Their languages are closely related to a number of others, such as Ngumba and Mabea in the west, So in enclaves along the Nyong, and a group of peoples in southeastern Cameroon. Guthrie called them A 80. Here they are referred to as the southern Cameroon group. Data on some Njem groups are particularly weak. Still, the reports in *Deutsches Kolonialblatt* of the German expeditions in the area allow one to conclude prudently that they were on the whole quite similar to the Djue, Makaa, and Njem from Congo, about whom monographs have been written.

10. For the meaning of this form, see C. Grégoire, "Le champ sémantique du thème bantou **-bánjá.*" She still misses some reflexes, among them the type *baa, abeny, banja, banjo* in the languages of Cameroon, which there designate the communal buildings for men. South of the Ogooué the reflex *mbanza* designates a village temple, and farther south and east the reflexes *mbánzá* (Kongo and Mboshi) and *mbéé* (Teke peoples) refer to "capital."

11. For southeastern Cameroon, see C. Koch, "Die Stämme des Bezirks Molundu," 286–304. High averages of inhabitants per village obtained there in 1910–1912 for the Kaka (325), Bokari (194), Bumbom (129.6), and Gunabemb (118.82). For the Bekwil villages, see Didier, "Le nomadisme des Sangas-sangas," 592 (150–200 people, but up to 1,000 people), and E. Zorzi, *Al Congo con Brazza,* 543 (the Bekwil village was the biggest village so far seen in Africa); their Bokiba (Kota) and Mboko neighbors to the south also had sizable villages, ibid., 525–27, 530, 573.

12. Reflexes occur in the Sanaga-Ntem, the southern Cameroon, the Kaka group of languages, and Sekyani (subgroup by itself), all class 5/6. Note that, within the southern Cameroon group, both to the west (Ngumba and Djieli) and to the east (in the Njem group of languages) of the present extent of the Sanaga-Ntem group, this form is preceded by **kwa-* meaning "at the place of So-and-So." This particular innovation presumes that the toponyms were derived from the name of leaders. It is itself older than the expansion of the Sanaga-Ntem group, hence pre-fifteenth century. Among the Sanaga-Ntem speakers and part of the Kaka group a second form refers to villages as **boga.*

13. CS 665 **-dongo:* e.g., *-long* (Saa), *bo-nong* (Nen), *ke-long* (Kpa?), *ko-long* (Kpa?), *joong* (Yambasa), *ayong* (Sanaga-Ntem group), and others. Cf. A1.

14. **-dom-.* All have Omaha cousin terminology. The precise system of terminology in Makaa remains unknown, however, and present knowledge of the terminology in the Njem set of languages remains rudimentary. Furthermore languages within the Saa group share a set of terms relating to patrilineal groups, and languages within the Sanaga-Ntem group another set. At least two other terms are shared by the Nen north of the Sanaga and the western languages of the Njem set.

15. The etymology of the innovations *ndog,* "patrilineage," and *lóg,* "patrilineage," in Nen and in the Saa group remains unclear. They are not related (tonal opposition). *Lóg* is not yet accepted by all Nen groups and may well be younger than *ndog.*

16. As seen on the maps in E. V. Thevoz, "Kamerun Eisenbahn," map 3 (present densities); R. Letouzey, "Végétation," 22–23 (savannas wooded or not, semideciduous forest recolonizing savannas abandoned in the late 1800s, and islands of semideciduous forests).

17. The innovation may well have diffused from the neighboring populations of the grasslands to the speakers of Nen and the Basaa group or to the Sanaga-Ntem group rather than the reverse, but conclusive evidence is not yet available.

18. J. M. W. Wognou, *Les Basaa du Cameroun*, 8–12, passim (patrilineal structures); S. B. Mandeng, "Traditional Healing of a 'Non-Ordinary' Disease (Kon) among the Basaa of Cameroun," 74–77 (Ngok Lituba), 77–80, 85–101 (social structure); C. Dikoume, "Les Elog-Mpoo," 20–23 (Ngok Lituba), 83–88 (terminology). Saa genealogies do not prove migration; they only claim it. Moreover they suffer from both telescoping and eponymic additions, as is shown by the absence of branching in most generations, and cannot be used to date a migration. The Saa occupied the site of Douala before the Duala settled there, in c. 1660 at the latest. Cf. E. Ardener, "Documentary and Linguistic Evidence for the Rise of the Trading Polities between Rio del Rey and Cameroons: 1500–1650," 81–116 (Van Leers and first evidence for the Duala language); idem, *Coastal Bantu of the Cameroons*, 17 (the toponym Ambos, known by c. 1507, could reflect the name Abo, a Saa related group) and 19 (six generations in the Duala ruling lineage before 1792).

19. R. Letouzey, *Etude phytogeographique*, 141–45 (*Lophira alata*); P. Foury, "Indications," 7–13.

20. S. B. Mandeng, "Tradional Healing," 87 (the naming of children by father is more rigid than among the Bamileke), and J. M. W. Wognou, *Les Basaa*, 40 (the kinship system was 8 generations deep, 10 with a "founder" and "a closure of patrilineal kinship"). On Nge associations, see n. 4, and J. M. W. Wognou, *Les Basaa*, 5, 6; C. Tastevin, "Société secrète du Gé chez les Ba Koko du Cameroun," 891–901; idem, "Société secrète féminine chez les Ba Koko," 901–6. On *mbog* and related concepts, see S. Epea, "Message chrétien et visage de l'homme chez les Basa, Bantie du sud Cameroun," 152–63; 163–79 (*mbombog*).

On segmentary terminology, J. M. W. Wognou, *Les Basaa*, 24, gives 15 terms of which 9 might refer to segments of different size. No other Basaa author does so. P. Lemb and F. de Gastines, *Dictionnaire Basaá-Français*, do not corroborate his claims either. Each of the terms cited means either a social group and is applied from family to ethnic group or has other meanings ("group," "company," "tomb," "camp," "patrimony," "father's domain"). *Dju*, "monogamous family," *mbai*, "courtyard (group)," and *sas*, "phratry," are not found in the dictionary. On balance it seems clear that there were neither clearly delineated segments nor a specific terminology to designate them.

21. M. Guthrie, *The Bantu Languages of Western Equatorial Africa*, 40–44, is the only general overview extant. Of the 10 languages recognized, 7 were spoken north of the Nyong, 5 of them around Nanga Eboko, 2 north of the Sanaga. The remnant speakers north of the Sanaga and west of Nanga Eboko

are all Fök and have always lived there. See J. C. Barbier, *Mimboo, reine d'Asem,* 15–17 and map.

22. P. Alexandre and J. Binet, *Le groupe dit Pahouin,* 40–49, 62–69, which is confirmed by monographs for all the (seven) ethnic groups studied.

23. P. Alexandre, "Proto-histoire du groupe Beti-Bulu-Fang," remains the best known of these; for a partial critique, see C. Chamberlin, "The Migration of the Fang into Central Gabon during the Nineteenth Century."

24. See n. 21. For the southern Cameroon languages, see M. Guthrie, *Bantu Languages,* 45–49 (the "northern Gabonese languages" are the group labeled B 20); ibid., 59–63; A. Jaquot, *Les classes nominales dans des langues bantoues des groupes B10, B20, B30,* 69–75, 295–97 (lexicostatistics show that Sekyani forms a group by itself). Speakers of these languages probably occupied most of northern Gabon before the first Fang expansion. They were split only by the second Fang migration, which began c. 1840.

25. Density figures in P. Alexandre and J. Binet, *Groupe dit Pahouin,* 10–11; J. C. Pauvert and J. L. Lancrey-Javal, "Le groupement d'Evodowa (Cameroun)," 11–12; G. Sautter, *De l'Atlantique,* endmaps.

26. A. Panyella, "Esquema de etnologia de los Fang Ntumu de la Guinea Equatorial desde el punto de vista etnológico," 15–17, map 1. Half of northeastern Rio Muní was no longer covered by primary forest in the 1950s. He erroneously concludes from this that the Ntumu were not adapted to life in the rainforests!

27. J. L. Wilson, *Western Africa,* 302 (scouts); F. Autenrieth, *Ins Inner Hochland von Kamerun,* 126–27, 138 (pioneer villages during expansion).

28. H. Bucher, "The Mpongwe of the Gabon Estuary," 128–29 (Mpongwe of the late 1700s); P. Alexandre and J. Binet, *Groupe dit Pahouin,* 14–15; P. Alexandre, "Proto-histoire," 532–35 (Fang after 1840s). Even in the rapid migrations after 1840 the Fang expanded continuously by drift of individual settlements over short distances rather than suddenly by large groups over long distances.

29. J. Vansina, "Peoples of the Forest," 80–81, for numerical evidence from Gabon and Cameroon. In these cases the movements had a purpose: to reach trading stations on the coast. That may have speeded up their march. The Sanaga-Ntem expansion may have been somewhat slower for lack of a specific objective. But the iron-producing district south of the Ntem may well have been known to the Ntumu. In addition the calculations assume a linear advance, not sideways movements, yet an eastern and the western movements occurred over a wide front. The total advance may have been slower than the 20–30 km attested for the 1800s.

30. On absorption, see P. Laburthe-Tolra, *Seigneurs de la forêt,* 101–2, 120–22 (most later Fang may well be "absorbed" populations; Ngovayang later was a stable migratory unit combining Ngumba and Fang). On large villages see n. 11.

31. Glottochronological dating yields: 78 percent or A.D. 1160 for Fang-Eton split and the total depth of all known Sanaga-Ntem languages; 83 percent or A.D. 1360 for Ntumu-Fang and Ewondo-Fang splits; 85 percent or A.D. 1440

for Ntumu-Ewondo and Ewondo-Eton splits; 87 percent or A.D. 1510 for Bulu-Ewondo split; and 90 percent or A.D. 1620 for Fang-Bulu split. P. Laburthe-Tolra's maps (seventeenth century), 108–9, in *Seigneurs de la forêt*, are too late because his calculations were based on genealogies which suffered from telescoping. See B. Clist, "Travaux archéologiques," 12 (sites A.D. 1590 +/−60, A.D. 1600 +/−70, and A.D. 1680 +/−60). Future ceramic studies may well show whether these were sites of new immigrants.

32. For distribution of crossbows (always named CS45 *bano* ["arrowshaft"] in eastern Bantu), see J. Vansina, "Deep Down Time," map "bow." For illustrations, see, e.g., G. Teßmann, *Die Pangwe*, 1:141; H. Koch, *Magie et chasse*, 127. For xylophone and harps, see, e.g., G. Teßmann, *Die Pangwe*, 2:322, 330.

33. The Ntumu even dropped the use of the term *mvog*, "lineage," for *etunga* used by their western neighbors. One should not forget that there was also resistance to change: e.g., the Sanaga-Ntem concept of *evus/evur* witch substance was not borrowed by autochthons. And some original features were abandoned by the emigrants, e.g., divination through the use of a spider common in the Saa group and among the Ewondo but not practiced by the Ntumu (G. Teßmann, *Die Pangwe*, 2:196). See A127.

34. P. Alexandre, "Proto-histoire," 535–37, cites some of these. For a recent example, see M. Ropivia, "Les Fangs dans les Grands Lacs et la vallée du Nil"; idem, "Migration Bantu et Tradition orale des Fang."

35. M. de Teran, *Síntesis geográfica de Fernando Poo*, 11, 58, 39, and in general for the natural background. The earliest full-fledged ethnographies about the Bubi are O. Baumann, *Eine Afrikanische Tropen-Insel: Fernando Poo und die Bube* (data from 1886–1887), A. Aymemi, *Los Bubis en Fernando Poo* (data from 1894–1939), and G. Teßmann, *Die Bubi auf Fernando Poo* (data 1915–1916). Among these Aymemi is by far the most reliable. In contrast Teßmann's data on social life are often unsound. Bubi institutions are often misrepresented in summary ethnographies. Contrary to the typical description, the Bubi were not organized in segmentary patrilineages, did not practice matrilineal succession, had no secret societies, no formal age-grading system, and did not live just in compact villages.

36. On unfavorable winds and currents, cf. P. de Marees, *Beschryvinghe ende historische verhael van het Gout Koninckrijck van Gunea*, 242; T. Boteler, *Narrative of a Voyage of Discovery to Africa and Arabia*, 412; M. de Teran, *Síntesis geográfica*, 9–26. On early Bubi-European relations, see C. Crespo Gil-Delgado, *Notas para un estudio antropológico y etnológico del Bubi de Fernando Poo*, 17, 170–72.

37. I. M. Rurangwa, "Nota sobre la investigación lingüística del Bubi," 141, argues that it is a single language. But T. R. H. Thomson, "The Bubis, or Edeeyah of Fernando Po," 106, claimed that the extreme dialects were mutually unintelligible in 1841. Bubi may have been a language cluster rather than a single language.

38. L. Silveira, *Descripción de la Isla de Fernando Poo en visperas del tratado de San Idelfonso*, 29, 30, 36, for the situation in 1772. The documentation from 1819 onward is rich enough to follow the breakdown of isolation step

by step. On trade and imports by 1846, see J. Clarke, *Introduction to the Fernandian Tongue*, v, and J. M. Usera y Alarcon, *Memoria de la Isla de Fernando Poo*, 32–33. By 1857 T. J. Hutchinson, *Impressions of Western Africa*, 192, reported on the last-known hoard of stone axes on the island.

39. A. Martin del Molino, "Secuencia Cultural en el Neolítico de Fernando Poo"; idem, *Etapas de la cultura Carboneras de Fernando Poo en el primer milenio de nuestra Era;* P. De Maret, "The Neolithic Problem in the West and South," 60–62; B. Clist, "1985 Fieldwork in Gabon," 7 (sites of similar ceramics: 930 B.P. on Bioko, 1150 +/–60 B.P. at Libreville).

40. T. J. Hutchinson, *Impressions*, 201, already reports Bubi origins on the Santa Isabel peak. Subsequent mountain climbers also report this, as does O. Baumann, *Eine Afrikanische Tropen-Insel*, 74. Traditions about the great migration are reported in some detail by A. Aymemi, *Los Bubis*, 13–22, and briefly by G. Teßmann, *Die Bubi*, 11–12. All authors and later descriptions cite various emblems, palladia, and the sacred fires.

41. Speculation as to a place of origin in Gabon is old (O. Baumann, *Eine Afrikanischen Tropen-Insel*, 73; G. Teßmann, *Die Bubi*, 12). The ceramic link found by Clist (n. 39) is still too tenuous as reported to build on. Spanish authors rather favored the coasts of Rio Muni or even the southern Cameroons. Further archaeological work and more systematic study of loaning between the mainland languages and southern Bubi speech will one day settle this issue.

The date for the earliest arrivals could, just possibly, correspond to the eleventh century, when inland settlement began in earnest. All the authors mentioned that if the migration had occurred after 1500 the earliest arrivals would have been reported by Europeans, especially on Saõ Tomé. But this argument from silence is suspect, if only because of the isolation of the island. Indeed a trickle of seventeenth- and eighteenth-century fugitives from the Portuguese islands to the south of Bioko was not reported before c. 1780 (O. Baumann, *Eine Afrikanische Tropen-Insel*, 74).

42. The reconstruction of institutions before the Great Migration is based on linguistic and ethnographic data. The reasoning used is the following: Innovations in vocabulary, common to all dialects but *not* shared by mainland languages, indicate presence in this early period. So does continuity with basic western Bantu terminology. The latter, however, is not foolproof. Some western Bantu terms died out and were later reimported from the coast. For instance, *boribo* ("spirit"), a synonym for *mmo*, is derived from CS 619. Reflexes of this root occur in all the mainland languages opposite the island. The fact that it is a duplicate for *mmo* alerts one to the likelihood that the term had been replaced by *mmo* in the deep past and was later reintroduced, presumably during the Great Migration.

Second, major original Bubi institutions—such as the opposition between married and unmarried men and the patterns of settlement—that are unknown anywhere on the mainland, show an original vocabulary in form, and are not linked to later institutional developments resulting from the Great Migration are presumed to antedate it. The data come from A. Aymemi, were compared with the information of G. Teßmann, and have been checked against earlier information from the 1840s and 1850s. In this summary it is not possible to cite the detailed evidence on each point.

43. The relevant traditions justified the position of the aristocracy and provided a social charter documenting their relative rights by conquest. The supposed order of arrival closely reflected their relative hierarchy in the 1880s.

44. For Tete and Bokoko, see A. Aymemi, *Los Bubis*, 14–18. On iron, note that Bubi *bojele*, "iron," derives from CS 800 *-geda* (and see Guthrie 1:138, topogram 25). Reflexes from this root occur among all the languages on the mainland from Mt. Cameroon to Rio Muni. The existence of the term reminds one that, although the Bubi did not use, work, or smelt iron, they knew of its existence. Whether the term was anterior to the arrival of the main body of immigrants or was introduced by them, it is a nice reminder that the immigrants arrived with iron weapons and tools.

45. The reconstruction of institutions in this period is based on the reasoning outlined in n. 42. Linguistic innovations, common on the mainland and present either in all Bubi dialects or in the main southern dialects only, have been used as evidence. Duplication in form sometimes suggests borrowing. Thus the terms *bese*, "central village," and *nse*, "district," share the same root, but in different classes. *Nse* classes 9/10 was the usual term on the whole coast and seems to have been imported to designate the new districts. Duplication of meaning (synonyms) may also indicate borrowing (see n. 47).

46. A. Aymemi, *Los Bubis*, 53–70 (social stratification and "government"), 84–85 (caste).

47. The term *botuku*, "lord," a true synonym of the earlier *etakio*, "ruler," both opposed to *bataki*, "dependent" or "servant" (Ayememi, *Los Bubis*, 53), is more frequent than the other term. One suspects it to be a loan in Bubi. It may well have been the designation for "leader"/"chief" among the immigrants. But the suspicion remains unconfirmed so far, because the term has not yet been found in any of the mainland languages.

48. A. Aymemi, *Los Bubis*, 37–50, 167, 173–74 (on marriage); ibid., 68, and C. Crespo Gil-Delgado, *Notas*, 155 (on the attempts of chiefs to control all virgin girls).

49. A. Aymemi, *Los Bubis*, 124–25 (priests of God), 57–63, 86–90, 142–48, 152–56 (major collective rituals), 165–66 (royal high priests).

50. O. Baumann, *Eine Afrikanischen Tropen-Insel*, 105–6; A. Aymemi, *Los Bubis*, 32, 115–22; C. Crespo Gil-Delgado, *Notas*, 156, 180.

51. Generally authors estimate his succession as c. 1850, which may be too late. The date suggested here rests on the following considerations. Moka died in 1899 reputedly 105 years old. He became first chief of Riabba as the senior of his generation, and only later achieved kingship. Given the existing practice of succession he was probably 30 or more when he became chief. Yet it seems unlikely that a person over 50 would succeed in unifying the island. Hence the

opinion that he unified the kingdom in his 40s, some five years after he became chief.

52. On historical laws, C. Crespo Gil-Delgado, *Notas,* 156, speaks of "the regular cycle common to the history of all peoples" which led to the rise of confederations and later of a kingdom. On p. 180 he says that this is "the normal development of the historical phenomenon [of centralization]." On previous kings, cf. A. Martin del Molino, "La familia real," 37–40 (a previous dynasty at Ureka, but O. Baumann, *Eine Afrikanischen Tropen-Insel,* 32–33, gives an alternative explanation); A. Aymemi, *Los Bubis,* 162 (the case of the Lombe Lagoon); O. Baumann, *Eine Afrikanischen Tropen-Insel,* 113 (a king's role in the ouster of the Spanish at Concepción Bay. But this event was followed by a Duala slave raid there against which the Bubi seemed helpless).

On wealthy chiefs near Clarence measured by the size of their harems, see T. R. H. Thomson, *Bubis,* 112 (the richest had 200 wives and many guns; Moka had only some 60 wives, late in his life).

On guns in the north, see C. Crespo Gil-Delgado, *Notas,* 174.

53. For the main events and publications, see A. de Unzueta y Yuste, *Historia geográfica de la isla de Fernando Poo.*

54. C. Crespo Gil-Delgado, *Notas,* 17, 170.

55. J. Vansina, "Deep Down Time" map 3: **-pika.* The map shows the extent of the meaning "slave," most of it stemming from Kongo as a result of the slave trade. Bobangi's skewed form is a good example. But some terms cannot be explained in this way. Thus the extension into Kasai (Luba group, Songye, and Kusu) and Shaba is not derived from Kongo. Neither are *bofika,* "slave woman," in Mongo and *mpika* in eastern Mongo (Mompono), nor are many Gabonese reflexes such as *nyeka* (Kota), *moyeka* (Ndaza, Shake), *oyiha* (Mbede, Ndumu), *oheka* (Mbosi, Koyo)—all designating "slave." The distribution suggests a term common to the whole southwestern block and the savanna languages derived from it, with a meaning such as "servant," "dependent." See J. Thornton, *The Kingdom of Kongo:* 21, P. P. Rey, *Colonialisme, néocolonialisme et transition au capitalisme,* 86–87. As a result of the slave trade the meaning changed in Kongo and diffused from there.

56. J. Vansina, "Antécédents des royaumes bateke (tio) et kongo," n. 12. The earliest reference to them is A. Battel, *Strange Adventures,* 59 (they already "pay tribute"). On dependency in the nineteenth century, see P. P. Rey, *Colonialisme,* 96–101.

57. See Appendix. Also see, e.g., J. Vansina, *The Tio Kingdom,* 47.

58. The Portuguese word *palavra,* "word," translates the ancestral western Bantu expression in African languages, CS 771 **-gambo* (CS 1919 is the same stem; cf. E. Meeussen, *Bantu Lexical Constructions,* 17): e.g., Kongo *mambu,* Lingala *likambo.* It refers to any "affair," court case, legislation, or discussion. See, e.g., J. Vansina, *Children of Woot,* 19, 252 n. 2, 305 n. 22.

59. W. MacGaffey, "The Religious Commissions."

60. On *nkindá,* see J. Vansina, *Children of Woot,* n. 15; the precise meaning "village charm" dates to the common southwestern language.

61. Based on cereals in the savannas and the AAB banana in the forests. Unfortunately no dated remains in the quadrant between A.D. 350 and 1300 have been found: B. Clist, "Pour une archéologie du royaume kongo." Still the distribution of the term *njale, nzadi,* covering the whole of this area is of interest here because it refers to the major routes of communication: H. A. Johnston, *A Comparative Study of the Bantu and Semi-Bantu Languages,* vol. 1. However, the area covered excludes the Ogooué and its affluents. Its distribution crosscuts the genetic divisions and forms a single block, so it spread *partly* by borrowing, well before the age of the slave trade (here c. 1525–1600), because it extends far beyond the area of this trade. The date and place of its appearance have not yet been ascertained.

62. This scenario is based only on analogy provided by later ethnographic descriptions.

63. See its distribution in J. Vansina, "Antécédents," n. 24, and idem, *Tio Kingdom,* 585.

64. J. Vansina, "Antécédents" nn. 18, 26, for the etymologies of "capital," **-pata* (CS 1455).

65. The term *mwéné* (CS 1971) is derived from an early Bantu form **-ényé,* "one-self" (CS 1970; E. Meeussen, *Bantu Lexical Constructions,* 13). Cf. also J. Vansina, "Antécédents," n. 27.

66. In all Kongo and Teke languages *mpu* designates both "hat" and "authority." The term **-bádí* (CS 28) with the meaning "court" is found in Tio, Mfinu, Boma, Kongo, and Mbosi. The etymology of the terms cannot be fixed with any certainty, and hence it is still unknown whether they are Teke or Kongo in origin. For *nlunga,* see J. Vansina, "Antécédents," n. 28; the origin of this term is Kongo. In Kongo only: **-yad-,* "to rule" (CS 1890), derives from CS 873 and 874, with the first meaning "leopard skin" (CS 1102) rather than "carpet." Kongo and Teke had terms of different origin for "to succeed": ibid., n. 29. The Teke term was shared by Bembe (northeastern Kongo), by the Mongo languages, and by those of the lower Kasai.

67. *Ngáá-* also occurs in Kongo, especially in northeastern Kongo, which seems to have borrowed it from the Teke group. On titles, see P. P. Rey, *Colonialisme,* 253–60, comparing the Tio and Loango kingdoms. Known Kongo and Loango titles date from the sixteenth and seventeenth centuries, known Tio titles, with one exception, only from the nineteenth century.

68. J. Daeleman, "A Comparison of Some Zone B Languages in Bantu"; map 5.5 is based on the extant vocabularies. See also J. Vansina, "Antécédents," n. 32. The phenomenon had already struck Europeans in the sixteenth century; F. Pigafetta and D. Lopes, *Description du Royaume de Congo et des Contrées environnantes,* 35.

69. J. Vansina, "Antécédents," n. 33.

70. J. Vansina, "The Bells of Kings." The linguistic terminology **-kungu,* for the twinned bells, and **-pam-,* for the single bell, is found in the Teke group, in Mbede-Obamba, and in the lower Kasai area (Yans, Mpur, Nswo, Ding, and Mbala). Only Boma, Saa, and Buma in the area of the linguistic phenomenon

have another form for twinned bell, *-lónjá, which is of Mongo origin and a later intrusion here, probably due to the influence of the *nkúmú* courts.

71. The later-known principalities (precursors of the kingdoms of Loango, Kongo, and neighbors) lay in Mayombe or on the adjacent coast with two exceptions only. This was also the area with the richest ecological diversity (forests, coastal and mountain savannas, coasts, the Zaire Estuary, and a diversity of mineral deposits).

72. For the chronology, see J. Vansina, "The Bells of Kings." The technology of these bells diffused from West Africa and reached known archaeological sites in Shaba and Zambia before 1400. At a diffusion speed of 11.75 km per year (which is quite fast) they were in the first Teke principalities by 1221. The speed of the diffusion is probably too high, and the archaeological dates are probably too late, because small single bells already appear in Shaba between A.D. 1100 and 1300. Hence the conclusion that they were in the Teke principalities before 1200 (probably in the eleventh or twelfth century).

73. J. Vansina, *Tio Kingdom,* 313–23, for the lower level squires c. 1880. The term *antsaana,* "plebeians," is also found in the lower Kasai area as well as among the Saa (*banshian*). In Buma the term means "orphan," clearly an older meaning.

74. CS 1175 *-kued, "to marry," has Kongo and Teke reflexes with several Kongo derivations (*nkwezi,* "wife's kin of her generation"; *kinkwezi,* "affine"; *ko,* "parent-in-law"). For the connection with bridewealth, see the discussion in chapter 3: p. 77 and n. 20.

75. J. Vansina, "Antécédents," n. 44 (Crow) and 45 (*ngwa nkhazi*).

76. Lineages make sense in terms of succession and/or inheritance: to acquire and defend property or position in society. They tend to appear as common, centralizing, overarching institutions appear and to grow as centralization grows, at least in social formations with "representative government," which was the Kongo as well as, for instance, the Yoruba case. Cf. P. C. Lloyd, "The Political Structure of African Kingdoms," 84, 98–102; *idem, Political Development of Yoruba Kingdoms,* pp. 1–9. It is not surprising, then, that Yoruba lineages are found only in centralized kingdoms and that undifferentiated groups occur where kingdoms do not exist. Whether or not lineage structures later break down depends on the further transformations occurring in the centralized body politic.

77. J. Vansina, "Antécédents," n. 46; n. 49 for the term *-bida* (*luvila* in Kongo) of doubtful status as a designation for "social group" before c. 1900. For these terms, see also A2.

78. F. Hagenbucher Sacripanti, *Les fondements spirituels du pouvoir au royaume de Loango,* 22–28, 62; P. P. Rey, *Colonialisme,* 251, 260. A. Hilton, *The Kingdom of Kongo,* 22–23, 29, tentatively proposes a similar scenario for Kongo.

79. J. Miller, *Kings and Kinsmen: Early Mbundu States in Angola,* 43–54, 59. Mother's brothers were called *lemba* after the *mulemba* fig tree, which stood

for the power of the heroes of the lineage. For Mai Ndombe, see Mpase Nselenge Mpeti, *L'évolution de la solidarité,* 89–95.

80. J. Vansina, "Antécédents," 51. Innovation included the adoption of throwing knives as well as body armor and battle axes, and the differentiation of spears into throwing and stabbing spears.

81. *Nkoli* (CS 1110) is western Bantu, not common Bantu as Guthrie has it. See also A23. The meaning "pawn" predominates over "captive," given by Guthrie. Maybe the widespread Mongo ethnic nickname *nkole,* which has a pejorative meaning, is another reflex? Cf. G. Van der Kerken, *L'ethnie Mongo* 2:710–11, 715–16, but G. Hulstaert does not have the term in his dictionary.

82. For terms relating to markets and the week, see J. Vansina, "Probing the Past of the Lower Kwilu," 349–53. The origin of most terms lies north of the lower Zaire and to the immediate south of the copper belt.

83. B. Clist, "Archéologie du royaume Kongo," map 3.

84. J. Vansina, "Antécédents," nn. 55 and 66.

85. For a list of the later provinces of Loango, F. Hagenbucher Sacripanti, *Fondements spirituels,* 64–70 (Chilongo, Mampili, Loandjili, NgaKanu, Mayombe, Makangu, and Makunyi); P. P. Rey, *Colonialisme,* 265–68; and P. Martin, *The External Trade of the Loango Coast,* 10–19 (Loangiri, Loango-mongo, Pili, and Chilongo were the inner provinces). One must add Mayumba to the north and the states of Ngoi, Kakongo, and Bungu farther south. A number of other principalities which later became five of the provinces of Kongo bordered on this core to the south and east. For these, see F. Pigafetta and D. Lopes, *Description,* 68–69.

86. F. Bontinck, ed., *Histoire du royaume du Congo (c. 1624),* 60, 84–87; F. Pigafetta and D. Lopes, *Description,* 69, 85–89.

87. For Loango: F. Hagenbucher Sacripanti, *Fondements spirituels,* 22–23; P. P. Rey, *Colonialisme,* 251, 264–65; P. Martin, *External Trade,* 5–9; O. Dapper, *Naukeurige Beschrijvinge,* 143–44, for an origin in Zarri in Kakongo, not far from Bungu. For the Tio state: J. Vansina, *Tio Kingdom,* 440 and map; F. Pigafetta and D. Lopes, *Description,* 168–70 n. 87 and 200 n. 275, for the old term Anziko and the surrounding lands, Anzicana; Ebiatsa-Hopiel-Obiele "Les Teke," 34–47, for an etymology of Anziko as *āsi* + *Nkoo,* "those of the Nkoo district." It is most probable that the name must be read *āsi* + *ōkoo,* "those of the king" (i.e., "the kingdom"). The first mention of Teke or rather *mundiquetes* in F. Pigafetta and D. Lopes, *Description,* 32, 65, 66, 84.

88. For tentative dates for Loango and Kongo, see P. Martin, *External Trade,* 9. For a review of opinions about Kongo, see J. Vansina, "Antécédents," n. 10. Dates vary from indeterminate but quite old, to 1300, to the latest proposed date "in the early fifteenth century," A. Hilton, *Kingdom of Kongo,* 31, which is barely tenable; O. Dapper, *Naukeurige Beschrijvinge,* 219, for the claim that the Tio kingdom was the oldest.

89. This broad comparison is based for the most part on the cited works of P. Martin, A. Hilton, J. K. Thornton, F. Hagenbucher Sacripanti, P. P. Rey, and

J. Vansina (*Tio Kingdom*), as well as on W. G. L. Randles, *L'ancien royaume du Congo des origines à la fin du XIXe siècle;* Y.-N. Gambeg, "Pouvoir politique et société en pays teke"; and F. Ewani, "Recul et stabilisation teke."

90. On associations, see n. 4.

91. See n. 10. The most famous of these are the Tsogo temples; cf. illustration in A. Raponda-Walker, and R. Sillans, *Rites et croyances,* 196, showing a construction similar to the public building for men elsewhere.

92. For the distribution of this bell, see map 5.7; the earliest references to it date from the Gabon Estuary in 1593 (J. H. Van Linschoten, *Itinerario,* 3:11–12) and Rio Muni in 1603 (A. Jones, *German Sources for West African History, 1599–1669;* 27 [English translation], 345 [original German; compare with W. Crecelius, "Josua Ulsheimer Reisen nach Guinea und Beschreibung des Landes," 104–5]). See illustration in T. Griffon du Bellay, "Le Gabon," 2:316.

93. The languages of the Ngounié province (Sira, Punu, Lumbu, and Sango) have *kazi/katsi* for both mother's brother and wife, except for Tsogo, which borrowed it for mother's brother but not for wife. See G. Dupré, *Un ordre et sa destruction,* 151–67, for a description of matrilineages and clans in one population.

94. For South Gabon and Congo, cf. G. Dupré, *Un ordre,* 163; P. P. Rey, *Colonialisme.* For Myene, Fang, and southern Gabon, see H. Bucher, "The Mpongwe of the Gabon Estuary," 28–30. Generally, see H. Deschamps, *Traditions orales,* 32, 34, 45, 52, 68–69, 88–89, 100.

95. For vocabulary, see G. Gaulme, *Le pays de Cama,* 102–14; for politics, ibid., 146–48; for the official Maramba association extending from Mayombe to Cape Lopez, see A. Battell, *Strange Adventures,* 56–58. In later centuries a "dance," *ivanga,* among the Myene and even all along the coast of Rio Muni reproduced part of a Loango-type titulature and appropriate roles; C. González Echegaray, *Estudios Guineos,* 183–99, and J. A. Avaro, *Un peuple gabonais à l'aube de la colonisation,* 107–14. Among the Myene the dance belonged to the Abulia and Apandji clans (109). The latter has the same name as the Buvandji clan which ruled Loango.

96. F. Pigafetta and D. Lopes, *Description,* 31, for the mention of the extension of Loango to Cape Lopez. See discussion in G. Gaulme, *Le pays de Cama,* 92–119. See also A. Battell, *Strange Adventures,* 58, who mentions lords of Sete and of Kesock, east and north of Mayumba, but does not make clear whether they still belonged to the realm of Loango. Given the political significance and extent of Maramba, it seems likely that they were dependent on Mayumba.

97. G. Gaulme, *Le pays de Cama,* 101–2, 114–16, 119; J. A. Avaro, *Un peuple gabonais,* 45–47.

98. These are the confederations of N. Metegue N'nah, *Economies et sociétés au Gabon dans la première moitié du XIXe siècle,* 18–20.

99. See n. 95 and K. D. Patterson, *The Northern Gabon Coast to 1875,* 20–23; G. Rossel, "Gewasinnovaties in Gabon" 1:125–26 (diffusion of crops), 2:238–59 maps.

100. M. Alihanga, *Structures communautaires traditionelles et perspectives cooperatives dans la société altogovéenne,* 89–156 (Mbede government), 58–72 (wars with Mbosi, Tege, and others); T. Obenga, *La cuvette congolaise,* 33–70 (government); J. Ollandet, "Les contacts Teke-Mbosi," 1:140–89, 226–67 (Mbosi government); I. Löffler, "Beiträge zur Ethnologie der Tege," 77–146 (Tege government); Y.-N. Gambeg, "Pouvoir politique et société en pays teke," 315–24 (Tege-Mbosi-Mbede wars); F. Ewani, "Recul et stabilisation teke," 230–36 (Tege-Mbosi wars).

101. H. Deschamps, *Traditions orales,* 74 (Shake); L. Perrois, *La circoncision Bakota,* 17–18, (Kota wars), 39–46 (circumcision), 72–81 (associations), n. 11 (villages); E. Darré, "Notes sur la tribu des Bomitaba," 314–16; E. Darré and Le Bourhis, "Notes sur la tribu Bomitaba," 25–27 (government, titles, emblems); E. Darré, "Notes sur les Kakas de la circonscription de l'Ibenga-Likouala," 16–17 (officials).

102. J. Vansina, "Probing the Past," 345–53, and the use of terms for "clan" related to Kongo *kanda.* For religious vocabulary, see J. F. Thiel, *Ahnen, Geister, Höchste Wesen,* 38–58, 92–98, 113–15, 122–23, 144–48, 154–56.

103. Ndaywell, "Organisation sociale," 253–57, 268–75, 318–409; J. Vansina, "Probing the Past," 340–45.

104. See n. 70.

105. As appears from the following preliminary statistic. Out of 21 known terms with a political meaning in Saa, the affiliation of 6 remains undetermined although most of these seem to be innovations. Of the 15 others: 3 are western Bantu, all with innovation in meaning; 4 relate to Teke languages (but 2 of these have the same root) with innovation in meaning, and 1 of these is shared with Buma; 3 relate to other lower Kasai languages; 2 are related and probably derived from Kongo, 2 are innovations; and 1 is derived from Mongo.

In Jia, *njuuwele* ("paramount chief") corresponds to *ndjuú* (Saa) + *wele* (Boma).

Out of 14 Boma terms, 4 remain undetermined, all with original meanings. Of the others, 3 relate to Mongo; 2 to lower Kasai; 1 each to Teke, Yans, and Saa; 1 is derived from Buma; and 1 related to Buma and Kongo.

Out of 22 Yans terms: 6 remain undetermined, mostly original; 6 are related western Bantu forms with identical meanings in Kongo or Tio; 3 to lower Kasai generally; 2 to Boma (one of which is also related to Mongo); 1 each to Kongo, Teke, Mongo, Buma, and western Bantu.

Out of 11 Buma terms: 3 remain undetermined; 2 are western Bantu; 2 are related to lower Kasai generally (one of which, however, is also related to Kongo); 2 to Teke (one of these is also related to Saa); 1 to Boma and Kongo; 1 to Yans.

106. R. Tonnoir, *Giribuma,* 261–312.

107. M. Storme, *Ngankabe,* and H. Hemeni, "Historique de la tribu des Banunu," 2–6. The earliest references to Mwene Mushie are on maps only.

108. R. Tonnoir, *Girubuma,* 103–217; E. Sulzmann, "Orale Tradition."

109. See n. 105.

110. In contradiction to Tonnoir, E. Sulzmann, "Orale Tradition," 543–45, 569, claims an origin for the Boma rulers among the Bolia *nkúmú.* This may be so, yet Boma political terminology contains several basic elements which are shared with other lower Kasai groups. For example, *nkesé,* "political domain," is in fact derived from Buma *ke-sé.* It seems as if a Mongo group founded a kingdom over existing principalities of the lower Kasai type. Later Mongo influences in the region are evident, especially among the Jia, whose dynasty came from Mai Ndombe (ibid., 546–47) and from Mongo-Boma wars, R. Tonnoir, *Giribuma,* 221–24. The use of the term *nkúm* in the Saa expression *kumemembe,* "chief of police," is also a Mongo loan (*mbe* being probably identical with Tio *mbéé,* "capital"). Toponyms such as Mushie or Mosenge are derived from Mongo *bosenge,* "capital"; J. Vansina, "Probing the Past," 353. Finally one should not forget the implantation of the Ngwi *nkúmú* farther upstream on the southern side of the lower Kasai, from where they influenced their neighbors.

111. The Ding, the Lwer, and the Mpur claim this. See Ndaywell, "Organisation sociale," 353–65, and esp. 368–69; J. Mertens, *Les Ba Dzing de la Kamtsha,* 9–13.

Chapter Six: The Eastern Uplands

1. F. Goffart, *Le Congo,* 94; M. Robert, "Considérations suggérées par l'étude du milieu physique centre-africain," population maps; P. Gourou, "Notice de la carte de densité"; C. Delhaise, *Les Warega,* 24, 39–40. The higher densities in eastern Maniema seem to be a demographic spillover from the very dense populations farther east, although culturally they do not belong to the great lakes.

2. E. Meeussen, "De talen van Maniema," and the lexicostatistic surveys. Nyanga and Tembo are languages of the great lakes group. Southern central Sudanic so strongly influenced the whole Komo group (Komo, Bira, Amba, Huku) and Bali that most of these were labeled "Sub Bantu" by M. Guthrie, *The Classification of the Bantu languages,* 18–19, 40, 83, 85 (Amba, Angba, Bali, Bira, Bua, Huku). For language contacts in these areas, see A. Vorbichler, "Sprachkontakte am Beispiel einiger Sprachen und Dialekte in Nordost-Zaire," 433–39.

3. J. Vansina, "The Past." The section has benefited from C. Keim's commentary and information, for which I am very grateful.

4. On language families see chapter 2. Besides these 28 languages another 4 at least had been spoken in the area before. Such a polyglot situation was preserved wherever extended households with their retainers were the basic ethnic referents, the usual situation among the non-Bantu speakers. Language then was part of the household identity. See B. Costermans, *Mosaique bangba.* Dominant languages spread and were replaced, but the speech of the home was clung to tenaciously. As a result the linguistic history of the area is remarkable for its unique detail. One day this will allow for the elaboration of a detailed institutional and cultural history based on relative "fine" linguistic chronology.

5. On the Uele Neolithic, cf. F. Van Noten, *The Uelian;* F. and E. Van Noten, "Het ijzersmelten bij de Madi"; A. de Calonne-Beaufaict, *Les Azande,* 135–38, 145. F. Van Noten, ed., *The Archaeology,* 58–59, holds the controversial view that the whole Uele Neolithic is of Iron Age date. The data do not mean that the smelting of iron was adopted only in the seventeenth century. The fabrication of hematite axes and the use of iron tools seem to have coexisted for almost two millennia.

6. Provisionally C. Ehret et al., "Some Thoughts on the Early History of the Nile-Congo Watershed," 87–90; N. David, "Prehistory and Historical Linguistics in Central Africa," 80–81; M. McMaster, "Patterns of Interaction." J. Goeyvaert's ongoing linguistic research is expected to clarify greatly the early history of the southern central Sudanic group.

7. Iron was introduced first from the west, later from the east, according to M. McMaster, "Patterns of Interaction," chap. 3, sec. 2.

8. On fishermen, M. McMaster, "Patterns of Interaction," chap. 5, sec. 2, argues that some Ngbandians (Sango) were fishermen on the Uele and the Bomokandi, and were later replaced on these rivers by Kango. On the Abarambo, cf. Bruggen, "Rapport constituant la chefferie Kiravungu," 1; I. Czekanowski, *Forschungen im Nil- Kongo-Zwischengebiet* 6 (2): 224.

9. D. E. Saxon, "Linguistic Evidence," 70–73, 75–76; N. David, "Prehistory," 88–91.

10. C. Ehret et al., "Early History of the Nile-Congo Watershed," 89–90, 99–102; N. David, "Prehistory," 81–82.

11. M. McMaster "Patterns of Interaction," chap. 3, on Buan. There is a vast literature on pygmies in Ituri, but it tends to be ahistorical; see J. Vansina, "Do Pygmies Have a History?"

12. M. McMaster, "Patterns of Interaction," chap. 6. On material culture, see C. Van Overberghe and E. De Jonghe, *Les Mangbetu,* 241–89.

13. M. McMaster, "Patterns of Interaction," chap. 7, secs. 2–4. On terminology in Mangbetu, cf. M. I. Hubbard, "In Search of the Mangbetu"; M. McMaster, "Patterns of Interaction," chap. 7, sec. 3. On Mangbetu expansion, cf. De Maeyer, "Etude générale sur la tribu des Makere," 1; N. Chaltin, "Exploration de la Lulu et de l'Aruwimi," 105–8 (Popoi); P. Schebesta, *Vollblutneger und Halbzwerge,* 44, 80, 152 (Abelu, Lombi, Meje); H. Van Geluwe, *Les Bira et les peuplades limitrophes,* 11, 12 (Lombi).

14. M. McMaster, "Patterns of Interaction," chap. 7, sec. 4, and illus. 7.7 and 7.8; C. Van Overberghe and E. de Jonghe, *Les Mangbetu,* 530–41; I. Czekanowski, *Forschungen,* 6 (2): 567.

15. On the lower social strata, see E. De Jonghe, *Les formes d'asservissement dans les sociétés indigènes du Congo Belge,* 79, 81, 83–85, 89, 98 n. 1, 105; on "leading fighters" and "mercenary warriors" (*mando* in Mangbetu), cf. Van Ermingen, "De l'organisation des Makere du territoire de Zobia," 1; "Les Bekeni," 4; H. Hackars, "Inspection du territoire d'Avakubi," 4; "Etudes sur

les pygmées: Territoire des Babali/Barumbi," 1, 5 (leading fighters among Bali, Lika, Bodo, and Mangbetu).

16. Despite the appearance of an Omaha system of kinship terminology, after marriage by delayed exchange with transfer of matrimonial goods became the preferred form of marriage over the original sister exchange (*lengbe*) in the Mamvu tradition a lineage structure still did not develop.

17. On legitimacy by the use of affinal links, see C. Keim, "Precolonial Mangbetu Rule," 41. On Manziga, see p. 176.

18. M. Siffer, "Note générale sur les Mabodu," 1–3; A. Winckelmans, "Histoire générale de la tribu Maha de la peuplade Mabudu"; H. Van Geluwe, *Les Bali et les peuplades apparentées,* 13–15. The emigration may perhaps be connected to repercussions in the upper Ituri region, caused by the expansion of the kingdom of Bunyoro in western Uganda. Bodo *letaka/etaka,* "land," is related to *butaka* with the same meaning in the languages of the great lakes.

19. M. Siffer, "Note générale," 4; H. Hackars, "Inspection du territoire d'Avakubi," 4–5; A. Bertrand, "Note sur les Mabudu-Madimbisa (dits Wasumbi)," 7; H. Van Geluwe, *Les Bali,* 78–80. There just might be a relation between Mamvu-Balese *embaa* and Mangbetu *ne* + *mba,* "tribute" or "metal." But tones, vowel length, and vowel quality are too poorly rendered in the sources to conclude.

20. I. Czekanowski, *Forschungen* 6 (2): 567. M. Siffer, "Note générale," 5, 7–9, underlines the importance of manpower and a temporary unified command in war (*gama,* "chief").

21. Bouccin, "Les Babali," 695. By 1900 the *mambela* chains (seven) did not yet encompass all Bali villages, and one chain used a rite different from the six others; see P. E. Joset, *Les sociétés secrètes des hommes-léopards en Afrique,* 98–106. H. Van Geluwe, *Les Bali,* 64–67, and 67 n. 1 gives a bibliography.

22. The term *mukama* for a political position also occurs among the Pere (D. Biebuyck, *The Arts of Zaire,* 2:247–48), perhaps among the Mbo and Ndaka, and among the Nande and Toro. On poisoned arrows in the region, see E. Perrot and E. Vogt, *Les poisons de flèches,* 100–103, and references to T. H. Parke and H. M. Stanley.

23. The earliest reference here to leopard men dates to 1895; see P. Salmon "Les carnets," 260; H. Van Geluwe, *Les Bali,* 85–88. Leopard men were known elsewhere in the region of Beni and in southern Maniema; cf. P. E. Joset, *Sociétés secrètes,* 17–91, 106–17 (Pakombe, Bali, and neighbors), who claims that *Aniota* (or *Anioto*) is actually a Bodo term (55 n. 1); E. Cordella, "Appunti sulla zona del Maniema," 976 (Lega).

24. C. Keim, "Precolonial Mangbetu Rule," 108–11. The Mabodo now coined the *bava-* neologism for the name of lineages after *mava-* coined by the Meje. Their ethnic name is *Ma-*bodo, rather than *Ba-*bodo, because its present form is a nineteenth-century Mangbetu name. By then such was the prestige of the Mangbetu that the Mabodo adopted the name Mabodo for themselves.

25. I. Czekanowski, *Forschungen* 6 (2): 413; H. Seidel, "Das Uele-Gebiet," 185. On the religious significance of the rocky outcrops, see B. Costermans, "Torè, God en Geesten bij de Mamvu en hun dwergen," 540–41, 546.

26. Van Ermingen, "Organisation," 1; A. Landeghem, "Etude préparatoire sur les Babua," 1–4; A. Hutereau, *Histoire des peuplades de l'Uele et de l'Ubangi*, 45–46; A. de Calonne-Beaufaict, *Les Azande*, 125–27. On Makere-Buan relations, see chapter 4 for developments on the Likati.

27. A. de Calonne-Beaufaict, *Les Azande*, 96–98, 137–39; A. Hutereau, *Histoire*, 246–48; F. Nys, *Chez les Abarambo*.

28. On the traditions collected since the 1860s, cf. C. Keim, "Precolonial Mangbetu Rule," 38–40; R. Bertrand, *Notes pour servir à l'étude des Mangbetu*, 27–80; P. Denis, *Histoire des Mangbetu et des Matschaga jusqu'à l'arrivée des Belges*, 7–20.

29. C. Keim, "Precolonial Mangbetu Rule," 51.

30. Ibid., 50–52, 60; R. Bertrand, *Notes*, 81–114; P. Denis, *Histoire des Mangbetu*, 21–46.

31. C. Keim, "Precolonial Mangbetu Rule," 72–77 (politics of kinship), 81–90 (ideology, magic, emblems), 97–101 (advisors).

32. Ibid., 93–97 (military organization), 119–59 (economic institutions).

33. Ibid., 52–63, 230–40; R. Bertrand, *Notes*, 115–26; P. Denis, *Histoire des Mangbetu*, 47–109.

34. On *nebeli*, cf. C. Keim, "Precolonial Mangbetu Rule," 90–92; L. Vincart, "Notes pour servir à l'histoire des peuplades environnant le poste de Massidjadet," 546; G. Casati, *Zehn Jahre in Aequatoria* 1:102; I. Czekanowski, *Forschungen*, 164–67; C. Delhaise-Arnould, "Les associations secrètes au Congo: Le Nebili ou Negbo," 284. For events after 1873, see C. Keim, "Precolonial Mangbetu Rule," 240–96; P. Denis, *Histoire des Mangbetu*, 111–28; R. Bertrand, *Notes*, 126–27.

35. D. Biebuyck, *Arts of Zaire*, 266–67, for quotations.

36. The earliest general overview is A. Moeller, *Les grandes lignes des migrations des Bantous de la province orientale du Congo Belge*. Governor Moeller summarized the traditions of origin and the general features of social and political structure of the populations as reported by his administrators. Readers must know administrative goals, thought, and practice of the period and have access to at least some of the original reports, as well as to earlier documents, to use the volume intelligently.

37. D. Biebuyck, *Arts of Zaire*, 267–68 (quote from 287).

38. Along the Lualaba, fishermen and traders speaking languages of this group went downstream and occupied the present site of Kisangani by or before c. 1750. Cf. A. Droogers, *The Dangerous Journey*, 31–33; idem, "Les Wagenia de Kisangani entre le fleuve et la ville," 155–57; T. Papadopoullos, *Cases of Tribal Differentiation*, 17–21, who documents an Enya settlement even farther among the Mba on the Lindi (41–42). By 1955 they had abandoned their language.

39. Mainly the people now called Nyanga and Tembo. For estimated dates, see map 2.8.

40. For associations in southeastern Zaire, cf. G. Wauters, *L'ésotérie des noirs dévoilée,* 97–111 (Songye); P. Colle, *Les Baluba,* 2:527–627, and T. Reefe, *The Rainbow and the Kings,* 13–14, 46–48 (Luba); A. F. Roberts, "Social and Historical Contexts of Tabwa Art," 35–36 ("Butwa" association). One could argue that they existed by 800 on the grounds that shell currency made sense only for social payments (see n. 43). Even if that was so, and the connection remains weak, that still dates the rise of associations more than half a millennium after people from the southeast settled in the forests of Maniema.

41. J. Druart, "Carte succincte du District du Maniema," notes on "Wagenia" and n. 38. The language was Enya and the common name was Genya north of Kindu; farther south the fishermen were called "Baluba."

42. Products traded included copper, palm products, iron products, salt, raffia cloth, raffia threads (to Kivu), red earth, red powder from the *Pterocarpus soyauxii* tree, lion teeth, bark cloth, beans, and fish (near the rivers). Major trade currents involved iron (mostly from Lega country and Manyara southeast of Kasongo), salt (Bushi near Lake Kivu, Micici, Kirundu, Nyangwe, the Malela district west of Nyangwe), raffia cloth (of Songye origin from the Lomami and beyond), palm products (areas near the confluence of the Elila and west of the Lualaba farther downstream from the confluences of the Ulindi and the Lowa), and copper. But no author has paid much attention to precolonial trade, and references are extremely scattered. In general, see E. Cordella, "Appùnti," 963–72. For details about the Lega, cf. C. Delhaise, "Chez les Wassongola du sud ou Babili," 165–66; L. Liétard, "Les Warega," 133–34; G. Ainti, "Les Mituku," 1–2. On quartz crystals, see D. Biebuyck, *Arts of Zaire,* 206–7, and R. Packard, *Chiefship and Cosmology,* 68–69.

43. D. Biebuyck, "La monnaie musanga des Balega," 676–84; J. Bettendorf, "Die Angst der Mituku vor den Mizimu under deren Vetretern, den raffinierten Mekota," 119; A. Moeller, *Grandes lignes,* 404, 427, 434; P. De Maret, *Fouilles archéologiques dans la vallée du Haut-Lualaba, Zaire* 1:165–66, 260–63 (A.D. 800 and later). De Maret mentions a possible connection with social payments to be made on entering an association.

44. D. Biebuyck, *Lega Culture,* 7–12, 82–84; idem, *Arts of Zaire:* 209–20, diagram 9. Yogolelo Tambwe ya Kasimba, *Introduction à l'histoire des Lega,* 26, is very specific: only the high dignitaries of the *bwámi* knew the history and genealogies of the Lega.

45. W. de Mahieu, *Qui a obstrué la cascade?* 31–42; idem, *Structures et symboles:* 1, 56–58, 115 n. 5; idem, "A l'intersection du temps et de l'espace, du mythe et de l'histoire, les généalogies," 415–37.

46. The ethnography of southern Maniema remains poorly known with the exception of the Lega and Bembe peoples studied by D. Biebuyck and Mulyumba. However, these constitute the two largest population groups of the area, and many different groups have evidently been incorporated under the

label Bembe and even Lega. The uncertainties of ethnic nomenclature are described by D. Biebuyck, *Lega Culture,* 3–8, and idem, *Statuary from the Pre-Bembe Hunters,* as well as by Mulyumba wa Mamba Itongwa, "La structure sociale des Balega Basile," 13–22.

47. A. Moeller, *Grandes lignes,* 421, 433, 443, 446, 450–64; D. Biebuyck, *Arts of Zaire:* 210–11; T. Papadopoullos, *Cases of Tribal Differentiation,* 22–25.

48. M. Piscicelli, *Nel Paese dei Bangobango,* 156–58 (Bembe: "La casta dei bwami è fra i bakombe, potentissima"); E. Cordella, *Verso l'Elila,* 41, 103–4; C. Delhaise, *Les Warega,* 337–45; D. Biebuyck, *Lega Culture,* 46–50, 85. On the privileges of *bakota* dignitaries among the Mituku, see J. Bettendorf, *Die Angst der Mituku,* 145–46. Along the Lualaba the Zanzibari called the chiefs they installed *mokota,* the title of the high dignitaries in the overarching associations, thus recognizing them as the previous government.

49. D. Biebuyck, *Lega Culture,* 7–8 and n. 12, 11–12, 82, and idem, *Arts of Zaire,* 205–11, for a tradition of Lega origins from the Lualaba to the north; C. Delhaise, *Les Warega,* 47–48, refers not to Lega origins (from the south) but to the Museme epic, as does A. S. Clarke, "The Warega," 66. But, given the genetic relationships of their language, the bulk of the Lega people clearly do not come from the northwest but from the south. Hence what do the traditions about the Lualaba refer to? The direction might be a logical cosmological conclusion, if the creation was in the absolute downstream (D. Biebuyck, *Lega Culture,* 11 n. 14). But there seems to be more than this. The tradition seems to tell of the origin of the lower *bwámi* ranks, despite the aphorism, "Bwami has no inventor; it is the fruit that came from above." Given the distribution of related associations this makes eminent sense.

50. D. Biebuyck, *Lega Culture,* 83–84, relates an opinion that *bwámi* was invented to do away with war.

51. C. Van Overberghe, *Les Basonge,* 475–76 (the groves were still recognizable in 1906; see end map); T. Reefe, *Rainbow and the Kings,* 130–31, 230 n. 10; A. Verbeken, "Accession au pouvoir chez certaines tribus du Congo par système électif," 654–57 (*Lwaba, ehata*); idem, "Institutions politiques indigènes," 1–3. The rotation was announced by a new circumcision cycle; see C. Wauters, *L'ésoterie,* 125–26, 159, 164–65. *Eata* is a reflex of **-pata* (like Kongo *libata*).

52. A. Moeller, *Grandes lignes,* 151–53, 508–11; T. Reefe, *Rainbow and the Kings,* 130–32, 149–50. *Eata* flourished before 1820 among the Hemba, Songye, and Kusu. Moeller gives the seven predecessors of Lusuna, which covers most of the eighteenth century (153). *Eata* antedates Luba influences on Songye political institutions which began c. 1700. A date for its emergence in the fifteenth and sixteenth centuries is derived from the date of arrival of *bwámi's* block of upper ranks among the Sile.

53. See n. 47. The term *mokota* may perhaps also be due to *eata* influence.

54. A. Moeller, *Grandes lignes,* 428.

55. Ibid., 435–50, 453–54; C. Delhaise, "Chez les Wasongola," 120–21, 134–35, 195–99; D. Biebuyck, *Arts of Zaire,* 235–38, 243–46; E. Cordella,

"Appunti," 971; Cdt. Borms, "Reconnaissance du pays Bango-bango et d'une partie de l'Uzimba," 256b.

56. A. Moeller, *Grandes lignes,* 421–35; D. Biebuyck, *Arts of Zaire,* 238–40; J. Jak, "Eenige ethnographica over deWalengola-Babira," 48–50; Van Belle, "Territoire des Walengola-Wasongola-Mituku," 4–9; J. Bettendorf, *Die Angst der Mituku,* 118–19, 145–47; H. Marmitte, "Baleka-Mituku," 3–8; J. Jak, "De bakota en hun grafhutten in Belgisch Congo," 37–39.

57. On the *ngodzi* and his lieutenant *moganda,* see A. Moeller, *Grandes lignes,* 433; Van Belle, "Territoire," 4. Note the stress on wealth and the acquisition of clients by giving them women to marry.

58. D. Biebuyck, *Arts of Zaire,* 241–43; K. Kudi, *Le Lilwakoy des Mbole du Lomami,* 4–32; V. Rouvroy, "Le'Lilwa'," 783–98; J. Tachelet, "De Montfortaanse missie in Belgisch Kongo," 44–49; R. V. Abbeloos, "De sekte lilwa," 311–31; R. Bouccin, "Au sujet du Lilwa"; J. F. Carrington, "Lilwaakoi-a Congo Secret Society," 237–44. For the *lilwá* as a boy's initiation, see n. 82; M. De Rijck, "Une société secrète chez les Lalia Ngolu," 2–7.

59. R. Philippe, *Inongo,* 8–108.

60. D. Biebuyck, *Lega Culture,* 82–84; ibid., 205, 209–16, 281–83 (origin of the Babongolo near Kirundu; "*kaluba*" sold the hat to the Babongolo); Yogolelo Tambwe ya Kasimba, *Introduction,* 22 (Kimbimbi). Mulyumba wa Mamba Itongwa, "Structure sociale," 309–19, shows that although in the decentralized western area, studied by Biebuyck, almost every head of a House held the highest rank (one man per 41.8; p. 318), in the east centralization was far greater, as there were four main kingdoms by the 1880s and hence there was one man of the highest rank for about 20,000 people!

61. *Mwámi* and *bwámi,* reflexes of **yáma,* an ancient root in the languages of the great lakes, are found in almost every language of the group, including all the languages adjacent to the forest.

62. Bishikwabo Chubaka, "Note sur l'origine de l'institution du 'bwami' et fondements de pouvoir politique au Kivu oriental," 6 (the Nyindu were then Lega), 5–13 (the acquisition of *bwámi* as told by the Nyindu and their neighbors), 13–17 (structure of the Nyindu *bwámi*), and idem, "Histoire d'un état shi en Afrique des grands lacs: Kaziba au Zaire," 243–49; Mulyumba wa Mamba Itongwa, *Structure sociale,* 319–29 (structure of Sile *bwámi*), 8–11 and 329–43 (*bwámi wa lusembe*), 343–47 (Nyindu and Shi traditions), 331 (succession list of the 'Alenga dynasty at 25 years per generation, starting in the third, yields c. 1670 for its onset; Shi calculations also yield a date well before 1700, despite Bishikwabo, "Note sur l'origine" 16). By rough reckoning a century would elapse before the *bwámi* reached this area from the Lualaba, and another century for the spread of the *eata* from the Lomami, which would then have started in the fifteenth century or c. 1500. Trees in the sacred groves of the Sile dynasty and in the *eata* groves can eventually be dated and yield a better chronology. Mugaruka bin-Mubibi, "Histoire clanique et évolution des états dans la région sud-ouest du lac Kivu," 425, gives c. 1240–1260 for the elaboration of *bwámi* on the Ulindi. Even corrected to 1300–1350 (leaving the Ulindi, cf. p. 400), the

dating seems early. It is ultimately derived from a spurious early chronology for Rwanda beginning in A.D. 906 (165–67, 371, 405–7).

63. R. Sigwalt, "The Early History of Bushi," 79–142, 187–339; Mugaruka bin-Mubibi, "Histoire clanique," 329–434, annexes. Bishikwabo Chubaka, "Histoire"; R. Sigwalt, pers. com. (1985), 17, now estimates that a large part of Maniema was occupied by speakers of great lakes languages before the Lega immigrated. This is untenable, except perhaps for the easternmost Lega groups (Sile, Mwenda, Nyindu).

64. For example, the *mpunju,* and *bubáké* rituals; cf. D. Biebuyck, *Lega Culture,* 82, 85 n. 7; idem, "Organisation politique des Nyanga," 313–15 (*bubáké*); idem, "La société kumu face au Kitawala," 33–34 (*mpunju*).

65. Although D. Biebuyck, *Arts of Zaire,* 6, says: "The *bwámi* association . . . dates from the beginnings of Lega society" and therefore gives no priority. On kinship, cf. D. Biebuyck, "Maternal Uncles and Sororal Nephews among the Lega; idem, *Les Mitamba: Sysèmes de mariages enchaînés chez les Bembe;* and idem, "De vorming van fiktieve patrilineaire verwantschapsgroepen bij de Balega" (unrelated groups attached as segments to patrilineages). For the territorial organization, cf. C. Delhaise, *Les Warega,* 339–47 (chiefs); D. Biebuyck, *Lega Culture,* 46–50. For *gúmi:* cf. E. Burke, *A Small Handbook of Kilega,* 36 (*bugumi*), 62 (*mugumi*).

66. The considerable differences between the accounts of D. Biebuyck, Mulyumba, and Bishikwabo relate to these differences in size. Biebuyck studied the western, decentralized Lega, the others the statelike social formations of the Sile and Nyindu.

67. D. Biebuyck, *Arts of Zaire,* 246–57, his "Organisation politique," "De Mumbo-instelling bij de Banyanga," and *Rights in Land and Its Resources among the Nyanga,* 8–11, 26–33; R. Hoffman, "Rapport sur la chefferie Bapere," 1–4; A. Moeller, *Grandes lignes,* 296 (Pere borrowed political titles from the Nande). So far no publications exist about the Tembo.

68. From the Hunde and Nande specifically. For the latter, see R. Packard, *Chiefship and Cosmology,* 28–52, 67–71, 125–26.

69. D. Biebuyck, *"Mumbira"* 42 (Pere, Mbali, Ndaka, Mbo, Mbuti, and hence Bira share aspects of this initiation); L. de Sousberghe, "Mumbira et Limombo des Nyanga," 42 n. 21.

70. *Mbuntsu, mambela, mondaa,* and *dokpo.* The latter two occur in W. de Mahieu, *Qui a obstrué la cascade?* 32. Of the *nsindi* initiation among the Pere, only the name is known. For the Nyanga and Pere, see D. Biebuyck, *Arts of Zaire,* 246–51; his "Nyanga Circumcision Masks and Costumes," *"Mumbira,"* and "Sculpture from the Eastern Zaire Forest Regions"; R. Hoffman, "Croyances et coutumes des Bapere," 1–8. From the Pere we know only that they had healing associations "like the Komo" (Hoffman, "Croyances et coutumes," 3), although one also found elements typical for the *nkumbi* initiation of Ituri such as occurred, e.g., among the Bira, cf. C. Turnbull, *Wayward Servants,* 63–65; H. Van Geluwe, *Les Bira,* 82–94. Almost every Nyanga House had its own rituals. D. Biebuyck, *"Mumbira,"* 42, notes the names of *mbuntsu, mangwe, mpande mukuki, ima*

nekukuya, ukanga, kakoka, kasindi, bubira, mwari, bundia, nyamosoku, and *mumbira, kasumba, lusumba,* and *esomba,* several of which are found in Ituri, northern or southern Maniema. Common vocabulary items related to brotherhoods abound in northern Maniema and Ituri in particular.

71. As seen from the retention of such terms as *kúmú* ("chief"), *etuka* ("House"), *noko* ("mother's brother"), and *gandjá* ("boy's initiation").

72. Because they have been the object of outstanding studies by W. de Mahieu, the Komo are privileged in this section. On their atomization, see W. de Mahieu, *Structures et symboles,* 5–17 and 17 n. 1; and F. Stradiot, "Rapport concernant l'organisation des populations Barumbi et Bakumu des territoires de Makale-Wandi, Lubutu et Ponthierville," whose results suggest that each clan counted on average perhaps 300 members and each House in it on average fewer than 40 (cf. W. de Mahieu, *Structures et symboles,* 8). Yet the House, coinciding with the village, was the only unit in physical reality. As a result of the atomization, it is nearly impossible to recover much history before 1876, apart from migrations and cosmology; see ibid., 6 (failure of the administration to regroup segments by common genealogies), 8 (genealogical memory was five to seven generations deep), and 15 (collective memory was mainly maintained by settlements over hunting grounds).

73. Although this description is derived from Komo data it applies also to the Mbuti (cf. C. Turnbull, *Wayward Servants,* and his *The Mbuti Pygmies,* 179–86) and to the Bira of the forest (cf. e.g., I. Czekanowski, *Forschungen,* 348–55; M. Siffer, "Note générale sur les Babira," 3; P. E. Joset, "Vie juridique et politique des Babombi," 4 [a–b]). After 1876 great changes occurred with the Zanzibari domination.

74. Apart from recently borrowed terms there was apparently no terminology for dependent statuses.

75. W. de Mahieu, *Structures et symboles,* 7. Houses split easily. Hence the technical name for segments, *osúkó,* i.e., "place where the generation of the grandchildren of X live"; W. de Mahieu, "Les Komo," 103 n. 10.

76. The Bira and Balese of Ituri were less mobile because farming was much more important to them than to the Komo; cf. H. Van Geluwe, *Les Bira,* 51–52, and idem, *Mamvu-Mangutu et Balese-Mvuba,* 129–30. The available data on the Bira and Balese, the "pygmy hosts," remain quite scanty, mostly byproducts of the research on hunters and gatherers. It may be briefly noted that chiefs here as in Komo land were a Zanzibari innovation, that the Bira advanced with the Zanzibari and later the Belgians into Balese lands, and were also quite mobile at that time. See M. Baltus, "Les Balese," 117–21, for the recent history of the farmers of Ituri.

77. W. de Mahieu, *Structures et symboles,* 55, 63, 73–74.

78. Ibid., 77, for the lack of congruence between conceptual and physical realities as the engine behind these dynamics of innovation. De Mahieu gives the example of *kaseá,* introduced from the Lengola to replace *kompómbo,* which was felt to be ineffective. On the introduction of *úmbá,* see W. de Mahieu, *Structures et symboles,* 86–88. Its rituals were inspired by the *esomba* rites, but

in turn the *gandjá* borrowed certain prerogatives from *úmbá;* see W. de Mahieu, *Qui a obstrué la cascade?* 9. In this area *yaba* diffused in the early 1930s from Komo land (where it was a ritual sequence) as far as the Uele; cf. W. de Mahieu, *Qui a obstrué la cascade?* 207, 310–13; E. Bock, "Trois notes sur la secte Biba"; Fivé, *Etudes Bamanga;* S. Kreutz, "Extrait du rapport trimestriel."

79. See nn. 70, 85.

80. *Gandjá, ganza, kandza, mu-kandá,* etc., "initiation for boys," are all reflexes of **-ganjá* found from Ubangi to Ituri and northern Maniema, as well as from the middle Kwango to the Lualaba and the middle Zambezi. W. de Mahieu, *Qui a obstrué la cascade?* 27–31, is the only author to give a wider semantic field, including "sperm" and "madness." These may be local derivations of meaning.

81. Cf. map 6.4. See n. 69 (diffusion of the *mambela* style with a bird sequence); W. de Mahieu, *Qui a obstrué la cascade?* 31–34, for *alútú* and *kentende.*

82. *Lilwá* is best known from the Lokele, Eso, and Mbole regions. The overall practices and rituals of initiation for boys found among the Bali, and there named *mambela,* were also common among their neighbors to the west as far as Basoko under the name of *lilwá.* Cf. H. Sutton Smith, *Yakusu, the Very Heart of Africa,* 8, 9, 28, 63–68; W. Millmann, "The Tribal Initiation Ceremony of the Lokele," 364–80; Van Dieren, "La circoncision chez les Bamanga"; J. Fräßle, *Meiner Urwaldneger,* 55 (So); idem, *Negerpsyche,* 85 (the name *Lilwá*).

83. The term *moámé* may have been introduced here only after c. 1876; see W. de Mahieu, *Structures,* 73. His *Qui a obstrué la cascade?* 141–378, details the initiation and the cycle of the *méná gandjá.* See also D. Biebuyck, *Arts of Zaire,* 233–35, but note that he gives *Umba* fathers as the highest rung (234) and perhaps other details are of "colonial" vintage. See n. 78.

84. W. de Mahieu, *Qui a obstrué la cascade?* 382–412.

85. The diffusion of two successive patterns of circumcision, the *bwadi* and the *-tende,* over areas stretching from the middle Kasai to the Lowa River and from Shaba to the Lindi River, respectively, both probably moving from south to north, confirms a complex and very dynamic history. Interchange from neighbor to neighbor affected enormous areas, and diffusions certainly took place in both directions, not just from south to north.

86. Seepage is indicated by the diffusion of emblematic objects such as bells and throwing knives, or by the still little-known diffusion of the lesser Asiatic crops such as taro and sugar cane. But, as the examples show, these kinds of innovations exerted at best a minor influence on the attitudes of peoples in the area and on their institutional developments.

Chapter Seven: Challenge from the Atlantic

1. A fully detailed history of the area has not yet been written. For the written sources see chapter 1. Over most of the affected area reliable oral traditions allow one to upstream well into the eighteenth century, and in some

cases into the seventeenth. After 1800 the oral record becomes especially detailed. Written sources for the nineteenth century have by no means been exhausted for the coastal areas, and there still are discoveries to be made even for the eighteenth century.

2. The exemplary systematic study of the Atlantic trading system is J. Miller, *Way of Death*. It deals with the Portuguese slave trade in the eighteenth century, is centered on Angola, and touches only incidentally on the forest areas. Still its discussion of the overall organization, the commercial mechanisms, and the institutions of the trade is invaluable and fully applies to the harbors on the Loango coast.

3. J. Vansina, *Kingdoms of the Savanna*, 41–46, 41–46; W. G. L. Randles, *L'ancien royaume du Congo*, 87–96.

4. R. Garfield, "A History of Saõ Tomé Island," 1–32. Slaves from the mainland were imported after 1493. The settlers acquired some 930 slaves between 1494 and 1499 (14).

5. J. Vansina, *Kingdoms of the Savanna*, 46–54; W. G. L. Randles, *L'ancien royaume du Congo*, 130–38; A. Hilton, *Kingdom of Kongo*, 50–68. On *nzimbu*, see F. Pigafetta and D. Lopes, *Description*, 157–58 n. 37. On the volume of slave exports, see P. Lovejoy, *Transformations in Slavery*, 38. B. Clist, "Pour une archéologie," map 3, indicates ceramic links between the Malebo Pool area and the lower Zaire in the sixteenth century (group 1 and 5 wares) and also the river upstream (group X ware found from Mai Ndombe to the banks of the lower Kwango and at sites in Kinshasa, including Ngombela). Ngombela has been dated in one instance to A.D. 1645; see D. Cahen, "Contribution à la chronologie de l'âge du fer dans la région de Kinshasa," 135, but clearly more dating is needed. On this site, see H. Van Moorsel, *Atlas de préhistoire de la plaine de Kinshasa*, 224–77, and the *nzimbu* treasure (256 bottom).

6. A. Hilton, *Kingdom of Kongo*, 69–141. The controversy among historians about the origin of these Jaga continues. For a caravan consisting of multiple parties, see A. Cavazzi de Montecúccolo, *Descriçaõ histórica dos três reinos, Congo, Matamba e Angola* 1:112 (ch. 1, sec. 229), 245–46 (ch. 2, sec. 245).

7. P. Martin, *External Trade*, 33–42.

8. Ibid., 43–68.

9. Ibid., 70, 130–31; O. Dapper, *Naukeurige Beschrijvinge*, 146, 157–59. The Ivili of Gabon now settled on the lower Ngounié are probably descendants of such Vili traders. Marriage with a close relative of a trading partner was the preferred strategy. It is often referred to, from Gabon to the Malebo Pool, from early times on and was still practiced in the nineteenth century. Bloodbrotherhood was the preferred link in the inner basin by the 1880s and was then spreading far and wide, but the practice may be quite old nevertheless; see H. Tegnaeus, *Bloodbrothers*, 104–18. For these and other ties among the Tio, see J. Vansina, *Tio Kingdom*, 87, 263–64.

10. An Ibare "kingdom" appears in texts of c. 1612 and 1620: A. Brasio, *Monumenta Missionaria Africana* 6:104, 438. Ibare refers to the name *ebale* for the Zaire River, common in languages of water people north of the Alima, and

its "kingdom" was the stretch of river upstream of the Alima confluence. The name Moenhemuge (Mwene Mushie) already appears on a map of 1561. This refers to Mushie on the Kwa and its lands inhabited by the Nunu; see E. Sulzmann, "Orale Tradition," 527.

11. O. Dapper, *Naukeurige Beschrijvinge*, 202, mentions cloth, metalware (especially copper basins), and shells or beads in the Kongo trade. Guns were in demand, but the Portuguese did not sell them. Textiles and guns, along with brass pans and other metal items, were to become the staples of the trade. By 1700 the composition of the packet for a slave already included the three categories of commodities described; see J. Barbot, Jr., and J. Casseneuve, "An Abstract of a Voyage to the Congo River or the Zaire and to Cabinde in the Year 1700," 509–12. Luxury textiles had been a sign and an instrument of social stratification before the Europeans arrived, and the role of foreign raiment and cloth as items of prestige and status was but a continuation of this habit (O. Dapper, *Naukeurige Beschrijvinge*, 199, for the wearing of imported cloth by the great). Leaders also wanted European guns, first as a symbol of power, then to arm elite guards, and again this affected local balances of power with the same results as described. Because gunpowder could not be made locally, the acquisition of guns created perforce a need for gunpowder. Meanwhile near the coast the importance of textiles or sundries as political weapons lessened as they became more common when the volume of such imports grew. The rulers on the coast constantly demanded different novelties. Hence such eccentric gifts as the two peacocks, the two white dogs, and the Dutch drum for the king of Loango in 1612 (S. Brun, *Schiffarten*, 10). Meanwhile the mass of earlier imports remained in demand by people of lesser status as they strove to emulate their lords. Finally textiles and guns gradually became necessities rather than luxuries on the Loango coast.

12. The figures given are estimates derived from data in P. Lovejoy, *Transformations in Slavery*, 52–54; P. D. Curtin, *The Atlantic Slave Trade: A Census*, 224–25 fig. 16, 266 fig. 26, tables 33, 34, 36, 63–67; P. Martin, *External Trade*, 73–92, 124, 137–38; K. D. Patterson, *The Northern Gabon Coast to 1875*, 32–38; R. A. Austen and K. Jacob, "Dutch Trading Voyages to Cameroun: 1721–1759," 10–13. Lovejoy and Curtin give totals only for the Angolan and Loango coast trade combined. J. Miller, *Way of Death*, 233, has slightly higher estimates than are given here for the northern coasts between 1650 and 1830.

13. K. D. Patterson, *Northern Gabon Coast*, 8, 14 (buying slaves), 32–38; H. Bucher, "The Mpongwe," 120; R. A. Austen and K. Jacob, "Dutch Trading Voyages."

14. The outer limits are described after S. W. Koelle, *Polyglotta Africana;* P. D. Curtin, *Atlantic Slave Trade*, 255–56 (maps), 289–90, 295–96, 298 (dates); T. E. Bowdich, *Mission from Cape Coast Castle to Ashantee*, 426–30; and the first European observers of the 1880s. Summary for Congo and southern Gabon, P. Martin, *External Trade*, 124–29; for Cameroon, see A. Wirz, *Vom Sklavenhandel zum Kolonialen Handel*, 82–91.

15. P. D. Curtin, *Atlantic Slave Trade*, 224–25 fig. 16, 226 fig. 26, tables 66, 69, 74; P. Lovejoy, *Transformations in Slavery*, 141, 144; J. Miller, *Way of Death*, 233; P. Martin *External Trade*, 138–42. After 1830 the data are quite deficient.

16. P. Martin, *External Trade*, 93–115. By 1700 this system was already firmly established. Cf. J. Barbot, Jr., and J. Casseneuve, "Voyage to the Congo River," 509–12.

17. P. Martin, *External Trade*, 102; P. de Marees, *Beschryvinghe*, 242–43 (fort on Corisco in 1600); P. Van den Broecke, *Reizen naar West Afrika*, 26 (temporary shop at Cape Lopez), 57 (a house for trade in Loango by 1610); L. Degrandpré, *Voyage à la côte occidentale d'Afrique fait dans les années 1786 et 1787*, 65–67.

18. P. Martin, *External Trade*, 70 (charms for protection), 118–22 (caravans). On canoes and flotillas, cf. R. M. Eggert, *Das Wirtschaftssystem*, 70–72, 118–20; C. Coquilhat, *Sur le Haut-Congo*, 85.

19. R. Harms, "Oral Tradition and Ethnicity."

20. For descriptions of currencies, see A. Mahieu, *Numismatique du Congo, 1484–1924* (Zaire); T. Obenga, *La cuvette congolaise*, 105–9, J.-F. Vincent, "Dot et monnaie de fer chez les Bakwele et les Djem" 283–91; J. Guyer, "Indigenous Currencies and the History of Marriage Payments"; J. Guyer, "The Iron Currencies of Southern Cameroon"; A. Cureau, *Les sociétés primitives*, 298–301. A study of the relevant terminologies and of their relative spatial extension has not yet been undertaken. For the "money market" at the Malebo Pool, see J. Vansina, *Tio Kingdom*, 282–88.

21. The notion of wealth has been little studied. But see P. Van Leynseele, "Les Libinza," 96–137, esp. 96–98 (*mosolo*, "wealth").

22. For slave status and terminologies, see E. de Jonghe, *Les formes d'asservissement*. See also n. 5. On the gradation of unequal statuses as reflected in terminology, see R. Austen, "Slavery among Coastal Middlemen," 307–20. Household slaves were employed on plantations by their owners in the seventeenth-century Kongo capital and in both the Gabon Estuary and the hinterland of Douala by the nineteenth centuries. On legal condemnation to slavery, see P. Martin, *External Trade*, 167–68.

23. For this subsection, see J.-L. Vellut, "Notes sur l'économie internationale des côtes de Guinée inférieure au XIXe siècle," 15–16, 22 (multiplication of posts), 39–49 (growth of trade between c. 1845 and 1890); A. Pinto, *Angola e Congo*, 234–37, 352–66, 370–400 (the Loango coast in 1882); A. Wirz, *Vom Sklavenhandel*, 96–99 (Kribi); C. Duparquet, "Etat commercial de la côte du Loango et du Congo," map of commercial stations from Sete to Ambriz in 1875; and the commentary published by F. Bontinck, "Etat commercial du littoral . . . Document inédit," 165–83.

24. P. Martin, *External Trade*, 149–57; J.-L. Vellut, "Notes sur l'économie," 22–24, 28 (ivory imports in London); A. Wirz, *Vom Sklavenhandel*, 60, 63–66; G. Dupré, "Le commerce entre sociétés lignagères," 625–26, 630–32 (Nzabi), 642 (Punu slave plantations); see n. 34 for special groundnut plantations in Gabon.

25. P. Du Chaillu, *Voyages et aventures dans l'Afrique équatoriale*, 44–50.

26. P. D. Curtin, *Atlantic Slave Trade*, 252, table 75, for the lower figure, which comes from ships known to the British Foreign Office; 30,000 is an estimate by Dutch traders based on the tonnage of slave ships leaving the Zaire Estuary (see J.-L. Vellut, "Notes sur l'économie," 40). No thorough quantitative research has yet been undertaken on these coasts in this period. For the general situation, see P. Martin, *External Trade*, 143–49.

27. J.-L. Vellut, "Notes sur l'économie," 23–24; A. Wirz, *Vorn Sklavenhandel*, 63.

28. See pp. 233–35.

29. On technology, see D. R. Headrick, "The Tools of Empire," 83–149, 165–79. On trade, travelers, and treaties, see N. Metegue N'nah, *L'implantation coloniale au Gabon*, 15–29, 32–35.

30. J. Vansina, "Esquisse historique" 26–32; G. Rossel, "Gewasinnovaties," 123–27; W. G. L. Randles, *L'ancien royaume du Congo* 66–67, for domestic animals. Pigs are first mentioned on the mainland c. 1575 (F. Pigafetta and D. Lopes, *Description*, 76) but were already kept on Saõ Tomé by c. 1500 (R. Garfield, "History of Saõ Tomé Island," 22). Later they were common only in the Kongo area. They may have been introduced from Europe. Sheep antedated the Europeans but disseminated more in the eighteenth and nineteenth centuries. Ducks were introduced by Europeans well after 1600.

31. R. M. Eggert, *Das Wirtschaftssystem* 11–17 (cassava in Equator Province), 16 (yields of about 20 tn./ha., slightly higher than about 15–18 tn./ha. for ABB plantains). Cassava bread was made at the Malebo Pool by 1698; tobacco was in great demand there, but still not cultivated (see F. Bontinck, *Diaire congolais*, 127). For the labor involved in preparing such bread, see J. Vansina, *Tio Kingdom*, 148–50.

32. R. Harms, *River of Wealth, River of Sorrow*, 53–54; G. Sautter, *De l'Atlantique* 1:272–74. See M. Miracle, *Agriculture*, 1–5, "A. Manioc," for the situation by 1950.

33. M. Miracle, *Agriculture*, map 1–5; idem, *Maize in Tropical Africa*, 82, 94–95; J. Vansina, *Children of Woot*, 176–78, for the advantages of maize over other cereals among the Kuba.

34. A. Raponda-Walker, "Enquête sur l'Agriculture noire au Gabon et sur certaines techniques utilisant des produits végétaux," 725–28, has the term *-boga*, "field for groundnuts," in the whole Ngounié area and among the Seki near Rio Muní. Among several peoples (Punu, Gisir, Wungu, and Tsogho) the term was used for a large field of groundnuts, smaller fields having special names. This situation testifies to the importance of groundnuts as a commercial crop in the nineteenth century. G. Le Testu, "Notes sur les cultures indigènes dans l'intérieur du Gabon," 547, confirms. He also mentions that only two species of beans were grown on the coast, and there they were planted on small surfaces only. Yet beans were important in the slave-trading era as food for

slaves on board ship; cf. N. Uring, *The Voyages and Travels*, 41, 47. Beans were also a major crop in the inner basin during the nineteenth century.

35. J. Vansina, *Tio Kingdom*, 266–310, 450; M. d'Atri, "Relations sur le royaume du Congo, 1690–1700," 64 (Malebo Pool); R. Harms, *River of Wealth*, (middle Zaire River); G. Le Testu, "Notes sur les cultures indigènes," 542 (grown in *falga*), 543 (Masango).

36. For examples of intensive agriculture, see G. Sautter, *De l'Atlantique* 1:262–64 (Bonga), 500–510 (Kongo), 606–11 and 617–18 (Kamba); and V. Drachousoff, *Essai sur l'agriculture indigène au Bas-Congo*, 127–55. For *kitemo*, working parties, and then associations, see G. Sautter, *De l'Atlantique*, 561–63; A. Thonnar, *Essai sur le système économique des primitifs*, 64–65; J. Vansina, *Tio Kingdom*, 81, 114.

37. P. Van Leynseele, "Les Libinza," 55–56; Mumbanza mwa Bamwele, "Histoire," 219–22, 254–58, 282–88, 312–14, 319–26.

38. G. Sautter, *De l'Atlantique* 1:259–64; P. Geisler, "Allgemeiner Bericht über die Kongo-Lobaje Expedition," 106.

39. See map 7.2 and also, e.g., P. Van Leynseele, "Les Libinza," endmap.

40. E. Zorzi. *Al Congo con Brazza*, 371, 376.

41. R. Harms, *River of Wealth*, 48–70, discusses the growing regional economy along the Zaire upstream of the Malebo Pool. See also J. Vansina, *Tio Kingdom*, 277–81.

42. P. D. Curtin, *Atlantic Slave Trade*, 116–26, 205–73, and summary fig. 26 (266); P. Lovejoy, *Transformations in Slavery*, 44–54, 144–46.

43. J. Miller, *Way of Death*, 151, 153, table 5.2 (165).

44. H. Klein, "The Portuguese Slave Trade from Angola in the Eighteenth Century," 914 n. 41; J. Miller, *Way of Death*, 159–64. Fewer than 10 percent of the slaves exported were children; see H. Klein, "Portuguese Slave Trade," 903–5. The loss of the reproductive capacity of 4,525.9 women (all presumed fertile) not compensated by the higher fertility of polygynous households amounts to $2,444,000 \div 6 = 407,333.33 = 0.11$ percent per year.

45. L. Degrandpré, *Voyage* 2:x, 25, 37 (1786–87 and earlier). He counted a sixth (16.6 percent) as from the Zaire River, a fourth (25 percent) as, or acquired by, Teke, and the rest (58.4 percent) as "Mayombe," including southern Gabonese. Slaves bought by Kongo, almost all from central Africa, were sold in Kabinda; at Malemba, the third harbor, both "Mayombe" and "Kongo" were sold. Equal weight in numbers is given here to the three harbors. In reality Loango had a smaller volume of slave exports then than the two others and hence Kongo are certainly underestimated. A third of the Kabinda exports is credited to Mondonge and two-thirds to Kongo and Sonho, which may again be an underestimate. There is something wrong with S. Koelle's sample of slaves c. 1830–1840 (P. D. Curtin, *Atlantic Slave Trade*, 295–98): there are no slaves at all from upstream on the Zaire farther than the confluence of the Kwa. On the other hand the relative numbers given for lower Zaire, lower Congo, Gabon, and Cameroon correspond to expectations.

46. Too many variables are involved here to allow for any useful calculation. Women's work increased during the period of heavy slave trading because they took over a portion of male tasks. Moreover the processing of cassava added greatly to the work load. For unfree women the work load may have been heavy enough to increase the chance of miscarriages. And as R. Harms, *River of Wealth*, 182–84, found among the Bobangi under these circumstances, many women resorted to abortion.

47. J. Vansina, *Kingdoms of the Savanna*, 48–50. King Affonso rejected the gist of the regimento of 1512, which proposed to model Kongo's administration, titulature, and laws after those of Portugal. A. Hilton, *Kingdom of Kongo*, passim, discusses the integration of foreign religion and foreign ideas into the social structure of Kongo before 1665. But her reconstruction of Kongo religion and of some social institutions before 1483 goes too far beyond what the evidence warrants (8–31).

48. A. Hilton, *Kingdom of Kongo*, gives perhaps the best-balanced account despite a tendency to overrate economic factors and underrate institutional innovation in Houses and matrilineal groups. See also J. Thornton, "Early Kongo-Portuguese Relations: A New Interpretation," 183–204.

49. J. Thornton, *The Kingdom of Kongo*, 85–121 (general), 117–19 (new oral tradition); J. Janzen, *Lemba*, 1650–1930, 49–51, 61–70.

50. Contrast the evidence in P. Martin, "Family Strategies in Nineteenth-Century Cabinda" with the idealized views in J. Martins Vaz, *No mundo dos Cabindas* 1:171–77 (kinship), 2:11–59, 151–75 (state of Ngoy), and 2:175–83 (dynastic history of Ngoy). On *ndunga*, see ibid., 1:50–58; Z. Volavka, "Le *Ndunga.*"

51. P. Martin, *External Trade*, 159–74. There was a regency already in 1701; cf. N. Uring, *Voyages*, 29; F. Hagenbucher Sacripanti, *Fondements spirituels*, 61–64, 70, 72, 75–76, 78–99. P. P. Rey, *Colonialisme*, 255–59; J. Janzen, *Lemba*, 46–49.

52. P. Martin, *External Trade*, 168–69, P. P. Rey, *Colonialisme*, 197–99, 266, 514.

53. J. Janzen, *Lemba*, 5 (map of trading routes); P. P. Rey, *Colonialisme*, 220–24; P. Martin, *External Trade*, 18 (Bungu destroyed in 1623 and "Jaga" in 1642).

54. J. Janzen, *Lemba*, 51–61, 70–79 (central *lemba* region), 95–272 (variants).

55. J. Vansina, *Tio Kingdom*, 455 (map 16), 456–63; P. Bonnafé, *Histoire sociale d'un peuple congolais*, 47–51; M.-C. Dupré, "Naissances et renaissances du masque kidumu," 27–45; I. Löffler, "Beiträge," 78–79; Y.-N. Gambeg, "Pouvoir politique," 464–94; J. Ollandet, "Les contacts Teke-Mbosi," 197–201; T. Obenga, *La cuvette congolaise*, 41. The contents of major Tio *nkobi* are said to stem in part from Loango and symbolize the ocean, wealth, peaceful relations, and power.

56. M. Alihanga, Structures, 151–53 (warlords), 240–41 (ancestral sanction), 259 (nkobi); L. Perrois et al., Gabon: Culture et techniques, 77–79 (carvings surmounting Mbede reliquaries); E. Andersson, Contribution à l'ethnographie des Kuta 1:169–71 (warlords).

57. R. Harms, River of Wealth, 30, 71–85, 126–42; J. Vansina, Tio Kingdom, 449; F. E. Dhanis, "District d'Upoto," 26, 27 (slave origins); 28 (trade language as far as Yalulema).

58. R. Harms, River of Wealth, 119–121, 143–59, 163–74 (older House), 175–96 (newer firm), 183–84 (population control); Mumbanza mwa Bamwele, "Histoire," 462–72. A. Thonnar, Essai sur le système économique, 17–27, 30–37 (both lower Zaire and inner basin); Mpase Nselenge Mpeti, L'évolution; 16, 94, 159–60 (the mbwayoyi leader of a firm among the Ntomba of Mai Ndombe and firms).

59. J. Vansina, Tio Kingdom, 74.

60. A. Thonnar, Essai sur le système économique, 37–39 (women's work and hierarchy. What he says of a lemba wife in lower Congo also applied to first wives in the firms of the inner basin). On social mobility, see R. Harms, River of Wealth, 157–58 (in Bolobo the slave Mobombo succeeded the chief Ebaka); M. Froment, "Trois affluents français du Congo," 467 (at Bonga the slave Ndombi succeeded to the paramount Mpakama, probably in the 1870s or earlier, but lost the paramountcy); J. Vansina, Tio Kingdom, 408–9 (Ngaliema); and other cases are known (Mumbanza mwa Bamwele "Histoire," 472–74). Ngankabe, "queen of the Nunu," was an example of a successful woman leader in the 1870s and 1880s; see M. Storme, Ngankabe, 66–76. In 1886 a woman, Combabéka, also exercised considerable influence in Bonga as an ally of now "old" chief Ndombi; see C. Coquery Vidrovitch, Brazza et la prise de possession du Congo, 1883–1885, 467.

61. For ezo and likundu, see R. Harms, River of Wealth, 200–203. The belief in likundu witch substance and the autopsy after death spread from the lower Congo and Gabon along the trade routes as far as Uele; see H. Baumann, "Likundu: Die Sektion der Zauberkraft."

62. G. Hulstaert, Le mariage des nkundo, 348–54, and a story of how a usurper died on the spot (348–49, bolumbu).

63. L. Siroto, "Masks and Social Organisation among the Bakwele People of Western Equatorial Africa," 294–314.

64. C. Coquilhat, Sur le Haut-Congo, 189–94, 198–212 (Mata Bwike); A. Thonnar, Essai sur le système économique, 26.

65. Mumbanza mwa Bamwele, "Histoire," 457–62; J. Vansina, Tio Kingdom, 74, 255–56. All figures given by contemporary visitors were estimates only, but they were internally consistent.

66. For Nkasa slave raiding on Momboyo-Tshuapa, Lulonga, cf. G. Van der Kerken, L'Ethnie Mongo, 469–71, and index "Nkasa" (1100); G. Hulstaert, Eléments, 70–71. For traditions in the Lobaye area: L. Bouquiaux and J. N. C. Thomas, "Le peuplement oubanguien," 810–12; S. Bahuchet, "Notes pour

l'histoire de la région de Bagandou," 54–55 (Ngando); J. M. C. Thomas, *Les Ngbaka de la Lobaye*, 255–58.

67. E. Sulzmann, "La soumission des Ekonda par les Bombomba," 5–11, 17; Colle, "Les Gombe," 162–67. E. J. Glave, *Six Years of Adventure in Congoland*, 188–205.

68. Almost every source comments on fortifications in these areas. For example, E. Froment, "Un voyage dans l'Oubangui," 211 (Monzombo and Lobala); Colle, "Les Gombe," 165–66, 167; E. J. Glave, *Six Years of Adventure*, 189; and remnants seen by M. Eggert, "Archäologische Forschungen," 3238–40 (Ngombe-Mongo); F. Thonner, *Dans la grande forêt de l'Afrique centrale*, 45, 64, 68; J. De Wilde, "Dans la Mongala," 187; S. Bahuchet, "Notes pour l'histoire," 54–55 (Ngando). However, the area completely escaped the attention of P. Briart, "Les fortifications indigènes au Congo."

69. H. Nicolai, *Le Kwilu*, 117–29; G. De Plaen, *Les structures d'autorité chez les Bayansi*, 3–12; H. Van Roy, *Les Byaambvu du Moyen Kwango*, 80–128; M. Plancquaert, *Les Yaka*, 110–18, 176; R. Tonnoir, *Giribuma*, 218–24; Ndaywell, "Organisation," 399–408.

70. J. Vansina, *Children of Woot*, 127–96.

71. J. H. Van Linschoten, *Itinerario*, 4–13; P. de Marees, *Beschryvinghe*, 243–45; K. D. Patterson, *Northern Gabon Coast*, 1–25; H. Bucher, "Mpongwe Origins," 60–61, 64–70; A. Raponda Walker, *Notes d'histoire du Gabon*, 49–59; E. Mbokolo, *Noirs et Blancs en Afrique Equatoriale*, 12–28. See also chapter 5, nn. 95 and 98.

72. P. de Marees, *Beschryvinghe*, 244–51; J. A. Avaro, *Un peuple gabonais*, 97–114, 143–46; G. Gaulme, *Le pays de Cama*, 89–175. See also chapter 5, nn. 95–97.

73. K. D. Patterson, *Northern Gabon Coast*, 26–67; H. Bucher, "The Mpongwe," 117–39; idem, "The Settlement of the Mpongwe Clans in the Gabon Estuary," 149–75; T. E. Bowdich, *Mission from Cape Coast Castle to Ashantee*, 424–39, for the hinterland of Gabon as it was then known to traders.

74. J. A. Avaro, *Un peuple gabonais*, 146–54 (Orungu), 219–29 (Galwa); A. Raponda Walker, *Notes d'histoire du Gabons*, 60–89; K. D. Patterson, *Northern Gabon Coast*, 68–89; Bodinga wa Bodinga, *Tradition orale de la race Eviya*, 10; H. Deschamps, *Traditions orales*, 21 n. 1, 40 n. 19, 42 n. 22 (kidnaping bird); M. Koumba-Manfoumbi, "Les Punu du Gabon, des origines à 1899," 241–50.

75. E. Ardener, "Rise of Trading Polities between Rio del Rey and Cameroons: 1500–1650"; J. Bouchaud, *La côte du Cameroun dans l'histoire et la cartographie*, 35–90. In 1603 Ulsheimer traded for ivory in the Cameroon Estuary. There was no major town, no trade language was known, and trade occurred on the river. Indeed the inhabitants first tried to storm the ship. Despite there not being a major town, there must have been an above-average density of population, given that they attacked with some 60 canoes; see W. Crecelius, "Josua Ulsheimers Reisen nach Guinea und Beschreibung des Landes," 102–3 (translated in A. Jones, *German Sources*, 25, 343–44).

76. R. Austen and K. Jakob, *Dutch Trading Voyages*, 24; J. Bouchaud, *La côte du Cameroun*, 91–123; L. Z. Elango, "Britain and Bimbia in the 19th Century (1833–1878)," 11–17. See E. Ardener, *Coastal Bantu of the Cameroons*, 27, for the expulsion of a major Duala leader, Bile, from Douala to Bimbia well before 1826 as the last break off. Earlier Duala leaders had left to try their luck as leaders in Kpe country or formed fishing settlements (Kole) west of Mt. Fako. G. Balandier, "Economie, société et pouvoir chez les Duala anciens," 361–79, stresses the role of the associations, but misses the genealogic irregularities which clearly betray that the Duala were, by 1800, a collection of Houses not strictly organized into lineages.

77. P. Laburthe-Tolra, *Les seigneurs de la forêt*, 127–96; P. Alexandre, "Protohistoire," 531–35, 557 (Bulu, Fang); J. F. Vincent, "Traditions historiques chez les Djem de Souanke," 65–67 (Bulu war); idem, "Dot et monnaie de fer," 276–78 (Djem and Bekwil).

78. C. Chamberlin, "The Migration of the Fang," 429–56; H. Deschamps, *Traditions orales*, 65–66 (Kota), 72 (Shake), 75–76 (Bekwil), 78–80 (Bichiwa), 83–86 (Fang), 91–92 (Ntumu), 103 (Fang Betsi). See chapter 5, n. 101.

79. G. Dupré, *Le commerce*, 645–57; E. Andersson, *Ethnographie*, 26–30 (30–35 is pure speculation).

80. E. Mbokolo, *Noirs et blancs*, 29–147; idem, "Le roi Denis," 73–95; H. Bucher, "The Mpongwe," 223–359. Ntoko was the best-known merchant prince, well in evidence by 1836, and the one who helped the Presbyterians to start a mission in 1842; see T. Omboni, "Viaggi nell'Africa Occidentale," 217–31 (219–20 for portrait of Songhey and Ntoko, "esteemed traders on these coasts entirely trustworthy in matters of business").

81. K. D. Patterson, *Northern Gabon Coast*, 108–49; J. A. Avaro, *Un peuple gabonais*, 152–73 (Orungu), 231–36 (Galwa); G. Gaulme, *Le pays de Cama*, 189–96; O. Lenz, *Skizzen aus West Afrika*, 193–205; idem, "Reise auf dem Okande in West Afrika," 250–52.

82. A. Wirz, *Vom Sklavenhandel*, 45–52; idem, "La rivière du Cameroun," 178–94; R. Austen, "Slavery among Coastal Middlemen," 305–33; E. Mveng, *Histoire du Cameroun*, 171–81; J. Bouchaud, *La côte du Cameroun*, 125–57; L. Z. Elango, "Britain and Bimbia," 25–33 and passim; C. Dikoume, "Les Elog Mpoo," 114 n. 6, 211–12.

83. A. Wirz, "La rivière de Cameroun," 176–78, for missionary influences in the matter.

84. J. Jacobs and J. Vansina, "Nshoong atoot: het koninklijk epos van de Kuba," 32–35.

85. Corrosive effects are not an inevitable law of nature. In many cases the first political impact of a world economy was to help produce a spatial scale of political organization to match the economic expansion. The Lunda state in central Africa grew into a slave-raiding empire after 1700 and began to feel "corroding effects" only by the 1850s. In West Africa the Asante and Danxome states established themselves in an area and era of intensive participation in the Atlantic trade. Rather than corroding or wilting away under the onslaught of

ever more massive trade, a series of states from Egypt to Madagascar blossomed in the nineteenth century as imperial expansions by economic proxy.

Chapter Eight: Death of a Tradition

1. This estimate was given in 1919 by the commission for the protection of the autochthons for the Belgian Congo (O. Louwers and A. Hoornaert, *La question sociale au Congi*, 23) and may well turn out to be an underestimate. The cases reported in note 13 may appear to be dramatic extremes, but there are many parallels especially from lower Zaire, lower Congo, Equateur province, and north Kasai, which explains why the commission gave its estimates. Equally dramatic losses were reported from north Congo (especially the lower Likouala, Alima, and Sangha areas), the lower Lobaye, and from most of Gabon. Major epidemics, a primary cause of mortality, tapered off only after the swine flu epidemic of 1918–1919, and when measures in the struggle against sleeping sickness became effective, also after 1920.

2. C. Keim, "Precolonial Mangbetu Rule," 232, 240–310; P. Ceulemans, *La question arabe et le Congo (1883–1892);* 326–31; R. D. Mohun, "Consular Dispatch from Basoko Camp," 36; P. Salmon, *La dernière insurrection de Mopoie Bangezegino.*

3. J. Vansina, *Kingdoms of the Savanna*, 235–41; P. Ceulemans, *La question arabe*, passim; F. Bontinck, *L'autobiographie de Hamed ben Mohammed el-Murjebi Tippo Tib (ca. 1840–1905).* On Zanzibari auxiliaries, cf. P. Salmon, "Les carnets de campagne," 272–73; R. D. Mohun, *Consular Dispatch*, 41. On Zanzibari influence just after their defeat (Fall 1894), see E. J. Glave, "New Conditions in Central Africa" 31:906–15, 32:699–705; and by May 1920, J. Druart, "Carte succincte," legend "arabisés."

4. J. Abemba, *Pouvoir politique traditionnel et Islam au Congo oriental*, 9–14; W. de Mahieu, "Les Komo," 99–100. On *mokota* chiefs, Zanzibari rule, and chiefs in lower Lomami, see L. Appermans, "Chefferie Kombe," 67, 69, 73.

5. N. Metegue N'nah, *L'implantation coloniale au Gabon*, 15–65; E. Mbokolo, *Noirs et blancs*, 41–218, esp. 151–75; O. Baumann, *Eine Afrikanische Tropen-insel:* 104–5.

6. A. Lejeune Choquet, *Histoire militaire; La Force Publique:* J. Meyers, *Le prix d'un empire.* On the 1897 mutiny, cf. P. Salmon, *La révolte des Batetela de l'expédition du Haut-Ituri;* J.-L. Vellut, "La violence armée dans l'État Indépendant du Congo."

7. Recent studies are D. Van Groenweghe, *Du sang sur les lianes;* J.-L. Vellut and D. Van Groenweghe, "Le rapport Casement"; R. Harms, "The World Abir Made." The military histories (see n. 6) carry reports of only the few more sizable military operations.

8. M. Denis, *Histoire militaire de l'Afrique equatoriale française.* For the rubber regime, see C. Coquery Vidrovitch, *Le Congo*, esp. 71–220.

9. H. Rudin, *Germans in the Cameroons*, 193–97; A. Rüger, "Die Aufstand der Polizeisoldaten"; individual reports on military expeditions mainly

in the issues of *Deutsches Kolonialblatt,* e.g., Scheunemann, "Die Unruhen im Südbezirk von Kamerun 1904 bis 1906" 18:347–52, 391–99. For the rubber regime, see A. Wirz, *Vom Sklavenhandel,* 107–47; and for a specific situation by 1914, see L. Haase, *Durch unbekanntes Kamerun,* 93–96.

10. For military operations against the Bekwil, cf. M. Denis *Histoire militaire;* Treichel, "Die Lage im Postenbereich Sembe von 1 Oktober 1912 bis 30 September 1913"; Heym, "Die Gefechte gegen die aufständige Ebaleute im Bezirk Sembe"; G. Teßmann, "Ethnologisches aus dem südöstlichen Kamerun," 91; C. Robineau, "Contribution à l'histoire du Congo," 302–13.

11. P. Salmon, "Les carnets de campagne," 244. The area was at war from 1886–1887 to 1906 with successive Zanzibari and Independent Congo State occupations, including two year-long uprisings (1894–1895 and 1906) against the rubber regime.

12. M.-C. Dupré, "La dualité du pouvoir politique chez les Teke de l'ouest," 80–90, esp. 88–89. The last campaign lasted from 1912 to 1916. The data for the three remaining villages are from 1933.

13. In general, see R. Headrick, "The Impact of Colonialism on Health in French Aequatorial Africa, 1880–1934." On sleeping sickness, see M. Lyons, "The Colonial Disease." On the lower Kwa, see A. De Backer, "Brief," 460–61 (Ebeke, arrival and destruction caused by the arrival of the Ponthier column); E. Costermans, "Le district du Stanley Pool," 26; idem, "Reconnaissance du pays entre le Congo, le Kassai et le Kwango," 40–42, 53–54 (still many people in 1897; Tua had 7,000 inhabitants); L. Anckaer, *De Evangelizatiemetode van de Missionarissen van Scheut in Kongo,* 110 (the mission was abolished in 1900 because the population was perishing as a result of sleeping sickness); L. Hamerlinck, "Un voyage chez les Bamfunuka," 17 (in 1932 sleeping sickness still ravaged the country and Tua counted only a few hundred inhabitants—maybe 5 percent of its former population). For a case in lower Zaire, see H. A. Johnston, *George Grenfell* 2:547–53.

14. See A. De Backer in n. 13.

15. R. H. Nassau, *Fetichism in West Africa,* 141–55 (cases in Corisco, Rio Muní, Batanga, and near Ndjole from the 1850s to 1879). Ibia j'Ikëngë, *Customs of the Benga and Neighboring Tribes,* with a motto on the title page: "The customs of the people are vain," quoting the prophet Jeremiah.

16. For the *Lilwá,* see H. Sutton Smith, *Yakusu,* 61–68; W. Millman, "The Tribal Initiation Ceremony of the Lokele," 365–68. The *mambela* of the Bali in the same area was eventually outlawed as a "front" for terrorist attacks, after missionaries such as J. Christen and Kawaters ("Reifezeremonien") pressed the government to "exile all authorities responsible for *mambela*" (J. Christen, *Mambela et Anyoto,* 54). Kuba initiation was strongly opposed by all missionaries and finally forbidden in the early years of the depression, because it lowered productivity. Although associations often continued in abbreviated and anemic forms in many cases, very few survived in their original richness, as happened among the Tsogo. For an introductory summary of their *bwiti,* see A. Raponda-Walker and R. Sillans, *Rites et croyances,* 171–214. R. Sillans and O. Gollnhofer have published many works about this *bwiti.*

17. A sharp increase in the rise of specific religious movements to cope with this repression occurred after 1920 as a last major reaction stemming from adherence to the principles of the old tradition. For examples of such movements, see G. Dupré, *Un ordre et sa destruction,* 354–85; J.-F. Vincent, "Le mouvement Croix Koma"; J. Vansina, "Lukoshi, Lupambula." These should not be confused with the rise of African churches or the Fang *bwiti,* which are attempts at the construction of a new tradition.

18. A. F. Roberts, "Social and Historical Contexts of Tabwa Art," 21 (Monsignor Roelens, bishop of upper Zaire). Such statements also occur in administrative reports. The curse of Cham was a virtual cliché among all missionaries, especially before 1940.

19. J. Vansina, "Ethnographic Account," 434–35.

20. A. de Calonne-Beaufaict, *Les Ababua.* The model was quickly adopted by the jurist F. Cattier and the administrators A. Bertrand ("Quelques notes sur la vie politique," 75–89) and G. Van der Kerken (*Les sociétés bantoues,* ii, 71–72, 78–79 [Ababua], 81–86), who were able to impose it as "the organization" to be found everywhere before 1920. For the Ngombe case, see A. Wolfe, *In the Ngombe Tradition.* "Patriarch" was a term invented by G. Van der Kerken (see *Lès sociétés bantoues,* 81), according to A. Bertrand. It was given legal substance as the "paternate" a legal neologism coined by E. Possoz, *Eléments du droit coutumier nègre,* 22–24, 65–75, 97–101.

21. The direct lines of the administrative imposition of the new rural structures remain to be traced for the French and German colonies. For French Equatorial Africa, see A. Cureau (*Les sociétés primitives*) and G. Bruel (*L'Afrique équatoriale française,* 186–99, and *La France équatoriale africaine,* 167–210), who shared the same "administrative" view of equatorial Africans as families living in villages. But how this view developed and who imposed it on the administrators remains unclear.

22. For Tio descent, see J. Vansina, *Tio Kingdom,* 29–40; J. Druart, "Carte succincte," "Basonge," still mentioned "a rather special system of an aristocratic republic with temporary sovereignty or presidency" in 1920. But then G. Van der Kerken, *Les sociétés bantoues,* 89, labeled this *eata* system as "a decadent conception, born from the loosening of tribal ties and, probably, of the disappearance in the clan or the tribe, of the family of the chiefs by right of blood." And since his book was authoritative, that was that. In the same way, he had also dismissed the existence of leaders of firms as "disaggregation" and not "the old organization" (84 n. 1).

23. A. Sohier, *Le mariage en droit coutumier congolais.* For *lengbe,* see R. Cleire, "Les bases socio-culturelles du mariage traditionnel au Congo," 60–62. On customary laws in general, see E. Possoz, *Eléments du droit coutumier nègre.*

24. J. Vansina, "The Bushong Poison Oracle," 245–60.

Chapter Nine: On History and Tradition

1. For instance, the largely arbitrary shapes of throwing knives allow one to attribute confidently a common origin to similar shapes in different localities. One such particular shape is the "hornbill head," now found in northeastern Gabon and neighboring areas of Congo, and c. 1610 also in Loango. That shape must have a single common origin. Mapping the names for throwing knives yields independent evidence. The "hornbill head" knives are all called -*sele*, usually *osele*. This makes the case for diffusion from a common origin practically a certainty. But shapes and names do not always match. Thus along the Lukenie River *woshele* indicates a throwing knife of a very different design, a design which itself extends, under various names, from the Ubangi River bend to the Kuba kingdom. In general, see J. Vansina, *Art History,* 168–73.

2. Such as guns adapted to shoot spears (J. Vansina, *Tio Kingdom,* 123) or Cabinda shipwrights building ships seaworthy enough for sailing to Brazil despite the lack of appropriate tools (J.-L. Vellut, "Notes sur l'économie," 11 n. 2).

3. The Tio Kingdom is an extreme example of decentralization. It was a kingdom only because the inhabitants held it to be one. There was no central administration, judicial system, army, or tribute system. Senior lords were practically autonomous, but there was only one king and no duplication of senior titles.

4. As the existence of "dead zones" shows. See chapter 3, n. 36.

5. See T. K. Earle, "Chiefdoms in Archaeological and Ethnohistorical Perspective," 279–308, for a recent bibliography and survey of social evolutionary theory. Africanists have always been allergic to its appeal; see, for example, I. Kopytoff, "The African Frontier," 77–78.

6. R. Harms, *Games against Nature,* 97–113.

7. G. Hulstaert, *Notes de botanique mongo;* A. Raponda-Walker and R. Sillans, *Les plantes utiles;* and to a lesser degree of completeness, E. De Wildeman, *Sur des plantes médicinales utiles du Mayumbe (Congo belge),* and A. Bouquet, *Féticheurs et médecines traditionelles.* I know of the inadequacy of anthropologists from personal experience among the Tio. I simply could not follow their instructions in the botany of their grasslands.

8. L. Fiedler and J. Preuss "Stone Tools from the Inner Zaire Basin," 182 (Ruki-Kwa stone tools). In general, see J. Vansina, "L'homme, les forêts et le passé en Afrique."

9. M. Sahlins, *Stone Age Economics,* 33–34 (hunter gatherers in general), R. Harms, *River of Wealth,* 182–83 (Bobangi). Among the Ntomba and Sengele of Lake Mai Ndombe, a woman was to abstain from intercourse after parturition until her child was old enough to walk (about two years of age). Then she presented the child to the leader of her House or firm and received formal permission to resume intercourse.

10. See map 2.4b, after a portion of R. Letouzey's map of Cameroon.

11. Thus the correlation between the length of the dry season and the size of the working party of men needed for slash-and-burn clearing is clear. But that

does not exclude a range of options to choose from. For variations, see L. E. Sponsel, "Amazon Ecology and Adaptation"; R. Mischung, "Seßhaftigkeit und Intensivierung beim Brandrodungsfeldbau" (Hmong).

12. E. Hobsbawm and T. Ranger, eds., *The Invention of Tradition;* D. Lowenthal, *The Past Is a Foreign Country.*

13. In African historiography, moreover, "tradition"—and even more, "traditional"—in colonial times meant a static precolonial situation and signaled a complete denial or disregard of precolonial history. Hence the terms became anathema to most later historians. Some nationalist authors, however, continued to used the terms in the same meaning as their colonialist opponents had done, but reversed their emotional polarity. They now implied African originality unsullied by foreign accretions.

14. P. Bellwood, *The Polynesians: Prehistory of an Island People;* I. Goldman, *Ancient Polynesian Society;* P. V. Kirch, *The Evolution of Polynesian Chiefdoms;* P. V. Kirch and R. C. Green, "History, Phylogeny, and Evolution in Polynesia"; F. Lichtenberg, "Leadership in Proto-Oceanic Society: Linguistic Evidence."

15. As is evident from the detailed studies in E. Rogers and F. Shoemaker, *Communication of Innovations,* and H. Barnett, *Innovation.*

16. E. Shils, *Tradition.*

17. I. Kopytoff, "African Frontier," 33–34.

18. I. Kopytoff, "African Frontier," 10, 15, for the citations. For a listing of the major precolonial traditions in Africa, see J. Devisse and J. Vansina, "Africa from the Seventh to the Eleventh Centuries," 750–93.

19. I. Kopytoff, "African Frontier," 22.

Works Cited

Acronyms

AIMO. Files *affaires indigènes et main-d'oeuvre*. In the ethnography section of the Royal Museum of Central Africa, Tervuren, Belgium.

ARSOM. *Académie royale des Sciences d'Outre-Mer*. Brussels. Unless otherwise noted, the primary series title for works cited with this abbreviation is Memoirs, Division of Moral and Political Science. The secondary, specific series designation is given with each title in the reference list. From 1955 to 1960 the institution was called Académie royale des Sciences coloniales. Before 1955 it was the Institut royal colonial belge. A new numbering of the memoirs began in 1955.

AT. *Administrateur territorial*. Official in charge of a "territory," Belgian Congo.

CEDAF. *Cahiers du centre d'étude et de documentation africaines*. Brussels. These are monographs.

CEMUBAC. *Centre scientifique et médical de l'Université Libre de Bruxelles en Afrique centrale*. Memoirs.

EHESS. *Ecole des Hautes Etudes en Sciences Sociales*. Centre de recherches historiques. Civilisation et Sociétés series.

K. Summary of archives of the former territory of Isangi made by Herman Jansen. Deposited in the archives of the congregation of Monfort, Kessel Lo, Belgium.

L. N. de Cleene and E. de Jonghe Collection. Library, Katolieke Universiteit van Leuven, Louvain, Belgium.

MRAC. *Musée royal de l'Afrique centrale* (Royal Museum of Central Africa, Tervuren, Belgium). Unless otherwise noted, the primary series title for works cited with this abbrevation is Human Sciences, Annals. The secondary, specific series designation is given with each title in the reference list.

ORSTOM. *Office de la recherche scientifique et technique d'Outre-Mer*. Paris. Unless otherwise noted, the acronym refers to memoirs.

W. M. De Ryck collection, Memorial Library, University of Wisconsin–Madison.

References

Abbeloos, R. V. "De sekte lilwa." *Band* 8 (1949): 311–13.

Abemba, J. *Pouvoir politique traditionnel et Islam au Congo oriental.* CEDAF 2. Brussels, 1971.

African Archaeological Review. 1983–.

Ainti, G. "Les Mituku." L. 89/2.

Alexandre, P. "Proto-histoire du groupe Beti-Bulu-Fang." *Cahiers d'études africaines* 20 (1965): 403–560.

Alexandre, P., and J. Binet. *Le groupe dit Pahouin (Fang-Boulou-Beti).* Paris, 1958.

Alihanga, M. *Structures communautaires traditionelles et perspectives coopératives dans la société altogovéenne.* Rome, 1976.

Almquist, L. A. "Symbolic Consensus in Ritual Practice: An Ethnography of Differentiation in Pagibeti Rites of Passage." Ph.D. diss., Indiana University, 1985. Ann Arbor.

Amat, C. "Ngovayang II. Une village du sud-Cameroun," Paris. Ecole pratique des Hautes Etudes, VI section 1972.

Anckaer, L. *De Evangelizatiemetode van de missionarissen van Scheut in Kongo.* ARSOM, n.s. 38, 1. Brussels, 1970.

Andersson, E. *Contribution à l'ethnographie des Kuta.* 2 vols. Uppsala, 1953.

Ankei, Y. "Connaissance populaire du poisson chez les Songola et les Bwari." *Senri Ethnological Studies* 15 (1984): 1–68.

Annaert, J. *Contribution à l'étude géographique de l'habitat et de l'habitation indigènes en milieu rural dans les provinces Orientale et du Kivu.* ARSOM, *Sciences médicales et naturelles,* n.s. 10, 3. Brussels, 1960.

Annaert Bruder, A. "La densité de la population du Congo-Kinshasa." *Revue belge de géographie* 91 (1967): 139–60.

Anttila, R. *An Introduction to Historical and Comparative Linguistics.* New York, 1972.

Appermans, L. "Chefferie Kombe." K. 62–79.

Ardener, E. *Coastal Bantu of the Cameroons.* London, 1956.

Ardener, E. "Documentary and Linguistic Evidence for the Rise of the Trading Polities between Rio del Rey and Cameroons: 1500–1650." In *History and Social Anthropology,* ed. I. M. Lewis, 81–126. London, 1968.

Austen, R. A. "Slavery among Coastal Middlemen: The Duala of Cameroon." In *Slavery in Africa: Historical and Anthropological Perspectives,* ed. S. Miers and I. Kopytoff, 305–34. Madison, 1977.

Austen, R. A., and K. Jacob. "Dutch Trading Voyages to Cameroun, 1721–1759: European Documents and African History." *Annales de la Faculté des lettres de l'université de Yaounde* 6 (1974): 1–27.

Autenrieth, F. *Ins Inner-Hochland von Kamerun: Eigene Reiseerlebnisse.* Stuttgart, 1913.

Avaro, J. A. *Un peuple gabonais à l'aube de la colonisation: Le Bas-Ogowe au XIXᵉ siècle.* Paris, 1981.

Avelot, R. "Notice historique sur les Ba-Kalé." *L'Anthropologie,* 24 (1913): 197–241.

Avelot, R. "Recherches sur l'histoire des migrations dans le bassin de l'Ogooué et la région littorale adjacente." *Bulletin de géographie historique et descriptive* 20, 3 (1905): 357–412.

Aymemi, A. *Los Bubis en Fernando Poo.* Madrid, 1942.

Bahuchet, S. "Etude écologique, d'un campement de pygmées Babinga." *Journal d'agriculture tropicale et de botanique appliquée* 19, 12 (1978): 509–59

Bahuchet, S. "Notes pour l'histoire de la région de Bagandou" In idem, *Pygmées de Centrafrique,* 51–76. Paris, 1979.

Bahuchet, S. *Les pygmées aka de la forêt centrafricaine: Ethnologie écologique.* Paris, 1985.

Bahuchet, S., and H. Guillaume. "Relations entre chasseurs-collecteurs pygmées et agriculteurs de la forêt du nord-ouest du bassin congolais." In *Pygmées de Centrafrique,* ed. S. Bahuchet, 109–39. Paris, 1979.

Bailey, R. C. "The Socioecology of Efe Pygmy Men in the Ituri Forest." Ph.D. diss., Harvard University, 1985. Ann Arbor.

Balandier, G. "Economie, société et pouvoir chez les Duala anciens." *Cahiers d'études africaines* 59 (1975): 361–80.

Baldi, P. "Archaeology and Language." *Current Anthropology* 29 (1988): 445–447.

Ballif, N. *Les danseurs de Dieu: Chez les pygmées de la Sangha.* Paris, 1954.

Baltus, M. "Les Walese." *Bulletin des juridictions indigènes et du droit coutumier congolais* 17, 4 (1949): 114–22.

Balz, H. *Where the Faith Has to Live: Studies in Bakossi Society and Religion.* 2 vols. Basel, 1984.

Barbier, J. C. *Mimboo, reine d'Asem,* Yaounde, 1978.

Barbot, J., Jr., and J. Casseneuve. "An Abstract of a Voyage to the Congo River or the Zaire and to Cabinde in the Year 1700." In *A Collection of Voyages and Travels,* ed. A. Churchill, vol. 5. London 1732.

Barnes, J. A. "African Models in the New Guinea Highlands." *Man* 1 (1962): 5–10.

Barnett, H. G. *Innovation: The Basis of Cultural Change.* New York, 1953.

Bassani, E. "I disegni dei Manoscritti Araldi del Padre Giovanni Antonio Cavazzi da Montecucolo." *Quaderni Poro* 4 (1987): 9–87.

Bastin, Y. *Bibliographie bantoue sélective.* MRAC Archives d'anthropologie 24. Tervuren, 1975

Bastin, Y., and A. Coupez. "Classification lexicostatistique des langues bantoues." Pers. com., 1985.

Bastin, Y., A. Coupez, and B. de Halleux. "Classification lexicostatistique des langues bantoues (214 relevés)." *Bulletin de l'ARSOM* 27, 2 (1983): 173–99.

Battell, A. See E. Ravenstein.

Baumann, H., ed. *Die Völker Afrikas und ihre traditionellen Kulturen.* 2 vols. Wiesbaden, 1975–1979.

Baumann, H. "Likundu: Die Sektion der Zauberkraft." *Zeitschrift für Ethnologie* 60 (1928): 73–85.

Baumann, H., and D. Westermann. *Les peuples et les civilisations de l'Afrique.* Translated from the German by L. Homburger. Paris, 1948.

Baumann, O. *Eine Afrikanische Tropen-Insel: Fernando Poo und die Bube.* Vienna, 1888.

Bayle des Hermens, R. "The Prehistory of Central Africa, Part 1." In *General History of Africa. Volume 1: Methodology and African Prehistory,* ed. J. Ki Zerbo, 530–50. UNESCO, Paris, 1981.

"Les Bekeni: Origines et migrations." AIMO, Bafwasende 2. Bafwaboli, 1925.

Bekombo-Priso, Manga. "Les classses d'âge chez les Dwala." In *Classes et associations d'âge en Afrique de l'ouest,* ed. D. Paulme, 286–307. Paris, 1971.

Bellwood, P. *The Polynesians: Prehistory of an Island People.* London, 1978.

Bengala, A. "Le noble des Booli." *Aequatoria* 25, 3 (1962): 105–11.

Bennett, P. B., and J. P. Sterk, "South Central Niger-Congo: A Reclassification." *Studies in African Linguistics* 8, 3 (1977): 241–73.

Bertrand, A. "Note sur les Mabudu-Madimbisa (dits Wasumbi)." AIMO, Kibali-Ituri 3. 1930.

Bertrand, A. "Notes pour servir à l'étude des mangbetu." Archives africaines du ministère des affaires étrangères. Brussels, c. 1932.

Bertrand, A. "Le problème 'Mongandu'." W. 20/1/2. Limba, 1925.

Bertrand, A. "Quelques notes sur la vie politique, le développement, la décadence des petites sociétés bantou du bassin central du Congo." *Revue de l'Institut de Sociologie de Bruxelles* 1 (1920): 75–91.

Bettendorf, J. "Die Angst der Mituku vor den Mizimu under deren Vertretern, den raffinierten Mekota." *Heimat und Mission* 31 (1957): 4:117–19, 5:145–48.

Bibeau, G. "De la maladie à la guérison: Essai d'analyse systémique de la médecine des Angbandi du Zaire." Ph.D. diss., Université Laval, Québec, 1979.

Biebuyck, D., *The Arts of Zaire. Vol. 11. Eastern Zaire.* Berkeley, 1986.

Biebuyck, D., *Lega Culture: Art, Initiation, and Moral Philosophy among a Central African People.* Berkeley, 1973.

Biebuyck, D., "Maternal Uncles and Sororal Nephews among the Lega." *Report of the Second Joint Conference on Research in the Social Sciences in East and Central Africa 1953,* 122–35. Kampala, 1954.

Biebuyck, D., *Les Mitamba: Systèmes de mariage enchaînés chez les Bembe.* ARSOM, n.s. 27, 2. Brussels, 1962.

Biebuyck, D., "La monnaie musanga des Balega." *Zaire* 7 (1953): 675–86.

Biebuyck, D., *"Mumbira: Musical Instrument of a Nyanga Initiation." African Arts* 7, 4 (1974): 42–45, 63–65, 96.

Biebuyck, D., "De Mumbo-instelling bij de Banyanga (Kivu)." *Kongo-Overzee* 21 (1951): 441–48.

Biebuyck, D., "Nyanga Circumcision Masks and Costumes." *African Arts* 6 (1973): 20–25, 86–92.

Biebuyck, D. "Organisation politique des Nyanga": La chefferie des Ihana." *Kongo-Overzee* 22, 4–5 (1956): 301–41; 23, 1–2 (1957): 58–98.

Biebuyck, D. "Répartition et droits du pangolin chez les Balega." *Zaire* 7 (1953): 899–924.

Biebuyck, D. *Rights in Land and Its Resources among the Nyanga.* ARSOM, n.s. 34, 2. Brussels, 1966.

Biebuyck, D. "Sculpture from the Eastern Zaire Forest Regions, Mbole, Yela and Pere." *African Arts* 10, 1 (1976): 54–61, 99.

Biebuyck, D. "La société kumu face au Kitawala." *Zaire* 11 (1957): 7–40.

Biebuyck, D. *Statuary from the Pre-Bembe Hunters: Issues in the Interpretation of Ancestral Figurines Ascribed to the Basikasingo-Bembe-Boyo.* Tervuren, 1981.

Biebuyck, D. "De vorming van fiktieve patrilineaire verwantschapsgroepen bij de Balega." *Band* 12, 4 (1953): 135–45.

Biebuyck, D., and K. Mateene. *The Mwindo Epic from the Banyanga (Republic Congo).* Berkeley, 1969.

Biffot, L. "Contribution à la connaissance et compréhension des populations rurales du nord-est du Gabon," Ph.D. diss., Université de Rennes, 1965.

Bishikwabo Chubaka. "Histoire d'un état shi en Afrique des grands lacs: Kaziba au Zaire (ca. 1850–1940)." Ph.D. diss., Université de Louvain, Louvain-la-Neuve, 1982.

Bishikwabo Chubaka. "Note sur l'origine de l'institution du 'bwami' et fondements de pouvoir politique au Kivu oriental." *Cahiers du CEDAF,* série 1, 8 (1979): 18–37.

Blakney, C. P. "On 'Banana' and 'Iron': Linguistic Footprints in African History." M.A. thesis, Hartford Seminary, Auburndale, 1963.

Bleek, W. H. I. *De nominum generibus linguarum Africae Australis.* Bonn, 1851.

Bock, E. "*Trois notes sur la secte Biba.*" AIMO, Zobia 2:1–5. 1933

Bodinga wa Bodinga. *Tradition orale de la race Eviya.* Touzet, 1969.

Boelaert, E. "Terminologie classificatoire des Nkundó." *Africa* 21 (1951): 218–23.

Bonnafé, P. *Histoire sociale d'un peuple congolais: Livre 1: La terre et le ciel.* Paris, 1987.

Bontinck, F. *L'autobiographie de Hamed ben Mohammed el-Murjebi Tippo Tib (ca. 1840–1905).* ARSOM, n.s. 42, 4. Brussels, 1974.

Bontinck, F. *Diaire congolais (1690–1701) de Fra Luca da Caltanisetta.* Louvain, 1970.

Bontinck, F. "Etat commercial du littoral . . . entre Sette et Ambriz en 1874. Document inédit." *Likundoli-O,* 5, 2 (1977): 165–83.

Bontinck, F., ed. *Histoire du royaume du Congo (c. 1624).* Special issue of *Etudes d'histoire africaine,* IV 4 (Louvain) 4 (1972).

Borms, Cdt. "Reconnaissance du pays Bango-bango et d'une partie de l'Uzimba." *Belgique coloniale* 8 (1902): 255–57, 268–90.

Born, K. "Nordkongo—Der Westen." In *Die Völker Afrikas und ihre traditionellen Kulturen,* ed. H. Baumann, 1:685–721. Wiesbaden, 1975.

Bosékônsombo. Letter to G. Hulstaert, 19/February/71, and supplement to this letter. Archives *Annales Aequatoria,* Mbandaka. See also G. Hulstaert, "Petite monographie des Bondombe" and "Encore Bondombe."

Boteler, T. *Narrative of a Voyage of Discovery to Africa and Arabia . . . under the Command of Captain F. Owen.* 2 vols. London, 1825.

Bouccin, R. "Les Babali." *Congo* 16, 2 (1935): 685–712;17, 1 (1936): 26–41.

Bouccin, R. "Au sujet du Lilwa." K. 156–83. Opala, 1946.

Bouchaud, J. *La côte du Cameroun dans l'histoire et la cartographie: Des origines à l'annexion allemande (1884).* Mémoires de l'Institut Français d'Afrique Noire 5. Paris, 1952.

Bouquet, A. *Féticheurs et médecines traditionelles du Congo (Brazzaville).* ORSTOM 36. Paris, 1969.

Bouquet, A., and A. Jacquot. "Essai de géographie linguistique sur quelques plantes médicinales du Congo Brazzaville." *Cahiers Orstom* 5, 3–4 (1967): 5–25.

Bouquiaux, L., and J. M. C. Thomas. "Le peuplement oubanguien: Hypothèse de reconstruction des mouvements migratoires dans la région oubanguienne d'après des données linguistiques, ethnolinguistiques et de tradition orale." In *L'expansion bantoue: Actes du Colloque International du CNRS. Viviers (France). 4–16 avril 1977,* ed. L. Bouquiaux, 3:807–24. Paris, 1980.

Bowdich, T. E. *Mission from Cape Coast Castle to Ashantee.* London, 1819.

Brasio, A. *Monumenta Missionaria Africana: Africa ocidental,* 14 vols. Lisbon, 1952.

Brausch, G., " 'Polyandrie' et 'mariage classique' chez les Bashi Lele." *Problèmes d'Afrique centrale* 12 (1951): 86–101.

Brausch, G. "La société N'Kutshu." *Bulletin des juridictions indigènes et du droit coutumier congolais* 13 (1945): 29–89.

Briart, P. "Les fortifications indigènes au Congo." *Le Congo illustré* 4 (1895): 12–14, 22–24, 28–30.

Brown, H. D., "The Nkumu of the Tumba." *Africa* 14 (1944): 431–47.

Bruel, G. *L'Afrique équatoriale française.* Paris, 1918.

Bruel, G. *La France équatoriale africaine.* Paris, 1925.

Bruggen. "Rapport constituant la chefferie Kiravungu, secteur Kembisa." AIMO, Poko 3: 1. 1914.

Brun, S. *Schiffarten: Welche er in etliche newe Länder und Insulen . . . gethan.* Basel, 1624.

Brunschwig, H. "Une histoire de l'Afrique noire est-elle possible?" *Méthodologie de l'histoire et des sciences humaines. Mélanges en l'honneur de Fernand Braudel,* 2:75–86. Toulouse, 1973.

Bucher, H. "The Settlement of the Mpongwe Clans in the Gabon Estuary: An historical Synthesis." *Revue française d'histoire d'outre-mer* 64, 2, #235 (1977): 149–75.

Bucher, H. "The Mpongwe of the Gabon Estuary: A History to 1860." Ph.D. diss., University of Wisconsin, 1977. Ann Arbor.

Bucher, H. "Mpongwe Origins: Historiographical Perspectives." *History in Africa* 2 (1975): 59–89.

Bultot, F. "Notice de la carte des zones climatiques du Congo Belge et du Ruanda-Urundi." *Atlas général du Congo,* 33. Brussels, 1954.

Bultot, H. "Saisons et périodes sèches et pluvieuses au Congo belge et au Ruanda-Urundi" *Communication du bureau climatique de l'INEAC,* 9. Brussels, 1954.

Burke, E. *A Small Handbook of Kilega.* Pittsburgh, 1940.

Burrows, G. *The Curse of Central Africa.* London, 1903.

Bylin, E. *Basakata: Le peuple du pays de l'entre-fleuves Lukenye-Kasai.* Studia ethnographica Upsaliensia 25. Lund, 1966.

Bynon, T. *Historical Linguistics.* Cambridge, 1977.

Cahen, D. "Contribution à la chronologie de l'âge du fer dans la région de Kinshasa (Zaire)." In *Préhistoire africaine. Mélanges offerts au doyen Lionel Balout,* ed. C. Roubet, J. Hugot, and G. Souville, 127–37. Paris, 1981.

Calvocoressi, D., and N. David. "A New Survey of Radiocarbon and Thermoluminescence Dates for West Africa." *Journal of African History* 20 (1979): 1–29.

Canisius, E. "A Campaign amongst Cannibals." In *The Curse of Central Africa,* ed. G. Burrows, 62–178. London, 1903.

Carrington, J. F. "Lilwaakoi—A Congo Secret Society." *Baptist Quarterly* 12, 8 (1947): 237–44.

Casati, G. *Zehn Jahre in Aequatoria.* 2 vols. Translated from the Italian by K. von Reinhardstöttner. Bamberg, 1891.

Cavalli-Sforza, l. L. *African Pygmies.* New York, 1986.

Cavazzi de Montecúccolo, A. *Descriçaõ historica dos três reinos, Congo, Matamba e Angola.* 2 vols. Translated from the Italian and annotated by G. M. de Leguzzano. Lisbon, 1965.

Ceulemans, P. *La Question arabe et le Congo (1883–1892).* ARSOM, n.s. 22, 1. Brussels, 1959.

Chaltin, N. "Exploration de la Lulu et de l'Aruwimi." *Le Congo illustré* 3 (1894): 105–8.

Chamberlin, C. "The Migration of the Fang into Central Gabon during the Nineteenth Century: A New Interpretation." *International Journal of African Historical Studies* 11, 3 (1978): 429–56.

Champaud, J. *Mom: terroir Bassa (Cameroun).* ORSTOM, Atlas des structures agraires au sud du Sahara, 9. Paris, 1973.

Chevalier, A. "Les rapports des Noirs avec la nature: Sur l'utilisation par les indigènes du Gabon d'une fougère pour piégeage, et d'un champignon pour la fabrication de ceintures de parure." *Journal de la société des Africanistes* 4 (1934): 123–27.

Chrétien, C. D. "The Mathematical Models of Glottochronology." *Language* 32 (1962): 11–37.

Christen, J. *Mambela et Anyoto.* Brussels, n.d. [1930?].

Clarke, A. S. "The Warega." *Man* 30, 48–49 (1930): 66–68.

Clarke, J. *Introduction to the Fernandian Tongue.* 2d ed. Berwick-on-Tweed, 1848.

Cleire, R. "Les bases socio-culturelles du mariage traditionnel au Congo." Report to the permanent committee of ordinary bishops in Congo. Kinshasa, 1966.

Cline, E. *Mining and Metallurgy in Negro Africa.* General Series in Anthropology 5) Menasha, 1937.

Clist, B. "Early Bantu Settlements in West-Central Africa: A Review of Recent Research." *Current Anthropology* 28, 1 (1987): 380–82.

Clist, B. "La fin de l'âge de la pierre et les débuts de la métallurgie du fer au Gabon: Résultats préliminaires 1986–1987." *Nsi* 2 (1987): 24–28.

Clist, B. "1985 Fieldwork in Gabon." *Nyame Akuma* 28 (1987): 6.

Clist, B. "Pour une archéologie du royaume kongo: Un exemple d'analyse systémique appliqué à la céramique africaine." *Muntu* (in press).

Clist, B. "Travaux archéologiques récents en République du Gabon, 1985–1986." *Nsi* 1 (1987): 9–12.

Clist, B. "Un nouvel ensemble néolithique en Afrique centrale: Le groupe d'Okala au Gabon." *Nsi* 3 (1988): 43–51.

Coart, E. *Les nattes.* MRAC, Annales in 4°, III, II, 2. Brussels, 1927.

Coart, E., and A. De Hauleville. *La céramique.* MRAC, Annales in 4°, III, II, 1. Brussels, 1907.

Coleman, R. "Archaeology and language." *Current Anthropology* 29 (1988): 449–53.

Colle (AT). "Les Gombe de l'Equateur: Histoire et migrations." *Bulletin de la société royale belge de géographie* 57 (1923): 141–69.

Colle, P. *Les Baluba.* 2 vols. Collection de Monographies ethnographiques, 10, 11. Brussels, 1913.

Comhaire-Sylvain, S. and J. "Les populations du Mai Ndombe." In *Mai Ndombe*, ed. J. Comhaire et al., 15–30. Bandundu, 1982.

Conradt, L. "Die Ngúmba in Südkamerun." *Globus* 81 (1902): 333–37, 350–54, 369–72.

Coquery Vidrovitch, C. *Brazza et la prise de possession du Congo, 1883–1885.* Paris, 1969.

Coquery Vidrovitch, C. *Le Congo au temps des grandes compagnies concessionnaires, 1898–1930.* Paris, 1972.

Coquilhat, C. *Sur le Haut-Congo.* Paris, 1888.

Cordell, D. "Throwing Knives in Equatorial Africa: A Distributional Study. *Ba-Shiru* 5, 1 (1973): 94–104.

Cordella, E. "Appunti sulla zona del Maniema (Riva sinistra del Lualaba)." *Bolletino de la societá de geographica italiana* 44 (1906): 963–78.

Cordella, E. *Verso l'Elila, affluente del Congo.* Rome, 1907.

Cordemans (AT). "Les Pama." Archives of Lukolela zone.

Cornet, J. "A propos des statues ndengese." *Arts d'Afrique noire* 17 (1976): 6–16.

Cornet, J. "Art Pygmée." In *Sura Dji: Visages et racines du Zaïre*, 97–103. Paris, 1982.

Cornet, J. "La société des chasseurs d'éléphants chez les Ipanga." *Annales Aequatoria* 1 (1980): 239–50.

Cornevin, R. *Histoire du Congo-Leo.* Paris, 1963.

Cornevin, R. *Histoire de l'Afrique.* 2 vols. Paris, 1962, 1966.

Costermans, B. *Mosaique bangba.* ARSOM 28, 3. Brussels, 1953.

Costermans, B. "Torè, God en Geesten bij de Mamvu en hun dwergen." *Congo* 1 (1938): 532–47.

Costermans, E. "Le district du Stanley Pool." *Bulletin de la société belge d'études congolaises* 2, 1 (1895): 25–76.

Costermans, E. "Reconnaissance du pays entre le Congo, le Kassai et le Kwango." *La Belgique coloniale* 3 (1897): 40–42, 53–54.

Crecelius, W., ed. "Josua Ulsheimer Reisen nach Guinea und Beschreibung des Landes." *Alemannia* 6 (1878): 90–126.

Crespo Gil-Delgado, C. *Notas para un estudio antropológico y etnológico del Bubi de Fernando Poo.* Madrid, 1949.

Crine, B. *La structure sociale des Foma.* CEDAF 4. Brussels, 1972.

Cureau, A. *Les sociétés primitives de l'Afrique équatoriale.* Paris, 1912.

Curtin, P. D. *The Atlantic Slave Trade: A Census.* Madison, 1969.

Czekanowski, J. *Forschungen im Nil- Kongo-Zwischengebiet.* Vol. 6, 2 (1924) of his *Wissenschaftliche Ergebnisse der deutschen Zentralafrika-Expedition unter Führung von A. Friedrich Herzog z. Mecklemburg, 1907–1908.* Leipzig, 1911–27.

Daeleman, J. "A comparison of Some Zone B Languages in Bantu." *Africana Linguistica VII* (1977): 93–143.

Dapper, O. *Naukeurige Beschrijvinge der Afrikaensche gewesten.* Amsterdam, 1668.

Darré, E., "Notes sur la tribu des Bomitaba." *Revue d'ethnographie et des traditions populaires* 3 (1924): 304–25.

Darré, E. "Notes sur les Kakas de la circonscription de l'Ibenga-Likouala." *Bulletin de la société de recherches congolaises* 1 (1922): 11–19.

Darre, E., and Le Bourhis. "Notes sur la tribu Bomitaba." *Bulletin de la société de recherches congolaises* 6 (1925): 15–38.

d'Atri, M. "Relations sur le royaume du Congo, 1690–1700." *Les cahiers Ngonge* 5 (1960): 1–115. Abbreviated translation by F. Bontinck.

David, N. "Prehistory and Historical Linguistics in Central Africa: Points of Contact." In *The Archaeological and Linguistic Reconstruction of African History,* ed. C. Ehret and M. Posnansky, 78–95. Berkeley, 1982.

De Backer, A. "Brief van den E.H. aan zijn familie." *Missions de Chine et du Congo,* 457–62. Scheut 1891.

De Bock (AT). "Nottes [sic] concernant la constitution politique des Basoo." L. 34/6. *N.D.* (c. 1922).

de Calonne-Beaufaict, A. "Les Ababua." *Mouvement sociologique international* 10, 2 (1909): 1–147.

de Calonne-Beaufaict, A. *Les Azande.* Brussels, 1921.

De Coster. "Coutume mongo." L. 89/1. *N.D.* (1920s?).

De Craemer, W., J. Vansina, and R. Fox. "Religious Movements in Central Africa: A Theoretical Study." *Comparative Studies in Society and History* 18, 4 (1976): 458–75.

de Dampierre, E. *Un ancien royaume bandia du Haut-Oubangui.* Paris, 1967.

Degrandpré, L. *Voyage à la côte occidentale d'Afrique fait dans les années 1786 et 1787; contenant . . .* 2 vols. Paris, 1801.

De Heusch, L. "Eléments de potlatch chez les Hamba." *Africa* 24 (1954): 337–48.

De Heusch, L. "Un Système de parenté insolite: Les Onga." *Zaire* 9 (1955): 1011–28.

De Jonghe, E. *Les formes d'asservissement dans les sociétés indigènes du Congo Belge.* Brussels, 1949.

De Langhe, E. "Bananas Musa spp." In *Outlines of Perennial Crop Breeding in the Tropics,* ed. F. P. Ferwerda and F. De Wit. Miscellaneous Papers 4. Wageningen, 1969.

De Langhe, E. "La taxonomie du bananier plantain en Afrique équatoriale." *Journal d'agriculture tropicale et botanique appliquée* 9, 10–11 (1961): 417–49.

Delhaise, C. "Chez les Wassongola du sud ou Babili." *Bulletin de la Société royale belge de géographie* 33 (1909): 34–58, 109–35, 159–214.

Delhaise, C. *Les Warega (Congo Belge).* Collection de monographies ethnographiques 5 Brussels, 1909.

Delhaise-Arnould, C. "Les associations secrètes au Congo: Le Nebili ou Negbo." *Bulletin de la Société d'études congolaises* 26 (1919): 283–90.

De Maeyer. "Etude générale sur la tribu des Makere." MRAC, musicology. Doromo, 1926.

de Mahieu, W. "A l'intersection du temps et de l'espace, du mythe et de l'histoire, les généalogies: L'exemple komo." *Cultures et développement* 11, 3 (1979): 415–37.

de Mahieu, W. "Les Komo." In *Kisangani, 1876–1976: Histoire d'une ville. Tome 1. La population,* ed. B. Verhaegen, 93–117. Kinshasa, 1975.

de Mahieu, W. *Qui a obstrué la cascade?: Analyse sémantique du rituel de la circoncision chez les Komo du Zaïre.* Paris, 1985.

de Mahieu, W. *Structures et symboles: Les structures sociales du groupe Komo du Zaïre dans leur élaboration symbolique.* Leuven, 1980.

de Marees, P. *Beschryvinghe ende historische verhael van het Gout Koninckrijck van Gunea.* The Hague, 1912. The original was published in Amsterdam, 1602.

De Maret, P. *Fouilles archéologiques dans la vallée du Haut-Lualaba, Zaire.* MRAC 120. 3 vols. Tervuren, 1985.

De Maret, P. "The neolithic problem in the west and south." In *The Archaeology of Central Africa,* ed. F. Van Noten, 59–65. Graz, 1982.

De Maret, P. "The Ngovo Group: An Industry with Polished Stone Tools and Pottery in Lower Zaire." *The African Archaeological Review* 4 (1986): 103–33.

De Maret, P. "Recent Archaeological Research and Dates from Central Africa." *Journal of African History* 26 (1985): 129–48.

De Maret, P. "Résultats des premières fouilles dans les abris de Shum laka et d'Abeke au nord-ouest du Cameroun: Belgian archaeological project in Cameroon." *L'Anthropologie* 91, 2 (1987): 521–58.

Demesse, L. *Techniques et économie des pygmées babinga.* Mémoire de l'Institut d'ethnologie, Muséum national d'histoire naturelle 20. Paris, 1980.

Denbow, J., A. Manima-Moubouha, and N. Sanviti. "Archaeological Excavations along the Loango Coast Congo." *Nsi* 3 (1988): 37–42.

Denis, M. See France.

Denis, P. *Histoire des Mangbetu et des Matschaga jusqu'à l'arrivée des Belges.* MRAC, Archives d'ethnographie 2. Tervuren, 1961.

De Plaen, G. *Les Structures d'autorité chez les Bayansi.* Paris, 1974.

De Rop, A., and E. Boelaert. *Versions et fragments de l'épopée Mongo: Nsong'a Lianja: Partie 2.* Etudes Aequatoria 1. Mbandaka, 1983.

De Ryck, M. "La chasse chez les Lalia-Ngolu." *Congo* (1932): 394–402.

De Ryck, M. *Les Lalia-Ngolu.* Antwerp, 1937.

De Ryck, M. "Une société secrète chez les Lalia Ngolu. Liloa." *Aequatoria* 3 (1940): 2–7.

Deschamps, H. *Traditions orales et archives au Gabon: Contribution à l'ethno-histoire.* Paris, 1962.

Deschamps, R., R. Lanfranchi, A. Le Cocq, and D. Schwartz. "Reconstitution d'environnements quaternaires par l'étude de macrorestes végétaux (Pays Bateke, R.P. du Congo)." *Palaeogeography, Palaeoclimatology, Palaeo-ecology* 66 (1988): 33–44.

De Sousberghe, L. *Don et contredon de la vie: Structure élémentaire de la parenté et union préférentielle.* Sankt Augustin, 1986.

De Sousberghe, L. "Mumbira et Limombo des Nyanga." *Africa-Tervuren* 21, 1–2 (1975): 36–38.

De Sousberghe, L., and J. Ndembe. "La parenté chez les Lokele." *Bulletin ARSOM* 4 (1967): 728–45.

de Teran, M. *Síntesis geográfica de Fernando Poo.* Madrid, 1962.

de Unzueta y Yuste, A. "Etnografía de Fernando Poo, Los Bubis." *Estudios geográficos* 8–9 (1947): 155–81.

de Unzueta y Yuste, A. *Historia geográfica de la isla de Fernando Poo.* Madrid, 1947.

Deutsches Kolonialblatt. 1889–1918.

Devisse, J., and J. Vansina. "Africa from the Seventh to the Eleventh Centuries." *Africa from the Seventh to the Eleventh Century.* ed. M. Al Fassi and I. Hrbek, 750–93. General History of Africa, vol. 3. Paris, 1988.

De Wilde, J. "Dans la Mongala." *Le Congo illustré* 4 (1895): 186–87.

De Wildeman. *Sur des plantes médicinales ou utiles du Mayumbe (Congo belge).* Brussels, 1938.

Dhanis, F. E. "Le district d'Upoto et la fondation du camp de l'Arouwimi." *Bulletin de la société royale belge de géographie* 14 (1890): 5–45.

Didier. "Le nomadisme des Sangas-sangas à la frontière sud du Cameroun." *Tropiques: Revue des troupes coloniales* (1911): 584–608.

Digombe, L., et al. "Early Iron Age Prehistory in Gabon." *Current Anthropology* 29, 1 (1988): 180–84.

Digombe, L., et al. "Recherches archéologiques au Gabon: Année académique 1986–1987." *Nsi* 2 (1987): 29–31.

Dikoume, C. "Etude concrète société traditionnelle: Les Elog-Mpoo." Ph.D. diss., troisième cycle, Université de Lille 2, 1979.

Dimandja Luhaka. "Le pays de Katako-Kombe à l'époque coloniale." Ph.D. diss., Université catholique de Louvain, 1974.

Douglas, M. "Animals in Lele Religious Symbolism." *Africa,* 27, 1 (1957): 46–58.

Douglas, M. "A Form of Polyandry among the Lele of Kasai." *Africa* 21, 1 (1951): 1–12.

Douglas, M. *The Lele of Kasai.* London, 1963.

Drachoussoff, V. *Essai sur l'agriculture indigène au Bas-Congo*. Brussels, 1947. Also in *Bulletin agricole du Congo belge* 38 (1947): 471–582, 783–880.

Droogers, A. *The Dangerous Journey: Symbolic Aspects of Boys' Initiation among the Wagenia of Kisangani, Zaire*. The Hague, 1980.

Droogers, A. "Les Wagenia de Kisangani entre le fleuve et la ville." In *Kisangani, 1876–1976: Histoire d'une ville. Tome 1. La population*, ed. B. Verhaegen, 153–77. Kinshasa, 1975.

Druart, J. "Carte succincte du District du Maniema." L. 27-1. 1920.

Du Chaillu, P. *Voyages et aventures dans l'Afrique équatoriale*. Paris, 1863.

Duffy, K. *Children of the Forest*. New York, 1984.

Du Fief, J. "Carte de l'Etat Indépendant du Congo." *Manuel du voyageur et du résident au Congo. Supplément*. 4 sheets. Brussels, 1900.

Dugast, I. "Banen, Bafia, Balom." In *Peoples of the Central Cameroons*, ed. M. McCulloch, M. Littlewood, and I. Dugast. Ethnographic Survey of Africa. Western Africa 9. London, 1954.

Dugast, I. *Monographie de la tribu des Ndiki*. 2 vols. Paris, 1955–1960.

Duparquet, C. "Etat commercial de la côte du Loango et du Congo." *Les Missions Catholiques* 6 (1874): 575–76, 586–88, 597–98; 7 (1875): 116–17, 128–29, 141–42. The map is on p. 116.

Dupré, G. "Le commerce entre sociétés lignagères: Les Nzabi dans la traite à la fin du XIXe siècle." -*Cahiers d'études africaines* 12, 4, #48 (1972): 616–58.

Dupré, G. *Un ordre et sa destruction*. ORSTOM, Mémoirs 93. Paris, 1982.

Dupré, M.-C. "La dualité du pouvoir politique chez les Teke de l'ouest: Pouvoir tsaayi et pouvoir nzinéké." 2 vols. Ph.D. diss., troisième cycle, Université de Lyon 2, 1972.

Dupré, M.-C. "Naissances et renaissances du masque kidumu: Art, politique et histoire chez les Teke Tsaayi. 3 vols. Ph.D. diss., University of Paris 5, 1984.

Dupré, M.-C. "Pour une histoire des productions de la métallurgie du fer chez les Téké, Ngungulu, Tio, Tsayi." *Cahiers ORSTOM* 18, 2 (1981–1982): 195–223.

Dupré, W. "Die Babinga-Pygmäen." *Annali del Pontificio museo missionario ethnologico* 26, 9 (1962–1963): 9–172.

Earle, T. K. "Chiefdoms in Archaeological and Ethnohistorical Perspective." *Annual Review of Anthropology* 16 (1987): 279–308.

Ebiatsa-Hopiel-Obiele. "Les Teke: Definition historique des hommes et de leur espace (avant le XVIIIe siècle)." *Muntu* 7 (1987): 33–47.

Eggert, M. "Archäologische Forschungen im zentralafrikanischen Regenwald." In *Die Großen Abenteuer der Archäologie*, ed. R. Pörtner and H. G. Niemayer, 9:3217–40. Salzburg, 1987.

Eggert, M. "Imbonga and Batalimo: Ceramic Evidence for Early Settlement of the Equatorial Rain Forest." *The African Archaeological Review* 5 (1987): 129–46.

Eggert, M. "Remarks on Exploring Archaeologically Unknown Rain Forest Territory: The Case of Central Africa." *Beiträge zur Allgemeinen und Vergleichenden Archäologie* 5 (1983): 283–322.

Eggert, M., and Misago Kanimba. "Recherches archéologiques et ethnographiques dans les régions de l'Equateur (Zaire), de la Cuvette de la Sangha et de la Likouala (Congo) Sangha, Djah, Likouala aux Herbes." *Annales Aequatoria* 8 (1987): 481–86.

Eggert, R. M. *Das Wirtschaftssystem der Mongo am Vorabend der Kolonisation: Eine Rekonstruktion.* Mainzer Afrika Studien 7. Berlin. 1987.

Ehret, C. "Sheep and Central Sudanic Peoples in Southern Africa." *Journal of African History* 9, 2 (1968): 213–21.

Ehret, C., et al. "Some Thoughts on the Early History of the Nile-Congo Watershed." *Ufahamu* 5, 2 (1974): 85–112.

Elango, L. Z. "Britain and Bimbia in the 19th Century (1833–1878): A Study in Anglo-Bimbian Trade and Diplomatic Relations." Ph.D. diss., Boston University, 1975. Ann Arbor.

Engels, A. *Les Wangata: Etude ethnographique.* Brussels, 1912.

Epea, S. "Message chrétien et visage de l'homme chez les Basa, Bantie du sud Cameroun." Ph.D. diss., Université de Strasbourg, Lille, 1978, 1982.

Ethnohistory. 1953–.

"Etudes sur les pygmées: Territoire des Babali/Barumbi." AIMO P.O. 1. 1934.

Evans Pritchard, E. E. *The Azande: History and Political Institutions.* Oxford, 1971.

Ewani, F. "Recul et stabilisation teke (Congo)." Ph.D. diss., troisième cycle, Université de Paris 1, 1979.

FAO, UNESCO. *Soil Map of the World.* Paris, 1977.

Fenton, W. N. "Ethnohistory and Its Problems." *Ethnohistory* 9 (1962): 1–23.

Fernandez-Fernandez, M. "Le rite et l'expérience: Les Bagba de Banalia (Zaire). Ph.D. diss., troisième cycle, Université de Paris 3, 1983.

Fiedler, L., and J. Preuss. "Stone Tools from the Inner Zaire Basin." *The African Archaeological Review* 3 (1985): 179–87.

Fiévez, L. "Le district de l'Equateur." *Le Congo illustré* 4, 10–12 (1895): 73–75, 84–87, 92–95, 97–99.

Fivé (AT). *Etudes Bamanga.* AIMO, Stanleyville 1. *N.D.* (c. 1930?)

Flenley, J. *The Equatorial Rain Forest: A Geological History.* London, 1979.

La Force Publique de sa naissance à 1914: Participation des militaires à l'histoire des premières années du Congo. ARSOM 27. Brussels, 1952.

Förster, Brix. "Aus dem Südostwinkel Kameruns." *Globus* 81, 10 (1902): 157–58.

Fournier, F., and A. Sasson. *Ecosystèmes forestiers tropicaux d'Afrique.* Paris, 1983.

Foury, P. "Indications données par l'état actuel de la végétation sur la répartition ancienne des groupements humains." *Bulletin de la société des études camerounaises* 2 (1937): 7–13.

Fräßle, J. *Fünf Jahre als Missionar im Herzen Afrikas.* Sittard, 1910.

Fräßle, J. *Meiner Urwaldneger Denken und Handeln.* Freiburg, 1923.

Fräßle, J. *Negerpsyche im Urwald am Lohali.* Freiburg, 1926.

Francart, M. "Note sur les institutions primitives des indigènes du territoire de Budjala." L. 34/5. 1922.

France, Etat Major de l'armée. "Les armées françaises d'outre-mer." *Histoire militaire de l'Afrique équatoriale française.* Paris, 1931.

Frobenius, L., and L. Ritter von Wilm. *Atlas africanus.* Munich, 1922–1933.

Froment, E. "Trois affluents français du Congo." *Bulletin de la société de géographie de Lille* 9 (1887): 457–74.

Froment, E. "Un voyage dans l'Oubangui." *Bulletin de la société de géographie de Lille* 11 (1889): 180–216.

Gambeg, Y.-N. "Pouvoir politique et société en pays teke (R.P. du Congo) de vers 1506 à 1957." 2 vols. Ph.D. diss., troisième cycle, *Université de Paris 1, 1984.*

Garfield, R. "A History of Saõ Tomé Island." Ph.D. diss., Northwestern University, 1971. Ann Arbor.

Gaulme, G. *Le pays de Cama: Un ancien état côtier du Gabon et ses origines.* Paris, 1981.

Geary, C. "Photographs as Materials for African History." *History in Africa* 13 (1986): 89–16.

Geisler, P. "Allgemeiner Bericht über die Kongo-Lobaje Expedition." *Mitteilungen der Deutschen Schutzgebieten* 9a (1914): 104–10.

Gilliard, L. "Les Bolia: Mort et intronisation d'un grand chef." *Congo* 5, 2 (1925): 223–38.

Glave, E. J. "New Conditions in Central Africa." *Century* 54, 4–5 (1897): 906–15, 699–715.

Glave, E. J. *Six Years of Adventure in Congo-land.* London, 1893.

Goebel. "Carte ethnographique de la zône Uere-Bili." Bambili, 1908. In possession of J. Vansina.

Goffart, F. *Le Congo.* 2d ed. Brussels, 1908.

Goffin, A. *Les pêcheries et les poissons du Congo.* Brussels, 1909.

Goldman, I. *Ancient Polynesian Society.* Chicago, 1970.

González Echegaray, C. *Estudios Guineos.* Madrid, 1959.

Gosse, J. P. "Les méthodes et engins de pêche des Lokele." *Bulletin du Congo ex Belge* 2 (1961): 335–85.

Gourou, P. *La densité de la population rurale au Congo belge.* ARSOM, Science: naturelles et médicales, n.s. 1, 2. Brussels, 1955.

Gourou, P. "Notice de la carte de densité de la population au Congo Belge et au Ruanda-Urundi." *Atlas général du Congo,* 624. Brussels, 1951.

Gourou, P. *Les pays tropicaux.* 4th ed. Paris, 1966.

Gräbner, F. *Methode der Ethnologie.* Heidelberg, 1911.

Grégoire, C. "Le champ sémantique du thème bantou *-bánjá." *African Language* 2 (1976): 1–12.

Griffon du Bellay, T. "Le Gabon: 1861–1864." *Le Tour du monde* 12, 2 (1865): 273–320.

Guilmin, M. "Proverbes des Ngombe." *Congo* 12, 1 (1932): 38–53.

Guthrie, M., *The Bantu Languages of Western Equatorial Africa.* London, 1953.

Guthrie, M. *The Classification of the Bantu languages.* London, 1948.

Guthrie, M. *Comparative Bantu.* 4 vols. Farnham, 1969–70.

Guyer, J., "Indigenous Currencies and the History of Marriage Payments." *Cahiers d'études africaines* 104 (1986): 577–610.

Haase, L. *Durch unbekanntes Kamerun.* Berlin, 1915.

Hackars, H. "Inspection du territoire d'Avakubi: Politique indigène organisation." AIMO, D. Stanleyville. Bafwasende, 1919.

Hagenbucher Sacripanti, F. *Les Fondements spirituels du pouvoir au royaume de Loango,* ORSTOM, Mémoires 67. Paris, 1973.

Hamerlinck, L. "Un voyage chez les Bamfunuka." *Revue missionnaire* 37 (1932): 14–17.

Harako, R. "The Mbuti as Hunters: A Study of Ecological Anthropology of the Mbuti Pygmies." *Kyoto University African Studies* 10 (1976): 37–99.

Harms, R. *Games against Nature: A History of the Nunu of Equatorial Africa.* Cambridge, 1987.

Harms, R. "Oral Tradition and Ethnicity." *Journal of Interdisciplinary History* 10, 1 (1979): 61–85.

Harms, R. *River of Wealth, River of Sorrow: The Central Zaire Basin in the Era of the Slave and Ivory Trade, 1500–1891.* New Haven, 1981.

Harms, R. "The World Abir Made: The Maringa-Lopori Basin, 1885–1903." M.A. thesis, University of Wisconsin–Madison, 1973.

Hart, T. B. *"The Ecology of a Single Species-Dominant Forest and Mixed Forest in Zaire."* Ph.D. diss., Michigan State University, 1985. Ann Arbor.

Hartweg, R. *La vie secrète des pygmées.* Paris, 1961.

Headrick, D. R., *The Tools of Empire: Technology and European Imperialism in the Nineteenth Century.* Oxford, 1981.

Headrick, R. "The Impact of Colonialism on Health in French Aequatorial Africa, 1880–1934." Ph.D. diss., University of Chicago, 1987. Ann Arbor.

Heine, B., H. Hoff, and R. Vossen. "Neuere Ergebnisse zur Territorialgeschichte der Bantu." In *Zur Sprachgeschichte und Ethnohistorie in Afrika*, ed. B. Heine, 57–70. Berlin, 1977.

Hemeni (AT). "Historique de la tribu des Banunu." L. 89.2. Mushie, 1923.

Henrotin. "Historique des Basoo." AIMO, Basoko 2. Basoko, 1916.

Hértier, F. *L'exercice de la parenté*. Paris, 1981.

Heym. "Die Gefechte gegen die aufständige Ebaleute im Bezirk Sembe." *Deutsches Kolonialblatt* (1914); 226–29.

Hiernaux, J. "Long-term Biological Effects of Human Migration from the African Savanna to the Equatorial Forest: A Case Study of Human Adaptability to a Hot and Wet Climate." In *Population Structure and Human Variation*, ed. G. A. Harrison. Cambridge, 1977.

Hiernaux, J. *The People of Africa*. New York, 1974.

Hilton, A. *The Kingdom of Kongo*. Oxford, 1985.

Hirschberg, W. "Das Crossflußgebiet und das Kameruner Grasland." In *Die Völker Afrikas und Ihre Traditionellen Kulturen*, ed. H. Baumann, 2:355–72. Wiesbaden, 1979.

Hobsbawm, E., and T. Ranger, eds. *The Invention of Tradition*. Cambridge, 1983.

Hock, H. H. *Principles of Historical Linguistics*. Berlin, 1986.

Hoffman, R. "Croyances et coutumes des Bapere." MRAC, Dossiers ethnographique 805. Luofu, 1932.

Hoffman, R. "Rapport sur la chefferie Bapere." AIMO, Lubero 1. 1932

Hubbard, M. I. "In Search of the Mangbetu." Los Angeles, 1973. Seminar paper.

Hulstaert, G. *Dictionnaire lomongo-français*. 2 vols. MRAC 16. Tervuren, 1957.

Hulstaert, G.*Eléments pour l'histoire Mongo ancienne*. ARSOM, n.s. 48, 2 Brussels, 1984.

Hulstaert, G. "Une lecture critique de *L'Ethnie Mongo* de G. Van der Kerken." *Etudes d'histoire africaine* 3 (1972): 27–60.

Hulstaert, G. "Lomongo en Ngbandi." *Aequatoria* 8 (1945): 153–55.

Hulstaert, G. *Le Mariage des Nkundo*. ARSOM 8. Brussels, 1938.

Hulstaert, G. *Les Mongo: Aperçu général*. MRAC, Archives d'ethnographie 5. Tervuren, 1961.

Hulstaert, G. "Nordkongo—Der zentrale Teil." In *Die Völker Afrikas und ihre traditionellen Kulturen*, ed. H. Baumann, 1:722–74. Wiesbaden, 1975.

Hulstaert, G. *Notes de botanique mongo*. ARSOM, n.s. 15, 3. Brussels, 1966.

Hulstaert, G. "Notes sur la langue des Bafóto." *Anthropos* 73, 1–2 (1978): 113–32.

Hulstaert, G. "Over de volkstammen van de Lomela." *Congo* 131, 1 (1931): 13–52.

Hulstaert, G. "Petite monographie des Bondombe." *Annales Aequatoria* 3 (1982): 7–106.

Hulstaert, G. *Au sujet de deux cartes linguistiques du Congo belge.* ARSOM 38, 1. Brussels, 1954.

Hulstaert, G. and Nakasa Bosékônsombo. "Encore Bondombe." *Annales Aequatoria* 7 (1986): 195–219.

Hutchinson, T. J. *Impressions of Western Africa.* London, 1858.

Hutereau, A. *Histoire des peuplades de l'Uele et de l'Ubangi.* Bibliothèque Congo 1. Brussels, 1922.

Hymes, D. H. "Lexicostatistics So Far." *Current Anthropology* 1, 1 (1960): 3–44.

Ibia j' Ikëngë. *Customs of the Benga and Neighboring Tribes.* Edited by R. H. Nassau. New York, 1902.

Irstam, T. *The King of Ganda: Studies in the Institutions of Sacral Kingship in Afrika.* Lund, 1944.

Ittmann, J. *Volkskundliche und religiöse Begriffe im Nördlichen Waldland von Kamerun.* Afrika und Uebersee, vol. 26. Berlin, 1953.

Jacobs, J., and J. Vansina. "Nshoong atoot: Het koninklijk epos der Bushoong." *Kongo Overzee* 22, 1 (1956): 1–33

Jacquot, A. *Les classes nominales dans les langues bantoues des groupes B10, B20, B30.* ORSTOM, travaux et documents. Paris, 1983.

Jadin, L., and M. Dicorato. *Correspondance de Dom Afonso roi du Congo: 1508–1543.* ARSOM, n.s. 41, 3. Brussels, 1974

Jak, J. "De bakota en hun grafhutten in Belgisch Congo." *Natuur en mensch* 60 (1940): 27–39.

Jak, J. "Eenige ethnographica over de Walengola-Babira." *Congo* 18, 1 (1938): 13–22; and 19, 2 (1939): 47–55.

Janzen, J. *Lemba, 1650–1930: A Drum of Affliction in Africa and in the New World.* New York, 1982.

Jean, S. *Les jachères en Afrique tropicale: Interprétation technique et foncière.* Mémoire de l'Institut d'ethnologie 14. Paris, 1975.

Jewsiewicki, B. "Etude analytique des archives administratives zairoises." Lubumbashi, 1973. Mimeograph.

Johnston, H. A. *A Comparative Study of the Bantu and Semi-Bantu Languages.* 2 vols. Oxford, 1919–1920.

Johnston, H. A. *George Grenfell and the Congo.* 2 vols. London, 1908.

Jones, A. *German Sources for West African History, 1599–1669.* Studien zur Kulturkunde 66. Wiesbaden, 1983.

Jones, A., and B. Heintze, eds. "European Sources for Sub-Saharan Africa before 1900: Use and Abuse." *Paideuma* 33 (1987): 1–444.

Jones, R. *The Rescue of Emin Pasha.* New York, 1972.

Jorissen. "Documentation ethnique: Tatouages." W. 20/4/3. Mbandaka, 1950.

Joset, P. E. *Les sociétés secrètes des hommes-léopards en Afrique.* Paris, 1955.

Joset, P. E. "Vie juridique et politique des Babombi." *Trait d'Union* 3 (July 1934): 3–4.

Kadima, K., et al. *Atlas linguistique du Zaire: Inventaire préliminaire.* Paris, 1983.

Kagame, A. *La philosophie Bantu comparée.* Paris, 1976.

Kawaters. "Reifezeremonien und Geheimbunde bei den Babali-Negern vom Ituri." *Erdball* 5 (1931): 454–64.

Keim, C. "Precolonial Mangbetu Rule: Political and Economic Factors in 19th-Century Mangbetu History (Northeast Zaire)." Ph.D. diss., Indiana University, 1979. Ann Arbor.

Kingsley, M. *Travels in West Africa, Congo Français, Corisco and Cameroons.* London, 1897 (1st ed.), 1965 (3d ed.).

Kirch, P. V. *The Evolution of Polynesian Chiefdoms.* Cambridge, 1984.

Kirch, P. V., and R. C. Green. "History, Phylogeny, and Evolution in Polynesia." *Current Anthropology* 28 4 (1987): 431–56.

Klein, H. "The Portuguese Slave Trade from Angola in the Eighteenth Century." *Journal of Economic History* 32 (1972): 894–918.

Koch, C. W. H. *Das Lied des Landes: Reiseerlebnisse aus Kamerun.* Leipzig, 1923.

Koch, C. W. H. "Die Stämme des Bezirks Molundu." *Bäßler-Archiv* 3 (1913): 257–312.

Koch, H. *Magie et chasse dans la forêt camerounaise.* Paris, 1968.

Koelle, S. *Polyglotta Africana.* London, 1854 (1st ed.), 1965 (2d ed.)

Koponen, J. "Written Ethnographic Sources and Some Problems Concerned with Their Use in African Historiography." *Scandinavian Journal of History* 11 (1986): 55–69.

Kopytoff, I. "The African Frontier." in *The African Frontier: The Reproduction of Traditional African Societies,* ed. I. Kopytoff, 1–80. Bloomington, 1987.

Koumba-Manfoumbi, M. "Les Punu du Gabon, des origines à 1899: Essai d'etude historique." Ph.D. diss., troisième cycle, Université de Paris 1, 1987.

Kreutz, S. "Extrait du rapport trimestriel: 18.5.1932. Objet: secte Biba." AIMO, Zobia 3: 6–7. Zobia, 1932.

Kroeber, A. *Anthropology.* New York, 1948.

Kudi, K. *Le Lilwakoy des Mbole du Lomami: Essai d'analyse de son symbolisme.* CEDAF 4. Brussels, 1979.

Laburthe Tolra, P. *Les seigneurs de la forêt.* Paris, 1981.

Laclavère, G., ed. *Atlas de la république unie du Cameroun.* Paris, 1979.

Landeghem, A. "Etude préparatoire sur les Babua." L. 181/15. Bambili, 1914.

Lanfranchi, R. "Recherches préhistoriques en République populaire du Congo: 1984–1986." *Nsi* 1 (1987): 6–8.

Lanfranchi, R., and B. Pinçon. "Résultats préliminaires des prospections archéologiques récentes sur les plateaux et collines Teke en R.P.du Congo." *Nsi* 3 (1988): 24–31.

Laumanns, G. U. *Verwandtschaftsnamen und Verwandtschaftsordnungen im Bantugebiet.* Lippstad i/ Westfalen, 1941.

Lehmann, W. *Historical Linguistics: An Introduction.* New York, 1962.

Lejeune-Choquet, A. *Histoire militaire du Congo.* Brussels, 1906.

Lemb, P., and F. de Gastines. *Dictionnaire Basaá-Français.* Douala, 1973.

Lenz, O. "Reise auf dem Okande in West Afrika." *Zeitschrift des Vereins der Gesellschaft für Erdkunde* 3 (1875): 236–65.

Lenz, O. *Skizzen aus West Afrika.* Berlin, 1878.

Le Testu, G., "Les coutumes indigènes de la circonscription de la Nyanga (Gabon)." *Bulletin de la Société de Recherches Congolaises* 11 (1930): 33–91.

Le Testu, G. "Notes sur les cultures indigènes dans l'intérieur du Gabon." *Revue de botanique appliquée et tropicale* 20 (1940): 540–56.

Le Testu, G. "La soumission des Bawanji." *Bulletin de la Société de Recherches congolaises* 15 (1931): 11–32.

Letouzey, R. *Contribution de la botanique au problème d'une éventuelle langue pygmée.* Paris, 1976.

Letouzey, R. *Etude phytogéographique du Cameroun.* Paris, 1968.

Letouzey, R. "Végétation." In *Atlas de la République unie du Cameroun,* ed. G. Laclavère, 22–23. Paris, 1979.

Lichtenberk, F. "Leadership in Proto-Oceanic Society: Linguistic Evidence." *Journal of the Polynesian Society* 95 (1986): 341–56.

Liétard, L. "Les Warega." *Bulletin de la société royale belge de géographie* 48 (1924): 133–45.

Lindblom, G. *Jakt- och Fangstmetoder bland afrikanska folk.* 2 vols. Stockholm, 1925–1926.

Liniger Goumaz, M. *Pygmées et autres races de petite taille (Bochimans, Hottentots, négritos etc.). Bibliographie générale.* Geneva, 1968.

Lloyd, P. C. *The Political Development of Yoruba Kingdoms in the Eighteenth and Nineteenth Centuries.* London, 1971.

Lloyd, P. C. "The Political Structure of African Kingdoms: An Explanatory Model." In *Political Systems and the Distribution of Power,* ed. M. Banton, 63–112. London, 1965.

Löffler, I. "Beiträge zur Ethnologie der Tege." Ph.D. diss., Mainz University, Frankfurt, 1975.

Loir, H. *Le tissage du raphia au Congo belge.* MRAC, Annales in 4º, III, I. Brussels, 1935.

Longman, K. A., and J. Jenik. *Tropical Forest and Its Environment.* London, 1974.

Louwers, O., and A. Hoornaert. *La question sociale au Congo.* Bibliothèque Congo 16. Brussels, 1924.

Lovejoy, P. *Transformations in Slavery: A History of Slavery in Africa.* African Studies Series 36. Cambridge, 1983.

Lowenthal, D. *The.Past Is a Foreign Country.* New York, 1985.

Lyons, M. "The Colonial Disease: Sleeping Sickness in the Social History of Northern Zaire, 1903–1930." Ph.D. diss., University of California, Los Angeles, 1987. Ann Arbor.

MacGaffey, W. *Religion and Society in Central Africa: The BaKongo of Lower Zaire.* Chicago, 1986.

MacGaffey, W. "The Religious Commissions of the BaKongo." *Man*, n.s. 5, 1 (1970): 27–38.

McMaster, D. N. "Speculations on the Coming of the Banana to Uganda." *Journal of Tropical Geography* 16 (1962): 57–69.

McMaster, M. "Patterns of Interaction: A Comparative Ethnolinguistic Perspective on the Uele Region of Zaire, c. 500 B.C. to A.D. 1900." Ph.D. diss., University of California, Los Angeles, 1988. Ann Arbor.

McNaughton, P. "The Throwing Knife in African History." *African Arts* 3, 2 (1970): 54–60.

Maes, J. "Armes de jet des populations du Congo Belge." *Congo* 3, 1 (1922): 181–93.

Maes, J. "Note sur les populations Lalia et Yasayama du territoire des Dzalia-Boyela." *Congo* 36, 1 (1934): 172–79.

Maes, J. "Les sabres et massues des populations du Congo Belge." *Congo* 33, 1 (1931): 351–67.

Maes, J. "Les Warumbi." *Anthropos* 4 (1909): 607–29.

Mahieu, A. *Numismatique du Congo, 1484–1924.* Brussels, 1925.

Maley, J. "Fragmentation de la forêt dense humide africaine et extension des biotopes montagnards au quaternaire récent: nouvelles données polliniques et chronologiques. Implications paléoclimatiques et biogéographiques." *Palaeoecology of Africa* 18 (1987): 307–34.

Mallart-Guimera, L. *Ni dos, ni ventre: Religion, magie et sorcellerie evuzok.* Paris, 1981.

Mandeng, S. B. "Traditional healing of a 'Non-Ordinary' Disease (Kon) among the Basaa of Cameroun: A Religious Anthropological Approach." Ph.D. diss., Emory University, 1984. Ann Arbor.

Maquet, E. *Outils de forge du Congo, du Rwanda et du Burundi.* MRAC, Annales in 4°, n.s. 5. Tervuren, 1965.

Marmitte, H. "Baleka-Mituku." AIMO, Ponthierville 6. Shabunda, 1934.

Martin, P. *The External Trade of the Loango Coast.* Oxford, 1972.

Martin, P. "Family Strategies in Nineteenth-Century Cabinda." *Journal of African History* 28 (1987): 65–86.

Martin del Molino, A. *Etapas de la cultura Carboneras de Fernando Poo en el Primer milenio de nuestra Era.* Madrid, 1968.

Martin del Molino, A., "La familia real." *Guinea Española* 59 (1962): 37–40.

Martin del Molino, A. "Secuencia Cultural en el Neolitico de Fernando Poo." In *Etapas de la cultura Carboneras de Fernando Poo en el primer milenio de nuestra Era.* Madrid, 1965.

Martins Vaz, J. *No mundo dos Cabindas.* 2 vols. Lisbon, 1970.

Martrou, P. L. "Le nomadisme des Fangs." *Revue de géographie* 3 (1909): 497–524.

Mbokolo, E. *Noirs et Blancs en Afrique Equatoriale: Les sociétés côtières et la pénétration française (vers 1820–1874).* EHESS 69. Paris, 1981.

Mbokolo, E. "Le roi Denis." In *Les africains,* ed. Julien et al., 6:69–95. Paris, 1977.

Meeussen, E. "Het aanleggen van kollekties met geluidsopnemingen." *Congo-Tervuren* 5, 1 (1959): 18–19.

Maeussen, E. *Bantu Lexical Reconstructions.* MRAC, Archief voor Anthropologie 27. Tervuren, 1980.

Meeussen, E. "De talen van Maniema." *Kongo Overzee* 19, 5 (1953): 385–91.

Meinhof, C. *Grundzüge einer vergleichenden Grammatik der Bantusprachen.* Berlin, 1906.

Mertens, J. *Les Ba Dzing de la Kamtsha. Première partie. Ethnographie.* ARSOM 4, 1. Brussels, 1935.

Metegue N'nah, N. *Economies et sociétés au Gabon dans la première moitié du XIXe siècle.* Paris, 1979.

Metegue N'nah, N. *L'implantation coloniale au Gabon: Résistance d'un peuple.* Paris, 1981.

Meyamm, A. "Zog Djo: Un puissant sorcier, un chef et une divinité bakwelé" *Réalités gabonaises* 33 (1968): 17–21.

Myers, J. *Le prix d'un empire.* Brussels, 1943.

Miller, J. *Kings and Kinsmen: Early Mbundu States in Angola.* Oxford, 1976.

Miller, J. *Way of Death: Merchant Capitalism and the Angolan Slave Trade, 1730–1830.* Madison, 1988.

Millman, W. "The Tribal Initiation Ceremony of the Lokele." *International Review of Missions* 16 (1927): 364–80.

Miracle, M. *Agriculture in the Congo Basin: Tradition and Change in African Rural Economy.* Madison, 1967.

Miracle, M. *Maize in Tropical Africa.* Madison, 1966.

Mischung, R. "Seßhaftigkeit und Intensivierung beim Brandrodungsfeldbau (Hmong)" *Paideuma* 30 (1984): 241–55.

Moeller, A. *Les grandes lignes des migrations des Bantous de la province Orientale du Congo Belge.* ARSOM 6. Brussels, 1936.

Möhlig, W. J. "Lehnwortforschung und Ethnohistorie." *Paideuma* 26 (1980): 7–20.

Mohun, R. D. "Consular Dispatch from Basoko Camp: June 21, 1893: 1–44." Consular Reports. U.S. Consulate, Boma, 1882–1893. Microfilm of the National Archives of the United States of America.

Moisel, Max. "Skizze zu den Berichten des Oberleutnants Frhr. v. Stein über seine Expedition im Jahre 1901 im Ssanga-Djah Gebiet, . . ." *Deutsches Kolonialblatt* 13 (1902): 42–43.

Mortier, R. "Ubangi onder linguistisch opzicht." *Aequatoria* 9 (1946): 104–112.

Motte, E. *Les plantes chez les pygmées aka et les Monzombo de la Lobaye.* Paris, 1980.

Mpase Nselenge Mpeti. *L'évolution de la solidarité traditionelle en milieu rural et urbain au Zaire: Le cas des Ntomba et des Basengele du Lac Mai-Ndombe.* Kinshasa, 1974.

Mugaruka bin-Mubibi. "Histoire clanique et évolution des états dans la région sud-ouest du lac Kivu." 2 vols. Louvain-la-Neuve, 1986.

Müller, E. W. "Das Fürstentum bei den Südwest-Mongo." Ph.D. diss., Mainz University, 1955.

Mulyumba wa Mamba Itongwa. "La structure sociale des Balega Basile." 2 vols. Ph.D. diss., Université Libre de Bruxelles, 1977.

Mumbanza mwa Bamwele. "Histoire des peuples riverains de l'entre Zaire-Ubangi." 2 vols. Ph.D. diss., Université du Zaire, Lubumbashi, 1980.

Mumbanza mwa Bamwele. "Les Ngombe de l'Equateur: Historique d'une identité. *Zaïre-Afrique* 18, 124 (1978): 229–49.

Munro Hay, S. "The Foreign Trade of the Aksumite Port of Adulis." *Azania* 17 (1982): 107–25.

Muntu. 1984–.

Murdock, G. P. *Africa: Its Peoples and Their Culture History.* New York, 1959.

Murdock, G. P. *Social Structure.* New York, 1949.

Mveng, E. *Histoire du Cameroun.* Paris, 1963.

Nassau, R. H. *Fetichism in West Africa.* London, 1904.

Ndaywell wa Ndaywell. "Organisation sociale et histoire: Les Ngwi et Ding du Zaire." 2 vols. Ph.D. diss., troisième cycle, Université de Paris 1, 1972.

Netting, R. Mc. *Cultural Ecology.* 2d ed. Prospect Heights, 1986.

Nicod, H. *La vie mystérieuse de l'Afrique noire.* Paris, 1948.

Nicolai, H. *Le Kwilu: Etude géographique d'une région congolaise.* CEMUBAC 69. Brussels, 1963.

Nsi. 1987–.

Nsuka-Nkutsi, F, and P. de Maret. "Etude comparative de quelques termes métallurgiques dans les langues bantoues." In *L'expansion bantoue,* ed. L. Bouquiaux, 3:731–41. Paris, 1980.

Nyame Akuma. 1972–.

Nys, F. *Chez les Abarambo.* Antwerp, 1896.

Nzenze, H. "Note sur les Pagabete." *Aequatoria* 13, 4 (1950): 135–37.

Obenga, T. *La cuvette congolaise: Les hommes et les structures: Contribution à l'histoire traditionelle de l'Afrique centrale.* Paris, 1976.

Obenga, T. *Littérature traditionelle des Mbochi.* Paris, 1984.

Ollandet, J. *"Les contacts Teke-Mbosi: Essai sur les Civilisations du Bassin Congolais."* Ph.D. diss., troisième cycle, Montpellier University, 1981.

Omboni, T. "Viaggi nell'Africa Occidentale." Milan, 1845.

Packard, R. *Chiefship and Cosmology: An Historical Study of Political Competition.* Bloomington, 1981.

Panyella, A. "Esquema de etnologia de los Fang Ntumu de la Guinea Equatorial desde el punto de vista etnológico." *Archivos del Institudo de Estudios Africanos* 34 (1957): 72–84.

Papadopoullos, T. *Cases of Tribal Differentiation.* London, 1971.

Parke, T. H. *My Personal Experiences in Equatorial Africa as Medical Officer of the Emin Pasha Relief Expedition.* New York, 1891.

Patterson, K. D. *The Northern Gabon Coast to 1875.* Oxford, 1975.

Pauvert, J. C., and J. L. Lancrey-Javal. "Le groupement d'Evodowa (Cameroun): Etude socio-économique." ORSTOM archives. Yaounde, 1957.

Pechuel Loesche, E. *Volkskunde von Loango.* Stuttgart, 1907.

Peeters, L. *Les limites forêt-savane dans le nord du Congo en relation avec le milieu géographique.* CEMUBAC 74. Brussels, 1965.

Pepper, H., and P. De Wolf. *Un mvet de Zwè Nguéma.* Classiques africains 9. Paris, 1972.

Perono, J. "Les Basa." *Bulletin de la Société d'Etudes Camerounaises* 4 (1943): 94–109.

Perrault, P. T. "Banana-Manioc Farming Systems of the Tropical Forest: A Case Study in Zaire." Ph.D. diss., Stanford University, 1979. Ann Arbor.

Perrois, L. "Chronique du pays kota." *Cahiers ORSTOM* 7, 2 (1970): 15–120.

Perrois, L. "La circoncision Bakota." *Cahiers ORSTOM* 5, 1 (1968): 1–109.

Perrois, L., et al. *Gabon: Culture et techniques.* Libreville, 1969.

Perrot, E., and E. Vogt. *Les poisons de flèches et les poisons de l'épreuve des indigènes de l'Afrique.* Paris, 1912.

Peyrot, B., and R. Olisly. "Paleoenvironment et archéologie au Gabon: 1985–1986." *Nsi* 1 (1987): 13–15.

Philippe, R. *Inongo: Les classes d'âge en région de la Lwafa (Tshuapa).* MRAC, Archives d'ethnographie 8. Tervuren, 1965.

Pigafetta, F., and D. Lopes. *Description du Royaume de Congo et des Contrées environnantes.* Translated and annotated by W. Bal. Louvain and Paris, 1965.

Pinto, A. *Angola e Congo.* Lisbon, 1888.

Piscicelli, M. *Nel Paese dei Bangobango.* Naples, 1906.

Piskaty, K. "Ist das Pygmäenwerk von Henri Trilles ein zuverlässige Quelle?" *Anthropos* 52 (1957): 33–48.

Plancquaert, M. *Les Yaka: Essai d'histoire.* MRAC 71. Tervuren, 1971.

Plisnier-Ladame, F. *Les pygmées.* Centre de documentation économique et sociale africaine. Enquêtes bibliographiques 17. Brussels, 1970.

Possoz. *Eléments du droit coutumier nègre.* Elisabethville, n.d. (1942).

Pouka, L. M. "Les Bassa du Cameroun." *Cahiers d'Outre-Mer* 3 (1950): 153–66.

Randles, W. G. L. *L'ancien royaume du Congo des origines à la fin du XIXe siècle.* EHESS 14. Paris, 1968.

Raponda-Walker, A. "Enquête sur l'Agriculture noire au Gabon et sur certaines techniques utilisant des produits végétaux." *Revue de botanique appliquée et d'agriculture tropicale* 20 (1940): 722–45.

Raponda-Walker, A. *Notes d'histoire du Gabon.* Mémoire de l'Institut d'Etudes Centrafricaines 9. Brazzaville, 1960.

Raponda-Walker, A., and R. Sillans. *Les plantes utiles du Gabon.* Paris, 1961.

Raponda-Walker, A., and R. Sillans. *Rites et croyances des peuples du Gabon.* Paris, 1962.

Ratelband, K., ed. *Reizen naar West Afrika van Pieter van den Broecke, 1605–1614.* Linschoten Vereniging 52. The Hague, 1950.

Ravenstein, E., ed. *The Strange Adventures of Andrew Battell of Leigh in Angola and the Adjoining Regions.* London, 1901.

Reed, M. C. "An Ethnohistorical Study of the Political Economy of Ndjole, Gabon. Ph.D. diss., Washington University, 1988. Ann Arbor.

Reefe, T. *The Rainbow and the Kings: A History of the Luba Empire to 1891.* Berkeley, 1981.

Renfrew, C. *Archaeology and Language: The Puzzle of Indo-European Origins.* London, 1987.

Réquier, F. "Rapport d'enquête: Chefferie des Nkole nki Yamba." AIMO, Ikela 9. Itoko, 1922.

Rey, P. P. *Colonialisme, neócolonialisme et transition au capitalisme: Exemple de la Comilog au Congo Brazzaville.* Paris, 1971.

Richards, P. "The Tropical Rain Forest." *Scientific American* 229 (1973): 58–67.

Robert, M. "Considérations suggérées par l'étude du milieu physique centreafricain." In *Deux études sur le Congo belge,* ed. M. Robert and J. Schwetz, 40–41. Brussels, 1945.

Roberts, A. F. "Social and Historical Contexts of Tabwa Art." In *Tabwa: The Rising of a New Moon: A Century of Tabwa Art,* ed. E. M. Maurer, 1–48. Ann Arbor, 1985.

Robertson, G. A. *Notes on Africa, Particularly Those Parts Which Are Situated between Cape Verd and the River Congo . . .* London, 1819.

Robineau, C. "Contribution à l'histoire du Congo: La domination européenne: L'exemple de Souanke (1900–1960)." *Cahiers d'études africaines* 7, 2, #26 (1967): 300–344.

Robyns, W. *Contribution à l'étude des formations herbeuses du district forestier central du Congo belge.* ARSOM, Sciences naturelles et médicales 5, 4. Brussels, 1936.

Rogers, E., and F. Shoemaker. *Communication of Innovations: A Cross-Cultural Approach.* New York, 1971.

Rood, N. "Lidoko et Mowea." *Aequatoria* 25 (1962): 125–39.

Rood, N. *Ngombe-Nederlands-Frans woordenboek.* MRAC, Linguistiek 21. Tervuren, 1958.

Ropivia, M. "Les Fangs dans les Grands Lacs et la vallée du Nil." *Présence africaine* 120, 4 (1981): 46–58.

Ropivia, M. "Migration Bantu et Tradition orale des Fang (Le Mvett): Interprétation critique." *Le mois en Afrique* (1983): 121–32.

Rossel, G. "Gewasinnovaties in Gabon: Van Prehistorie to koloniale tijd." Scriptie: Tropische plattelandsgeschiedenis LUW Wageningen. 2 vols. 1987.

Rouvroy, V. "Historique des Bobango et de quelques tribu voisines." AIMO, Basoko 3. Yahila, 1930.

Rouvroy, V. "Le 'Lilwa.' " *Congo* 31 (1929): 783–98.

Rouvroy, V. "Le Lilwa: Quelques notes." L. 181/46. Opala, 1928.

Rudin, H. *Germans in the Cameroons.* New Haven, 1938.

Rüger, A. "Der Aufstand der Polizeisoldaten (Dezember 1893)." In *Kamerun unter Deutscher Kolonialherrschaft,* ed. H. Stöcker, 97–147. Berlin, 1960.

Rurangwa, I. M. "Nota sobre la investigación lingüística del Bubi." *Muntu* 3 (1985): 137–44.

Rusillon, J. "Le rôle social d'une société d'Afrique équatoriale." *Genêve-Afrique* 7, 2 (1968): 51–59.

Sahlins, M. *Stone Age Economics.* Chicago, 1972.

Salmon, P. "Les carnets de campagne de Louis Leclercq." *Revue de l'université de Bruxelles* 22 (1969–70): 233–302.

Salmon, P. *La dernière insurrection de Mopoie Bangezegino (1916).* CEMUBAC 86. Brussels, 1969.

Salmon, P. *La révolte des Batetela de l'expédition du Haut-Ituri: Témoignages inédits.* ARSOM, n.s. 44, 3. Brussels, 1977.

Samarin, W. J. "Bondjo Ethnicity and Colonial Imagination." *Canadian Journal of African Studies* 18 (1984): 345–65.

Sapir, E. "Time Perspective in Aboriginal American Culture: A Study in Method." In *Selected Writings of Edward Sapir,* ed. D. G. Mandelbaum, 389–462. Berkeley, 1963.

Sautter, G. *De l'Atlantique au fleuve Congo: Une géographie du sous-peuplement.* 2 vols. Paris, 1966.

Sautter, G. "Le plateau de Mbe." *Cahiers d'études africaines* 2 (1960): 27–30.

Saxon, D. E. "Linguistic Evidence for the Eastward Spread of Ubangian Peoples." *The Archaeological and Linguistic Reconstruction of African History,* ed. C. Ehret and M. Posnansky, 66–77. Berkeley, 1982.

Schadeberg, T. C. "The Lexicostatistic Base of Bennett and Sterk's Reclassification of Niger-Congo with Particular Reference to the Cohesion of Bantu." *Studies in African Linguistics* 17 (1986): 69–83.

Schatzberg, M. *Dialectics of Oppression.* Bloomington, 1988.

Schebesta, P. *Vollblutneger und Halbzwerge: Forschungen unter Waldnegern und halbpygmäen am Ituri in Belgisch Kongo.* Salzburg, 1934.

Scheub, H. *African Oral Narratives, Proverbs, Riddles, Poetry and Song: An Annotated Bibliography.* Boston, 1977.

Scheunemann. "Die Unruhen im Südbezirk von Kamerun 1904 bis 1906." *Deutsches Kolonialblatt* 18 (1907): 347–52, 391–99.

Schilde, W. *Orakel und Gottesurteile in Afrika.* Leipzig, 1940.

Schmidt, W. *The Culture Historical Method of Ethnology: The Scientific Approach to the Racial Question.* Translated from the German by S. A. Sieber. New York, 1939.

Schmitz, C. A., ed. *Historische Völkerkunde.* Frankfurt am Main, 1967.

Schultze, A. "German Congo and South Cameroons." In *From the Congo and the Niger to the Nile,* ed. A. F. Duke of Mecklenburg, 2:75–223. London, 1913.

Scohy, A. "A propos des Nkumu du lac Tumba: Le dernier écho d'une tradition indigène." *Brousse* 3, 4 (1946): 23–29.

Seidel, H. "Das Uele-Gebiet." *Globus* 56, 11 (1889): 161–65; 56, 12 (1989): 185–88.

Seitz, S. *Die zentralafrikanischen Wildbeuterkulturen.* Studien. Wiesbaden, 1977.

Sheppard, W. H. *Presbyterian Pioneers.* Richmond, 1917.

Shils, E. *Tradition.* Chicago, 1981.

Siffer, M. "Note générale sur les Babira." L. 81/17. Irumu, 1915.

Siffer, M. "Note générale sur les Mabodu." AIMO, Wamba 2. Irumu, 1916.

Sigwalt, R. "The Early History of Bushi: An Essay in the Historical Use of Genesis Traditions." Ph.D. diss., University of Wisconsin, 1975. Ann Arbor.

Silveira, L. *Descripción de la Isla de Fernando Poo en visperas del tratado de San Idelfonso.* Madrid, 1939.

Simmonds, N. W. *Bananas.* New York, 1966.

Siroto, L. "Masks and Social Organisation among the Bakwele People of Western Equatorial Africa. Ph.D. diss., Columbia University, 1969. Ann Arbor.

Sohier, A. *Le mariage en droit coutumier congolais.* ARSOM 11, 3. Brussels, 1943.

Soupart, J. "Les coutumes budja." *Bulletin des juridictions indigènes et du droit coutumier congolais* 6, 10–11 (1938): 269–74; 299–310.

Soupart, J. "Les tatouages chez les Budja." *Bulletin des juridictions indigènes et du droit coutumier congolais* 6, 12 (1938): 317–25.

Sponsel, L. E. "Amazon Ecology and Adaptation." *Annual Review of Anthropology* 15 (1986): 67–97.

Stanley, H. M. *In Darkest Africa.* 2 vols. New York, 1890.

Stanley, H. M. *Through the Dark Continent.* 2d ed. London, 1890.

Stas, J. B. "Le nkumu chez les Ntomba de Bikoro." *Aequatoria* 2, 10–11 (1939): 109–23.

Steward, J. *Theory of Culture Change: The Methodology of Multilinear Evolution.* Urbana, 1955.

Storme, M. *Ngankabe, la prétendue reine des Baboma d'après H.-M. Stanley.* ARSOM, n.s. 7, 2. Brussels, 1956.

Stradiot, F. "Rapport concernant l'organisation des populations Barumbi et Bakumu des territoires de Makale-Wandi, Lubu et Ponthierville." AIMO, D. Stanleyville 2. Stanleyville, 1931.

Sulzmann, E. "Die bokopo-Herrschaft der Bolia." *Archiv für Rechts-und Sozialphilosophie* 45, 3 (1959): 389–417.

Sulzmann, E. "Orale Tradition und Chronologie: Der Fall Baboma-Bolia." In *Mélanges de culture et de linguistique africaines, publiés à la mémoire de Leo Stappers,* ed. P. de Wolf et al. Berlin, 1983.

Sulzmann, E. "La soumission des Ekonda par les Bombomba." *Annales Aequatoria* 6 (1985): 3–17.

Sulzmann, E. "Zentralafrikanische Keramik aus voreuropäischer Zeit." *Keramos* 8 (1960): 19–30.

Sundstrom, L. *The Exchange Economy of Pre-Colonial Africa.* London, 1974.

Suret Canale, J. *Afrique noire.* 3 vols. Paris, 1961–1972.

Sutton Smith, H. *Yakusu, the Very Heart of Africa.* London, n.d. (1912?).

Swadesh, M. "Lexicostatistical Dating of Prehistoric Ethnic Contacts." *Proceedings of the American Philosophical Society* 96 (1952): 452–63.

Swadesh, M. "Towards Greater Accuracy in Lexicostatistical Dating." *International Journal of American Linguistics* 21 (1955): 121–37.

Tachelet, J. "De Montfortaanse missie in Belgisch Kongo 1933–1958. Licentie Missiologische wetenschappen, Katolieke universiteit, Leuven, 1975.

Talbot, P. A. *The Peoples of Southern Nigeria.* 2d ed. 4 vols. London, 1969.

Tanghe, B. *Le culte du serpent chez les Ngbandi.* Brugge, 1927.

Tanghe, B. *De Ngbandi: Geschiedkundige bijdragen.* Congo Biblioteek 30. Brugge, 1929.

Tanghe, B. *De Ngbandi naar het leven geschetst.* Congo Biblioteek 29. Brugge, n.d. (1929).

Tastevin, C. F. "Société secrète du Gé chez les Ba Koko du Cameroun." *16ᵉ Congrès international d'Anthropologie et d'Archéologie Préhistorique,* 891–901. Brussels, 1935.

Tastevin, C. F. "Société secrète féminine chez les Ba Koko (Cameroun)" *16ᵉ Congrès international d'Anthropologie et d'Archéologie Préhistorique,* 901–6. Brussels, 1935.

Tegnaeus, H. *Bloodbrothers.* Ethnographic Museum of Sweden, Publications, n.s. 10. Stockholm, 1952.

Teßmann, G. *Die Bubi auf Fernando Poo: Völkerkundliche Einzelbeschreibung einer westafrikanischen Negerstammes.* Hagen in Westfalen und Darmstadt, 1923.

Teßmann, G. "Ethnologisches aus dem südöstlichen Kamerun." *Mitteilungen aus dem Deutschen Schutzgebieten.* Erganzungsheft 9a (1914): 90–92.

Teßmann, G. *Die Pangwe: Völkerkundliche Monographie eines Westafrikanischen Negerstammes.* 2 vols. Berlin, 1913.

Thevoz, E. V. "Kamerun Eisenbahn-Erkundigungs-Expedition Bevölkerungsdichte." *Mitteilungen der Deutschen Schutzgebieten* 32 (1919): map 3.

Thiel, J. F. *Ahnen, Geister, Höchste Wesen: Religionsethnologische Untersuchungen im Zaïre-Kasai-Gebiet.* Studia Instituti Anthropos 26. St. Augustin, 1977.

Thomas, J. M. C. "Emprunt ou parenté? A propos de parlers des populations forestières de Centrafrique." In *Pygmées de Centrafrique,* ed. S. Bahuchet, 141–69. Paris, 1979.

Thomas, J. M. C. *Les Ngbaka de la Lobaye.* Le monde d'outre-mer 2, 11. Paris, 1963.

Thomson, T. R. H. "The Bubis, or Edeeyah of Fernando Po." *Journal of the Ethnological Society of London* 2 (1850): 105–18.

Thonnar, A. *Essai sur le système économique des primitifs d'après les populations de l'Etat Indépendant du Congo.* Brussels, 1901.

Thonner, F. *Dans la grande forêt de l'Afrique centrale: Mon voyage au Congo et à la Mongala en 1896.* Translated from the German. Brussels, 1898.

Thornton, J. "Early Kongo-Portuguese Relations: A New Interpretation." *History in Africa* 8 (1981): 183–204.

Thornton, J. *The Kingdom of Kongo: Civil War and Transition, 1641–1718.* Madison, 1983.

Thornton, R. "Narrative Ethnography in Africa, 1850–1920: The Creation and Capture of an Appropriate Domain Anthropology." *Man* 18, 3 (1983): 503–20.

Tonnoir, R. *Giribuma: Contribution à l'histoire et à la petite histoire du Congo-équatorial.* MRAC Archives d'ethnographie 14. Tervuren, 1970.

Torday, E. "Der Tofoke." *Mitteilungen der Anthropologischen Gesellschaft in Wien* 41 (1911): 189–202.

Torday, E., and T. A. Joyce. *Notes ethnographiques sur les peuples communément appelés Bakuba, ainsi que sur les peuplades apparentées. Les Bushongo.* MRAC, Annales 4º III, II, I. Brussels, 1910.

Treichel. "Die Lage im Postenbereich Sembe von I Oktober 1912 bis 30 September 1913." *Deutsches Kolonialblatt* 24 (1914): 223–25.

Tucker, A. N., and M. A. Bryan. *The Non-Bantu Languages of North-Eastern Africa.* Handbook of African Languages 3. Oxford, 1956.

Turnbull, C. "Forest Hunters and Gatherers: The Mbuti Pygmies." *The Ecology of Man in the Tropical Environment*, 38–43. Proceedings of the International Union for the Conservation of Nature and of Its Resources, 9th meeting, Nairobi 1963. Morges, Switz., 1964.

Turnbull, C. "The Mbuti Pygmies: An Ethnographic Survey." *Anthropological Papers of the American Museum of Natural History* 50, 3 (1965): 139–282.

Turnbull, C. "The Molimo: A Men's Religious Association among the Ituri Bambuti." *Zaïre* 14, 4 (1960): 307–40.

Turnbull, C. *Wayward Servants: The Two Worlds of the African Pygmies.* New York, 1965.

Uring, N. *The Voyages and Travels of Captain Nathaniel Uring.* London, 1726; 2d ed. 1928.

Usera y Alarcón, J. M. *Memoria de la Isla de Fernando Poo.* Madrid, 1848.

Valentin, P. *Jujus of the Forest Areas of West Cameroon.* Basel, 1980.

Van Belle, A. "Territoire des Walengola-Wasongola-Mituku." AIMO, Ponthierville 3. Lowa, 1932.

Van Bulck, G. *Les deux cartes linguistiques du Congo Belge.* ARSOM 25, 2. Brussels, 1952.

Van Bulck, G. *Mission linguistique, 1949–1951.* ARSOM 31, 5. Brussels, 1954.

Van Bulck, G. *Les recherches linguistiques au Congo Belge: Résultats acquis. Nouvelles enquêtes à entreprendre.* ARSOM 16. Brussels, 1948.

Van de Capelle. "Populations de Mondombe et Yolombo." W. 20/1/3. Gombe-Isongu, 1924.

Van de Capelle. "Note and map." W. 36/5 and 20/4/9. N.d.

Van den Broecke, P. See K. Ratelband.

Vanden Plas, H. "La langue des Azande: Introduction historico-géographique" In *La langue des Azande*, ed. C. R. Lagae, 1:9–65. Bibliothèque Congo 6/8. Gent, 1921.

Van der Kerken, G. *L'ethnie Mongo.* 2 vols. ARSOM 13, 1–2. Brussels, 1944.

Van der Kerken, G. *Les sociétés bantoues du Congo belge et les problèmes de la politique indigène.* Brussels, n.d. (1920).

Van der Merwe, N. "The Advent of Iron in Africa." In *The Coming of the Age of Iron,* ed. T. A. Wertime and J. R. Muhly, 473–506. New Haven, 1980.

Van de Woude, E. "Documents pour servir à la connaissance des populations du Congo Belge." Archives du Congo Belge 2. Léopoldville, 1958. Mimeograph.

Van Dieren. "La circoncision chez les Bamanga." AIMO, Banalia 4. Banalia, 1933.

Van Ermingen. "De l'organisation des Makere du territoire de Zobia." L. 181/11. Kaima, 1913.

Van Everbroeck, N. *Mbomb'Ipoku: Le seigneur à l'abîme.* MRAC, Archives d'ethnographie 3. Tervuren, 1961.

Van Geluwe, H. *Les Bali et les peuplades apparentées.* MRAC, Monographies etnnographiques 5. Tervuren, 1960.

Van Geluwe, H. *Les Bira et les peuplades limitrophes.* MRAC, Monographies ethnographiques 2. Tervuren, 1956.

Van Geluwe, H. *Mamvu-Mangutu et Balese-Mvuba.* MRAC, Monographies ethnographiques 3. Tervuren, 1957.

Van Groenweghe, D. *Bobongo: La grande fête des Ekonda (Zaire).* Mainzer Afrika Studien 9. Berlin, 1988.

Van Groenweghe, D. *Du sang sur les lianes: Léopold II et son Congo.* Brussels, 1986.

Van Grunderbeek, M. C., E. Roche, and H. Doutrelepont. "L'âge du fer ancien au Rwanda et au Burundi." *Journal des Africanistes* 52, 1–2 (1982): 5–58.

Van Grunderbeek, M. C., E. Roche, and H. Doutrelepont. *Le premier âge du fer au Rwanda et au Burundi: Archéologie et environnement.* Brussels, 1983.

Van Houteghem, A. "Overzicht der Bantu dialekten van het gewest Lisala." *Aequatoria* 10, 2 (1947): 41–53.

Van Leynseele, P. "*Les Libinza de la Ngiri.*" Ph.D. diss., University of Leiden, 1979.

Van Linschoten, J. H. *Itinerario: Voyage* . . . Linschoten vereniging 2. The Hague, 1598; 2d ed. 1934.

Van Moorsel, H. *Atlas de préhistoire de la plaine de Kinshasa.* Kinshasa, 1968.

Van Noten, F. "The Early Iron Age in the Interlacustrine Region: The Diffusion of Iron Technology." *Azania* 14 (1979): 61–80.

Van Noten, F. *The Uelian: A Culture with a Neolithic Aspect, Uele-Basin (N. E. Congo Republic): An Archaeological Study.* MRAC 64. Tervuren, 1968.

Van Noten, F., ed. *The Archaeology of Central Africa.* Graz, 1982.

Van Noten, F., and E. Van Noten. "Het ijzersmelten bij de Madi." *Africa-Tervuren* 20, 3–4 (1974): 57–66.

Van Noten, F., et al. "The Prehistory of Africa, Part 2." In *General History of Africa,* Vol. 1: *Methodology and African Prehistory,* ed. J. Ki Zerbo, 550–66. UNESCO, Paris, 1981.

Van Overberghe, C. *Les Basonge.* Collection de monographies ethnographiques 3. Brussels, 1908.

Van Overberghe, C., and E. De Jonghe. *Les Mangbetu.* Collection de monographies ethnographiques 4. Brussels, 1909.

Van Roy, H. *Les Byaambvu du Moyen Kwango: Histoire du royaume luwayaka.* Collectanea Instituti Anthropos 37. Berlin, 1988.

Vansina, J. "Antécédents des royaumes bateke (tio) et kongo." *Muntu* 9 (in press).

Vansina, J. *Art History in Africa.* London, 1984.

Vansina, J. "The Bells of Kings." *Journal of African History* 10, 2 (1969): 187–97.

Vansina, J. "The Bushong Poison Oracle." In *Man in Africa,* ed. P. Kaberry and M. Douglas, 245–60. London, 1969.

Vansina, J. *The Children of Woot: Essays in Kuba History.* Madison, 1978.

Vansina, J. "Deep Down Time." *History in Africa* (in press).

Vansina, J. "Do Pygmies Have a History?" *Sprache und Geschichte in Afrika* 7, 1 (1986): 431–45.

Vansina, J. "Esquisse historique de l'agriculture en milieu forestier." *Muntu* 2 (1985): 5–34.

Vansina, J. "The Ethnographic Account as a Genre in Central Africa." *Paideuma* 33 (1987): 433–44.

Vansina, J. *Geschiedenis van de Kuba van ongeveer 1500 tot 1904.* MRAC 44. Tervuren, 1963.

Vansina, J. *Habitat, Economy, and Society in Equatorial Africa.* London, in press.

Vansina, J. "The History of God among the Kuba." *Africa* (Rome) 28, 1 (1983): 17–39.

Vansina, J. "L'homme, les forêts et le passé en Afrique." *Annales: Economies, Sociétés, Civilisations* 40, 6 (1985): 1307–34.

Vansina, J. "Initiation Rituals of the Bushong." *Africa* 25, 1 (1956): 138–55.

Vansina, J. *Kingdoms of the Savanna: A History of the Central African States until European Occupation.* Madison, 1966.

Vansina, J. "Lignage, idéologie et histoire en Afrique équatoriale." *Enquêtes et documents d'histoire africaine* 4 (1980): 133–55.

Vansina, J. "Lukoshi, Lupambula: Histoire d'un culte religieux dans les régions du Kasai et du Kwango (1920–1970)." *Etudes d'histoire africaine* 5 (1973): 51–97.

Vansina, J. *Oral Tradition as History.* Madison, 1985.

Vansina, J. "The Past." In *African Reflections: Art from Northeastern Zaire,* ed. E. Schildkrout and C. Keim. New York, in press.

Vansina, J. "Peoples of the Forest." In *History of Central Africa* ed. D. Birmingham and P. Martin, 1:75–117. London, 1983.

Vansina, J. "Probing the Past of the Lower Kwilu Peoples (Zaire)." *Paideuma* 19, 20 (1974): 332–64.

Vansina, J. "Le régime foncier dans la société kuba." *Zaire* 9 (1956): 899–926.

Vansina, J. *Le royaume kuba.* MRAC 49. Tervuren, 1964.

Vansina, J. *The Tio Kingdom of the Middle Congo: 1880–1892.* London, 1973.

Vansina, J. "Vers une histoire des sociétés mongo." *Annales Aequatoria* 8 (1987): 9–57.

Vansina, J. "Western Bantu Expansion." *Journal of African History* 25, 2 (1984): 129–45.

Védy, L. "Les Ababuas." *Bulletin de la société royale belge de géographie* 28 (1904): 191–205, 265–94.

Vellut, J.-L. "Notes sur l'économie internationale des côtes de Guinée inférieure au XIXᵉ siècle." *Reunião Internacional: História de Africa. Relação Europa-Africa no 3º quartel do Séc XIX,* 1–50. Lisbon, 1988.

Vellut, J.-L. "La violence armée dans l'Etat Indépendant du Congo." *Cultures et développement* 16, 3–4 (1984): 671–707.

Vellut, J.-L., and D. Van Groenweghe "Le rapport Casement." *Enquêtes et documents d'histoire africaine* 6 (1985): 1–175.

Vennetier, P. *Atlas de la République populaire du Congo.* Paris, 1977.

Verbeken, A. "Accession au pouvoir chez certaines tribus du Congo par système électif." *Congo* 35, 2 (1933): 653–57.

Verbeken, A. "Institutions politiques indigènes: Accession au pouvoir . . ." *Bulletin des juridictions indigènes et du droit coutumier congolais* 3, 1 (1935): 1–3.

Verdcourt, A. "Organisation coutumière des juridictions indigènes dans le territoire de Bomboma." *Bulletin des juridictions indigènes et du droit coutumier congolais* 11, 1 (1943): 11–29.

Vermassen. "La chefferie des Basengere." L. 23, 5. Gandja, 1931.

Verstraeten, A. "Les tatouages." *Belgique coloniale* 3 (1897): 89–91, 113–14, 316–18, 330–31, 377–78.

Vincart, L. "Notes pour servir à l'histoire des peuplades environnant le poste de Massidjadet." *Belgique coloniale* 5 (1899): 521–23, 529–33, 544–46.

Vincent, J. F. "Dot et monnaie de fer chez les Bakwele et les Djem." *Objets et Mondes* 3 (1963): 273–92.

Vincent, J. F. "Le mouvement Croix Koma." *Cahiers d'études africaines* 6, 4, #21 (1966): 527–63.

Vincent, J. F. "Traditions historiques chez les Djem de Souanke." *Revue française d'Histoire d'Outre-mer* 178 (1963): 64–73.

Volavka, Z. "Le *Ndunga:* Un masque, une danse, une institution sociale au Ngoyo" *Arts d'Afrique noire* 18 (1976): 28–43.

Von Skopp, E. "Sitten und Gebräuche der Bakoko in Kamerun." *Beiträge zur Kolonialpolitik und Kolonialwirtschaft* 4 (1902–3): 482–90, 510–18, 523–31, 551–59.

Von Stein, F. "Expedition des Freiherrn von Stein." *Deutsches Kolonialblatt* 12 (1901): 518–21, 742–46.

Vorbichler, A. "Linguistische Bemerkungen zur Herkunft der Mamvu-Balese." *Zeitschrift der Deutschen Morgenländische Gesellschaft,* Supplementa 1, 3 (1969): 1145–54.

Vorbichler, A. *Die Phonologie und Morphologie des Balese (Ituri-Urwald, Kongo).* Afrikanische Forschungen 2. Gluckstadt, 1965.

Vorbichler, A. *Die Sprache der Mamvu.* Afrikanische Forschungen 5. Gluckstadt, 1971.

Vorbichler, A. "Sprachkontakte am Beispiel einiger Sprachen und Dialekte in Nordost-Zaire." *Anthropos* 74, 3–4 (1979): 433–42.

Vorbichler, A. "Die Sprachliche Beziehungen zwischen den Waldnegern und Pygmäen in der Republik Kongo-Leo." *Actes du VIᵉ Congrès international des sciences anthropologiques et ethnologiques,* 2:85–91. Paris, 1960.

Vorbichler, A. "Zu dem Problem der Klasseneinteilung in Lebendiges und Lebloses in den Pygmäen- und Waldnegerdialekten des Ituri, Congo." In *Festschrift Paul Schebesta,* 25–34. Studia Instituti Anthropos 18. Vienna-Mödling, 1963.

Wainwright, G. A., "The Coming of the Banana to Uganda." *Uganda Journal* 16, 1 (1952): 145–47.

Walter, R., and J. Barret, eds. *Géographie et cartographie du Gabon: Atlas illustré.* Paris, 1983.

Watson, M. *Agricultural Innovation in the Early Islamic World: The Diffusion of Crops and Farming Techniques, 700–1100.* Cambridge, 1983.

Wauters, G. *L'ésotérie des noirs dévoilée.* Brussels, 1949.

White, F. *The Vegetation of Africa.* UNESCO Natural Resources Research 20. Paris, 1983.

White, P. T. "Tropical Rainforests." *National Geographic* 163, 1 (1983): 2–46.

Wijnant, D. "De Doko's." *Congo* 7, 2 (1925): 410–26.

Wijnant, D. "Eene bladzijde uit de geschiedenis van Boela. *Congo* 9, 1 (1927): 605–8.

Wijnant, D. "Het Doko volk." *Congo* 7, 1 (1925): 206–15.

Wijnant, D. "Het Doko volk in hun handel en wandel." *Congo* 8, 1 (1926): 584–95.

Willey, G. R. "Archaeological Theories and Interpretations: New World." In *Anthropology Today*, ed. A. Kroeber, 361–85. New York, 1953.

Wilson, J. L. *Western Africa: Its History, Conditions and Prospects.* London, 1856.

Windels, A. "Chefferie des Pama-Bakutu." Archives of the zône of Lukolela. Lukolela, n.d. (c. 1939). Copy courtesy of R. Harms.

Winkelmans, A. "Histoire générale de la tribu Maha de la peuplade Mabudu." Archives of zône of Wamba. Wamba, 1937. Copy courtesy of C. Keim.

Wirz, A. "La rivière du Cameroun: Commerce pré-colonial et contrôle du pouvoir en société lignagére." *Revue française d'Histoire d'Outre-mer* 40, 219 (1973): 172–95.

Wirz, A. *Vom Sklavenhandel zum Kolonialen Handel: Wirtschaftsräume und Wirtschaftsformen in Kamerun vor 1914.* Zurich, 1972.

Wognou, J. M. W. *Les Basaa du Cameroun.* Paris, 1974.

Wolfe, A. "The dynamics of the Ngombe Segmentary System." In *Continuity and Change in African Cultures,* ed. W. Bascom and M. Herskovits, 168–86. Chicago, 1959.

Wolfe, A. *In the Ngombe Tradition: Continuity and Change in the Congo.* Evanston, 1961.

Wrigley, C. "Speculations on the Economic Prehistory of Africa." *Journal of African History* 1, 2 (1960): 189–203.

Wurm, P. *Die Religion der Küstenstämme in Kamerun.* Bäßler Missions-Studien 22. Basel, 1904.

Yogolelo Tambwe ya Kasimba. *Introduction à l'histoire des Lega: Problèmes et méthode.* CEDAF 5, 2. Brussels, 1975.

Zenker, G. "Die Mabea." *Ethnologisches Notizblatt* 3, 3 (1904): 1–24.

Zorzi, E. *Al Congo con Brazza.* Rome, 1940.

Index

Ababua (people), 371*n20*. *See also* Boa
Abala, 314*n51*
Abandia, 116, 176
Abarambo (people), 171, 176
Abelu (people), 173–76
Abo (people), 337*n5*, 339*n18*
abortion, 219, 227, 365n46
Adamawa languages, 65
Adulis, 64
Aduma (people), 206
age, grouping by, 79–80, 117, 130;
   among the Bubi, 140–41, 143; among
   the Komo, 189
age grades, 79–80, 171, 183, 341*n35*
agriculture. *See* crops; farming; planta-
   tion
Aka (people), 309*n71*
Aka-Mbati languages, 50–52, 312*n31*
Akan (peoples), 256
'Alenga dynasty, 356*n62*
Alima-Likouala area, 147, 161
Alima River, 52, 55, 103, 360–61*n10;*
   and Atlantic trade, 202, 206, 214, 227
alliance: of Houses, 81–83; of villages,
   105, 109, 113, 175; of towns, 114; with
   colonial powers, 240; with Zanzibari
   and Sudanese, 240–42. *See also* clan;
   marriage
Amaya Mokini, 224
Amazon rainforests, 257
Ambaquistas (people), 236
Ambos (ethnonym), 339*n18*
ambush, 107, 130
Ambwila, battle of, 204, 220
Americas, 201, 202, 210, 218, 314*n42*
anachronism, 8, 10, 50
analogy, 156, 261–62
ancestor. *See* hero; spirit
ancestor, common, 82, 132, 134–35, 159,
   187, 233
Angola, 3, 154; and the slave trade, 201,
   218, 230, 236, 360*n2*
Angumu, 47
anthill: as emblem of power, 120; as symbol of House, 328*n6*
anthropology: theoretical, 6–7, 27–28,
   72; historical, 10; and rules of evi-

dence, 17, 18, 24–25, 81, 246; comparative, 31–33, 260–63; and history,
   249; African, 253
Anziko (ethnonym), 347*n87*
Apagibeti (people), 317*n65*
arbitration and rule, 146, 189, 228, 235,
   252
archaeology, 8, 18, 26; and the notion of
   tradition, 6–7; and glottochronology,
   16; of the Bantu expansion, 47, 49, 53,
   54, 57; of the early iron age, 59, 60,
   68; in the Inner Basin, 102–4, 121; on
   Bioko, 139, 140; in the southwest quadrant, 155, 156; as a test, 250. *See also*
   ceramics
archers, 41, 111, 173, 174, 175
Arnhemland, 8
Aruwimi River area, 39; confluence, 62,
   126, 106–10, 194; lower, 118, 244; upper, 167, 169, 173, 175
Asante (kingdom), 368*n85*
Asia, 87, 232, 256, 257
assimilation: and Bantu expansion, 57,
   65; and Bantu and Ubangian speakers,
   66; and Sanaga Ntem expansion, 134–
   37; on Bioko, 142–44; in Uele, 172–73
associations, 80, 191–92, 236; in Cameroon and northern Gabon, 25, 130–36,
   232–35, 245; in southern Gabon and
   lower Congo, 25, 158–59, 221, 224, 232;
   in northern Congo, 161, 229; in southern Maniema, 177–86, 191, 194, 241; on
   Bioko, 341*n35;* in Shaba, 354*n43;* and
   colonial rule, 370*n16*. *See also* brotherhood; *bwámi;* dance association
Atlantic trade, 159, 196–237, 252, 254.
   See also slave trade
Australia, 261
Austro-Hungarian Empire, 217
autochthons: before Bantu expansion,
   47–49, 83, 91, 325*n61;* and Bantu
   speakers, 56–58, 65, 69, 88; Bantu
   speaking, 126, 136–37, 142, 164
autonomy, 73, 237, 252–54; of village in
   district, 109; of the House, 119, 188;
   within a kingdom, 225. *See also* egali-
   tarianism

411

DATE DUE